AF506322

Growth and Cycle in the Eurozone

Growth and Cycle in the Eurozone

Edited by

Gian Luigi Mazzi

and

Giovanni Savio

This edition published 2007 by
PALGRAVE MACMILLAN
Houndmills, Basingstoke, Hampshire RG21 6XS and
175 Fifth Avenue, New York, N.Y. 10010
Companies and representatives throughout the world

PALGRAVE MACMILLAN is the global academic imprint of the Palgrave
Macmillan division of St. Martin's Press, LLC and of Palgrave Macmillan Ltd.
Macmillan® is a registered trademark in the United States, United Kingdom
and other countries. Palgrave is a registered trademark in the European
Union and other countries.

ISBN-13: 978–0–230–00790–1
ISBN-10: 0–230–00790–2

This book is printed on paper suitable for recycling and made from fully
managed and sustained forest sources.

A catalogue record for this book is available from the British Library.

Library of Congress Cataloging-in-Publication Data
    Growth and cycle in the Eurozone / edited by Gian Luigi Mazzi
  and Giovanni Savio.
        p. cm.
    Conference papers.
    Includes bibliographical references and index.
    ISBN 0–230–00790–2 (cloth)
    1. Business cycles – European Union countries – Statistics – Congresses.
  2. Business cycles – European Union countries – Econometric models –
  Congresses. 3. European Union countries – Economic conditions – Congresses
  I. Mazzi, Gian Luigi, 1951– II. Savio, Giovanni, 1961– III. Eurostat/TACIS.
HB3782.G76 2006
338.5′42094–dc22   2006047456

10 9 8 7 6 5 4 3 2 1
16 15 14 13 12 11 10 09 08 07

Printed and bound in Great Britain by
Antony Rowe Ltd, Chippenham and Eastbourne

Contents

**Part IV   Composite Indicators and Forecasting of
Economic Activity**

Part V   Turning Points Dating and Detection

List of Tables and Figures

Tables

Figures

Preface

This volume contains shorter and revised versions of the papers presented at the 4th Eurostat and DG ECFIN Colloquium on Modern Tools for Business Cycle Analysis, Luxembourg, 20–22 October 2003. The main objectives of the Colloquium were to discuss recent developments in theoretical and empirical business cycle analysis; to identify possible applications of sophisticated tools by private and public institutions involved in the analysis of economic fluctuations; and to facilitate the interaction among academics, researchers and institutions in the area of business cycles.

The papers contained in this volume encompass recent methodological advances in several important areas for business cycle analysis, such as multivariate statistical methods, synchronization and convergence, composite indicators, turning points dating and detection, output gap measurement, as well as innovative applications of the existing theories and methods to the economy of the Eurozone.

The chapters have been ideally divided into seven Parts. The first Part is dedicated to the links between business cycle studies and the provision of short-term statistics by national and supra-national statistical agencies. This part analyses in detail strong points and shortcomings of data for short-term analysis actually produced by the European Statistical System, and identifies areas where major efforts are needed, such as the availability of long time series of coherent data.

The second Part contains chapters on multivariate techniques and other recent advances in business cycle analyses, amongst these Bayesian approaches to the study of business fluctuations. There is no doubt that multivariate statistical techniques have deeply contributed in the last few years to the understanding of business cycle fluctuations, as they allow for the simultaneous modelling of growths and cycles for a large set of series whilst taking into account all their likely interactions.

The third Part concerns convergence and synchronization among variables and countries. Convergence and synchronization are at the core of Burns and Mitchell's classical definition of business cycles, where a clear relationship in terms of common movements among different economic series is required. This Part of the book analyses different but complementary aspects of co-movements and convergence, both at the Eurozone and the international level.

The fourth Part of the book contains chapters on composite indicators and forecasting of economic activity, and deals with indicators that synthesize the dynamics of cyclical fluctuations and which are used for their capacity to detect in advance turning points of business cycles.

The fifth Part deals with the definition and identification in real time of turning points, a point obviously at the core of almost all business cycle theories and analyses. Though the classical approach to the definition and location of turning points still remains the most commonly used in theoretical and empirical research, alternative definitions of turning points based either on growth cycles, acceleration cycles or recovery-cycles are also discussed in a univariate and multivariate context.

The sixth Part of the book includes chapters which consider the historical or real-time estimates of output gap, the deviation of current output from its long-term trend, and discusses the relationship of these deviations with monetary and budgetary impulses.

The direction and intensity of policy interventions, especially monetary ones, are usually determined following the latest developments of business cycle. Chapters in the last Part of the book focus on monetary factors and business fluctuations. This Part touches on various issues of interest, from the Nairu and Phillips curve, to the credibility of monetary policy in the Eurozone and the transmission of monetary and fiscal shocks, and finally to the saving and financing gaps.

We would like to express our appreciation to all the authors and participants in the Colloquium, whose contributions and stimulating comments helped to make – we hope – this volume interesting for theoreticians and practitioners of the discipline.

GIAN LUIGI MAZZI
GIOVANNI SAVIO

Notes on the Contributors

Bas van Aarle, Faculty of Economics and Applied Economics, Catholic University of Leuven, Leuven, Belgium.

Jacques Anas, Centre d'Observation Economique, Paris, France.

Toichiro Asada, Faculty of Economics, Chuo University, Tokyo, Japan.

Roberto Astolfi, Direzione Centrale della Contabilità Nazionale, ISTAT, Rome, Italy.

Michael U. Bergman, Department of Economics, University of Copenhagen, Copenhagen, Denmark.

Monica Billio, Dipartimento di Economia, Università di Venezia, Venice, Italy.

Maurizio Bovi, Institute for Studies and Economic Analyses, ISAE, Rome, Italy.

Roberto Casarin, Dipartimento di Economia, Università di Venezia, Venice, Italy.

Nuno Cassola, Directorate General Economics, European Central Bank, Frankfurt am Main, Germany.

José Luis Cendejas Bueno, Departamento de Análisis Económico, Universidad Autónoma de Madrid, Madrid, Spain.

Marco Centoni, Dipartimento SEGeS, Università del Molise, Campobasso, Italy.

Carl Chiarella, School of Finance and Economics, University of Technology Sydney, Sydney, Australia.

Marco Crivellini, Dipartimento di Economia, Università Politecnica delle Marche, Ancona, Italy.

Gianluca Cubadda, Dipartimento SEFEMEQ, Università di Roma 'Tor Vergata', Rome, Italy.

Herman K. van Dijk, Econometric Institute, Erasmus University, Rotterdam, The Netherlands.

Juan Del Hoyo Bernat, Departamento de Análisis Económico, Universidad Autónoma de Madrid, Madrid, Spain.

Antoni Espasa, Departamento de Métodos Cuantitativos para la Economía, Universidad San Pablo-CEU and Univ. Carlos III, Madrid, Spain.

Laurent Ferrara, Centre d'Observation Economique, Paris, France.

Gebhard Flaig, Department of Business Cycle Analyses and Financial Markets, Ifo Institute for Economic Research, Munich, Germany.

Peter Flaschel, Department of Economics, Bielefeld University, Bielefeld, Germany.

Reiner Franke, Technische Universität Wien, Wien, Austria.

Federico Galizia, European Investment Bank, Luxembourg, Luxembourg.

Marco Gallegati, Dipartimento di Economia, Università Politecnica delle Marche, Ancona, Italy.

Mauro Gallegati, Dipartimento di Economia, Università Politecnica delle Marche, Ancona, Italy.

Harry Garretsen, Utrecht School of Economics, Utrecht University, Utrecht, The Netherlands.

Niko Gobbin, Department of Economics, Universiteit Gent, Gent, Belgium.

Dominique Guégan, Departement d'Economie et Gestion, MORA-CNRS, Cachan, France.

Andrew C. Harvey, Department of Economics and Politics, University of Cambridge, UK.

Alain Hecq, Department of Quantitative Economics, Universiteit Maastricht, The Netherlands.

Göran Hjelm, National Institute of Economic Research, Stockholm, Sweden.

Matthieu Lemoine, Observatoire Français des Conjonctures Economiques, Paris, France.

Marco Lo Duca, GRETA Associati, Venice, Italy.

Camille Logeay, Institut für Makroökonomie und Konjunkturforschung (IMK), Düsseldorf, Germany.

Marco Marini, Direzione Centrale della Contabilità Nazionale, ISTAT, Rome, Italy.

Antonio Matas-Mir, Directorate General Statistics, European Central Bank, Frankfurt am Main, Germany.

Gian Luigi Mazzi, Statistical Office of the European Communities, Eurostat, European Commission, Luxembourg, Luxembourg.

Roman Minguez, Departamento de Métodos Cuantitativos para la Economía, Universidad San Pablo-CEU and Univ. Carlos III, Madrid, Spain.

James Mitchell, National Institute of Economic and Social Research, London, UK.

Claudio Morana, Dipartimento di Scienze Economiche e Metodi Quantitativi, Università del Piemonte Orientale, Novara, Italy.

Kostas Mouratidis, National Institute of Economic and Social Research, London, UK.

Alberto Musso, Directorate General Economics, European Central Bank, Frankfurt am Main, Germany.

Simon van Norden, Department of Finance, HEC Montréal, Montréal, Canada.

Denise R. Osborn, Centre for Growth and Business Cycle Research, School of Economic Studies, University of Manchester, UK.

Antonio Palestrini, Dipartimento di Economia, Università di Teramo, Teramo, Italy.

Pedro J. Perez, Economic Analysis Department, University of Valencia, Valencia, Spain.

Domenico Sartore, Dipartimento di Economia, Università di Venezia, Venice, Italy.

Giovanni Savio, Senior Statistician in the United Nations Economic and Social Commission for Western Asia.

Nikolaos Sdrakas, Directorate-General Economics and Finance, European Commission, Bruxelles, Belgium.

Marianne Sensier, Centre for Growth and Business Cycle Research, School of Economic Studies, University of Manchester, UK.

Jan-Egbert Sturm, Center for Economic Studies, University of Munich, Munich, Germany.

Silke Tober, Institut für Makroökonomie und Konjunkturforschung (IMK), Düsseldorf, Germany.

Thomas M. Trimbur, US Census Bureau, Washington, DC, USA.

Ulrich Woitek, Department of Economics, University of Munich, Munich, Germany.

Part I
The Business Cycle and Official Statistics

1
Official Statistics for Business Cycle Analysis

Gian Luigi Mazzi and Giovanni Savio

Introduction

Infra-annual macro-economic statistics represent, nowadays, a key tool for economic policy-making and business cycle analyses. The demand for such timely and good quality statistics for the Eurozone has strongly increased since the advent of the monetary union in 1999. Although considerable progress has been made over recent years in this area, further improvements are needed for many EU/Eurozone statistics as far as concerns timeliness, coverage, convergence of revision practices and policies, and appropriate length of time series. In effect, the traditional approach based on harmonization has serious drawbacks, at least in the short–medium period, as it can induce breaks in the series and may cause delays in the provision of final estimates at the aggregated level. Difficulties could sharply increase in the near future as a consequence of the EU enlargement process. At this stage, statistical and econometric methods can play an important role to get timely figures, long time series, and to construct new indicators. These methods can provide users with estimates until the usual process based on harmonization is able to give more reliable and complete figures. This chapter, after a review of the institutional framework, analyses projects and research conducted by Eurostat in numerous fields relevant for business cycle analyses.

Since its establishment in 1953, Eurostat, the Statistical Office of the European Communities, has essentially focused its efforts on the release of structural and well-harmonized figures for the European Union. In effect, for a long time the main statistical activity of Eurostat has consisted in the harmonization of national statistics through a set of legal acts covering different areas. These acts were essentially concerned with structural statistics, and accuracy rather than timeliness has been the keyword of Eurostat's actions in the various fields of interest. This approach was justified by the need to support relevant political decisions, including the attribution of structural funds, and regional and agricultural intervention policies. Therefore, for a number of years short-term statistics were considered to be only a useful complement to structural statistics. From the end of the 1980s the situation gradually changed. Due to the creation of a common market and the adoption of the Maastricht criteria, several legal acts concerning infra-annual statistics were adopted (for example the Intrastat Directive of 1993 for external trade statistics; the European System of Accounts 1995 Regulation; the Regulation for the Harmonized Index of Consumer Prices in January 1997; the Regulation for setting up a common framework for Short-term Business Statistics in May 1998).

Pressure towards improvements of the short-term statistical information system came from the requests of the European Central Bank, DG ECFIN and other institutional and non-institutional users. In the meantime, the interest of financial market analysts and newspapers towards the statistics released by Eurostat increased, accompanied by pressures for more timely, accurate and reliable statistics useful for short-term analyses and interventions.

Eurostat, as other international statistical agencies, has in recent years put great effort into defining and implementing a quality framework for the statistics released. While a clear definition of the term 'quality' has now been reached, the implementation of such a quality framework is still in development, though important improvements have been made over recent years.

Notwithstanding the considerable efforts made, an analysis of the availability of short-term information shows some problems related to specific aspects of data quality, in particular timeliness, the length of time series, and availability of some key short-term indicators for the Eurozone.

Nowadays, Eurostat has a doubly challenging mission regarding infra-annual statistics. Firstly, it has to provide users with a complete set of reliable short-term indicators for member states as well as for the Eurozone and the EU. Secondly, it has to assist and help economic policy/decision-makers and business cycle analysts by providing them with quasi-real time estimates and high quality statistical analyses. In these respects, the two major outcomes of Eurostat activity are the Euro-indicators webpages, in part dedicated to business cycle analysis, and the Euro-IND database, which aims to give a synthetic but complete picture of the economic short-term situation of the Eurozone, European Union and member states.

The regular monitoring of the Euro-IND database in recent years has shown that, notwithstanding numerous improvements, several quality problems still persist. A series of actions have been launched by Eurostat to investigate areas where official statistics can benefit from recent advances in statistical and econometric techniques (for example backward calculation, nowcasting, construction of proxies for some unavailable indicators). These methodological activities constitute a natural complement to traditional data production actions, which take time to have effect, especially in a complex and integrated system. The creation of a methodological *presidium* within Eurostat serves to give an impulse to some of these non-traditional methods of data production.

The statistical actions launched by Eurostat in recent years to improve availability and timeliness of short-term statistics will be analysed in this chapter, whose plan is as follows. The next section details the institutional framework, whose aims consist in putting in place measures (from more formal legal acts to simple 'gentleman agreements') with member states in order to improve data quality of short-term statistics in various respects. We then consider statistical methods which are directly used to improve the quality of infra-annual statistics and on which Eurostat at the moment concentrates. Other mathematical and statistical methods to improve the data-presentation of infra-annual series are then analysed, followed by a final concluding section.

The institutional role of Eurostat in the improvement of infra-annual statistics

Over recent years, the Commission, the Council, the ECB and the European Statistical System (ESS) as a whole have substantially improved the quality of statistics, notably with respect to their comparability, coverage, timeliness and coherence. Since the signature of the Maastricht Treaty in 1992, several important legal initiatives have been undertaken to enhance European macroeconomic statistics. Some of these have been cited in the Introduction. However, many EU/Eurozone statistics lack timeliness, and the comparison between the best EU member states and the USA is particularly striking. Moreover, the quality of some of these statistics has been criticized. In this respect, the Commission's main objective is to accelerate the release of a set of key EU/Eurozone infra-annual macroeconomic statistics and to improve other quality features. These notably include complete statistical coverage, consistency between the different sets of data, transparency of the methods applied, sound monitoring, and detailed explanations of data revisions and the accessibility of statistical information.

To these ends, an important instrument used in recent years has been the so-called EMU Action Plan. The Action Plan covers a number of areas: quarterly national accounts, quarterly accounts for the government sector, statistics on labour markets, short-term business statistics, and statistics on external trade. For each member state, the Action Plan has identified areas where progress is needed in the compilation of national indicators, and a list of action points has been established for Eurostat and for each member state (National Action Plans). The Action Plans require member states to accelerate the production of national data series to permit timely compilation of reliable EU/Eurozone indicators.

In parallel to the Action Plan, an intra-EU and EU–USA benchmark study was carried out in September 2000. It confirmed that the Action Plan, although very substantial, might not be enough to match the US timeliness and best practices worldwide. A list of more focused infra-annual macroeconomic indicators (the so-called Principal European Economic Indicators, PEEIs) has therefore been set up, with more challenging target release dates for EU/Eurozone indicators (see Table 1.1).

The Commission should compile and release the set of PEEIs based on member states' contributions. This does not mean that all member states have to produce representative indicators nationally with the same timeliness, but member

Table 1.1   List of PEEIs, periodicity, target and actual delays

Set	Indicator	Periodicity	EU delay target	EU delay actual
Set 1: consumer price indicators				
1.1	Harmonized consumer price index: MUICP flash estimate	monthly	0	2
1.2	Harmonized consumer price index: actual indices	monthly	17	17
Set 2: national accounts indicators				
2.1	Quarterly national accounts: first GDP estimate	quarterly	45	n.a.
2.2	Quarterly national accounts: first GDP release with more breakdowns	quarterly	60	70/120
2.3	Quarterly national accounts: household and company accounts	quarterly	90	n.a.
2.4	Quarterly national accounts: government finance statistics	quarterly	90	100
Set 3: business indicators				
3.1	Industrial production index	monthly	40	48
3.2	Industrial output price index for domestic markets	monthly	35	35
3.3	Industrial new orders index	monthly	40/50	Preliminary data
3.4	Industrial import price index	monthly	45	n.a.
3.5	Production in construction	monthly/ quarterly	45	75
3.6	Turnover index for retail trade and repair	monthly	30	60
3.7	Turnover index for other services	quarterly	60	Partial data
3.8	Corporate output price index for services	quarterly	60	n.a.
Set 4: labour market indicators				
4.1	Unemployment rate	monthly	30	30
4.2	Job vacancy rate	quarterly	45	n.a.
4.3	Employment	quarterly	45	70/75
4.4	Labour cost index	quarterly	70	90
Set 5: foreign trade indicators				
5.1	External trade balance: intra and extra for MU and EU	monthly	45	50

n.a. = not available (not published yet at EU level).

states – in particular those whose economies have the most significant impact on EU/Eurozone aggregates – are expected to give the information needed to produce and release timely and representative indicators at the EU/Eurozone level (the so called First for Europe principle).

For each PEEI, ambitious objectives have been set up regarding timeliness and other quality aspects. The commitments planned under this concerted approach are made voluntarily, which means that no new regulatory instruments are needed since requests to member states are based on either already existing EU legislation or on voluntary arrangements (generally referred to in the statistical field as 'gentleman agreements').

Improving data quality through statistical techniques

The traditional instruments depicted above have two serious drawbacks. Firstly they can generate breaks in series, for example when a new country joins the European Union. Secondly, they might cause delays as the indicators are generally released by National Institutes with different release lags. Moreover, the compilation of a new statistical indicator is often likely to be a long and difficult task, and series are sometimes unavailable for years. As the usual process based on harmonization cannot quickly fulfill these new needs, Eurostat is changing its strategy: statistical methods and econometric models are now playing a greater role to get timely figures, long time series, and to obtain new indicators. These models will provide users with estimates until the usual process, based on harmonization, is able to give more reliable figures. Moreover, other statistical analyses will be carried out on some important indicators to make interpretation and analysis easier for economists.

Ideally, the Euro-IND database aims at providing series spanning over 15 years, that is covering at least two complete economic cycles, and real-time updated. Unfortunately the situation is much less satisfactory for the Eurozone, and varies substantially from one domain to another. Even if it is difficult to evaluate the punctuality of the series in the Euro-IND database, it clearly appears that there are several delays to updating the database which cumulate with the well-known production delays (lack of timeliness). Backward recalculation and flash estimates of data for this area have become a priority for Eurostat as discussed below. Moreover, the pressure from users to obtain data with a higher frequency for macroeconomic indicators requires the use of sophisticated interpolation and extrapolation techniques.

Temporal disaggregation

It is often said that the analysis of business cycle should be conducted on time series spanning a sufficiently long time, with a 'golden rule' given either by a minimum of two complete business cycles (10–15 years), or by a sufficient number of observations to conduct efficient statistical analyses. In many situations, these conditions are not fulfilled by many series: for example, 20.4 per cent of the active series of the Euro-IND database cover 15 years or more, and 72.1 per cent cover at least 10 years. The problem can be circumvented, at least partially, by the use of temporal disaggregation/benchmarking techniques. These techniques interpolate or distribute economic time series observed at low frequency into compatible higher frequency data, generally using related time series, and can also be useful for extrapolation of the target series over the sample period. Temporal disaggregation/benchmarking techniques can also increase data quality in terms of forecasting the actual series according to the evolution of the indicator series. Their use can also be relevant in backcasting exercises (see below).

While interpolation refers to the estimation of missing observations of stock variables, a distribution problem occurs for flow and time averages of stock variables. In the distribution case, for example, the problem concerns the estimation of intra-period values for a given time series subject to the constraint that their sums (or averages) equal the aggregates over the lower frequency.

Temporal disaggregation has been extensively considered in the econometric and statistical literature and numerous solutions have been proposed (see for example, Eurostat (1999, ch. 6) for a survey and taxonomy of temporal disaggregation methods). Over the last 5–10 years, developments in this field have essentially followed two distinct lines of research: (a) use of univariate dynamic regression models – usually represented as autoregressive distributed lag (ADL) models, possibly using non-linearly transformed data; and (b) univariate or multivariate approaches that use formulations in terms of unobserved components and structural time series models (and possibly non-linearly transformed data) and Kalman filtering techniques to get optimal estimates of missing observations by a smoothing algorithm. The first line of research comprises the work of, for example, Santos Silva and Cardoso (2001) and Mitchell *et al.* (2005). The second line of research, originally developed by Harvey and Pierce (1984), has been exploited by, for example, Gudmundsson (1999), Hotta and Vasconcellos (1999) and Proietti (1999), and has been further developed in the framework of structural time series models by Durbin and Quenneville (1997), Harvey (1989), Harvey and Chung (2000) and Moauro and Savio (2005). Other fields of research at the border of the two lines discussed above are the use of nonlinear transformations of the data (Proietti, 2004, and Di Fonzo, 2003) and the contemporaneous disaggregation and seasonal adjustment of time series in multivariate structural models (Moauro and Proietti, 2005).

It has been under consideration whether to extend the Ecotrim programme for temporal disaggregation developed by Eurostat to introduce into it some of the major disaggregation methods cited above. Empirical applications of temporal disaggregation techniques to themes relevant for our purposes have received attention in recent years at Eurostat, and are now going to be finalized. We only cite here the estimation of a monthly disaggregation for quarterly GDP at the Eurozone level, with preliminary results discussed in Astolfi *et al.* (2002). A similar approach has been used to build a monthly indicator of activity in the Construction sector, but the results are still under evaluation due to the lack of stability and timeliness of the original series.

Backward calculation

The need for economic time series that are homogeneous and, at the same time, defined over the longest possible period, is a central issue for statisticians, econometricians and economic analysts. Unfortunately, due to changes in definitions

Table 1.2   Backward recalculated time series

Series	Freq.	Actual time span	Retrapolated sample
Industrial production index and MIGs	M	1985M1–present	1970M1–1984M12
GDP, GVA and components	Q	1991Q1–present	1970Q1–1990Q4
Industrial turnover index	M	1995M1–present	1975M1–1994M12
Consumer prices index (HICP)	M	1990M1–present	No retrap.
Consumer prices index (CPI)	M	1960M1–present	No retrap.
Deflated retail trade index	M	1995M1–present	1970M1–1994M12
Producer prices index	M	1981M1–present	1970M1–1980M12
Unemployment	M	1991M6–present	1970M1–1991M5

and/or new basic data availability, the available series very often show inconsistencies and breaks in their dynamic profile. In some cases the partial availability of information prevents the calculation of the series, but estimation techniques which make use of all the available information to get 'reasonable' estimates of the series of interest can offer a valid solution, with a quality and usefulness strictly linked to the amount of basic information processed and to the way in which the various 'pieces' of information are combined.

Eurostat is currently working in the framework of backward calculations for a set of relevant economic variables for the Eurozone: Quarterly GDP and its main components; an Industrial Production Index and its disaggregation by main industrial groupings (MIGs); an Industrial Turnover Index; Total Employment; a Deflated Retail Trade Index; a Producer Price Index; and Unemployment. The objective is to carry out retrapolations of the above series back to 1970 at a fine detail level. Periods covered and other information on the series analysed are reported in Table 1.2.

A number of alternative methodologies can be used for back-calculating a time series, from simple univariate interpolation and/or extrapolation, up to very complex statistical models. The back-recalculation of disrupted time series requires a number of steps, the first being the search for the relevant (related) information and its statistical analysis. Other important aspects are the choice of the retrapolation approach (and the comparison of direct versus indirect strategies), statistical testing of the available related series, model choice, and finally back-calculation of the series.

In general, the statistical characteristics of the available information and the relationships between the target series and information set drastically affect the choice of the model and the strategy used in the back-recalculation exercises. Furthermore, the methodology used varies case-by-case, though the philosophy of the approach used generally belongs to the regression approach family, possibly extended with ARIMA structures on residuals. Multi-step procedures have been used intensively by combining direct and indirect reconstructions, together with the appropriate use of disaggregation (balancing) techniques. Further details on the alternative methods for back-recalculation used by Eurostat can be found in Mazzi and Savio (2003).

Table 1.3   Release lag for some key aggregates

	USA	Eurozone	France	Germany	Italy
Industrial production	15	45	41	40	45
GDP	24	45	50	45	40
Producer prices	10	38	30	27	28

Nowcasting techniques and early estimation of Europen aggregates

As previously noted, the target is to provide users with initial estimates before the results of the usual calculations for the indicator are available. This problem has of course numerous similarities with retrapolation issues, and with general forecasting as well. Thus, the reference statistical background includes the class of univariate forecasting models, dynamic regression or transfer functions, VAR, and non-linear models.

Eurostat is currently working on a comparative analysis of these techniques for providing quick estimates. An important step in this project relates the Eurozone data to a US timetable: the project starts with the consideration that data on industrial production, GDP and producer prices are published considerably later in the Eurozone than in the United States (Table 1.3).

This project aims to explore whether by using auxiliary data available, it may be possible to produce estimates with the same timetable as the USA. In fact, it is always possible to produce estimates using modelling methods of one sort or other. The key question is whether estimates generated using plausible techniques are likely to be reliable enough to make Eurostat comfortable in releasing them, and users happy to use them. The main auxiliary variables available to the required timetable are the business survey results produced by DG ECFIN. They are published at the end of the month to which they relate and thus the estimates produced using them would be available with no delay. For the production of estimates of quarterly GDP growth two months' industrial production figures are available 15 days after the end of the quarter. These have been included in our data-set, so that the estimates of GDP would be available with a delay of 15 days. Use is also made of data on oil prices and the Eurozone real exchange rate available in real time. All possible models have been explored which could be constructed using relevant survey variables and the other auxiliary variables. The best performing model (identified by a standard statistical criterion) has been selected and used to make a prediction of one period ahead. The exercise has been repeated recursively in order to identify the performance of forecasts generated using the model which would have been selected at each point in time. The simulation has been conducted using the survey data as published. We have also looked at the performance of our models when the data are adjusted using Tramo-Seats, a widely-used seasonal adjustment package. The results are summarized in Table 1.4.

Starting from the institutional framework discussed above, and in the context of the general improvement of quarterly European accounts, Eurostat has recently

Table 1.4   Forecast errors for nowcasting

Variable	RMSE (%)		RMSE (%) of rolling quarterly estimates	
	Original data	Tramo-Seats	Original data	Tramo-Seats
Industrial production	0.61	0.61	0.35	0.35
GDP	0.33	0.27	–	–
Producer prices	0.22	0.22	0.12	0.12

developed a methodology for the compilation of a flash estimate of quarterly GDP for the Eurozone and the European Union at 45 days after the end of the reference quarter. The methodology has been developed on the basis of the results of a project on flash estimates coordinated and supervised by Eurostat in the framework of the European Union Fifth Research Programme (see Eurostat, 2003, for details).

An indirect approach to the compilation of the European GDP has been taken into consideration using member states data as a basis of constructing indicators. In order to assess the performance of the model, a simulation under real conditions has been carried out. The flash estimate figures for GDP of Germany, Italy, the Netherlands and the UK (and only recently Greece), usually available within 45 days from the end of the reference quarter, together with the indicators for France and Spain, have been used to produce a flash estimate of the European GDP under real conditions. The nowcasting performance of the models has been tested by comparing the flash estimation with the 'traditional' Eurostat estimations over nine quarters from 2000Q4 to 2002Q4, both for the Eurozone and the European Union. Results are quite satisfactory as far as quarterly growth rates are concerned, with a root-mean-squared error calculated by comparing the first Eurostat estimate (60–70 days) with the flash estimate equal to 0.04 per cent both for the Eurozone and the European Union. The success rate in predicting an acceleration/slowdown of growth is satisfactory: eight out of nine cases for both the Eurozone and the European Union (compared with the 60–70 days estimate). The forecasting performance remains almost unchanged when results are compared with the second and third release of Eurostat estimates (100 and 120 days). The model is also good in capturing annual growth rates: the root-mean-squared error calculated with respect to the first Eurostat estimate is around 0.10 per cent for both European aggregates and it becomes even smaller with respect to the second and third estimates.

Improving the informative content of the data

Here we consider areas for improvement of the informative content of the data released, most notably in the field of what is called 'data presentation and interpretation'. In this context we will consider seasonal adjustment and business cycle estimation issues.

Seasonal adjustment

The European Central Bank and Eurostat have recently presented specific reports – including recommendations – on seasonal adjustment. Two problems should be mentioned here. Firstly, Tramo-Seats and X12-Regarima are the software packages recommended in the reports. Empirical studies have shown that the choice of one or other method is not clear-cut and depends, amongst other things, on the characteristics of the series to be seasonally adjusted. Secondly, seasonal adjustment of European series, calculated by aggregating the national series, can in theory be carried out in four different ways: (a) seasonal adjustment of aggregated raw series (direct approach); (b) aggregation of seasonally adjusted national series (indirect approach); (c) aggregation of national series seasonally adjusted by the member states (mixed indirect approach) and (d) simultaneous seasonal adjustment of national series (multivariate approach).

Some empirical studies have shown that differences in multivariate versus univariate approaches are relatively small. The empirical results show that direct and indirect approaches produce equivalent results only under very restrictive assumptions, that is when no trading day or outlier correction is made, when the decomposition is additive, and no forecasts are produced (see Ladiray and Mazzi, 2003). In practice, such conditions are met rarely. Some criteria to discriminate between direct and indirect approach can be put forward: smoothness of seasonally adjusted series, minimization of revision errors, stability of the seasonal component, quality assessment of seasonal adjustment, analysis of the irregular component and out-of-sample forecast accuracy.

A comparison between the direct and the indirect approach has been presented by Ladiray and Mazzi (2003) with reference to the Eurozone GDP. The results obtained show that the direct approach produces smoother figures than the indirect one, and these estimates do not show significant evidence of residual seasonality in the irregular components. This comparative analysis will be extended to other relevant areas in order to assess a common seasonal adjustment strategy for Eurozone figures.

The direct approach seems to be preferred, in particular when estimation and nowcasting are carried out. However, the use of a direct approach implies the loss of additivity between national and Eurozone totals; users should be aware of this situation. From the producers' point of view, it is essential to monitor that Eurozone seasonally adjusted figures, obtained through a direct approach, deliver the very same message. The aggregation of national series seasonally adjusted by member states has the advantage that the additivity of seasonally adjusted series is guaranteed, but this is hampered by the fact that member states generally do not use the same method. Thus, the seasonally adjusted series for Europe are tainted by the use of different filters. It is highly recommended that member states move towards a harmonization of seasonal adjustment policies and practices. This implies not only a convergence of methods, but also several other aspects such as trading-day correction, revisions, consistency between seasonally adjusted and non-seasonally adjusted totals, and so on.

Table 1.5   Turning points in quarterly GDP for the
Eurozone, classical cycle

	Tramo-Seats		X12-Regarima	
	Direct	*Indirect*	*Direct*	*Indirect*
Through	1981Q1	1981Q1	1981Q1	1981Q1
Peak	1992Q3	1992Q1	1992Q1	1992Q1
Through	1993Q1	1993Q1	1993Q1	1993Q1
Peak	–	–	2001Q1	2001Q1
Through	–	–	2001Q3	2001Q4

Another important line of research is the role of seasonal adjustment in the measurement of the business cycle, from both the classical and the deviation cycle perspectives. Regarding the former, one could aim at evaluating the uncertainty in the detection of turning points arising from the application of different seasonal adjustment techniques and, possibly, different aggregation procedures. Concerning the latter point, one could investigate ways of assessing how and by how much different seasonal adjustments affect the level of output gap estimates. Another line for future research is the analysis of the combined effects on turning points identification of different seasonal adjustment and detrending techniques.

Preliminary results obtained within studies conducted by Eurostat show that the impact of seasonal adjustment can be substantial in the identification of turning points, as evidenced in Table 1.5. In particular, a complete cycle seems to be missing when Tramo-Seats is used instead of the X12-Regarima software, and some turning points are shifted using the indirect instead of the direct seasonal adjustment approach.

Another important aspect of seasonal adjustment, namely the performance and quality of different adjusting procedures when the series span a short time period, is at the core of another project recently started. In effect, most of the filters actually used for seasonal adjustment are asymmetric. Under these circumstances, quality statistics tend to be flawed by the use of a limited number of observations. It is widely recognized that seasonal adjustment should be performed using a sample period of at least five–six years, but unfortunately that is not the case in many real-life situations. In the context of the statistical activities carried out by Eurostat, raw infra-annual statistics seldom span a sample of more than 10 years. This situation can arise for a number of reasons, amongst them we cite breaks in the component (country-specific) series, changes in the base year for constant price evaluations, and changes in the definitions, sources and methods used for the compilation of the micro-aggregates. There is no doubt that future enlargements of the EU will be another important factor of risk in this respect. The project tries to shed some lights on the issue of the dependency of the results of seasonal adjustment on the length of infra-annual time series. The issue of seasonal adjustment/length of time series is under study with reference to both real (external trade statistics, national accounts, industrial production indices) and simulated data-sets. Preliminary results show that both seasonal adjustment programmes suffer for a deterioration of quality indicators for progressively shorter time series, but that this deterioration is (fortunately) less severe at the end of the series, the most scrutinized by users.

Business cycle estimation, dating and detection of turning points

The business cycle has an importance in popular debate which can tend to run ahead of the problems in measuring it. For example, before discussing whether there is a European business cycle, or whether output is above or below its trend, we must confront the logically prior step of the appropriate way of measuring the business cycle or, equivalently, the trend level of output.

Business cycle analysis has thus developed into a prominent sub-discipline and, accordingly, there is a vast literature on the subject. Among the variety of different questions that have been treated in this context, two important ones stand out, namely how a cycle should be extracted from a given data series and, more generally, how the turning points of the cycle should be identified. Many different measures of the business cycle have been proposed in the literature. Indeed, there is a fundamental dichotomy between so-called 'growth' and 'classical' business cycles. Eurostat recently turned its attention to two questions: (a) is there a European business cycle, and how do national business cycles relate to this; and (b) how should we measure the 'output-gap', that is the difference between actual and potential output?

Regarding the analysis of synchronization of business cycles, an eclectic approach has been taken within the current debate considering a range of different measures of the business cycle. These measures are assumed to be complementary in the sense that they may all provide relevant information about the state of the business cycle. A comparison has been carried out among the complementary measures of the business cycle in an empirical application to the Eurozone business cycle. It is important to reconsider the question of Eurozone convergence as the literature has not yet reached a consensus on whether Eurozone business cycles have converged. Differences are explained in part by the use of different data, but other reasons include the use of different methods of both identifying business cycles and gauging convergence.

The starting point is the controversy initiated by Artis and Zhang (1997, 1999) and Inklaar and de Haan (2001). While Artis and Zhang (1997, 1999) conclude that European business cycles have become more synchronized, Inklaar and de Haan (2001), using the same but updated data, reach the opposite conclusion. The evidence that sparked this controversy has been reconsidered and in so doing some important stylized facts about the nature of the Eurozone business cycle have been assessed. The work has been characterized by the following five developments.

1 Using the same raw data as Artis-Zhang and Inklaar–de Haan, again appropriately updated, one can identify business cycles using a range of trend-cycle decompositions, as well as by parametric and nonparametric turning point

rules. This is in contrast to the selective de-trending methods considered by Artis-Zhang and Inklaar–de Haan. This lets us ascertain whether inference on convergence is contingent on the measure of the cycle.

2 In order to test whether Eurozone business cycles actually have converged, and there is evidence for a common cycle, the distribution of bivariate correlation coefficients between the 12 countries' business cycles has been analysed. This extends previous work that has tested for convergence in a similar manner by focusing on correlation, but has not considered the entire distribution, instead focusing on the mean correlation coefficient or particular bivariate correlation coefficients. The distribution-based measure of convergence is related to the economic growth literature, specifically the concepts of β and σ convergence; see Quah (1993, 1996).

3 Since one can imagine the situation where Eurozone business cycles, for example, are uncorrelated but are moving 'closer' together, due to less pronounced cyclical volatility, the further step consisted in the examination of whether Eurozone business cycles have moved closer together over time. Specifically, a measure of closeness the root-mean-squared difference between the Eurozone growth business cycles is proposed, expressed as a percentage of potential or trend output.

4 The evolution of the estimates over time using a series of rolling windows has been considered, rather than just two or four windows of fixed width as in Artis-Zhang and Inklaar–de Haan.

5 A measure of uncertainty associated with our estimates has been provided by estimating the correlation coefficients using a generalized method of moments estimation.

The empirical findings about the Eurozone are that, although empirical inference about individual Eurozone business cycles is found to be sensitive to the measure of the business cycle considered, the proposed measure of convergence between the Eurozone business cycles exhibits common features across the alternative measures of the business cycle. Interestingly, it is found that there have been periods of convergence, identified by the distribution tending to unity, and periods of divergence. Although further data are required to corroborate the story, there is evidence to suggest that the Eurozone entered a period of convergence after the clear period of divergence in the early 1990s in the aftermath of German unification and at the time of the currency crises in Europe. This is encouraging for the successful operation of a common monetary policy in the Eurozone.

Regarding the question of how we should measure the 'output-gap', that is the difference between actual and potential output, both multivariate and univariate measures of the output gap have been considered. It is widely recognized that multivariate estimators offer a more economic interpretation to the output gap as they essentially combine the estimators of the growth cycle with additional economic information. The Phillips Curve, for example, suggests that inflation data contain information about the output gap while Okun's Law suggests unemployment is important. These economic variables may contain useful

Table 1.6   The correlation of real-time estimates with final estimates

Model	Correlation
Hodrick–Prescott	0.273
Univariate unobserved components	0.179
Bivariate unobserved components	0.457
Bivariate Hodrick–Prescott	0.688
Trivariate unobserved components	0.455
SVAR – no cointegration	0.901 and 0.153
SVAR – cointegration	0.575

information about the supply side of the economy and the stage of the business cycle. Three multivariate models have been analysed: (1) unobserved components models, (2) Hodrick–Prescott models, and (3) structural VAR models. A simulated out-of-sample experiment has been used in this context to analyse the real-time performance of these alternative output gap estimators, as well as some representative univariate estimators. The real-time behaviour of output gap estimates is of importance given that policy-makers require estimates in real-time. Across a range of widely used univariate and multivariate estimators of the output gap we have found significant differences between real-time and final output gap estimates for the Eurozone – real-time estimates are unreliable. As the future becomes the present, output gap estimates are revised. It is not just in the USA that real-time measurement of the output gap is difficult. Nevertheless, the change from univariate to multivariate measures of the output gap does lead to real-time estimates better correlated with the final estimates. Adding 'economic information' appears to help. The correlation of two univariate and five multivariate estimators of the output gap computed in real-time against the final estimates is summarized in Table 1.6. Note that even for a given measure the correlation is sensitive to the specification chosen. This is illustrated for the SVAR with no cointegration where two numbers are reported, the first for a VAR with lag order one, the second for a higher-order VAR: SVAR estimates of the output gap are sensitive to the lag order chosen. An important finding is that a low lag order, as is typically selected by information criteria such as the BIC, can lead to implausible looking output gap estimates. Given the unreliability of real-time output gap estimates for the Eurozone, this begs the question, should we be surprised by this unreliability? As forecasters know, the fact that forecasts are wrong does not mean they are misleading or useless. If within the bounds of what was expected the forecast can remain useful, similarly for output gap estimates which we view analogously to a forecast.

To capture fully the uncertainty associated with the real-time estimates, or forecasts, of the output gap, density forecasts have been constructed. Density forecasts of the realization of a random variable at some future point in time provide an estimate of the probability distribution of the possible future values of that variable. Two approaches have been used to construct density estimates of the output gap in real time. The first relies on a state-space representation for the output gap estimator, while the second quantifies the degree of uncertainty through forecasting. One important finding is that the real-time measures of uncertainty do not prove to offer reliable indications of the degree of uncertainty associated with real-time estimates. This provides a serious challenge to users of output gap estimates.

Finally, given that output gap estimates are frequently used to forecast inflation, one could examine whether the unreliability of output gap estimates in real-time impacts upon the quality of forecasts. In this respect it has been found that, although real-time output gap estimates often have little forecasting power over inflation relative to simple autoregressive alternatives, this does not appear to be due to the unreliability of output gap estimates but rather the difficulties of forecasting inflation *per se.*

An application of the multivariate Hodrick–Prescott (HPMV) filter to estimation of the Eurozone output gap has been also carried out. The analysis investigates the impact of using alternative economic relationships on the output gap estimates of the Eurozone. Comparison with the univariate HP filter shows that this can significantly modify the appreciation of the output gap level of the Eurozone in some specific periods. The study also proposes to estimate the HPMV models with the methodology adopted for the estimation of state-space models. This strategy provides an alternative to the calibration of the parameters and allows us to assess the reliability of the HPMV output gap estimates. Estimated weights associated to the economic relationships in the optimization program of the HPMV are generally coherent with the calibrated values usually retained in the literature. The assessment of the reliability of the alternative output gaps and of the revision properties have shown a substantial superiority of some HPMV models over the univariate HP filter. Another important finding of this project is that the integration of macro-economic information generally improves the accuracy of the inflation forecasts.

In another project, an analytical framework for the estimation of potential output and output gaps for the Eurozone is used by combining multivariate filtering techniques with the production function approach. The potential advantage of this methodology consists in combining a model-based approach to estimate potential output with explicit statistical assumptions concerning the estimation of the potential values of the components of the production function.

The need for a cycle turning-point chronology is now widely recognized by experts and practitioners of economic analysis. As an example of application, it may help to compare the cycles among countries or to point out the links between the cycles and diverse macroeconomic aggregates. However, it turns out that the most important use of the turning-point chronology consists in establishing a reference cycle dating for a given country or an economic area. Regarding the USA, the NBER's Business Cycle Dating Committee is widely recognized as the authority for determining peaks and troughs in the classical business cycle. In other

Table 1.7   Turning-point chronology

Phase	Industrial production		GDP	
	Class. cycle	*Growth cycle*	*Class. cycle*	*Growth cycle*
Trough		1971M11		
Peak	1974M4	1974M1	1974Q2	1974Q1
Trough	1975M5	1975M6	1975Q1	1975Q3
Peak		1976M11		1977Q1
Trough		1978M3		1978Q2
Peak	1980M2	1980M2	1980Q1	1979Q4
Trough	1981M1	1981M1	1980Q4	1981Q1
Peak	1981M10	1981M10	1981Q4	1981Q4
Peak			1982Q4	
Trough	1982M12	1982M12		1982Q2
Peak		1985M11		1986Q1
Trough		1987M10		1987Q2
Peak	1992M1	1992M1	1992Q1	1992Q1
Trough	1993M5	1993M6	1993Q1	1993Q3
Peak		1995M2		1995Q1
Trough		1996M10		1996Q4
Peak		1998M2		1998Q1
Trough		1999M4		1999Q1
Peak	2000M12	2000M11		2000Q3
Trough	2001M12			

countries, in our context in the Eurozone, there is no official dating of business cycles, and therefore reference dates which could be considered as a benchmark are not available for theoretical and empirical studies.

The definition of a turning point chronology is now a central theme for Eurostat, which some years ago started a project aimed at identifying turning points for a number of key indicators of economic activity.

A comparison has been made among different methods for identification of turning points, namely univariate *versus* multivariate methods and parametric *versus* non parametric approaches. Further, the effects of aggregation and seasonal adjustment and the detrending methods used have been studied in great detail by applying the various procedures to the Industrial Production, GDP and Employment data. The preliminary chronology, extended to both classical and growth cycles, is synthesized for the Eurozone in Table 1.7.

Conclusions

The availability of good quality Eurozone statistics is essential for the coordination of economic policies, the assessment of convergence, and the conduct of monetary and fiscal policies. This particularly applies to infra-annual macroeconomic statistics which represent a key instrument for business cycle analyses and short-term economic interventions. Over recent years the Commission, the Council, the ECB and the ESS as a whole have made substantial improvements to the quality of statistics, notably with respect to comparability, coverage, timeliness and coherence. However, the limitations of the actual procedures for calculating European aggregates are evident, especially where data freshness and revisions are concerned. There is a risk that the enlargement of the European Union and the Eurozone could aggravate these problems in the near future. The use of econometric models in response to economists' needs for business cycle analyses offers an interesting and promising complement to traditional methods.

The quality of the Euro-IND database of Eurostat has shown a marked improvement thanks to the help of many users and researchers. At the moment, tremendous efforts are being made to cut the time it takes to supply national and European data. The Eurostat methodological projects are still in a start-up phase, but concrete results have been achieved and now await routine application to everyday statistical life. The organization of an annual Colloquium on the business cycle can be viewed in this context. In addition, several studies have been launched in various relevant fields. Eurostat plans to make rapid progress on the various subjects referred to in this chapter, and to do so with an open mind and with a genuine desire for transparency.

Several of the results presented in the chapter, such as back recalculation and flash estimates as well as estimates of high-frequency data, could become with only a short delay an integral part of the Eurostat production and dissemination system. Other results, such as estimation of output gaps and turning-points chronology, could represent a useful starting point in an open and constructive discussion with our economic partners, such as the DG ECFIN and ECB. Several projects need to be further developed, namely the definition of harmonized policies for seasonal adjustment, data revision and estimation. More sophisticated research such as estimation of multivariate leading indicators, construction of a multivariate chronology of turning points and real-time detection of turning points need further development. The extension of convergence and synchronization studies also represents an activity to which Eurostat is giving high priority. Most of the tools recently developed by Eurostat could be fruitfully used by member states to improve their statistical production and to enhance the informative content of short-term statistics.

Users will have a major role to play in improving our European system of infra-annual indicators. The success of all these approaches will depend to a large extent on the full cooperation and active participation of member states, research centres and academics. In the medium–long term, for the European Statistical System to become a centre of excellence a quantum leap is needed. This will be best achieved, *inter alia*, through implementing the First for Europe Principle with member states focusing on the provision of the information required for compiling timely and high quality European statistics.

References

Artis, M. and Zhang, W. (1997) 'International business cycle and the ERM: is there a European business cycle?', *International Journal of Finance and Economics*, 2: 1–16.

Artis, M. and Zhang, W. (1999) 'Further evidence on the international business cycle and the ERM: is there a European business cycle?', *Oxford Economic Papers*, 51: 120–32.

Astolfi, R., Ladiray, D., Mazzi, G.L., Sartori, F. and Soares, R. (2002) 'A monthly indicator of GDP for the Euro-zone', *Working Papers and Studies*, Luxembourg: European Commission.

Di Fonzo, T. (2003) 'Temporal disaggregation using related series: log-transformation and dynamic extension', *Rivista Internazionale di Scienze Economiche e Commerciali*, 50: 371–400.

Durbin, J. and Quenneville, B. (1997) 'Benchmarking by state space models', *International Statistical Review*, 65: 23–48.

Eurostat (1999) *Handbook on Quarterly National Accounts*, Methods and Nomenclatures, Theme 2. Luxembourg: European Commission.

Eurostat (2003) *Flash Estimation of the Quarterly Gross Domestic Product for the Euro-zone and the European Union: Eurostat Methodology*, Methods and Nomenclatures, Theme 2. Luxembourg: European Commission.

Gudmundsson, G. (1999) 'Disaggregation of annual flow data with multiplicative trend', *Journal of Forecasting*, 18: 33–7.

Harvey, A.C. (1989) *Forecasting, Structural Time Series Models and the Kalman Filter*. Cambridge: Cambridge University Press.

Harvey, A.C. and Chung, C. (2000) 'Estimating the underlying change in unemployment in the UK', *Journal of the Royal Statistical Society Series A*, 163: 303–39.

Harvey, A.C. and Pierce, R.G. (1984) 'Estimating missing observations in economic time series', *Journal of the American Statistical Association*, 79: 125–31.

Hotta, L.K. and Vasconcellos, K.L. (1999) 'Aggregation and disaggregation of structural time series models', *Journal of Time Series Analysis*, 20: 155–71.

Inklaar, R. and de Haan, J. (2001) 'Is there really a European business cycle? A comment', *Oxford Economic Papers*, 53: 215–20.

Ladiray, D. and Mazzi, G.L. (2003) 'Seasonal adjustment of European aggregates: direct versus indirect approach', in M. Manna and R. Peronaci (eds), *Seasonal Adjustment*. Frankfurt am Main: European Central Bank, 37–65.

Ladiray, D. and Mazzi, G.L. (2003) 'Common factor versus Baxter–King cycle in the Euro-zone', *Working Papers and Studies*. Luxembourg: European Commission.

Mazzi, G.L. and Savio, G. (2003) 'Statistical analysis of cyclical fluctuations: the role of official statisticians', *Working Papers and Studies*. Luxembourg: European Commission.

Mitchell, J., Smith, R.J., Weale, M.R., Wright, S. and Salazar, E.L. (2005) 'An indicator of monthly GDP and an early estimate of quarterly GDP growth', *The Economic Journal F 115*, F108–29.

Moauro, F. and Proietti, T. (2005) 'Temporal disaggregation and seasonal adjustment', Paper presented at the joint Eurostat–OECD Workshop on *Frontiers in Benchmarking Techniques and their Application to Official Statistics*, 7–8 April, Luxembourg.

Moauro, F. and Savio, G. (2005) 'Temporal disaggregation using multivariate structural time series models', *The Econometrics Journal*, 8: 214–34.

Proietti, T. (1999) 'Distribution and interpolation revisited: a structural approach', *Statistica*, 58: 411–32.

Proietti, T. (2004) 'On the estimation of nonlinearly aggregated mixed models', *Working Papers and Studies*. Luxembourg: European Commission.

Quah, D. (1993) 'Galton's fallacy and tests of the convergence hypothesis', *Scandinavian Journal of Economics*, 95: 427–43.

Quah, D. (1996) 'Empirics for economic growth and convergence', *European Economic Review*, 40: 1353–75.

Santos Silva, J.M.C. and Cardoso, F.N. (2001) 'The Chow–Lin method using dynamic models', *Economic Modelling*, 18: 269–80.

Part II

Multivariate Statistical Methods and Recent Advances in Business Cycle Analysis

2
Bayesian Inference on Dynamic Models with Latent Factors

Monica Billio, Roberto Casarin and Domenico Sartore

Introduction

In time series analysis, latent factors are often introduced to model the heterogeneous time evolution of the observed processes. The presence of unobserved components makes the maximum likelihood estimation method more difficult to apply. A Bayesian approach can sometimes be preferable since it allows us to treat general state space models and makes the simulation-based approach to parameters estimation and latent factors filtering easier. The chapter examines economic time series models in a Bayesian perspective focusing, through some examples, on the extraction of the business cycle components. We briefly review some general univariate Bayesian dynamic models and discuss the simulation based techniques, such as Gibbs sampling and adaptive importance sampling, and finally suggest the use of the particle filter for parameter estimation and latent factor extraction.

The analysis of dynamic phenomena is a common problem to many fields like engineering, physics, biology, statistics and econometrics. A time varying system can be represented through a *dynamic model*, defined by an observable component and an unobservable state. The hidden state vector represents the desired information that we want to extrapolate from the observations.

In the literature on business cycle analysis, dynamic models are used to capture two well known features of the economic cycle: comovement and asymmetry. Asymmetry denotes an heterogeneous dynamics of the economic variable. If the behaviour of the economic time series depends on the phase of the economic cycle, then asymmetry arises. To capture asymmetry Goldfeld and Quandt (1973) introduced Markov Switching (MS) models for serially uncorrelated data, while Hamilton (1989) applies MS to serially correlated time series. In these models parameters are allowed to depend on the hidden state, representing the economic cycle.

The state usually assumes two values, interpreted as either a positive growth trend as a negative growth trend.

All above cited approaches, and in particular the original work of Hamilton (1989), have been successively extended in many directions. Kim (1994) applies MS to a dynamic linear model, Kim and Nelson (1999) analyse general MS dynamic models and provide Bayesian inference tools together with Markov chain Monte Carlo (MCMC) simulation techniques. Kim and Murray (2001) and Anas and Ferrara (2004) suggest dividing the business cycle into three phases: recession, high-growth and normal-growth. Another kind of extension concerns the duration of the phases of the business cycle, for example Sichel (1991), Watson (1994) and Diebold and Rudebusch (1996) assume that the transition probability of the Markov chain depends on the duration of the current phase of the cycle. Finally, multivariate extensions have been suggested by Diebold and Rudebusch (1996) and Krolzig (1997).

The seminal work of Kalman (1960) and Kalman and Bucy (1960) introduces filtering techniques (Kalman–Bucy filter) for continuous valued, linear and Gaussian dynamic systems. Harvey (1989) extensively studies state space representation of dynamic models for time series and treats the use of the Kalman filter for states and parameters estimation. Hamilton (1989) introduces a filter (Hamilton–Kitagawa filter) for discrete time and discrete valued dynamic systems with a finite number of states. Bauwens, Lubrano and Richard (1999) compare maximum likelihood inference with Bayesian inference on static and dynamic econometric models. Harrison and West (1997) treat the problem of the dynamic model estimation in a Bayesian perspective. Kim and Nelson (1999) analyse Monte Carlo simulation methods for non-linear discrete valued (MS) models. Recently, Durbin and Koopman (2001) propose an updated review on MCMC methods for the estimation of general dynamic models, with both a Bayesian and a maximum likelihood approach. The main aim of this chapter is to suggest the use of sequential simulation methods for filtering and smoothing in business cycle dynamic models. These methods have been recently developed to overcome some problems of the traditional MCMC methods. As pointed out by Liu and Chen (1998), the Gibbs sampler is less attractive when considering on-line data processing. Furthermore, the Gibbs sampler may be inefficient when simulated states are very sticky and the sampler has difficulties in moving in the state space. In these situations, the use of sequential Monte Carlo techniques and in particular of particle filter algorithms may be more efficient. Doucet, Freitas and Gordon (2001) provide the state of the art on sequential Monte Carlo methods and discuss both applications and theoretical convergence results for these algorithms, with special attention to particle filters.

The chapter is structured as follows. The next section introduces the general representation of a dynamic model in a Bayesian framework and deals with conditionally normal linear models. We then review simulation-based methods, including MCMC methods, an adaptive importance sampling algorithm, and particle filter algorithms. The final sections provide an application of the particle filter to business cycle models and a conclusion.

Bayesian dynamic models

We consider a quite general formulation of a probabilistic *dynamic model* and review some fundamental relations for Bayesian inference on it. This definition includes time series models analysed in Kalman (1960), Hamilton (1989), Harrison and West (1997) and in Doucet, Freitas and Gordon (2001).

We denote $\{x_t; t \in \mathbb{N}\}, x_t \in \mathcal{X}$, the hidden state vectors of the system, $\{y_t; t \in \mathbb{N}_0\}, y_t \in \mathcal{Y}$, the observable variables and $\theta \in \Theta$ the parameter vector. We assume that the state space, observation space and parameter space are $\mathcal{X} \subset \mathbb{R}^{n_x}, \mathcal{Y} \subset \mathbb{R}^{n_y}$ and $\Theta \subset \mathbb{R}^{n_\theta}$, respectively. n_x, n_y and n_θ represent the dimensions of the state, observable variable and parameter vectors. This general Bayesian state space representation accounts also for nonlinear and non-Gaussian components and is given by an *initial distribution* $p(x_0|\theta)$, a *measurement density* $p(y_t|x_t, y_{1:t-1}, \theta)$ and a *transition density* $p(x_t|x_{0:t-1}, y_{1:t-1}, \theta)$:

$$y_t \sim p(y_t|x_t, y_{1:t-1}, \theta) \tag{2.1}$$

$$x_t \sim p(x_t|x_{0:t-1}, y_{1:t-1}, \theta) \tag{2.2}$$

$$x_0 \sim p(x_0|\theta), \quad \text{with } t = 1, \ldots, T \tag{2.3}$$

where $p(x_0|\theta)$ can be interpreted as the prior distribution on the initial state of the system. By $x_{0:t} \triangleq (x_0, \ldots, x_t)$ we denote the collection of vectors up to time t, while by $x_{-t} \triangleq (x_0, \ldots, x_{t-1}, x_{t+1}, \ldots, x_T)$ we denote the collection of all the vectors without the t-th element.

If the transition density depends on the past only through the last value of the hidden state vector, the dynamic model is defined as *Markovian* of the first-order, that is:

$$(y_t|x_t) \sim p(y_t|x_t, y_{1:t-1}, \theta) \tag{2.4}$$

$$(x_t|x_{t-1}) \sim p(x_t|x_{t-1}, y_{1:t-1}, \theta) \tag{2.5}$$

$$x_0 \sim p(x_0|\theta), \quad \text{with } t = 1, \ldots, T \tag{2.6}$$

The first-order Markov property is not restrictive because a Markov model of order p can always be rewritten as a first-order Markovian model.

Let us now see the three main issues necessary for inference: filtering, prediction and smoothing.

State estimation

We are interested in estimating the density $p(x_t|y_{1:s}, \theta)$ when parameters are known. If $t = s$ the density of interest is called the *filtering density*, if $t < s$ it is called the *smoothing density* and if $t > s$ it is called the *prediction density*. We assume that at time t the density $p(x_{t-1}|y_{1:t-1}, \theta)$ is known.[1] By applying the Chapman–Kolmogorov transition density, we obtain the one-step-ahead *prediction density*:

$$p(x_t|y_{1:t-1}, \theta) = \int_{\mathcal{X}} p(x_t|x_{t-1}, y_{1:t-1}, \theta)p(x_{t-1}|y_{1:t-1}, \theta)dx_{t-1}$$

When a new observation $\mathbf{y}_t$ becomes available, using the Bayes theorem, it is possible to update the prediction density and to filter the current state of the system. The *filtering density* is:

$$p(\mathbf{x}_t|\mathbf{y}_{1:t},\theta) = \frac{p(\mathbf{y}_t,\mathbf{x}_t|\mathbf{y}_{1:t-1},\theta)}{p(\mathbf{y}_t|\mathbf{y}_{1:t-1},\theta)} = \frac{p(\mathbf{y}_t|\mathbf{x}_t,\mathbf{y}_{1:t-1},\theta)p(\mathbf{x}_t|\mathbf{y}_{1:t-1},\theta)}{\int_{\mathcal{X}} p(\mathbf{y}_t|\mathbf{x}_t,\mathbf{y}_{1:t-1},\theta)p(\mathbf{x}_t|\mathbf{y}_{1:t-1},\theta)d\mathbf{x}_t}$$

where $p(\mathbf{x}_t|\mathbf{y}_{1:t-1},\theta)$ is the prediction density obtained at the previous step.

At each date t, it is possible to determine the *K-steps-ahead prediction density* of the state vector, conditional on the available information $\mathbf{y}_{1:t}$. It can be evaluated iteratively, as follows:

$$\text{first step} \qquad p(\mathbf{x}_{t+1}|\mathbf{y}_{1:t},\theta) = \int_{\mathcal{X}} p(\mathbf{x}_{t+1}|\mathbf{x}_t,\mathbf{y}_{1:t},\theta)p(\mathbf{x}_t|\mathbf{y}_{1:t},\theta)d\mathbf{x}_t \qquad (2.7)$$

$$\text{k-th step} \quad p(\mathbf{x}_{t+k}|\mathbf{y}_{1:t},\theta) = \int_{\mathcal{X}} p(\mathbf{x}_{t+k}|\mathbf{x}_{t+k-1},\mathbf{y}_{1:t},\theta)p(\mathbf{x}_{t+k-1}|\mathbf{y}_{1:t},\theta)d\mathbf{x}_{t+k-1}$$

$$(2.8)$$

where

$$p(\mathbf{x}_{t+k}|\mathbf{x}_{t+k-1},\mathbf{y}_{1:t},\theta) = \int_{\mathcal{Y}^{k-1}} p(\mathbf{x}_{t+k}|\mathbf{x}_{t+k-1},\mathbf{y}_{1:t+k-1},\theta)p(d\mathbf{y}_{t+1:t+k-1}|\mathbf{y}_{1:t},\theta)$$

and $\mathcal{Y}^k = \otimes_{i=1}^k \mathcal{Y}_i$ is the k-times Cartesian product of the state space, with $k = 1,\ldots,K$. Similarly, the *K-steps-ahead prediction density* of the observable variable $\mathbf{y}_{t+K}$ conditional on the available information is determined as follows:

$$p(\mathbf{y}_{t+K}|\mathbf{y}_{1:t},\theta) = \int_{\mathcal{Y}} p(\mathbf{y}_{t+K}|\mathbf{x}_{t+K},\mathbf{y}_{1:t+K-1},\theta)p(d\mathbf{y}_{t+1:t+K-1}|\mathbf{y}_{1:t},\theta)p(d\mathbf{x}_{t+K}|\mathbf{y}_{1:t},\theta)$$

$$(2.9)$$

With general dynamics, due to the high number of integrals that must be solved, previous densities may be very difficult to evaluate. From a numerical point of view, simulation methods, like MCMC algorithms or particle filters, allow us to overcome these difficulties. From a modelling point of view, to obtain analytical relations we need to introduce some simplifying hypothesis on the dynamics of the variables. For example, if we assume that the evolution of the dynamic model does not depend on the past values of the observable variable $\mathbf{y}_{1:t}$, then equations (2.4), (2.5) and (2.6) become:

$$(\mathbf{y}_t|\mathbf{x}_t) \sim p(\mathbf{y}_t|\mathbf{x}_t,\theta) \qquad (2.10)$$

$$(\mathbf{x}_t|\mathbf{x}_{t-1}) \sim p(\mathbf{x}_t|\mathbf{x}_{t-1},\theta) \qquad (2.11)$$

$$x_0 \sim p(x_0|\theta), \quad \text{with } t = 1,\ldots,T \qquad (2.12)$$

The causality structure of this model is represented through the Directed Acyclic Graph (DAG) of Figure 2.1. Under the previous assumptions the filtering and

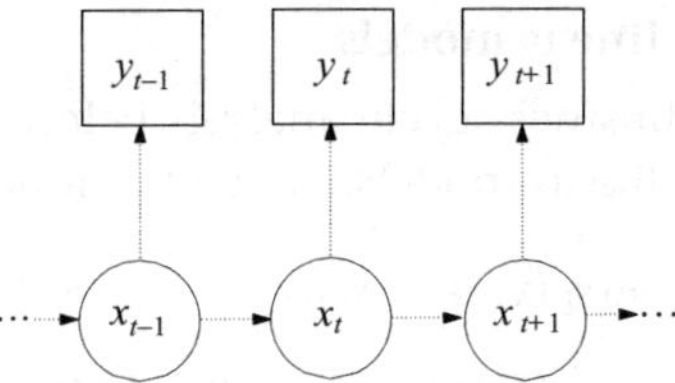

Figure 2.1   The causality structure of a Markov dynamic model with hidden states. A box indicates that the variable is known, while a circle indicates that the variable is hidden

prediction densities simplify as follows:

$$p(\mathbf{x}_t|\mathbf{y}_{1:t-1},\theta) = \int_{\mathcal{X}} p(\mathbf{x}_t|\mathbf{x}_{t-1},\theta)p(\mathbf{x}_{t-1}|\mathbf{y}_{1:t-1},\theta)d\mathbf{x}_{t-1} \tag{2.13}$$

$$p(\mathbf{x}_t|\mathbf{y}_{1:t},\theta) = \frac{p(\mathbf{y}_t|\mathbf{x}_t,\theta)p(\mathbf{x}_t|\mathbf{y}_{1:t-1},\theta)}{p(\mathbf{y}_t|\mathbf{y}_{0:t-1},\theta)} \tag{2.14}$$

$$p(\mathbf{x}_{t+K}|\mathbf{y}_{1:t},\theta) = \int_{\mathcal{X}} p(\mathbf{x}_{t+K}|\mathbf{x}_{t+K-1},\theta)p(\mathbf{x}_{t+K-1}|\mathbf{y}_{1:t},\theta)d\mathbf{x}_{t+K-1} \tag{2.15}$$

$$p(\mathbf{y}_{t+K}|\mathbf{y}_{1:t},\theta) = \int_{\mathcal{X}} p(\mathbf{y}_{t+K}|\mathbf{x}_{t+K},\theta)p(\mathbf{x}_{t+K}|\mathbf{y}_{1:t},\theta)d\mathbf{x}_{t+K} \tag{2.16}$$

We conclude this section with two important recursive relations, both of which can be proved starting from the definition of joint smoothing density and assuming that the Markov property holds. The first relation is the sequential filtering equation:

$$p(\mathbf{x}_{0:T}|\mathbf{y}_{1:T},\theta) = p(\mathbf{x}_{0:T-1}|\mathbf{y}_{1:T-1},\theta)\frac{p(\mathbf{y}_T|\mathbf{x}_T,\theta)p(\mathbf{x}_T|\mathbf{x}_{T-1},\theta)}{p(\mathbf{y}_T|\mathbf{y}_{1:T-1},\theta)} \tag{2.17}$$

which is particularly useful when processing data sequentially and is fundamental in implementing particle filter algorithms. The second relation provides the factorization of the *smoothing density* of the state vectors given the information available at time T:

$$p(\mathbf{x}_{0:T}|\mathbf{y}_{1:T},\theta) = p(\mathbf{x}_T|\mathbf{y}_{1:T},\theta)\prod_{t=0}^{T-1} p(\mathbf{x}_t|\mathbf{x}_{t+1},\mathbf{y}_{1:t},\theta) \tag{2.18}$$

Note that the density $p(\mathbf{x}_t|\mathbf{x}_{t+1},\mathbf{y}_{1:t},\theta)$, which appears in the joint smoothing density, can be represented through the filtering and the prediction densities[2]:

$$p(\mathbf{x}_t|\mathbf{x}_{t+1},\mathbf{y}_{1:t},\theta) = \frac{p(\mathbf{x}_{t+1}|\mathbf{x}_t,\mathbf{y}_{1:t},\theta)p(\mathbf{x}_t|\mathbf{y}_{1:t},\theta)}{p(\mathbf{x}_{t+1}|\mathbf{y}_{1:t},\theta)} \tag{2.19}$$

This factorization of the smoothing density is also relevant when inference is carried out through simulation methods.[3] We now introduce an important class of dynamic models, which do not admit a tractable analytical representation of the filtering, prediction and smoothing densities. These are *conditional normal linear models* and are widely used in business cycle analysis (see Kim and Nelson (1999)).

Conditionally Gaussian linear models

Usually, models used in business cycle analysis belong to the class of the conditionally normal dynamic linear models, defined as follows:

$$\mathbf{y}_t = F(s_t)\mathbf{x}_t + V(s_t)\epsilon_t \qquad \epsilon_t \sim N(0, I)$$

$$\mathbf{x}_{t+1} = G(s_t)\mathbf{x}_t + W(s_t)\eta_t \quad \eta_t \sim N(0, I) \tag{2.20}$$

where ϵ_t is independent of η_t and s_t is a sequence of random variables. Harrison and West (1997) call this a multi-process model: in their classification, if $s_t = s_{t-1} = s$, $\forall t$ the model is a multi-process model of the first kind, while if s_t is a stochastic process it is a multi-process model of the second kind. Note that if s_t is a discrete time and finite state Markov chain with known transition probabilities, the model is also called a *jump Markov linear system* or *Markov switching linear model* with parameters evolving over time.

Example 1   The stochastic latent factor model with Markov switching. Economic phases can be represented through a Markov switching hidden process. Let y_t be the observable variable and x_t the latent factor. The switching model is:

$$y_t = \alpha x_t + \sigma_\epsilon \epsilon_t \qquad\qquad \epsilon_t \sim N(0, 1) \tag{2.21}$$

$$x_{t+1} = \mu(s_{t+1}) + \rho\, x_t + \sigma_\eta \eta_{t+1} \quad \eta_{t+1} \sim N(0, 1) \tag{2.22}$$

$$s_t \sim Markov(\mathbb{P}), \qquad\qquad \text{with } s_t \in \{0, 1\} \tag{2.23}$$

where $\mu(s_t) = \mu + \nu s_t$, $\mathbb{P}$ is the transition matrix and ε_t is independent of η_t $\forall t$.

This kind of model can be found in Kim and Nelson (1999). The absence of analytical filtering densities makes Bayesian-simulation-based inference a possible solution to the filtering problem. Figure 2.2 exhibits simulation paths of $1,000$ observations[4] of the Markov switching process, the latent factor and the observable variable, respectively.

Simulation-based filtering

In the following, we focus on the Bayesian approach and on simulation-based methods for nonlinear and non-Gaussian models. First, MCMC methods are reviewed, then some basic sequential Monte Carlo simulation methods are introduced. Mainly, we refer to sequential importance sampling algorithm and to more advanced sequential Monte Carlo algorithms called Particle Filters. Finally we investigate the problem of estimation of the parameter vector both in a Bayesian MCMC-based approach and in a sequential data-processing approach.

The Gibbs sampler

In previous sections we examined some estimation algorithms for filtering, predicting and smoothing the state vector of a quite general probabilistic dynamic model.

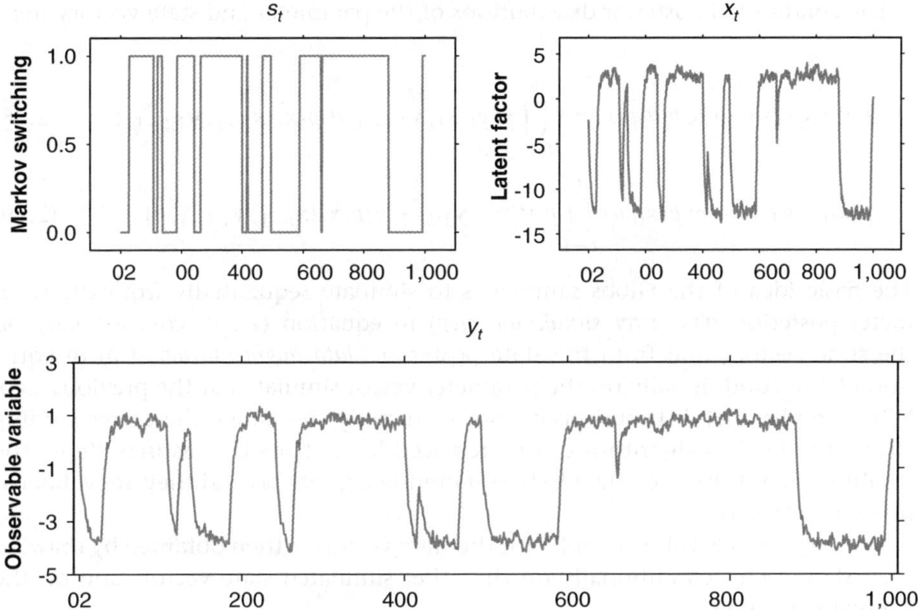

Figure 2.2   Simulation from the Markov switching stochastic trend model given in Example 1. Parameters are set to $\alpha = 0.3$, $\sigma_\varepsilon = 0.1$, $\rho = 0.8$, $\mu_0 = -2.5$, $\mu_1 = 0.5$, $\sigma_\eta = 0.1$, $p_{11} = 0.97$ and $p_{22} = 0.99$

To show how Gibbs sampling applies, we consider the following dynamic model:

$$(\mathbf{y}_t | \mathbf{x}_t) \sim p(\mathbf{y}_t | \mathbf{x}_t, \mathbf{y}_{1:t-1}, \theta) \tag{2.24}$$

$$(\mathbf{x}_t | \mathbf{x}_{t-1}) \sim p(\mathbf{x}_t | \mathbf{x}_{t-1}, \mathbf{y}_{1:t-1}, \theta) \tag{2.25}$$

$$x_0 \sim p(\mathbf{x}_0 | \theta) \tag{2.26}$$

$$\theta \sim p(\theta), \quad \text{with } t = 1, \ldots, T \tag{2.27}$$

The estimation problem is solved in a Bayesian perspective by evaluating the mean of the joint posterior density of the state and parameter vectors $p(\mathbf{x}_{0:T}, \theta | \mathbf{y}_{1:T})$. Tanner and Wong (1987) motivate this solution by the *data augmentation principle*, which consists in considering the hidden state vectors as nuisance parameters.

If an analytical evaluation of the posterior mean is not possible, then simulation methods and in particular MCMC apply. The most simple solution is to implement a *single-move* Gibbs sampler (see Carlin, Polson and Stoffer, 1992, and Harrison and West, 1997). This method generates the states one at a time using the Markov property of the dynamic model and conditional on the neighbouring states.

The conditional posterior distributions of the parameter and state vectors are:

$$p(\theta|\mathbf{x}_{0:T}, \mathbf{y}_{1:T}) \propto p(\theta)p(\mathbf{x}_0|\theta) \prod_{t=1}^{T} p(\mathbf{y}_t|\mathbf{x}_t, \mathbf{y}_{1:t-1}, \theta)p(\mathbf{x}_t|\mathbf{x}_{t-1}, \mathbf{y}_{1:t-1}, \theta) \qquad (2.28)$$

$$p(\mathbf{x}_{0:T}|\mathbf{y}_{1:T}, \theta) \propto p(\mathbf{x}_0|\theta) \prod_{t=1}^{T} p(\mathbf{y}_t|\mathbf{x}_t, \mathbf{y}_{1:t-1}, \theta)p(\mathbf{x}_t|\mathbf{x}_{t-1}, \mathbf{y}_{1:t-1}, \theta) \qquad (2.29)$$

The basic idea of the Gibbs sampler is to simulate sequentially from the parameter posterior (*parameter simulation step*) in equation (2.28), conditionally on the state vectors, and from the state posterior (*data augmentation step*) in equation (2.29), conditionally on the parameter vector simulated at the previous step. When conditional distributions cannot be directly simulated, the corresponding steps in the Gibbs algorithm can be replaced by Metropolis–Hastings steps. The resulting algorithms are called hybrid sampling algorithms and they are validated in Tierney (1994).

The single-move Gibbs sampler for the state vectors is then obtained by drawing each state vector conditionally on the other simulated state vectors and on the simulated parameter vector.

Altorithm 1: Single-move Gibbs sampler

(i) Simulate $\theta^{(i)}$ through a generic Gibbs sampler; and (ii) given $\theta^{(i)}$ and $\mathbf{x}_{0:T}^{(i)}$, simulate state vectors as follows:

1 $\mathbf{x}_0^{(i+1)} \sim p(\mathbf{x}_0|\mathbf{x}_{2:T}^{(i)}, \mathbf{y}_{1:T}, \theta^{(i+1)})$
2 $\mathbf{x}_1^{(i+1)} \sim p(\mathbf{x}_1|\mathbf{x}_0^{(i+1)}, \mathbf{x}_{2:T}^{(i)}, \mathbf{y}_{1:T}, \theta^{(i+1)})$
3 ...
4 $\mathbf{x}_T^{(i+1)} \sim p(\mathbf{x}_T|\mathbf{x}_{0:T-1}^{(i+1)}, \mathbf{y}_{1:T}, \theta^{(i+1)})$

The single-move algorithm can be implemented for general dynamic models. Moreover, note that the dynamic model given in equations (2.24)–(2.27) satisfies the Markov property. In this case the full posterior density of the state vector, given in the single-move Gibbs sampler (see Algorithm 1), is simply:

$$p(\mathbf{x}_t|\mathbf{x}_{-t}, \mathbf{y}_{1:T}, \theta) \propto p(\mathbf{y}_t|\mathbf{x}_t, \mathbf{y}_{1:t-1}, \theta)p(\mathbf{x}_t|\mathbf{x}_{t-1}, \mathbf{y}_{1:t-1}, \theta)p(\mathbf{x}_{t+1}|\mathbf{x}_t, \mathbf{y}_{1:t}, \theta) \quad (2.30)$$

and the implementation of the algorithm becomes easier. For a proof see Billio, Casarin and Sartore (2004).

Although the simplification due to the Markov property makes the single-move Gibbs sampler easier to implement, some problems arise. In particular, the Markovian dependence between neighbouring states generates correlation between outputs of the Gibbs sampler and leads to slower convergence to the posterior distribution (see Carter and Köhn, 1994). As a consequence, if an adaptive importance sampling is carried out by running parallel single-move Gibbs samplers, the number of replications before convergence of the parameter estimates could be very high.

A general method to solve this autocorrelation problem in the output of the Gibbs sampler is to group parameters (or states) and to simulate them simultaneously. This idea has been independently applied by Carter and Köhn (1994) and by Frühwirth-Schnatter (1994) to dynamic models and the resulting algorithm is the multi-move Gibbs sampler. The main idea of this method is to simultaneously generate all the state vectors using analytical filtering and smoothing relations. Their approach is less general than that of Carlin, Polson and Stoffer (1992), but for linear dynamic models with Gaussian mixture innovations in the observation equation, it is more efficient. In particular, the multi-move Gibbs sampler has a faster convergence to the posterior distribution and the posterior moment estimates have smaller variance. These results are supported theoretically by Liu, Wong and Kong (1995) and Müller (1992), who show that generating variables simultaneously produces faster convergence.[5] Furthermore, Frühwirth-Schnatter (1994) shows how the use of the multi-move Gibbs sampler improves the convergence rate of an adaptive importance sampling algorithm and makes a comparison with a set of parallel single-move Gibbs samplers.

The implementation of the multi-move Gibbs sampler depends on the availability of the analytical form of filtering and smoothing densities. We give here a general representation of the algorithm, but its implementation is strictly related to the specific dynamic model.

Altorithm 2: multi-move gibbs sampler

(i) Simulate $\theta^{(i)}$ through a generic Gibbs sampler; and (ii) Given $\theta^{(i)}$ and $\mathbf{x}_{0:T}^{(i)}$, run analytical filtering relations to estimate prediction and filtering densities for each $t = 0, \ldots, T$:

1 $\hat{p}(\mathbf{x}_t | \mathbf{y}_{1:t-1}, \theta^{(i+1)})$
2 $\hat{p}(\mathbf{x}_t | \mathbf{y}_{1:t}, \theta^{(i+1)})$

(iii) Simulate state vectors by means of the recursive factorization of the smoothing density:

1
3 $\mathbf{x}_T^{(i+1)} \sim p(\mathbf{x}_T | \mathbf{y}_{1:T}, \theta^{(i+1)})$
4 $\mathbf{x}_{T-1}^{(i+1)} \sim p(\mathbf{x}_{T-1} | \mathbf{x}_T^{(i+1)}, \mathbf{y}_{1:T-1}, \theta^{(i+1)})$
5 $\ldots$
6 $\mathbf{x}_1^{(i+1)} \sim p(\mathbf{x}_1 | \mathbf{x}_2^{(i+1)}, \mathbf{y}_1, \theta^{(i+1)})$

The algorithm has been derived through the recursive smoothing relation given in equation (2.18). Moreover, at each simulation step the posterior density is obtained by means of the estimated prediction and filtering densities. By applying the fundamental relation given in equation (2.19) we obtain:

$$p(\mathbf{x}_t | \mathbf{x}_{t+1}^{(i+1)}, \mathbf{y}_{1:t}, \theta^{(i+1)}) = \frac{p(\mathbf{x}_{t+1}^{(i+1)} | \mathbf{x}_t, \theta^{(i+1)}) \hat{p}(\mathbf{x}_t | \mathbf{y}_{1:t}, \theta^{(i+1)})}{\hat{p}(\mathbf{x}_{t+1}^{(i+1)} | \mathbf{y}_{1:t}, \theta^{(i+1)})} \tag{2.31}$$

We stress once more that the multi-move Gibbs sampler does not easily apply to nonlinear and non-Gaussian models. Thus in a MCMC approach, the single-move Gibbs sampler remains the only numerical solution to the estimation problem.

A sequential sampling approach represents another possible solution to this problem and sequential Monte Carlo algorithms allow us to make inference on general dynamic models.

Adaptive importance sampling

The adaptive sequential importance sampling scheme is a sequential stochastic simulation method which adapts progressively to the posterior distribution. It also uses the information contained in the samples which are simulated in the previous steps. The adaptation mechanism is based on the discrete posterior approximation and on the kernel density reconstruction of the prior and posterior densities. West (1992) proposed this technique to estimate parameters of static models. West (1993) and West and Harrison (1997) successively extended the method to estimate parameters and states of dynamic models.

The first key idea is to use importance sampling (see Casella and Robert (1999)) to obtain a weighted random grid of evaluation points in the state space. Let $\{x_t^i, w_t^i\}_{t=1}^{n_t}$ be a sample drawn from the posterior $p(x_t|y_{1:t}, \theta)$ through an importance density g_t. The prediction density, given in equation (2.13), can be approximated as follows:

$$p(x_{t+1}|y_{1:t}, \theta) \approx \sum_{i=1}^{n_t} w_t^i p(x_{t+1}|x_t^i, \theta) \tag{2.32}$$

Algorithm 3: adaptive sequential importance sampling

Given a weighted random sample $\{x_t^i, w_t^i\}_{t=1}^{n_t}$, for $i = 1, \ldots, n_t$:

1 Simulate $\tilde{x}_{t+1}^i \sim p(x_{t+1}|x_t^i, \theta)$
2 Calculate $m_t = \sum_{i=1}^{n_t} w_t^i \tilde{x}_{t+1}^i$, $V_t = \sum_{i=1}^{n_t} w_t^i (\tilde{x}_{t+1}^i - m_t)'(\tilde{x}_{t+1}^i - m_t)$
3 Generate from the Gaussian kernel $x_{t+1}^i \sim \sum_{i=1}^{n_t} w_t^i N(x_{t+1}|(m_t a + x_t^i(1 - a)), h^2 V_t)$
4 Update the weights $w_{t+1}^i \propto w_t^i \dfrac{p(y_{t+1}|x_{t+1}^i)p(x_{t+1}^i|x_t^i)}{N(x_{t+1}^i|(m_t a + (1-a)x_t^i), h^2 V_t)}$

The second key idea is to propagate points of the stochastic grid by means of the transition density and to build a smoothed approximation of the prior density. This approximation is obtained through a kernel density estimation. West (1993) suggested to use Gaussian or Student-t kernels due to their flexibility in approximating other densities. For example, the Gaussian kernel reconstruction is:

$$p(x_{t+1}|y_{1:t}, \theta) \approx \sum_{i=1}^{n_t} w_t^i N(x_{t+1}|m_t a + x_t^i(1 - a), h^2 V_t) \tag{2.33}$$

The final step of the algorithm consists in updating the prior density and in producing a random sample, $\{x_{t+1}^i, w_{t+1}^i\}_{i=1}^{n_{t+1}}$, from the resulting posterior density. The sample is obtained by using the kernel density estimate as importance density.

The main advantage of this algorithm lies in the smoothed reconstruction of the prior density. This kernel density estimate of the prior allows us to obtain adaptive importance densities and to avoid information loss, which comes from cumulating numerical approximation over time. However, adaptive importance sampling requires the calibration of parameters a and h, which determine the behaviour of the kernel density estimate. The choice of these shrinkage parameters influences the convergence of the algorithm and heavily depends on the complexity of the model.

Adaptive importance sampling belongs to a more general class of sequential simulation algorithms, called particle filters, which will be reviewed in the next section.

Particle filters

In the following we focus on Particle filters, also referred in the literature as Bootstrap filters, Interacting particle filters, Condensation algorithms or Monte Carlo filters and on the estimation of the states.[6]

Assume that the parameter vector, θ is known. At each step $t + 1$, as a new observation y_{t+1} becomes available, we are interested in predicting and filtering the hidden variables and the parameters. In particular, we want to approximate the prediction and filtering densities given in equations (2.13) and (2.14) by means of sequential Monte Carlo methods.

Assume that a weighted sample $\{x_t^i, w_t^i\}_{i=1}^N$ has been drawn from the filtering density at time t:

$$\hat{p}(x_t|y_{1:t}, \theta) = \sum_{i=1}^N w_t^i \delta_{\{x_t^i\}}(dx_t) \tag{2.34}$$

Each simulated value x_t^i is called *particle* and the particles set, $\{x_t^i, w_t^i\}_{i=1}^N$, can be viewed as a random discretization of the state space $\mathcal{X}$, with associated weights w_t^i. It is possible to approximate, by means of this particle set, the prediction density given in equation (2.13) as follows:

$$p(x_{t+1}|y_{1:t}, \theta) = \int_{\mathcal{X}} p(x_{t+1}|x_t, \theta)p(x_t|y_{1:t}, \theta)dx_t \simeq \sum_{i=1}^N w_t^i p(x_{t+1}|x_t^i, \theta) \tag{2.35}$$

which is called the *empirical prediction density* and is denoted by $\hat{p}(x_{t+1}|y_{1:t}, \theta)$. By applying the Chapman–Kolmogorov equation, it is also possible to obtain an approximation of the filtering density given in equation (2.14):

$$p(x_{t+1}|y_{1:t+1}, \theta) \propto p(y_{t+1}|x_{t+1}, \theta)p(x_{t+1}|y_{1:t}, \theta)$$

$$\simeq \sum_{i=1}^N p(y_{t+1}|x_{t+1}, \theta)p(x_{t+1}|x_t^i, \theta)w_t^i \tag{2.36}$$

which is called *empirical filtering density* and is denoted by $\hat{p}(x_{t+1}|y_{1:t+1}, \theta)$.

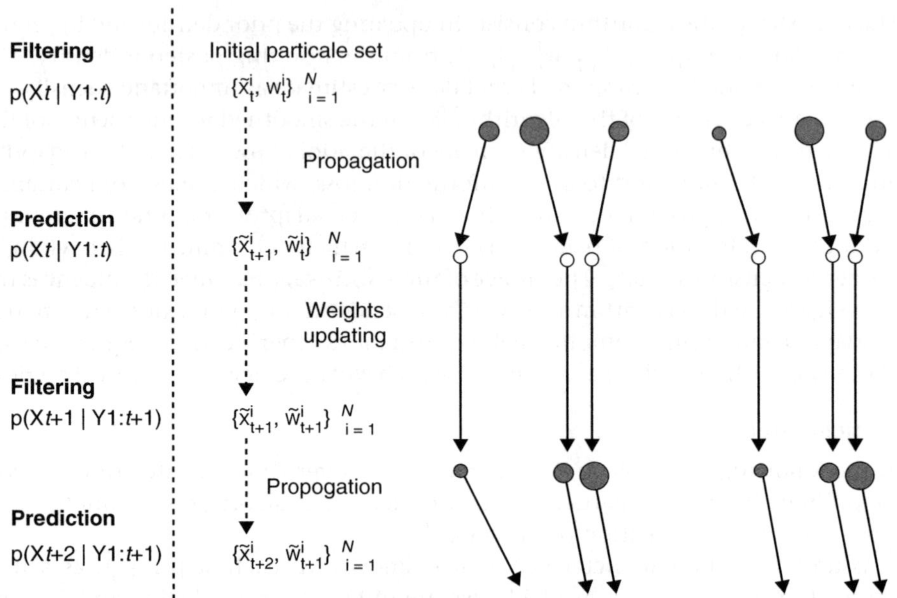

Figure 2.3   Evolution of the particle set in the Sequential Importance Sampling algorithm

Assume now that the quantity $\mathbb{E}(f(\mathbf{x}_{t+1})|\mathbf{y}_{1:t+1})$ is of interest. It can be numerically evaluated by a Monte Carlo sample $\{\mathbf{x}_{t+1}^i, w_{t+1}^i\}_{i=1}^N$, drawn from the filtering distribution:

$$\mathbb{E}(f(\mathbf{x}_{t+1})|\mathbf{y}_{1:t+1}) \simeq \frac{(1/N)\sum_{i=1}^N f(x_{t+1}^i)w_{t+1}^i}{(1/N)\sum_{i=1}^N w_{t+1}^i} \tag{2.37}$$

A simple way to obtain a weighted sample from the filtering density at time $t+1$ is to apply importance sampling to the empirical filtering density given in equation (2.36). This step corresponds to propagating the initial particle set (see Figure 2.3) through the importance density $q(\mathbf{x}_{t+1}|\mathbf{x}_t^i, \mathbf{y}_{t+1}, \theta)$. Moreover, if we propagate each particle through the transition density $p(\mathbf{x}_t|\mathbf{x}_{t-1}^i, \theta)$, then the particle weights update as follows:

$$w_{t+1}^i \propto \frac{p(\mathbf{y}_{t+1}|\mathbf{x}_{t+1}, \theta)p(\mathbf{x}_{t+1}|\mathbf{y}_{1:t}, \theta)w_t^i}{q(\mathbf{x}_{t+1}|\mathbf{x}_t^i, \mathbf{y}_{t+1}, \theta)} = w_t^i p(\mathbf{y}_{t+1}|\mathbf{x}_{t+1}^i, \theta) \tag{2.38}$$

This is the natural choice for the importance density, because the transition density represents a sort of prior at time t for the state x_{t+1}. However, as underlined in Pitt and Shephard (1999), this strategy is sensitive to outliers.[7] The basic particle filter developed through the previous equations is called *Sequential Importance Sampling* (SIS). In Algorithm 4, we give a pseudo-code representation of this method.

Sequential importance sampling permits us to obtain recursive updating of the particle weights and is based on the sequential decomposition of the joint filtering density and on a particular choice of the importance density. To highlight these aspects, we consider the smoothing density $p(x_{0:t+1}|y_{1:t+1}, \theta)$ of the state vectors and approximate it as follows:

$$p(x_{0:t+1}|y_{1:t+1}, \theta) \simeq \sum_{i=1}^{N} \tilde{w}_{t+1}^{i} \delta_{\{x_{0:t+1}^{i}\}}(dx_{0:t+1}) \qquad (2.39)$$

by simulating $\{x_{0:t+1}^{i}\}_{i=1}^{N}$ from a proposal distribution $q(x_{0:t}|y_{1:t}, \theta)$ and by correcting the weights of the resulting empirical density. The correction step comes from an importance sampling argument, thus the *unnormalized particle weights*[8] are defined as follows:

$$w_{t+1}^{i} \triangleq \frac{p(x_{0:t+1}^{i}|y_{1:t+1}, \theta)}{q(x_{0:t+1}^{i}|y_{1:t+1}, \theta)} \qquad (2.40)$$

The key idea used in the SIS algorithm consists in obtaining a recursive relation for the weights updating. This property makes them particulary appealing for on-line applications. Assume that the dynamic model of interest is the one described in equations (2.10), (2.11) and (2.12) and choose the importance density to factorize as follows: $q(x_{0:t+1}|y_{1:t+1}, \theta) = q(x_{0:t}|y_{1:t}, \theta)q(x_{t+1}|x_{0:t}, y_{1:t+1}, \theta)$, then the weights can be rewritten in the following recursive form:

$$w_{t+1}^{i} = w_{t}^{i} \frac{p(y_{t+1}|x_{t+1}^{i}, \theta)p(x_{t+1}^{i}|x_{t}^{i}, \theta)}{q(x_{t+1}^{i}|x_{t+1}^{i}, y_{t+1}, \theta)} \qquad (2.41)$$

This relation is a direct consequence of the Bayes rule and the Markov property of the system.

Algorithm 4: the SIS particle filter

Given the initial set of particles $\{x_{t}^{i}, w_{t}^{i}\}_{i=1}^{N}$, for $i = 1, \ldots, N$:

1 Simulate $x_{t+1}^{i} \sim q(x_{t+1}|x_{t}^{i}, y_{t+1}, \theta)$
2 Update the weights:

$$w_{t+1}^{i} \propto w_{t}^{i} \frac{p(y_{t+1}|x_{t+1}^{i}, \theta)\, p(x_{t+1}|x_{t}^{i}; \theta)}{q(x_{t+1}|x_{t}^{i}, y_{t+1}, \theta)}$$

It is well-known in the literature (see for example Arulampalam *et al.*, 2001), that basic SIS algorithms have a degeneracy problem. After some iterations the empirical distribution degenerates into a single particle, because the variance of the importance weights is non-decreasing over time (see Doucet *et al.*, 2000). In order to solve this degeneracy problem, the *Sampling Importance Resampling* (SIR) algorithm was introduced by Gordon *et al.* (1993). This algorithm belongs to a wider class of bootstrap filters which use a re-sampling step to generate a new set of particles with uniform weights. This step introduces diversity in the particle set, avoiding degeneracy.

Algorithm 5: SIR particle filter

Given the initial set of particles $\{\mathbf{x}_t^i, w_t^i\}_{i=1}^N$, for $i = 1, \ldots, N$:

1 Simulate $\mathbf{x}_{t+1}^i \sim q(\mathbf{x}_{t+1}|\mathbf{x}_t^i, \mathbf{y}_{t+1}, \theta)$
2 Update the weights: $\tilde{w}_{t+1}^i \propto p(\mathbf{y}_{t+1}|\mathbf{x}_{t+1}^i, \theta)$
3 Normalize the weights: $\bar{w}_{t+1}^i = \tilde{w}_{t+1}^i \left(\sum_{j=1}^N \tilde{w}_{t+1}^j\right)^{-1}$, for $i = 1, \ldots, N$.
4 Simulate $\{x_{t+1}^i\}_{i=1}^N$ from the empirical density $\{\mathbf{x}_t^i, \bar{w}_t^i\}_{i=1}^N$
5 Assign $w_{t+1}^i = 1/N$, for $i = 1, \ldots, N$.

Note that in the SIR particle filter, we assumed $q(\mathbf{x}_{t+1}|\mathbf{x}_t^i, \mathbf{y}_{t+1}, \theta) = p(\mathbf{x}_{t+1}|\mathbf{x}_t^i, \theta)$. Moreover, due to the resampling step, the weights are uniformly distributed over the particle set: $w_t^i = 1/N$. Thus, the weights updating relation becomes: $\tilde{w}_{t+1}^i \propto w_t^i p(\mathbf{y}_{t+1}|\mathbf{x}_{t+1}^i, \theta) \propto p(\mathbf{y}_{t+1}|\mathbf{x}_{t+1}^i, \theta)$.

However, the basic SIR algorithm produces a progressive impoverishment of the information contained in the particle set, because of the resampling step and of the fact that particles do not change over the filter iterations. Many solutions have been proposed in the literature. We recall the *Regularized Particle Filter* proposed by Musso *et al.* (2001), which is based on a discretization of the continuous state space. Gilks and Berzuini (2001) propose the SIR-Move algorithm, which moves particles after the re-sampling step. Thus, the particle value changes and impoverishment is partially avoided. Finally, Pitt and Shephard (1999) introduce the *Auxiliary Particle Filter* (APF) and applied it to a Gaussian ARCH-type stochastic volatility model. They found that the auxiliary particle filter works well and that the sensibility to outliers is lower than in the basic filters.

In order to avoid re-sampling, the APF algorithm uses an auxiliary variable to select most representative particles and to mutate them through a simulation step. Then, weights of the regenerated particles are updated through an importance sampling argument. In this way, particles with low probability do not survive the selection and the information contained in the particle set is not wasted. In particular, the auxiliary variable μ_t^i contains and resumes the information on the previous particle set and it is used in the selection step to sample the random particle index. Note that the empirical filtering density given in equation (2.36) is a mixture of distributions, which can be reparameterized by introducing an auxiliary variable $i \in \{1, \ldots, N\}$, which indicates the component of the mixture. The joint distribution of the hidden state and of the index i is then:

$$p(\mathbf{x}_{t+1}, i|\mathbf{y}_{1:t+1}, \theta) = \frac{p(\mathbf{y}_{t+1}|\mathbf{y}_{1:t}, \mathbf{x}_{t+1}, i)}{p(\mathbf{y}_{t+1}|\mathbf{y}_{1:t}, \theta)} p(\mathbf{x}_{t+1}, i|\mathbf{y}_{1:t}, \theta)$$

$$= \frac{p(\mathbf{y}_{t+1}|\mathbf{x}_{t+1}, \theta)}{p(\mathbf{y}_{t+1}|\mathbf{y}_{1:t}, \theta)} p(\mathbf{x}_{t+1}|\mathbf{x}_t^i, \theta) w_t^i \tag{2.42}$$

The basic idea of the APF is to refresh the particle set while reducing the loss of information due to this operation. Thus, the algorithm generates a new set of particles by jointly simulating the particle index i (*selection step*) and the selected particle value $\mathbf{x}_{t+1}$ (*mutation step*) from the reparameterized empirical filtering density, according to the following importance density:

$$q(\mathbf{x}_{t+1}^j, i^j | \mathbf{y}_{1:t+1}, \theta) = q(\mathbf{x}_{t+1}^j | \mathbf{y}_{1:t+1}, \theta) q(i^j | \mathbf{y}_{1:t+1}, \theta)$$

$$= p(\mathbf{x}_{t+1}^j | \mathbf{x}^{i^j}, \theta)(p(\mathbf{y}_{t+1} | \mu_{t+1}^{i^j}, \theta) w_t^{i^j}) \qquad (2.43)$$

for $j = 1, \ldots, N$. Note that the index is sampled using weights which are proportional to the observation density conditional on a summary statistics of the initial particle set. In this way, less informative particles are discarded. The information contained in each particle is evaluated with respect to both the observable variable and the initial particle set. By following the usual importance sampling argument, the updating relation for the particle weights is:

$$w_{t+1}^j \triangleq \frac{p(\mathbf{x}_{t+1}^j, i^j | \mathbf{y}_{1:t+1}, \theta)}{q(\mathbf{x}_{t+1}^j, i^j | \mathbf{y}_{1:t+1}, \theta)} = \frac{p(\mathbf{x}_{t+1}^j | \mathbf{x}^{i^j}, \theta) p(\mathbf{y}_{t+1} | \mathbf{x}_{t+1}^j, \theta) w_t^{i^j}}{p(\mathbf{x}_{t+1}^j | \mathbf{x}^{i^j}, \theta) p(\mathbf{y}_{t+1} | \mu_{t+1}^{i^j}, \theta) w_t^{i^j}} = \frac{p(\mathbf{y}_{t+1} | \mathbf{x}_{t+1}^j, \theta)}{p(\mathbf{y}_{t+1} | \mu_{t+1}^{i^j}, \theta)}$$

$$(2.44)$$

Algorithm 6: auxiliary particle filter

Given the initial set of particles $\{\mathbf{x}_t^j, w_t^j\}_{j=1}^N$, for $j = 1, \ldots, N$,

1 Calculate $\mu_{t+1}^j = \mathbb{E}(\mathbf{x}_{t+1} | \mathbf{x}_t^j, \theta)$
2 Simulate $i^j \sim q(i | \mathbf{y}_{1:t+1}, \theta) \propto w_t^i p(\mathbf{y}_{t+1} | \mu_{t+1}^i, \theta)$ with $i \in \{1, \ldots, N\}$
3 Simulate $\mathbf{x}_{t+1}^j \sim p(\mathbf{x}_{t+1} | \mathbf{x}_t^{i^j}, \theta)$
4 Update particles weights:

$$\tilde{w}_{t+1}^j \propto \frac{p(\mathbf{y}_{t+1} | \mathbf{x}_{t+1}^j, \theta)}{p(\mathbf{y}_{t+1} | \mu_{t+1}^{i^j}, \theta)}.$$

5 Normalize the weights:

$$w_{t+1}^i = \tilde{w}_{t+1}^i \left(\sum_{j=1}^N \tilde{w}_{t+1}^j \right)^{-1}, \qquad \text{for } i = 1, \ldots, N.$$

We conclude this section with a brief discussion of the problem of parameter estimation, for dynamic models with hidden variables, in a sequential data-processing approach. Note that following the engineering literature, a common way to solve the parameter estimation problem is to treat parameters θ as hidden state of the system (see Berzuini *et al.*, 1997). The model is restated assuming time-dependent parameter vectors θ_t, and imposing the constraint: $\theta_t = \theta_{t-1}$ on its dynamic.

In principle, parameter estimation and state filtering can be treated separately (see Storvik, 2002). In many applications of particle filter techniques, parameters are treated as known and MCMC parameter estimates are used instead of the true parameter values. But in this way parameter estimate are not continuously updated as the hidden states. MCMC is typically an off-line approach, in that it does not allow sequential updating of parameter estimates as new observations arrive. Moreover, when applied sequentially, the MCMC estimation method is more time-consuming than particle filter algorithms.

One of the main issue in research on particle filters is the inclusion of the parameter estimation procedure in the state filtering algorithm. See for example Berzuini *et al.* (1997) and Storvik (2002) for a general discussion of the problem, and Liu and West (2001) for the joint application of adaptive importance sampling for parameter estimation and APF for hidden state filtering. See also Casarin (2004a, 2004b) for an updated review and an application to heavy-tail stochastic volatility models.

An application to business cycle models

The aim of this section is to show how particle filter algorithms apply to a widely used class of business cycle models: *Markov switching stochastic latent factor models.* We apply the APF algorithm to synthetic data in order to verify the efficiency of the algorithm and to detect possible degeneracy of the APF algorithm.

We refer to the model of Example 1 and apply the algorithm of Liu and West (2001). This algorithm combines adaptive importance sampling for sequential estimation of the parameter vector with the auxiliary particle filter for filtering and predicting the hidden state. Observe that the latent structure of the MS model in the example exhibits two levels. The first is given by the stochastic latent factor x_t, and the second is given by the regime switching process s_t.

We adapt the algorithm of Liu and West (2001) and obtain the following particle filter algorithm.

Algorithm 7

Given an initial set of particles $\{x_t^i, s_t^i, \theta_t^i, w_t^i\}_{i=1}^N$, the tuning parameters a and b are equal to $(3\delta - 1)/2\delta$ and $\sqrt{1 - a^2}$ respectively, where we chose $\delta = 0.99$ as suggested in West (1993).

Figure 2.4 shows on-line estimation of parameters α, σ_ε, ρ, μ_0, μ_1, σ_η, p_{11}, p_{22} obtained by running the APF algorithm on the synthetic dataset exhibited in Figure 2.2. We use a set of $N = 1,000$ particles to obtain the empirical filtering and prediction densities. All computations have been carried out on a Pentium IV 2.4 Ghz, and the APF algorithm has been implemented in GAUSS 4.0. Figure 2.5 shows on-line estimation of the latent factor x_t. To detect the absence of degeneracy in the output of the APF algorithm we evaluate at each step the Survival Rate as the number of particles survived to the selection step over the total number of particles. The particle set degenerates when persistently exhibiting a high number of dead particles from a generation to the subsequent one. The survival rate is calculated as follows:

$$SR_t = \left\{ N - \sum_{i=1}^N \mathbb{I}_{\{0\}}(Card(I_{i,t})) \right\} N^{-1} \tag{2.45}$$

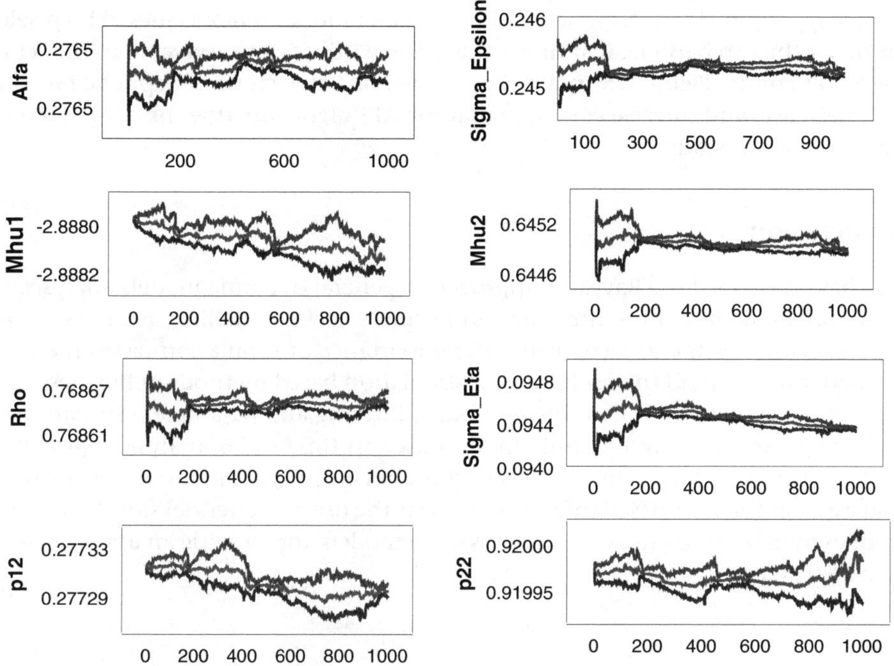

Figure 2.4   On-line parameter estimates.

At each date, graphs exhibit the empirical mean and quantiles at 0.275 and 0.925 of the parameters

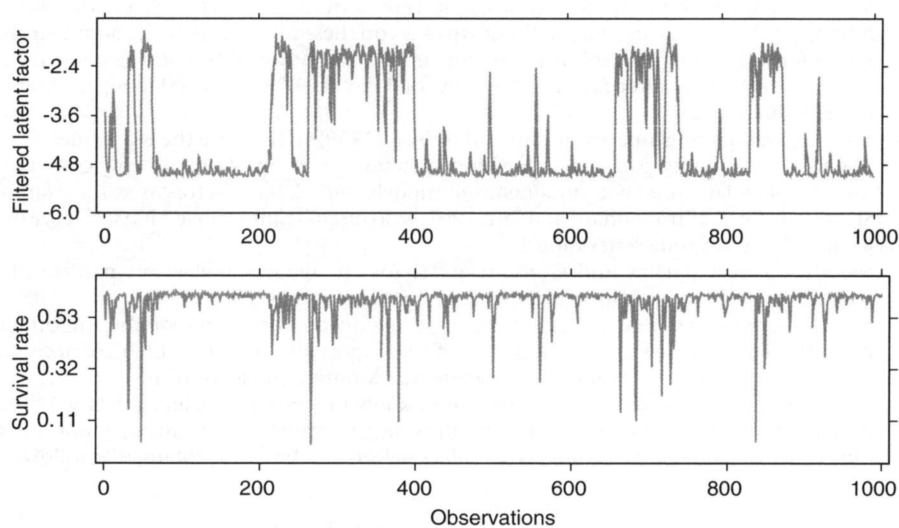

Figure 2.5   Sequentially filtered latent factor and survival rate of the particle set, over $T = 1{,}000$ observations

where $I_{i,t} = \{j \in \{1, \ldots, N\} | i_t^j = i\}$ is the set of all random index values, which select at time t the i-th particle. If at time t the particle k does not survive, then the set $I_{k,t}$ becomes empty. Figure 2.5 shows the survival rate at each time step. The rate does not decrease, and thus we conclude that the APF algorithm does not degenerate in our simulation study.

Conclusion

We have described the Bayesian approach to general dynamic models analysis. We have briefly reviewed the literature on business cycle modelling, focusing on the Bayesian approach and recognizing the importance of simulation-based methods. To better understand the usefulness of simulation based methods in business cycle analysis, we analysed the problems of state filtering and parameter estimation for a quite general class of dynamic models used in time series analysis that exhibit general filtering, predicting and smoothing relations. Furthermore, our focus on Bayesian simulation-based inference suggests the use of sequential simulation techniques to make inferences on business cycle models and provide an application on synthetic data.

Notes

1 Observe that if $t = 1$ the density $p(\mathbf{x}_0|\mathbf{y}_0, \theta) = p(\mathbf{x}_0|\theta)$ is the initial distribution of the dynamic model.
2 For proofs see Billio, Casarin and Sartore (2004).
3 See, for example, the multi-move Gibbs sampler of Carter and Köhn (1994) and the particle filter algorithms. Only in some well-known cases do these filtering densities admit an analytical form. For the normal linear dynamic model, filtering and smoothing densities are given by the Kalman filter. See also Harrison and West (1997) for a Bayesian representation of the Kalman filter.
4 We use parameters estimated in Kim and Nelson (1999) to simulate the MS model.
5 The idea of grouping parameters (or hidden states) when simulating is now commonly used in Bayesian inference on stochastic models with latent factors (see for example Shephard, 1994, and Shephard and Pitt, 1997, who discuss multi-move MCMC algorithms for non-Gaussian time series models).
6 See also Doucet, Freitas and Gordon (2001) for an updated review on particle filter techniques, their applications and the main convergence results.
7 See also Crisan and Doucet (2000) for a discussion on the choice of the importance densities. They focused on the properties of the importance density, which are necessary conditions for the convergence of the sequential Monte Carlo algorithm.
8 Note that importance sampling requires us to know the importance and the target distributions up to a proportionality constant, thus the unnormalized weights may not sum to one. However *normalized importance sampling weights* can be easily obtained as follows:

$$\tilde{w}_t^i = \frac{w_t^i}{\sum_{j=1}^{N} w_t^j} \quad i = 1, \ldots, N \text{ and } t = 1, \ldots, T$$

The normalization procedure causes the loss of the unbiasness property.

References

Anas, J. and Ferrara, L. (2004) 'Detecting cyclical turning points: the ABCD approach and two probabilistic indicators', *Journal of Business Cycle Measurement and Analysis*, 1: 193–226.

Arulampalam, S., Maskell, S., Gordon, N. and Clapp, T. (2001) 'A tutorial on particle filters for on-line nonlinear/non-gaussian bayesian tracking', *Technical Report*. Cambridge: QinetiQ Ltd., DSTO.

Bauwens, L., Lubrano, M. and Richard, J.F. (1999) *Bayesian Inference in Dynamic Econometric Models*, New York: Oxford University Press.

Berzuini, C., Best, N.G., Gilks, W.R. and Larizza, C. (1997) 'Dynamic conditional independence models and Markov chain Monte Carlo methods', *Journal of the American Statistical Association*, 92: 1403–41.

Berzuini, C. and Gilks, W.R. (2001) 'Following a moving average-Monte Carlo inference for dynamic bayesian models', *Journal of the Royal Statististical Society Series B*, 63: 127–46.

Billio, M., Casarin, R. and Sartore, D. (2004) 'Bayesian inference on dynamic models with latent factors', *Working Paper*. Venice: GRETA.

Carlin, B.P., Polson, N.G. and Stoffer, D.S. (1992) 'A Monte Carlo approach to nonnormal and nonlinear state-space modelling', *Journal of the American Statistical Association*, 87: 493–500.

Carter, C.K. and Köhn, R. (1994) 'On Gibbs sampling for state space models', *Biometrika*, 81: 541–53.

Casarin, R. (2004) 'Bayesian Monte Carlo filtering for stochastic volatility models', *Cahier du CEREMADE*, 0415.

Casarin, R. (2004) 'Bayesian Inference for Markov Switching Stochastic Volatility Models', *Cahier du CEREMADE*, 0414.

Casella, G. and Robert, C.P. (1999) *Monte Carlo Statistical Methods*. New York: Springer Verlag.

Crisan, D. and Doucet, A. (2000) 'Convergence of sequential Monte Carlo methods', *Technical Report*, 381, CUED-F-INFENG.

Diebold, F.X. and Rudebusch, G.D. (1996) 'Measuring business cycles: a modern perspective', *The Review of Economics and Statistics*, 78: 67–77.

Doucet, A., Freitas, J.G. and Gordon, J. (2001) *Sequential Monte Carlo Methods in Practice*. New York: Springer Verlag.

Doucet, A., Godsill, S. and Andrieu, C. (2000) 'On sequential Monte Carlo sampling methods for Bayesian filtering', *Statistics and Computing*, 10: 197–208.

Durbin, J. and Koopman, S.J. (2001) *Time Series Analysis by State Space Methods*. New York: Oxford University Press.

Frühwirth-Schnatter, S. (1994) 'Data augmentation and dynamic linear models', *Journal of Time Series Analysis*, 15: 183–202.

Goldfeld, S.M. and Quandt, R.E. (1973) 'A Markov model for switching regression', *Journal of Econometrics*, 1: 3–16.

Gordon, N., Salmond, D. and Smith, A.F.M. (1993) 'Novel approach to nonlinear and non-gaussian bayesian state estimation', *IEE Proceedings-F*, 140: 107–13.

Hamilton, J.D. (1989) 'A new approach to the economic analysis of nonstationary time series and the business cycle', *Econometrica*, 57, 357–84.

Harvey, A.C. (1989) *Forecasting, Structural Time Series Models and the Kalman Filter*. Cambridge: Cambridge University Press.

Harrison, J. and West, M. (1997) *Bayesian Forecasting and Dynamic Models*. New York: Springer Verlag.

Kalman, R.E. (1960) 'A new approach to linear filtering and prediction problems', *Journal of Basic Engineering, Transaction ASME* , Series D, 82: 35–45.

Kalman, R.E. and Bucy, R.S. (1960) 'New results in linear filtering and prediction problems', *Transaction of the ASME-Journal of Basic Engineering Series D*, 83: 95–108.

Kim, C.J. (1994) 'Dynamic linear models with Markov switching', *Journal of Econometrics*, 60: 1–22.

Kim, C.J. and Nelson, C.R. (1999) *State-Space Models with Regime Switching*, Cambridge: MIT Press.

Kim, C.J. and Murray, C.J. (2002) 'Permanent and transitory components of recessions', *Empirical Economics*, 27: 163–83.

Krolzig, H.M. (1997) *Markov-Switching Vector Autoregressions. Modelling, Statistical Inference and Applications to Business Cycle Analysis*. Berlin: Springer.

Liu, J.S. and Chen, R. (1998) 'Sequential Monte Carlo methods for dynamical system', *Journal of the American Statistical Association*, 93, 1032–44.

Liu, J. and West, M. (2001) 'Combined parameter and state estimation in simulation based filtering', in A. Doucet, J.G. Freitas and J. Gordon (eds), *Sequential Monte Carlo Methods in Practice*. New York: Springer Verlag.

Liu, J.S., Wong, W.H. and Kong, A. (1994) 'Covariance structure of the Gibbs sampler with applications to the comparison of estimators and augmentation schemes', *Biometrika*, 81: 27–40.

Liu, J.S., Wong, W.H. and Kong, A. (1995) 'Correlation structure and convergence rate of the Gibbs sampler with various scans', *Journal of the Royal Statistical Society Series B*, 57: 157–69.

Müller, P. (1992) 'Alternatives to the Gibbs sampling scheme', *Technical Report*, Duke University: Institute of Statistics and Decision Sciences.

Musso, C., Oudjane, N. and LeGland, F. (2001) 'Improving regularised particle filters', in A. Doucet, J.G. Freitas and J. Gordon (eds), *Sequential Monte Carlo in Practice*. New York: Springer Verlag.

Pitt, M. and Shephard, N. (1999) 'Filtering via simulation: auxiliary particle filters', *Journal of the American Statistical Association*, 94: 590–9.

Shephard, N. (1994) 'Partial non-gaussian state space', *Biometrika*, 81: 115–31.

Robert, C.P. (2001) *The Bayesian Choice*. New York: Springer Verlag.

Shephard, N. and Pitt, M.K. (1997) 'Likelihood analysis of non-Gaussian measurement time series', *Biometrika*, 84: 653–67.

Sichel, D.E. (1991) 'Business cycle duration dependence: a parametric approach', *Review of Economics and Statistics*, 73: 254–6.

Storvik, G. (2002) 'Particle filters for state space models with the presence of unknown static parameters', *IEEE Transactions on Signal Processing*, 50: 281–9.

Tanner, M. and Wong, W. (1987) 'The calculation of posterior distributions by data augmentation', *Journal of the American Statistical Association*, 82: 528–50.

Tierney, L. (1994) 'Markov chains for exploring posterior distributions', *Annals of Statististics*, 22: 1701–86.

Watson, J. (1994) 'Business cycle durations and postwar stabilization of the U.S. economy', *American Economic Review*, 84: 24–46.

West, M. (1992) 'Mixture models, Monte Carlo, bayesian updating and dynamic models', *Computer Science and Statistics*, 24: 325–33.

West, M. (1993) 'Approximating posterior distribution by mixtures', *Journal of the Royal Statistical Society Series B*, 55: 409–42.

3
Output Fluctuations in G7 Countries: A Time-Scale Decomposition Analysis

Marco Crivellini, Marco Gallegati, Mauro Gallegati and Antonio Palestrini

Introduction

In this chapter we apply the wavelets methodology to the analysis of business cycle fluctuations. The analysis is performed using the industrial production index of G7 countries between 1961M1 – 2002M12. We produce an orthogonal decomposition of industrial output series by time scale over seven different time scales and analyse the basic characteristics (volatility, frequency and asymmetry) and the co-movements of these time-scale components across countries and over time. The results show no convincing evidence of a decrease in output variability, different correlation patterns at the different time-scale components, and the emergence of increasing relationships between two groups of countries: the Euro-area and the Anglo countries.

Most macroeconomists share the view that the business cycle is characterized by '*co-movements* among different aggregative time series' which are common to all decentralized market economies with no restriction 'to particular countries or time period', and therefore they are *all alike* (Lucas, 1977, p. 217). This notion replaces the National Bureau of Economic Research (NBER) view that the business cycle 'consists of expansion occurring at about the same time in many economic activities, followed by similarly general recessions, contractions, and revivals which merge into the expansion phase of the next cycle' (Burns and Mitchell, 1946).

These opposite approaches share the view that the underlying cyclical component can be represented by a data generation process of an approximate length between two and eight (10) years. This view is not without exceptions, however. Recently, Blanchard (1997) and Comin and Gertler (2003) have pointed out the existence of a 'medium run' cycle between 10 and 40 years, together with a shorter cycle below 10 years. This last approach can be traced back to Schumpeter (1939) who disentangled business cycle movements into several minor components.[1]

From an econometric point of view this approach may be pursued by the *wavelet methodology*. Wavelets are particular types of function $\omega(x)$ that are localized both in time and frequency and are used to decompose a function $f(x)$, that is a signal, a surface, a series and so on, into more elementary functions which include information about the same $f(x)$. The main advantage of wavelet analysis is its ability to decompose macroeconomic time series, and data in general, into their time-scale components. Several applications of wavelet analysis in economics and finance have recently been provided by Ramsey and Lampart (1998a, 1998b), Ramsey (2002), and Kim and Haueck In (2003) among others, but no attempts have been made to apply this methodology to the analysis of business cycle fluctuations.

There is no need to make any *a priori* assumptions about the underlying cause of the business cycle (*impulse-response function* versus a *deterministic approach*); rather one should recognize that the different *causae causantes* (supply of and demand for durable-, non-durable-, or investment-goods, as well as different economic policies and shifts of factors' revenues) systematically display their effects on very different time scales. According to this view, in order to understand the business cycle behaviour one has to fully understand what is going on at a disaggregated level.

The underlying assumption of this chapter is that economic activity may undergo different time-scale periods, and they coexist within the time period of interest to business cycle analysts. It follows that the aggregate cyclical movement is nothing but the sum of each single component, which is displaced at different time horizons. It is therefore possible to analyse the relative importance of the various components and appreciate why the cycle has changed.[2] In this chapter we apply wavelet methodology to the analysis of the output series of G7 countries between 1961M1 and 2001M12. For each time-scale component of the industrial production series of G7 countries, we explore: (a) the moderation of volatility; (b) the linkages between countries; and (c) the evolution of the synchronization pattern.

The main properties of the wavelets and the analytical differences with other filtering methods are dealt with in the next section, where the characteristics of our data-set are also illustrated. We then report and discuss the main empirical findings, before a final conclusion.

Methodology and data

The analysis was conducted using the monthly production index (OECD source; 1961–2001) for Canada, France, Germany, Italy, Japan, the UK and the USA.[3] The series were filtered with a *non-decimated discrete wavelet transform* that is a relatively new (at least for economists) statistical tool that, roughly speaking, decomposes a given series into orthogonal components, as in Fourier approach, but according to scale (time components) instead of frequencies. The comparison with Fourier analysis is useful because wavelet analysis uses a similar strategy. First, it finds some orthogonal objects (wavelet functions instead of sines and cosines) and uses them to decompose the series. Second, since Fourier analysis is a common tool in economics, it may be useful in understanding the methodology and also in the interpretation of results. Saying that, we have to stress the main difference between the two tools. Wavelet analysis does not need the stationary assumption in order to decompose the series. This is because the Fourier approach that decomposes in frequency space may be interpreted as events of time-period T (where T is the number of observations). Put differently, spectral decomposition methods perform a global analysis whereas, on the other hand, wavelets methods act locally in time and so do not need stationary cyclical components.

Recently, to relax the stationary frequencies assumption a *windowing Fourier decomposition* has been developed that essentially uses, for frequencies estimation, a time-period M (the window) event less than the number of observations T. The problem with this approach is the right choice of the window and, more important, its constancy over time.

For a natural comparison of the wavelet filter the well-known Hodrick–Prescott (HP) and Baxter–King (BK) filters are usually used in business cycles analysis. According to the BK definition business cycles are 'cyclical' components with a frequency higher than 18 months and less than 96. Failure of the stationary assumption ends up with biased estimated business cycles. For example, the weight of the different time-scale components characterizing the series cannot, in general, be considered constant[4] causing a difficult interpretation of band-pass filter estimations that are mixed objects of such time-scale components. In fact, recent investigations (Guay and St-Amant, 1997) seem to show that HP and BK filters have a correct interpretation only when the frequencies that have a peak in the spectrum belong to the *ideal filter* band. Unfortunately, as shown by Granger (1966), this does not happen for many macroeconomic time series since they seem to have most of their power at low frequencies and decrease monotonically moving towards higher frequencies. The consequence of this problem is the extraction of spurious cyclical components as shown also by Harvey-Jaeger (1993) and Cogley-Nason (1995).

Going into some mathematical detail, there are different types of wavelet functions belonging to two classes: the *father-wavelet* and the *mother-wavelet*. The former integrates to 1 and reconstructs the longest time-scale component of the series (trend). The latter integrates to 0 (similar to sine and cosine) and extracts the cyclical components around the trend.

The formal definition of the father wavelets is the function:

$$\Phi_{J,k} = 2^{-J/2}\Phi\left(\frac{t - 2^J k}{2^J}\right)$$

defined non-zero over a finite time length support that corresponds to given mother wavelets:

$$\Psi_{J,k} = 2^{-J/2}\Psi\left(\frac{t - 2^J k}{2^J}\right)$$

with $j = 1, \ldots, J$ in a J-level wavelets decomposition.

These functions represent a basis for a projection space of the signal with father wavelets projection coefficients s_{Jk} and mother wavelets projection coefficients d_{Jk}, decomposing a time series $f(t)$ as:

$$f(t) = S_J + D_J + D_{J-1} + \cdots + D_j + \cdots + D_1 \tag{3.1}$$

where S_J denotes cycles with periodicity greater that 2^{J+1} periods (say the 'trend') and the D_j components capture cycles between 2^j and 2^{j+1}.

The mother wavelets, as said above, play a role similar to sines and cosines in the Fourier decomposition. They are compressed or dilated, in time domain, to generate cycles fitting actual data. To compute the decomposition we need to calculate wavelet coefficients at all scales representing the projections of the time series onto the basis generated by the chosen family of wavelets. That is,

$$d_{j,k} = \int f(t)\Psi_{j,k}$$

$$s_{J,k} = \int f(t)\Phi_{J,k}$$

where d_{jk} and s_{Jk} represent, respectively, the projection onto mother and father wavelets.

Finally, the components in equation (3.1) are computed as weighted averages of the wavelets fitting the series with weight given by the above coefficients,

$$f(t) = \sum_k s_{J,k}\Phi_{J,k}(t) + \sum_k d_{J,k}\Psi_{J,k}(t) + \cdots + \sum_k d_{j,k}\Psi_{j,k}(t) + \cdots + \sum_k d_{1,k}\Psi_{1,k}(t)$$

$$(3.2)$$

We decompose each aggregate monthly industrial production series into its time-scale components according to the *non-decimated Symmlet discrete wavelet transform*, designated as 'S8'.[5] The non-decimated discrete wavelet transform is a non-orthogonal variant of the discrete wavelet transform that is translation invariant, as shifts in the signal do not change the pattern of the coefficients. After the application of the translation invariant wavelet transform we obtain eight different time-scale components: $D1$ (2–4 months); $D2$ (4–8 months); $D3$ (8–16 months); $D4$ (16–32 months); $D5$ (32–64 months); $D6$ (64–128 months), $D7$ (128–256 months). Of course, the first three components are the very short-run elements, $D4$ to $D6$ refer to the standard business cycle time period (Stock and Watson, 2000), while $D7$ and the trend components refer, respectively, to medium-run[6] and long-run elements.

Basics characteristics of the different time-scale components of output

In recent years there has been a renewed interest in the volatility of economic activity following the 'reduction in the volatility of output growth, and a concomitant moderation of business cycle fluctuations in the past two decades' (Stock and Watson, 2003)[7] and in the international synchronization of cyclical fluctuations (Doyle and Faust, 2002, De Haan *et al.*, 2002, Kose *et al.*, 2003, and Bordo and Helbling, 2003). In this section, using the time scale components of the industrial production series of G7 countries, we explore at different time-scales: (a) the moderation of volatility; (b) the links between countries; and (c) the evolution of the pattern of synchronization.

Volatility

A simple measure of economic volatility may be represented by the standard deviation of the single time-scale component of industrial production. In Table 3.1 we present the values of the standard deviations of the most significant time-scale components, $D3$ to $D7$, for the whole period (1961–2001) as well as for four sub-periods, that is before the Bretton Woods' collapse (1961–71), the oil shocks (1972–82), the slow recovery (1983–92) and the irrational euphoric years (1992–2001). The very

Table 3.1   Standard deviations of the time-scale components $D3$–$D7$

		D3	D4	D5	D6	D7
Canada	1961–2001	0.004	0.008	0.016	0.020	0.024
	1961–71	0.003	0.006	0.013	0.014	0.018
	1972–82	0.004	0.011	0.017	0.021	0.018
	1983–92	0.004	0.008	0.021	0.027	0.021
	1993–2001	0.002	0.005	0.010	0.014	0.034
France	1961–2001	0.007	0.008	0.011	0.014	0.017
	1961–71	0.013	0.010	0.011	0.012	0.014
	1972–82	0.005	0.012	0.017	0.017	0.014
	1983–92	0.003	0.003	0.005	0.013	0.011
	1993–2001	0.003	0.006	0.009	0.013	0.019
Germany	1961–2001	0.005	0.007	0.015	0.019	0.021
	1961–71	0.005	0.006	0.018	0.021	0.023
	1972–82	0.005	0.009	0.015	0.019	0.016
	1983–92	0.005	0.006	0.011	0.019	0.022
	1993–2001	0.003	0.007	0.012	0.019	0.021
Italy	1961–2001	0.007	0.011	0.015	0.016	0.013
	1961–71	0.009	0.010	0.013	0.011	0.017
	1972–82	0.009	0.017	0.024	0.018	0.005
	1983–92	0.004	0.004	0.007	0.020	0.010
	1993–2001	0.003	0.008	0.012	0.011	0.014
Japan	1961–2001	0.004	0.010	0.020	0.022	0.038
	1961–71	0.004	0.011	0.018	0.019	0.058
	1972–82	0.005	0.014	0.028	0.029	0.040
	1983–92	0.002	0.006	0.014	0.019	0.019
	1993–2001	0.004	0.010	0.019	0.018	0.013
UK	1961–2001	0.005	0.007	0.012	0.014	0.014
	1961–71	0.004	0.005	0.012	0.010	0.013
	1972–82	0.008	0.012	0.019	0.017	0.011
	1983–92	0.004	0.006	0.007	0.017	0.015
	1993–2001	0.002	0.003	0.006	0.008	0.012
USA	1961–2001	0.004	0.007	0.015	0.018	0.024
	1961–71	0.003	0.006	0.014	0.014	0.021
	1972–82	0.007	0.011	0.021	0.024	0.007
	1983–92	0.003	0.007	0.014	0.017	0.013
	1993–2001	0.002	0.004	0.006	0.016	0.035

short-term components, from $D1$ to $D3$, are quite erratic and country-specific (no country is inside the interval confidence of 10 per cent of the average standard deviation in any time span, except for $D3$ in the last decade), while the traditional business cycle components, $D4$ to $D6$, are more uniform, at least in the first two decades, especially for the continental European countries and the USA.

The main results for the whole period may be summarized as follows:

- the standard deviation increases as one goes from the $D3$ to $D7$ scales;
- the $D7$ component looks very country-specific in its dynamics, but with a common amplitude: exceptions are Japan with a very high standard deviation, as well as Italy and the UK with the lowest standard deviation values.
- at the time scales corresponding to the usual definition of the business cycle[8] there are no significant differences among countries. Exceptions are Japan (highest volatility for all time scales), Italy (high volatility at the $D4$ scale), and France and the UK (lowest volatilities at the $D6$ and $D5$ scales).

Heterogeneity in business cycles is not a country-specific characteristic, but also involves different periods of time. For each country, rows 2 to 5 in Table 3.1 report the standard deviation at different time scales and for different decades. It is quite evident that during the oil shocks years the volatility of the business cycles' time-scale components increased by about 50 per cent (the main exception is Germany where it decreased at the $D5$ and $D6$ scales). Regarding the second decade, the years 1983–92 show a sharp decline in the variability at the $D4$ and $D5$ scales for all countries (except for Canada at $D5$) and at $D6$ only for France, Japan and the USA. In the last decade, the volatility rises at the $D4$ and $D5$ time-scale components for France, Italy and Japan, while at $D6$ it collapses for Canada, Italy and the UK.

The results stemming from the recent ample literature on the evidence and the cause of the moderation of the business cycle (Mc Connel and Perez Quiros, 2000; Kim and Nelson, 1999; Stock and Watson, 2002; Chauvet and Potter, 2001) provide twofold evidence:

- stabilization occurred after the 1983 trough;
- there is evidence of lower (higher) volatility at business cycle (lower) frequencies.

According to our analysis, these hypotheses are not without caveats. From the results in Table 3.1 it is quite clear that the stabilization claimed by the literature is an artefact of the aggregation procedure. In fact, if we compare the first and the third or last decade in the period under analysis, we do not find any change in variability. The volatility decreases only by aggregating the years 1960–82, but only because it increased markedly during the oil shocks. The scaling analysis does not show any sign, of moderation (except perhaps at the $D4$ scales). The decline in volatility during the 'roaring 90s' is almost entirely due to the decline for the $D4$ and $D5$ time-scale components.

All in all, we may say that there is no convincing evidence of a decrease in output variability if we analyse the standard deviations of G7 countries at different time scales over different time periods (the only reduction seems to be confined to the very short run and the demand components).

Of course there are exceptions, and Japan is the main case in point. At the $D3$ and $D4$ scales there is no evidence of a decrease in volatility, and at the $D4$–$D7$ scales Japan is more volatile than any other G7 country. In the USA after 1983 the 'monetary policy' impulses collapsed, while in France the French May dominates the fluctuations of the pre-Bretton Woods collapse years. In the UK (USA) at the $D6$ ($D5$) component the volatility decreased by more than 50 per cent (70%) in the 1980s (see Blanchard, 1997) while Italy experienced a reduction by two-thirds in the last decade of the past century when an income policy was adopted.

Co-movements

The most commonly used measure to analyse co-movements in the level of economic activity across countries and over time is, undoubtedly, correlation analysis. Cross-country correlations have been widely used to obtain a static estimate of the linkages in output movements across countries (amongst others, Backus and Keho, 1992, Christodoulakis *et al.*, 1995, and Comin and Gertler, 2003). In the following sub-sections we analyse the relationships among output variables at different time scales computing the cross-country correlation coefficients for the $D7$, $D6$, $D5$ and $D4$ time-scale components of G7 countries. Figure 3.1 plots the cross-country correlations between the USA and the other G7 countries.

Analysis of the plots of cross-correlation coefficients for the different time-scale components between the USA and other G7 countries in the top two panel Figure 3.1 suggests that while the correlation pattern differs markedly for the longest time-scale components $D7$ and $D6$, it shows a remarkable similarity for the medium and shortest business cycle time-scale components, $D5$ and $D4$.[9] In particular, over the medium term the USA displays both positive significant contemporaneous relationships with Canada (very high) and the UK (high), and positive significant leading relationships with the other G7 countries, with a lead between 1 (Italy) and 2 years (France and Germany). At the longest business cycle time scale the relationships are qualitatively similar, even if highly significant only with Canada, Italy and the UK. On the other hand, both for the medium and the shortest business cycle time-scale components the plot of the cross-country correlation coefficients for the USA in the bottom two panel of Figure 3.1 suggests that the co-movements between the USA and other G7 countries are highly synchronized, particularly at the $D5$ scale.[10]

$D7$ and $D6$ time-scales

There is evidence of high synchronization between Canada, the UK and the USA at for longest time-scale components $D7$ and $D6$, with values of the contemporaneous cross-correlation coefficients between .80 and .90 (the lowest value is between the UK and the USA with a contemporaneous coefficient value of .60 at $D7$). At the longest time scale, $D7$, a positive significant relationship (about .75) emerges between the Anglo (namely, Canada, the UK and the USA) and the Euro area (namely, France, Germany and Italy) countries, with Italy lagging by 1 year and France and Germany by 2 years the Anglo countries.

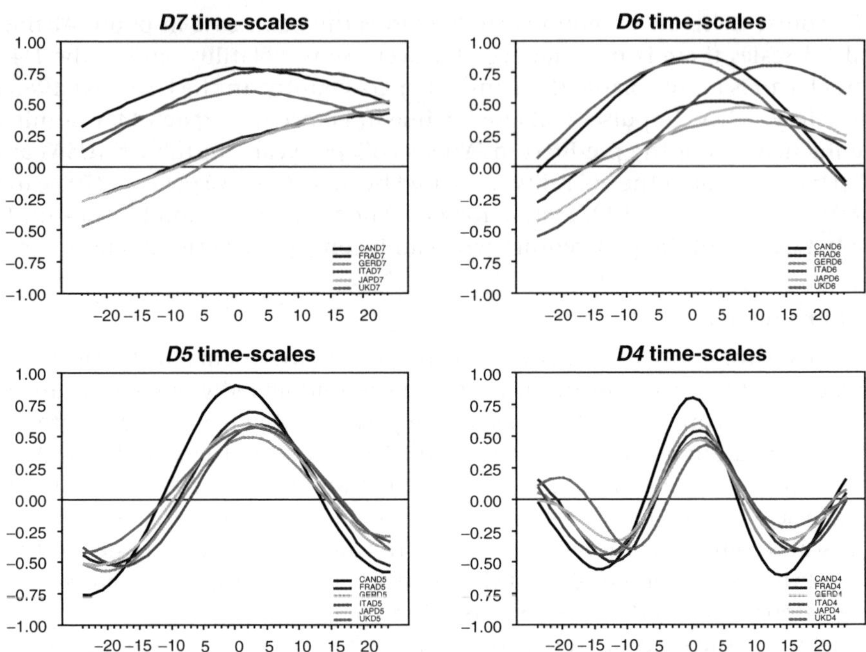

Cross-country correlations between USA and other G7 countries

Figure 3.1   Cross-country correlations between the USA and other G7 countries
Notes:
*D*4 : 16–32 months component
*D*5 : 32–64 months component
*D*6 : 64–128 months component
*D*7 : 128–256 months component

Moreover, even Germany and France, like Canada and the USA, show a very high and stable contemporaneous relationship at all time-scales, with the contemporaneous correlation coefficients ranging from .90 to .75. With the other countries the patterns of France and Germany change according to the time scale considered. In particular, if at the longest time scale *D*7 there is a significant lagged relationship with the Anglo countries, at the longest business cycle time scale, that is *D*6, there is evidence of a strong lagged relationship with Japan at *D*6 for both countries (about .75).

Thus, for the longest time-scale components there is evidence of a high linkage between the Anglo countries, that is Canada, the UK and the USA, and between the core G7 European countries, that is France and Germany, with Italy lagging the first group and Japan leading the latter.

*D*5 and *D*4 time scales

For the medium business cycle time-scale components all countries show a remarkable level of synchronization, with the maximum correlation coefficient values at the $D4$ scale generally lower than the corresponding values at the $D5$ scale (particularly for Japan and the UK). Indeed, the analysis of the cross-correlation coefficients at different leads and lags shows, particularly at the $D5$ scale, the existence of a positive significant relationships among all G7 countries, with the highest values of the contemporaneous cross-correlation coefficients (.80 to .90) characterizing the relationships between Canada and the USA, and between France and Germany.

Summary of results

The analysis of the cross-country correlation coefficients between G7 countries at different time scales may be summarized as follows:

- For the time-scale component $D7$, all countries are highly correlated with values between .50 and .80. In particular, a high contemporaneous positive correlation exists between the USA, Canada and the UK, and between France and Germany, with Italy correlated with all other countries lagging the Anglo countries and leading the other Euro-area countries by 1 year, and Japan more correlated with the Euro-area than with the Anglo countries.
- For the longest business cycle time-scale component $D6$, there is again evidence of a very high positive contemporaneous relationship between Canada, the UK and the USA, a lagged relationship between the Anglo countries and Italy (with Italy lagging by 1 year), and between France, Germany and Japan with Japan leading the Euro-area countries by about a quarter.
- For the medium business cycle time-scale component $D5$, all countries show a remarkable level of synchronization with the highest cross-correlation values between Canada and the USA (.90), France and Germany, France and Italy (.75), and between Japan and the Euro-area countries (around .70).
- For the shortest business cycle time-scale component $D4$, the values of the cross-correlation coefficients, even if they denote a good level of synchronization, are generally lower than the corresponding values at the $D5$, scale, particularly for Japan and the UK. Again, the highest cross-correlation coefficient values are between Canada and the USA (.80), and between France with Canada, Germany and Italy (.70).

Thus, the analysis of the overall linkage between the different time-scale components among G7 countries based on the maximum lead/lag cross-correlation coefficients shows a different correlation between groups of countries and across time scales. In particular, strong and stable relationships, in the sense that they hold across time scales, emerge among the Anglo countries, and between France and Germany at each time scale, with Italy displaying the closest links to the Anglo or to the Euro-area countries according to the different time-scales.[11]

Synchronization

Synchronization refers to the tendency of recessions and expansions in one country occurring at about the same time as in other countries. Recent empirical studies on business cycle synchronization in G7 countries have shown no (Stock and Watson 2003), little (Doyle and Faust, 2002, Kose *et al.*, 2003) or mixed (De Haan *et al.*, 2002) evidence towards increasing international synchronization of business cycle fluctuations. Moreover, there appears to be evidence of the emergence of two cyclical groups, the Eurozone (Euro-area) countries and the English-speaking (or Anglo) countries (Artis and Zhang, 1999, Duarte and Holden, 2003, Stock and Watson, 2003).

The degree of synchronization between two countries, and their evolution over time, may be measured by the contemporaneous cross-correlation of the cyclical component of the output series (see Artis and Zhang, 1999, and De Haan *et al.*, 2002). Recently, Harding and Pagan (2002) have proposed the use of a statistic, the index of concordance, which measures the fraction of time spent in the same phase by two countries and allows one to test whether two series are synchronized or not. The index or degree of concordance is defined as:

$$IC_{ij} = \frac{1}{T} \sum_{t=1}^{T} \left[S_t^i S_t^j + \left(1 - S_t^i\right)\left(1 - S_t^j\right) \right]$$

where S_t is a state variable which equals one in recession phases, the year after a peak date to the date of the trough, and zero in expansion phases, and indexes i and j refer to the countries for which the index is computed.

In our case, in order to analyse the issue of synchronization through the index of concordance, it is first necessary to establish the chronology of the time-scale components. The turning points chronology provides a collection of dates at which the time-scale components of industrial production reaches a peak or a trough, and then defines periods of contractions and expansions in economic activity with declining and increasing growth rates, respectively. So far, we have established a cycle chronology with reference to the longest time-scale components, $D7$ and $D6$, using the 'growth'-rate cycle definition, which delineates periods of cyclical upswings and downswings around an underlying trend.

In Tables 3.2 and 3.3 we present the values of the index of concordance for the time scale components $D7$ and $D6$ of G7 countries. In order to determine the evolution over time of the degree of synchronization between countries, we computed the index of concordance for two sub-samples: 1961–81 and 1982–2001. The results from the sub-sample 1961–81 are presented in the lower diagonal of

Table 3.2   Index of concordance $D7$, 1961–81 (lower diagonal) and 1982–2001 (upper diagonal)

	Canada	France	Germany	Italy	Japan	UK	USA
Canada	–	.70	.62	.75	.75	.87	.93
France	.71	–	.91	.90	.78	.75	.71
Germany	.77	.79	–	.89	.71	.67	.63
Italy	.71	.57	.77	–	.77	.80	.76
Japan	.58	.66	.72	.68	–	.66	.68
UK	.68	.54	.67	.96	.65	-	.79
USA	.63	.29	36	.67	.37	.70	–

Table 3.3   Index of concordance $D6$, 1961–81 (lower diagonal) and 1982–2001 (upper diagonal)

	Canada	France	Germany	Italy	Japan	UK	USA
Canada	–	.62	.71	.80	.58	.95	.97
France	.76	–	.74	.78	.87	.64	.64
Germany	.63	.83	–	.75	.74	.72	.71
Italy	.62	.55	.45	–	.64	.82	.80
Japan	.62	.85	.92	.52	–	.60	.58
UK	.86	.71	.63	.57	.56	–	.95
USA	.86	.67	.55	.67	.62	.66	

Tables 3.2 and 3.3, while the results from the sub-sample 1981–2001 are presented in the upper diagonal.

The comparison of the average values of the index of concordance for each sub-period may provide evidence about the extent to which G7 countries have become more synchronized over time. The average values of the index of concordance[12] document an increase in the overall degree of synchronization between G7 countries in both time-scale components. But the comparison of the values of the index of concordance between two countries suggests that the pattern of synchronization has changed over time. In particular, from the 1980s there is evidence of the emergence of clusters of countries characterized by a very high degree of synchronization between them: the Anglo and the Euro-area countries. Indeed, between 1982–2001 for the $D7$ and $D6$ components the Anglo countries present values of the index of concordance of .86 and .96, and the Euro-area countries present values of .90 and .76, respectively. Thus, if the Anglo countries show an almost perfect synchronization between them for the longest business cycle time-scale component $D6$, the Euro-area countries show a very high level of synchronization at the longest time-scale component $D7$.

Not surprisingly, given the results of the previous section, Italy seems to show a behaviour that is changing across time-scales, as it shows higher synchronization with the Anglo than with the other Euro-area countries at the $D6$ time-scale component.

Trend components

Finally, we look at the trend components, shown in Figure 3.2 as measured by the first difference (monthly rate of growth of trend) for all the countries. It is evident that the decline in the growth rate of the industrial production index, particularly for the European countries and Japan, is due to the well-known catching-up, productivity slowdown and structural transformations (decline in industrial ratio to GNP). The continental European countries, that is France, Germany and Italy, behave in a similar way, while Japan, after the extraordinary growth of the first years, is almost stationary in the last period. Over the whole period, not one of the European countries reduced its distance from the USA, as the gains obtained from

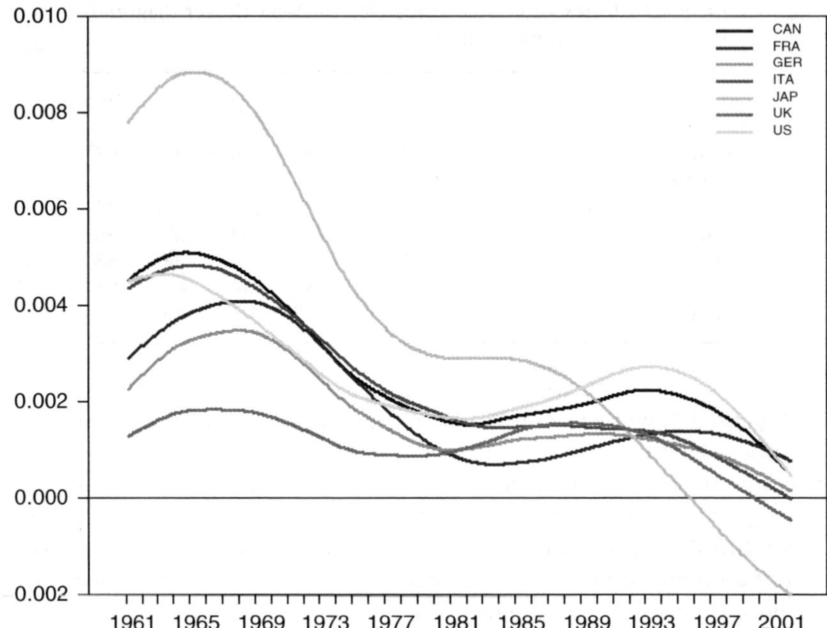

Figure 3.2   First differences of the trend components for G7 countries

the first years following the second world war up to the mid-1970s by the European countries have been more than made up by the USA in recent years. Moreover, Figure 3.2 shows that G7 countries, even if characterized by similar tendencies, display very different average growth rates that are changing throughout the period. In particular, countries' growth rates converge downwards until the early 1980s, then diverge upwards throughout the 1990s, and finally converge downwards again at the beginning of the twenty-first century.

Conclusions

In this chapter we have applied wavelets to analyse the characteristics of the time scale components of output as well as the relationships between pairs of countries across time scales for G7 countries.

Our analysis of volatility, co-movements and synchronization for G7 countries at different time scales suggests the following main results:

1   There is no convincing evidence of a decrease in output variability if we analyse the standard deviations of G7 countries at different time scales over different time periods (the only reduction seems to be confined to the very short run and the demand components).
2   Our analysis of the overall linkage between the different time-scale components among G7 countries based on the maximum lead/lag cross-correlation

coefficients highlights a different correlation between groups of countries and across time scales. In particular, strong and stable relationships, in the sense that they hold across time scales, emerge among the Anglo countries, and between France and Germany at each time scale, with Italy displaying the closest links to the Anglo or to the Euro-area countries according to the different time scales.

3   There is evidence of an increase in the overall degree of synchronization between G7 countries in both time-scale components analysed ($D7$ and $D6$), particularly between the Anglo countries at the $D6$ time-scale, and between the Euro-area countries at the $D7$ time-scale.

Our results seem to suggest that time-scale decomposition through wavelet analysis may reveal very different aspects in the characteristics and correlations of business cycle fluctuations that may have important implications for economic policy. In particular, the growing international business cycle uniformity, associated to the most recent divergence of individual growth rates, suggests an instruments/targets relationship where structural economic policies are assigned to individual countries, as they may steadily affect a country's growth rate, and countercyclical monetary and fiscal policies are assigned to supranational authorities, as aggregate demand policies may be ineffective at a national level for problems of coordination.

Notes

1   Schumpeter 'described short cycles under the Kitchin–Crun terminology; then the good old business cycle of allegedly eight to ten years' periodicity was labelled Juglar cycles; and of course there were also the long waves of Kondratieff ... Between Juglar's and Kondratieff's came Kuznets' intermediate cycles in construction and immigration, with an alleged approximate periodicity of 18 to 20 years', Samuelson, 1998: 33–4. The wavelet approach is able to disentangle the components with different periodicities. Let's note that this methodology violates the individualistic methodology of the mainstream approach in favour of a holistic view which claims that the aggregate is the outcome of the interaction of several different components.

2   Of course, since the different time periods merge into each other, and the impulses of the different components propagate through time, exact identification would be impossible. Moreover, the inexistence of a single source of recession (such as oil prices, interest rates) is erroneous (Zarnovitz, 1998). A holistic, cliometric approach would be more appropriate (Temin, 1998).

3   Only for Canada do we use real GDP data.

4   In a sense, this assumption requires time series homogeneity properties.

5   There are many possible choices for wavelet functions (see Gencay *et al.* (2001)). In this work we use the nearly symmetric wavelets or symmlet with 8 vanishing moments, meaning that polynomial of an order less than 8 will be passed through by the mother wavelets.

6   See Blanchard (1997) and Caballero and Hammour (1998) for a notion of the medium term business cycle.

7   Following the papers by Kim and Nelson (1999) and McConnell and Perez-Quiros (2000) many other papers have analysed both this decline in volatility and its causes (see Stock and Watson, 2002, for a review of the recent literature on the moderation of business cycle fluctuations).

 8 We maintain the traditional time interval for business cycle fluctuations (from 1.5 to 8 or 10 years, that is $D4$ to $D6$ in terms of time-scale components).
 9 We do not report here for brevity the results of the cross-country relationships of the other G7 countries.
10 The values of the contemporaneous cross-correlation coefficients between the two series may be used as a measure of their degree of synchronization.
11 These results do not contrast with those obtained in previous studies using different methodologies (see Duarte and Holden, 2003, and Stock and Watson, 2003).
12 Average values of the index of concordance are .64 and .76 for the $D7$ component, and .67 and .74 for the $D6$ component in 1961–81 and 1982–2001, respectively.

References

Artis, M.J. and Zhang, W. (1999) 'Further evidence on the international business cycle and the ERM: is there a European business cycle', *Oxford Economic Papers*, 51: 120–32.

Backus, D.K. and Kehoe, P.J. (1992) 'International evidence on the historical properties of business cycles', *American Economic Review*, 82: 864–88.

Blanchard, O. (1997) 'The medium run', *Brookings Papers on Economic Activity*, 2: 89–158.

Bordo, M.D. and Helbling, T. (2003) 'Have national business cycles become more synchronized?', *Working Paper*, no. 10130. New York: National Bureau of Economic Research.

Burns, A.F. and Mitchell, W.C. (1946) *Measuring Business Cycles*. New York: National Bureau of Economic Research.

Caballero, R. and Hammour, M. (1998) 'Jobless growth: appropriability, factor substitution and unemployment', *Carnegie-Rochester Conference Series on Public Policy*, 48: 51–94.

Chauvet, M. and Potter, S. (2001) 'Recent changes in the US business cycle', *The Manchester School*, 69: 481–508.

Christodoulakis, N., Dimelis S.P. and Kollintzas, T. (1995) 'Comparisons of business cycles in the EC. Idiosyncracies and regularities', *Economica*, 62: 1–27.

Cogley, T. and Nason, J.M. (1995) 'Effects of the Hodrick–Prescott filter on trend and difference stationary series implications for business cycle research', *Journal of Economic Dynamics and Control*, 19: 253–78.

Comin, D. and Gertler, M. (2003) 'Medium term business cycle', *Working Paper*, no. 10003. New York: National Bureau of Economic Research.

De Haan, J.D., Inklaar, R. and Sleupen, O. (2002) 'Have business cycles become more synchronized?', *Journal of Common Market Studies* , 40: 23–42.

Doyle, B. and Faust J., (2002) 'An investigation of co-movements among the growth rates of the G-7 countries', *Federal Reserve Bulletin*, October: 427–37.

Duarte, A. and Holden, K. (2003) 'The business cycle in the G7 economies', *International Journal of Forecasting*, 19: 685–700.

Gencay, R., Selcuk, F. and Whitcher, B. (2001) *An Introduction to Wavelets and Other Filtering Methods in Finance and Economics* : San Diego: Academic Press.

Granger, C.W.J. (1966) 'The typical spectral shape of an economic variable', *Econometrica*, 34: 150–61.

Guay, A. and St-Amant, P. (1997) 'Do the Hodrick–Prescott and Baxter–King filters provide a good approximation of business cycles?', *Cahiers de Recherche CREFE Working Papers*, no. 53.

Harding, D. and Pagan, A. (2002) 'Dissecting the cycle: a methodological investigation', *Journal of Monetary Economics*, 49: 365–81.

Harvey, A.C. and Jaeger, A. (1993) 'Detrending, stylized facts and the business cycle', *Journal of Applied Econometrics*, 8: 231–47.

Kim, C.J. and Nelson, C.R. (1999) 'Has the US economy become more stable', *Review of Economics and Statistics*, 81: 608–16.

Kim, S. and Haueck, F. (2003) 'The relationship between financial variables and real economic activity: evidence from spectral and wavelet analyses', *Studies in Nonlinear Dynamics and Econometrics*, 7, article 4.

Kose, M.A., Prasad, E.S. and Terrones, M.E. (2003) 'How does globalization affect the synchronization of business cycles?', *IZA Discussion Paper*, no. 72.

Lucas, R.E. (1977) 'Understanding business cycles', in D. Brunner and A.H Meltzer (eds), *Stabilization of the Domestic and International Economy*. Amsterdam: North Holland.

Mc Connel, M.M. and Perez Quiros, G. (2000) 'Output fluctuations in the United States: what has changed since the early 1980s?', *American Economic Review*, 90: 1464–76.

Ramsey, J.B. and Lampart, C. (1998a) 'The decomposition of economic relationship by time scale using wavelets: money and income', *Macroeconomic Dynamics*, 2: 49–71.

Ramsey, J.B. and Lampart, C. (1998b) 'The decomposition of economic relationship by time scale using wavelets: expenditure and income', *Studies in Nonlinear Dynamics and Econometrics*, 3: 23–42.

Ramsey, J.B. (2002) 'Wavelets in economics and finance: past and future', *Studies in Nonlinear Dynamics and Econometrics*, 6, article 1.

Samuelson, P. (1998) 'Summing up on business cycles: opening address', in J.C. Fuhrer and S. Schuh (eds), *Beyond Shocks: What Causes Business Cycles?* Boston: The Federal Reserve Bank of Boston Conference Series, 42.

Schumpter, J. (1939) *Business Cycles*. New York: Mc-Graw Hill.

Stock, J.H. and Watson, M.W. (2000) 'Business cycle fluctuations in US macroeconomic time series', in B. Taylor and M. Woodford (eds), *Handbook of Macroeconomics*, Vol.1. Amsterdam: North Holland, pp. 3–64.

Stock, J.H. and Watson, M.W. (2002) 'Has the business cycle changed and why', *NBER Macroeconomics Annual*: 159–218.

Stock, J.H. and Watson, M.W. (2003) 'Understanding changes in international business cycle dynamics', *Working Paper*, no. 9859. New York: National Bureau of Economic Research.

Temin, P. (1998) 'The causes of American business cycles: an essay in economic historiography', J.C. Fuhrer and S. Schuh (eds), *Beyond Shocks: What Causes Business Cycles?* Boston: The Federal Reserve Bank of Boston Conference Series, 42.

Zarnovitz, V. (1998) 'Has the business cycle been abolished', *Working Paper*, no. 6367. New York: National Bureau of Economic Research..

4
Trend Estimation, Signal–Noise Ratios and the Frequency of Observations

Andrew C. Harvey and Thomas M. Trimbur

The implied signal extraction filters in unobserved components models depend on key signal–noise ratios. This chapter examines how these ratios change with the observation interval. The analysis is based on continuous time models and is carried out for both stocks and flows. As a byproduct, a connection is established between continuous time flow models and the canonical decomposition.

Introduction

Unobserved components (UC) models with a stochastic trend form the basis for a class of flexible procedures for trend estimation and detrending. The behaviour of the extracted series depends on key signal–noise ratios. These signal–noise ratios are sometimes pre-specified, as in the Hodrick–Prescott (HP) filter or when a trend is assumed to be deterministic. More generally they may be estimated by maximum likelihood (ML) applied to a fully specified model. Bayesian procedures may also be used and these have the attraction that prior information on plausible values may be taken on board. Most Bayesian treatments of UC models, such as those in Frühwirth–Schnatter(1994) and Harvey, Trimbur and van Dijk (2003), are based on non-informative priors for variances. The ability to employ proper priors provides a bridge between a full model-based approach, where all parameters are freely estimated, and a more restricted approach where particular values are imposed. A Bayesian treatment with proper priors may also be appealing on pragmatic grounds when ML fails to converge to a plausible solution.

A concern with values of signal–noise ratios leads on to the issue of comparability over different sampling periods. This issue can be addressed by constructing models at a fine sampling interval and then deducing the corresponding models at a coarser frequency. A more elegant approach is to set up a base model in continuous time. Such models provide a good statistical framework in which to analyse the effects of detrending procedures for both stock and flow variables. Some interesting new results emerge from tackling the problem in this way. In particular, setting up a continuous time model for a flow variable and using this as the basis for signal extraction from discretely sampled observations leads to a weighting kernel that tends to produce a relatively smoother trend than that obtained from an analogous model initially formulated at the discrete time observation interval. Furthermore, it can be shown that there is a connection between signal extraction in continuous time models and the canonical decomposition in which the variance of the irregular component is maximized; see Tiao and Hillmer (1978), Box *et al.* (1978), and Pierce (1979). This provides an important link between structural time series models, as implemented in the STAMP package of Koopman *et al.* (2001), and procedures based on the canonical decomposition like Tramo-Seats of Gomez and Maravall (2000). Results concerning the issue of adapting the HP filter to different frequencies was also be obtained using this approach and can be found in an extended version of this chapter, published as a Euroindicators working paper.

Signal extraction implies a weighting of the observations. Exposing the weighting pattern provides insight into what the procedures are doing and how they compare. It also allows a comparison with nonparametric methods of signal extraction where the weights are explicit. Such methods are based on weighted moving averages, the shapes of which are called kernels; see, for example, Härdle (1990). The implied signal extraction weights from a fitted unobserved component time series model constitute a kernel and signal–noise ratios concerning the relative variation in trend and stationary components play a similar role to kernel bandwidths. For simple UC models' expressions for the signal extraction weights may be obtained by the Wiener–Kolmogorov filter, as described in Whittle (1982). More generally, numerical values for the weights can be calculated for any model in state space form by using the algorithm of Koopman and Harvey (2003). When an expression for the Wiener–Kolmogorov filter can be obtained, a complementary analysis is provided by the frequency domain. The Fourier transform of the Wiener–Kolmogorov filter gives the frequency response function. Its absolute value, the gain, is useful for comparing the properties of different filters. Thus it can be used for assessing how well one filter might approximate another and for determining a suitable value for the signal–noise ratio. However, because the gain shows the effect on a stationary time series, some care has to be taken in deducing the implications for detrending where the series are, by the very nature of the problem, nonstationary. Many of the arguments in the literature are flawed because they fail to adequately address this point.

The plan of this chapter is as follows. The next section reviews discrete unobserved components models for stochastic trends, including the model for the canonical decomposition, and analyses the effect of detrending filters in the frequency domain. We then look at corresponding models in continuous time and note the relationship between signal extraction and the canonical decomposition. A final section presents conclusions.

Discrete time models for stochastic trends

The simplest time series models for trend analysis are made up of a *stochastic trend* component, μ_t, and a random irregular term. Other components, such as seasonals and cycles, may be added, and the implications of doing this will be discussed later.

In the *local level* model the trend is just a random walk. Thus,

$$y_t = \mu_t + \varepsilon_t, \quad \varepsilon_t \sim NID\,(0, \sigma_\varepsilon^2), \quad t = 1, \ldots, T \tag{4.1}$$

$$\mu_t = \mu_{t-1} + \eta_t, \quad \eta_t \sim NID(0, \sigma_\eta^2) \tag{4.2}$$

where the irregular and level disturbances, ε_t and η_t, respectively, are mutually independent and the notation $NID(0, \sigma^2)$ denotes normally and independently distributed with mean zero and variance σ^2. The signal–noise ratio, $q = \sigma_\eta^2/\sigma_\varepsilon^2$, plays the key role in determining how observations should be weighted for prediction and signal extraction. The higher is q, the more past observations are discounted in forecasting the future. Similarly a higher q means that the closest observations receive a higher weight when signal extraction is carried out.

The *local linear trend* model is more general in that the trend component in (4.1) has a stochastic slope, β_t, which itself follows a random walk. Thus:

$$\begin{aligned} \mu_t &= \mu_{t-1} + \beta_{t-1} + \eta_t & \eta_t &\sim NID(0, \sigma_\eta^2) \\ \beta_t &= \beta_{t-1} + \zeta_t, & \zeta_t &\sim NID(0, \sigma_\zeta^2) \end{aligned} \tag{4.3}$$

where the irregular, level and slope disturbances, ε_t, η_t and ζ_t, respectively, are mutually independent. Setting σ_η^2 to zero gives an *integrated random walk* trend, which when estimated tends to be relatively smooth. The model is often referred to as the 'smooth trend' model. The signal–noise ratio for this model is given by $q = \sigma_\zeta^2/\sigma_\varepsilon^2$.

State space form and the Kalman filter

The statistical treatment of unobserved component models is based on the state space form (SSF). Once a model has been put in SSF, the Kalman filter yields estimators of the components based on current and past observations. Signal extraction refers to estimation of components based on all the information in the sample. Signal extraction is based on smoothing recursions which run backwards from the last observation. Predictions are made by extending the Kalman filter forward. Root-mean-square errors (RMSEs) can be computed for all estimators and prediction or confidence intervals constructed.

The unknown variance parameters are estimated by constructing a likelihood function from the one-step-ahead prediction errors, or innovations, produced by the Kalman filter. The likelihood function is maximized by an iterative procedure. The calculations can be done with the STAMP package of Koopman *et al.* (2000). Once estimated, the fit of the model can be checked using standard time series diagnostics such as tests for residual serial correlation.

Reduced form

If the local level model is differenced, it can be seen that the autocorrelations are zero beyond the first lag. The reduced form is therefore an *ARIMA*(0, 1, 1) model:

$$\Delta y_t = \xi_t + \theta \xi_{t-1}, \qquad \xi_t \sim NID(0, \sigma^2) \tag{4.4}$$

and by equating the autocorrelations at lag one it can be shown that:

$$\theta = (-q - 2 + \sqrt{q^2 + 4q})/2 \tag{4.5}$$

Note that θ is restricted to the range $-1 \leq \theta \leq 0$.

The local linear trend model is made stationary by differencing twice. It can be shown that the reduced form is *ARIMA*(0, 2, 2), but only part of the invertibility region is admissible; see Harvey (1989, p69).

Prediction

The expression for the optimal predictor of a future observation in a local level model depends only on θ which is a function of q as in (4.5). It is the same for all lead times and is equal to the filtered estimator of the level at time T, $\tilde{\mu}_T$. Thus:

$$\tilde{y}_{T+l|T} = \tilde{\mu}_T = (1 + \theta) \sum_{j=0}^{\infty} (-\theta)^j y_{T-j}, \quad l = 1, 2, 3 \ldots \tag{4.6}$$

which is an exponentially weighted moving average (EWMA). A negative θ, as implied by (4.5), means that all weights are positive.

Signal extraction

As already noted, the calculations for prediction and signal extraction are generally carried out using state space methods. However, analysing the implied weighting patterns for the observations in making predictions and extracting trends is important in acquiring an understanding of what exactly the models are doing and how they relate to other methods.

If a Gaussian model consists of two stochastic components, μ_t and υ_t, the Wiener–Komogorov (WK) formula for finding the weights to extract the optimal (minimum mean square error) estimator[1] of μ_t in a doubly infinite sample, is:

$$\tilde{\mu}_{t|\infty} = w(L) y_t = \sum_{j=-\infty}^{\infty} w_{-j} L^j y_t = \sum_{j=-\infty}^{\infty} w_j y_{t+j} \tag{4.7}$$

$$w(L) = \frac{\gamma_{\mu y}(L)}{\gamma_y(L)} = \frac{\gamma_\mu(L)}{\gamma_y(L)} + \frac{\gamma_{\mu \upsilon}(L)}{\gamma_y(L)} \tag{4.8}$$

where L is the lag operator, $\gamma_\mu(L)$ is the autocovariance generating function (ACGF) of μ_t and $\gamma_{\mu y}(L)$ is the cross-covariance generating function of μ_t and y_t. The ACGF of y_t is usually evaluated in terms of the reduced form parameters. For a stationary ARMA process, written $\phi^{-1}(L)\theta(L)\xi_t$, where $\phi(L)$ and $\theta(L)$ are polynomials in the lag operator and ξ_t is white noise with variance σ^2, the ACGF is given directly by:

$$\gamma(L) = \{|\theta(L)|^2 / |\phi(L)|^2\} \sigma^2 \tag{4.9}$$

where we follow Whittle[2] in adopting the convention that $|\theta(L)|^2 = \theta(L)\theta(L^{-1})$ and similarly for $\phi(L)$. Formula (4.7) can still be used for nonstationary models even though expressions like (4.9) are no longer strictly ACGFs.

Local level model

Provided $q > 0$, the WK formula for estimating μ_t yields:

$$\tilde{\mu}_{t|\infty} = w(L)y_t = \frac{\sigma_\eta^2/|1-L|^2}{\sigma^2|1+\theta L|^2/|1-L|^2}y_t = \frac{(1+\theta)^2}{|1+\theta L|^2}y_t \tag{4.10}$$

as $\sigma_\eta^2 = (1+\theta)^2\sigma^2$. On recognizing that $1/|1+\theta L|^2$ is the ACGF of an AR(1) model with autoregressive parameter $-\theta$ and unit disturbance variance, it can be seen that the weights decline symmetrically and exponentially, that is:

$$w_j = \{(1+\theta)/(1-\theta)\}(-\theta)^{|j|}, \qquad j = 0, 1, 2, \ldots. \tag{4.11}$$

with $-1 < \theta \leq 0$. Setting $L = 1$ in (4.10) shows that the weights sum to unity.

Local linear trend

The WK formula shows that when σ_η^2 is zero the weights decay according to a damped sine wave; see Harvey and Koopman (2000). The initial slow decline of the weights contrasts with the exponential decline of the weights for a random walk trend in (4.11). Hence the smooth trend.

Canonical decomposition

An alternative approach to trend estimation is to begin with a model for the observations and then break it down into components. The canonical decomposition of Pierce (1979) and Hillmer and Tiao (1978) can be applied to any ARIMA(p, d, q) model provided that $q \geq p + d$. Here we will concentrate on the ARIMA$(0, 1, 1)$ model so as to compare the canonical decomposition with the random walk plus noise. The ARIMA$(0, 1, 1)$ model can be decomposed as in (4.1), but with level:

$$\mu_t = \mu_{t-1} + \eta_t + \theta^\dagger \eta_{t-1}, \qquad \eta_t \sim NID(0, \sigma_\eta^2) \tag{4.12}$$

where $|\theta^\dagger| \leq 1$ and $E(\varepsilon_s\eta_t) = 0$ for all s, t. Note that the θ parameter in the reduced form, (4.4), is no longer restricted to being negative as it is for a random walk plus noise.

As it stands, the model is not identifiable and so restrictions must be placed on it. Instead of setting $\theta^\dagger$ equal to zero so as to give a random walk plus noise, the idea in the canonical decomposition is to minimize the signal–noise ratio for a given value of θ, thereby determining the value of $\theta^\dagger$. Box *et al.* (1978) show that this means setting $\theta^\dagger = 1$. In this case, we find, by equating the variance and lag one autocorrelation of the first differences, that $\sigma_\eta^2 = (1+\theta)^2\sigma^2/4$, $\sigma_\varepsilon^2 = (1-\theta)^2\sigma^2/4$.

The WK signal extraction formula gives:

$$w^\dagger(L) = \frac{\sigma_\eta^2}{\sigma^2}\frac{|1+L|^2}{|1+\theta L|^2} = \frac{(1+\theta)^2}{|1+\theta L|^2}\frac{|1+L|^2}{4} \tag{4.13}$$

This yields:[3]

$$w_0^\dagger = (1+\theta)/2, \tag{4.14}$$

$$w_j^\dagger = [(1+\theta)(1-\theta)/4](-\theta)^{|j|-1}, \qquad j = \pm 1, \pm 2, \dots. $$

for $-1 < \theta \le 1$. Thus the weights start their exponential decline at $j = \pm 1$ and w_0 is less dominant than in the random walk plus noise.

If $\tilde{\eta}_T$ denotes the MMSE of η_T, the forecast function for the trend, which is also the forecast function for the observations, is:

$$\tilde{\mu}_{T+l|T} = \tilde{\mu}_T + \eta_T, \qquad l = 1, 2, \dots \tag{4.15}$$

The implications of the fact that the forecasts are not equal to $\tilde{\mu}_T^\dagger$ are brought home most clearly in the special case where y_t is a random walk. The forecast function for $l \ge 1$ is just y_T, but $\tilde{\mu}_T = (3/4)y_T + (1/4)y_{T-1}$; see Box *et al.* (1978: 319). Similarly the estimates of the trend within the sample, given by:

$$\tilde{\mu}_{t|T} = \frac{1}{4}y_{t-1} + \frac{1}{2}y_t + \frac{1}{4}y_{t+1}, \qquad t = 2, \dots, T-1 \tag{4.16}$$

reflect an attempt to smooth a process that would appear to inherently unsmoothable.

For more general models, the key feature of a canonical decomposition is that the MA polynomial in the trend, $\theta^\dagger(L)$, should have at least one root on the unit circle; see Box *et al.* (1978: 317). Hence $w^\dagger(e^{-i\lambda}) = 0$ for some λ. In the case of the *ARIMA*(0, 1, 1) above, the factor of $1 + L$ in (4.12) means that $w^\dagger(e^{-i\lambda}) = 0$ at $\lambda = \pi$. The canonical decomposition of the *ARIMA*(0, 2, 2) model also has a root of minus one – a factor of $1 + L$ – in the moving average; see Maravall (1993). As an interesting corollary it follows that when the $1 + L$ factor is present:

$$w(-1) = \sum_{j=-\infty}^{\infty} (-1)^i w_i = w_0 + 2\sum_{i=1}^{\infty}(-1)^i w_i = 0 \tag{4.17}$$

The local linear trend model can be modified to produce a canonical decomposition simply by replacing η_t by $\zeta_t/2$ in the level equation, so that:

$$\Delta^2 \mu_t = \zeta_t + \zeta_{t-1} \tag{4.18}$$

Unlike (4.12), this does not require an extra element in the state vector.

Frequency domain analysis and Butterworth filters

The effect of any linear filter, $w(L)$, can be obtained from the frequency response function, which is found by replacing L by $exp(-i\lambda)$, where λ denotes frequency in radians. The gain is the modulus of the frequency response function. Assuming the original series to be stationary, the gain shows how the amplitude at each frequency is affected. Squaring the gain gives the factor by which the spectrum of the original series must be multiplied to give the spectrum of the filtered series. When the filter is symmetric, the frequency response function is real and if it is nowhere negative it is the same as the gain. A comparison of gains can be used to give an indication of the closeness of two filters.

Writing $w(e^{-i\lambda})$ somewhat more compactly as $w(\lambda)$, the gain for extracting an mth order stochastic trend, as defined in (5.3), from a trend plus noise model (4.1), can be expressed as:

$$w(\lambda) = \frac{1}{1 + q^{-1}(2 - 2\cos\lambda)^m} = \frac{1}{1 + q^{-1}2^{2m}\sin^{2m}(\lambda/2)}, \qquad 0 \le \lambda \le \pi \qquad (4.19)$$

where $m = 1$ for the random walk while $m = 2$ gives the integrated random walk.

If $\lambda_{0.5}$ is the frequency for which the gain equals one-half, the corresponding signal–noise ratio is:

$$q(\lambda_{0.5}) = [2\sin(\lambda_{0.5}/2)]^{2m}, \qquad 0 < \lambda_{0.5} < \pi \qquad (4.20)$$

A frequency of $\lambda_{0.5} = 0.1583$ corresponds to a period of 39.70 quarters or 9.93 years. Hence, with $m = 2$, $q(\lambda_{0.5}) = q(0.1583) = 0.000625$ and its reciprocal is $1,600$, which is the HP filter smoothing constant for quarterly data.

The gain for the canonical local level model, (4.12), is:

$$w^{\dagger}(\lambda) = \frac{(2 + 2\cos\lambda)}{(2 + 2\cos\lambda) + (\sigma_\eta^2/\sigma_\varepsilon^2)(2 - 2\cos\lambda)} = \frac{1}{1 + (\sigma_\eta^2/\sigma_\varepsilon^2)\tan^2(\lambda/2)} \qquad (4.21)$$

As noted by Gomez (2001: 366), this is the Butterworth tangent filter; the Butterworth sine filter has a gain given by (4.19). Now suppose the trend is of the form:

$$\Delta^m \mu_t = (1 + L)^m \zeta_t, \qquad m = 1, 2$$

This implies the more general Butterworth tangent filter with a gain of:

$$w^{\dagger}(\lambda) = \frac{1}{1 + (2^{2m}/q^{\dagger})\tan^{2m}(\lambda/2)} \qquad (4.22)$$

where $q^{\dagger}$ is ratio of the long-run variance[4] of $\Delta^m \mu_t$, namely $4^m\sigma_\zeta^2$, to σ_ε^2. For the filter to be one-half at $\lambda_{0.5}$:

$$q^{\dagger}(\lambda_{0.5}) = [2\tan(\lambda_{0.5}/2)]^{2m}, \qquad 0 < \lambda_{0.5} < \pi \qquad (4.23)$$

If $\lambda_{0.5}$ is reasonably close to zero, this gives a value similar in magnitude to that of q for the sine filter. Thus for $m = 2$ and $\lambda_{0.5} = 0.1583$ we get 0.000629. A plot of the gains shows them to be very close. Similarly the gain for the canonical model of (4.18), with one unit root in the MA(2) disturbance for the trend, is also very close if the signal–noise ratio is determined on the basis of the long-run variance of $\Delta^2 \mu_t$, that is using σ_ζ^2.

Continuous time models and the frequency of observations

Now suppose observations are generated by a stochastic trend model, but are observed every δ time periods, where δ is an integer. For a stock variable, this leads to a model for the observations in which the level and slope disturbances are correlated. For variables observed as a flow, that is aggregated over the δ time periods, the level, slope and irregular disturbances are all correlated with each other; see Harvey (1989: 309–26). The implications are best explored by working with models set up in continuous time. If the observations are irregularly spaced, δ need no longer be an integer.

Stochastic trends in continuous time

The local level component, $\mu(t)$, is defined by $d\mu(t) = \sigma_\eta dW_\eta(t)$, where $W_\eta(t)$ is a standard Wiener process. Thus the increment $d\mu(t)$ has mean zero and variance $\sigma_\eta^2 dt$.

The linear trend component is:

$$\begin{bmatrix} d\mu(t) \\ d\beta(t) \end{bmatrix} = \begin{bmatrix} 0 & 1 \\ 0 & 0 \end{bmatrix} \begin{bmatrix} \mu(t)dt \\ \beta(t)dt \end{bmatrix} + \begin{bmatrix} \sigma_\eta dW_\eta(t) \\ \sigma_\zeta dW_\zeta(t) \end{bmatrix} \tag{4.24}$$

where $W_\eta(t)$ and $W_\zeta(t)$ are mutually independent Wiener processes. Further discussion can be found in Harvey (1989, ch. 9).

We suppose that observations, y_τ, $\tau = 1, \ldots, T$, are made at intervals δ apart. Let t_τ denote the time at which the τth observation is made and let μ_τ and β_τ denote $\mu(t_\tau)$ and $\beta(t_\tau)$ respectively.

Stocks

For the local level model it follows almost immediately that:

$$\mu_\tau = \mu_{\tau-1} + \eta_\tau, \qquad Var(\eta_\tau) = \delta\sigma_\eta^2 \tag{4.25}$$

since

$$\eta_\tau = \mu(t_\tau) - \mu(t_{\tau-1}) = \sigma_\eta \int_{t_{\tau-1}}^{t_\tau} dW_\eta(t) = \sigma_\eta(W_\eta(t_\tau) - W_\eta(t_{\tau-1}))$$

The discrete model is therefore a random walk for equally spaced observations. If the observation at time τ is made up of $\mu(t_\tau)$ plus a white-noise disturbance term, ε_τ, with variance σ_ε^2, the discrete time measurement equation can be written:

$$y_\tau = \mu_\tau + \varepsilon_\tau, \qquad Var(\varepsilon_\tau) = \sigma_\varepsilon^2, \qquad \tau = 1, \ldots, T \tag{4.26}$$

and the set-up corresponds exactly to the familiar random walk plus noise model with signal–noise ratio $q_\delta = \delta\sigma_\eta^2/\sigma_\varepsilon^2 = \delta q$.

The local linear trend model may be handled in similar fashion. When $\sigma_\eta^2 = 0$, signal extraction with this model yields a cubic spline. Letting $\beta_\tau^* = \delta\beta_\tau$ gives a form analogous to (4.3), namely:

$$\begin{bmatrix} \mu_\tau \\ \beta_\tau^* \end{bmatrix} = \begin{bmatrix} 1 & 1 \\ 0 & 1 \end{bmatrix} \begin{bmatrix} \mu_{\tau-1} \\ \beta_{\tau-1}^* \end{bmatrix} + \begin{bmatrix} \eta_\tau \\ \zeta_\tau^* \end{bmatrix} \tag{4.27}$$

with

$$Var\begin{bmatrix} \eta_\tau \\ \zeta_\tau^* \end{bmatrix} = \delta^3 \sigma_\zeta^2 \begin{bmatrix} \frac{1}{3} & \vdots & \frac{1}{2} \\ \cdots\cdots\cdots\cdots & \vdots & \cdots\cdots \\ \frac{1}{2} & \vdots & 1 \end{bmatrix} \tag{4.28}$$

The correlation between the level and slope disturbances is $\rho = 0.866$. The most appropriate discrete time signal–noise ratio for capturing the behaviour of the trend extraction filter is $q_\delta = Var(\zeta_\tau^*)/Var(\varepsilon_\tau) = \delta^3 \sigma_\zeta^2/\sigma_\varepsilon^2 = \delta^3 q$.

Flows

For a flow, the irregular is assumed to be aggregated over the observation interval in the same way as the trend. Thus:

$$y_\tau = \int_{t_{\tau-1}}^{t_\tau} \mu(t)dt + \sigma_\varepsilon \int_{t_{\tau-1}}^{t_\tau} dW_\varepsilon(t)$$

where $W_\varepsilon(t)$ is a Wiener process, independent of $W_\eta(t)$.

Local level model

If the level is redefined as $\mu_\tau^* = \delta\mu(t_{\tau-1})$, it follows from (9.3.15) of Harvey (1989: 495) that the model can be cast in the standard future state form:

$$y_\tau = \mu_\tau^* + \varepsilon_\tau^*$$
$$\mu_{\tau+1}^* = \mu_\tau^* + \eta_\tau^* \tag{4.29}$$

with covariance matrix

$$Var\begin{bmatrix} \eta_\tau^* \\ \varepsilon_\tau^* \end{bmatrix} = \begin{bmatrix} \delta^3 \sigma_\eta^2 & \frac{1}{2}\delta^3 \sigma_\eta^2 \\ \frac{1}{2}\delta^3 \sigma_\eta^2 & \frac{1}{3}\delta^3 \sigma_\eta^2 + \delta\sigma_\varepsilon^2 \end{bmatrix}$$

Now

$$q_\delta^* = \frac{Var(\eta_\tau^*)}{Var(\varepsilon_\tau^*)} = \frac{\delta^3 \sigma_\eta^2}{\delta^3 \sigma_\eta^2/3 + \delta\sigma_\varepsilon^2} = \frac{\delta^2 q}{\delta^2 q/3 + 1} \tag{4.30}$$

If σ_η^2 is much smaller than σ_ε^2, this discrete time signal–noise ratio is approximately δ^2 times the continuous time ratio, q. However, the question is whether the correlation between the disturbances will now lead to the weights for filtering and smoothing having a very different pattern from those for a standard orthogonal discrete time model. If this is the case it may be misleading to interpret q_δ^* as a signal–noise ratio in the same way as for (4.1).

Local linear trend

It follows from (9.3.6) of Harvey (1989: 494) that after defining the level and slope as $\mu_\tau^* = \delta\mu(t_{\tau-1})$ and $\beta_\tau^* = \delta^2\beta(t_{\tau-1})$ respectively, the model with σ_η^2 zero is:

$$y_\tau = \mu_\tau^* + (1/2)\beta_\tau^* + \varepsilon_\tau^*, \qquad \tau = 1,\ldots,T \tag{4.31}$$

$$\mu_{\tau+1}^* = \mu_\tau^* + \beta_\tau^* + \eta_\tau^*$$

$$\beta_{\tau+1}^* = \beta_\tau^* + \zeta_\tau^*$$

with covariance matrix

$$Var\begin{bmatrix}\eta_\tau^*\\\zeta_\tau^*\\\varepsilon_\tau^*\end{bmatrix} = \begin{bmatrix}\frac{1}{3}\delta^5\sigma_\zeta^2 & \frac{1}{2}\delta^5\sigma_\zeta^2 & \frac{1}{8}\delta^5\sigma_\zeta^2\\[4pt]\frac{1}{2}\delta^5\sigma_\zeta^2 & \delta^5\sigma_\zeta^2 & \frac{1}{6}\delta^5\sigma_\zeta^2\\[4pt]\frac{1}{8}\delta^5\sigma_\zeta^2 & \frac{1}{6}\delta^5\sigma_\zeta^2 & \frac{1}{20}\delta^5\sigma_\zeta^2 + \delta\sigma_\varepsilon^2\end{bmatrix}$$

Although $Var(\eta_\tau^*)$ is not zero, its effect is dominated by that of $Var(\zeta_\tau^*)$. Hence

$$q_\delta^* = \frac{\delta^5 q}{\delta^5 q/20 + \delta} \simeq \delta^4 q \tag{4.32}$$

is an appropriate signal–noise ratio. If the continuous time signal noise ratio, $q = \sigma_\zeta^2/\sigma_\varepsilon^2$, is relatively small, the discrete time ratio is $q_\delta^* \simeq \delta^4 q$. Again the issue is whether the weighting pattern is significantly affected by the correlations induced by temporal aggregation.

Signal extraction for a flow

For the future state model as formulated in (4.29), let $\bar{\sigma}_\varepsilon^2 = Var(\varepsilon_\tau^*)$ and $\alpha^2 = q_\delta^* = \sigma_\eta^2/\bar{\sigma}_\varepsilon^2$. Then

$$\tilde{\mu}_\tau^* = w(L)y_\tau, \qquad w(L) = \frac{(1+\theta)^2}{|1+\theta L|^2}\frac{1+L}{2} \tag{4.33}$$

where, from Harvey and Koopman (2000) and (4.30), it can be seen that $\theta = f(q,\delta)$ since

$$\theta = \frac{2 - \alpha\sqrt{4-\alpha^2}}{\alpha^2 - 2} = \frac{2 - \delta\sqrt{q/(\delta^2 q/3 + 1)}\sqrt{4 - \delta^2 q/(\delta^2 q/3 + 1)}}{\delta^2 q/(\delta^2 q/3 + 1) - 2} \tag{4.34}$$

When $q = 0, \theta = -1$ and when $q = \infty$, $\alpha^2 = 3$ so $\theta = 2 - \sqrt{3} = 0.268$.

The weights in $w(L)$ do not decline symmetrically about zero. The weights assigned to y_τ and $y_{\tau-1}$ in (4.33) are the same, but since $\mu_\tau^* = \delta\mu(t_{\tau-1})$ this is as it should be because y_τ and $y_{\tau-1}$ are temporal aggregates over the periods $t_{\tau-2}$ to $t_{\tau-1}$ and $t_{\tau-1}$ to t_τ respectively. If, on the other hand, an estimator of $\delta\mu(t)$ is located midway between $t_{\tau-1}$ to t_τ, at time $t = (t_\tau + t_{\tau-1})/2 = t_\tau - \delta/2$, a symmetric filter centred on y_τ is obtained.

The smoothed estimator of the signal at a point midway between observations can be calculated by setting up a state space model in which the state vector is augmented by a cumulator variable as described in Harvey (1989, ch. 9). Unfortunately, this gives us little insight into the weights. However, Chambers and McGarry (2002: 396) show that the continuous time flow model can be represented by a state space model in which the disturbance driving the level is an MA(1) process with variance $2\delta^3\sigma_\eta^2/3$ and first-order autocovariance $\delta^3\sigma_\eta^2/6$. Thus the model has a level similar to (4.12) but with $\theta^\dagger = 0.268$ rather than one. Hence:

$$w(L) = \frac{(1+\theta)^2}{|1+\theta L|^2}\frac{|1+0.268L|^2}{1.268^2} \tag{4.35}$$

and explicit expressions for the weights may be obtained as was done for (4.13). If the strength of the signal is measured by the long-run variance, the signal–noise ratio is

$$q_\delta^{**} = \delta^3\sigma_\eta^2(2/3 + 2/6)/\delta\sigma_\varepsilon^2 = \delta^2\sigma_\eta^2/\sigma_\varepsilon^2 = \delta^2 q \tag{4.36}$$

The canonical connection

As was noted in the previous sub-section, the asymmetric estimator in (4.33) is of $\mu_\tau^* = \delta\mu_{\tau-1}$. Shifting the weights forward one time period gives an estimator of $\delta\mu_\tau$, that is:

$$\widetilde{\delta\mu_\tau} = \widetilde{\mu}_{\tau+1}^* = w(L)L^{-1}y_\tau$$

This expression is also asymmetric but with the weights a mirror image of those for $\widetilde{\mu}_\tau^* - 1 + L$ is replaced by $1 + L^{-1}$. What this gives us is an estimator of $\delta\mu(t_\tau)$, while $\widetilde{\mu}_\tau^*$ is an estimator of $\delta\mu(t_{\tau-1})$. An estimator of $\delta\mu(t)$ located midway between these points, at time $t = (t_\tau + t_{\tau-1})/2 = t_\tau - \delta/2$, can be constructed by taking the average of $\widetilde{\mu}_{\tau+1}^*$ and $\widetilde{\mu}_\tau^*$. The weighting function is then:

$$\frac{w(L) + w(L)L^{-1}}{2} = \frac{(1+\theta)^2}{|1+\theta L|^2}\frac{1+L+1+L^{-1}}{4}$$

and this is the same as the signal extraction formula for the canonical decomposition given earlier in (4.13). The implied reduced-form parameter is somewhat restricted, though, since, as noted below (4.33), it must lie in the range $-1 \le \theta \le 0.268$. The result is interesting as it provides a rationale for the canonical decomposition starting from a continuous time STSM. The paradox in forecasting with the canonical decomposition model is now resolved since it can be seen that $\widetilde{\mu}_T$ is the estimated level at time $t_{T-\delta/2}$ rather than at time t_T. The forecast function is as in (4.6).

A comparison of (4.13) with (4.35) shows that the former is not the MMSE estimator of $\delta\mu(t_\tau - \delta/2)$. Nevertheless it is useful to regard the signal extracted from the canonical model as being an approximation to the one obtained from the continuous time model. The canonical signal–noise ratio for observations at an interval of δ can then be expressed in terms of the continuous time signal–noise ratio, q. If the signal noise ratio is measured in terms of the long-run variance, as in (4.22), then:

$$q_\delta^\dagger = 4(1+\theta)^2/(1-\theta)^2 \tag{4.37}$$

Table 4.1 MMSE and canonical weights for extracting the level between observation times for $q = 0.5$

j	0	1	2	3	4
MMSE	.302	.180	.087	.042	.021
Canonical	.257	.191	.093	.045	.022
RW + noise	.346	.168	.082	.040	.019

Substituting for θ from (4.34) gives:

$$q_\delta^\dagger = \frac{4\{\delta^2 q/(\delta^2 q/3 + 1) - \delta\sqrt{q/(\delta^2 q/3 + 1)}\sqrt{4 - \delta^2 q/(\delta^2 q/3 + 1)}\}^2}{\{\delta^2 q/(\delta^2 q/3 + 1) - 4 + \delta\sqrt{q/(\delta^2 q/3 + 1)}\sqrt{4 - \delta^2 q/(\delta^2 q/3 + 1)}\}^2}$$

If q is reasonably small then $q_\delta^\dagger \simeq \delta^2 q$; compare (4.36).

Table 4.1 compares the MMSE and canonical weights for $q = 0.5$ and $\delta = 1$, and hence $\theta = -0.485$. For the MMSE weights, the criterion in (4.17), $w(-1)$, is 0.060. The random walk plus (uncorrelated) noise weights, obtained from (4.10), are also shown. The weights for the continuous time model lie between those for the canonical model and the random walk plus noise; the weights converge as σ_η^2 goes towards zero (θ goes towards minus one) and the level becomes deterministic.[5]

The signal–noise ratios for the continuous time model are $q_\delta^* = 0.429$ and $q_\delta^{**} = 0.5$, while for the canonical form, $q_\delta^\dagger = 0.480$ and for the random walk plus noise, $q_\delta = -(1 + \theta)^2/\theta = 0.549$.

A good and well-known example of series following a local level model, drawn from social life, is the series of Chicago purse-matching data, with q estimated as 0.208. (Harvey (1989: 89–90). Setting $q_\delta = 0.208$ corresponds to $\theta = -.636$ and a continuous time signal–noise ratio of $q = 0.2$. Figure 4.1 shows smoothed estimates at and between observations obtained from the augmented state space form, together with the canonical estimates obtained by averaging.

Repeating the above arguments for the local linear trend is more difficult. Table 4.2 shows the two sets of weights for the local linear trend, the MMSE weights obtained from the augmented state space form and canonical ones obtained by averaging the weights for extracting the trend at the two adjacent observations.[6] The weights are fairly close and $w(-1) = 0.0013$ for the MMSE weights. Although q might seem small, it will become apparent in later sections that much smaller values are likely to pertain for real macroeconomic time series. Chambers and McGarry (2002: 396) show that the model can be expressed in state space form with the level and slope disturbances following a vector MA(1). The long-run variance of the slope disturbance is $\delta^5 \sigma_\zeta^2$, so the slope to irregular signal–noise ratio is $\delta^4 q$; compare (4.36) and (4.36).

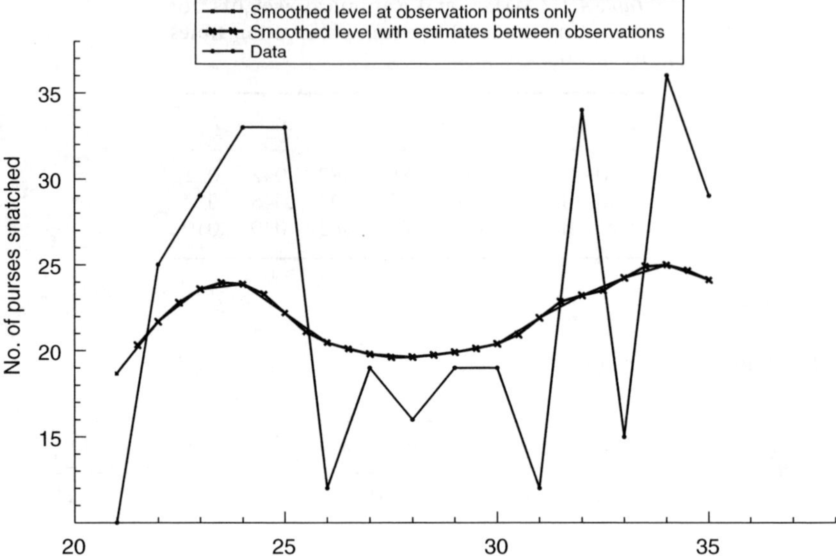

Figure 4.1   Smoothed estimates for Chicago purse-snatching data

Table 4.2   MMSE and canonical weights for extracting the level between observation times for the local linear trend with $q = 0.1$

j	0	1	2	3	4
MMSE	.198	.175	.128	.079	.040
Canonical	.192	.172	.128	.080	.042

Comparison of gains

For a *stock*, the continuous time local level signal extraction gain is exactly the same as the Butterworth sine filter with $m = 1$. For $m = 2$ the gain is:

$$w(\lambda) = \frac{\delta^3 + \delta^3(2 - 2\cos\lambda)/3}{\delta^3 + q^{-1}(2 - 2\cos\lambda)^2 + \delta^3(2 - 2\cos\lambda)/3} \qquad (4.38)$$

$$= \frac{1 + [2\sin(\lambda_{0.5}/2)]^2}{1 + [2\sin(\lambda_{0.5}/2)]^2 + (q\delta^3)^{-1}[2\sin(\lambda_{0.5}/2)]^4}$$

Figure 4.2 shows this gain and the HP gain for $\delta = 1$ (quarterly) and 4 (annual), with $q = 1/1,600$ in both cases. The gains are almost indistinguishable for $\delta = 1$ and are still close for annual data when the HP smoothing constant is 25. As δ increases they move further apart.

Turning to *flows*, a given value of q in the continuous time local level model implies a particular value of θ in the ARIMA(0,1,1) reduced form. It follows from

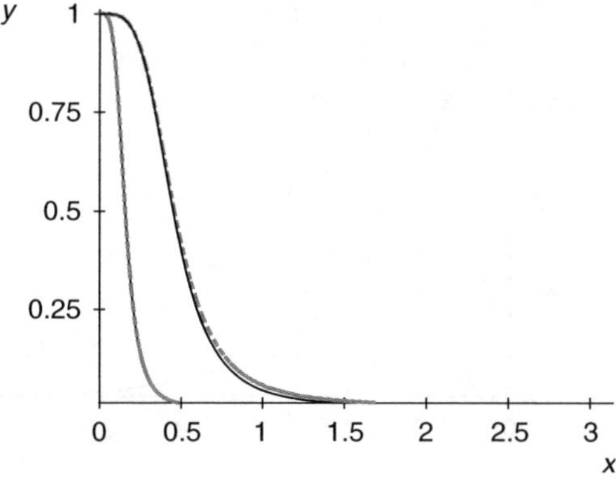

Figure 4.2   Gains for continuous time local linear trend model and HP (1,600 and 25) filter (continuous lines) gains for quarterly (lower lines) and annual data

the results of the previous section, that the gain functions for continuous time, random walk plus noise and canonical models are of the form:

$$w(\lambda) = \frac{(1+\theta)^2}{|1+\theta e^{-i\lambda}|^2}\frac{|1+\bar\theta e^{-i\lambda}|^2}{(1+\bar\theta)^2} = \frac{(1+\theta)^2}{1+\theta^2+2\theta\cos\lambda}\frac{1+\bar\theta^2+2\bar\theta\cos\lambda}{(1+\bar\theta)^2}$$

with $\bar\theta$ set to 0.268, 0 and 1 respectively. This expression can also be written in terms of the original components rather than using the reduced form. For the continuous time model, working directly with the variance and autocovariances of the MA disturbance in the Chambers and McGarry (2002) representation gives:

$$w(\lambda) = \frac{(2+\cos\lambda)}{(2+\cos\lambda)+(6/\delta q)(1-\cos\lambda)} \tag{4.39}$$

Figure 4.3 shows the gains for $q = 0.5$, and hence $\theta = -0.485$, corresponding to the weights in Table 4.1. As can be seen, the continuous time model gain lies between the other two. If q is increased (decreased), the lines move to the right (left) and become further apart (closer together).

If the reduced form parameter is allowed to differ for the three filters, they can be made closer by setting the signal–noise ratios so that the gains are the same when they are 0.5.

Conclusion

The focus of this chapter has been on the way in which signal–noise ratios in unobserved components models change as the observation interval changes. The most elegant way of analysing this problem is by setting up an underlying model in continuous time and then deducing the discrete time representation. This shows how changing the observation interval can change the form of the model, for example by inducing correlations between components, and so changes in the

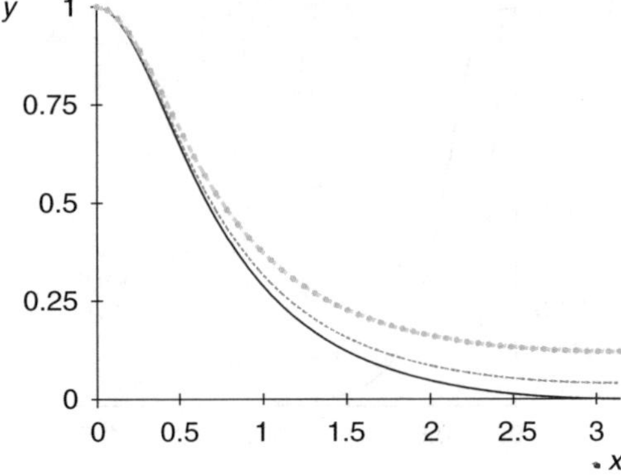

Figure 4.3   Local level model gains for $q = 0.5$, $\theta = -.485$. Solid line is canonical, dot-dash is RW plus noise

shape of signal extraction filters must be considered in order to interpret signal–noise ratios in a meaningful way.

One result to emerge from our analysis is that there is a connection between signal extraction in continuous time models and the canonical decomposition in which the variance of the irregular component is maximized. Specifically, if a continuous time local level model is observed as a flow, then estimates of the level constructed at the mid-point of the flow period coincide with estimates of the level obtained from a canonical model. These estimates are not MMSEs, but are a simple weighted average of the smoothed estimates for the observation in question and the one in the previous time period. A similar result appears to hold for the local linear trend model, though so far we have only demonstrated this by numerical computation of the weights. The gain functions for the exact MMSE weights lie between those for the standard models with mutually uncorrelated disturbances, for which the gain is a Butterworth sine filter, and those for canonical models. The practical implication of these findings is that, other things being equal, smoother trends will tend to be extracted from models for flows set up in continuous time.

Notes

1   Without Gaussianicity we would still have minimum mean-square error estimators within the class of linear estimators.
2   Whittle (1982: 12) writes 'Our arguments so often concern real γ_j, and z on $|z| = 1$, that we are scarcely guilty of inconsistency if we use $\ldots|\gamma(z)|^2$ to denote $\gamma(z)\gamma(z^{-1})$.'
3   This can be obtained by noting that $w(L)$ is the ACGF of an ARMA(1,1) process with AR parameter $-\theta$ and MA parameter one.
4   That is the variance plus the sum of the autocovariances (at negative and positive lags).
5   On the other hand, when $\sigma_\varepsilon^2 = 0$, so that $\theta = 0.268$, the MMSE estimator has all the weight on y_t.
6   Giving adjacent observations the same weight automatically leads to $w(-1)$ being zero.

References

Box, G.E.P., Hillmer, S.C. and Tiao, G.C. (1978) 'Analysis and modelling of seasonal time series', in A. Zellner (ed.), *Seasonal Analysis of Economic Time Series*. Washington DC: US Department of Commerce, pp. 309–34.

Chambers, M.J. and McGarry, J. (2002) 'Modeling cyclical behaviour with differential-difference equations in an unobserved components framework', *Econometric Theory*, 18: 387–419.

Gomez, V. (2001) 'The use of Butterworth filters for trend and cycle estimation in economic time series', *Journal of Business and Economic Statistics*, 19: 365–73.

Gomez, V. and Maravall, A. (2000) 'Seasonal adjustment and signal extraction in economic time series', in D. Pena, G.C. Tiao and R.S. Tsay (eds), *A Course in Time Series Analysis*. New York: John Wiley & Sons, pp. 202–46.

Härdle, W. (1990) *Applied Nonparametric Regression*. Cambridge: Cambridge University Press.

Harvey, A.C. (1989) *Forecasting, Structural Time Series Models and the Kalman Filter*. Cambridge: Cambridge University Press.

Harvey, A.C., and Koopman, S.J. (2000) 'Signal extraction and the formulation of unobserved components models', *Econometrics Journal*, 3: 84–107.

Harvey, A.C., Trimbur, T. and Van Dijk, H. (2003) 'Cyclical components in economic time series: a Bayesian approach', *Discussion Paper*, no. 0302. Cambridge: Department of Applied Economics.

Koopman, S.J., Harvey, A.C., Doornik, J.A. and Shepard, N. (2000) *STAMP 6: Structural Time Series Analysis Modeller and Predictor*. London: Timberlake Consultants Ltd.

Maravall, A. (1993) 'Stochastic linear trends, models and estimators', *Journal of Econometrics*, 58: 5–37.

Pierce, D.A. (1979) 'Signal extraction error in nonstationary time series', *Annals of Statistics*, 7: 1303–20.

Tiao, G.C. and Hillmer, S.C. (1978) 'Some consideration of decomposition of a time series', *Biometrika*, 65: 497–502.

Whittle, P. (1983) *Prediction and Regulation*. Oxford: Blackwell.

5

Bayes Estimates of the Cyclical Component in Twentieth Century US Gross Domestic Product

*Andrew C. Harvey, Thomas M. Trimbur and Herman K. van Dijk**

Introduction

In this chapter, cyclical components in economic time series are analysed in a Bayesian framework, thereby allowing prior notions about periodicity to be used. The method is based on a general class of unobserved component models that encompasses a range of dynamics in the stochastic cycle. This allows, for instance, relatively smooth cycles to be extracted from time series. Posterior densities of parameters and estimated components are obtained using Markov-chain Monte Carlo methods, which we develop for both univariate and multivariate models. Features such as time-varying amplitude may be studied by examining different functions of the posterior draws for the cyclical component and parameters. The empirical application illustrates the method for annual USA real GDP over the last 130 years.

Decomposing time series into trends and cycles is fundamental to a good deal of macroeconomic analysis. The Hodrick–Prescott (HP) filter is often used to detrend series, but as shown in Harvey and Jaeger (1993) and Cogley and Nason (1995), using it inappropriately can result in the creation of spurious cycles. The same

* Earlier versions of this chapter were presented at the Cambridge PhD Workshop in Econometrics and at the NAKE conference at the Netherlands Central Bank. Trimbur wishes to thank the Cambridge Commonwealth Trust and the Richard Kahn Fund for financial support, and is grateful to the Tinbergen Institute for its hospitality and financial support in autumn 2001. Harvey thanks the Economic and Social Research Council (ESRC) for support as part of a project on Dynamic Common Factor Models for Regional Time Series, grant number L138 25 1008. We would like to thank Bill Bell and Simon Godsill for helpful comments. A more extended version of this chapter is available as 'Trends and Cycles in Economic Time Series: A Bayesian Approach', forthcoming in *Journal of Econometrics*.

is true of the bandpass filter recently proposed by Baxter and King (1999) for extracting cyclical movements over the range two to ten years; see Murray (2003).

Harvey and Jaeger (1993) argued that detrending is best accomplished by fitting a structural time-series model consisting of trend, cycle and irregular unobserved components. In the classical approach, the model is estimated in state space form with the components extracted by the Kalman filter and associated smoother. However, fitting the model to series like GDP usually results in the irregular component nearly disappearing with the result that the cycle is quite noisy. The class of higher order stochastic cycles introduced in Harvey and Trimbur (2003) enables one to overcome this feature. Trimbur (2006) provides the exact characterization of this class of models, showing analytical expressions for the time and frequency domain properties.

Using higher order cycles in the unobserved components model for the series yields implicit filters that concentrate on extracting relatively more power from a narrower band of frequencies. More high frequency noise is forced into the irregular, thereby yielding a smoother cycle. A perfectly sharp bandpass filter, typically referred to as the 'ideal' filter, emerges as a limiting case. In empirical work it has often been taken for granted that such a filter naturally provides the best basis for extracting cycles – this view is implicit in the terminology itself – and the 'ideal' filter has been emulated in numerous applications with time-series data. Examining the models that underpin different types of filters provides insight as to their relative appropriateness. In the general case, the gain tapers off gradually at the band edges, in contrast to the 'ideal' filter which exhibits discontinuity at the boundaries, a shape that is in some sense less natural, particularly in economic applications. The biggest concern, however, remains the potential for distortions of the type demonstrated in Murray (2003).

The model-based estimators of cyclical components, introduced in Harvey and Trimbur (2003), enable one to mitigate such distortions. These classical estimators are referred to as generalized Butterworth bandpass filters, given their close links with the Butterworth filters commonly used in engineering. The goal of this chapter is to develop the complementary Bayesian analysis of models with higher order cycles so that parameter uncertainty is accounted for, with the estimated posterior densities providing compact and informative summaries of trend and cyclical dynamics. We show empirical application with the annual USA real GDP series. Essentially, the chapter introduces Bayesian bandpass filters for economic time series.

Prior knowledge on periodicity is readily available in the area of business cycle analysis. We introduce a Bayesian approach, whereby parameter uncertainty in accounted for and expectations about cyclical dynamics are updated optimally, producing a posterior probability density of the model parameters and component series. In a classical framework, fixed estimates for the parameters in structural time-series models are usually obtained by maximum likelihood (ML) using the Kalman filter. Harvey and Trimbur (2003) found that this works well for series like investment where the cycle is pronounced. For some cases, however, it may be difficult to obtain plausible parameter estimates on the basis of the likelihood surface alone. In any case, the classical approach is unable to provide a satisfactory way to implement any prior knowledge that may be available about the period of oscillation.

In estimating economic cycles, prior information on the frequency range of interest has clearly played a role in a good deal of empirical work. Typically, however, such information has been implemented by imposing stringent conditions on the desired pattern of the gain function of the filter, for instance in Baxter and King (1999) where an approximation to an 'ideal' filter with prespecified boundaries is proposed. The concerns associated with the use of 'ideal' filters in economics were noted above. By using prior knowledge in a more consistent manner, a model-based framework is able to address these concerns. Specifically, one may construct a Bayesian prior for the frequency parameter of the cyclical component as part of the model; the prior distribution is then updated, following Bayes rule, conditional on the information in the data. Prior information on other parameters may also be used, though this will typically be rather more vague. The resulting joint posterior density of parameters and components may then be used to provide a great deal of insight on many different aspects of the time series dynamics.

The Bayesian approach also has the practical advantage that it allows one to address potential finite sample problems. In particular, for any given model and series of limited length, the likelihood surface may exhibit some irregularities, with reasonable parameter estimates impossible to attain in an unrestricted classical framework. In Harvey and Trimbur (2003), difficulties were sometimes experienced in obtaining a sensible period for the cycle in real GDP; in such cases, estimation with a fixed period led to acceptable results. However, the use of suitable priors, within a Bayesian framework, enables one to address the problem more effectively in a consistent manner. Greater flexibility is provided, and, generally, a Bayesian approach may be feasible for a broader range of applications with different model structures and sample sizes.

In this chapter we present a Markov-chain Monte Carlo (MCMC) algorithm for a Bayesian analysis of stochastic cycles in time series. The method we develop is a new composite of the Gibbs sampler and Metropolis–Hastings algorithms. With the aid of state space modelling techniques, we set out an efficient procedure for computing the joint posterior density of parameters and components. This provides a great deal of information that may be used to study a variety of features of cyclical dynamics. For instance, one may characterize the complete distribution of the cyclical component series. As the algorithm allows for the computation of marginal posteriors of the trend and cyclical component at different points in time, based on the percentiles of the estimated distributions, bands showing the highest posterior density regions of the cycle and trend may be constructed.

The area of Bayesian analysis of dynamic econometric models has benefitted from developments in state space and MCMC methods in recent years. Some important contributions have been Carter and Kohn (1994), Fruhwirth-Schnatter (1994), deJong and Shephard (1995), and Durbin and Koopman (2002). The paper by Huerta and West (1999) sets out a Bayesian treatment of cyclical behaviour indirectly through autoregressive models. However, there has been no attempt to conduct a Bayesian analysis of cycles in an unobserved components framework.

Frühwirth-Schnatter (1994) and Koop and van Dijk (2000) analyse trends and seasonals in various macroeconomic series. The treatment of cycles leads to a number of new technical issues which we address, and the Bayesian approach allows us to present the results of model fitting in an informative way. As outlined in Harvey, Trimbur and van Dijk (2005), the analysis may be naturally extended to multivariate unobserved components models. Again this has not been attempted previously in a Bayesian framework and it introduces a number of issues that require careful consideration.

The rest of the chapter is arranged as follows. The next section describes the extension of the class of structural time-series models to include higher order cyclical components. The Bayesian treatment is the developed and the method illustrated with an applications to an annual USA macroeconomic series. Technical details on the state space form and the Markov-chain Monte Carlo algorithms for the univariate and multivariate cases are set out in Harvey, Trimbur, and van Dijk (2005).

Cyclical and trend components in time series

We consider a class of unobserved component (UC) models in which the observations y_t, $t = 1,\ldots, T$, are made up of a nonstationary trend component μ_t, a cyclical component $\psi_{n,t}$, and an irregular term ε_t. Thus:

$$y_t = \mu_t + \psi_{n,t} + \varepsilon_t, \quad t = 1,\ldots T \tag{5.1}$$

where the irregular is white noise, that is $\varepsilon_t \sim WN(0, \sigma_\varepsilon^2)$, the stochastic trend is an integrated random walk:

$$\mu_t = \mu_{t-1} + \beta_{t-1} \tag{5.2}$$

$$\beta_t = \beta_{t-1} + \zeta_t, \quad \zeta_t \sim WN(0, \sigma_\zeta^2) \tag{5.3}$$

while the nth order cycle is defined by:

$$\begin{bmatrix} \psi_{1,t} \\ \psi_{1,t}^* \end{bmatrix} = \rho \begin{bmatrix} \cos\lambda_c & \sin\lambda_c \\ -\sin\lambda_c & \cos\lambda_c \end{bmatrix} \begin{bmatrix} \psi_{1,t-1} \\ \psi_{1,t-1}^* \end{bmatrix} + \begin{bmatrix} \kappa_t \\ \kappa_t^* \end{bmatrix}$$

$$\begin{bmatrix} \kappa_t \\ \kappa_t^* \end{bmatrix} \sim WN\left(\begin{bmatrix} 0 \\ 0 \end{bmatrix}, \begin{bmatrix} \sigma_\kappa^2 & 0 \\ 0 & \sigma_\kappa^2 \end{bmatrix} \right) \tag{5.4}$$

$$\begin{bmatrix} \psi_{i,t} \\ \psi_{i,t}^* \end{bmatrix} = \rho \begin{bmatrix} \cos\lambda_c & \sin\lambda_c \\ -\sin\lambda_c & \cos\lambda_c \end{bmatrix} \begin{bmatrix} \psi_{i,t-1} \\ \psi_{i,t-1}^* \end{bmatrix} + \begin{bmatrix} \psi_{i-1,t-1} \\ \psi_{i-1,t-1}^* \end{bmatrix}, \quad i = 2,\ldots,n \tag{5.5}$$

The parameter λ_c denotes frequency in radians while ρ is a damping factor lying between zero and one; if it is equal to one, the cycle is nonstationary. The disturbances driving the trend and cycle are assumed to be uncorrelated with each other and with the irregular. The specification in (5.1) is well-suited for trend-cycle decompositions. The assumption in using model (5.1) directly is that the seasonal component has been removed. Alternatively, the raw (non-seasonally adjusted) data could be used, with the model augmented by adding a seasonal component.

Each type of stochastic cycle is defined in terms of a number of processes. The nth order stochastic cycle $\psi_{n,t}$ has periodic movements centred around a frequency of λ_c. The stochastic movements stem from the two disturbances, κ_t and κ_t^* in (5.4). Suppressing κ_t^* in the model specification yields a class of bandpass filters that generalizes the Butterworth class of filters; see Gomez (2001) and Harvey and Trimbur (2003). Our preference here is to work with the 'balanced form' of (5.4); for $n = 1$ this is identical to the stochastic cycle in (Harvey, 1989: 39) and as shown in Trimbur (2005), analytical expressions for key properties are available for all n. The different spectral shapes for different orders give an illustration of the range of dynamics of the class of higher order cycles. With the cyclical parameters fixed, the spectrum becomes sharper as the order increases, concentrating around the central frequency. Further details and illustrations may be found in Trimbur (2006).

State space methods play a key role in both classical and Bayesian treatments of the class of models (5.1). The state space formulation and dynamic characteristics of the higher order cycles are set out in Trimbur (2006). In the next section, we devise an efficient Bayesian approach, where components are estimated in a way that accounts for parameter uncertainty. This allows for an informative analysis of cyclical behavior with flexible expectations on periodicity.

Bayesian treatment

The three variance parameters and two cyclical parameters are arranged in the vector $\theta = \{\sigma_\zeta^2, \sigma_\kappa^2, \sigma_\varepsilon^2, \rho, \lambda_c\}$. The model is assumed to have Gaussian disturbances throughout. Given a sample $\mathbf{y} = \{y_1, \ldots, y_T\}$, the likelihood function is specified by the model structure. Below we introduce a flexible set of priors for θ.

The goal is then to analyse the properties of the posterior distribution, $p(\theta|\mathbf{y})$. Since this is not a member of a class of densities which has known analytical properties, a new Markov-chain Monte Carlo routine is developed. The method produces draws from the posterior density of the parameters and components, giving smoothed estimates of the cycle as a byproduct. The approach can be adapted to different kinds of priors, and in the next section we also set out the extension to multivariate model structures.

Priors and likelihood

We start by summarizing the elicitation of priors. The direct interpretation of the cycle parameters makes it straightforward to design suitable priors; they are linked to economic intuition and previous experience of studying business cycles. The parameter λ_c represents a central frequency; the annual sample we investigate below includes cyclical swings that vary a great deal in their duration, and the expectation is that, on average, fluctuations in the cycle will have a period of around ten years. A standard peaked distribution for λ_c may be used by the researcher to reflect this expectation in a consistent and adaptable framework.

For annual macroeconomic data we consider priors for λ_c centred around $2\pi/10$, based on the class of beta distributions; such priors are flexible, covering a variety of possibilities, and they are easy to work with analytically. We consider different degrees of concentration in the prior around the mean. The least informative prior covers a wide range of frequencies, while the sharpest density focuses attention narrowly around a period of ten years. Other priors, with different spreads and locations, may be implemented in this framework. If a particular shape of prior were desired, then another class of densities could be used and the algorithm would be constructed in the same way as shown below. The informative priors we implement all reflect an emphasis on average business cycle periodicity of ten years.

For technical details on the class of priors we use, see appendix A in Harvey, Trimbur and van Dijk (2005). The approach taken by Huerta and West (1999) uses priors for the autoregressive parameters implied by the reduced form of the first-order cycle. We find it more useful to focus on λ_c. In any case, adapting the Huerta and West approach to higher order cycles would not be straightforward. The parameter ρ is linked to the order of the cycle. In the first-order case ρ is the rate of decay of the cycle, but for higher orders the interpretation of ρ changes somewhat so that different values are appropriate. However, since the precise form of the relationship between ρ and n is not clear, we use a uniform prior on ρ over the interval $[0,1]$.

For the variance parameters, we use inverted gamma prior densities with shape and scale set to near zero, which effectively serve as noninformatives. The class of inverted gamma priors are conditionally natural conjugate so that the conditional posteriors are also inverted gamma, and thus one has the advantage of direct simulation within the Gibbs sampler routine. Also, the flexibility of this class of density allows for implementing any prior knowledge that may be available for the variance parameters. Thus, for instance, if there is the expectation of stochastic trend dynamics, such an expectation may be expressed as a prior with positive mean and a degree of dispersion to reflect uncertainty in the exact value of the disturbance variance.

Next, we summarize the evaluation of the likelihood and posterior of our unobserved components model. The sample $\mathbf{y}$ represents the observed realization of the data-generating process, which is a multivariate density $p(Y|\theta)$ over all possible realizations Y. As normality of the disturbances is assumed, the likelihood function, $L(\theta; \mathbf{y}) = p(\mathbf{y}|\theta)$, can be evaluated for any permissible value of θ using the Kalman filter. This relies on the prediction error decomposition as described in Harvey (1989: 126). With an appropriate initialization, the density $p(Y|\theta)$ is multivariate Gaussian so that computation of the likelihood for a given sample is straightforward.

The densities $\{p(\theta), p(Y|\theta)\}$ give the full description of the model in the Bayesian context. Given the data $\mathbf{y}$, the prior-likelihood pair $\{p(\theta), L(\theta; \mathbf{y})\}$ defines the analysis. The expectations reflected in $p(\theta)$ are updated using the information in the $\mathbf{y}$, through $L(\theta; \mathbf{y})$. By studying the characteristics of the posterior, the analysis addresses various questions about cyclical and trend dynamics.

Posterior

The posterior $p(\theta|\mathbf{y})$ is proportional to the product of the prior and likelihood. However, the expression for the product $p(\theta)L(\theta;\mathbf{y})$ does not represent the kernel of a known distribution. The normalizing constant (equal to the marginal likelihood) required for evaluating the posterior ordinate is not known in terms of elementary functions (like $\sqrt{2\pi}$ in the case of the normal distribution).

A strategy is needed for analysing the properties of $p(\theta|\mathbf{y})$. With a five-dimensional parameter vector, MCMC methods offer an efficient way to sample (pseudo-random) parameter drawings from the posterior. This may be used to produce drawings of regular functions of the parameters. Thus for instance, finite sample results on posterior moments may be compared with ML estimates.

The strategy for posterior analysis is based on extending the parameter space to include the components and associated auxiliary processes in (5.1), which together form the basis for the state space form of the model. As described in Harvey, Trimbur and van Dijk (2005), we design an MCMC routine that is able to capitalize on recent developments in state space modelling. Thus, the simulation smoothing techniques developed, for instance, in deJong and Shephard (1995) and Durbin and Koopman (2001), may be efficiently used in a Gibbs sampling setup. In this way, the algorithm is set up to produce drawings from the expanded density of both the parameters and unobserved components. This provides an efficient route for obtaining draws from $p(\theta|\mathbf{y})$, and it also gives additional information that is useful for studying the trend and cycle.

Signal extraction

The MCMC method produces drawings from the joint density of the two unobserved components, the cycle and trend, over the sample period. These high-dimensional variates, conditional on the data, can be used to compute a Bayesian analogue of the classical smoother. As they form part of the Gibbs sampler, no additional effort is required to obtain them. Classical estimates correspond to the conditional means of the cyclical component, given the sample, assuming the parameters are fixed at estimated values. The *Bayesian smoother* incorporates parameter uncertainty (the parameter vector is integrated out) and accounts for prior knowledge about the period.

The Bayesian analysis produces drawings from the joint posterior of the trend and cyclical components, $p(\mu_1, \ldots, \mu_T, \psi_{n,1}, \ldots, \psi_{n,T}|\mathbf{y})$. We note that the posterior mean is the optimal estimator for a quadratic loss. The estimated component series are obtained by averaging over the J state draws, that is:

$$\widehat{\mu}_t = \frac{1}{J}\sum_{j=1}^{J}\mu_t^{(j)}, \qquad \widehat{\psi}_{n,t} = \frac{1}{J}\sum_{j=1}^{J}\psi_{n,t}^{(j)}, \quad t = 1,\ldots,T$$

where $\mu_t^{(j)}$ denotes the jth draw for the trend at time t and similarly for the cyclical component. The standard deviation of the trend estimate at each time point is given by $\sqrt{\sum \mu_t^{2(j)}/J - \widehat{\mu}_t^2}$ and other higher-order moments, for the various components, may be computed in a similar way.

Drawings of regular functions of the trend, cycle and other state vector elements over the sample are directly obtained. This enables properties of the time-varying cycle, such as amplitude, to be studied. The amplitude of the cycle at time t is estimated by:

$$A_t = \frac{1}{J}\sum_{j=1}^{J}\sqrt{\psi_{n,t}^{2(j)} + \psi_{n,t}^{*2(j)}}, \quad t = 1,\ldots,T$$

Other features of interest of the unobserved components may be studied in an analogous fashion.

Annual USA GDP

Annual time series are available over a fairly long period of time and this allows one to investigate issues concerning long-term changes in the business cycle. We examine annual USA real GDP data from 1870 to 1998 compiled from the OECD publications *Monitoring the World Economy* and *The World Economy: A Millennial Perspective*. The enormous swing from the beginning of the Great Depression to the end of the Second World War constitutes a much longer and more pronounced cycle than is found in postwar data. The priors we consider for λ_c have a mean of $2\pi/10$; thus we allow for relatively long periods with an average of around ten years. In addition we assume that the variance of the cyclical disturbances from 1929 to 1946 is ten times what it is elsewhere. The state space model has no difficulty handling such an extension. (A similar device could have been adopted for the frequency, that is the period from 1929 to 1946 could have been assumed to be double what it is elsewhere.)

The results for $n = 1$ with the least informative prior on λ_c show that the posterior distribution of period concentrates around 17.5 years, owing to the dominating influence of the Great Depression and the subsequent Second World War recovery. It may be preferable, therefore, to use a sharper prior. The posterior densities for frequency and period are shown in Figure 5.1 for intermediate and very informative priors, and the resulting trend and cycle for the very informative prior is shown in Figures 5.2 and 5.3. Note that the data are in logarithms.

The series of trend and cycle estimates over the sample period are computed as posterior means, obtained by averaging over the J state draws as described in the previous sub-section. The HPD (highest posterior density) regions for the estimated series are shown as well.

The HPD regions in Figures 5.2 and 5.3 are obtained by taking the 2.5 and 97.5 percentiles, and we will refer to the series of HPD regions as HPD bands.[1] These resemble classical 95 per cent confidence intervals but their interpretation is distinct; the bands in Figures 5.2 and 5.3 give exact finite sample measures of uncertainty. The Bayesian smoother refers to the actual distribution of the trend and cycle conditional on the data-set. The associated HPD bands incorporate the posterior

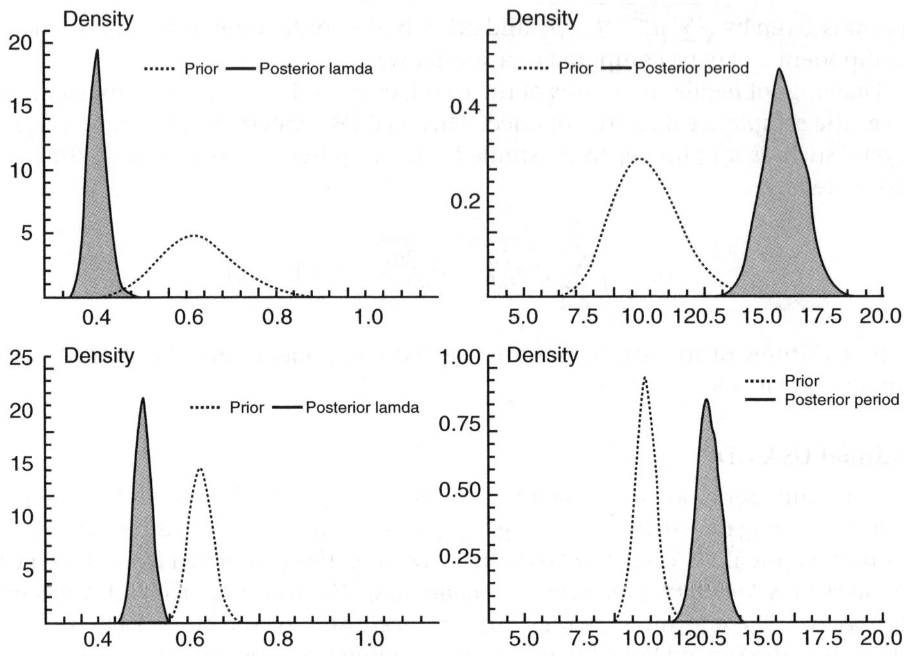

Figure 5.1 Marginal posterior densities of frequency and period with intermediate and very informative priors on λ_c for annual USA real GDP (logarithms) from 1870 to 1998

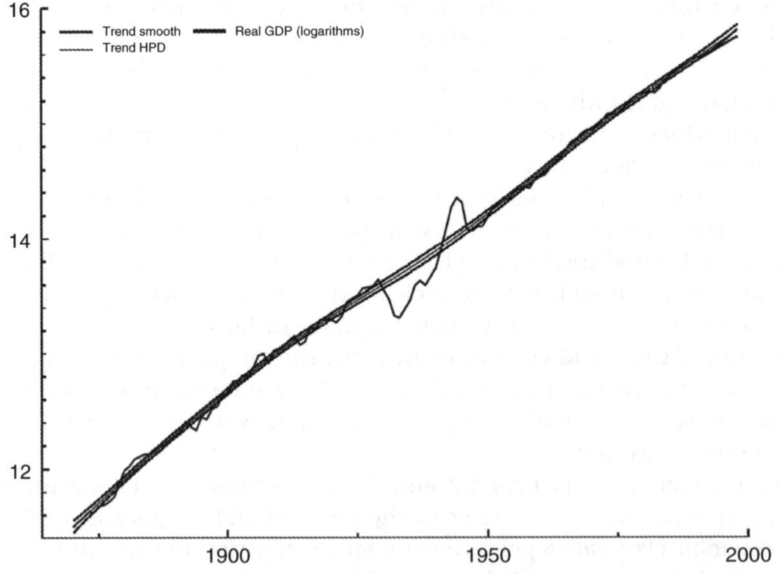

Figure 5.2 Estimated trend in annual USA real GDP (logarithms) from 1870 to 1998 for $n = 1$ with most informative prior on λ_c

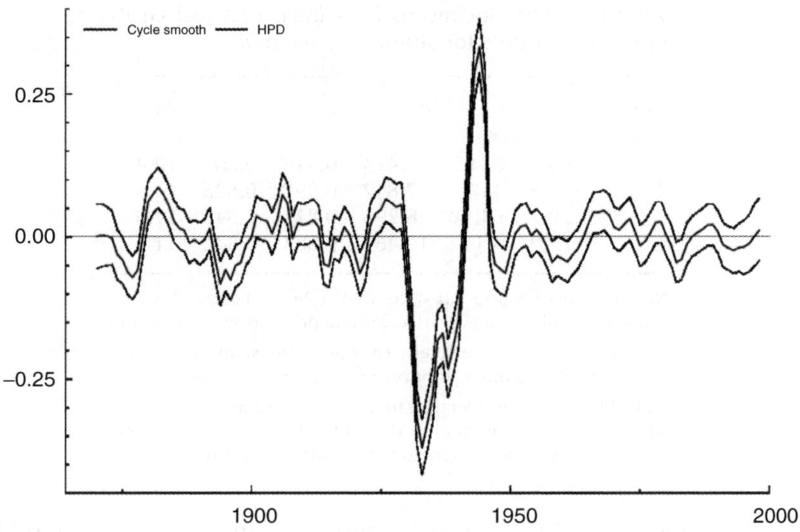

Figure 5.3   Estimated cycle in annual USA real GDP (logarithms) from 1870 to 1998 for $n = 1$ with most informative prior on λ_c

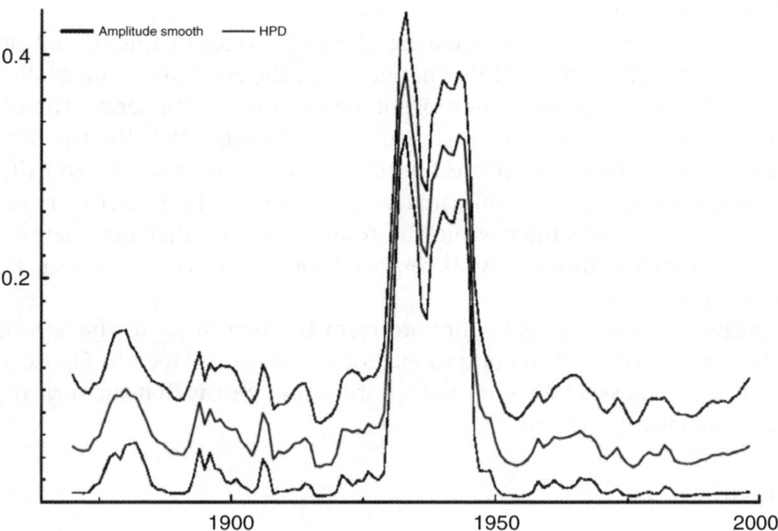

Figure 5.4   Evolving amplitude of the cyclical component in annual USA real GDP (logarithms) from 1870 to 1998 for $n = 1$ with most informative prior on λ_c

uncertainty in components and parameters. To our knowledge, no one has given, so far, finite sample confidence bands around the trend and cycle components.

An interesting question is whether business cycles have generally declined in intensity since the Second World War. Figure 5.4 displays the evolving amplitude.

Table 5.1   Posterior means for annual USA real GDP from 1870 to 1998 for different values of n

Order n	σ_ζ^2	σ_κ^2	σ_ε^2	ρ	λ_c	$2\pi/\lambda_c$
1	60.7	5416	3,413	0.918	0.507	12.4
2	18.8	417	7,847	0.897	0.525	11.9
3	20.7	64.4	8,296	0.872	0.549	11.5
4	12.9	3.11	10,469	0.883	0.542	11.6

Note: Informative prior on λ_c centred at $2\pi/10$. For $n = 2, 3$ the shape and scale of the inverted gamma prior on σ_ζ^2 were set to 20 and 2×10^{-5}, respectively. For $n = 4$, the shape and scale of the inverted gamma prior on σ_ζ^2 were set to 100 and 10^{-4}, and additionally a moderately informative prior on σ_ε^2 was used with shape and scale equal to 10 and 10^{-5}. The period in years is $2\pi/\lambda_c$. All variance parameters are multiplied by 10^7.

The graph is dominated by the Great Depression and the Second World War, but there is some indication that the average amplitude of the cycle is smaller in the postwar period as compared with the period before 1929. This contradicts the findings of Backus and Kehoe (1992) from a study based on detrending with the Hodrick–Prescott filter.[2]

There is some difficulty in estimating plausible cycles in the annual series for higher order models; with noninformative priors the cyclical variance falls to near zero so that the trend accounts for most of the variation in the series. Therefore, for $n > 1$ more informative priors on σ_ζ^2 were used to ensure that the trend does not change too rapidly. Posterior means for different values of n are shown in Table 5.1 for the sharp prior; with less informative priors on λ_c the posterior mass of the period shifts to higher values while the results for the other parameters remain similar. Considerably more noise is removed for $n > 1$, as can be seen from the higher estimates for σ_ε^2.

The biggest change occurs in moving from the first-order to the second-order cycle. The estimated cyclical component for $n = 2$ is displayed in Figure 5.5. The increased smoothness relative to the first order case means that the turning points become more clearly defined.

Conclusion

A structural time-series model provides a consistent framework for extracting trends and cycles. This chapter has investigated the Bayesian treatment of such a model, paying particular attention to the cyclical component and the way in which prior information on periodicity can be used. Markov-chain Monte Carlo routines are successfully designed for univariate and multivariate models, including those with higher order cycles of the kind introduced recently by Harvey and Trimbur (2003). Smooth cycles were successfully extracted from the annual US GDP time series. These cycles have a simple interpretation in terms of the percentage by which they

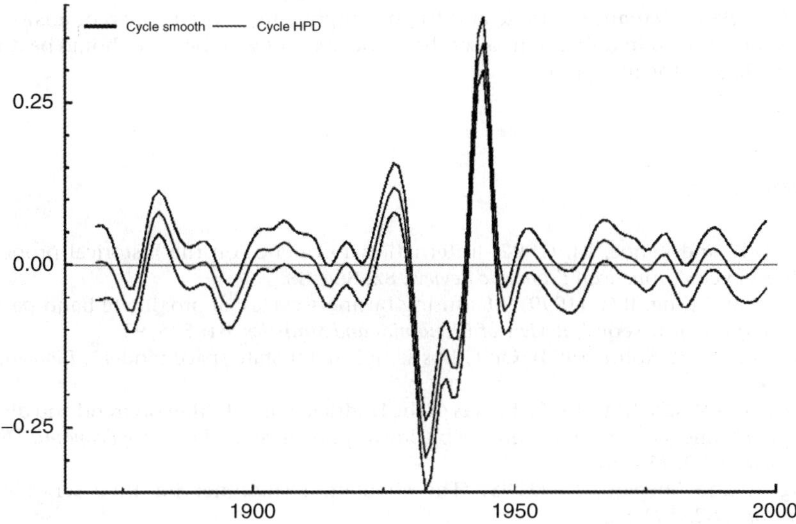

Figure 5.5   Estimated cycle in annual USA real GDP (logarithms) from 1870 to 1998 for $n = 2$ with most informative prior on λ_c

exceed or fall below the long-term level. The series of smoothed Bayesian estimates give more information about the relative position of the business cycle over time, along with measures of uncertainty.

Two key incentives for exploring a Bayesian approach are, on the practical side, the possibility of addressing a broader range of problems including those with limited sample sizes, and from a theoretical perspective the more consistent and flexible use of prior knowledge on periodicity. Bayesian analysis in an unobserved components framework provides a direct and informative approach to studying cyclical dynamics. Cyclical turning points and features such as changing amplitude are assessed while accounting for parameter uncertainty. Multivariate applications provide the capacity to combine the information in sets of economic indicators and to study underlying business cycle components and relationships across different series.

Notes

1   The precise definition of the 95% highest posterior density (HPD) region is the minimum interval that contains 95% of the probability mass. For symmetric distributions this gives a result identical to the 2.5 to 97.5 percentile interval as defined in the chapter. For posteriors with a limited degree of asymmetry, the HPD region is approximately given by the percentile-based definition.
2   Backus and Kehoe (1992) are concerned with the volatility of macroeconomic time series in different historical periods, but in fixing the HP smoothing constant (the inverse of the signal–noise ratio), they effectively make an assumption about the very thing they are trying to determine! Ravn and Uhlig (2002) show that the result is overturned if a more plausible value of the HP smoothing constant is used. A model-based approach, focusing

on the relative variance of cycle and trend components, gives a coherent answer to the question, though in doing so it raises the whole issue of whether one should be doing HP detrending in the first place.

References

Backus, D.K. and Kehoe, P.J. (1992) 'International evidence on the historical properties of business cycles', *American Economic Review*, 82: 864–88.

Baxter, M. and King, R.G. (1999) 'Measuring business cycles: approximate band-pass filters for economic time series', *Review of Economics and Statistics*, 81: 575–93.

Carter, C.K. and R. Kohn (1994) 'On Gibbs sampling for state space models', *Biometrika*, 81: 541–53.

Cogley, T. and Nason, J.M. (1995) 'Effects of the Hodrick–Prescott filter on trend and difference stationary time series: implications for business cycle research', *Journal of Economic Dynamics and Control*, 19: 253–78.

DeJong, P. and Shepard, N. (1995) 'The simulation smoother for time series models', *Biometrika*, 82: 339–50.

Doornik, J.A. (1999) *Ox: An Object-Oriented Matrix Programming Language*. London: Timberlake Consultants Ltd.

Durbin, J. and Koopman, S.J. (2002) 'A simple and efficient simulation smoother', *Biometrika*, 89: 603–16.

Fruhwirth-Schnatter, S. (1994) 'Data augmentation and dynamic linear models', *Journal of Time Series Analysis*, 15: 183–202.

Gomez, V. (2001) 'The use of Butterworth filters for trend and cycle estimation in economic time series', *Journal of Business and Economic Statistics*, 19: 365–73.

Harvey, A.C. (1989) *Forecasting, Structural Time Series Models and the Kalman Filter*. Cambridge: Cambridge University Press.

Harvey, A.C. and Jaeger, A. (1993) 'Detrending, stylised facts and the business cycle', *Journal of Applied Econometrics*, 8: 231–47.

Harvey, A.C. and Koopman, S.J. (1997) 'Multivariate structural time series models', in C. Heij *et al.* (eds), *System Dynamics in Economic and Financial models*. Chichester: Wiley & Sons.

Harvey, A.C. and Koopman, S.J. (2000) 'Signal extraction and the formulation of unobserved component models', *Econometrics Journal*, 3: 84–107.

Harvey, A.C. and Trimbur, T.M. (2003) 'General model-based filters for extracting trends and cycles in economic time series', *Review of Economics and Statistics*, 85: 244–55.

Harvey, A.C., Trimbur, T.M. and van Dijk, H.K. (2005) 'Cyclical components in economic time series: a Bayesian approach', *Journal of Econometrics*, forthcoming.

Hodrick, R.J. and Prescott, E.C. (1997) 'Postwar US business cycles: an empirical investigation', *Journal of Money, Credit and Banking*, 24: 1–16.

Huerta, G. and West, M. (1999) 'Priors and component structures in autoregressive time series models', *Journal of the Royal Statistical Society Series B*, 61: 881–99.

Kass, R.E. and Raftery, A.E. (1995) 'Bayes factors', *Journal of the American Statistical Association*, 24: 773–95.

Kitagawa, G. and Gersch, W. (1996) *Smoothness Priors Analysis of Time Series*. Berlin: Springer-Verlag.

Kohn, R., Ansley, C. and Wong, C.H. (1992) 'Nonparametric spline regression with autoregressive moving average errors', *Biometrika*, 79: 335–46.

Koop, G. and van Dijk, H.K. (2000) 'Testing for integration using evolving trend and seasonals models: a Bayesian approach', *Journal of Econometrics*, 97: 261–91.

Koopman, S.J. and Harvey, A.C. (2003) 'Computing observation weights for signal extraction and filtering', *Journal of Economic Dynamics and Control*, 27: 1317–33.

Koopman, S.J., Harvey, A.C. Doornik, J.A. and Shepard, N. (2000) *STAMP 6.0 Structural Time Series Analysis Modeller and Predictor*. London: Timberlake Consultants Ltd.

Koopman, S.J., Shepard, N. and Doornik, J.A. (1999) 'Statistical algorithms for models in state space using SsfPack 2.2', *Econometrics Journal*, 2: 113–66.

Murray, C.J. (2003) 'Cyclical properties of Baxter–King filtered time series', *Review of Economics and Statistics*, 85: 471–6.

Trimbur, T.M. (2006) 'Properites of higher order stochastic cycles', *Journal of Time Series Analysis*, 27: 1–17.

Young, P. (1984) *Recursive Estimation and Time Series Analysis*. Berlin: Springer-Verlag.

6
The Extent of Seasonal/Business Cycle Interactions in European Industrial Production

*Denise R. Osborn and Antonio Matas-Mir**

Introduction

Recent literature has uncovered evidence that the seasonal pattern in industrial production changes over the business cycle, with seasonality typically being less pronounced in periods of high growth than in the low growth (or recession) business cycle phase. Matas-Mir and Osborn (2003) examined this effect using monthly data for various OECD countries, finding that the change in the seasonal pattern is typically concentrated in the summer months. This chapter extends this analysis in a specifically European context, by presenting measures of the extent of seasonal/business cycle interactions for industrial production series from the countries of the European Union. The analysis is undertaken using a nonlinear threshold model that allows the overall mean and seasonal characteristics to change with the regime. The extent of seasonality in each regime is represented as the average absolute deviation of the steady-state growth in each month from the overall steady-state mean growth in that regime. Seasonal/business cycle interaction is then measured in two ways, namely as the difference and the ratio of the regime-dependent seasonality. These measures are computed over all months, and also separately for the summer and non-summer months. The results reinforce previous findings of reduced seasonality in higher growth periods, with the seasonal pattern sometimes being moderated by 20 per cent or more (both over the year and in the summer months).

* Support from the Economic and Social Research Council (UK) under grant number L138251030 is gratefully acknowledged by the first author. The opinions expressed are those of the authors and do not necessarily reflect the views of the European Central Bank or the European System of Central Banks.

There is no doubt that nonlinear models have provided a whole class of new tools for business cycle analysis. These nonlinear models have been embraced and further developed, both theoretically and empirically, by economists over the last decade or so. Their popularity is partly because they typically fit historical data better than linear models. More importantly, however, nonlinear models are popular because they provide practical tools that allow economists to investigate issues concerned with how economic responses vary over business cycle phases in a way that is not possible within the confines of a linear framework.

This chapter uses nonlinear models to examine an issue that is important to statisticians working in official statistical agencies, but (for reasons that are not immediately obvious) has attracted relatively little interest among economists. This issue is the nature of seasonality, specifically seasonality in industrial production for the countries of the European Union. It is well-documented that seasonality dominates the short-term (month-to-month or-quarter to-quarter) movements in such series; see, for example, Miron and Beaulieu (1996) or Matas-Mir and Osborn (2003). Nevertheless, the widespread view among economists is that these movements associated with seasonality contain no economic information, and hence they prefer to estimate models using seasonally adjusted data. It is, therefore, not surprising that virtually all the key papers developing nonlinear models for business cycle analysis (including the seminal study of Hamilton, 1989) have been set in a nonseasonal context, either explicitly or implicitly using seasonally adjusted data.

Despite the predominance of the use of seasonally adjusted data, there has recently been a strain of literature that has found evidence of interactions between seasonality and the business cycle, with contributions including Ghysels (1993, 1994), Canova and Ghysels (1994), Cecchetti and Kashyap (1996), Miron and Beaulieu (1996), Cecchetti, Kashyap and Wilcox (1997), Carpenter and Levy (1998), Krane and Wascher (1999), van Dijk, Strikholm and Teräsvirta (2003), Teräsvirta, Strikholm and van Dijk (2003), and Matas-Mir and Osborn (2003, 2004). Perhaps the most compelling theoretical case for anticipating a seasonal/business cycle interaction is that of Cecchetti and Kashyap (1996), who argue that the seasonal slowdown in production during the summer months should be less marked at business cycle peaks compared with troughs, because when there are capacity constraints due to high demand around the peak of the cycle it will be cost-effective for producers to utilize the spare capacity that occurs in the summer months in order to meet this demand.

In Matas-Mir and Osborn (2003) we took up this issue, using a nonlinear threshold model to capture the business cycle regimes while allowing the seasonal parameters (as well as the intercept) to change with the regime. Applying the model to monthly industrial production series for 16 OECD countries, using data from 1960 to 1995, we found evidence of a significant seasonal/business cycle interaction in about a third of the 74 series analysed. Further, examining the seasonal patterns by month for each business cycle regime, our evidence supports the arguments of Cecchetti and Kashyap (1996) that changes in seasonality associated with the business cycle are evident primarily in the summer months, when seasonality is muted during the upper regime (where growth is above a threshold) in comparison with the seasonality exhibited in the lower regime.

This chapter again examines this issue, but now focusing exclusively on the countries of the European Union. Further, here we provide measures of the change in seasonality over the business cycle, comparing changes for all months of the year to changes for the summer months alone, in order to examine the extent to which seasonal/business cycle interactions are confined to the summer months. The outline of the remainder of the chapter is that the next section outlines the particular version of the nonlinear threshold model we employ, followed by a presentation of the substantive results, with a final concluding section.

Modelling and measuring seasonal/business cycle interactions

The model we employ here is almost identical to that used in our earlier study, Matas-Mir and Osborn (2003). As discussed below, however, we now take a simpler approach to testing for significance of the nonlinearity. The model is of the threshold autoregressive (TAR) class, which is particularly appropriate in the context of business cycle phases, as it allows the parameters to change when growth exceeds some threshold. In the present context the specific parameters permitted to change with the threshold are the (nonseasonal and seasonal) intercept coefficients, thereby allowing the underlying seasonal pattern to vary over business cycle regimes.

First we outline the model we employ, before considering estimation and inference issues, and, finally, the measures we employ for the extent of seasonal/business cycle interactions.

The model

As in Matas-Mir and Osborn (2003), the model we employ has the form:

$$\phi(L)\Delta y_t = \delta_0 + \eta_0 t + \gamma_0 I_t + \sum_{j=1}^{11} \delta_j s_{jt} + \sum_{j=1}^{11} \eta_j s_{jt} t + \sum_{j=1}^{11} \gamma_j I_t s_{jt} + \varepsilon_t \qquad (6.1)$$

where Δy_t is the monthly growth in industrial production with disturbance process $\varepsilon_t \sim NID(0, \sigma^2)$. The autoregressive operator $\phi(L)$, defined in terms of the usual lag operator L, is assumed to have all roots strictly outside the unit circle. Seasonality is captured through the variables s_{jt} which are defined by $s_{jt} = D_{jt} - D_{12t}, j = 1, \ldots, 11$ where D_{jt} are the conventional monthly seasonal dummy variables. In the lower regime at time $t (I_t = 0)$, the coefficients $\delta_j (j = 1, \ldots, 11)$ measure the seasonal intercept shift in each of 11 months compared with the overall intercept δ_0, with the intercept shift for the final month computed as $\delta_{12} = -\sum_{j=1}^{11} \delta_j$.

We define the regime indicator I_t by:

$$I_t = \begin{cases} 1 \text{ if } (1 + L + L^2)\Delta_{12} y_{t-1}/3 \geq r \\ 0 \text{ if } (1 + L + L^2)\Delta_{12} y_{t-1}/3 < r \end{cases} \qquad (6.2)$$

Equations (6.1) and (6.2) then define a restricted TAR model, where r is the (single) threshold parameter.[1] The coefficients γ_j ($j = 0, \ldots, 12$) give the amount by which the overall intercept and seasonal intercept terms shift in the upper regime ($I_t = 1$) compared with the lower, where the seasonal intercept shift omitted from (6.1) can be computed as $\gamma_{12} = -\sum_{j=1}^{11} \gamma_j$. Through the specification of (6.1), combined with the regime shift defined in (6.2), we can separate monthly regime-dependent seasonal patterns around the mean from the overall steady-state mean growth within the regime. This is discussed below.

From a behavioural perspective (6.2) allows seasonality to change when, over the previous three months, the average increase in production is more than some threshold amount r compared with a year earlier. For many European countries, production peaks during the spring and early summer, before falling (sometimes dramatically) during July or August; see, for example, the monthly growth rate patterns in Miron and Beaulieu (1996, table 3). The business cycle indicator in (6.2) then allows the possibility that the seasonal pattern in July/August may alter as a consequence of conditions that have operated in the spring. However such changes are not restricted to the summer, since changes in the seasonal pattern may occur in (6.1) for any month of the year that the business cycle regime shifts.

It may be noted that our model restricts changing seasonal behaviour to the seasonal intercepts, with no effect operating through the dynamics in $\phi(L)$. This keeps the parameterization simple, but nevertheless captures the essential feature of any relationship between seasonality and the business cycle.

Seasonal trend terms are included in (6.1) to allow for the trends over time in the seasonal pattern that occurs for many series in at least some months of the year. Although van Dijk *et al.* (2003) model changing seasonality as logistic time trends, we prefer the simpler approach of linear seasonal trends. In Matas-Mir and Osborn (2003) we report the joint significance of these seasonal trends. Although we do not do so in this chapter, they are highly significant for almost all series examined.

Estimation and inference

Estimation of a threshold model, such as (6.1), can be undertaken through a grid search over values of the threshold r with ordinary-least-squares (OLS) applied conditional on its value. This is implemented by searching over the empirical distribution function of the threshold variable defined in (6.2), excluding its extremes. For the present analysis we search over the central 50 per cent of the distribution, thereby not allowing the threshold to be in the upper or lower quartiles of the distribution of the average annual growth rate threshold variable. This is to avoid the problem that one 'regime' may correspond to only a small number of observations and hence we hope to obtain reliable estimates of the regime-dependent monthly seasonal coefficients δ_j and γ_j in (6.1).

Chan (1993) shows that, for a given order of $\phi(L)$, searching over all possible values of r to minimize the sum of squared residuals produces a super-consistent estimate of the threshold. In practice we use a fixed autoregressive order of 24 for $\phi(L)$, thereby allowing for dynamics of up to two years.

Conventional inference cannot be applied in (6.1) for the coefficients related to the business cycle nonlinearity, namely γ_j ($j = 0, 1, \ldots, 11$), since these depend on the unobserved threshold r. The solution adopted in Matas-Mir and Osborn (2003) is to use a simulation procedure to obtain finite sample p-values corresponding to a test of the null joint hypothesis $\gamma_j = 0$ ($j = 0, 1, \ldots, 11$). Such a test is important since it provides information on whether there is any business cycle nonlinearity in (6.1), and hence whether there could be a seasonal/business cycle interaction. However the simulation method is very costly in computing time. Therefore in the present paper we take the simpler approach of testing the joint significance of these terms using the Hansen (1997) approximation to the asymptotic distribution of tests for structural change, where in our context the structural change is associated with values of the threshold variable rather than with time. The number of parameters of (6.1) subject to potential structural change over the business cycle is $m = 12$, namely the intercept and eleven seasonal intercept coefficients.

Measuring seasonal/business cycle interactions

As already noted, the model of (6.1) allows the separation of the overall mean from the deterministic seasonal effects. The overall steady-state mean for Δy_t corresponding to the lower regime (with $I_t = I_{t-1} = \cdots = 0$) is given by $\mu_0 = \phi^{-1}(1)\delta_0$. As shown in Matas-Mir and Osborn (2003), the implied deviation in steady state for each month in relation to this overall mean can be calculated from the parameters of (6.1), and here we denote these monthly steady-state mean deviations in the lower regime by λ_{0j} ($j = 1, \ldots, 12$). [2] These monthly mean deviations provide a convenient measure of the nature and extent of seasonality over the year.

Within the upper regime, the overall steady state mean is given by $\mu_1 = \phi^{-1}(1)[\delta_0 + \gamma_0]$, while corresponding steady-state deviations from this mean in each month of the year can also be computed. These upper regime steady-state monthly deviations are denoted by λ_{1j} ($j = 1, \ldots, 12$). Matas-Mir and Osborn (2003) provide a graphical analysis of these lower and upper regime steady-state seasonal deviations. Here, however, we present numerical measures of the extent of seasonal/business interaction based on these.

In the context of our model, an obvious measure of the extent of seasonality within a regime is the average absolute value of these monthly mean deviations, namely:

$$S_i = \frac{\sum_{j=1}^{12} |\lambda_{ij}|}{12} \qquad i = 0, 1 \tag{6.3}$$

Similarly, the corresponding average over the summer months ($j = 7, 8, 9$) provides a measure of the extent of summer seasonality in each regime. Note that the summer production decline occurs in either July or August depending on the specific country, but that seasonal decline is then followed by a rebound in production in the following month (August or September). Therefore, averaging over these three months allows for both the summer decline and the subsequent recovery to more normal production levels. In an analogous way, we also measure the extent of seasonality over the non-summer months, that is excluding July, August and September.[3]

Building on (6.3), there are then two natural measures of the interaction of seasonality and the business cycle, namely the difference between the seasonality measure of (6.3) for the upper regime compared with the lower regime, namely $S_1 - S_0$, and the ratio S_1/S_0. Both of these measures are reported below, with these computed over all months, and also separately over the summer and non-summer months.

The only other study of which we are aware that provides any measure of such interaction between seasonality and the business cycle is Cecchetti and Kashyap (1996), who use the ratio of the estimated variance of the seasonal effects at given stages of the business cycle for this purpose. This is clearly a measure similar in spirit to the ratio S_1/S_0 that we present. However we believe that it is important to supplement this with information about the extent of seasonality, captured in our case by S_0 and the difference $S_1 - S_0$, since the ratio is a dimensionless measure and by itself does not reflect the practical relevance of the seasonal/cyclical interaction.

Results

We analyse seasonally unadjusted monthly indexes of industrial production for the 15 countries of the European Union, as available from the OECD *Main Economic Indicators* database. Since we need to have sufficient observations available for individual months to estimate intercept parameters associated with each of two regimes, we require data covering a long time span. Therefore, the specific variables analysed are those available from the 1970s. The analysis here uses the period from the beginning of 1970, or the earliest date for which the series is available.[4] Typically, our sample period ends in April or May 2003. Only one series (total industrial production) is available for Germany, so that we supplement this by including series for the former West Germany, despite the fact that these finish in December 1994. Information about the sample period used for all series can be found in the Appendix. Prior to analysis, all series are transformed to monthly percentage growth rates by taking first differences of the (natural) logarithms and multiplying by 100.

Some series exhibit a small number of outliers, which may be associated with strikes or other one-off events. Outliers are removed prior to analysis, with the Appendix providing details of the number of outliers removed from each series.[5]

The discussion below considers first the nonlinear business cycle characteristics uncovered and then the extent of seasonal/business cycle interactions.

Business cycle regime characteristics

Table 6.1 provides the results of the test of the joint null joint hypothesis $\gamma_j = 0$ $(j = 0, 1, \ldots, 11)$ in (6.1), which (as discussed above) is a test of the null hypothesis of linearity. The information presented includes the p-values obtained using the approximation of Hansen (1997) to the asymptotic distribution of the test statistic, together with the percentile (between 25 and 75) of the distribution of

Table 6.1 Data and nonlinear characteristics of the threshold model

	Nonlinearity p-value	Threshold	
		Percentile	Value
Austria			
Industrial production	.831	38	2.45
Manufacturing	.997	44	3.45
Belgium			
Construction	.064	39	−2.42
Total inc. construction	.187	71	4.32
Industrial production	.053	64	3.39
Manufacturing	.211	63	3.48
Consumption durables	.087	75	5.03
Consumption non-durab.	.001	65	3.45
Intermediate goods	.965	29	0.14
Investment goods	.282	25	−3.95
Germany			
Industrial production	.542	53	2.60
West Germany			
Industrial production	.440	25	−0.73
Consumer goods	.014	25	−1.99
Intermediate goods	.376	69	4.60
Investment goods	.003	45	2.47
Denmark			
Manufacturing	.273	71	5.00
Consumption durables	.035	75	6.80
Investment goods	.001	26	−1.15
Spain			
Industrial production	.000	75	5.84
Manufacturing	.000	73	5.83
Naval construction	.254	28	−26.06
Consumer goods	.598	50	2.66
Intermediate goods	.662	53	3.54
Investment goods	.101	36	0.31
Finland			
Industrial production	.000	42	3.67
Manufacturing	.000	69	7.14
Consumer goods	.056	75	5.62
Intermediate goods	.176	34	2.34
Investment goods	.139	65	12.22
France			
Construction	.230	54	1.33
Energy	.879	71	4.92
Industrial production	.272	30	0.46
Manufacturing	.056	49	1.89
Agriculture & food	.147	74	2.74
Consumer goods	.843	25	−0.86
Intermediate goods	.000	41	0.70
Investment goods	.798	25	−0.38

(Continued)

Table 6.1 Continued

	Nonlinearity p-value	Threshold	
		Percentile	Value
United Kingdom			
Industrial production	.018	75	3.75
Manufacturing	.066	47	0.94
Intermediate goods	.001	69	3.49
Investment goods	.083	65	3.24
Greece			
Industrial production	.358	74	7.09
Manufacturing	.331	25	−0.50
Consumption durables	.517	75	10.43
Consumption non-durab.	.260	73	7.48
Investment goods	.266	63	4.44
Ireland			
Industrial production	.157	73	11.56
Manufacturing	.233	70	11.62
Consumer goods	.202	74	6.03
Intermediate goods	.777	69	14.24
Capital goods	.854	619	14.44
Italy			
Industrial production	.029	39	1.12
Consumer goods	.621	33	−0.39
Intermediate goods	.000	67	3.06
Investment goods	.016	28	−2.73
Luxembourg			
Construction	.259	72	7.17
Industrial production	.299	68	5.20
Manufacturing	.519	41	1.75
Netherlands			
Industrial production	.032	28	−0.23
Manufacturing	.848	75	5.09
Portugal			
Industrial production	.684	25	0.02
Manufacturing	.347	25	−0.01
Sweden			
Mining manufacturing	.011	69	5.56
Manufacturing	.022	68	5.35

the threshold variable that minimizes the residual sum of squares of (6.1) and the corresponding threshold value, r, of (6.2).

Of the 64 European industrial production series that we analyse, 25 evidence significant nonlinearity at the 10 per cent level. Indeed, 17 are significant at 5 per cent, including 9 at 1 per cent or lower. Therefore, these European series overall shown substantial evidence of nonlinearity associated with the business cycle. The proportion of rejections at this level (40 per cent) is higher than that found in our previous study, Matas-Mir and Osborn (2003), that covered a wider range of countries.

In common with our previous results, the nonlinearity is particularly notable in some countries. The extreme significance of this nonlinearity for total industrial production and manufacturing production for Spain and Finland is particularly noteworthy. Further, the evidence of nonlinearity is strong at the aggregate level of industrial production or manufacturing overall, with 6 from 13 and 5 from 13 series, respectively, significant at 10 per cent for these two categories.[6] Also echoing our previous results, there is again substantial evidence of nonlinearity in the production of Intermediate goods, with this significant at 1 per cent for three countries (France, UK, Italy), and in addition significant at 10 per cent for West Germany.

Of the 64 series included in Table 6.1, the threshold value occurs at the 30th percentile or lower for 14 series and at the 70th percentile or higher for 18 series. In the former case, the lower regime can be associated with recession, with the associated threshold value almost always negative. In the latter case, the lower regime identified is negative or 'normal' growth, compared with the upper regime of high growth. In the remaining cases, the threshold is in the intermediate interval of the observed distribution of the average annual growth threshold variable. In these cases, the regimes may be described as distinguishing higher from lower growth. Although Cecchetti and Kashyap (1996) argue that the seasonal/business cycle interaction will be particularly associated with business cycle peaks, the threshold percentiles and values in Table 6.1 suggest that such interactions may be spread over the business cycle, depending on the specific characteristics of the industry and country.

Seasonal/business cycle interactions

The results of principal interest, namely the measures of the extent of interaction between seasonality and the business cycle, are shown in Table 6.2. The results in this table based on differences $S_1 - S_0$ confirm the hypothesis of Cecchetti and Kashyap (1996) that seasonality is less marked in the upper regime of the business cycle, with 46 values negative when this difference is calculated over all months of the year. Indeed, when the summer months alone are considered, the figure rises to 50, while only 33 of the 64 series exhibit an average decline in seasonality in the upper regime over the non-summer months. Thus, in terms of the number of series for which seasonality is reduced in the upper business cycle regime, the reduction is concentrated in the summer months rather than being spread over all months.

When examined through the average reduction in seasonality across all 64 series, as presented in the bottom row of Table 6.2, the summer reduction in the seasonal pattern in the upper regime is approximately $2\frac{1}{4}$ percentage points of the level of the series. This is substantially stronger than the average reduction over all months of 0.49 and compares with a small average increase of 0.09 in the non-summer months. In terms of the ratio of seasonality in the two regimes averaged across all 64 series, the summer reduction is around 9 per cent.

Alongside these general statements about averages across all series, it should be noted that the interaction with the business cycle sometimes leads to seasonality, as captured by our measure in (6.3), to be reduced dramatically. This is the case, for example, for total industrial production in both Spain and Finland, where seasonality in the upper regime is 60 to 70 per cent of its magnitude in the lower regime. While seasonality in industrial production for both countries is much stronger in the summer than in other months (compare the magnitude of seasonality in the lower regime for the summer and non-summer months), nevertheless the effect of reduced seasonality in the upper regime occurs across all months of the year in these cases. Indeed, it is worth remarking that for these two aggregate industrial production series, the proportional reduction is quite similar for the summer and non-summer months.

Another feature of Table 6.2 is that, irrespective of significance of the business cycle nonlinearity in Table 6.1, seasonality over all months is reduced in the upper regime for all series in the Scandinavian countries of Finland and Sweden, although this is not the case in Denmark. In terms of the ratio S_1/S_0, the reduction for the first two countries is particularly marked in the summer, with the ratio then being on average approximately 0.70. In terms of magnitude, these changes in seasonality over the business cycle are not trivial. In the case of Finland, for example, the difference $S_1 - S_0$ for the summer months is approximately 10 on average, implying a reduction in the magnitude of seasonal movements by around 10 percentage points of the level series in the upper regime. Interestingly, according to Table 6.2, seasonality often appears to increase in the upper (compared to the lower) regime for the non-summer months in these two countries. However, given that the magnitude of seasonality in these months is relatively small, these results may not be reliable.

Overall, the scale of cyclical change in the seasonal pattern for some months, and specifically the summer, may be substantially larger than the typical size of a business cycle fluctuation. The threshold values in Table 6.1 present one measure of the size of a business cycle fluctuation, by showing the average annual growth rate that triggers the regime shift for each series. It is clear that if these are scaled to monthly averages by dividing by 12, these threshold values would generally be much smaller in magnitude than the extent of the change in summer seasonality over regimes. An extreme example is industrial production in Spain, where the threshold of Table 6.1 corresponds to a monthly average growth of 0.49, whereas the average monthly change in the seasonal pattern over regimes for the summer is larger than 15. As a result of the extent of such interaction, standard seasonal adjustment methods, which assume that seasonal and cyclical fluctuations are orthogonal, may produce misleading results for such months.

Although the general pattern is of reduced summer seasonality in the upper business cycle regime, there are some exceptions to this. For example, for consumer non-durables for Belgium and consumer goods for West Germany, significant (at 5 per cent) nonlinearity is indicated in Table 6.1, while Table 6.2 shows seasonality to be increased in the summer in this regime. Indeed, the pattern of interactions for West Germany consumer goods is unusual, because here

Table 6.2   The extent of seasonality and the seasonal/business cycle interaction

	Average lower regime seasonality			Relative seasonality upper compared to lower regime					
				Difference			Ratio		
	All months	Summer	Non-summer	All months	Summer	Non-summer	All months	Summer	Non-summer
Austria									
Industrial production	5.60	11.17	3.74	0.06	−0.66	0.30	1.01	0.94	1.08
Manufacturing	6.17	12.20	4.16	0.20	−0.18	0.32	1.03	0.99	1.08
Belgium									
Construction	26.91	66.65	13.66	−4.48	−7.62	−3.44	0.83	0.89	0.75
Total inc. construction	9.41	26.78	3.62	−0.50	−0.84	−0.39	0.95	0.97	0.89
Industrial production	7.48	19.79	3.37	−0.38	−1.05	−0.16	0.95	0.95	0.95
Manufacturing	7.91	21.65	3.32	−1.49	−3.28	−0.90	0.81	0.85	0.73
Consumption durables	11.82	31.64	5.22	1.41	0.47	1.72	1.12	1.02	1.33
Consumption non-durab.	5.61	11.46	3.66	0.88	3.17	0.11	1.16	1.28	1.03
Intermediate goods	7.82	20.81	3.48	−0.84	−2.19	−0.40	0.89	0.89	0.89
Investment goods	10.68	26.10	5.53	−2.45	−1.76	−2.68	0.77	0.93	0.52
Germany									
Industrial production	5.38	9.30	4.07	−0.55	−0.30	−0.63	0.90	0.97	0.84
West Germany									
Industrial production	5.42	8.55	4.38	−0.66	0.88	−1.18	0.88	1.10	0.73
Consumer goods	7.56	9.25	6.99	−1.85	0.89	−2.76	0.76	1.10	0.61
Intermediate goods	4.09	4.82	3.85	−0.28	−1.53	0.14	0.93	0.68	1.03
Investment goods	7.43	14.32	5.14	−0.48	0.60	−0.84	0.93	1.04	0.84
Denmark									
Manufacturing	11.59	27.39	6.32	−1.06	−1.35	−0.96	0.91	0.95	0.85
Consumption durables	13.37	34.01	6.49	5.38	9.58	3.98	1.40	1.28	1.61
Investment goods	17.12	34.88	11.19	0.11	2.94	−0.83	1.01	1.08	0.93
Spain									
Industrial production	13.05	35.92	5.43	−5.49	−15.54	−2.15	0.58	0.57	0.60
Manufacturing	12.92	40.34	3.78	−1.49	−12.13	2.05	0.88	0.70	1.54
Naval construction	16.82	36.44	10.27	6.22	25.97	−0.36	1.37	1.71	0.96
Consumer goods	13.90	34.70	6.97	−3.09	−5.82	−2.18	0.78	0.83	0.69
Intermediate goods	11.81	30.32	5.64	−2.33	−4.29	−1.68	0.80	0.86	0.70
Investment goods	30.21	89.18	10.56	−2.20	−10.09	0.43	0.93	0.89	1.04

Finland									
Industrial production	11.11	32.57	3.96	−3.84	−11.91	−1.15	0.65	0.63	0.71
Manufacturing	10.50	33.99	2.66	−1.79	−16.48	3.10	0.83	0.52	2.17
Consumer goods	10.59	30.94	3.81	−0.58	−7.24	1.64	0.95	0.77	1.43
Intermediate goods	10.14	22.43	6.05	−2.61	−4.38	−2.02	0.74	0.80	0.67
Investment goods	15.37	52.24	3.08	−1.73	−15.64	2.90	0.89	0.70	1.94
France									
Construction	12.58	34.28	5.35	−0.92	−3.67	−0.00	0.93	0.89	1.00
Energy	7.42	8.01	7.23	−0.10	−1.86	0.49	0.99	0.77	1.07
Industrial production	8.60	26.17	2.75	−0.25	−1.71	0.24	0.97	0.93	1.09
Manufacturing	9.38	28.19	3.11	−0.64	−1.72	−0.28	0.93	0.94	0.91
Agriculture & food	7.42	5.46	8.08	0.03	−2.78	0.97	1.00	0.49	1.12
Consumer goods	10.65	31.12	3.82	−0.09	−1.79	0.48	0.99	0.94	1.13
Intermediate goods	13.11	37.59	4.94	−2.00	−5.70	−0.76	0.85	0.85	0.85
Investment goods	8.08	13.14	6.39	1.80	4.32	0.96	1.22	1.33	1.15
United Kingdom									
Industrial production	4.99	8.10	3.96	0.69	−0.14	0.97	1.14	0.98	1.24
Manufacturing	5.43	9.29	4.15	0.78	−1.02	1.38	1.14	0.89	1.33
Intermediate goods	5.29	8.26	4.30	0.13	−1.32	0.62	1.02	0.84	1.14
Investment goods	7.56	10.46	6.59	0.40	−2.66	1.42	1.05	0.75	1.22
Greece									
Industrial production	4.62	7.95	3.51	−0.66	−1.66	−0.32	0.86	0.79	0.91
Manufacturing	5.94	10.14	4.53	−0.85	−1.00	−0.80	0.86	0.90	0.82
Consumption durables	15.33	45.57	5.25	3.64	−2.68	5.74	1.24	0.94	2.09
Consumption non-durab	4.46	5.71	4.05	0.33	−0.34	0.55	1.07	0.94	1.14
Investment goods	7.72	19.08	3.93	0.23	−3.56	1.49	1.03	0.81	1.38
Ireland									
Industrial production	6.13	13.80	3.57	−0.35	−2.17	0.26	0.94	0.84	1.07
Manufacturing	6.56	14.97	3.75	−0.11	−1.42	0.33	0.98	0.90	1.09
Consumer goods	6.02	7.89	5.40	−0.28	1.85	−1.00	0.95	1.23	0.82
Intermediate goods	8.38	18.73	4.93	−0.13	−3.69	1.05	0.98	0.80	1.21
Capital goods	10.08	17.89	7.47	−0.83	−0.23	−1.03	0.92	0.99	0.86

(Continued)

Table 6.2 Continued

	Average lower regime seasonality			Relative seasonality upper compared to lower regime					
				Difference			*Ratio*		
	All months	*Summer*	*Non-summer*	*All months*	*Summer*	*Non-summer*	*All months*	*Summer*	*Non-summer*
Italy									
Industrial production	17.90	53.13	6.15	−4.01	−7.29	−2.92	0.78	0.86	0.53
Consumer goods	17.46	48.79	7.02	−0.78	2.80	−1.97	0.96	1.06	0.72
Intermediate goods	18.51	55.90	6.05	−2.66	−4.50	−2.04	0.86	0.92	0.66
Investment goods	24.72	79.79	6.37	−5.79	−16.73	−2.14	0.77	0.79	0.66
Luxembourg									
Construction	20.92	43.72	13.32	9.25	25.83	3.72	1.44	1.59	1.28
Industrial production	7.13	20.21	2.77	−0.29	−4.58	1.15	0.96	0.77	1.41
Manufacturing	8.31	23.22	3.34	−1.64	−6.09	−0.16	0.80	0.74	0.95
Netherlands									
Industrial production	8.14	12.60	6.65	−3.62	−2.15	−4.11	0.56	0.83	0.38
Manufacturing	4.78	10.56	2.85	0.92	1.86	0.61	1.19	1.18	1.21
Portugal									
Industrial production	8.35	23.86	3.18	−0.83	−1.11	−0.74	0.90	0.95	0.77
Manufacturing	9.11	24.68	3.98	−0.33	1.18	−0.83	0.96	1.05	0.79
Sweden									
Mining manufact.	15.52	51.09	3.66	−2.96	−17.85	2.00	0.81	0.65	1.55
Manufacturing	15.70	51.29	3.83	−3.04	−16.45	1.43	0.81	0.68	1.37
Average									
All series	9.87	23.76	5.24	−0.49	−2.25	0.09	0.95	0.91	1.05

seasonality is increased in the upper regime during the summer, but it is lower in the non-summer months and is lower overall compared with the lower regime.

Conclusions

In this chapter we have provided numerical measures of the extent of the interaction of seasonality and the business cycle. In order to focus on whether changes in the seasonal pattern over the business cycle are concentrated in the summer months, in addition to seasonality measured over the year, we have separately considered seasonality in the summer and non-summer months.

Our results confirm the extent of the reduction in seasonality in the upper regime of the business cycle, with this reduction being as much as 30 per cent or more in some cases when measured in terms of average seasonality over the year. More generally, however, the reductions are of the order of 10 to 20 per cent. Seasonality in the lower regime can imply substantial average month to month movements. However, seasonality changes over business cycle regimes may moderate these movements by the order of 10 percentage points of the level of the series, thus having the potential of being larger than the average monthly business cycle variation.

In general, our findings also confirm that the seasonal/business cycle interaction effects are concentrated primarily in the summer months, with the summer slowdown being muted in the upper (higher growth) regime of the business cycle. In addition to showing their importance in terms of statistical significance, with the interaction being significant at the 10 per cent level for 40 per cent of our series, our results here also establish the practical importance in terms of the magnitudes of changes in seasonality over the business cycle. We believe that these are of sufficient importance to merit further investigation, to see what economic information is conveyed by the changes in these seasonal effects.

Appendix: Data and outliers

	Sample period	Outliers removed
Austria		
Industrial production	1970M1-2002M12	1
Manufacturing	1970M1-2002M12	1
Belgium		
Construction	1970M1-2003M4	1
Total inc. construction	1970M1-2003M4	1
Industrial production	1970M1-2003M4	0
Manufacturing	1970M1-2003M4	0
Consumption durables	1970M1-2003M4	2
Consumption non-dur.	1970M1-2003M4	1

(Continued)

Appendix: Continued

	Sample period	*Outliers removed*
Intermediate goods	1970M1-2003M4	1
Investment goods	1970M1-2003M4	2
Germany		
Industrial production	1970M1-2003M4	1
West Germany		
Industrial production	1970M1-1994M12	1
Consumer goods	1970M1-1994M12	0
Intermediate goods	1970M1-1994M12	0
Investment goods	1970M1-1994M12	1
Denmark		
Manufacturing	1976M2-2003M4	0
Consumption durables	1976M2-2003M4	3
Investment goods	1976M2-2003M4	1
Spain		
Industrial production	1970M1-2003M4	0
Manufacturing	1970M1-2003M4	0
Naval construction	1977M2-2002M12	1
Consumer goods	1970M1-2003M4	2
Intermediate goods	1970M1-2003M4	1
Investment goods	1970M1-2003M4	3
Finland		
Industrial production	1970M1-2003M5	0
Manufacturing	1970M1-2003M5	1
Consumer goods	1970M1-2003M5	0
Intermediate goods	1970M1-2003M5	1
Investment goods	1970M1-2003M5	0
France		
Construction	1970M1-2003M4	0
Energy	1970M1-2003M4	0
Industrial production	1970M1-2003M4	0
Manufacturing	1970M1-2003M4	0
Agriculture & food	1970M1-2003M4	0
Consumer goods	1970M1-2003M4	1
United Kingdom		
Industrial production	1970M1-2003M4	1
Manufacturing	1970M1-2003M4	1
Intermediate goods	1970M1-2003M4	1
Investment goods	1970M1-2003M4	0

(Continued)

Appendix: Continued

	Sample period	*Outliers removed*
Greece		
Industrial production	1970M1-2003M3	1
Manufacturing	1970M1-2003M3	2
Consumption durables	1974M2-2003M3	0
Consumption non-dur.	1970M1-2003M3	1
Investment goods	1970M1-2003M3	2
Ireland		
Industrial production	1977M8-2003M3	0
Manufacturing	1977M8-2003M3	0
Consumer goods	1977M8-2003M3	0
Intermediate goods	1977M8-2003M3	0
Capital goods	1977M8-2003M3	0
Italy		
Industrial production	1970M1-2003M4	2
Consumer goods	1979M2-2003M4	1
Intermediate goods	1979M2-2003M4	1
Investment goods	1973M2-2003M4	1
Luxembourg		
Construction	1970M1-2003M3	3
Industrial production	1970M1-2003M3	1
Manufacturing	1970M1-2003M3	1
Netherlands		
Industrial production	1970M1-2003M4	1
Manufacturing	1970M1-2003M4	1
Portugal		
Industrial production	1970M1-2003M5	1
Manufacturing	1970M1-2003M5	1
Sweden		
Mining manufacturing	1970M1-2003M4	2
Manufacturing	1970M1-2003M4	2

Notes

1 In Matas-Mir and Osborn (2003) we removed a linear trend from the threshold variable to allow for the possibility that Δy_t trends over time. We do not do so in the present analysis, however, since the overall trend η_0 was rarely significant in (6.1).

2 Matas-Mir and Osborn (2003) show that each monthly seasonal mean deviation in steady state will depend on all seasonal intercepts in (6.1) with weigths that are nonlinear functions of the autoregressive parameters.

3 Seasonality over all months is then, of course, an appropriate weighted average of the summer and non-summer seasonality measures.

4 In Matas-Mir and Osborn (2003) we use data from 1960. Here, however, we start later as a graphical analysis indicated the possiblity of a structural break in some series around 1970.
5 Outlier removal was based on a linear version of (6.1) , namely an AR(24) model with seasonal dummy variables and seasonal trends. Any observation for which the corresponding residual was greater than 4 standard errors was replaced by the forecast value from this linear specification. Although 4 standard errors is a relatively conservative criterion, we wish to avoid the removal of observations associated with seasonal/business cycle interactions that may appear to be outliers in a linear model.
6 In counting the number of significant industrial production series, West Germany is not counted separately from Germany, although results for both are presented in Table 6.1.

References

Beaulieu, J.J. and Miron, J.A. (1993) 'Seasonal unit roots in aggregate U.S. data', *Journal of Econometrics*, 55: 305–28.

Canova, F. and Ghysels, E. (1994) 'Changes in seasonal patterns – are they cyclical?', *Journal of Economic Dynamics and Control*, 18: 1143–71.

Carpenter, R.E. and Levy, D. (1998) 'Seasonal cycles, business cycles and the comovement of inventory investment and output', *Journal of Money, Credit, and Banking*, 30: 331–46.

Cecchetti, S.G. and Kashyap, A.K. (1996) 'International cycles', *European Economic Review*, 40: 331–60.

Cecchetti, S.G., Kashyap, A.K. and Wilcox, D.W. (1997) 'Interactions between the seasonal and business cycles in production and inventories', *American Economic Review*: 884–92.

Chan, K.S. (1993) 'Consistency and limiting distribution of the least squares estimator of a threshold autoregressive model', *Annals of Statistics*, 21: 520–33.

Ghysels, E. (1993) 'On scoring asymmetric periodic probability models of turning point forecasts', *Journal of Forecasting*, 12: 227–38.

Ghysels, E. (1994) 'On the periodic structure of the business cycle', *Journal of Business and Economic Statistics*, 12: 289–98.

Hamilton, J.D. (1989) 'A new approach to the economic analysis of nonstationary time series and the business cycle', *Econometrica*, 57: 357–84.

Hansen, B.E. (1997) 'Asymptotic *P* values for structural change tests', *Journal of Business and Economic Statistics*, 15: 60–7.

Krane, S. and Wascher, W. (1999) 'The cyclical sensitivity of seasonality in US employment', *Journal of Monetary Economics*, 44: 523–53.

Matas-Mir, A. and Osborn, D.R. (2004) 'Does seasonality change over the business cycle? An investigation using monthly industrial production series', *European Economic Review*, 48: 1309–32.

Matas-Mir, A. and Osborn, D.R. (2004) 'Seasonal adjustment and the detection of business cycle phases', *Working Paper*, 357. Frankfurt am Main: European Central Bank.

Miron, J.A. and Beaulieu, J.J. (1996) 'What have macroeconomists learned about business cycles from the study of seasonal cycles?', *Review of Economics and Statistics*, 78: 54–66.

Teräsvirta, T., Strikholm, B. and van Dijk, D. (2003) 'Changing seasonal patterns in quarterly industrial production in Finland and Sweden', in R. Höglund, M. Jäntti and G. Rosenqvist (eds), *Statistics, Econometrics and Society: Essays in Honour of Leif Nordberg*. Helsinki: Statistics Finland, pp. 229–46.

van Dijk, D., Strikholm, B. and Teräsvirta, T. (2003) 'The effects of institutional and technological change and business cycle fluctuations on seasonal patterns in quarterly industrial production series', *Econometrics Journal*, 6: 79–98.

Part III
Synchronization and Convergence

7
Interacting Two-Country Business Fluctuations: Euroland and the USA

Toichiro Asada, Carl Chiarella, Peter Flaschel and Reiner Franke

Introduction

In this chapter we briefly present a model of business cycle fluctuations between two interacting open economies within the disequilibrium or non-market clearing paradigm[1]. We discuss the main feedback mechanisms (Keynes, Mundell, Rose and Dornbusch) driving the dynamics and the conflict between their stabilizing and destabilizing tendencies and how these depend on certain key speeds of adjustment in the real and foreign exchange sectors. We numerically explore some situations of interacting price cycles in the two countries, where the steady state is locally repelling, but where the overall dynamics are bounded in an economically meaningful domain by means of a kinked money wage Phillips curve.

We reconsider the model structure and the analysis of two large interacting open economies, like Euroland and the USA, as provided in Asada, Chiarella, Flaschel and Franke (ACFF) (2003, ch. 10). We discuss their model of the transmission of inflation between Euroland and the USA directly on the intensive form level and present basic stability results obtained by detailed matrix calculations in their chapter 10. Thereafter we tame the generally explosive dynamics of this model type by the assumption that money wages may rise, but do not fall. On this basis we obtain persistent fluctuations in demand and, therefrom, resulting inflation or disinflation that can only be briefly illustrated here by means of some numerical simulations of the model.

In this note we simplify the 14D Keynes–Metzler–Goodwin (KMG) two-country dynamics of ACFF (2003, ch. 10), which included Keynesian quantity dynamics, to 10D Keynes–Wicksell–Goodwin (KWG) growth and inflation dynamics. The results achieved should therefore be viewed as an initial attempt to gauge the potential of the proposed model type to analyse the international transmission of the business cycle through positive or negative phase synchronization and other mechanisms that arise in the literature on coupled economic oscillators.

The core 10D KWG growth dynamics

The model we are going to present and discuss in this short note can be compactly presented on the intensive form level in terms of 10 state variables and their laws of motion. It represents a nonlinear autonomous dynamical system in the 10 variables $\omega = w/p$, the real wage, $l = L/K$, full-employment labour intensity, p, the price level, π, the inflationary climate, and $\omega^* = w^*/p^*$, $l^* = L^*/K^*$, p^*, π^* for the foreign economy, and finally e, the nominal exchange rate and ϵ, the expected rate of depreciation.

In this condensed form of the model we first have, in equation (7.1), the law of motion for domestic real wages the growth rate of which depends positively on excess demand X^w in the labour market ($\kappa_p \in (0, 1)$) and negatively on excess demand X^p in the goods market ($\kappa_w \in (0, 1)$), the first excess driving money wages and the second the price level. This equation is a reduced form equation based on money-wage and price Phillips curves which besides these demand pressure terms contain cost pressure terms that use the κ parameters as weights. Equation (7.2) gives the growth law for labour intensity l which depends solely on investment per unit of capital $i(\cdot)$, in turn driven by the excess of the profit rate ρ over the real rate of interest $r - \pi$, since trend terms in investment and labour force growth are assumed to be the same for reasons of simplicity. Due to the assumed money wage and price level Phillips curves, we moreover get as a reduced form expression for the rate of price inflation, in equation (7.3), a dependence on both the excess demand in the labour as well as in the goods market, augmented by the inflationary climate in which the economy is currently operating. This reduced form expression is a direct generalization of the one that is generally employed in the empirical literature, using two types of excess demand expressions here, with a specific mixture of the coefficients characterizing labour and goods market dynamics. Equation (7.4) finally assumes that the inflationary climate π is updated in an adaptive way. Note that we have myopic perfect foresight with respect to both wage and price inflation (of crossover type) in this model, which however is removed from sight when reduced form expressions are calculated.

Of course, the corresponding laws of motion (7.7)–(7.10) for the foreign economy are motivated in the same way and thus need not be discussed here any further. The equations in between, equations (7.5) and (7.6), represent the links between the two economies here considered. The trade link is given by net exports nx per unit of capital which depends in the usual way on the real exchange rate η in particular. We denote in equation (7.5) by $\beta(\cdot)$ the international flow of capital – measured in terms of the domestic currency – which is here made dependent solely on the risk premium $r^* + \epsilon - r$ of foreign bonds over domestic ones. This currency flow must be augmented by the one deriving from net exports nx in order to obtain total currency flows, which in turn determine exchange rate depreciation or appreciation $\hat{e}$ on the basis of a speed of adjustment parameter β_e. The expected depreciation rate ϵ is then determined in equation (7.6) as a weighted average of backward looking, here adaptive expectations, and forward looking regressive expectations. In the present version of the model we neglect steady-state inflation and de- or appreciation of the currency and thus have that regressive expectations expect the rate of depreciation ϵ to return to zero with a certain speed.

For the domestic economy:

$$\widehat{\omega} = \kappa[(1 - \kappa_p)\beta_w X^W + (\kappa_w - 1)\beta_p X^p] \tag{7.1}$$

$$\widehat{l} = -i(\rho - (r - \pi)) \tag{7.2}$$

$$\widehat{p} = \kappa[\beta_p X^p + \kappa_p \beta_w X^W] + \pi \tag{7.3}$$

$$\dot{\pi} = \beta_\pi(\hat{p} - \pi) \tag{7.4}$$

Financial and trade links between the two economies are described by:

$$\hat{e} = \beta_e(\beta(r^* + \epsilon - r) - nx(\eta)), \quad \eta = \left(\frac{ep^*}{p}\right)^{-1} \tag{7.5}$$

$$\dot{\epsilon} = \beta_\epsilon[\alpha_\epsilon(\hat{e} - \epsilon) + (1 - \alpha_\epsilon)(-\epsilon)] \tag{7.6}$$

For the foreign economy:

$$\widehat{\omega}^* = \kappa^*[(1 - \kappa_p^*)\beta_W^* X^{W*} + (\kappa_w^* - 1)\beta_p^* X^{p*}] \tag{7.7}$$

$$\widehat{l}^* = -i^*(\rho^* + \pi^* - r^*) \tag{7.8}$$

$$\widehat{p}^* = \kappa^*[\beta_p^* X^{p*} + \kappa_p^* \beta_w^* X^{W*}] + \pi^* \tag{7.9}$$

$$\dot{\pi}^* = \beta_\pi^*(\hat{p}^* - \pi^*) \tag{7.10}$$

We give a brief graphical summary of the assumed two-country interaction by way of the essential links for trade in commodities and in financial assets. Figure 7.1 shows the consumption demands for foreign goods, the way the financial markets determine the real exchange rate via the Dornbusch exchange-rate dynamics, and finally the repercussions back from commodity markets to the financial markets via the interest rates implied by the transactions in the two economies. The model is traditional insofar as we have a stabilizing Keynes or nominal rate of interest rate effect, but also a destabilizing feedback channel via the expected rate of inflation π which, when increased, increases activity and thus gives a further push to the inflation that is already in existence. This is the so-called Mundell effect based on inflationary expectations and the expected real rate of interest. We briefly mention another feedback channel of the considered economic dynamics, a real wage channel in fact, which can be stabilizing or destabilizing depending on the adjustment speed of wages and prices and on whether investment or consumption demand is

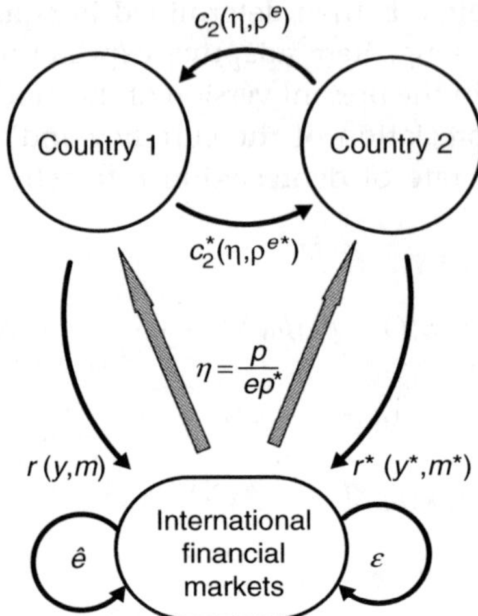

Figure 7.1 The two country KWG framework (*m, y* real balances and real output per capital)

the dominant force in the case of real wage increases. This so-called Rose effect is discussed in detail in ACFF (2003), where also a variety of other topics related to open economy macrodynamics are considered.

In this framework, output and real balances per unit of capital determine the domestic as well as the foreign interest rate by way of Keynesian liquidity preference theory. These in turn – together with expected currency depreciation or appreciation and the currency demand originating in the trade account – determine the actual rate of currency depreciation or appreciation (and on this basis also the expected change). Given price levels in the two countries imply a certain real exchange rate whose rate of change is determined by inflation at home and abroad and the just determined actual exchange rate dynamics. Inflation at home and abroad are simultaneously determined by demand pressures in the markets for goods and for labour and give rise in this way to an international transmission of inflation. We have wage dynamics in addition and also investment and growth, leading in sum to a dynamic structure where two Keynes effects, two Mundell effects, and two Rose effects interact with the Dornbusch exchange rate dynamics on the foreign exchange market. The generally accelerating foreign exchange rate dynamics is illustrated in Figure 7.2. The overall effect of all these feedback channels is to create a fairly complex situation of two business cycle mechanisms that interact via trade and via what happens on international financial markets.

In the next section we show that the feedback structure in the foreign exchange market is such that a tendency towards cumulative instability is established. This instability may, however, be overcome by the interaction with the real sectors of the two economies. There are of course other possible mechanisms that can tame an, in principle, unstable financial accelerator of this type, which however must be left for future research.

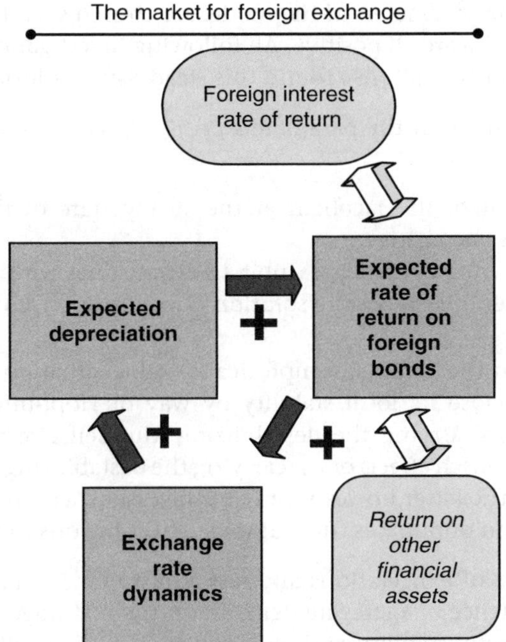

Figure 7.2   The Dornbusch exchange rate link of the model

Local stability and loss of stability

In this section we briefly characterize the stability properties of the unique interior steady state of the considered two-country dynamics (7.1)–(7.10). For the proofs of these stability results we refer the reader to ACFF (2003, ch. 10). Here we will confine ourselves to just observing that the strategy for obtaining the asymptotic stability results for such a high-dimensional system starts from considering the dynamical system with most speeds of adjustment set equal to zero. The speeds of adjustment are then successively 'switched on' (that is, set to a small positive value). By this approach, and relying on the continuous dependence of eigenvalues on model parameters, it is possible in particular to obtain the stability results given in Theorem 2 below.

Let us first consider whether there is a uniquely determined interior steady state solution of the 10D dynamics (7.1)–(7.10) of the preceding section. We disregard the boundary solutions $\omega, l, p = 0$, caused by the growth rate formulation of their laws of motion. These values of the variables ω, l, p are economically meaningless and never appear as attractors in the numerical investigations performed later. Furthermore, the achieved theoretical results will all be constrained to a neighbourhood of the unique interior steady state considered below.

Theorem 1   There is a unique steady–state solution or point of rest of the dynamics (7.1)–(7.10) fulfilling $\omega_0, l_0, p_0 \neq 0$.

We assume that the parameters of the model are chosen such that the steady state values for $\omega, l, p, \rho, r, \eta$ are all positive. All following investigations will be confined to local stability considerations around this steady-state solution.

Theorem 2   Assume that the parameters β_ϵ, β_e, β, β_π, β_π^*, β_p , β_p^* are all chosen sufficiently small; then:

1 The determinant of the Jacobian at the steady state of the considered 10D dynamics is always positive.
2 The considered 10D dynamics exhibit 10 eigenvalues with negative real parts, that is their interior steady state solution is locally asymptotically stable.

Theorem 3   From the locally asymptotically stable situation of Theorem 2, the steady state must lose its local stability by way of Hopf-bifurcations if one of the parameters β_π (carrying the destabilizing Mundell effect), β_ϵ (carrying the destabilizing Dornbusch effect) or β_p (carrying the destabilizing Rose effect) is made sufficiently large, the latter however only in the case where the real wage effect in investment demand dominates the real wage effect in consumption demand.

Fast adjustments of expectations and fast adjustments of prices (in the case of a negative dependence of aggregate demand on the real wage level) are thus dangerous for asymptotic stability and will lead to loss of stability which is always accompanied by business fluctuations, possibly persistent ones if a supercritical Hopf-bifurcation occurs, but generally explosive ones as long as only intrinsic non-linearities are present in the considered dynamical system. Numerical simulations have then to be used to gain insights into the global dynamics. These indicate that stable limit cycle situations or persistent cycles can be generated by the additional assumption of extrinsic nonlinearities, such as asymmetries (kinks) in the money wage Phillips curve.

Some numerical investigation of the dynamics

In this section we provide some numerical illustrations of the two-country KWG growth dynamics. It is not difficult to provide numerical examples of damped oscillations or even monotonic adjustment back to the steady state based on what has been asserted for the speed of adjustment parameters in the preceding section. Increasing such speed of adjustment parameters may then provide examples of supercritical Hopf-bifurcations where – after the loss of local stability–stable limit cycles and thus persistent economic fluctuations will be born for a certain parameter range. However, there will often simply be purely explosive behavior after such a loss of stability, indicating that the intrinsic nonlinearities are generally too weak to bound the dynamics within economically meaningful ranges. The addition of extrinsic or behavioural nonlinearities is thus generally unavoidable in order to arrive at an economically meaningful dynamic behaviour.

In the following we will make use of one prominent behavioural nonlinearity, already discussed in Keynes' General Theory, namely a kinked money wage

Phillips curve, expressing in stylized form the fact that wages are much more flexible upwards than downwards. This nonlinearity can be shown to be sufficient to limit the dynamics to economically viable domains. Downward nominal wage rigidity is indeed often sufficient to overcome the destabilizing feedback channels of Mundell-type (working through the real interest rate) or Rose-type (working through the real wage rate) effects, and thus succeeds in stabilizing the economy in a certain area outside the steady state. Note that the simulations presented in this section now allow for steady-state inflation and thus do not imply stable depressions when money wages are assumed to be completely rigid in the downward direction.

In Figure 7.3 we show with the time series in the top graph that increasing the speed of exchange rate adjustment produces increasing volatility, here shown for the inflationary climate variable π. The final outcome shown is convergence to a persistent business cycle (stable limit cycle) in both countries, yet – as the lower time series (with $\beta_e = 2.3$) show – with nearly perfect negative correlation. This figure demonstrates that business fluctuations need not at all be synchronized in a flexible exchange rate system with respect to upswings and downswings, though they are clearly synchronized here with respect to phase length.

Figure 7.4, by contrast, shows for a fixed exchange rate system that phase synchronization can in this case be considered a compelling outcome, since there are

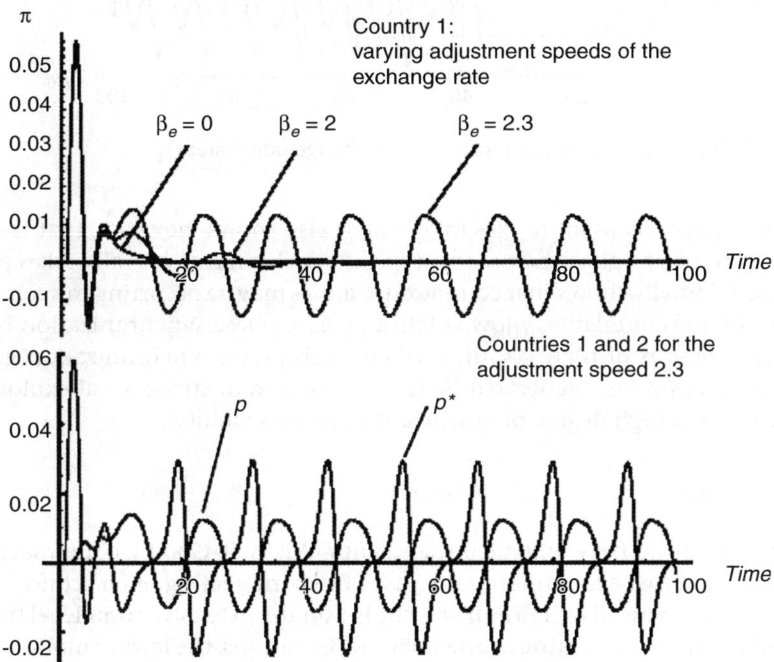

Figure 7.3   The occurrence of limit cycles and of negative transmission of inflation

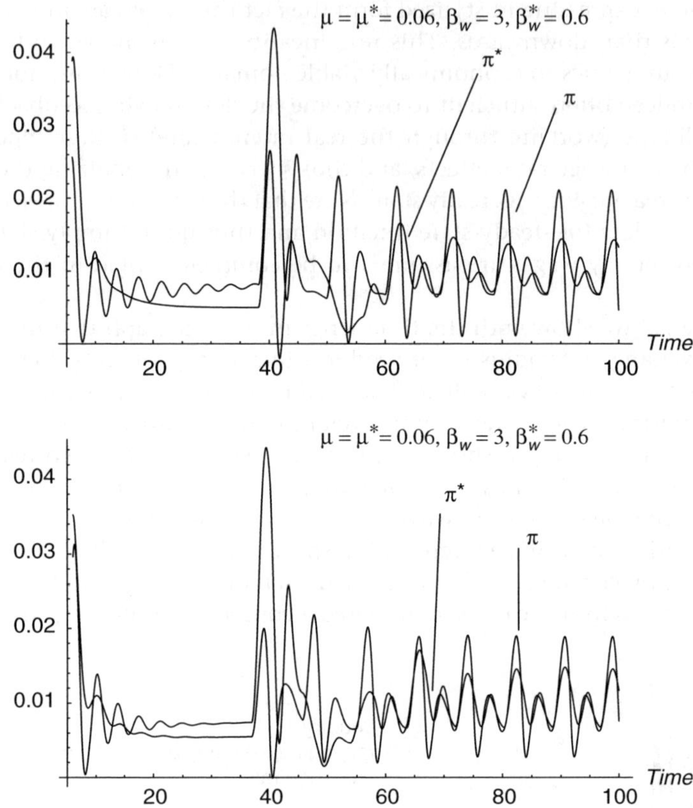

Figure 7.4   Phase synchronization in a fixed exchange rate system

then no longer any asymmetries involved. It also shows, however, that there may be a long transient phase before this type of synchronization really takes place.

Figure 7.5 finally shows that complex dynamics may be occurring in such dynamics with periods of relatively low volatility where phase synchronization is taking place and periods of high volatility where such phase synchronization gets lost. Such dynamics is here generated by the assumption of strong local explosiveness coupled with a high degree of downward wage inflexibility.

Conclusions

In this chapter we have extended the Keynes–Wicksell–Goodwin approach to the dynamics of closed economies to the case of two interacting open economies. The model was introduced in ACFF (2003, ch. 10) on the extensive form level by way of nine submodules, presenting the behavioural equations, the laws of motion and the budget equations of the sectors and markets. On the basis of simplifying assumptions we there derived the 10D core dynamics, here briefly presented in the second

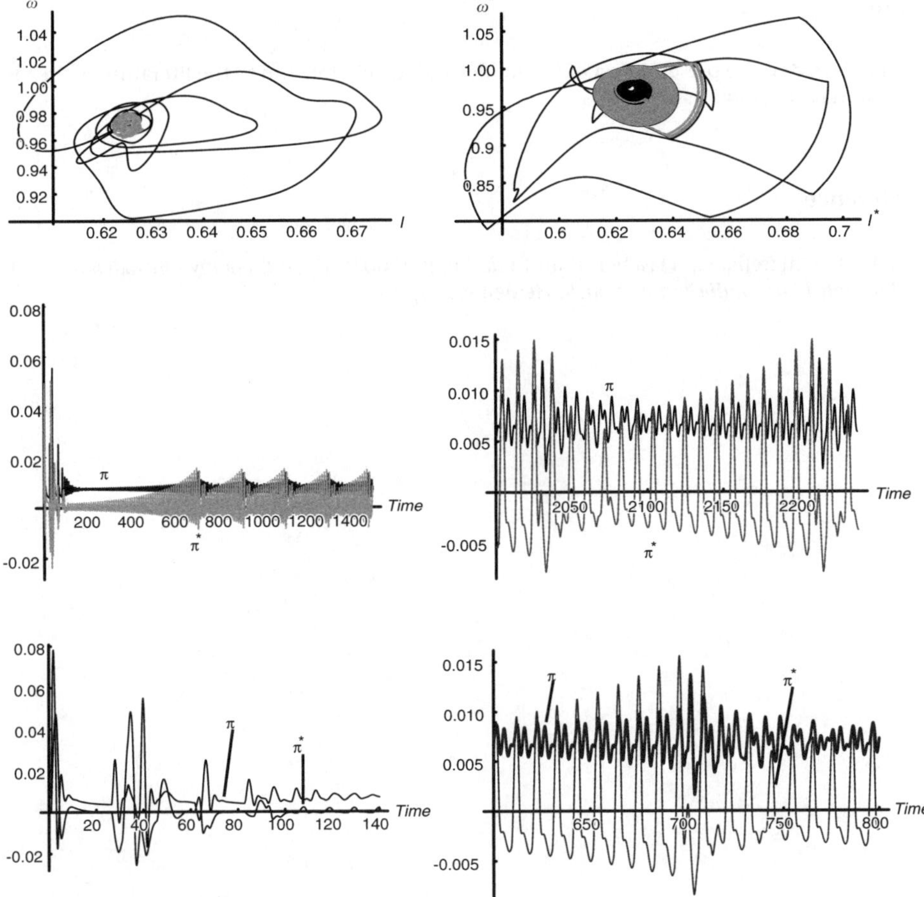

Figure 7.5   Complex dynamics with recurrent loss of phase synchronization under flexible exchange rates

main section. The uniquely determined interior steady state of the dynamics, its stability and the loss stability by way of Hopf-bifurcations was discussed. In the case of local explosiveness of the dynamics around the steady state we have bounded them by an institutionally determined kink in the money-wage Phillips curve of the model (adding downward wage rigidity to it). This behavioural nonlinearity restricts the dynamics around the interior steady state to economically meaningful domains. Numerical simulations of the dynamics show interesting features of more or less coupled oscillators and thus indicate that interesting dynamics may be obtained from the coupling of models of monetary growth of the KWG and of the more general KMG type when applied to the case of two interacting open economies.

Note

1   For an extensive presentation of the model and its relationship to the literature the reader can refer to Asada *et al.* 2003.

Reference

Asada, T., Chiarella, C., Flaschel, P. and Franke, R. (2003) *Open Economy Macrodynamics. An Integrated Disequilibrium Approach.* Heidelberg: Springer.

8
How Does the Eurozone Respond to Shocks? A Common Trends and Common Cycles Analysis

Roberto Astolfi

Introduction

Recent theoretical and empirical research proposed by Vahid and Engle (1993 and 1997), Engle and Kozicki (1993) and Issler and Vahid (2001) has revived interest in the co-movement of macroeconomic time series. In those papers authors extend results already achieved by Engle and Granger (1987) and Johansen (1995) in the field of common trend identification (cointegration). They demonstrate that a similar approach can be applied to the stationary part of the series in a VAR system in order to identify common cyclical movements. As a consequence, they demonstrated that a joint application of the two methodologies could lead to a simultaneous decomposition of the series into common trend and cycle. By applying this methodology we investigate the degree of short-run and long-run co-movement among Eurozone economies. Multivariate co-integration and common features (cycles) tests are performed in order to verify the hypotheses that EMU countries share common trends and common cycles. Once this hypothesis is verified, relevant consequences can arise for applied economic and statistical analysis of the Eurozone. These might be applied in the construction of synthetic and leading indicators as well as in turning point detection of the business cycle. Next the dynamic effects of permanent and transitory shocks on the Eurozone system were studied applying the 'generalized' impulse response analysis proposed by Pesaran and Shin (1998). Unlike the traditional impulse response analysis, this approach does not require orthogonalization of shocks and is invariant to the ordering of the variables in the VAR. On that basis, we measured the speed of convergence to equilibrium with persistence profiles.

The chapter is organized as follows: the next section briefly presents the data-set used, followed by the empirical results and a concluding final section.

The data

The data-set includes quarterly observations on gross domestic product of Eurozone member states and was extracted from New Cronos. Data are seasonally adjusted at constant 1995 prices, covering from 1991Q1 to 2003Q2. Although our first intention was to retain all 12 countries who joined the European Monetary Union (EMU), we had to reduce our sample to the following seven countries: Belgium, Germany, Spain, France, Italy, Netherlands and Austria. The choice was due in some cases to the lack of quarterly national accounts (Greece and Luxembourg), in others to the shortness of the series published (Portugal) or even to exceptional performance recorded by some countries (Ireland and Finland) which made their growth pattern completely different from the rest of the partners. All series are in logarithm form. All computations have been carried out using GAUSS.

Empirical analysis

We started our analysis by investigating the degree of integration of each series. In order to do that, we made use of the Augmented Dickey–Fuller, the Schmidt–Phillips and the Phillips–Perron integration tests. All three tests suggested that the totality of our series is well-approximated by an $I(1)$ process. Next we tested for the presence of serial correlation in the first differences of our variables. Using both Box–Pierce and Ljung–Box statistics, we found evidence of serial correlation in all the series.

In the following stage we focused our attention on the estimation of the VAR system. At the very beginning we retained in the system all the series available, but the first results we reached following this strategy did not allow us to draw any clear conclusions on the structure of the model. In particular, we could not detect a co-integration relationship among all member states. Therefore, we decided to restrict our system by marginalizing those countries whose behaviour is notably different from the majority of member states (that is Ireland and Finland).

Following Vahid and Engle (1993), we paid particular attention to the selection of the maximum lag (p) to be included in the system. The Akaike, Hannan-Quinn and Schwarz information criteria were all used, and coherently suggested a maximum lag equal to four.

Conditional on these results, the presence of common trends was investigated. The likelihood-based co-integration tests of Johansen (1995) and Johansen and Juselius (1990) were employed to investigate for cointegration in a vector error-correction model (VECM). Since four lags were retained in the unrestricted VAR system of the levels of the variables, we included here three lags. Table 8.1 shows the results obtained by applying both the trace test and the maximum eigenvalue test: as can be seen, both tests provide clear evidence that the rank of the matrix $\alpha\beta'$ (see Johansen 1995) is six at the 99 per cent significance level.

Table 8.1   Johansen cointegration test

Eigenv.	$H_0R =$	$N - R =$	L-Max	Cv L95%	Trace	Cv Tr95%
0.87637	0	7	79.19**	29.12	259.21**	123.04
0.68235	1	6	65.93**	25.24	180.01**	93.92
0.57379	2	5	37.19**	21.47	114.09**	68.68
0.46917	3	4	28.60**	17.83	76.90**	47.21
0.40452	4	3	26.90**	14.04	48.30**	29.38
0.25318	5	2	19.42**	11.50	21.40**	15.34
0.04764	6	1	1.97	3.84	1.97	3.84

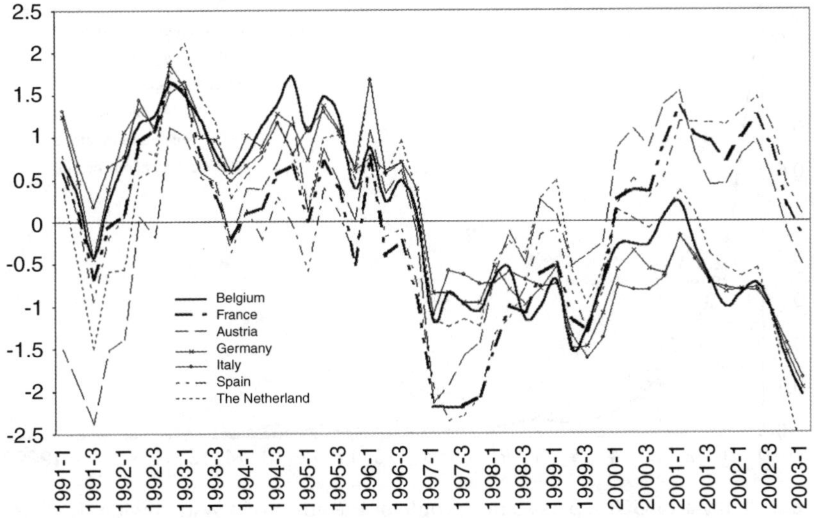

Figure 8.1   Euro-area GDPs: common cycles

Therefore, conditional to the hypothesis that the rank is six, we again tested the significance of the deterministic components previously included in the model, retaining in the VAR system an unrestricted constant term (included among the I(0) variables) and no deterministic trend.

Conditional on the estimates of the VECM model (results are not reported to save space), we tested for the presence of serial correlation common features in the member states' GDP series using the canonical correlation-based test proposed by Vahid and Engle (1993). The test examines canonical correlation between Δy_t and its relevant history $\Delta \hat{y}_t$, determined as the dependent variables in the estimated VECM representation of the system. The canonical correlations that are not significantly different from zero represent linear combinations of $\beta \Delta y_t$ that are uncorrelated with the past. As stated by Vahid and Engle, this can be viewed as evidence of a common cycle (Figure 8.1). Ordering the squared canonical correlation

Table 8.2   Co-feature test results

H_0:	H_1:	χ_i^2	$C(p, s)$	χ^2 Test d.o.f.:	Crit.values
$s > 0$	$s = 0$	0.537	34.66**	21	39.67
$s > 1$	$s = 1$	0.669	84.47	44	55.76
$s > 2$	$s = 2$	0.718	141.44	69	79.08
$s > 3$	$s = 3$	0.779	209.45	96	101.9
$s > 4$	$s = 4$	0.844	292.94	125	124.3
$s > 5$	$s = 5$	0.907	399.76	156	124.3
$s > 6$	$s = 6$	0.935	522.42	189	124.3

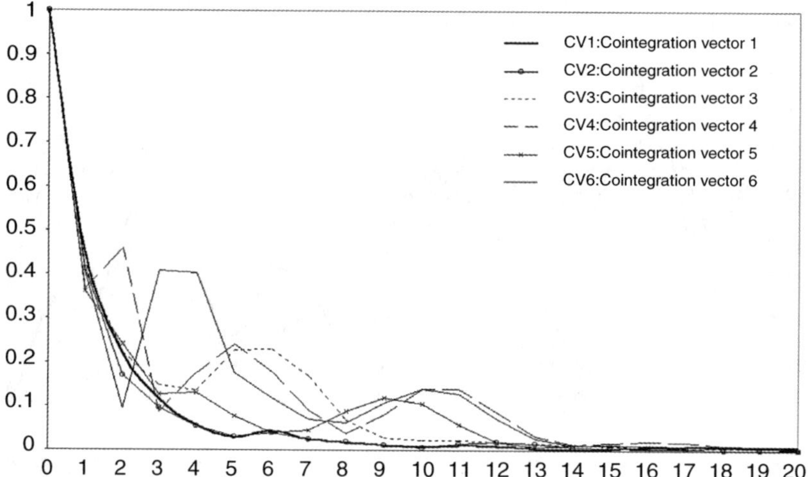

Figure 8.2   Euro-area GDPs: persistence profile of the effect of a system-wide shock to CVs

from lowest to highest, the null hypothesis for the test is that the first j correlation are zero but the $(j + 1)^{\text{th}}$ is nonzero. The squared canonical correlation and the value of the test statistic for the dimension of the co-feature vector are reported in Table 8.2. The data support the existence of one co-feature vector s at the 5 per cent level of significance. It has to be noted that in our example the number of co-feature vectors s and co-integration vectors r sum up to the number of variables included in the model ($r + s = n$) which represents the 'special case' mentioned in Vahid and Engle (1993).

Our analysis proceeds by applying the 'generalized impulse response analysis' proposed by Pesaran and Shin (1998). Since our interest is mainly on how the Eurozone responds to shocks, we focus on the persistence profile which allows us to investigate the speed of convergence to equilibrium. The persistence profile (Figure 8.2) suggests that the effect of a system-wide shock persists for many years (14 quarters).

Conclusions

In this chapter we have examined the dynamics of Eurozone economies by applying the methodology proposed by Engle, Kozicki and Vahid in order to test for the presence of common trends and common cycles. Our results suggest that Euro-area economies share both long and short-run co-movements. Furthermore, we found that the dimension of the co-integration space and the co-feature space sum up to the number of variables retained in the model. This corresponds to the so-called 'special case' discussed by Vahid and Engle (1993). As suggested by those authors, such a result may be used to reduce the complexity of a multivariate system in the European framework. The presence of a common trend and of six common cycles among the seven member states in the present analysis seems to us particularly interesting: in fact, since our sample ranges from 1991Q1 to 2003Q2, our results suggest that during the period characterized by the various steps (the so called 'convergency criteria') towards the creation of EMU in 1999, European economies had already started moving together. Unfortunately, the lack of quarterly data for Germany before 1991 does not enable us to apply the Vahid and Engle methodology to a longer period and to analyse whether an acceleration in the convergence process occurred.

Our analysis also investigated the speed of convergence to equilibrium by applying the 'generalized' impulse response analysis proposed by Pesaran and Shin (1998). The results suggest that the effect of a system-wide shock persists for many years (14 quarters).

We believe our results may be considered encouraging for further research in analysing Eurozone economies.

References

Engle, R.F. and Granger, C.W.J. (1987) 'Cointegration and error correction: representation, estimation and testing', *Econometrica*, 55: 251–76.

Engle, R.F. and Issler, J.V. (1995) 'Estimating common sectoral cycle', *Journal of Monetary Economics*, 35: 83–113.

Engle, R.F. and Kozicki, S.(1993) 'Testing for common features', *Journal of Business and Economic Statistics*, 11: 369–80.

Issler, J.V. and Vahid, F. (2001) 'Common cycles and the importance of transitory shocks to macroeconomics aggregates', *Journal of Monetary Economics*, 47: 449–75.

Johansen, S. (1995) *Likelihood-Based Inference in Cointegrated Vector Autoregressive Models*. New York: Oxford University Press.

Johansen, S. and Juselius, K. (1990) 'Maximum likelihood estimation and inference on cointegration – with applications to the demand for money', *Oxford Bulletin of Economics and Statistics*, 52: 169–210.

Pesaran, M.H. and Shin, Y. (1998) 'Generalized impulse response analysis in linear multivariate models', *Economics Letters*, 58: 17–29.

Stock, J.H. and Watson, M.W. (1998) 'Testing for common trends', *Journal of the American Statistical Association*, 83: 1097–107.

Vahid, F. and Engle, R.F. (1993) 'Common trends and common cycles', *Journal of Applied Econometrics*, 8: 341–60.

Vahid, F. and Engle, R.F. (1997) 'Codependent cycles', *Journal of Econometrics*, 80: 199–221.

9

How Similar are European Business Cycles?

*Michael U. Bergman**

Introduction

In this chapter, we focus on how European economic integration has affected the synchronization and the magnitude of business cycles among participating countries. We measure, based on bandpass filtered data, the characteristics of European business cycles analysing to what extent they have become more similar over time. We also consider the role of other factors such as differences in fiscal and monetary policy, border effects and trade intensity. Our main finding is that European business cycles are highly synchronized, although we also find that synchronization is higher during periods with highly flexible exchange rates. In addition we find a positive tradeoff between timing and magnitude such that more synchronization coincides with larger relative magnitude. These results raise concern about the consequences of a common monetary policy within EMU.

Linkages between European countries have become more prevalent in the postwar period as a result of the efforts of integrating national markets. These efforts include the removal of trade barriers, the implementation of the Single European Act in 1986, the Maastricht Treaty in 1992, the introduction of the Single European Market in 1993, the Stability and Growth Pact in 1997, and the creation of the European Monetary Union with a common currency and monetary policy. An

* This is a short version of the Working Paper with the same title. I have received valuable comments from Marianne Baxter, Roel Beetsma, Andrew Hughes Hallett, Lars Jonung, Katarina Juselius, Finn Østrup, Christian Richter, Clas Wihlborg, seminar participants at Lund University, University of Copenhagen, and conference participants at the 4th Eurostat and DG ECFIN Colloquium on Modern Tools for Business Cycle Analysis, the 6th Swedish Network for European Studies in Economics and Business Conference on European Economic Integration in Swedish Research, the ECFIN Research Conference 'Business Cycles and Growth in Europe' and the CEPR and CEBR workshop on Labour Markets, Fiscal Policy and Structural Reform. Financial support from the Swedish Research Council is gratefully acknowledged.

important question is whether these efforts of economic and monetary integration have led to a higher degree of similarity of European business cycles in recent years.

Such a development is also desirable since the loss of the option of using an independent monetary policy and giving up the value of changing the exchange rate when desired would otherwise constitute a major cost for the EMU countries. These options are especially important if countries are facing asymmetric shocks, in which case exchange rate adjustments and separate monetary policies could help to stabilize nation-specific aggregate fluctuations. A common monetary policy therefore requires that the timing of business cycles is similar among the members of the monetary union. However, even if the timing of business cycles is similar, the magnitude may differ, in which case the intensities of policies may have to be different.

There are theoretical reasons for both the view that economic integration will lead to more synchronized business cycles, and the opposite view that increased economic integration will lead to less synchronized business cycles. Kalemli-Ozcan *et al.* (2001) argue that increased economic integration leads to better income insurance through greater capital integration which in turn will lead to a more specialized production structure and an increase in trade and therefore less syn-chronized business cycles. A similar argument has also been proposed by Krugman (1993). Alternatively, it could be argued, as Coe and Helpman (1995) and Frankel and Rose (1998) suggest, that the removal of trade barriers will lead to more trade such that demand shocks are more easily transmitted across national borders. Economic and monetary integration, will according to this view, lead to more symmetry of structural shocks and knowledge and technology spillovers which will lead to a higher degree of synchronization of national business cycles.

Given these theoretical ambiguities over the effects of economic and monet-ary integration on the behaviour of business cycles, empirical evidence must be brought to bear on the issue. Indeed, there are several papers suggesting that busi-ness cycles are more synchronized when exchange rate variability is low (Fatás, 1997; Artis and Zhang, 1997, 1999; Dickerson, Gibson and Tsakalotos, 1998; and Rose and Engel, 2002). However, there are also papers suggesting the opposite, that business cycles are more synchronized during periods with higher exchange rate volatility (Gerlach, 1988; Inklaar and De Haan, 2001; and De Haan, Inklaar and Sleijpen, 2002). A few authors report evidence suggesting no relationship between the exchange rate regime and business cycle synchronization (Baxter and Stockman, 1989; Sopraseuth, 2003; and Baxter and Kouparitsas, 2005).[1] In addition, there seems to be at most only weak evidence supporting the view that increased economic integration leads to a higher degree of synchronization. Indeed, Doyle and Faust (2002) and Kose, Prasad and Terrones (2003) find no strong evidence supporting this idea.

With few exceptions, earlier papers focus on the relationship between exchange rate regimes and the timing of European business cycles disregarding any effects of the magnitude of cycles.[2] This is in part surprising since there is a direct relationship between the correlation and the variance. For example, holding everything else constant, a lower variance would imply a higher correlation coefficient. Dickerson, Gibson and Tsakalotos (1998) find that the magnitude of business cycles in general is lower for core EU countries, but they provide no analysis of the relationship between magnitude and exchange rate regimes. Sopraseuth (2003), however, found that the magnitude of European business cycles was unrelated to membership of the EMS.

The purpose of this chapter is to shed light on the question whether European business cycles have become more similar as a result of economic and monetary integration. We measure, based on bandpass filtered data, the characteristics of European business cycles analysing to what extent they have become more synchronized over time and test whether, for example, EU membership and the Single Market programme can account for a higher degree of synchronization. We then consider the role of other factors that have received considerable attention in the literature, such as differences in fiscal and monetary policy, border effects and trade intensity. Can these factors explain the lack of full synchronization among European business cycles?

The chapter is organized as follows: in the next section we describe the method used to extract the business cycle component from the data and perform a first preliminary analysis of the data. Section 3 contains the empirical analysis and there is a concluding section.

Methodology

Data

The data-set consists of quarterly observations on industrial production for the EU-14 countries (Austria, Belgium, Denmark, Finland, France, Germany, Greece, Ireland, Italy, Netherlands, Portugal, Spain, Sweden and the United Kingdom) for the sample 1961M1 to 2001M4.[3] The data are taken from the IFS CD-Rom except industrial production for Ireland and Portugal taken from OECD *Main Economic Indicators*.

Measuring domestic business cycles

Prior to our empirical analysis we must extract the cyclical component from the macroeconomic time series; that is, the natural logarithm of industrial production. Recently, Baxter and King (1999) have developed a bandpass filter that isolates cyclical components of economic time series, and this filter can be designed to isolate cyclical components of economic time series conforming to a certain definition of business cycles. In particular, we isolate cyclical components of the data with durations conforming to the Burns–Mitchell definition of the business cycle. We use a 12-order two-sided filter following Baxter and King (1999) to extract all fluctuations at frequencies between six and 32 quarters (1.5 year and eight years) from the logarithm of industrial production in each country.[4] When applying this filter, we lose observations at both ends of our sample. We use forecasts and backcasts based on a twelfth-order univariate autoregressive model to add these observations to the sample prior to applying the bandpass filter. This same method is used by Stock and Watson (1999) and Bergman *et al.* (1998) amongst others.

Empirical work

The first step in our analysis is to examine whether the degree of synchronization has changed over time and if these changes are related to other developments, for example the exchange rate regime. We therefore divide our sample into five sub-samples reflecting different monetary regimes and different degrees of economic integration: the Bretton–Woods period 1961Q1–1973Q1, the flexible exchange rate regime 1973Q2–1978Q4, the EMS period 1979Q1–1987Q2, the implementation of the Single European Act period 1987Q3–1992Q4, and the implementation of the common market and preparations for monetary union 1993Q1–2001Q4.[5] We will focus on the general pattern, that is, we distinguish between EU members and EU-14 countries that were not members of the EU at the time we measure the cross-correlations. In addition, we test for a EU-membership effect conditional on other factors that could explain the observed changes in the degree of synchronization. Following Clark and van Wincoop (2001) who study the border effect on the synchronization of business cycles, we consider in addition to a border effect the role played by trade intensity, distance between countries, the size of countries, differences in monetary and fiscal policy, and exchange rate volatility.

One potential problem when estimating a regression equation using the cross-correlation as dependent variable is that we do not observe the true bilateral cross-correlations. It is most likely that there is a high correlation in estimated cross-correlations within each sub-sample due to measurement errors. Two different solutions to this potential problem have been suggested in the earlier related literature. Clark and van Wincoop (2001) and Imbs (2003) use random effects models, whereas Baxter and Kouparitsas (2005) suggest fixed effects models to correct for this problem. We follow the latter approach and estimate fixed effects models.

We define trade intensity (following Frankel and Rose, 1998) as the natural logarithm of the value of bilateral trade between two countries (w_{ij}) divided by sum of the value of total trade in both countries. We then take the average of these trade intensities over the five sub-samples. The distance (D) between countries is measured as the great circle between largest cities in each country taken from Fitzpatrick and Modlin (1986).[6] The size is measured as the natural logarithm of the product of real GDP per capita measured in current \$US taken from World Penn Tables.[7] To account for differences in monetary and fiscal policy, we use the standard deviation of the money market (or equivalent measures) interest-rate differential (σ_{r-r*}) and the standard deviation of the budget deficit (as a percentage of GDP) differential (σ_{D-D*}), respectively. Finally, the exchange rate volatility is measured as the standard deviation of the first log difference of bilateral exchange rates ($\sigma_{\Delta s}$). All variables are taken from IFS unless otherwise stated.

Table 9.1 The synchronization of business cycles. Is there a EU-membership effect?

	OLS	OLS	IV	IV	IV	IV
EUM	0.090	0.073	0.058	0.048	0.056	0.068
	(0.036)	(0.037)	(0.039)	(0.041)	(0.040)	(0.040)
Border		0.139				
		(0.054)				
Distance		0.005				
		(0.040)				
Size		0.128	0.076	0.111	0.008	0.048
		(0.072)	(0.072)	(0.071)	(0.084)	(0.070)
w_{ij}			0.028	0.038	0.043	0.046
			(0.012)	(0.012)	(0.014)	(0.013)
σ_{r-r*}				0.067		
				(0.026)		
σ_{D-D*}					0.092	
					(0.054)	
$\sigma_{\Delta s}$						0.188
						(0.054)

Note: EUM is a dummy variable equal to one for EU members. The instruments we use are discussed in the text. HAC standard errors are shown in parentheses below each parameter estimate. All regression equations include country-specific fixed effects.

In Table 9.1 we show the role of these factors in explaining the synchronization of business cycles within the EU-14 countries. All results are based on running a standard regression with a constant, country-specific fixed effects and adding the various explanatory variables mentioned above. When including trade and the policy variables, we estimate the regression using instrumental variables as discussed below.

As can be seen from the first column of this table, there is a significant EU-membership effect. EU members tend to have somewhat more synchronized business cycles compared to non-members. The second column in Table 9.1 reports the results when including border, distance and size as additional explanatory variables besides the constant and the EU membership dummy. As is evident, there is a very strong border effect; bordering EU countries tend to have more synchronized business cycles compared to non-bordering countries. This result is consistent with evidence provided by Clark and van Wincoop (2001) who report very strong border effects between France, Germany, Italy and the UK. The distance between the countries seems to play no role in explaining synchronization; the parameter is not significantly different from zero. The size effect is highly significant suggesting that the size of the countries play an important role for explaining the degree of business cycle synchronization. The cross-correlation between large countries tends to be higher compared to between two small countries. Controlling for border, distance and size has some effect on the importance of EU membership. The coefficient drops from 0.095 to 0.073, it is still statistically significant at the 5 per cent level suggesting that border, distance and size explain parts but not all of the co-movements of business cycles in EU member states.

Next, we add trade intensity to the regression. To avoid multicollinearity between the regressors, we now exclude both border and distance from our regression. Since trade may be endogenous (as argued by Frankel and Rose, 1998) we estimate the regression using instrumental variables. Countries that border usually trade more and therefore have more synchronized business cycles. A similar argument holds for distance, the longer the distance is between two countries, the more likely it is that the volume of trade is smaller. At the same time, as argued by both Frankel and Rose (1998) and Clark and van Wincoop (2001), countries with highly synchronized business cycles are better candidates for currency unions, which in turn could increase trade. We use instruments that often are used in gravity models: border, distance, linguistic distance, and an interaction term equal to the product of size and distance.

The results when including trade as an explanatory variable are shown in the third column of Table 9.1. The parameter associated with the EU dummy is further reduced and is not statistically different from zero when adding the policy variables. Trade, on the other hand, is positively related to the synchronization of business cycles. The reason why the business cycle is more synchronized between EU member states is, according to these estimates, that they trade more not that they are members of the EU.

In the last three columns of Table 9.1 we also include the three policy variables, differences in monetary and fiscal policy and exchange rate volatility. We still use instrumental variables when estimating the parameters. Trade is instrumented using the same set of instruments as indicated above. To instrument the policy variables, we use the absolute inflation differential, the sum of interest rates, the absolute difference between the ratios of government spending to GDP and the sum of the ratios of government spending to GDP. These same instruments were used in a similar context by Clark and van Wincoop (2001). From these columns we observe that trade intensity is always significantly different from zero and positive. As the parameter associated to the EU membership dummy is not statistically significant at conventional levels, our results suggest that trade and the policy variables explain the co–movements of business cycles in these countries. A surprising result, however, is that the three policy variables all exert a positive influence on the degree of synchronization. It is often assumed that a more similar economic policy, a lower value of the policy variables, should to lead to a higher degree of business cycle synchronization.

Looking at the particular estimates, we find that larger differences in monetary policy and a higher bilateral exchange rate volatility implies a higher degree of synchronization. Differences in fiscal policy is not statistically different from zero. These results are different from the evidence presented by Clark and van Wincoop (2001). In their empirical application, policy variables were often found to be positively related to the degree of synchronization but very seldom statistically significant. The positive relationship between synchronization and exchange rate

Table 9.2   The magnitude of the business cycle

	Mean of absolute difference of standard deviations					
	1961–2001	*1961–72*	*1973–78*	*1979–87*	*1987–92*	*1993–2001*
EU-14	0.749	0.595	0.759	0.678	0.767	0.948
	(0.031)	(0.056)	(0.091)	(0.062)	(0.043)	(0.055)
EU members	0.792	0.682	0.717	0.682	0.575	0.948
	(0.043)	(0.132)	(0.118)	(0.074)	(0.077)	(0.055)

Note: Newey-West HAC standard errors are shown in parentheses below each cross-correlation.

volatility in Table 9.1 is, however, consistent with results provided by, for example, De Haan, Inklaar and Sleijpen (2002).

The magnitude of business cycles

The analysis above shed some light on the timing of business cycles in the EU where the main argument was that the implementation of a common monetary policy and the synchronization of fiscal policy within the EU area is a concern if the timing of business cycles differs considerably. A similar argument holds for the magnitude of business cycles as a common economic policy could lead to too small effects in countries with highly variable cycles and too large effects in countries with less variable cycles. For countries with similar amplitudes, a common economic policy raises no such concerns. In other words, the intensity of economic policies has to differ among countries with different amplitudes of its business cycles.

In the upper panel of Table 9.2 we report estimates of the absolute difference of the standard deviation of national business cycles both for all EU14 countries and for the EU member states. According to these estimates, the amplitude for all EU14 countries have increased considerably over the sample from 0.6 to 0.95. This suggests that the magnitude of business cycles were more similar during the Bretton–Woods period compared to all other sub-samples we examine. This result does not fully carry over to EU member states. According to the results shown in the table, differences in the amplitude for these countries fell somewhat during the implementation of the Single European Act period compared to the earlier EMS period.

It is surprising that the relative magnitude of European business cycles tends to increase, in particular, towards the end of our sample. Our result is, however, consistent with earlier empirical findings in the literature. There is a general consensus that the volatility of business cycle in the USA and in the G-7 countries has been dampened even though there is a debate on the date of the structural break in the amplitude and, of course, whether there has been more than one structural break, see for example van Dijk, Osborn and Sensier (2002), Doyle and Faust (2002) and Stock and Watson (2003). Indeed, looking at the underlying data we use to compute the relative magnitudes, we find that the volatility of the bandpass filtered data tend to be lower for the more recent sub-samples for some but not all EU14 countries compared to earlier periods.

How should we interpret our results that both the cross–correlations and the relative magnitude have increased during the most recent period. First, we recognize that these changes are related. Holding everything else constant, an increase in the volatility implies a reduction in the co-movement of the two time series we examine. As shown by Doyle and Faust (2002) there is one case when both the correlation and the relative standard deviation increase, when the variance of foreign idiosyncratic shocks is falling. This prediction is also consistent with recent empirical results provided by Stock and Watson (2003) who showed that the increase in synchronization among the G7 countries could be explained by lower volatility in idiosyncratic shocks.

To shed some light on these issues, we run a regression with the contemporaneous cross-correlations ρ as a function of a constant, country–specific fixed effects, the absolute difference between standard deviations of national business cycles and the corresponding measure for EU member states. It is important to notice that we are not discussing any causal relationship between these variables, we are only interested in whether synchronization and the relative magnitudes are correlated and if there is a difference between all EU countries and EU member states. These regression results are shown in panel A of Table 9.3. As can be seen from these estimates, we find a negative point estimate (although not statistically significant) of the parameter associated to the absolute difference in the magnitude. What is

Table 9.3   The tradeoff between synchronization and magnitude

Dep.var.	$|\sigma_i - \sigma_j|$	$|\sigma_i - \sigma_j| * EUM$
Panel A: tradeoff between synchronization and magnitude		
ρ	−0.028	0.105
	(0.035)	(0.034)

$|\sigma_i - \sigma_j|$	$|\sigma_i - \sigma_j| * EUM$	σ_{r-r*}	σ_{D-D*}	$\sigma_{\Delta s}$
Panel B: can policy variables explain the tradeoff? Dependent variable: ρ				
−0.051	0.107	0.058		
(0.034)	(0.033)	(0.026)		
−0.040	0.116		0.047	
(0.036)	(0.036)		(0.055)	
−0.052	0.126			0.146
(0.033)	(0.033)			(0.045)

Note: Newey–West HAC standard errors are shown in parentheses below each cross-correlation. All regression equations include country–specific fixed effects.

indeed surprising is that we obtain a positive and significant point estimate for EU members. According to this regression result, a lower absolute difference in the magnitude is associated with a lower degree of business cycle synchronization for EU members only.

To answer the question whether similarities in economic policy and whether the exchange rate regime can explain the significant EU-membership effect, we run additional regression of the cross-correlations on a constant, country-specific fixed effects, the magnitude and the magnitude for EU members adding one policy variable at a time. These results are shown in panel B in Table 9.3. We use the same instruments for the policy variables as in our earlier regressions. The overall impression from these tests is that the policy variables cannot explain the positive tradeoff. Neither differences in monetary policy nor differences in fiscal policy are statistically significant in these regressions and the parameter associated to the magnitude for EU members does not change much. It is still significant and positive. We also reach the same conclusion when adding exchange rate volatility. Our results suggest that a higher degree of exchange rate volatility is associated with a higher degree of synchronization, the same result as we obtained earlier.

To interpret these empirical results and to be able to speculate about future developments and the consequences of the common monetary policy in Europe, we have to look more closely at the exchange rate volatility we have measured for the five sub-samples. For the EU member states, exchange rate volatility was highest during the flexible exchange rate period and the most recent period. It is also for these two sub-samples we obtain a positive tradeoff between the relative magnitude and synchronization. This implies that a higher degree of exchange rate volatility is associated with more synchronization and larger differences in the magnitude of the business cycle. This would imply, if these relations are stable over time and over different monetary regimes, that business cycles in EU member states will become less synchronized but also display less differences in the magnitude which would constitute a potential problem when implementing a common monetary policy and the common currency.

Conclusions

It is widely argued that the success of the common currency area in Europe rests on the uniformity of business-cycle fluctuations. Our results suggest that European business cycles are synchronized to a high degree but we also find that the degree of synchronization has changed considerably since the early 1960s. In particular, we find that synchronization is higher during periods with more flexible exchange rates and lower when exchange rate volatility is low. These results question earlier findings that European business cycles became more synchronized during the EMS period. Our evidence further suggests that there are several contradicting forces affecting the degree of synchronization, a lower exchange rate volatility and smaller differences in monetary policy leading to less synchronized cycles and increases in trade leading to more synchronization. As a major objective of the

EU is economic and monetary integration, one would anticipate that the linkages should strengthen over time, maybe also offset the negative effects from the common monetary policy and lower exchange rate volatility.

When adding the analysis of the magnitude of European business cycles, the picture becomes more complex. Our estimates suggest that differences in the magnitude of European business cycles have risen over time and have never been so large for EU members. This result raises concern about the common monetary policy as it is likely that the policy will be too expansive for some member states and too restrictive for others. The tradeoff between synchronization and differences in magnitude is positive such that larger differences coincide with a higher degree of synchronization. These empirical results highlight the potential problem when implementing a common policy in Europe. If business cycles become more synchronized and the relative magnitude less similar, then the timing of the common policy tends to be optimal but the intensity tends to be wrong for some member states. Our results, therefore, raises concern about the implementation of a common monetary policy in the EMU area.

A major objective of the EU is to foster stronger economic ties between members and this process will tend to increase the degree of compatibility between the member states. If this also leads to more synchronization and convergence of the amplitude of the business cycle in member countries is an open question and cannot be answered by looking at historical relationships. The analysis in this chapter supports this view. We find that business cycle behaviour change over time in response to new economic environments. This point, which is a version of the Lucas critique, implies that it is not possible to draw too strong policy conclusions from our empirical analysis. It may well be the case that economic integration leads to more similar business cycles within the EMU area even though our empirical analysis of historical data suggests the opposite.

Notes

1 Baxter and Stockman (1989) found that synchronization and monetary regimes were unrelated for linear trend adjusted data but not for first log difference data where synchronization was higher when exchange rate volatility was low. Sopraseuth (2003) also found that even though membership of the EMS did not result in a higher degree of synchronization, business cycles in EMS countries became more synchronized to the German cycle and less synchronized to the US cycle. Baxter and Kouparitsas (2005) find that currency union is not robust, i.e., that there is no relationship between business cycle co-movements and currency unions.
2 The literature usually focuses on the G-7 countries documenting shifts in the volatility and in the synchronization of cycles, see e.g. Doyle and Faust (2002), van Dijk, Osborn and Sensier (2002) and Stock and Watson (2003). The consensus from this literature is that the business cycle has been dampened recently but there is disagreement on the number of shifts, the dates of the breaks and the magnitude of these breaks.
3 We use industrial production as our business cycle indicator rather than GDP, since quarterly GDP data for all these countries is only available for a shorter sample period making it difficult to study changes in business cycle behaviour over time.

4 The results below are essentially unaffected when using the Hodrick–Prescott filter to extract the business cycle component of industrial production instead of the Baxter–King filter.
5 It would have been interesting to divide the last period into two sub-periods allowing us to also study the effects of EMU. This is, unfortunately, not possible since our estimates of co-movements would be highly uncertain given the few available observations on industrial production and other variables used in the analysis below for the EMU-period. The sub-samples we use roughly correspond to the ones used in the earlier literature.
6 We have also considered alternative measures of distance such as the distance in radians of the unit circle between country centroids. The empirical results below are essentially unaffected when using this measure.
7 Another approach to measure size is to use the natural logarithm of the sum of population. In general, the significance of the parameters associated to this measure of size was lower (although statistically significant at conventional levels) compared to the significance of the log of the product of real GDP. All other results were essentially unaffected.

References

Artis, M.J. and Zhang, W. (1997) 'International business cycles and the ERM: is there a European business cycle?', *International Journal of Finance and Economics*, 2: 1–16.

Artis, M.J. and Zhang, W. (1999) 'Further evidence on the international business cycle and the ERM: is there a European business cycle?', *Oxford Economic Papers*, 51: 120–32.

Baxter, M. and King, R.G. (1999) 'Measuring business cycles: approximate band-pass filters for economic time series', *Review of Economics and Statistics*, 81: 575–93.

Baxter, M. and Kouparitsas, M.A. (2005) 'Determinants of business cycle movement: a robust analysis', *Journal of Monetary Economics*, 52: 113–57.

Baxter, M. and Stockman, A.C. (1989) 'Business cycles and the exchange-rate regime', *Journal of Monetary Economics*, 23: 377–400.

Bergman, U.M., Bordo, M.D. and Jonung, L. (1998) 'Historical evidence on business cycles: international experience', in J.C. Fuhrer and S. Schuh (eds), *Beyond Shocks: What Causes Business Cycles?* Boston: Federal Reserve Bank of Boston, Conference Series no. 42.

Clark, T.E. and van Wincoop, E. (2001) 'Borders and business cycles', *Journal of International Economics*, 55: 59–85.

Coe, D. and Helpman, E. (1995) 'International R&D spillovers', *European Economic Review*, 39: 859–87.

De Haan, J., Inklaar, R. and Sleijpen, O. (2002) 'Have business cycles become more synchronized?', *Journal of Common Market Studies*, 40: 23–42.

Dickerson, A.P., Gibson, H.D. and Tsakalotos, E. (1998) 'Business cycle correspondence in the European Union', *Empirica*, 25: 51–77.

Doyle, B. and Faust, J. (2002) 'Breaks in the volatility and co-movement of G-7 economic growth', *manuscript*, Federal Reserve Board.

Fatás, A. (1997) 'EMU: Countries or regions? Lessons from the EMS experience', *European Economic Review*, 41: 743–51.

Fitzpatrick, G.L. and Modlin, M.J. (1986) *Direct-Line Distances: International Edition*, Lanham, MD: Scarecrow Press.

Frankel, J.A. and Rose, A.K. (1998) 'The endogeneity of the optimum currency area criteria', *Economic Journal*, 108: 1009–25.

Gerlach, H.S. (1988) 'World business cycle under fixed and flexible exchange rates', *Journal of Money, Credit, and Banking*, 20: 621–32.

Inklaar, R. and De Haan, J. (2001) 'Is there really a european business cycle? A comment', *Oxford Economic Papers*, 53: 215–20.

Kalemli-Ozcan, S., Sørensen, B.E. and Yosha, O. (2001) 'Economic integration, industrial specialization, and the asymmetry of macroeconomic fluctuations', *Journal of International Economics*, 55: 107–37.

Kose, M.A., Prasad, E.E. and Terrones, M.E. (2003) 'How does globalization affect the synchronization of business cycles?', *IZA Discussion Paper*: 702.

Krugman, P. (1993) 'Lessons of Massachusetts for EMU', in F. Giavazzi and F. Torres (eds), *The Transition to Economic and Monetary Union in Europe*. New York: Cambridge University Press.

Rose, A.K. and Engel, C. (2002) 'Currency unions and international integration', *Journal of Money, Credit, and Banking*, 34: 1067–89.

Sopraseuth, T. (2003) 'Exchange rate regimes and international business cycles', *Review of Economic Dynamics*, 6: 339–61.

Stock, J.H., and Watson, M.W. (1999) 'Business cycle fluctuations in U.S. macroeconomic time series', in J. Taylor and M. Woodford (eds), *Handbook of Macroeconomics*. Amsterdam: North Holland.

Stock, J.H. and Watson, M.W. (2003) 'Understanding changes in international business cycle dynamics', NBER Working Paper no. 9859.

van Dijk, D., Osborn, D.R. and Sensier, M. (2002) 'Changes in variability of the business cycle in the G-7 countries', *Discussion Paper Series* no. 016, University of Manchester.

10
A Nonparametric Analysis of International Business Cycles

Maurizio Bovi

Introduction

In this chapter I examine the emergence of economic clubs and their coherence with European commitments. To this end, I analyse business cycle co-movements in six industrialized economies, which are pooled into several clusters. Unlike the mainstream literature, which frequently analyses correlations, the proposed empirical framework tests the relative cyclical association via the marginal homogeneity in 2×2 contingency tables. Under very few assumptions, the results indicate that an English-speaking club (Canada, the UK, the USA) is emerging in the last decades, whereas explicit and formal commitments seem to have had a relatively weaker power in determining Eurozone business cycles comovements.

There are several reasons for taking an interest in the international business cycles for both economists and politicians[1]. Just to mention a few issues, it is important to gather information about the relative contributions of domestic and international shocks to recessions, or about how synchronized cycles need to be for countries to form a monetary union. On this latter topic, Artis and Zhang (1997, 1999) report evidence supporting the view that business cycles are more synchronized when exchange rate variability is low. However, Inklaar and De Haan (2001) and De Haan *et al.* (2002) suggest the opposite, while Baxter and Stockman (1989) conclude that there is no relationship between exchange rate regime and business cycle similarity. Also, over recent years there have been a number of studies focusing on the dynamics of their co-movements. Results suggest widespread reduction in volatility (Carvalho and Harvey, 2004; Stock and Watson, 2003; Canova *et al.*, 2004) but not a clear tendency towards increasing international synchronization of cyclical fluctuations (Doyle and Faust, 2002a, 2002b; Heathcoate and Perri, 2002; Kose *et al.*, 2003; Massmann and Mitchell, 2003). Instead, there appears to have been an emergence of at least one cyclically coherent group, the major countries in the Eurozone (Carvalho and Harvey, 2004; Artis, 2003; Del Negro and Otrok, 2003; Luginbuhl and Koopman, 2003; Lumsdaine and Prasad, 2003), and possibly a second English-speaking group consisting of Canada, the UK, and the USA (Helbling and Bayoumi, 2003; Stock and Watson, 2003).

My aim is to shed light on the presence/emergence of economic clubs with a special focus on their relationship with European commitments. My main contribution lies in analysing the *relative* groupwise synchronization within a new empirical framework. The cyclical affiliation has often been conceptualized by comparing over time within and across correlations among national business cycles. If the former are increasing while the latter are decreasing, one concludes for the emergence of different clubs (De Haan *et al.*, 2002; Artis, 2003; Stock and Watson, 2003). In other words, the business cycles of different (groups of) countries are compared over different time periods. However, if globalization is strong (see Artis, 2003), it could be hard to disentangle different clubs because across-correlations are not decreasing. I analyse the presence/emergence of a *relative* economic club by comparing the within-groupwise synchronization between two clusters of countries over the same time period. Thus, I may detect an economic club even if across-correlations are not decreasing. On the other hand, it has been emphasized (Mitchell and Mouratidis, 2002) that any reduction in the cyclical disparity between business cycles need not be associated with increased correlation.

Without using correlations as a measure of association, the analysis I present appears to be particularly suitable for the questions of interest here. Moreover, I perform group by group comparisons without taking any of them as benchmark for the others (as done, for example, by Mitchell and Mouratidis, 2002). In addition, the literature on globalization and/or on Europeanization (Mansour, 2003; Del Negro and Otrok, 2003; Canova *et al.*, 2004; and, especially, Forni *et al.*, 2001, 2004), computes the world/European business cycle by assuming from the beginning that this cycle exists. Then, it tries to calculate if and how much the common cycle explains the country-specific movements. I do not impose any kind of such *a priori* requirements. Finally, the nonparametric statistical tool I use can address both linear and non-linear relationships (it is well-known that the correlation coefficient may not be a good measure of association), it can be validly applied even to classical cycles (and in that avoiding the issue of detrending), and it does not suffer from data scarcity (nonparametric tests are usefully and validly applied when there are few observations). Altogether, it means that under very few assumptions the exercises I propose can offer additional insights that can be combined with those of the earlier literature.

From the methodological point of view I follow to some extent the suggestions of Artis *et al.*, (1997), where a classical business cycle chronology is used to create a binary (expansion=1; contraction=0) time series variable for each country. The scores are then organized into 2×2 contingency tables recording pairwise expansion/contraction frequencies, which form the bases for Pearson's independence tests. Similarly, in order to test the relative groupwise similarities in the most industrialized countries' business cycles, I start from turning-point chronologies. Then, I make use of McNemar's (1947) test to statistically analyse the marginal homogeneity of 2×2 contingency tables which, in the present context, allows the relative groupwise synchronization to be addressed. I focus exclusively on *whether* business cycles co-move, throughout several periods and across some macro area. This is an admittedly less ambitious target compared, for example, to the 'holy grail of business cycle research' (Harding and Pagan, (2002a, p. 2), that is understanding *why* there is (not) synchronization in the level of economic activity across countries.

Hopefully, useful insights can emerge in this simple 'measurement-without-theory' approach as well. The results suggest that troughs and peaks tend to take place at the same time with a greater frequency in groups formed by English-speaking countries (Canada, the UK, the USA) than in clusters collecting core Eurozone economies (France, Germany, Italy). These findings hold for different concepts of business cycles (classical and growth rate) and are not a constant feature in international business cycles, but are emerging one recent decades. *Ad hoc* experiments suggest that in the aftermath of three potentially path-breaking events (the European Monetary System, EMS, the Maastricht Treaty, and the euro's inception), the core Eurozone countries formed a less coherent club than the English-speaking one. In other words it seems that the 'treatment' does not matter, at least in the expected direction, because the UK seems to belong more and more to the North American continent than to the European one, despite (or because of? – see Kontolemis and Samiei, 2000) the European arrangements. Then, loosely speaking, one can wonder whether a common language is a stronger attractor than a common currency. The chapter is organized as follows. In the next section I describe the data. The statistical framework and the empirical results are reported, respectively, in the third and in the fourth section. Concluding remarks close the chapter.

Data

To test the coherence in international business cycles in the present context I need a business cycle chronology for each country. There is a large amount of literature dealing with the problem of dating business cycles (Artis *et al.*, 2002), and it can roughly be grouped into two research approaches (Harding and Pagan, 2003). One (nonparametric) approach is the traditional way of distinguishing between different phases of the business cycle by picking peaks and troughs with the Bry and Boschan (1971) procedure. This approach is related directly to the methodology of Burns and Mitchell (1946) and the NBER Business Cycle Dating Committee. The other dominant (parametric) approach stems from the influential work of Hamilton (1989). It takes the form of regime switching models that assume the economy is to be found in one of a number of different states, and where the probability of moving from the current state to another is contingent on the current state. As argued by Harding and Pagan (2002b), the traditional approach is more robust and transparent. I avoid the problem of dating business cycles by using two different chronologies[2] as computed by the Economic Cycle Research Institute (ECRI). I deal with the most industrialized countries,[3] which can be grouped into two clusters: (1) the Eurozone (EZ = France, Germany, Italy); (2) English-speaking (ES = Canada, the UK, the USA).

Although the NBER–ECRI method and dates have sometimes aroused controversy, they are widely accepted and frequently used as a standard of comparison[4] (Boldin, 1994; Artis *et al.*, 1997; Canova *et al.*, 2004). ECRI determines the reference cycle chronologies for several economies using the same methodology used to establish the official business cycle dates for the United States. The data are monthly, cover the period January 1956 –November 2003, and the reference aggregate variable is not a single one. In the ECRI approach, the business cycle cannot be defined by any single variable (such as the GDP or the industrial output, just to mention the most frequently used), but by the consensus of key measures of output, income, employment and sales. These coincident indices define 'the economy' and constitute ECRI's reference series for each country. To identify business cycle recessions and expansions and the turning points (peaks and troughs) that demarcate them, ECRI applies an algorithm to the reference series (Bry and Boschan, 1971) codifying the judgmental procedures used by classical business cycle analysts. Basically, according to this routine each cyclical movement (peak-to-peak or trough-to-trough) should not be less than 15 months, each phase (peak-to-trough or trough-to-peak) should have a minimum of 6 months, and troughs always follow peaks and vice versa. As Watson (1994) has pointed out, the Bry–Boschan procedure provides a good way to define turning points, since it is based on objective criteria for determining cyclical peaks and troughs.

ECRI offers two kinds of chronologies. The first deals with the classical business cycle, the other with the growth rate cycle. As Harding and Pagan (2004) pointed out, the latter is a special case of the cycle identified from the detrended (for example by bandpass filters) reference series. The dating procedure is the same except that it is applied to the levels, in the former case, and to the growth rates of the same time series, in the latter case. It implies that classical cycles refer to alternating periods of expansion and contraction, while growth rate cycles refer to alternating periods of rising and declining growth rates. The average expansion probability (the fraction of time that the economy is in expansion) is roughly 0.5 in the growth rate case, while it is likely to be higher in the classical one. This is so because in a trending series (Stock and Watson, 1999): (1) classical cycle peaks come later in time than growth rate cycle peaks; (2) classical cycles become more and more asymmetric over time: a long period of positive growth is followed by a short downturn; and (3) classical cycles tend to vanish over time if the trend growth rises steadily from zero: in the long run the length of the classical contractions become shorter and shorter compared to the expansions so classical turning points will ultimately disappear. As a matter of fact, in many political circles the main focus seems to be on declines in the growth rate of aggregate economic activity as the primary way to monitor cyclical fluctuations in the economic system. On the other hand, even if many countries saw long periods of virtually uninterrupted growth, in recent years there have been a number of instances of absolute decline in GDP, which have renewed the conceptual appeal of classical business cycle contractions (Banerji, 2001). Finally, an important difficulty with any growth cycle analysis is that it is based on a definition of trend and such definitions are essentially arbitrary and can affect the results (Canova, 1998a; 1998b). For instance, Baxter and Stockman (1989) found that cyclical synchronization and monetary regimes were unrelated for linear-trend adjusted data but not for first-log-difference data, where synchronization was higher when exchange rate volatility was low. Summing up, in this chapter I use both concepts of the cycle because they can tell different stories about the economy and can increase the robustness of the findings.

The statistical procedure

In this section I broadly follow the methodology suggested by Artis *et al.* (1997) to study the synchronous nature of business cycles.[5] Given that my cycles are defined by the ECRI turning points, my business cycle phases are simply $0, 1$ (recession, expansion) binary series, S_{ti} for each country i, with periods within overall expansions taking the value unity. With $i = 1, \ldots, j$ and $t = 1, \ldots, N$, I have $jN \times 1$ binary column country-vectors. By pooling them I generate [6] an $N \times j$ 'macro-area matrix' (or macro-area cluster), and the degree of groupwise synchronization in the international business cycles can be measured by the fraction of time the national cycles are in the same phase (expansion/recession). With this macro-area matrix/cluster in mind, I define *groupwise synchronization* as the situation in which all the countries included in a cluster are in the same phase. That is, a group is synchronous in the periods in which the relative macro-area-matrix show rows with only zeros or only ones. It is worth noting that even if an economic club is emerging, in the sense that its groupwise synchronization is increasing, one must control whether there is globalization, that is a tendency towards a world business cycle. In other words, it is important to study the internal coherence of a group as compared to the rest of the world (or to other groups). To this end, I select a period and two sets of countries to form two macro-area matrices. Then, I create a 2×2 contingency table (Table 10.1) according to the four possible combinations.

A useful test for comparing the proportions in Table 10.1 is McNemar's test (McNemar, 1947). Basically, it examines marginal homogeneity and consists in analysing the off-diagonal terms of Table 10.1, because marginal homogeneity implies that row totals are equal to the corresponding column totals, or $(N_{11} + N_{12}) = (N_{11} + N_{21}); (N_{21} + N_{22}) = (N_{12} + N_{22})$. This implies $N_{12} = N_{21}$, which is the basis of the test. In fact, with $(N_{12} + N_{21}) > 9$, McNemar offered a chi-square test with 1 degree of freedom:[7] $(\chi^2)_1 = (N_{12} - N_{21})^2/(N_{12} + N_{21})$. Intuitively, when the

Table 10.1   The contingency table

		Cluster 2	
		In-phase	*Out-of-phase*
Cluster 1	In-phase	$N_{in,in} \equiv N_{11}$	$N_{in,out} \equiv N_{12}$
	Out-of-phase	$N_{out,in} \equiv N_{21}$	$N_{out,out} \equiv N_{22}$

focus is on different behaviours it seems logic to concentrate on situations in which the 'subjects' behave differently. The frequency of these situations is mirrored in the magnitude of the off-diagonal terms, namely $N_{in,out} \equiv N_{12}$ and $N_{out,in} \equiv N_{21}$. The latter is the number of periods spent in the same phase by the countries forming cluster 2 when cluster 1 is out-of-phase. Vice versa, N_{12} is the number of groupwise synchronized periods in cluster 1 when the cluster 2 is internally asynchronous. The more the two clusters are relatively homogeneous, the more the off-diagonal terms are similar. If $N_{12} = N_{21}$, McNemar's statistic is zero and one cannot reject the null of marginal homogeneity. Otherwise stated, a zero McNemar's statistic implies that the two groups have the same degree of intra-cluster synchronization.

Thus, in the present context the marginal homogeneity is a useful statistical concept in order to analyse the relative groupwise synchronization. A significant result implies that the two clusters are not homogeneous, that is that the probability[8] of groupwise cyclical similarity is statistically different across clusters. In particular, when N_{12} is significantly larger (smaller) than N_{21}, one can conclude that the countries included in cluster 1 constitute a more (less) coherent group than those in cluster 2. Note that $N_{12} = N_{21}$ can be realized with very different values of N_{11}, this is an interesting feature of this framework. In fact, since national classical business cycles will very often show $Sti = 1$ (as noted earlier in the chapter), frequencies will be so heavily clustered on the upper left cell that a χ^2 test like Pearson's contingency coefficient will likely reject the null of independence. A test of marginal homogeneity focusing only on the off-diagonal proportions does not suffer from this. Thus, it can be validly applied to classical cycles as well. Also, the mainstream literature on globalization and/or on Europeanization (Mansour, 2003; Del Negro and Otrok, 2003; Forni *et al.*, 2001, 2004; Canova *et al.*, 2004), computes the world/European business cycle by assuming from the beginning that this cycle exists. Then, it tries to calculate if and how much the common cycle explains the country-specific movements. For instance, Canova *et al.* (2004) find that this common business cycle explains about 30 percent of the fluctuations in each country.

I do not impose any kind of such *a priori* requirements. Furthermore, the emergence of economic clubs has often been conceptualized by showing that, over time, *within* correlations increase, while *across* correlations decrease[9] (De Haan *et al.*, 2002; Stock and Watson, 2003; Artis, 2003). In other words, the business cycles of different (groups of) countries are compared over different time periods. However, if globalization is strong (see Artis, 2003), it could be hard to disentangle different clubs because across correlations are not decreasing. I analyse the presence/emergence of a *relative* economic club by comparing the within groupwise synchronization between two clusters of countries over the same time period. Thus, I may detect an economic club even if across correlations are not decreasing. On the other hand, it has been emphasized (Mitchell and Mouratidis, 2002) that any reduction in the cyclical disparity between business cycles need not be associated with increased correlation. Not using correlations as a measure of association, the analysis I present appears to be particularly suitable for the questions of interest here.

Finally, I perform group by group comparisons without taking any of them as benchmark for the others (as done, for example, by Mitchell and Mouratidis, 2002). Admittedly, the empirical design ignores the magnitude of change, considering only the direction of underlying movement implied by the chronologies, and can offer only qualitative answers. Regarding the former, the problem is that even if the timing of business cycles is similar, the magnitude may differ and countries in a cluster could be recorded in the same cyclical phase even if their economic performances are very different. However, the decreased volatility shown by the GDP of the G7 countries (Carvalho and Harvey, 2004; Stock and Watson, 2003; Canova *et al.*, 2004) could somewhat reduce this issue. In addition, in European political circles the focus is often on relative behaviours and, regardless of quantitative aspects, the mantra seems to be 'our country is moving side-by-side with our partners'. On the positive side and to sum up, McNemar's test is not based on correlations and allows us to deal with: (1) group by group comparisons without imposing any benchmark; (2) linear and non-linear relationships; (3) short samples; and moreover, (4) it can be validly implemented to classical cycles (in that, avoiding the issues of detrending) and, most importantly, because of its features and its distribution-free nature, (5) it works under very few assumptions. Taken together, the proposed analysis can offer additional and complementing evidence on the presence/emergence of economic clubs.

Empirical results

The following tables are organized according to the concept of the cycle (Tables 10.2, 10.3, 10.4 and 10.2a, 10.3a, 10.4a respectively for the classical and growth rate cycles). To aid the detection of patterns in the data I shade the most important rows (involving English Speaking [ES] countries *vs* Eurozone [EZ] countries) and columns (for example the 'Maastricht experiment'). Also, in reporting all the possible trials I focus especially on the UK.[10] This is why I replicate the experiments for the two tri-variate clusters that are of particular interest here, the ES and the EZ.

Consistent with recent findings, the picture emerging from the empirical exercises leads us to conclude that over the last 50 years, the major Eurozone countries (France, Germany, Italy) formed less coherent economic clubs than those made up by combinations of English-speaking economies (Canada, the UK, the USA). Comparing over the entire sample pairs of EZ countries *vs* pairs of ES countries, all the resulting signs are '–' or '=' (see the shaded cells in the last column of Tables 10.2 and 10.2a). In the former case, it means that the probability of the event 'the ES bivariate clusters are synchronized' is significantly greater than the probability of the event 'the EZ bivariate clusters are synchronized'. Clearly, it does not imply that the EZ couples are not synchronized at all, but only that they constitute a *relatively* less coherent group than that formed by an Anglo-Saxon pair. This result is even stronger when the employed concept of cycle is the growth rate (Table 10.2a). In this case the ES couples seem to share a stronger gravitational force than that linking the EZ ones with no exemptions. Validating

Table 10.2 Analysis of relative homogeneity in classical business cycles

Clusters		Sample period										
1	*2*	*1956M1–1966M12*	*1960M12–1970M12*	*1965M12–1975M12*	*1970M12–1980M12*	*1975M12–1985M12*	*1980M12–1990M12*	*Maastr. (1992)*	*PRE EMS*	*POST EMS*	*Euro 1999*	*1956 2003*
GE&IT	US&CA	−	−	=	=	=	−	−	−	−	−	−
FR&IT	US&CA	−	=	=	=	−	−	−	−	−	−	−
GE&FR	US&CA	−	−	=	=	−	−	−	−	−	−	−
GE&UK	US&CA	−	=	=	+	−	−	−	=	−	−	−
FR&UK	US&CA	−	−	=	+	−	−	−	=	−	−	−
IT&UK	US&CA	−	=	=	=	−	−	−	=	−	−	−
GE&IT	UK&CA	−	=	=	=	=	−	−	−	−	−	−
FR&IT	UK&CA	=	+	+	−	−	−	−	=	−	−	−
GE&FR	UK&CA	=	+	+	=	−	−	−	=	−	−	−
GE&US	UK&CA	+	+	+	=	−	−	−	+	−	=	=
FR&US	UK&CA	=	+	+	+	−	=	−	+	−	−	=
IT&US	UK&CA	=	+	+	−	=	+	−	=	−	−	−
GE&IT	UK&US	−	−	−	=	+	−	−	−	−	=	−
FR&IT	UK&US	=	=	−	−	−	−	−	=	−	=	−
GE&FR	UK&US	=	=	−	=	=	−	=	=	−	=	−
GE&CA	UK&US	+	=	−	=	+	−	−	=	−	=	−
FR&CA	UK&US	=	+	−	=	=	=	−	=	−	=	−
IT&CA	UK&US	=	=	−	=	+	+	−	−	−	−	−

Continued

143

Table 10.2   Continued

Clusters		Sample period										
1	2	1956M1–1966M12	1960M12–1970M12	1965M12–1975M12	1970M12–1980M12	1975M12–1985M12	1980M12–1990M12	Maastr. (1992)	PRE EMS	POST EMS	Euro 1999	1956 2003
GE&FR	UK&IT	=	–	=	=	=	–	=	–	=	–	–
GE&CA	UK&IT	=	=	+	=	–	–	=	=	–	=	=
FR&CA	UK&IT	=	=	=	=	=	=	=	–	=	=	=
GE&US	UK&IT	+	=	=	=	=	–	=	=	=	=	=
FR&US	UK&IT	=	–	=	+	=	=	–	=	=	–	=
GE&IT	UK&FR	–	–	–	=	+	–	+	–	=	=	–
GE&CA	UK&FR	=	–	–	=	+	–	=	=	=	=	=
IT&CA	UK&FR	=	–	–	–	+	+	–	–	=	–	–
GE&US	UK&FR	+	=	=	=	=	–	=	=	=	=	=
IT&US	UK&FR	–	–	–	–	=	+	–	–	–	–	–
FR&IT	UK&GE	=	=	=	–	–	+	–	=	=	–	=
FR&CA	UK&GE	=	=	=	–	=	+	=	=	+	=	=
IT&CA	UK&GE	=	–	–	–	+	+	=	–	+	–	=
FR&US	UK&GE	=	–	=	+	=	+	=	=	+	–	=
IT&US	UK&GE	–	–	=	–	=	+	–	–	=	–	=

Note: Following the logic of Table 10.1, if $(N_{12} - N_{21}) < 0$ then I write '–'. This means that the number of periods spent in the same phase by the countries included in cluster 2 (UK&GE = the UK and Germany), when the countries included in the cluster 1 (IT&US = Italy and the USA) are not in the same phase (N_{21}), is significantly larger than the number of in-phase periods in cluster 1, when cluster 2 is out-of-phase (N_{12}). That is, cluster 2 is more homogeneous (at the 5% level) than cluster 1. A similar logic holds for '+' ('='), which means that cluster 2 is less (equally) homogeneous relatively to cluster 1. The cutting date for 'EMS' (European Monetary System) is 1979M3; the sample period for 'Maastr.' (the Maastricht Treaty) is 1992M1–2003M11, and for 'Euro' is 1999M1–2003M11.

Table 10.2a Analysis of relative homogeneity in growth-rate business cycles

Clusters		Sample period										
1	*2*	*1956M1–1966M12*	*1960M12–1970M12*	*1965M12–1975M12*	*1970M12–1980M12*	*1975M12–1985M12*	*1980M12–1990M12*	*Maastr. (1992)*	*PRE EMS*	*POST EMS*	*Euro 1999*	*1956 2003*
GE&IT	US&CA	−	−	=	=	=	−	−	−	−	−	−
FR&IT	US&CA	−	=	=	=	−	−	−	−	−	−	−
GE&FR	US&CA	−	−	=	=	−	−	−	−	−	−	−
GE&UK	US&CA	−	=	=	+	−	−	−	=	−	−	−
FR&UK	US&CA	−	−	=	+	−	−	−	=	−	−	−
IT&UK	US&CA	−	=	=	=	−	−	−	=	−	−	−
GE&IT	UK&CA	−	=	=	=	=	−	−	−	−	−	−
FR&IT	UK&CA	=	+	+	−	−	−	−	=	−	−	−
GE&FR	UK&CA	=	+	+	=	−	−	−	=	−	−	−
GE&US	UK&CA	+	+	+	=	−	−	−	+	−	=	=
FR&US	UK&CA	=	+	+	+	−	=	−	+	−	−	=
IT&US	UK&CA	=	+	+	−	=	+	−	=	−	−	+
GE&IT	UK&US	−	−	−	=	+	−	−	−	−	=	−
FR&IT	UK&US	=	=	−	−	−	−	−	=	−	=	−
GE&FR	UK&US	=	=	−	=	=	−	=	=	−	=	−
GE&CA	UK&US	+	=	−	=	+	−	−	=	−	=	−
FR&CA	UK&US	=	+	−	=	=	=	−	=	−	=	−
IT&CA	UK&US	=	=	−	=	+	+	−	−	−	−	−
GE&FR	UK&IT	=	−	=	=	=	−	=	−	=	−	−
GE&CA	UK&IT	=	=	+	=	−	−	=	=	−	=	=
FR&CA	UK&IT	=	=	=	=	=	=	=	−	=	=	=
GE&US	UK&IT	+	=	=	=	=	−	=	=	=	=	=
FR&US	UK&IT	=	−	=	+	=	=	−	=	=	−	=
GE&IT	UK&FR	−	−	−	=	+	−	+	−	=	=	−
GE&CA	UK&FR	=	−	−	=	+	−	=	=	=	=	=
IT&CA	UK&FR	=	−	−	−	+	+	−	−	=	−	−
GE&US	UK&FR	+	=	=	=	=	−	=	=	=	=	=
IT&US	UK&FR	−	−	−	−	=	+	−	−	=	−	−
FR&IT	UK&GE	=	=	=	−	−	+	−	=	=	−	−
FR&CA	UK&GE	=	=	=	−	=	+	=	=	+	=	=
IT&CA	UK&GE	=	−	−	−	+	+	=	−	+	−	=
FR&US	UK&GE	=	−	=	+	=	+	=	=	+	−	=
IT&US	UK&GE	−	−	=	−	=	+	−	−	=	−	=

Note: See Table 10.2.

Table 10.3   Recursive analysis of relative homogeneity in classical business cycles

Clusters*	Sample	N12	N21	P-value	Sign*
1 = EZ; 2 = ES	1956M1–1960M12	21	12	0.12	=
1 = EZ; 2 = ES	1956M1–1965M12	23	26	0.67	=
1 = EZ; 2 = ES	1956M1–1970M12	33	41	0.86	=
1 = EZ; 2 = ES	1956M1–1975M12	43	52	0.36	=
1 = EZ; 2 = ES	1956M1–1980M12	45	52	0.48	=
1 = EZ; 2 = ES	1956M1–1985M12	51	77	0.02	−
1 = EZ; 2 = ES	1956M1–1990M12	57	77	0.08	=
1 = EZ; 2 = ES	1956M1–1995M12	58	87	0.02	−
1 = EZ; 2 = ES	1956M1–2000M12	58	87	0.02	−
1 = EZ; 2 = ES	1956M1–2003M11	63	87	0.05	−

* Clusters and frequencies follow the logic of Table 10.1.
EZ = cluster 1 = (France, Germany, Italy); ES = cluster 2 = (Canada, UK, USA). Other details as under Table 10.2.

Table 10.3a   Recursive analysis of relative homogeneity in growth-rate business cycles

Clusters*	Sample	N12	N21	P-value	Sign*
1 = EZ; 2 = ES	1956M1–1960M12	0	35	0.00	−
1 = EZ; 2 = ES	1956M1–1965M12	1	40	0.00	−
1 = EZ; 2 = ES	1956M1–1970M12	8	48	0.00	−
1 = EZ; 2 = ES	1956M1–1975M12	23	62	0.00	−
1 = EZ; 2 = ES	1956M1–1980M12	29	80	0.00	−
1 = EZ; 2 = ES	1956M1–1985M12	32	108	0.00	−
1 = EZ; 2 = ES	1956M1–1990M12	33	144	0.00	−
1 = EZ; 2 = ES	1956M1–1995M12	41	159	0.00	−
1 − EZ; 2 − ES	1956M1–2000M12	55	182	0.00	−
1 = EZ; 2 = ES	1956M1–2003M11	58	191	0.00	−

* See Table 10.3.

what has already pointed out in a different empirical framework (Artis, 2003), the less synchronized couple appears to be GE&FR (Germany and France), which takes home nine minus[11] signs and three '=' in the 12 experiments (six for each concept of cycle, some of them unreported)[12]. On the other side, somewhat surprisingly, the most 'winning' couple is UK&US, which seems to be at least as mutually adherent as the North American block (US&CA). In the 12 competitions, UK&US is relatively superior to nine couples and equally homogeneous in three cases; the numbers for US&CA are, respectively, eight and four. As expected, UK&CA seems to be the less exclusive ES couple, although it never loses a match against EZ clusters.

There are several reasons to expect that the cyclical affiliations of the economies might have changed over time (worldwide shocks, international agreements, and

Table 10.4   A sub-sample analysis of relative homogeneity in classical business cycles

Clusters*	Sample	N12	N21	P-value	Sign*
1 = EZ; 2 = ES	1956M1–1966M12	23	26	0.67	=
1 = EZ; 2 = ES	1960M12–1970M12	13	29	0.01	–
1 = EZ; 2 = ES	1965M12–1975M12	20	26	0.38	=
1 = EZ; 2 = ES	1970M12–1980M12	12	12	1.00	=
1 = EZ; 2 = ES	1975M12–1985M12	8	25	0.00	–
1 = EZ; 2 = ES	1980M12–1990M12	12	25	0.03	–
1 = EZ; 2 = ES	1985M12–1995M12	7	10	0.47	=
1 = EZ; 2 = ES	1990M12–2003M11	6	10	0.32	=
1 = EZ; 2 = ES	Pre-EMS	43	52	0.36	=
1 = EZ; 2 = ES	Post-EMS	20	35	0.04	–
1 = EZ; 2 = ES	Maastricht	6	8	0.59	=
1 = EZ; 2 = ES	Euro	5	0	0.02[a]	+

Note: See Table 10.3. [a] The cumulative binomial (see text) gives a similar exact probability.

Table 10.4a   A sub-sample analysis of relative homogeneity in growth-rate business cycles

Clusters*	Sample	N12	N21	P-value	Sign*
1=EZ; 2=ES	1956M1–1966M12	1	40	0.00	–
1 = EZ; 2 = ES	1960M12–1970M12	8	14	0.20	=
1 = EZ; 2 = ES	1965M12–1975M12	22	22	1.00	=
1 = EZ; 2 = ES	1970M12–1980M12	22	32	0.17	=
1 = EZ; 2 = ES	1975M12–1985M12	9	46	0.00	–
1 = EZ; 2 = ES	1980M12–1990M12	25	44	0.01	–
1 = EZ; 2 = ES	1985M12–1995M12	9	52	0.00	–
1 = EZ; 2 = ES	1990M12–2003M11	25	44	0.01	–
1 = EZ; 2 = ES	Pre-EMS	28	68	0.00	–
1 = EZ; 2 = ES	Post-EMS	30	123	0.00	–
1 = EZ; 2 = ES	Maastricht	23	46	0.01	–
1 = EZ; 2 = ES	Euro	13	16	0.58	=

* See Table 10.3.

so on). Working with monthly data on industrial production over the last 40 years, Doyle and Faust (2002) and Massmann and Mitchell (2003) suggest that the degree of synchronization is not constant over time and that the particular sub-periods used in the analysis can affect the results. The sub-sample analysis performed here corroborates their hint. There were periods during which the cycles of GE&IT were more synchronized than those of ES pairs, while UK&US was a less strong contender (see the several '+' signs in the left-hand side of Tables 10.2 and 10.2a). These findings are congruent with those of somewhat comparable exercises reported by Stock and Watson (2003), despite those authors analysing correlations and employ national GDPs as reference series. The 1970s, characterized by two worldwide oil shocks, show the greatest degree of homogeneity (66% of '='). This result broadly supports Canova *et al.* (2004: 9) who claim that 'declines in economic activity tend to have common timing and similar dynamics, both within and across countries'. Also, Massmann and Mitchell (2003) note that all the countries experiencing the first recession of the 1970s, showed the peak in 1974. Using the words of Helbling and Bayoumi (2003), all these countries were in the same boat.

The other question of interest here is if the European agreements, such as the EMS, the Maastricht Treaty, and the euro's inception, have induced a common cycle in the Eurozone. *Ad hoc* experiments suggest that in the aftermath of their formal commitments, Eurozone countries constitute less coherent clubs than those of the linguistically-homogeneous economies. This finding can be drawn once again by looking at the signs reported in the shaded cells corresponding to the three European appointments (post-EMS, Maastr., Euro in Tables 10.2 and 10.2a) and to the EZ *vs* ES trials. In 54 contests (27 for each definition of cycle) the Anglo-Saxon groups lose just twice and, especially referring to the growth-rate business cycles, they appear to be unbeatable as compared to EZ competitors. Moreover, UK& IT and UK&FR, if anything, do not seem to be affected by the EMS, while the affinity of UK&GE results even smaller than that of 'mixed couples' such as FR&US (see the lower-right side of Tables 10.2 and 10.2a). The relative similarity of UK&IT and UK&FR classical cycles seems to be reinforced in the aftermath of the Maastricht Treaty and of the euro's inception, while this cannot be said for the growth-rate concept. Once again, UK&GE seems to be the relatively weaker pair.

All the outcomes achieved so far are ratified by contrasting altogether the three Eurozone countries against the three English-speaking economies (Tables 10.3–10.4a). Recursive experiments show that classical cycles were relatively homogeneous until the end of the 1970s. Henceforth troughs and peaks have tended to take place at the same time with a statistically significant greater frequency in the ES circle. The behaviour of growth-rate cycles supports the stronger adherence of this group, but the result is even more extreme because of the uninterrupted tendency of English-speaking countries to co-move more closely than the EZ ones. Rolling tests point out that the greater tendency of ES countries to form a more consistent club is not monotonic over time. A common feature of both concepts of cycles is the systematically superior Anglo-Saxon interaction as compared to the Eurozone situation, especially in the last decades. In other words it seems that the 'European treatment' did not attract the UK towards European countries.

Concluding remarks

This chapter has presented a nonparametric analysis of the most industrialized countries' business cycles as identified by the NBER–ECRI in search of some stylized facts. A non-conventional statistical design adds new evidence on the cyclical affiliation in some economic clubs, whose emergence has been pointed out by recent works. Data suggest that the English-speaking countries business cycles are more synchronous than the core Eurozone ones. This outcome is enforced in the last decades, and thus one can say that the recent European commitments failed to pass the 'English exam' and we may wonder whether a common language is more important than a common currency in establishing the cyclical affiliation. Unlike the mainstream literature, in this chapter the relative emergence of economic clubs is not based on correlations, but it is verified by analysing the marginal homogeneity in 2×2 contingency tables. Also, the reference series is not a single series such as the frequently used GDP, but the ECRI composite index which tries to capture the economic activity as a whole. The group by group comparisons are performed without imposing any leading country and the relative groupwise synchronization is tested by using both concepts of cycle, classical and growth rate. The 'Euro experiment' is somewhat fragile and the proposed non-parametric statistical tool deals only with qualitative information. On the positive side, the empirical framework works under very few assumptions, it can be validly applied to short samples, to classical cycles, and can discover even non-linear relationships. Finally, while this chapter offers some new results, the comparable findings are coherent with mainstream literature suggestions. Taken together, it means that the reported results are robust and can be thought of as complementing earlier evidence on the presence/emergence of economic clubs.

Notes

1 See, for instance, 'Is there an Anglo-Saxon cycle?', *Herald Tribune*, 22 January 1997.
2 Available via the Internet http://www.businesscycle.com/research/intlcycledates.php
3 I exclude Japan because it is outside the main purpose of this work.
4 ECRI claims that its international chronologies can be used for international comparisons, because they are based on the same standard approach applied to analogous sets of variables across countries. They use a proprietary procedure to incorporate any quarterly data, but no lower-frequency data than quarterly are used. I thank Lakshman Achuthan (ECRI) for support in the interpretation of the ECRI data.
5 Harding and Pagan (2002b) is another work on synchronization based on binary variables. As in the present work, they test the null of no synchronization, but their method is based on pairwise correlation while I focus on groupwise comparisons. Moreover, as known, pairwise correlation does not imply groupwise correlation.
6 Given that I analyse six countries ($N = 6$) and since the proposed test must compare clusters with the same number of countries, the macro-area matrices (the clusters) can only be bi- or tri-variate.
7 When $(N_{12} + N_{21}) < 10$, a two-tailed exact test, based on the cumulative binomial distribution with $p = q = 0.5$, can be used instead. A continuity correction, reflected in the numerator as $(|N_{12} - N_{21}| - 1)^2$, could be included to improve the approximation (Sheskin (2000)).
8 It is easily seen that the contingency table is made up by proportions based on 0/1 data.
9 In the literature this approach leads to distinguish between core and periphery countries, where the core countries have higher synchronized business cycles.
10 The goal here is to stress the relative performance between the English-speaking countries and the Eurozone countries.
11 GE&FR is in the column 'Cluster 1' and thus, as should be clear, the sign '–' implies that GE&FR is a less similar cluster than the corresponding couple in the column 'Cluster 2'.

12 Even if this could be due to German (re)unification, it remains to be explained why GE&IT results as a stronger contender. These considerations are beyond the focus of this chapter.

References

Artis, M.J. (2003) 'Is there a European business cycle?', CESifo (Centre for Economic Studies) Working Paper Series, No 1053, Munich.

Artis, M.J., Kontolemis, Z.G. and Osborn, D.R. (1997) 'Business cycles for G7 and European countries', *Journal of Business*, 70: 249–79.

Artis, M.J. and Zhang, W. (1997) 'International business cycle and the ERM: is there a European business cycle?', *International Journal of Finance and Economics*, 2: 1–16.

Artis, M.J. and Zhang, W.(1999) 'Further evidence on the international business cycle and the ERM: is there a European business cycle?', *Oxford Economic Papers*, 51: 120–32.

Artis, M.J., Marcellino, M. and Proietti, T. (2002) 'Dating the Euro area business cycle', *Working Paper*, ECO N. 24: European University Institute Florence.

Banerji, A. (2001) 'The Resurrection of risk', ECRI Working Paper no. 2001/11A.

Basu, S. and Taylor, A.M. (1999) 'Business cycles in international historical perspective', *Journal of Economic Perspectives*, 13: 72–6.

Baxter M. and King, R.G. (1999) 'Measuring business cycles: approximate band-pass filters for economic time series', *Review of Economics and Statistics*, 81: 575–93.

Baxter, M. and Stockman, A.C. (1989) 'Business cycles and the exchange rate system', *Journal of Monetary Economics*, 23: 377–400.

Boldin, M.D. (1994) 'Dating turning points in the business cycle', *Journal of Business*, 41: 97–131.

Bry, G. and Boschan, C. (1971) *Cyclical Analysis of Time Series.Selected Procedures and Computer Programs*. New York: Columbia University Press.

Burns, A.F. and Mitchell, W.C. (1946) *Measuring Business Cycles*. New York: Columbia University Press.

Canova, F. (1998a) 'Detrending and business cycle facts', *Journal of Monetary Economics*, 41: 475–512.

Canova, F. (1998b) 'Detrending and business cycle facts: a user's guide', *Journal of Monetary Economics*, 41: 533–40.

Canova, F., Ciccarelli, M. and Ortega, E. (2004) 'Similarities and convergence in G-7 cycles', Working Paper no.312. Frankfurt am Main: European Central Bank.

Carvalho, V.M. and Harvey, A.C. (2004) 'Convergence and cycles in the Euro-zone', in G.L. Mazzi and G. Savio (eds), *Monographs of Official Statistics*. Luxembourg: European Commission, pp. 122–46.

Del Negro, M. and Otrok, C. (2003) 'Time-varying European business cycles', mimeo: University of Virginia.

De Haan, J., Inklaar, R. and Sleijpen, O. (2002) 'Have business cycles become more synchronized?', *Journal of Common Market Studies* , 40: 23–42.

Doyle, B. and Faust, J. (2002a) 'An investigation of co-movements among the growth rates of the G-7 countries', *Federal Reserve Bulletin*, October: 427–37.

Doyle, B. and Faust, J. (2002b) 'Breaks in the variability and co-movement of G-7 economic growth', mimeo: Federal Reserve Board.

Forni, M., Hallin, M., Lippi, M. and Reichlin, L. (2001) 'The generalized dynamic factor model: one-sided estimation and forecasting', Discussion Paper Series no. 3432: Centre for Economic Policy Research.

Forni, M., Hallin, M., Lippi, M. and Reichlin, L. (2004), 'The generalized dynamic factor model: consistency and rates', *Journal of Econometrics*, 119, 231–55.

Harding D. and Pagan, A.R. (2001) 'Some econometric problems with regressions using constructed state variables', mimeo.

Harding D. and Pagan, A.R. (2002a) 'Dissecting the cycle: a methodological investigation', *Journal of Monetary Economics*, 49: 365–81.

Harding D. and Pagan, A.R. (2002b) 'Synchronisation of cycles', mimeo.

Harding D. and Pagan, A.R. (2003) 'A comparison of two business cycle dating methods', *Journal of Economic Dynamics and Control*, 27: 9.

Harding D. and Pagan, A.R. (2004) 'A suggested framework for classifying the modes of cycle research', mimeo.

Heathcoate, J. and Perri, F. (2002) 'Financial globalization and real regionalization', Working Paper no. 9292: National Bureau of Economic Research, Cambridge, MA.

Helbling, T. and Bayoumi, T. (2003) 'Are they all in the same boat? The 2000–2001 growth slowdown and the G-7 business cycle linkages', mimeo: International Monetary Fund.

Inklaar R. and de Haan, J. (2001) 'Is there really a common euro-zone business cycle? A comment', *Oxford Economic Papers*, 53: 215–20.

Kontolemis, Z. and Samiei, H. (2000) 'The UK business cycle, monetary policy and EMU entry', Working Paper no. WP/00/210: Internation Monetary Fund.

Kose, M.A., Prasad, E.S. and Terrones, M.E. (2003) 'How does globalization affect the synchronization of business cycles?', *American Economic Review*, 93: 52–62.

Luginbuhl, R. and Koopman, S.J. (2003) 'Convergence in European GDP series: a multivariate common converging trend-cycle decomposition', Tinbergen Institute, Discussion Paper no. 2003–031/4.

Lumsdaine, R.L. and Prasad, E.S. (2003) 'Identifying the common component of international economic fluctuations: a new approach', *Economic Journal*, 113: 101–27.

Mansour, J.M. (2003) 'Do national business cycles have an international origin?', *Empirical Economics*, 28: 223–47.

Massmann, M. and Mitchell, J. (2003) 'Reconsidering the evidence: are Eurozone business cycles converging?', Discussion Paper no. 210, London: National Institute of Economic and Social Research, London.

McNemar, Q (1947) 'Note on the sampling error of the difference between correlated proportions or percentages', *Psychometrika*, 12: 153–7.

Mitchell, J. and Mouratidis, K. (2002) 'Is there a common euro-zone business cycle?', Paper presented at the Colloquium on Modern Tools for Business Cycle Analysis, 28–29 November, Luxemburg.

Sheskin, D.J. (2000) *Handbook of Parametric and Nonparametric Statistical Procedures*. Boca Raton, Florida: Taylor & Framcis/CRC Press.

Stock, J.H. and M.W. Watson (1999) 'Business cycle fluctuations in U.S. macroeconomic time series', in J.B. Taylor and M. Woodford (eds), *Hanbook of Macroeconomics*, Vol. 1. Amsterdam: Elsevier, pp. 3–64.

Stock, J.H. and M.W. Watson (2003) 'Understanding changes in international business cycle dynamics', Working Paper no. w9859: National Bureau of Economic Research.

Watson, M.W. (1994) 'Business cycle durations and postwar stabilization of the U.S. economy', *American Economic Review*, 84: 24–46.

11
Measuring the Sources of Cyclical Fluctuations in the G7 Economies

*Marco Centoni, Gianluca Cubadda and Alain Hecq**

Introduction

In this chapter we analyse the importance of four types of shocks in contributing to the business cycles of the G7 economies. After disentangling the common permanent and transitory shocks in the G7 outputs, we identify the domestic and foreign components of such shocks for each country. This provides us with quite a flexible palette for understanding the degree of openness of the G7 countries, useful information for the analysis of the strengths and weaknesses of each national economy. Our empirical analysis reveals that the cycles of most of the G7 outputs are dominated by their domestic components and that the foreign components are almost entirely due to permanent shocks.

For many years, applied econometricians have been developing tools with a view to extracting common components in a set of economic time series. Among these components, the presence of common trends and common cycles (Vahid and Engle, 1993) brings important information both from a statistical and economic point of view. For instance, the existence of such co-movements provides support for some types of convergence or the sustainability of an optimal currency area (Beine *et al.*, 2000). This chapter shows that the output series of the G7 economies are governed by five common trends and three common cycles, thus providing support for the existence of co-movements both in the long and short run. Given the relative heterogeneity of the G7 economies, we cannot hope to obtain a single source of long-term fluctuations and it is likely there is a multitude of growth factors

* A previous draft of this chapter was presented at the 4th Eurostat Colloquium on Modern Tools for Business Cycle Analysis in Luxembourg. We thank the participants for their useful comments. Marco Centoni and Gianluca Cubadda gratefully acknowledge the financial support from MIUR. Alain Hecq gratefully acknowledges the financial support from METEOR through the research project 'Macroeconomic Consequences of Financial Instability'.

determining the dynamics of national outputs, a phenomenon documented *inter alia* in Bernard and Durlauf (1996). Using also the G7 output series but over a different sample period, Cheung and Westermann (2002) uncover six common trends. However, they find a single common cycle, thus indicating a stronger short-term integration than in this study, which utilizes data post the first oil shock.

However, to be instructive for policy-making, these descriptive statements concerning co-movements should be accompanied by a deeper analysis of the contribution of different shocks to the cyclical fluctuations of output series. In this chapter, after having determined the number of common components we further decompose cyclical output fluctuations into four elements. Using the approach of Centoni *et al.* (2004), we first assess the relative importance of foreign and domestic shocks in contributing to national business cycles. Indeed, it is important for policy-makers to know whether cyclical output fluctuations are mainly generated by shocks of domestic or foreign origin. For both foreign and domestic shocks, we then determine whether they have a predominant permanent or transitory effect. To touch on the huge literature on the latter distinction, allow us to recall that this additional information is crucial to understanding whether national business cycles are affected by permanent supply shocks or transitory demand shocks. For instance, if demand shocks are largely responsible for fluctuations, there may be a role for aggregate Keynesian-type policies.

Based on Centoni *et al.* (2004), our strategy differs from the usual strategy consisting of extracting from the outputs of several countries a common dynamic factor summarizing the worldwide component (see *inter alia* Gregory *et al.*, 1997, and Kose *et al.*, 2004). Indeed, we obtain a pair of domestic (foreign) permanent-transitory (hereafter, PT) shocks for each of the G7 countries. However, unlike a number of recent papers, Dufourt (2005) and Galí (2004) for example, we do not want to resort to a particular economic theory, such as a real business cycle model, in order to further identify these shocks as monetary or productivity in nature. This will be either the weakness or the strength of our chapter depending on the reader's point of view.

The chapter is organized as follows. In the next section we briefly review the PT decomposition by Centoni and Cubadda (2003), the notion of serial correlation common feature by Engle and Kozicki (1993), and the measures of the importance of domestic and foreign components of the PT shocks in explaining business cycles by Centoni *et al.* (2004). We then present our empirical analysis of the G7 output series. Similar to most studies (see for example King *et al.*, 1991), the empirical results indicate that permanent shocks are the main source of business cycles. But in contrast to Canova and Marrinan (1998) and Mellander *et al.* (1992), we find that foreign shocks account for a small portion of the cyclical fluctuations of the non-European G7 countries (about 13% for Japan and 25% for the USA). Ahmed *et al.* (1993) and Kwark (1999) reached a similar conclusion for the US economy using a structural VAR approach. This portion is around 53 per cent for the European countries. Moreover, we show that the domestic component is responsible for most of the business cycle effects of transitory shocks for all the G7 countries, whereas the foreign component dominates the cyclical variability which is due to permanent shocks in France, Germany and Italy.

Statistical methodology

Let us assume that an n-vector X_t of cointegrated series of order $(1,1)$ is generated by the following vector error-correction model (VECM):

$$\Gamma(L)\Delta X_t = \alpha\beta' X_{t-1} + \varepsilon_t, \quad t = 1,\ldots,T \tag{11.1}$$

for fixed values of $X_{-p+1},\ldots,X_0$, where $\Gamma(L) = I_n - \sum_{i=1}^{p-1}\Gamma_i L^i$, α and β are both $(n\times r)$ matrices of full rank r, the matrix $\alpha'_\perp \Gamma(1)\beta_\perp$ has rank equal to $(n-r)$, and ε_t are i.i.d. $N_n(0,\Omega)$ innovations. Series X_t also admit the following Wold representation:

$$\Delta X_t = C(L)\varepsilon_t$$

where $C(L) = I_n + \sum_{i=1}^{\infty} C_i L^i$ is such that $\sum_{j=1}^{\infty} j|C_j| < \infty$ (see for example Johansen, 1996).

Assuming hereafter that series X_t represent the outputs of n different countries, a possible source of the cyclical comovements across countries is the presence of common shock transmission mechanisms. In order to explore this possibility, we resort to the notion of Serial Correlation Common Feature (hereafter, SCCF) by Engle and Kozicki (1993), according to which series ΔX_t have s SCCF relationships if and only if there exists a $n \times s$ matrix δ with full column rank and such that $\delta'C(L) = \delta'$. Hence, the impulse response functions of series ΔX_t are collinear. As shown by Vahid and Engle (1993), the existence of s SCCF relationships is also equivalent to the presence of $(n - s)$ common cycles in the multivariate decomposition by Beveridge and Nelson (1981). Optimal statistical inference on SCCF is obtained by either canonical correlation analysis or full information maximum likelihood, see Vahid and Engle (1993) for details.

Another popular explanation for the existence of international business cycles is the presence of common shocks across different national economies. As shown by Centoni and Cubadda (2003), series X_t admit a PT decomposition where the common permanent and transitory shocks are respectively given by:

$$u_t^P = \alpha'_\perp \varepsilon_t \quad \text{and} \quad u_t^T = \alpha'\Omega^{-1}\varepsilon_t \tag{11.2}$$

the permanent and transitory components of series X_t are respectively P_t and T_t, $X_t = P_t + T_t$, $\Delta P_t = P(L)u_t^P$, $\Delta T_t = T(L)u_t^T$, and

$$P(L) = C(L)\Omega\alpha_\perp(\alpha'_\perp \Omega\alpha_\perp)^{-1}$$

$$T(L) = C(L)\alpha(\alpha'\Omega^{-1}\alpha)^{-1}$$

It is easy to verify that the shocks u_t^P only have permanent effects on series X_t, and the components P_t and T_t are uncorrelated at all lags and leads.

Centoni *et al.* (2004) further decomposed the PT shocks (11.2) into their domestic and foreign components. In particular, the permanent [transitory] domestic shock of the jth country $u_{jt}^{P,D}$ [$u_{jt}^{T,D}$] is defined as the component of the common permanent [transitory] shocks u_t^P [u_t^T] which is explained by the permanent [transitory] shock which has contemporaneous effect on the jth country output. Consequently, the permanent [transitory] foreign shock of the jth country $u_{jt}^{P,F}$ [$u_{jt}^{T,F}$] is the component of the common permanent [transitory] shocks u_t^P [u_t^T] which is independent from jth country permanent [transitory] domestic shocks.

Building on Centoni and Cubadda (2003), Centoni *et al.* (2004) proposed measuring the business cycle effect of PT foreign shocks by the portion of the spectral mass of the jth country output at the business cycle frequencies which is explained by the jth country permanent [transitory] foreign shocks. Similarly, the business cycle effects of PT domestic shocks is measured by the portion of the spectral mass of the jth country output at the business cycle frequencies, which is explained by the jth country permanent [transitory] domestic shocks. Remarkably, although these measures are conceptually formulated in the frequency domain, they can be easily computed after having estimated the parameters of model (11.1), see Centoni *et al.* (2004) for details.

Empirical analysis

We applied the methods presented in the previous section to the gross domestic product (hereafter, GDP) in volume of the G7 countries, that is Canada, the USA, the UK, Germany,[1] Italy, France and Japan. Quarterly, seasonally adjusted indexes (1995 = 100) were taken from OECD databases. Canova and Dellas (1993), *inter alia*, documented that after 1973 (that is, the first oil shock) the presence of common disturbances plays a role in accounting for international output comovements. We then used the sample that spans 1974Q1 to 2002Q3, namely $T = 115$ observations.

There exists a positive trend in the log-levels of all series, so we first tested for the presence of common permanent and transitory shocks by a cointegration analysis. A VAR(3) seems to appropriately characterize the covariance structure of the data according to the Akaike Information Criterion (AIC). Indeed, we do not reject the null of no autocorrelation in all the individual equations of the VAR.[2] We used Johansen's trace test for cointegration with a deterministic trend included in the error-correction term (Johansen, 1996) in order to capture the differences among the average growth rates of the various national outputs. Table 11.1 gives the values of the so-called trace test statistics (*Trace*) as well as the associated p-values. We do not reject the presence of two cointegrating vectors. This implies that the G7 outputs are driven by five common permanent shocks and two common transitory shocks.

The output growth rates exhibit a cyclical pattern the similarity of which is tested through a SCCF analysis. Having fixed $r = 2$, Table 11.2 gives the results of the likelihood ratio test for SCCF, and the degrees of freedom (df) as well as the p-values associated with both the asymptotic test statistic and a small-sample corrected test statistic (p-values^{SS}) considered by Hecq (2005). It emerges that we cannot exclude

Table 11.1   Johansen's
trace test for cointegration

	Trace	*p-values*
$r = 0$	183.54	0.00
$r \leq 1$	134.17	0.00
$r \leq 2$	88.02	0.06
$r \leq 3$	60.23	0.10
$r \leq 4$	35.96	0.21
$r \leq 5$	18.54	0.32
$r \leq 6$	6.58	0.40

Table 11.2   LR test for SCCF

	LR	*df*	*p-values*	*p-values*^{ss}
$s \geq 1$	6.43	10	0.77	0.85
$s \geq 2$	21.37	22	0.49	0.68
$s \geq 3$	38.25	36	0.36	0.61
$s \geq 4$	65.99	52	0.09	0.30
$s \geq 5$	117.07	70	<0.001	0.01

the presence of four SCCF vectors. Information criteria also indicate $s = 4$. We conclude that there are three common cycles across the G7 economies.[3]

In order to asses the relative importance of common PT domestic and foreign shocks in contributing to national business cycles, we applied the measures proposed by Centoni *et al.* (2004). We estimated the VECM model (11.1) fixing $r = 2$ and $s = 4$ and derived from the estimated parameters the spectra of each output and its components at the frequencies corresponding to 8–32 quarter periods. In particular, these spectra are computed for frequencies $\omega_k = (\pi)/16((199 - k)/199) + (\pi)/4(k/199)$ and $k = 0, 1, \ldots, 199$. Table 11.3 gives the estimated measures along with the 95 bootstrapped confidence bounds in brackets.

First, the results clearly indicate the dominant role of permanent shocks in explaining business cycles. From Table 11.3 we see that permanent shocks account for about 85 per cent of cyclical variations in GDP for European countries and Japan, and up to 94 per cent for the USA and Canada.

Second, we turned to evaluating the importance of the domestic and foreign shocks on the different economies at the business cycle frequencies. Indeed, it emerges that for Japan, Canada and the USA the foreign component of the business cycle is small, ranging from 11 per cent to 30 per cent. Due to their higher degree of openness, European countries are more sensitive to foreign shocks with proportions around 35 per cent for UK and reaching 50 per cent for France and Italy.

Third, for all the G7 economies, the foreign component of the business cycle is almost entirely generated by permanent shocks. This result is consistent with

Table 11.3   Measures of the BC effects of domestic-foreign PT shocks ($s = 4$)

		Permanent	*Transitory*	*Total*
Canada	Domestic	0.826	0.046	0.872
		[0.545–0.892]	[0.017–0.073]	[0.587–0.927]
	Foreign	0.112	0.014	0.127
		[0.059–0.397]	[0.004–0.033]	[0.072–0.412]
	Total	0.939	0.061	
		[0.907–0.972]	[0.028–0.092]	
USA	Domestic	0.614	0.067	0.682
		[0.330–0.781]	[0.028–0.096]	[0.385–0.831]
	Foreign	0.312	0.005	0.317
		[0.163–0.605]	[0.001–0.016]	[0.168–0.613]
	Total	0.926	0.073	
		[0.896–0.965]	[0.034–0.103]	
Japan	Domestic	0.650	0.161	0.811
		[0.421–0.822]	[0.062–0.202]	[0.556–0.918]
	Foreign	0.184	0.004	0.184
		[0.078–0.437]	[0.001–0.011]	[0.081–0.442]
	Total	0.834	0.166	
		[0.792–0.936]	[0.063–0.207]	
France	Domestic	0.372	0.130	0.502
		[0.147–0.642]	[0.044–0.156]	[0.237–0.722]
	Foreign	0.497	0.000	0.497
		[0.275–0.762]	[0.000–0.001]	[0.276–0.762]
	Total	0.869	0.130	
		[0.843–0.954]	[0.045–0.157]	
Germany	Domestic	0.414	0.135	0.549
		[0.227–0.660]	[0.053–0.154]	[0.327–0.752]
	Foreign	0.445	0.004	0.450
		[0.245–0.669]	[0.000–0.007]	[0.247–0.672]
	Total	0.860	0.139	
		[0.840–0.945]	[0.054–0.159]	
Italy	Domestic	0.408	0.101	0.509
		[0.234–0.661]	[0.033–0.126]	[0.307–0.724]
	Foreign	0.488	0.002	0.490
		[0.272–0.691]	[0.001–0.004]	[0.275–0.692]
	Total	0.897	0.103	
		[0.871–0.964]	[0.035–0.128]	
UK	Domestic	0.506	0.124	0.631
		[0.254–0.720]	[0.055–0.153]	[0.360–0.801]
	Foreign	0.343	0.026	0.368
		[0.182–0.611]	[0.009–0.036]	[0.198–0.638]
	Total	0.849	0.150	
		[0.820–0.932]	[0.068–0.179]	

the view that international technology diffusion is an important propagation mechanism of permanent shocks across countries. An important force generating technology spillovers among countries is the international trade of input goods, see for example Coe and Helpman (1995) and Eaton and Kortum (2001).[4] Frankel and Rose (1997), *inter alia*, argued that closer international trade links result in more coherent national business cycles.

Fourth, the domestic component clearly dominates the cyclical effects of transitory shocks, especially for European countries. This finding is in line with the interpretation that transitory shocks are mainly connected to country-specific monetary and fiscal policies.

Remarkably, previous analyses based on dynamic factor models by Gregory *et al.* (1997) and Kose *et al.* (2003) attributed a more limited role to country-specific shocks in contributing to national business cycles.[5] A possible explanation of these differences is that our identification of the domestic and foreign shocks was not obtained by imposing a factor structure to the data.

Notes

1   The data for Germany for the period 1974:Q1–1990:Q4 were reconstructed by using the GDP of West Germany.
2   The *p*-values associated to the Lagrange multiplier test statistics for fourth-order residual autocorrelation are 0.61, 0.81, 0.87, 0.29, 0.11, 0.07, 0.51 for respectively $\ln Can_t$, $\ln US_t$, $\ln Jap_t$, $\ln Fr_t$, $\ln Ger_t$, $\ln It_t$ and $\ln UK_t$.
3   In order to check whether the estimated common feature relationships really correspond to international linkages, we tested in a FIML framework (see Vahid and Engle, 1993, for details) for the existence of a SCCF vector with a single element equal to unity and the others equal to zero. The presence of such trivial SCCF vectors is rejected with *p*-values less than 0.001 for each country. We also rejected at the conventional significance levels the null hypothesis that one variable can simultaneously be excluded from the four common feature vectors.
4   See e.g. Keller (2004) for a detailed survey of the importance of various channels of international technology diffusion.
5   However, our ranking for the degree of each country's openness is very similar to that of Gregory *et al.* (1997), according to which the countries with the highest share of output variance accounted for by country factors are respectively Japan, Canada, the UK, the USA, Germany, Italy and France.

References

Ahmed, S., Ickes, B., Wang, P. and Yoo, B. (1993) 'International business cycles', *American Economic Review*, 83: 335–59.

Bernard, A.B. and Durlauf, S.N. (1995) 'Convergence in international output', *Journal of Applied Econometrics*, 10: 97–108.

Beveridge, S. and Nelson, C.R. (1981) 'A new approach to decomposition of economic time series into permanent and transitory components with particular attention to measurement of the business cycle', *Journal of Monetary Economics*, 7: 151–74.

Canova, F. and Dellas, H. (1993) 'Trade interdependence and international business cycle', *Journal of International Economics*, 34: 23–49.

Canova, F. and Marrinan, J. (1998) 'Sources and propagation of international output cycles: common shocks or transmission?', *Journal of International Economics*, 46: 133–66.

Centoni, M. and Cubadda, G. (2003) 'Measuring the business cycle effects of permanent and transitory shocks in cointegrated time series', *Economics Letters*, 80: 45–51.

Centoni M., Cubadda, G. and Hecq, A. (2004) 'Common shocks, common dynamics, and the international business cycle', *Working Papers and Studies*, Cat. no. KS-DT-04–003-EN-N, Luxembourg: Eurostat.

Cheung, Y.-W. and Westermann, F. (2002) 'Output dynamics of the G7 countries – stochastic trends and cyclical movements', *Applied Economics*, 34: 2239–47.

Coe, D.T. and Helpman, E. (1995) 'International R&D spillovers', *European Economic Review*, 39: 859–87.

Dufourt, F. (2005) 'Demand and productivity components of business cycles: estimates and implications', *Journal of Monetary Economics*, 52: 1089–105.

Eaton, J. and Kortum, S. (2001) 'Trade in capital goods', *European Economic Review*, 45: 1195–235.

Engle, R.F., and S. Kozicki (1993) 'Testing for common features (with comments)', *Journal of Business and Economic Statistics*, 11: 369–95.

Frankel, J.A. and Rose, A.K. (1997) 'Is EMU more justifiable ex post than ex ante?', *European Economic Review*, 41: 753–60.

Galí, J. (2004) 'On the role of technology shocks as a source of cusiness cycles: some new evidence', *Journal of the European Economic Association*, 2: 372–80.

Gregory, A., Head, A. and Raynaud, J. (1997) 'Measuring word business cycles', *International Economic Review*, 38: 677–701.

Hecq, A. (2005) 'Testing for cointegration and common cyclical features in VAR models: a 2-step vs. an iterative approach', mimeo, Maastricht: Universiteit Maastricht RM.

Johansen, S. (1996) *Likelihood-Based Inference in Cointegrated Vector Autoregressive Models.* Oxford: Oxford University Press.

Keller, W. (2004) 'International technology diffusion', *Journal of Economic Literature*, 42: 752–82.

King, R., Plosser, C., Stock, J. and Watson, M. (1991) 'Stochastic trends and economic fluctuations, *American Economic Review*, 81: 819–40.

Kose, M.A., Otrok, C. and Whiteman, C.H. (2003) 'International business cycles: world, region, and country-specific factors', *American Economic Review*, 93: 1216–39.

Kwark, N.S. (1999) 'Sources of international business fluctuations: country-specific shocks or worldwide shocks?', *Journal of International Economics*, 48: 367–85.

Mellander, E., Vredin, A. and Warne, A. (1992) 'Stochastic trends and economic fluctuations in a small open economy', *Journal of Applied Econometrics*, 7: 369–94.

Vahid, F. and Engle, R.F. (1993) 'Common trends and common cycles', *Journal of Applied Econometrics*, 8: 341–60.

12
Synchronization of National Business Cycles in Europe?

Gebhard Flaig, Jan-Egbert Sturm and Ulrich Woitek

Introduction

In this chapter we explore the extent to which co-movement in business cycles in European countries has changed over the last fifty years. Several complementary methods are applied to check the robustness of the findings. The most important result is that the correlation between the national business cycles was already quite high during the 1950s and early 1960s declined in the late 1960s to in some cases even negative values, and reached a peak after the first oil price shock. Since the 1980s we have observed a stable or even steadily increasing co-movement of the national business cycles.

In an open economy, business cycle developments not only depend upon internal supply and demand factors, but also shocks originating in other countries. The European integration of goods, capital and factor markets suggests that economic dynamism in a European country is more responsive to external influences as used to be the case. This suggests increasing business cycle affiliations at least within Europe. On the other hand, however, economic and financial integration allows countries to exploit comparative advantage through specialization, which leads to increased macroeconomic asymmetry (Krugman, 1991).

Following the European Commission (2001: 7), the transmission channels of the external shocks can be grouped into four: international trade, the corporate channel, confidence effects and financial linkages. Ideally, one needs a structural model to be able to differentiate between these channels and to test whether at least one of these channels has changed over time. There is a general feeling that all four channels have indeed become more important in recent history. Removal of trade barriers has boosted international trade, especially between European countries, and recent years have witnessed exponentially increasing flows of foreign direct investment. Confidence indicators throughout the world have moved in tandem in recent years. As confidence influences business cycles, the increased international co-movement of confidence indicators could suggest a larger transmission of shocks. Finally, linkages through financial markets have become stronger as investors have increased the international diversification of their portfolio.

The often mentioned intensification of international business cycle co-movement has clear implication for economic policy. For instance, many economists argue that divergence among the EMU member countries is still so high and the flexibility of labour markets so low, that the Eurozone common currency area is not optimal from an economic point of view (De Grauwe, 2000; Eijffinger and De Haan, 2000). Various studies have, in that respect, pointed out that business cycles in the Eurozone countries diverged considerably in the past (see, for example, Christodoulakis, Dimelis and Kollintzas, 1995). However, in assessing the economic case for EMU the crucial question is how likely is it that business cycles will diverge in the future.[1]

The next section will discuss the data and present some descriptive statistics. We then use rolling correlation coefficients for the cyclical component generated by an Unobserved Components Model, followed by an application of spectral analysis to the problem. We end with some conclusions.

Data

In order to analyse business cycles across countries and over time, we need to observe the evolution of a measure of production both comparable across countries and over time. The latter implies focusing on a measure like real GDP. Cross-country comparison forces us to convert real GDP into one unit of measure. As we do not want the data to be influenced by the relatively volatile movements of exchange rates, we turn to purchasing power parities (PPPs), and we use GDP measures based on constant PPPs.[2]

These time series have a very convenient property: they exactly replicate the relative movements of volume GDP growth of each country, which facilitates the use and interpretation of PPPs over time. Another advantage is that the resulting series is unaffected by methodological changes relating to the calculation of PPPs. For these reasons, the OECD recommends indices based on constant PPPs for the analysis of relative business cycle performance between countries and over time.[3]

The GDP data comes from the GGDC Total Economy Database at the University of Groningen and the Conference Board.[4] This database is strongly rooted in the work of Angus Maddison (2001). We use the tables for OECD countries expressed in 1999 US dollars, for which 'EKS' purchasing power parities (as published by the OECD, 2002) have been used. For all European countries, the data cover the period 1950 until 2002.[5]

To analyse the issue of business cycle synchronization, it is necessary to determine the cyclical component of output. The problem we face here is that the widely used filtering methods cause artificial cyclical structure when applied to a series based on a data generating process different from the assumptions underlying the chosen filter.[6] Following Canova (1998), we choose the pragmatic way of comparing the results for different filters; for example, the difference filter, the Hodrick–Prescott filter (HP, Hodrick and Prescott, 1997), the Baxter–King filter (Baxter and King, 1999) and the filter generated by an Unobserved Components Model.[7]

Correlation coefficients

Arguably the most commonly used measure of co-movement is correlation analysis. A high coefficient of correlation indicates that countries tend to be in similar states of cyclical movement. The degree of synchronization itself is determined on the basis of contemporaneous cross-correlation, while the overall linkage between cyclical movements is measured by the maximum coefficient, which emerges from cross-correlation at different lags and leads. This allows for a fairly comprehensive analysis. Developments in synchronization over time are examined on the basis of the contemporaneous cross-correlation coefficients for rolling 10-year periods.[8]

While evidence of increasing or decreasing synchronization may emerge, there is uncertainty as to whether this is due to generally higher or lower linkages in cyclical developments or simply due to a phase shift of the cycles, effectively reducing the number of lag and lead periods during which the maximum correlation occurs. Evidence of increased synchronization may thus be considered most convincing if the contemporaneous correlation is increasing over time and tends to be equal to the maximum correlation at a zero lag or lead (ECB, 1999).

In this section we restrict our attention to a correlation analysis for the period 1950 until 2002. In a first step we explore the association between the growth rate of GDP of each country and the growth rate of GDP of the rest of the European countries.

The left-hand side of Table 12.1 shows the highest cross-correlation coefficients between the growth rates of single countries versus the growth rate of the remaining European countries. As the first column indicates, except for Greece, Spain and the United Kingdom the contemporaneous correlation coefficient is the highest among all lead/lag-relationships. Whereas the United Kingdom leads the European business cycle by one year, Spain and Greece have a lag of respectively one and two years. We observe strikingly low correlations for Ireland and Norway. Also the United Kingdom, Greece and Denmark have correlation coefficients below 0.5. Except for maybe Denmark, this list is not really surprising. The United Kingdom and Ireland traditionally have rather strong economic relationships with the USA and other Commonwealth nations. Norway – as an oil-producing non-EU country – has probably been affected by oil price developments – which underlie most major international business cycle shocks – in a rather different way than most European countries. Greece's peripheral location within the EU together with its relatively low degree of economic development might be able to explain its low business cycle correlation with the rest of Europe.

Using the cyclical component extracted by using the Hodrick–Prescott filter the picture changes slightly. The right-hand side of Table 12.1 shows that in this case Norway, Denmark, Finland and the UK lead the other European countries

Table 12.1 Maximum cross-correlations for single countries versus European countries

	Growth rates		HP filtered series	
	lead/lag	*corr.*	*lead/lag*	*corr.*
Austria	0	0.75	0	0.67
Belgium	0	0.77	0	0.87
Denmark	0	0.49	3	0.53
Finland	0	0.57	1	0.54
France	0	0.85	0	0.87
Germany	0	0.64	−1	0.48
Greece	−2	0.47	0	0.60
Ireland	0	−0.08	0	0.48
Italy	0	0.70	0	0.69
Netherlands	0	0.71	0	0.77
Norway	0	0.26	4	0.44
Portugal	0	0.67	0	0.82
Spain	−1	0.65	0	0.77
Sweden	0	0.62	0	0.59
Switzerland	0	0.76	0	0.65
United Kingdom	1	0.41	1	0.69

by respectively four, three and one year; Germany on the other hand lags the other European countries by one year. Except for Ireland and the United Kingdom, the differences in correlation coefficients are not large. Whereas Belgium, France, the Netherlands, Portugal and Spain all report correlation coefficients of around 0.8, for Germany, Ireland and Norway its magnitude is below 0.5. With the clear exception of Germany, the initiators of European integration all belong to the group of countries with the highest correlations.

Synchronization in the time domain

The unobserved components model

In this section we employ an Unobserved Components Model in order to extract the cyclical component from the yearly GDP series for single countries and the rest of the European countries, respectively. In a second step, we use rolling correlation coefficients to analyse the changing pattern of synchronization between the national and international business cycles.

The basic assumption underlying unobserved components models is that an observed time series y_t can be decomposed into several interpretable components.[9] In the following, we decompose the logarithm of the yearly GDP series into the unobserved components trend T, cycle C, and the irregular I:

$$y_t = T_t + C_t + I_t \qquad (12.1)$$

The *trend component* represents the long-run development of GDP and is specified as a random walk with a possibly time-varying drift rate μ_t: $T_t = T_{t-1} + \mu_t + \varepsilon_t,$

where $\mu_t = \mu_{t-1} + \xi_t$. The level impulse ε_t is a white noise variable with mean zero and variance σ_ε^2, and the drift impulse ξ_t is a white-noise variable with variance σ_ξ^2. This model implies that the trend component follows an IMA(2,1)-process. Special cases emerge when we set the variance of the shocks to zero. If both are zero, we get a deterministic linear trend. If σ_ξ^2 is zero and σ_ε^2 is strictly positive, the model collapses to a random walk with a constant drift rate. The opposite case – with a strictly positive σ_ξ^2 and σ_ε^2 equal to zero – gives an integrated random walk with a usually smooth trend component.

The *cycle component* C captures the business cycle fluctuations around the trend component and is modelled as the sum of M subcycles with different frequencies each specified as a vector AR(1) process:[10]

$$C_t = \sum_{i=1}^{M} C_{t,i}, \text{ where } \begin{pmatrix} C_{t,i} \\ C_{t,i}^* \end{pmatrix} = \rho_i \begin{pmatrix} \cos \lambda_i^C & \sin \lambda_i^C \\ -\sin \lambda_i^C & \cos \lambda_i^C \end{pmatrix} \begin{pmatrix} C_{t-1,i} \\ C_{t-1,i}^* \end{pmatrix} + \begin{pmatrix} \kappa_{t,1} \\ \kappa_{t,i}^* \end{pmatrix} \quad (12.2)$$

The specification of the total cycle as the superposition of subcycles with different frequencies is able to represent some ideas of classical business cycle theory (for example, the existence of Kitchin or Juglar cycles) and to capture several forms of business cycle asymmetries.[11]

The period of subcycle i is $2\pi/\lambda_i^C$ with λ_i^C the frequency in radians. The damping factor ρ_i with $0 < \rho_i \leq 1$ ensures that $C_{t,i}$ is a stationary ARMA(2,1) process with complex roots in the AR-part (see Harvey, 1989). This guarantees a quasi-cyclical behaviour of $C_{t,i}$. The shocks $\kappa_{t,i}$ and $\kappa_{t,i}^*$ are assumed to be uncorrelated white-noise variables with common variance $\sigma_{\kappa_i}^2$. They induce a stochastically varying phase and amplitude of the wave-like process. The total cycle C_t is an ARMA($2M, 2M - 1$) process with restricted MA-parameters.

The *irregular component* is specified as a pure white-noise process: $I_t = u_t$. It is assumed that all disturbances are normally distributed and are independent of each other. This is the usual assumption to assure the identification of the parameters (see, for example, Watson (1986)).

Estimation of the model parameters is carried out by maximum likelihood in the time domain. The initial values for the stationary cycle components are given by the unconditional distribution and for the nonstationary trend and drift components by a diffuse prior. The filtered and smoothed values of the unobserved components are generated by the Kalman filter (for details see Harvey, 1989).

Empirical results

After an intensive specification search we choose a model with two subcycles. This model passes all specification tests and delivers plausible estimates for the trend and cycle components. The short subcycle varies between 3.5 and 5 years, the long subcycle between 9 and 12 years.

Using the cyclical components of both the unobserved components model and the Hodrick–Prescott filter (as used earlier), we then calculate the rolling contemporaneous correlation coefficients between each country and the rest of Europe. Each value of the correlation coefficient is computed over a window of the past 10 years. Due to lack of space, we do not comment in detail on the results for each individual country. However, by graphical inspection we are able to distinguish five groups (Figure 12.1) within our set of 16 European countries. Within each group the time pattern of the correlation coefficients is rather similar. Furthermore, the results are quite robust across the different filtering techniques we apply.[12]

The first two graphs of Figure 12.1 show the contemporaneous cross-correlation coefficients for Belgium, France and the Netherlands (group 1). In general, these three countries show correlation coefficients well above 0.5 throughout. Furthermore, these three countries show a relatively stable pattern over time.

The second group consists of the two oil-producing countries in our sample–the United Kingdom and Norway. In the 1950s and early 1960s, these two countries move in clear concordance with the rest of Europe, but the abruptly changed at the end of the 1960s. Especially for Norway, its correlation with the rest of Europe remained low – and often even negative – until the end of the 1990s. Only in recent years have both countries witnessed a sharp increase in concordance with other European countries.

Austria, Denmark and Germany, the third group we distinguish, depict a steady increase in correlation until the 1970s after which it starts deteriorating again – reaching their low at the end of the 1980s/early 1990s. From then on we observe that these countries start moving in line with the rest of Europe again. For Germany we can identify the sluggish behaviour of the German economy between 1982 and 1987, when other countries experienced a more or less strong recovery from the 1981/82 recession and the idiosyncratic unification boom in Germany in the years 1990/91.

The countries in the fourth group, Belgium, Finland, Ireland, Sweden and Switzerland, start from a level above 0.6 in the 1950s. However, these cross-correlation coefficients then slowly decline and – except for Sweden – reach their lows during the late 1970s/early 1980s. When using the unobserved components model, Sweden's turning point was already noticeable in the early 1970s. During the 1990s, all correlation coefficients are on a high and relatively stable level again.

The last group, containing the southern European countries Greece, Italy, Portugal and Spain, show lows in the late 1960s and early 1980s. Except for Portugal – which already started from a very high level – we see a clear rise in concordance of these countries with the rest of Europe. For Portugal and Spain this pattern is interrupted during the late 1970s and early 1980s. In recent years, we see some slight regress for all countries within this group.

Both (GDP-) weighted and unweighted average contemporaneous cross-correlations across our group of 16 European countries using the unobserved components model and the Hodrick–Prescott filter reveal that the correlation between the national business cycles was already quite high during the 1950s and early 1960s (not shown). For countries in groups 2 and 5 we observe a sharp decline in the business cycle synchronization during the late 1960s, sometimes even leading to negative correlations. The first oil price shock induced a high synchronization between the national business cycles. Consequently, the correlation coefficients show a sharp increase from the mid-1970s to the early

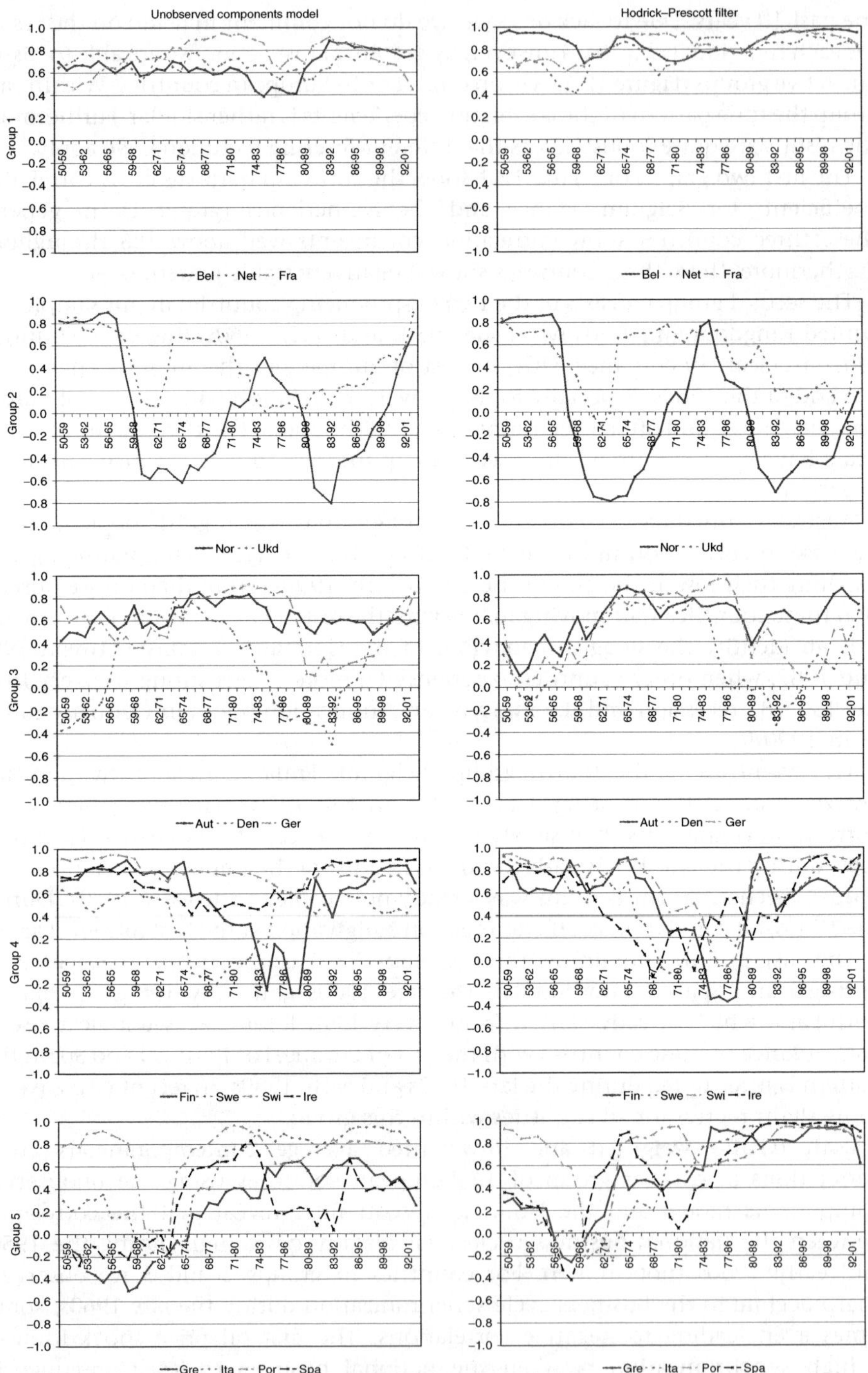

Figure 12.1 Average correlation coefficients across different groups

1960s and remain then fairly stable on a high level. There is some evidence – especially when focusing on the unobserved components model – that the strength of the co-movement of national business cycles further increased during the 1990s.

The last few years have exhibited a tendency to a stronger co-movement of, especially, the British and German business cycles with those of the remaining European countries. So – except for the southern European countries (group 5) in which European integration has probably indeed led to a higher business cycle concordance with the rest of Europe – we have a convergence to a situation which is 'normal' for most other countries – in particular those from the first (and third) group – over the last two or three decades. 'Normal' means that we observe a correlation coefficient in the range of 0.5 to 0.8 between the national and the European business cycle, respectively. There is a significant association among the cycle in different countries, but the co-movement is far from a perfect synchronization.

Synchronization in the frequency domain

To go a step further and check the results in the time domain for robustness, we employ spectral analysis techniques. This method has the advantage that it allows us to derive a measure for synchronization frequency by frequency, which enables us to focus on the relevant business cycle frequency intervals. The measures are based on those developed in A'Hearn and Woitek (2001). We focus on three cycle ranges: the 7–10 years range (Juglar cycle), the 5–7 years range, and the 3–5 years range (Kitchin cycle). The dominant cycle band is identified by calculating the share of total variance attributable to cycles in these intervals. To address the issue of synchronization, we decompose the variance for each frequency band into an explained and an unexplained part. In addition, we adopt the dynamic correlation measure suggested by Croux, Forni and Reichlin (2001) to distinguish between in-phase and out-of-phase movements.[13]

The time path for the in-phase proportion of explained variance for the European countries is displayed in Figure 12.2 (data in logs). Explained variance is calculated as the proportion of variance of a European member explained by the variance of the rest in the business cycle intervals (7–10 years, 5–7 years and 3–5 years). The results are summarized for the five groups identified above by taking averages over the group members. Note that the time paths are smoothed to facilitate the identification of overall patterns.

It is obvious that for Belgium, France and the Netherlands, in-phase explained variance is highest, that is above 50 per cent in all three business cycle intervals for almost the entire observation period, with the exception of the 7–10 years range, where it is below 50 per cent before 1955. Compared with the other four groups, the United Kingdom and Norway exhibit the lowest link to the European cycle: explained variance is constantly below 50 per cent. Austria, Germany and Denmark have an average explained variance above 50 per cent, with the exception of short periods at the end of the 1960s and the beginning of the 1990s. Group 4 (Finland, Ireland, Sweden and Switzerland) starts with explained variance above 50 per cent. After 1965, the measure declines, and increases again after 1985, at

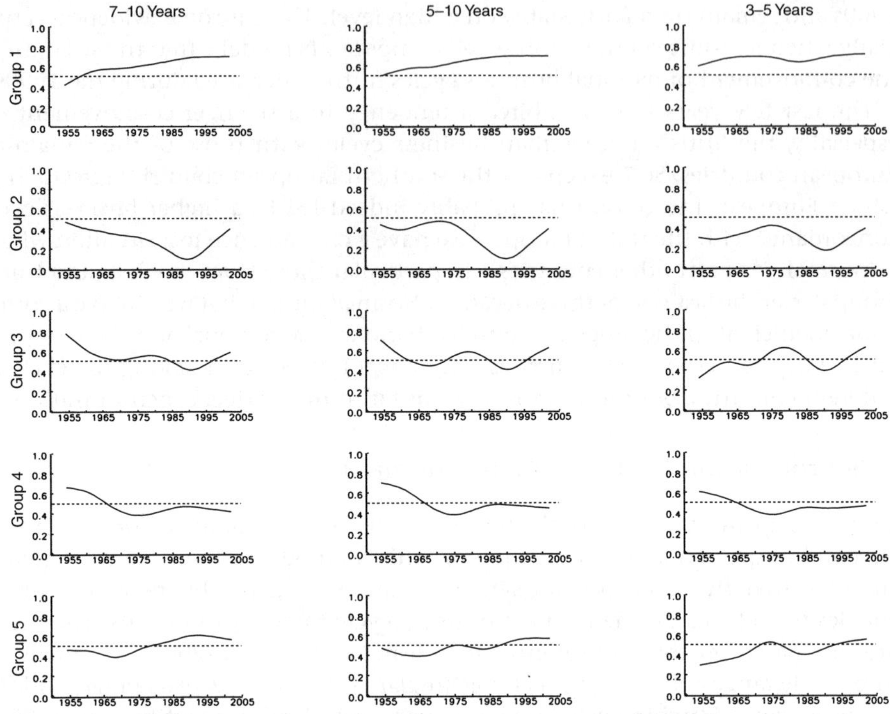

Figure 12.2   Synchronization of European business cycles

least in the 3–5 years range. Finally, Greece, Italy, Portugal and Spain start with an average explained variance below 50 per cent, which in the 5–7 and 7–10 years range decreases until about 1965. After 1965, the measure increases again to reach values above 50 per cent around 1980 in the 7–10 years range. For the other two business cycle ranges it does not cross the 50 per cent line before the start of the 1990s. A comparison with the outcome for the difference filter shows that with the exception of group 4, these results are robust.

Ahmed, Levin, and Wilson (2002) interpret synchronization in the high frequency ranges as due to converging business practices like improved inventory management, while synchronization in the lower frequency range is caused by fiscal and monetary policies aimed at smoothing out the business cycle. Reducing the variance of innovations would affect all frequencies. Since our results do not favor a particular range, and are also not entirely the same over all three ranges, there seems to be a mixture of causes responsible for the synchronization process of the European cycles.

Concluding remarks

This chapter has presented an exploratory study concerning the strength of business cycle co-movements of the European countries from 1950 to 2002. Special emphasis has been given to the question of whether the correlation between the national business cycles has changed over time. We find that the association between the national and the European business cycle was already quite high during the 1950s and early 1960s. Since the mid-1960s we see a dramatic decrease in the strength of co-movement with even negative correlation coefficients for some countries. The first oil price shock induced a closer co-movement of the national cycles. Since then we observe over more than 20 years a stable or even steadily increasing correlation. However, there is no clear evidence that the co-movement is higher than in the 1950s or 1970s. These findings are generally corroborated by an analysis in the frequency domain. Looking at co-movement in three different frequency bands (7–10 years, 5–7 years, 3–5 years) reveals additional insights. It turns out that especially Norway can be seen as an outlier with respect to synchronization with the aggregate European business cycle. For the main part of the observation period, the Norwegian cycle is not in phase with the European cycle.

Notes

1 Arthis and Zhang (1999) found evidence that business cycles are becoming more synchronous across Europe. This view is challenged by Inklaar and De Haan (2001).

2 This approach to generate time series of PPPs is to fix a 'base' year and to extrapolate PPPs for other years. Extrapolation is done by applying the relative rates of inflation observed in different countries to the base year PPPs. GDP series in national currency and at current prices can now be converted with these PPPs to yield volume measures that are comparable across countries. The resulting measures of GDP comparisons are volume indices at constant prices and PPPs.

3 For the latest 'snapshot' comparisons of GDPs and therefore business cycles across countries, the OECD recommends the use of indices based on current (benchmark) PPPs.

4 http://www.eco.rug.nl/ggdc.

5 Our set of European countries includes Austria, Belgium, Denmark, Finland, France, (West-) Germany, Greece, Ireland, Italy, the Netherlands, Norway, Portugal, Spain, Sweden, Switzerland and the United Kingdom.

6 See the discussion in Cogley and Nason (1995), King and Rebelo (1993) and Harvey and Jaeger (1993).

7 Note that, Arthis and Zhang (1997, 1999) and De Haan *et al.* (2002) report that their results are not dependent on the choice of the detrending method.

8 There are drawbacks when using 'moving windows'. For instance, the results might be quite dependent on the size of the window. For example, if the moving window covers a common shock (such as the oil price shock in the 1970s), correlation is very high, and immediately drops once this common shock is no longer covered.

9 For a general discussion see, e.g., Harvey (1989) or Maravall (1995).

10 C^* appears only by the construction of the recursion and has no intrinsic interpretation.

11 For some alternative specifications see, e.g., Harvey (2004) and Harvey and Trimbur (2001).

12 Besides an unobserved components model and the Hodrick–Prescott filter, we have also used annual growth rates and the Baxter–King filter. The results are similar to those presented and are available upon request.

13 For technical detail, refer to Flaig, Sturm and Woitek (2003).

References

A'Hearn, B. and Woitek, U. (2001) 'More international evidence on the historical properties of business cycles', *Journal of Monetary Economics*, 47: 299–319.

Ahmed, S., Levin, A. and Wilson, B. (2002) 'Recent U.S. macroeconomic stability: good policies, good practice, or good luck?', *International Finance Division Discussion Paper* no. 730: Board of Governors of the Federal Reserve System.

Arthis, M. and Zhang, W. (1997) 'International business cycles and the ERM: is there a European business cycle?', *International Journal of Finance and Economics*, 2: 1–16.

Arthis, M. and Zhang, W. (1999) 'Further evidence on the international business cycle and the ERM: is there a European business cycle?', *Oxford Economic Papers*, 51: 120–32.

Baxter, M. and King, R. (1999) 'Measuring business cycles. approximate band-pass filters for economic time series', *Review of Economics and Statistics*, 81: 575–93.

Canova, F. (1998) 'Detrending and business cycle stylized facts', *Journal of Monetary Economics*, 41: 475–512.

Christodoulakis, N., Dimelis, S. and Kollintzas, T. (1995) 'Comparisons of business cycles in Greece and the EC: idiosyncrasies and regularities', *Economica*, 62 (245): 1–27.

Cogley, T. and Nason, J.M. (1995) 'Effects of the Hodrick–Prescott filter on trend and difference stationary time series: implications for business cycle research', *Journal of Economic Dynamics and Control*, 19: 253–78.

Croux, T., Forni, M. and Reichlin, L. (2001) 'A measure of comovement for economic variables: theory and empirics', *Review of Economics and Statistics*, 83: 232–41.

De Grauwe, P. (2000) *The Economics of Monetary Integration*. Oxford: Oxford University Press.

De Haan, J., Inklaar, R. and Sleijpen, O. (2002) 'Have business cycles become more synchronized?', *Journal of Common Market Studies*, 40: 23–42.

Eijffinger, S. and De Haan, J. (2000) *European Monetary and Fiscal Policy*. Oxford: Oxford University Press.

European Central Bank (1999) 'Longer-term developments and cyclical variation in key economic indicators across euro area countries', *ECB Monthly Bulletin*, July: 33–54.

European Commission, Directorate-General for Economic and Financial Affairs (2001) *Supplement A, Economic Trends*, October–November. Bruxelles: European Commission.

Flaig, G., Sturm, J.-E. and Woitek, U. (2003) 'International synchronization of national business cycles?', *Applied Economics Quarterly*, 54: 21–40, Supplement.

Harvey, A. (1989) *Forecasting, Structural Time Series Models and the Kalman Filter*, Cambridge: Cambridge University Press.

Harvey, A.C. (2004) 'Test for cycles', in *State Space and Unobserved Component Models*, in A.C. Harvey, S.J. Koopman and N. Shepard (eds) Cambridge: Cambridge University Press: pp. 102–19.

Harvey, A. and Jaeger, A. (1993) 'Detrending, stylized facts and the business cycle', *Journal of Econometrics*, 8: 231–47.

Harvey, A. and Trimbur, T. (2001) 'General model-based filters for extracting cycles and trends in economic time series', mimeo.

Hodrick, R. and Prescott, E. (1997) 'Postwar U.S. business cycles: an empirical investigation', *Journal of Money, Credit and Banking*, 29: 1–16.

Inklaar, R. and De Haan, J. (2001) 'Is there really a European business cycle: a comment', *Oxford Economic Papers*, 53 (2): 215–20.

King, R. and Rebelo, S. (1993) 'Low frequency filtering and real business cycles', *Journal of Economic Dynamics and Control*, 17: 207–31.

Krugman, P. (1991) *Geography and Trade*. Cambridge, Mass.: MIT Press.

Maddison, A. (2001) *The World Economy. A Millennial Perspective*. Paris: OECD.

Maravall, A. (1995) 'Unobserved components in economic time series', in H. Pesaran and T. Wickens (eds), *Handbook of Applied Econometrics – Macroeconomics*. Oxford: Blackwell, pp. 12–77.

Organization for Economic Cooperate and Development (2002) *Purchasing Power Parities and Real Expenditures 1999 Benchmark Year*. Paris: OECD.

Ravn, M.O. and Uhlig, H. (2002) 'On adjusting the Hodrick-Prescott filter for the frequency of observations', *Review of Economics and Statistics*, 84: 371–6.

Watson, M. (1986) 'Univariate detrending methods with stochastic trends', *Journal of Monetary Economics*, 18: 49–75.

13
Modelling the Dynamic Convergence of Business Cycles

*Matthieu Lemoine**

Introduction

In this chapter, I propose a new non-linear parametric model, called the Dynamic Cyclical Convergence Model (DCCM), to measure and test the convergence between two cycles. This model combines unobserved component models with time-varying parameter models. The convergence is characterized by two time-varying indicators, the shift and the amplitude ratios between the two cycles. A Kalman filter-based iterative procedure is developed for the model estimation, and the procedure is assessed on simulated time series. The time-domain approach is compared with a frequency-domain approach, using techniques from the bivariate spectral analysis. DCCM models are applied to British, German and American business cycles over a period ranging from 1970 to 2003. The empirical results of this method will be seen to be twofold: on the one hand, since 1996, the British cycle progressively synchronizes with the German one: at the end of the period, both cycles have a lag equal to four quarters relative to American fluctuations. On the other hand, it appears that the British cycle amplitude has stood at around 40 per cent of the German one since 1996: shocks have asymmetric effects and the euro adoption would require an improved fiscal co-ordination.

Since the seminal paper 'A theorem of optimal currency areas' (Mundell, 1961), the degree of cyclical convergence in a group of countries has become a key criterion to assess whether a currency area is feasible. The evaluation of this criterion influences the overall organization in a currency area. In particular, a lack of cyclical convergence might increase the role of other criteria such as labour market flexibility or fiscal coordination.

---

* I am grateful to Severine Candelier and Guilhem Bentoglio for their comments and suggestions.

In order to analyse the convergence between cycles, many approaches are possible. For example, to assess if British and Eurozone cycles have converged, four approaches have been followed by HM Treasury (2003): analysing how close the main macro-economic variables have been in the recent period; assessing the degree of cyclical convergence during the last decades, measuring the risk of cyclical divergence in the future (Artis and Zhang, 1997); considering structural factors like the commercial balance structure, oil production asymmetry or housing markets differences; or assessing endogenous factors like trade effects associated with integration in a currency area (Rose, 1999).

In this chapter, I propose a new model and its estimation methodology, which are useful for studying the historical convergence of business cycles (second approach). Even if many cyclical models have been proposed, cyclical convergence is generally studied with *ad hoc* indicators applied to estimated cycles. As far as I know, few models have been developed for studying cyclical convergence dynamics. Common cycle models have been proposed by Vahid and Engle (1993), but do not allow the dynamics of convergence to be studied. More recently, Koopman and Azevedo (2003) modelled convergence dynamics with logistic functions, but such a mechanism does not allow convergence and divergence movements to occur successively. This chapter proposes a new bivariate model, called the Dynamic Cyclical Convergence Model (DCCM) for convenience, in which the shift and the amplitude ratio between the two cycles follow random walk dynamics. Contrary to the logistic function specification, the random walk allows for successive convergence and divergence. Cycles are modelled in an unobserved components framework. The random walk processes allow some reversible dynamics. As this model is non-linear, a specific procedure is also proposed for the estimation.

After a short description of the unobserved component models, the model DCCM and its estimation procedure are presented in the next second. The estimation procedure is than assessed on simulated data, and DCCM models are applied to British, American and German cycles from 1970Q1 to 2003Q1. The analysis of historical divergences might provide indications about the first test proposed by the Chancellor of the Exchequer for UK entry into the Eurozone.

Modelling the dynamic cyclical convergence

Unobserved components model of shifted cycles

For modelling the cyclical dynamics of a stationary vectorial time series y_t , we first consider a multivariate cycle model developed by Harvey and Koopman (1997) and extended by Rünstler(2004), in which cycles might be shifted between each other.

The bivariate case will be sufficient for the analysis carried on in this article. y_t is a (2×1) vector of observations that depends on two unobserved components that are also (2×1): a cycle ψ_t, and an irregular term ε_t. Measurement equations are written as follows:

$$y_{i,t} = \left[\cos(\lambda\xi_i)\psi_{i,t} + \sin(\lambda\xi_i)\psi_{i,t}^*\right] + \varepsilon_{i,t} \tag{13.1}$$

where $i = 1, 2$ is the index of the two variables and with $\varepsilon_{i,t}$ white independent Gaussian noises, with standard errors $\sigma_{i,\varepsilon}$. Parameters λ and ξ_i are the frequency and the shifts of both cycles. The normalization $\xi_1 = 0$ is imposed. The first equation is the decomposition of the first series into cycle and irregular components. The second equation has the same structure, but the cyclical component is expressed as a function of hidden cycles $\psi_{2,t}$ and $\psi_{2,t}^*$. As shown further, $\psi_{1,t}$ and $\psi_{2,t}$ are synchronized, but the transformation of $\psi_{2,t}$ and $\psi_{2,t}^*$ creates a 'shift' equal to ξ_2 periods between the second cycle and the first. State equations have a similar iterative equation for both time series:

$$\begin{bmatrix} \psi_{i,t} \\ \psi_{i,t}^* \end{bmatrix} = \rho \begin{bmatrix} \cos \lambda & \sin \lambda \\ -\sin \lambda & \cos \lambda \end{bmatrix} \begin{bmatrix} \psi_{i,t-1} \\ \psi_{i,t-1}^* \end{bmatrix} + \begin{bmatrix} \kappa_{i,t} \\ \kappa_{i,t}^* \end{bmatrix} \tag{13.2}$$

where i=1,2. Models of this kind are called *seemingly unrelated time series equations* (see Harvey, 1989). The (2×1) disturbance vectors κ_t, κ_t^* are bivariate normal disturbances, which are mutually uncorrelated in all time periods and have (2 × 2) covariance matrices Σ_κ:

$$\begin{bmatrix} \kappa_{1,t} \\ \kappa_{2,t} \end{bmatrix} \sim N(0, \Sigma_\kappa), \quad \begin{bmatrix} \kappa_{1,t}^* \\ \kappa_{2,t}^* \end{bmatrix} \sim N(0, \Sigma_\kappa) \quad \text{and} \quad \Sigma_\kappa = \begin{bmatrix} \sigma_{\kappa,1} & \sigma_{\kappa,12} \\ \sigma_{\kappa,12} & \sigma_{\kappa,2} \end{bmatrix} \tag{13.3}$$

Then one can verify that the cycles are stationary ARMA(2,1) processes (when the coefficient ρ is strictly inferior to one) and have the following autocovariance function:[1]

$$\Gamma(\tau) = (1 - \rho^2)^{-1} \rho^\tau \begin{pmatrix} \sigma_{\kappa,1}^2 \cos(\lambda\tau) & \sigma_{\kappa,12} \cos[\lambda(\tau + \xi_2)] \\ \sigma_{\kappa,12} \cos[\lambda(\tau - \xi_2)] & \sigma_{\kappa,2}^2 \cos(\lambda\tau) \end{pmatrix} \tag{13.4}$$

The cross-covariance functions show that the covariance between both cycles is maximized when the lag operator is applied ξ_2 times on the second cycle. It is assumed that $0 < \rho < 1$, which implies that ψ_t is stationary. The roots of the autoregressive part are constrained to lie in the complex region, which is the usual condition of cyclical behaviour. In the particular case where the frequency λ takes the value 0 or π, the cycle ψ_t degenerates into an autoregressive process of order one.

The damping factor ρ and the frequency λ are the same in both series. Cycles with the same coefficients ρ and λ are called *similar cycles*. The shape of such similar cycles can be different between series, because it depends on the variance of its disturbance which is specific to each series. Similar cycles are not necessarily synchronized among series, because the sequence of its disturbances is also peculiar to each series. When cycles are perfectly synchronized despite of a possible shift ($\psi_{2t} = \theta.\psi_{1t}$), cycles are called *common cycles*. The only difference is in the strength of the cycles: each cycle is proportional to the others. Common cycles embody much stronger restrictions than similar cycles.

Dynamic cyclical convergence model (DCCM)

A traditional approach, initiated by Vahid and Engle (1993), has studied the convergence of cycles in a group of countries by testing the presence of common components in vector error-correction models (VECM). However this test only shows whether the convergence had already occurred before the sample period, that is often before the 1960s. Moreover, VECM models provide transitory components which do not show enough persistence, a property that is generally expected from a cycle. Koopman and Azevedo (2003) have proposed a multivariate unobserved components model that tries to deal with these two problems: cycles are modelled as Harvey cycles with shifts; the convergence is associated with a progressive reduction of the shift and an increase in the correlation between the two cycles. But these evolutions are adjusted with logistic functions, which are monotonous functions and do not allow transitory divergences. Indeed, each turning point is an opportunity of divergence, for example some countries might have begun their recoveries, while others remain in deeper recession. Such recurrent divergences require a stochastic model of shift and amplitude coefficients, for example a random walk model.

In this chapter, a multivariate unobserved components framework is also used, but the convergence mechanism has been changed. First, the two series play different roles in the DCCM model. As a convention are distinguished a *reference cycle* from a *cycle of interest*, and properties of the cycle of interest are studied relative to the reference cycle. The cycle of interest is characterized by two main properties: its shift and its amplitude. The shift is the lag relative to the reference cycle. The amplitude is the amplitude ratio of the cycle of interest relative to the reference one. Second, each property is modelled with a time-varying (tv) parameter: the *tv-shift* and the *tv-amplitude*. These tv-parameters are both modelled as random walk processes. Finally, the *cyclical convergence* at a date t requires two necessary conditions: the tv-shift should not differ significantly from 0, and the tv-amplitude should not differ significantly from 1.

The normalization conditions $\xi_{2,t} = 0$ and $\phi_{2,t} = 1$ are imposed. The tv-shift $\xi_{2,t}$ and the tv-amplitude $\phi_{2,t}$ might be modelled as time-varying coefficients in a regression of $y_{2,t}$ on the reference cycle $\psi_{1,t}$.[2] The Dynamic Cyclical Convergence Model (DCCM) is written as follows:

$$
\begin{bmatrix} y_{1,t} \\ y_{2,t} \end{bmatrix} = \begin{bmatrix} \phi_{1,t}\cos(\lambda\xi_{1,t}) & \phi_{1,t}\sin(\lambda\xi_{1,t}) \\ \phi_{2,t}\cos(\lambda\xi_{2,t}) & \phi_{2,t}\sin(\lambda\xi_{2,t}) \end{bmatrix} \begin{bmatrix} \psi_{1,t} \\ \psi_{1,t}^* \end{bmatrix} + \begin{bmatrix} \varepsilon_{1,t} \\ \varepsilon_{2,t} \end{bmatrix}
$$

$$
\begin{bmatrix} \psi_{1,t} \\ \psi_{1,t}^* \end{bmatrix} = \rho \begin{bmatrix} \cos\lambda & \sin\lambda \\ -\sin\lambda & \cos\lambda \end{bmatrix} \begin{bmatrix} \psi_{1,t-1} \\ \psi_{1,t-1}^* \end{bmatrix} + \begin{bmatrix} \kappa_{1,t} \\ \kappa_{1,t}^* \end{bmatrix} \tag{13.5}
$$

$$
\begin{bmatrix} \phi_{1,t} \\ \xi_{1,t} \end{bmatrix} = \begin{bmatrix} 1 \\ 0 \end{bmatrix}, \begin{bmatrix} \phi_{2,t} \\ \xi_{2,t} \end{bmatrix} = \begin{bmatrix} \phi_{2,t-1} \\ \xi_{2,t-1} \end{bmatrix} + \begin{bmatrix} \gamma_t \\ \delta_t \end{bmatrix}
$$

with $\varepsilon_{i,t}$, κ_t, κ_t^*, γ_t and δ_t white independent Gaussian noises, with standard errors σ_ε, Σ_κ, σ_γ and σ_δ. In this form, the second cycle is generated by the propagation of the first cycle. This propagation is characterized by the tv-shift ($\xi_{2,t}$) and the tv-amplitude ($\phi_{2,t}$).

Estimation methodology

The difficulty in estimating the DCCM model comes from the non-linear transformation of time-varying parameters $\xi_{2,t}$ and $\phi_{2,t}$. The model cannot be written in a linear state-space form and a linear Kalman filter cannot be directly applied to approximate maximum likelihood estimates.

Thus, an iterative procedure is used (for details, see Lemoine, 2004), in which the equation is linearly approximated at each step n with a Taylor development[3] of order 1 around previous step estimates: (a) the reference cycle is pre-modelled in an unobserved components model and the tv-shift is initialized with the frequency-domain estimate; (b) estimates are recursively updated, by estimating a linearized model with Kalman filters and EM algorithms.

The estimation is iterated until the estimates are stabilized, that is until the iteration error $e^{(n)}$ is lower than a fixed value. The iteration error is computed as the standard error of the difference between estimates at iteration $(n - 1)$ and (n).

Simulation results

The Dynamic Cyclical Convergence Model (DCCM) and the estimation procedure proposed in the previous section are now assessed with simulated time series. First I describe the simulated data-set (see also Table 13.1, Figures 13.1, 13.2 and 13.3). The sample period goes from 1 to 180. A reference cycle is simulated with an unobserved component model: the frequency equal to 0.28 imply a period equal to 40; the damping factor (0.97) and the innovation standard deviation imply a standard deviation of the cycle equal to 1. Tv-shifts and tv-amplitudes are simulated as random-walk processes. A second cycle is generated as a transformation of the reference cycle, using these respective tv-shifts and tv-amplitudes. This generated cycle should show a tv-shift which varies from 3 at the beginning of the sample to 7 for $t = 70$. Its tv-amplitude is very dampened for t around 120.

Given the two cycles, the estimation procedure already described is applied to these simulated cycles: the reference cycle is modelled; the tv-shift and the tv-amplitude are estimated. Estimated cycle parameters are generally close to real values of the simulated DCCM. Concerning propagation parameters estimates, we might notice that they are underestimated: tv-shift and tv-amplitude estimates are

Table 13.1   Parameters of the simulated cyclical convergence model

Parameter	Symbol	Value	Estimate
damping factor	ρ	0.97	0.98
frequency	λ	0.28	0.31
innovation std. dev.	σ_κ	0.06	0.05
tv-shift std. dev.	σ_δ	0.15	0.04
tv-amplitude std. dev.	σ_γ	0.09	0.06

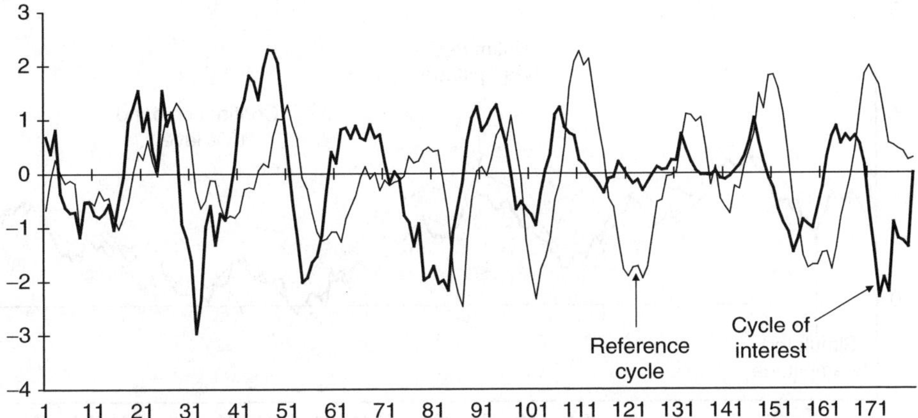

Figure 13.1   Simulated cycles

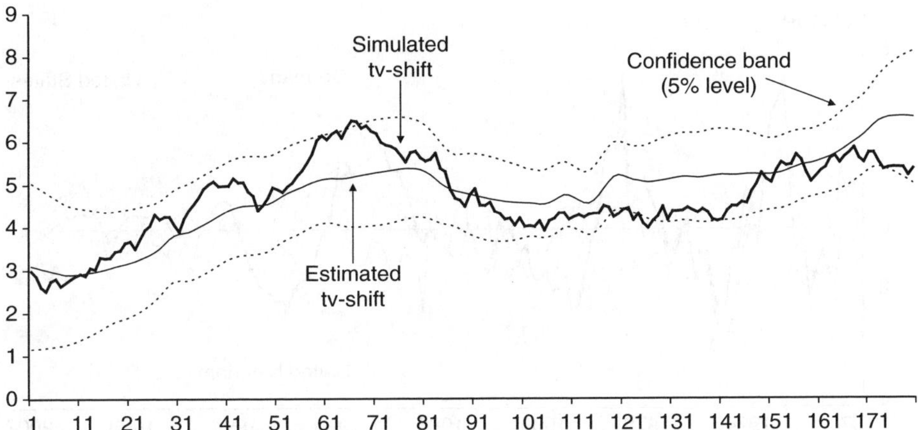

Figure 13.2   Simulated and estimated tv-shifts

smoother than their real values. However, the results seem satisfactory, as estimated values are rarely significantly different from real values at the 5 per cent level (Figures 13.2 and 13.3).

Empirical results

In this section we use DCCM models as outlined above, in order to study if the British cycle has diverged from the American cycle during the 1990s, to become anchored to the German one. After a short presentation of data sources, estimated models are presented jointly and compared. The convergence is then described in its two dimensions, the tv-shift and the tv-amplitude.

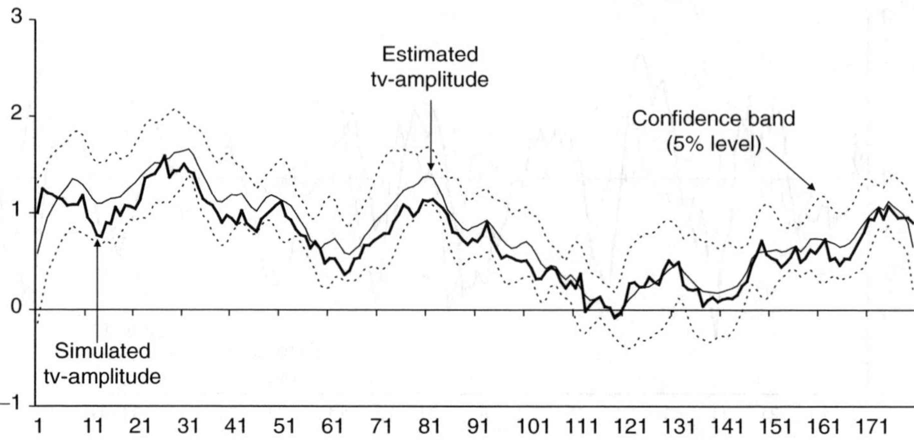

Figure 13.3   Simulated and estimated tv-amplitudes

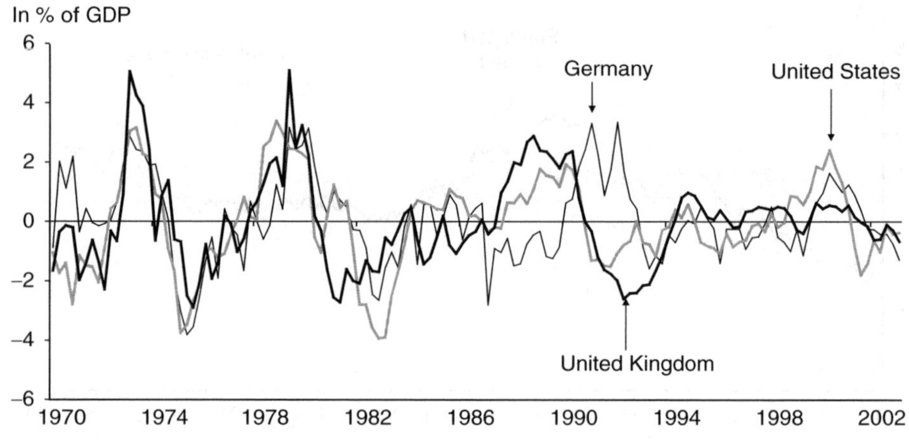

Figure 13.4   American, British and German cycles

Data sources

GDP time series come from Eurostat and have been retropolated to 1970 with the OECD *Business Sector Database* (BSDB). Series are expressed in 1995 euros and have a quarterly frequency. They have been seasonally adjusted and they have been de-trended with HP filters with the lambda parameter fixed equal to 1,600 (Figure 13.4). Estimation of DCCM models have been proceeded using algorithms and routines written on Eviews.

Has the British cycle converged towards the German one?

To analyse the position of the British cycle relative to the American and the German cycles, two DCCM models (1 and 2) are built and estimated in this section. In both

Table 13.2   Parameters estimates for models 1 and 2

Parameter	Symbol	Model 1	Model 2
Damping factor	ρ	0.95	0.95
Frequency	λ	0.20	0.20
Innovation std.dev.	σ_κ	0.14	0.14
Tv-shift std.dev.	σ_δ	0.24	0.24
Tv-amplitude std.dev.	σ_γ	0.14	0.23

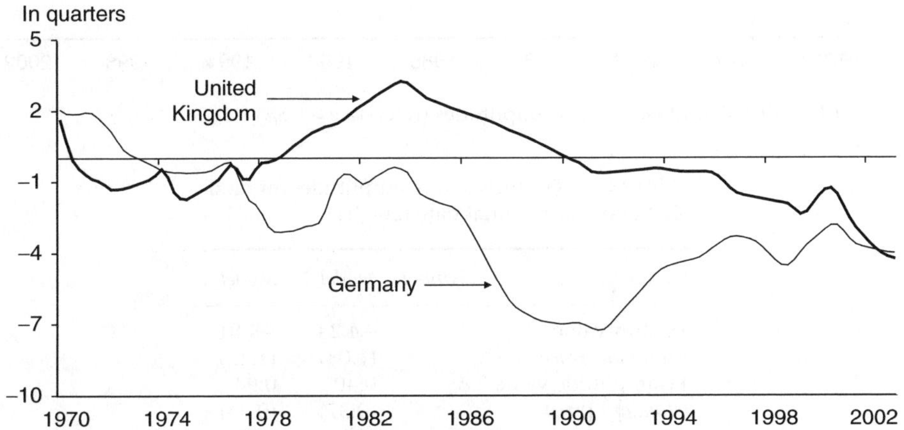

Figure 13.5   British and German tv-shifts (reference = USA)

cases, the American cycle is chosen as a reference cycle. In model 1, the British cycle is the cycle of interest,while model 2 the German cycle plays this role. Parameter estimates of models 1 and 2 are reported in Table 13.2. Parameters of the American cycle are standard (see Bentoglio, Fayolle and Lemoine, 2001). In particular, the estimated frequency implies a period equal to 32 quarters, that is 8 years.

Concerning the two tv-shifts estimated in models 1 and 2 (Figure 13.5), they were generally both lower than two quarters during the 1970s; they diverge from 1980 to 1995 and converge afterwards. German and British recessions were well synchronized with the American one during the 1970s, because of major symmetric oil shocks. At the beginning of the 1980s the British recovery leads the American and the German ones by one year. Then, the German slowdown occurred almost two years later (in 1993) than the American one because of the re-unification consequences. The United Kingdom follows the United States in the recession. Finally, after the high growth at the end of the 1990s, the United Kingdom and Germany moved together through a slowdown in 2001, while the American slowdown began in 2000. The British–German synchronization seems to have been reinforced at the end of the 1990s.

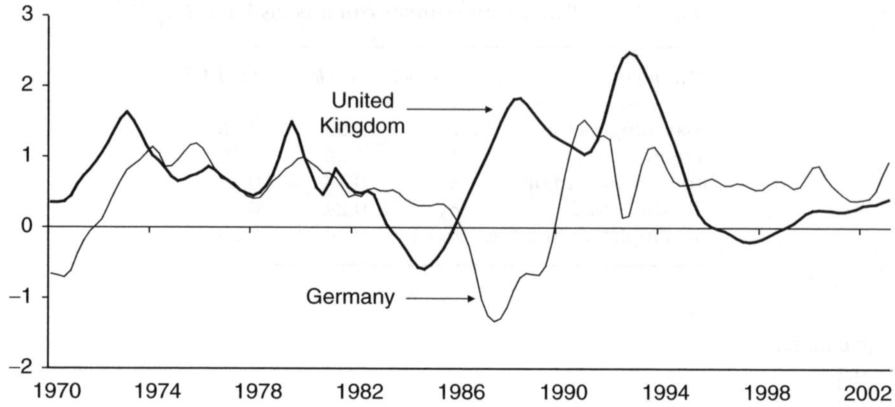

Figure 13.6   British and German tv-amplitudes (reference = USA)

Table 13.3   Tv-shifts and tv-amplitudes for models 1 and 2 at the final date (2003:1)

Parameter	Symbol	Model 1	Model 2
Tv-shift value	ξ	−4.24	−4.01
(standard error)		(1.03)	(1.17)
Tv-amplitude value	ϕ	0.40	0.94
(standard error)		(0.37)	(0.44)

Concerning the two tv-amplitudes estimated in models 1 and 2 (Figure 3.6), they measure the ratios of British and German cycles relative to the American one at each date t. They were quite stable around 1 during the 1970s (symmetric oil shock). The British amplitude has known strong movements from 1980 to 1995 with negative values in the 1980s (opposite fluctuations) and values over 1 in the 1990s. These strong unsynchronized cyclical fluctuations might be related to the specific development of financial services in the United Kingdom (Micolet, 1998). Finally, since 1996, despite the cyclical synchronization, amplitudes have diverged: the British cycle is particularly dampened relative to the others. This might be related to the British contra-cyclical policies.

Now, the convergence of the UK towards the USA or Germany can be tested at the end of the sample with final values of tv-shifts and tv-amplitudes and their associated standard errors (Table 13.3). Two hypotheses are tested for each couple: are the cycles synchronized ($\xi = 0$) and do they have the same amplitude ($\phi = 1$)?

This synchronization is tested by comparing final values of tv-shifts (Table 13.3): the British cycle has a lag equal to 4.24 in 2003Q1 relative to the American one; the German cycle has a lag equal to 4.01. As standard errors are approximately equal to one quarter, for a level equal to 5 per cent, these two lags are significantly different from 0 and are not significantly different from each other. In other words, both cycles are synchronized and have a significant lag relative to the United States (one year).

Concerning final amplitudes, the German amplitude is very close to the American one (0.94) and the British one is dampened (0.40). But standard errors are large (around 0.4) and the equality of American and British amplitudes cannot be rejected at a 5 per cent level.

If we come back to the issue raised by the British government about entry in the Eurozone, this indicator shows positive results concerning synchronization and mixed results concerning amplitude convergence in recent years.

Conclusion

The main innovation of this chapter concerns the dynamic property of the DCCM model: it formalizes the stochastic evolution of the relation between two cycles. Moreover, the DCCM model formalizes both dimensions of this relation, by distinguishing the tv-shift from the tv-amplitude.

Two DCCM models have been applied on British, American and German cycles, on a sample going from 1970Q1 to 2003Q1. During the 1970s, oil shocks provoked synchronized recessions with similar amplitudes. From 1980 to 1995, the United Kingdom underwent an early recovery and was then synchronized with the United States, despite of a higher amplitude. Since 1996, the British cycle became very dampened and progressively synchronized with the German cycle. Hence, although the synchronization test seems to have been validated recently, the risk of asymmetric shocks remains and the entry of the United Kingdom into the Eurozone would require an improved fiscal coordination.

Even if our convergence model has proved to be an interesting starting point for assessing in a probabilistic framework the dynamic convergence of business cycles, some improvements have been signposted for future research. The estimation procedure of such a non-linear model could become more precise with importance-sampling techniques. We could also try to explain the convergence by integrating into the convergence mechanism exogenous variables, for example economic policies indicators (interest rates, exchange rates and fiscal indicators).

Notes

1   Proof of the auto-covariance expression is given by Rünstler (2004, Appendix).
2   Boone (1997) used such time-varying regressions for measuring convergence of supply and demand shocks, in a SVAR model. The idea came from an application on exchange rates (Hall *et al.*, 1992). The DCCM model can also be compared with the stochastic covariance model proposed in Harvey and Shepard (1994).
3   For estimating non-linear models, Durbin and Koopman (2001) proposed such a method. However, they also recommend improving the estimation with importance sampling techniques. This improvement remains for further research.

References

Artis, M. and Zhang, W. (1997) 'International business cycles and the ERM: is there a European business cycle?', *International Journal of Finance and Economics*, 2: 1–16.

Bentoglio, G., Fayolle, J. and Lemoine, M. (2001) 'Unité et pluralité du cycle européen', *Revue de l'OFCE*, 78. Paris: Observatoire Français des Conjonctures Économiques.

Boone, L. (1997) 'Symétrie des chocs en Union Européenne: une analyse dynamique', *Economie Internationale*, 70.

Durbin, J. and Koopman, S.J. (2001) *Time Series Analysis by State Space Methods*. Oxford: Oxford University Press.

Hall, S.G., Robertson, D. and Wickens, M. (1992) 'Measuring convergence of the EC economics', *The Manchester School*, LX, Supplement.

Harvey, A.C. (1989) *Forecasting, Structural Time Series Models and the Kalman Filter*. Cambridge: Cambridge University Press.

Harvey, A.C. and Koopman, S.J. (1997) 'Multivariate structural time series models', in C. Heij, H. Schumacher, B. Hanzon and C. Praagman (eds), *Systematic Dynamics in Economic and Financial Models*. Chichester: John Wiley & Sons, pp. 269–98.

Harvey, A.C., Ruiz, E. and Shepard, N. (1994) 'Multivariate Stochastic Variance Models', *Review of Economic Studies*, 61, issue 2.

HM Treasury (2003) 'UK membership of the single currency: an assessment of the five economic tests', Report presented to Parliament by the Chancellor of the Exchequer.

Iacobucci, A. (2003) 'Spectral analysis for economic time series', OFCE Working Paper, 2003–07. Paris: Observatoire Français des Conjonctures Économiques.

Koopman, S.J. and Azevedo, J.V. (2003) 'Measuring synchronisation and convergence of business cycles', Tinbergen Institute Discussion Paper, no. 03-052/4.

Lemoine, M. (2004) 'Modelling the dynamic convergence of business cycles', Working Paper and Studies. Luxembourg: Eurostat.

Micolet, P.-E. (1998) 'Positionnement conjoncturel du Royaume-Uni et UEM', *Revue de l'OFCE*, 66. Paris: OFCE.

Mundell, R. (1961) 'A theory of optimal currency areas', *American Economic Review*, 51.

Rose, A.K. (1999) 'One money, one market: estimating the effect of common currencies on trade', CEPR Discussion Paper no. 2329.

Rünstler, G. (2004) 'Modelling phase shifts among stochastic cycles', *Econometrics Journal*, 7: 232–48.

Vahid, F. and Engle, R.F. (1993) 'Common trends and common cycles', *Journal of Applied Econometrics*, 8: 341–60.

14
The Economic Integration of Candidate Countries in the European Union: An Analysis with a Three-Level Dynamic Factor Model

Marco Marini

Introduction

The process of convergence across different regions and countries is generally intended as the reduction of economic inequality. The issue has become of particular interest because of the enlargement process experimented within the European Union, capturing the attention of policy-makers and researchers. Indeed, one of the main important goals included in the Maastricht Treaty is the reduction of disparities between member states and acceding countries. From the initial six countries in the 1950s, the EU has grown to the current 25 states and this process of enlargement is still continuing. Ten countries joined the European Union on 1 May 2004 (Cyprus, the Czech Republic, Estonia, Hungary, Latvia, Lithuania, Malta, Poland, Slovenia, the Slovak Republic), Bulgaria and Romania are negotiating their accession by 2007, while Turkey is still involved in political problems which delay its integration.

Doubts about the real effectiveness of economic integration of poorer countries into the EU have been expressed by many economists. Economic theory identifies a set of convergence and divergence mechanisms on economic integration across countries and regions with different income levels: see, for example, De La Fuente (2002). The presence of similar macroeconomic fluctuations assumes a significant role in such theoretical models, especially in the recent literature on endogenous growth; a climate of macroeconomic stability favours decisions of investment in all those kind of capital assets required to achieve a sustained economic growth, as stressed by Martin and Sanz (2001).

The aim of this work is to measure and compare real and nominal fluctuations in former acceding countries and member states (MS) of the European Union (EU) in the decade before the integration. The empirical analysis is centred on the fluctuations of the industrial production index for three main industrial groupings (mining, manufacturing and electricity) and of the consumer price index for 12 consumption functions. Such indices are regarded as barometers of the state of the real and nominal economic activity. A dynamic factor model with three additive orthogonal components is assumed: each variable is decomposed into a European component, a specific component and an idiosyncratic component. Such an approach relies on the empirical work of Forni and Reichlin (2001), in which the second-level component is referred to geographical entities (regions, counties). This component is here called *specific* since it refers specifically to each industrial grouping and consumption function considered.

A first result of the analysis is the variance decomposition for each country; the spectral shape for the three components is also shown for some countries. For the real activity, co-movements of candidate countries and member states are measured at different frequencies through the cohesion measure. Finally, the phase shift for each candidate country is computed with respect to a weighted average of the estimated European components of the member states, so as to classify them into leading, coincident and lagging with respect to the EU business cycle.

The chapter is organized as follows. In the next section I present the theoretical factor model and the estimation procedure. The data are then described and the results discussed for the industrial production index and the consumer price index. Some conclusions are finally given.

The three-level dynamic factor model

The dynamic factor model (or index-model) introduced by Sargent and Sims (1977) and Geweke (1977) has been widely applied to macroeconomic analysis. Recently, Forni, Hallin, Lippi and Reichlin (2000) have proposed a generalization of the index model: the mutual orthogonality assumed for the idiosyncratic components is relaxed, allowing for a limited amount of dynamic cross-correlation.

The dynamic property of the model is needed to catch the different dynamic responses of individual units to common factors (or shocks) characterizing the business cycle. This feature perfectly fits this application. In fact, countries may be affected in different ways by the same common shock, with different lags or even with opposite magnitude. Furthermore, each sector is likely to be linked to other sectors of the same country or to the same sector of other countries; in other words, the idiosyncratic components cannot be considered mutually orthogonal.

At an aggregated level, the factor model can be expressed as:

$$x_{it} = \chi_{it} + \xi_{it} \tag{14.1}$$

where χ_{it} and ξ_{it} are called the common component and the idiosyncratic component of x_{it}, respectively. Forni and Reichlin (2001) introduce a third level of factor which is neither common nor idiosyncratic. Their study analyses regional output for Europe and the USA assuming that each variable can be decomposed into a European (USA) component, a national (state for the USA) component and a regional component (county for the USA). Based on a similar idea, the model proposed here is a three-level factor model with an intermediate sectorial component. We assume the existence of a common source of fluctuation, in a wide sense, at the European level. Output fluctuation of a sector can also depend on shock which are specific within the sector it belongs to. The remaining part of variability is left unexplained by this two factors and is called idiosyncratic or local.

Let x_t^{ij} be the growth rate of output for the ith sector of nation j. The factor model is expressed as:

$$x_t^{ij} = E_t^{ij} + S_t^{ij} + I_t^{ij} \tag{14.2}$$

for $j = 1, \ldots, n$ and $i = 1, \ldots, s$, where E_t^{ij} is the European component, S_t^{ij} is the sectorial component and I_t^{ij} is the idiosyncratic component.

The same estimation procedure outlined in Forni and Reichlin (2001), with some modifications, is applied. The steps are briefly reported below. In the first step, a linear combination is computed for each sector i:

$$x_t^i = \sum_{j=1}^{n} w^{ij} x_t^{ij}$$

using the dynamic principal components estimator proposed in Forni *et al.* (2000a). The aggregates x_t^i represent the sectorial shocks. As a second step, the European shock is computed as:

$$x_t = \sum_{i=1}^{s} w^i x_t^i$$

where the weights w^{ij} are found solving the generalized principal components problem. It can be shown that this linear combination is the one which minimizes the ratio of the variance of the idiosyncratic component over the total variance expressed by x_t^{ij} (Forni *et al.*, 2003). The estimate of the European shock is used in a set of ordinary least-squares (OLS) regressions for each sector (step 3):

$$x_t^i = a^i(L)x_t + S_t^i$$

with $a^i(L)$ specified as a third-order moving average filter. In the fourth step the idiosyncratic component is derived as the residual of the OLS equation:

$$x_t^{ij} = a^{ij}(L)x_t + b^{ij}(L)x_t^i + I_t^{ij}$$

Estimates for the European component E_t^{ij} and the sectorial component S_t^{ij} are provided by the following relationships:

$$x_t^{ij} = a^{ij}(L)x_t + b^{ij}(L)(a^i(L)x_t + S_t^i) + I_t^{ij}$$
$$x_t^{ij} = E_t^{ij} + S_t^{ij} + I_t^{ij}$$

with

$$E_t^{ij} = a^{ij}(L)x_t + b^{ij}(L)\, a^i(L)x_t$$

$$S_t^{ij} = b^{ij}(L)S_t^i$$

Following this procedure it is possible to obtain an estimate for the three components of the factor model (14.2). Because of the method of construction, the components are mutually orthogonal; the variance of x_t^{ij} can then be decomposed into the sum of three variances. The next sections show the decomposition for each country and distinguish for some of them between long-run and short-run fluctuations by looking at the estimated spectral density matrix.

Analysis on the industrial production index[1]

The data

The estimation method used requires both a large number of variables and observations. Consistent estimation of the factor space can only be achieved when both n (the number of variables) and T (the number of observations) tend to infinity. Unfortunately, the system of official statistics in candidate countries is not as developed as in member states. Quarterly national accounts aggregates, which represent the most comprehensive source for the economic analysis, are only available from the second part of the 1990s.

The empirical analysis on the real activity is thus based on the monthly industrial production indices. The data spans the period 1993M1 to 2002M12 and are available for the three main industrial groupings: mining, manufacturing and electricity. The indices by industries were not found for Bulgaria and Malta, while for Latvia and Estonia the series start only from 1996: these countries are thus excluded from the analysis. Therefore, the data-set includes production indices for the 15 EU member states along with the remaining 9 candidate countries ($n = 72$ and $T = 120$).

Raw data are collected in order to avoid different treatments of the seasonal components by data producers. To this end, the whole set of raw indices have been adjusted by Tramo-Seats using the automatic model identification option.

The seasonal adjusted indices show the typical components of an economic time series: trend, cycle and irregular. The dynamic factor model considered holds only for stationary time series. Morever, only the cyclical fluctuations of the industrial production are of interest. To eliminate trend and high-frequency fluctuations a band-pass filter is applied to the series. The filter suggested by Baxter and King (1995) is used with periodicity from 6 to 32 quarters (the bilateral moving average filter is set to 6, so 12 months are lost in the sample analysed).

The results

Table 14.1 reports the percentage of variance explained by the three components for each sector/country. Moreover, average values are shown in boldface for each

Table 14.1 Industrial production index: variance explained by the European component, the sectorial component and the idiosyncratic component

Country	σ_E^2/σ_x^2				σ_S^2/σ_x^2				σ_I^2/σ_x^2				$\sigma_x^2 10^4$		
	Min	*Man*	*Ele*	**Ave**	*Min*	*Man*	*Ele*	**Ave**	*Min*	*Man*	*Ele*	**Ave**	*Min*	*Man*	*Ele*
Cyprus	0.16	0.30	0.21	**0.22**	0.26	0.13	0.07	**0.15**	0.58	0.57	0.72	**0.62**	0.67	0.09	0.22
Czech Rep.	0.14	0.46	0.32	**0.30**	0.25	0.05	0.45	**0.25**	0.62	0.49	0.23	**0.45**	0.36	0.21	0.65
Hungary	0.33	0.46	0.37	**0.39**	0.15	0.06	0.26	**0.16**	0.52	0.48	0.37	**0.46**	0.95	0.13	0.56
Lithuania	0.50	0.33	0.37	**0.40**	0.26	0.25	0.07	**0.19**	0.24	0.42	0.56	**0.41**	0.55	0.75	3.80
Poland	0.12	0.50	0.51	**0.38**	0.18	0.12	0.18	**0.16**	0.69	0.38	0.31	**0.46**	0.67	0.15	0.33
Romania	0.10	0.11	0.09	**0.10**	0.29	0.13	0.16	**0.20**	0.61	0.76	0.75	**0.71**	0.55	0.06	2.07
Slovenia	0.04	0.17	0.15	**0.12**	0.13	0.08	0.12	**0.11**	0.82	0.74	0.72	**0.76**	6.18	0.24	0.09
Slovak Rep.	0.32	0.53	0.26	**0.37**	0.15	0.15	0.15	**0.15**	0.53	0.32	0.59	**0.48**	0.72	0.16	0.66
Turkey	0.30	0.28	0.18	**0.26**	0.27	0.05	0.07	**0.13**	0.43	0.67	0.75	**0.61**	1.11	0.30	0.16
Belgium	0.36	0.54	0.16	**0.35**	0.24	0.08	0.18	**0.16**	0.40	0.38	0.67	**0.48**	3.05	0.06	0.37
Denmark	0.19	0.20	0.20	**0.17**	0.08	0.09	0.05	**0.07**	0.73	0.71	0.75	**0.76**	2.03	0.55	0.65
Germany	0.26	0.52	0.33	**0.37**	0.05	0.11	0.25	**0.13**	0.68	0.37	0.43	**0.49**	0.29	0.03	0.10
Greece	0.21	0.34	0.34	**0.29**	0.18	0.34	0.10	**0.21**	0.62	0.32	0.56	**0.50**	1.02	0.23	0.22
Spain	0.18	0.29	0.20	**0.22**	0.47	0.15	0.46	**0.36**	0.35	0.56	0.34	**0.42**	0.36	0.05	0.39
France	0.17	0.63	0.29	**0.36**	0.40	0.03	0.15	**0.19**	0.43	0.34	0.55	**0.44**	0.36	0.04	0.43
Ireland	0.10	0.31	0.27	**0.23**	0.10	0.09	0.09	**0.09**	0.80	0.60	0.65	**0.68**	8.51	0.62	0.23
Italy	0.36	0.30	0.36	**0.34**	0.15	0.04	0.23	**0.14**	0.49	0.65	0.41	**0.52**	0.61	0.03	0.22
Luxemb.	0.27	0.44	0.16	**0.29**	0.21	0.07	0.08	**0.12**	0.52	0.50	0.75	**0.59**	0.51	0.30	0.04
Netherl.	0.34	0.15	0.15	**0.21**	0.16	0.12	0.36	**0.21**	0.50	0.73	0.50	**0.58**	2.75	0.10	0.39
Austria	0.20	0.45	0.08	**0.24**	0.12	0.20	0.24	**0.18**	0.69	0.35	0.69	**0.57**	0.37	0.04	1.29
Portugal	0.11	0.25	0.12	**0.16**	0.18	0.20	0.07	**0.15**	0.72	0.55	0.81	**0.69**	0.57	0.01	1.77
Finland	0.06	0.19	0.19	**0.15**	0.21	0.08	0.13	**0.14**	0.73	0.73	0.68	**0.71**	15.67	0.24	0.75
Sweden	0.47	0.28	0.13	**0.29**	0.18	0.06	0.31	**0.18**	0.34	0.67	0.56	**0.52**	0.09	0.07	0.61

sector and country. The estimated standard deviations of the output growth x_t^{ij} are shown in the last three columns of the table.

The manufacturing sector is the most affected by the European shock on average. For the Slovak Republic, Poland, Hungary and the Czech Republic the European-wide component accounts for about 50 per cent of the total variance of the manufacturing sector. Lithuania is the country showing the highest average European commonality (40 %), Romania the lowest (10%); among the EU member states, France, Belgium and Germany present the highest percentages (63%, 54% and 52%, respectively).

The sectorial component is stronger for mining and electricity activities, with peaks for Spain and the Czech Republic. According to these estimates, much of the variance remains unexplained by the two factors; among the candidate countries, Romania and Slovenia present the highest level of idiosyncratic variance (71% and 76% on average).

To better appreciate the factor decomposition, it is useful to take a look at the spectral density matrix of each component. Figure 14.1 shows the estimated spectrum of the three factor components for the manufacturing sector of German, France, Belgium, Poland, the Czech Republic and Hungary. The dynamic profiles of German, France and Belgium are quite similar: the long-run fluctuations are mainly explained by the European component, while the variance of the idiosyncratic component is mostly concentrated at business cycle frequencies. The sectorial components are almost absent over the whole range of frequencies. Similar considerations can be applied for the candidate countries. Hungary appears to be the most influenced by the European shock. The spectral shape for the idiosyncratic components is very close to that seen for the EU member states.

The sectorial component assumes a significant role for the electricity sector. The spectra for the electricity sector in Spain and, to a lesser extent, in the Netherlands have a typical business cycle shape. A similar pattern can be noted for the sectorial component of the Czech Republic (see Marini, 2003, for more results).

It is now interesting to evaluate cohesion among the states. This measure has been proposed in Croux, Forni and Reichlin (1999). Given a $T \times n$ matrix $\mathbf{x} = (\mathbf{x}_1, \ldots, \mathbf{x}_n)$ and a $T \times m$ matrix $\mathbf{y} = (\mathbf{y}_1, \ldots, \mathbf{y}_m)$ with no common elements, the cross-cohesion between $\mathbf{x}$ and $\mathbf{y}$ is given by:

$$coh_{\mathbf{xy}}(\lambda) = \frac{\sum_{i=1}^{n} \sum_{j=1}^{m} w_{\mathbf{x}_i} w_{\mathbf{y}_j} \rho_{\mathbf{x}_i \mathbf{y}_j}(\lambda)}{\sum_{i=1}^{n} \sum_{j=1}^{m} w_{\mathbf{x}_i} w_{\mathbf{y}_j}} \qquad (14.3)$$

where $\rho_{\mathbf{x}_i \mathbf{y}_j}(\lambda)$ is the dynamic cross-correlation,[2] and $w_{\mathbf{x}_i}$ and $w_{\mathbf{y}_j}$ represent the weighting system. In this case, the weights are given by the 1999 production levels at constant prices. Figure 14.2 shows graphically the cross-cohesion for the three components. The European component shows the greatest cohesion level for the manufacturing sector, especially in the long run. The electricity sector and, to a lesser extent, the mining sector present the highest level of cohesion for the sectorial component, even if this is spread out over the whole range

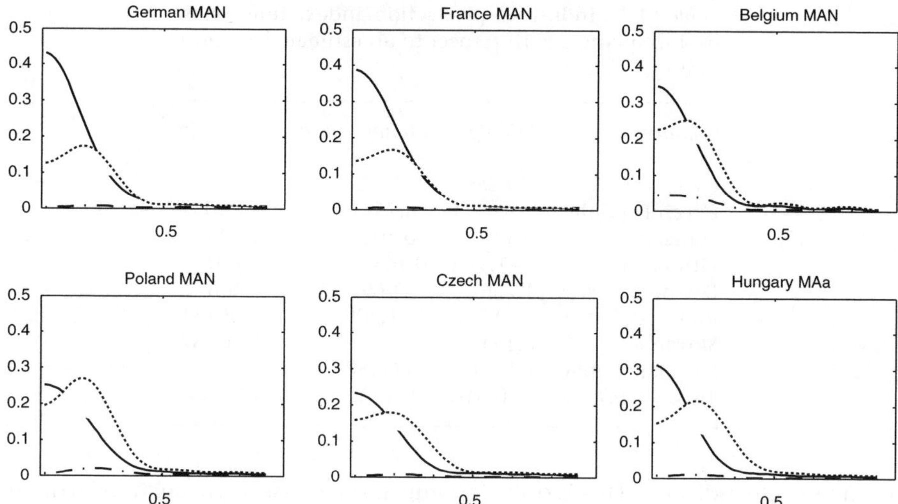

Figure 14.1 The spectral shape of some EU member states and candidate countries: manufacturing sector

European component: solid line; sectorial component: dot-dashed line; idiosyncratic component: dotted line.

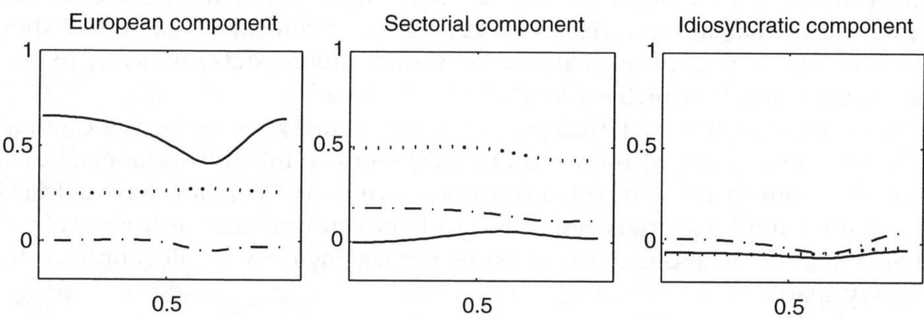

Figure 14.2 Cross-cohesion between candidate countries and member states for the three components

Manufacturing sector: solid line; electricity sector: dotted line; mining sector: dot-dashed line.

of frequencies. The idiosyncratic component, as expected, does not present any dynamic correlation in the three sectors.

Finally, the phase shifts between each candidate country and the EU considered as a whole have been computed. To this end, an aggregated EU business cycle is estimated. We derive this measure as the weighted average of the European components estimated for the EU member states. Then, the procedure described in Forni and Reichlin (2001) is applied. Firstly, I determine if the European component of the candidate countries is in phase or in phase opposition with respect to the EU

Table 14.2   Industrial production index: time phase lead in quarters with respect to an estimated EU business cycle index

Country	Mining	Manufacturing	Electricity
Cyprus	−0.259	*−3.727	2.513
Czech Republic	*−0.594	*0.754	*−2.631
Hungary	0.135	*0.102	2.493
Lithuania	*−1.929	0.163	3.140
Poland	1.756	*0.969	2.406
Romania	*−0.390	*−1.309	*−2.111
Slovenia	0.191	*−0.586	*−1.337
Slovak Republic	−1.001	*−0.158	0.405
Turkey	*−0.516	*0.572	−3.343

business cycle indicator. This is done looking at the phase angle delay at frequency zero: this can be 0 or π depending on whether long-run correlation is positive or negative. Then, the phase angle delay is computed at the frequency of $\theta^* = \pi/24$, corresponding to a period of four years for monthly series. Now, it is possible to see which sector/country is found to be coincident, lagging and leading with the EU business cycle in the last decade. Leading sectors are those with time phase lead larger than a quarter, lagging sectors as those which lag by more than the same delay and the remaining variables are considered as coincident. Table 14.2 shows the time lead expressed in quarters; the starred numbers also indicate, for each sector, the countries which are found to be in phase.

With the exception of Lithuania, the manufacturing sector for the candidate countries are in phase with the estimated EU index. While this sector can be considered as coincident in the other countries, Cyprus and Romania have a delay of 3.7 quarters and 1.3 quarters, respectively. All the countries that are leading of more than a quarter are also procyclical, while the lagging ones are all countercyclical (Turkey apart).

Analysis on the consumer price index

The data

The three-level dynamic factor model is now applied to the EU harmonized consumer prices index. Monthly time series from 1995M1 to 2003M12 have been collected for the 15 EU member states and nine acceding countries (Cyprus, Czech Republic, Estonia, Hungary, Lithuania, Latvia, Polonia , Slovenia, Slovak Republic). The series are available for 12 consumption functions, according to the COICOP (Classification of Individual Consumption by Purpose) classification.

Missing values are found in 1995 for Cyprus, Latvia and Polonia for some function; these are estimated using the general consumer price index. The general index is used to replace the Education function for Belgium, not present in the database. The data-set consists of 288 time series with 108 observations.

The harmonized index of consumption prices is used to measure inflation in the context of international, mostly inner-European, comparisons. The computation of this index is based on concepts, methods and procedures established at the EU level. The harmonized index often presents jumps in the series due to, for example, temporary price reductions. Such jumps might have a seasonal pattern in the series. To eliminate such seasonal peaks, the series have been adjusted for seasonal effects using Tramo-Seats. Again, the option of automatic ARIMA model identification has been used.

Stationarity of the series is obtained again by the application of the Baxter and King's filter. The periodicity has been fixed between 18 and 96 months.

The results

Table 14.3 shows the variance decomposition for each country for three consumption functions: f1-food and non-alchoolic beverages, f2-alcoholic beverages and tobacco, and f8-communication. The complete results of this exercise are reported in Marini (2004).

On average, the variance explained by the European component is high for f8-communication (44% of the total variance), f1-food and non alchoolic beverages (38%) and f5-furnishings, household equipment and maintenance (31%), low for f12-miscellaneous goods and services (17%) and f11-hotels, cafes and restaurants (18%). The sectorial component accounts for a larger portion of variance than the European component, except for f8-communication, f1-food and non alchoolic beverages and f5-furnishings, household equipment and maintenance. In particular, for f2-alcoholic beverages and tobacco and f9-Recreation and culture the sectorial component explains 38 per cent and 37 per cent of the total variance, respectively.

The highest percentages of variance are, however, explained by the idiosyncratic components. The peaks can be found for f6-health (55%), f12-miscellaneous goods and services (55%) and f11-hotels, cafes and restaurants (53%).

Three interesting consumption functions are now analysed in-depth: f1-food and non alchoolic beverages, f2-alcoholic beverages and tobacco, and f8-communication. Figures 14.3 and 14.4 show the spectral density for the three components of six countries (member states in the upper side, candidate countries in the lower side). The analysis for f1-food and non alchoolic beverages is performed for the UK, Italy, France, Slovenia, Cyprus and Poland. Figure 14.3 shows that the European component is much stronger than the sectorial component over the whole range of frequencies for the three member states; UK and France also present a common peak at high frequency. A similar shape can be found in the candidate countries, even if the local component is more important, especially for Cyprus and Poland. Slovenia shows a spectral decomposition of the components very close to that of Italy.

As far as f8-communication is concerned, the spectral shape (Figure 14.4) is displayed for the UK, Finland, Sweden, the Czech Republic, Estonia and Hungary. The European component is still the largest one for all countries. Again, the UK show the two-peak shape seen for function f1. The European component

Table 14.3 Consumer price index: variance and percentage explained by the three components for f1, f2, and f8 consumption functions

	f1				f2				f8			
	Eur	*Fun*	*Idio*	*Var*	*Eur*	*Fun*	*Idio*	*Var*	*Eur*	*Fun*	*Idio*	*Var*
Cyprus	0.38	0.07	0.54	0.18	0.07	0.12	0.81	3.91	0.30	0.26	0.45	0.84
Czech Republic	0.36	0.16	0.48	0.40	0.51	0.23	0.26	2.02	0.55	0.19	0.26	2.69
Estonia	0.23	0.61	0.16	0.69	0.39	0.34	0.27	3.38	0.56	0.22	0.21	1.95
Hungary	0.25	0.24	0.51	0.42	0.43	0.17	0.40	2.45	0.43	0.19	0.38	1.84
Latvia	0.21	0.26	0.53	0.29	0.18	0.30	0.52	0.94	0.10	0.08	0.82	0.46
Lithuania	0.16	0.51	0.33	0.91	0.28	0.37	0.35	3.19	0.14	0.17	0.69	4.41
Poland	0.37	0.03	0.60	0.35	0.46	0.22	0.33	1.61	0.51	0.10	0.40	3.89
Slovenia	0.52	0.23	0.24	0.44	0.29	0.37	0.33	1.30	0.48	0.04	0.48	0.99
Slovak Republic	0.16	0.17	0.67	0.83	0.18	0.08	0.75	0.83	0.24	0.16	0.59	1.46
Belgium	0.47	0.05	0.48	0.02	0.11	0.59	0.29	0.40	0.45	0.22	0.33	0.60
Denmark	0.52	0.21	0.27	0.03	0.31	0.07	0.62	0.16	0.21	0.28	0.51	0.34
Germany	0.22	0.17	0.60	0.02	0.15	0.76	0.09	0.38	0.53	0.05	0.41	0.29
Greece	0.47	0.19	0.34	0.06	0.14	0.31	0.56	0.09	0.53	0.09	0.38	1.74
Spain	0.59	0.12	0.29	0.02	0.19	0.40	0.41	0.40	0.50	0.35	0.15	1.34
France	0.69	0.10	0.21	0.03	0.24	0.50	0.26	0.43	0.58	0.35	0.08	0.26
Ireland	0.39	0.12	0.49	0.12	0.17	0.25	0.58	0.32	0.30	0.33	0.38	2.65
Italy	0.51	0.11	0.38	0.03	0.16	0.36	0.49	0.18	0.54	0.24	0.22	0.22
Luxembourg	0.55	0.18	0.26	0.04	0.04	0.64	0.31	0.20	0.39	0.29	0.32	1.17
Netherlands	0.14	0.17	0.68	0.07	0.18	0.52	0.29	0.43	0.45	0.29	0.26	0.29
Austria	0.40	0.08	0.52	0.03	0.25	0.39	0.35	0.30	0.42	0.33	0.25	0.53
Portugal	0.21	0.17	0.62	0.06	0.25	0.31	0.43	0.69	0.23	0.21	0.56	0.13
Finland	0.50	0.12	0.39	0.03	0.10	0.45	0.45	0.23	0.77	0.10	0.13	0.52
Sweden	0.10	0.20	0.70	0.08	0.44	0.23	0.34	0.67	0.52	0.25	0.23	0.27

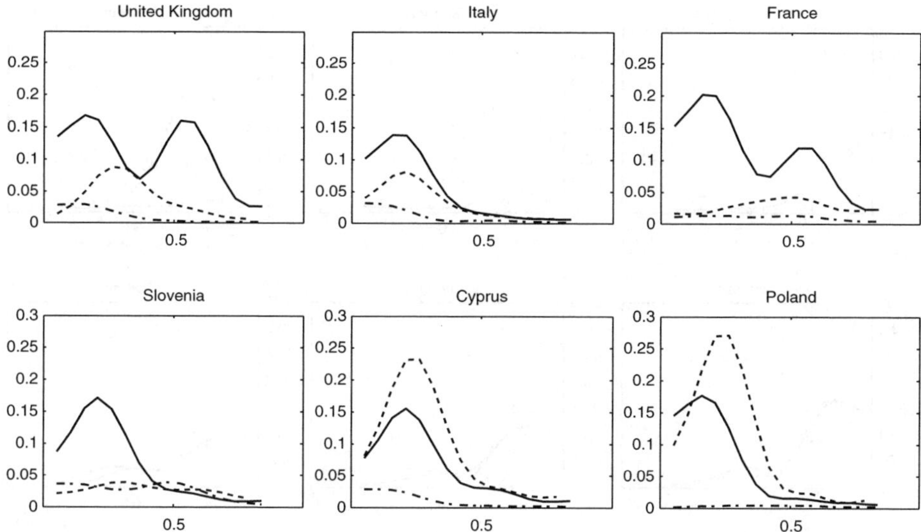

Figure 14.3 The spectral shape of some EU member states and acceding countries: food and non-alcoholic beverages

European component: solid line; sectorial component: dot-dashed line; idiosyncratic components: dotted line.

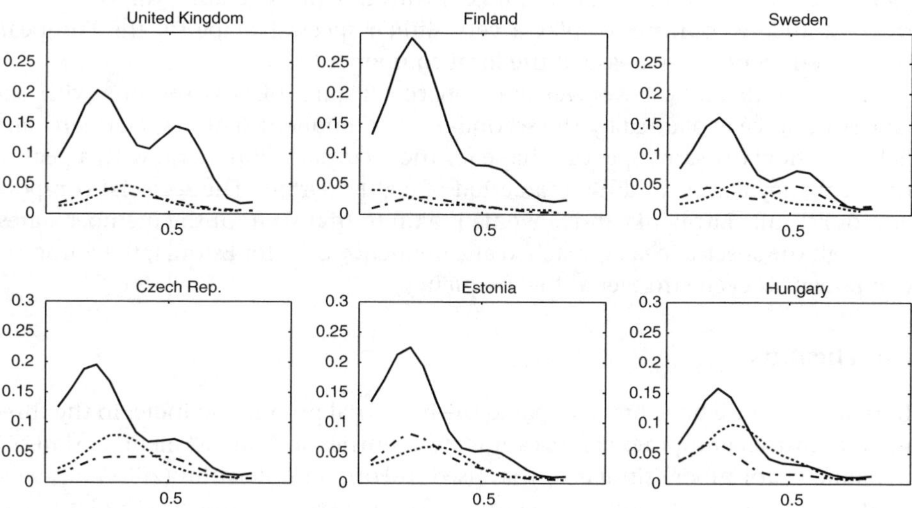

Figure 14.4 The spectral shape of some EU member states and acceding countries: communication

European component: solid line; sectorial component: dot-dashed line; idiosyncratic components: dotted line.

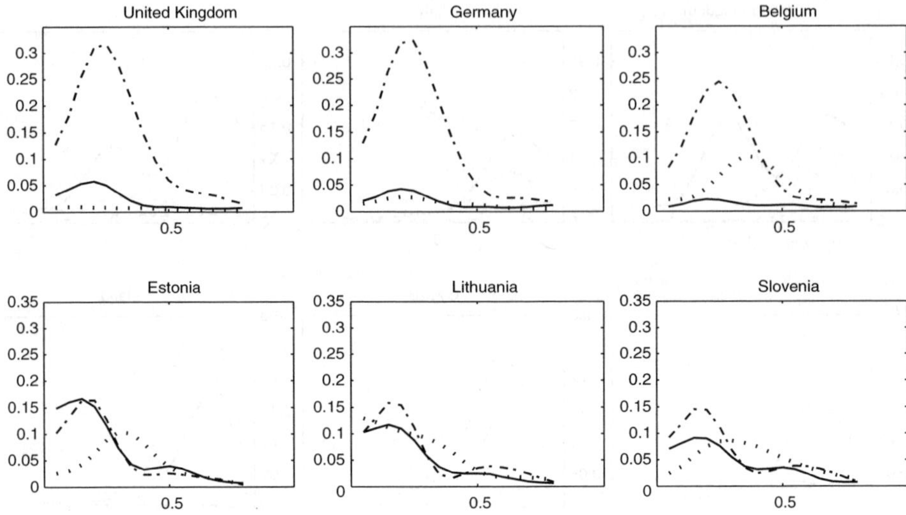

Figure 14.5   The spectral shape of some EU member states and acceding countries: alcoholic beverages and tobacco

European component: solid line; Sectorial component: dot-dashed line; idiosyncratic components: dotted line.

of Finland exhibits a peak around the business cycle frequencies. The sectorial component remains rather flat and mixed with the idiosyncratic component. The three candidate countries display a very similar spectral shape for the European component, with an increase of the local component.

Finally, f2-alcoholic beverages and tobacco (Figure 14.5) is the one with the largest variance explained by the second-level component. The UK, Germany and Belgium show the same spectral shape for the sectorial component, with a peak at the frequency corresponding to a period of eight quarters. The sectorial component for Estonia, Lithuania and Slovenia is akin to that seen for the member states, although the spectral peak is reached at a frequency of $\frac{\pi}{6}$ (for Estonia, the European component is even stronger at low frequency).

Conclusions

In this chapter we have first compared the industrial production index in the three main industrial groupings across candidate countries and the EU member states. A dynamic factor model similar to that used in Forni and Reichlin (2001) has been used to decompose the output growth rate for each sector/country into a European component, a sectorial component and an idiosyncratic component.

We find that, on average, the manufacturing sector is the most represented by the European shock. For the Slovak Republic, Poland, Hungary and the Czech Republic the European-wide component accounts for about 50 per cent of the total variance of manufacturing output growth. Lithuania is the country showing the highest average commonality (40%). The sectorial shocks explain lower variability. Some evidence is found only for the electricity sector which shows the highest level of cohesion across candidate countries and member states.

Finally, an analysis on the time phase lead of each candidate country is done with respect to a business cycle index for the EU. The manufacturing sector, which represents about 90 per cent of the total production in the candidate countries, are found to be coincident and in phase with the European index.

The same model has been applied to the consumer price index disaggregated for 12 consumption functions. Differently from the analysis on the real activity, the sectorial component is found to explain a large fraction of variance for both groups of countries.

Notes

1   This section is based on Marini (2003), a work presented at the Eurostat Colloquium on Modern Tools for Business Cycle Analysis, October 2003, Luxembourg.
2   The dynamic correlation between two real stochastic processes x and y is defined as the ratio between the co-spectrum $C_{xy}(\lambda)$ and the square root of the product of their spectral density functions $S_x(\lambda)$ and $S_y(\lambda)$.

References

Baxter, M. and King, R.G. (1995) 'Measuring business cycles. Approximate band-pass filters for economic time series', Working Paper Series no. 5022. New York: National Bureau of Economic Research.

Croux, C , Forni, M. and Reichlin, L. (1999) 'A measure of comovements for economic variables: theory and empirics', Discussion Paper no. 2339. London: Centre for Economic Policy Research (CEPR).

De la Fuente, A. (2002) 'Convergence across countries and regions: theory and empirics', Discussion Paper no. 2465. London: CEPR.

Forni, M. and Reichlin, L. (2001) 'Federal policies and local economies: Europe and the US', *European Economic Review*, 45: 109–34.

Forni, M., Hallin, M., Lippi, M. and Reichlin, L. (2000a) 'The generalised dynamic factor model: identification and estimation', *Review of Economics and Statistics*, 82: 540–54.

Forni, M., Hallin, M., Lippi, M. and Reichlin, L. (2000b) 'Reference cycles: the NBER methodology revisited', Discussion Paper no. 2400. London: CEPR.

Forni, M., Hallin, M., Lippi, M. and Reichlin, L. (2005) 'The generalized dynamic factor model: one-sided estimation and forecasting', *Journal of the American Statistical Association* 100: 830–40.

Geweke, J. (1977) *The Dynamic Factor Analysis of Economic Time Series*. Amsterdam: North-Holland.

Marini, M. (2003) 'Convergence of candidate countries to European Union: an analysis on industrial production index using dynamic factor model', Working Paper and Studies 2004. Luxembourg: Eurostat.

Marini, M. (2004) *'Dynamic factor models for the analysis of large panels of time series: theory, estimation and applications to macroeconomic analysis'*, PHD thesis. Rome: University of Rome 'RomeTre' .

Martin, C. and Sanz, I. (2001) 'Real convergence and European integration: the experience of the less developed EU members', Interim Report of the project *'Catching up and EU Accession – Prospects for First and Second Wave Countries*.
Sargent, T. and Sims, C. (1977) 'Business cycle modeling without pretending to have too much a priori economic theory'. Minneapolis: Federal Reserve Bank of Minneapolis.

15
European Business Cycle Affiliations with the USA

*Pedro J. Perez, Denise R. Osborn and Marianne Sensier**

Introduction

In this chapter we study the changing nature of affiliations for major Euro-area countries (Germany, France, Italy and Spain) with the USA. The analysis is based on correlations for Hodrick–Prescott (HP) filtered real GDP, with lead–lag relations considered in addition to contemporaneous correlations. Our results, computed both over sub-samples and using rolling correlations, show that the business cycle in the USA has retained a leading role for that in European countries throughout the period from 1960, with this role being especially strong since 1993. Our analysis corrects the fallacy that the European business cycle became disjoint from the USA during the 1990s. The view of disjoint business cycles is attributed to the occurrence of abnormal observations in 1991–92, possibly associated with a temporary disruption of USA–Europe relationships consequent on German reunification.

In the period of increasing economic integration for the countries of Europe, especially since the commencement of the European Monetary System (EMS) in 1979, a number of authors have noted a generally increasing correlation between European countries, alongside a reduced correlation of these countries with the USA. For example, Artis and Zhang (1997, 1999) document increased integration with Germany since 1979 for the member countries of the European

* This research was partially supported through a European Community Marie Curie Fellowship (programme 'Improving Human Research Potential and the Socio-Economic Knowledge Base' IHP-MCFI-99-1), under which the first author visited the University of Manchester. The second and third authors gratefully acknowledge financial assistance from the Economic and Social Research Council (UK) under grant number L138251030. This research does not necessarily reflect the views of the funding bodies. The authors also gratefully acknowledge the contribution to this research of stimulating discussions with Mike Artis.

Exchange Rate Mechanism (ERM) and lower correlation with the USA. Some authors find this reduced correlation with the USA to be particularly evident during the 1990s, leading to the view that the business cycle in the countries of mainland Europe has become 'disjoint' from the USA. In this context, the almost simultaneous occurrence of recessions in the USA and major European economies in 2000 was considered to be a surprise (IMF, 2001; OECD, 2002; Doyle and Faust, 2002).

In contrast to the view of diverging business cycle movements just outlined, in this chapter we argue that the appearance of Europe being 'disjoint' from the USA is due to a relatively small number of abnormal observations, with these observations reflecting the temporary disruption of relationships following German reunification. Further, we believe that the literature to date has placed undue importance on contemporary correlations. When lead/lag relations are allowed, the role of the US business cycle in leading Europe does not disappear during the 1980s/1990s. Indeed, this relationship is especially strong in the period since 1993, so that the apparent transmission of the USA recession of 2000 to European countries is not a surprise.

In this chapter we examine the business cycle relationships between each of Germany, France, Italy and Spain and the USA. We consider these countries since they are the principal countries of the Euro-area, and hence may be expected to play an important role in the future evolution of the business cycle in Europe. The UK is frequently seen to have distinctive relationships compared with other large European countries, which is also evidenced by its not being a member of the Euro-area. Consequently, we do not include the UK in our analysis. However, Perez, Osborn and Sensier (2003) present a more detailed analysis than that included here, with that analysis including more countries and also comparing relationships of individual countries with the USA to those with Germany.

In the next section we discuss the data used in this study, including the sub-periods analysed, followed by the substantive results, and a concluding section.

Data

As just noted, we analyse France (FRA), Germany (DEU), Italy (ITA) and Spain (ESP) in relation to the USA. With the exception of Spain, we employ real GDP data over the period 1960Q1 to 2002Q1 or 2001Q4. The sample period for Spain commences in 1970Q1. All series are seasonally adjusted. Full details of all data, including sources, can be found in Perez *et al.* (2003).

As already mentioned, our analysis is based on correlations of HP detrended data.[1] Following Artis and Zhang (1997, 1999) and Inklaar and de Haan (2001), we use the end of 1979 to define sub-periods for analysis, with this date chosen because the commencement of the EMS 1979 is a defining period in European integration. Although the post-1980 period is sometimes considered to be homogeneous, in fact a number of important events in European integration occur during this period. Therefore, we separate 1980Q1–1990Q4 and 1991Q1–2002Q1. The 1990 date is

Table 15.1   Correlation of HP filtered GDP with respect to USA

		Whole sample	*1960–79*	*1980–90*	*1991–2002*	*1993–2002*
DEU	Contem. corr.	0.33	0.36	0.47	−0.05	0.57
	Maximum corr.	0.41	0.44	0.48	0.16	0.71
	Lead/lag	1	1	1	5	2
FRA	Contem. corr.	0.34	0.51	0.09	0.20	0.62
	Maximum corr.	0.37	0.52	0.19	0.33	0.85
	Lead/lag	1	1	5	2	2
ITA	Contem. corr.	0.27	0.23	0.51	−0.02	0.31
	Maximum corr.	0.42	0.43	0.62	0.41	0.50
	Lead/lag	3	4	2	5	2
ESP	Contem. corr.	0.28	0.47	0.19	0.02	0.64
	Maximum corr.	0.39	0.66	0.31	0.39	0.75
	Lead/lag	2	2	-3	5	2

Note: For each variable the first row contains the contemporary correlation; the second row the maximum (positive) correlation for a window of five leads and five lags. The number in the third row shows, for the maximum correlation, the lead (lag) of USA if the value is positive (negative).

selected due to the decision in December 1990 to introduce a single currency for the European Union and the reunification of Germany that took place in October 1990. However, the period 1991–92 was one of considerable uncertainty in Europe, due to the effects of German reunification and the Exchange Rate mechanism (ERM) crisis of 1992. To avoid potential temporary instabilities associated with these events, we also examine separately the sub-period 1993–2002.

Business cycle affiliations

Table 15.1 shows the correlations of HP detrended GDP for the USA with each of the four major Euro countries considered. Correlations are presented for the whole data period and for each sub-period 1960–79, 1980–90, 1991–2002 and 1993–2002. In addition to the conventional contemporaneous correlation, we also show the maximum correlation calculated over leads and lags of one to five quarters, together with the corresponding lead time[2]. Since we wish to examine leadership for business cycle movements, this maximum correlation is sought over positive correlation values and not over the strength of the correlation measured by the absolute value. A lead of, say, 2 implies that the maximum positive correlation occurs with the USA leading that country by two quarters.

From even a superficial examination of Table 15.1, it is clear that business cycle movements in the USA have consistently led those of the European countries considered. In terms of the overall period since 1960, the lead time has been one quarter for the largest countries, namely Germany and France. Although the lead time for the maximum correlation with Italy and Spain is a little longer (at three and two quarters, respectively), nevertheless the general pattern is of business cycle movements in these European countries following those of the USA with a relatively short lag. The maximum correlation for all countries with the USA is similar, at around 0.4.

Consider, now, the relationship between Germany and the USA over time. Positive contemporaneous correlations of 0.36 and 0.47 for 1960–80 and 1980–90, respectively, are evident. Further, it appears that the US growth led that in Germany by a quarter throughout these decades, with the maximum correlation being relatively constant at 0.44–0.48. However, the correlation of −0.05 for 1991–2002 suggests that the growth relationship between these countries was severed completely and abruptly in the 1990s. This impression is apparently confirmed by the maximum correlation, which declines to 0.16 for this sub-period. Further, the lead time for the USA extends to five quarters, so that even this relatively modest US influence appears slow to take effect.

However, the elimination of the two years 1991 and 1992 has a dramatic effect on the US/German correlations. Indeed, for the 1993–2002 period, both the contemporaneous and maximum correlations increase to their highest values over the sub-periods considered, namely to 0.57 and 0.71 respectively, with the US business cycle again leading Germany by a relatively short interval, namely two quarters. This does not accord with the severance of the business cycle relationship.

Turning to other countries, the sub-period patterns for France and Spain in Table 15.1 are similar. Both countries show strong positive correlations of their business cycles with the USA to 1980, whether the contemporaneous or maximum correlations are considered. At least in terms of the contemporaneous values, however, this relationship is largely absent when the decades of the 1980s or 1990s are considered. Nevertheless, the maximum correlation implies that the USA led both countries during the 1990s, with moderate correlations of 0.33 and 0.39. As with Germany, when the period from 1993 is considered, a historically strong leading role is once again evident for the USA in relation to the business cycles of these countries.

The maximum correlation with the USA is relatively constant over time for Italy. This constancy is, indeed, in contrast to the contemporaneous correlation, which changes markedly, depending on the specific sub-period analysed.

The more detailed results in Perez *et al.* (2003) confirm that, qualitatively, the pattern of results shown here in Table 15.1 for the major countries extends also to the smaller countries of the European Union. In particular, the exclusion of the two years 1991 and 1992 has a substantial effect on the correlations with the USA, with the results implying that the US business cycle plays a strong role for that of European countries in the period from 1993. There, we also examine correlations of business cycle movements in these countries with Germany. In this case the exclusion of 1991–1992 has little substantive impact, implying that the abnormal effect of these years can be associated with events in Germany.

In order to further consider the evolution of the correlations over time, Figure 15.1 shows the rolling contemporary correlations for detrended GDP of the USA with each of Germany, France, Spain and Italy. These rolling correlations are calculated using a window of 40 observations (10 years), with the value shown being centred at the mid-point of the window. For convenience, our discussion

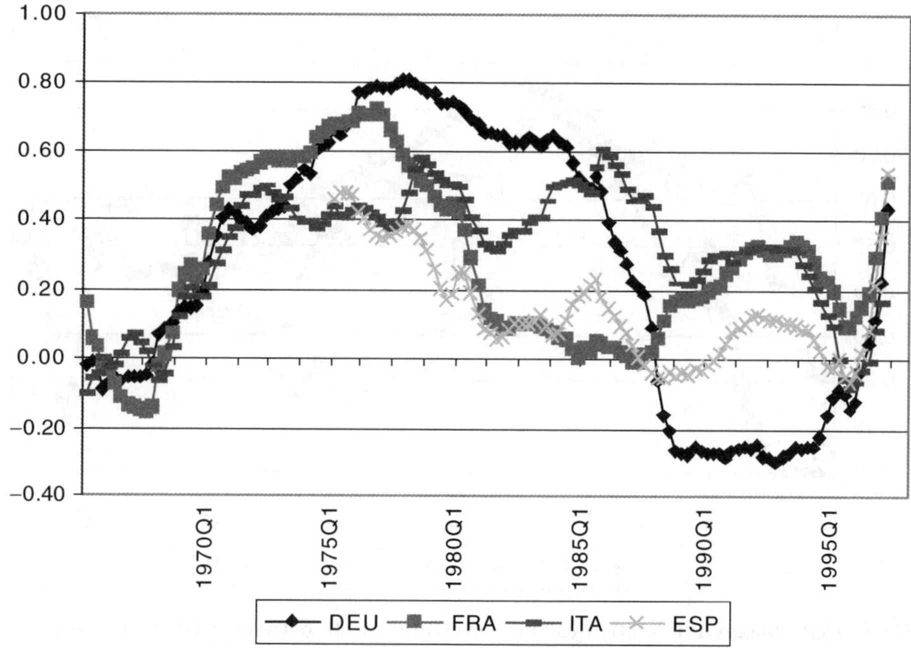

Figure 15.1 Contemporary rolling correlation of HP detrended GDP with respect to the USA
Note: Rolling correlations are calculated for a temporal window of 10 years.

often refers to this mid-point as the date to which the correlation relates. Figure 15.2 shows corresponding information for the maximum correlation with the USA.

These figures reinforce the comments made above about the business cycle relationships between these countries and the USA. In each case, the rolling contemporaneous correlation (Figure 15.1) peaks around 1980 and then declines. The changing pattern for Germany after this date is the most dramatic, with the decline in the correlation being particularly marked from around 1985 and the correlation is negative for around ten years from the late 1980s. However, this is precisely the period when the relevant rolling window includes he observations of 1991 and 1992. A historically more typical business cycle correlation is restored at the end of the period considered, when these observations effectively drop out of the window used for calculation of the correlations.

The patterns in Figure 15.2 for the maximum correlations are broadly similar to those of the contemporaneous correlations. Nevertheless, it is also evident from Figure 15.2 that the typical maximum business cycle correlation for each country with the USA during the 1990s is in the interval 0.4 to 0.6. The correlations fall below this band for only a relatively small number of quarters, generally centred on 1996. However, these values are reflected in the sub-period maximum correlations in Table 15.1 for the period 1991–2002, with that for Germany being especially small at this point.

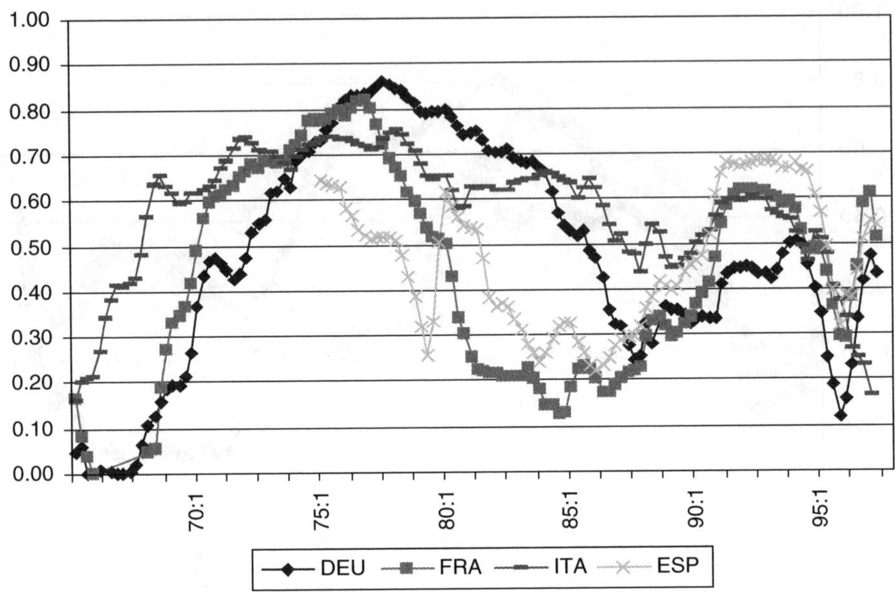

Figure 15.2   Maximum positive rolling correlation of HP detrended GDP with respect to the USA

Note: Rolling correlations are calculated for a temporal window of 10 years. Maximum correlation is computed over a range of five leads and five lags.

Concluding remarks

Based on the analysis of this chapter, we argue that the business cycle in major Euro-area European countries did not become 'disjoint' from that of the USA during the 1990s. Consequently, we believe that the conclusion of IMF (2001), Doyle and Faust (2002) and others to this effect is mistaken. Indeed, the striking effect of excluding the years 1991 and 1992 from calculations for the 1990s implies that it is these observations that are abnormal. It is plausible that these abnormal relationships with the USA may be due to the economic problems experienced by Germany in the wake of reunification, with some of these effects transmitted to closely allied European countries.

In general, the business cycle of the USA is shown to consistently lead that of the major Euro countries by one or two quarters over the period from 1960. In this context, the apparent transmission of the US recession of 2001 to these countries is not surprising. Our more detailed results in Perez *et al.* (2003) discuss this further, where we also show that our principal findings are robust to different measures of the business cycle. The mechanisms for the international transmission (and non-transmission) of business cycle movements remains an important research topic, and we suggest that the potential role of interest rate linkages in this context is worthy of further examination (see Perez *et al.*, 2003).

Notes

1   We use $\lambda = 1,600$ in the HP filter, which is the conventional value for quarterly data. The filter is applied to the series after taking logarithms.
2   That is, for each t, we compute the correlation of the business cycle with that of the USA for quarters $t-5, \ldots, t, \ldots, t+5$. Among these 11 correlations, the one with the maximum positive value is shown.

References

Artis, M.J. and Zhang, W. (1997) 'International business cycles and the ERM: is there a European business cycle?', *International Journal of Finance and Economics*, 2: 1–16.

Artis, M.J. and Zhang, W. (1999) 'Further evidence on the international business cycle and the ERM: is there a European business cycle?', *Oxford Economic Papers*, 51: 120–32.

Doyle, B.M. and Faust, J. (2002) 'An investigation of co-movements among growth rates of the G-7 countries', *Federal Reserve Bulletin*, 88: 427–37.

Hodrick, R.J. and Prescott, E.C. (1997) 'Postwar US business cycles: an empirical investigation', *Journal of Money, Credit and Banking*, 29: 1–16.

Inklaar, R. and de Haan, J. (2001), 'Is there really a European business cycle?: a comment', *Oxford Economic Papers*, 53: 215–20.

International Monetary Fund (2001) 'International linkages: three perspectives', *World Economic Outlook*: 65–104.

Organisation for Economic Cooperation and Development (2002) *OECD Economic Outlook*. Paris: OECD; pp. 141–57.

Perez, P., Osborn, D.R. and Sensier, M. (2003) 'Business cycle affiliations in the context of European integration', Discussion Paper no. 29. Manchester: Centre for Growth and Business Cycle Research, University of Manchester.

16
VAR Modelling of the Euro-Area GDP on the Basis of Principal Component Analysis

*Nikolaos Sdrakas**

Introduction and background

This study outlines how the Principal Component technique can be useful in the short-run economic analysis and forecasting of Euro-area GDP growth. With reference to a previous work, we examined a restricted vector autoregressive (VAR) model based on selected components from industry and consumer confidence indicators of Business and Consumer surveys (BCS) to forecast the quarterly year-on-year growth of GDP in the Euro-area. One of the main conclusions was that this restricted VAR model outperforms a single autoregressive model in short-term forecasting, since we excluded all noise variables which do not help to explain GDP growth.

The derived forecasts of these new models are compared with those of the old VAR. The predictive performance of VAR and autoregressive models has been improved by including the first principal component based in all questions from the four main domains (Industry, Consumption, Construction, and Retail Trade).

With reference to previous work we assessed univariate autoregressive models in short-run economic analysis and forecasting by using traditional tools with different data (quarterly national accounts, business surveys). In particular, we have shown that autoregressive single equations models can perform reasonably well in terms of forecasting ability when compared with more complicated econometric models, such as the BUSYIII model developed by DG ECFIN (see progress report

* The findings and conclusions expressed in this chapter are those of the author and they do not necessary represent the views of the European Commission. The author thanks Cedric Viguie for assistance in the elaborations presented in the chapter.

presented on Workshop on BCS, Brussels, November 2002). Moreover, the inclusion of the Economic Sentiment Indicator (ESI) in this baseline model clearly improved the results, showing that people's opinions (expectations) derived from the business and consumer surveys could lead by 1 quarter the quantitative data (GDP growth).

In a latter stage, our objective was the specification of more complicated models, like Vector Autoregressive Models (VAR). We examined a vector autoregressive (VAR) model based on the BCS results to forecast the quarterly year-on-year growth of GDP in the Euro-area for two quarter ahead. In particular, the four main components[1] of the ESI were initially considered. The results from the Granger causality test led us to reduce the VAR model to four variables; a Retail Trade Confidence Indicator was excluded. According to the results of the Diebold Mariano test, we showed that the restricted VAR did not outperform a single equation model in the short run. Even thought the results from the shock analysis were interesting in understanding the structural shocks hitting the European economy, some improvements had to be made.

In a more recent work, we focused on a VAR approach based on a deeper approach. The specific components of the industry and consumer confidence indicators were considered.[2] The two components of the construction confidence indicator have been excluded, due to non-stationarity and high volatility. The derived forecasts of the new restricted VAR model are compared with those of the single autoregressive model. The predictive value of VAR models has been improved by excluding all the noise variables (balances of opinions) whose past values cannot explain GDP growth. In particular, we selected specific components of the industrial and consumer confidence indicator which might be leading indicators for GDP growth. Order books, production expectations, financial situation over the next 12 months, unemployment over the next months and savings over the next months, are the five variables introduced. Moreover, we showed that this restricted VAR model outperformed a single autoregressive model in short-term forecasting.

In this chapter we focus on VAR and autoregressive estimations based on the principal component analysis, which will remove the noise factor from the various shocks among variables (that is, extracting only the common trend). The derived forecasts of these new models are compared with those of the old VAR.

Data analysis

The real GDP series for the Euro-area was taken from the quarterly national accounts in a non-seasonally adjusted form and was transformed into quarterly year-on-year growth (GDPg hereafter). The series is available from 1991Q1 to 2002Q4. The balances of opinions from the monthly business and consumer surveys concerning Euro-area countries were used. In particular, all the questions (272) from the four main domains (Industry, Consumption, Construction and Retail Trade) were considered[3]. Before introducing the balances of opinion within the models, we had to transfer these monthly data into quarterly data, that is taking the three-month average.

Principal component analysis

In order to reduce the dimensionality of the data-set and to remove all the idiosyncratic shocks in each variable, the technique of principal component analysis was used. Principal component analysis (PCA) involves a mathematical procedure that transforms a number of (possibly) correlated variables into a (smaller) number of uncorrelated variables called *principal components*. The first principal component accounts for as much of the variability in the data as possible, and each succeeding component accounts for as much of the remaining variability as possible.

According to our empirical results derived from SAS software programme, the first principal component (PC) explained more than 30 per cent of the total variance.

Unit roots

With a constant term, two tests–Augmented Dickey–Fuller and Philips–Perron– rejected the null hypothesis of a unit root in the GDPg. The first principal component had to be converted into quarterly year-on-year differences (d) in order to become stationary.

Cross-correlation

Cross-correlation analysis was used in order to test whether the quarterly year-on-year differences of the first principal component (x) can be considered as a leading indicator of GDPg (y). There is evidence to suggest that x appears to be a leading indicator for y at the first lag (see Table 16.1).

Model analysis

AR model selection and estimation

A first step was to estimate a model for y by using its own past values as predictors. We started the estimation process with nine lags as explanatory variables, reducing step-wise the number of lags. Finally, a model with five lags was chosen. Excluding

Table 16.1   Cross correlations of GDPg(y) and PCd(x)

i	$y, x(-i)$	$y, x(+i)$
	lag	lead
1	0.70	0.70
2	0.67	0.47
3	0.64	0.17
4	0.45	−0.19
5	0.22	−0.47

Table 16.2   AR estimates: sample (adjusted)1993:2–2002:4

Equations/variables	y
y(−1)	0.47
	(0.14)
	[3.5]
y(−4)	−0.32
	(0.13)
	[−2.55]
y(−5)	0.43
	(0.14)
	[3.13]
x(−1)	0.08
	(0.02)
	[3.46]
c	0.74
	(0.22)
	[3.31]
Adj. R^2	0.77

Note: Standard errors are in ( ) and t statistics in [ ].

the non-significant lags in this model (that is, lags 2 and 3) resulted in the new fitted model.

Since the baseline model is a function of the past values of GDP growth, quarterly y-o-y differences of the first Principal Component (x) were included. Since x is a leading indicator of y we estimated a model for y, consisting of its own past values at lags 1, 4 and 5, and x at the first lag. OLS regression was used as estimation method. The estimated sample period is 1993Q2–2002Q4 (see Table 16.2).

VAR model selection and estimation

A standard VAR with two variables is presented below:

$$Y_t = c + \sum_{i=1}^{p} \Theta Y_{t-i} + \varepsilon_t$$

where c is a constant and $Y_t = (y_t, x_t)'$.

The sample period begins in 1992Q1 and finishes in 2002Q4. As Y_t is stationary, Zellner's theorem allows as to estimate the system with ordinary least-squares (OLS) equation by equation. According to the Schwarz Information Criterion based on the likelihood ratio, the optimal lag number is 3. However, for reasons of parsimony a second model was estimated excluding also the 2nd and 3rd lag (see Table 16.3).

AR roots

The following test (Table 16.4) reports the inverse roots of the characteristic AR polynomial; see Lutkepohl (1991). The estimated VAR is stable (stationary) if all

Table 16.3 VAR estimates: sample (adjusted) 1992Q2–2002Q4

Equations/ variables	x	y
$x(-1)$	1.06	0.07
	(0.09)	(0.01)
	[11.1]	[3.95]
$y(-1)$	−1.82	0.41
	(0.66)	(0.12)
	[−2.74]	[3.42]
c	3.35	0.99
	(1.36)	(0.25)
	[2.47]	[3.95]
Adj. R^2	0.81	0.69

Table 16.4 VAR stability conditions check

Roots of characteristic polynomial	
Endogenous variables:	x, y
Exogenous variables:	c
Lag specification:	1
Root	Modulus
$0.749861 - 0.169375i$	0.768752
$0.749861 + 0.169375i$	0.768752

roots have modulus less than one and lie outside the unit circle. The table shows that the restricted VAR satisfies the stability condition, since no root lies outside the unit circle.

Forecasting

With the new VAR model, dynamic short-term forecasts of GDP growth were calculated (1 quarter following the release of the quarterly national accounts). In order to forecast the quarterly year-on-year GDP growth one quarter ahead from the last release of national accounts–the current quarter (t)–we used the new VAR based on the first principal component. This form allows us to take into account the information available at an early stage from the business surveys. For instance, at the moment the study was conducted, the business surveys are available up to 2003Q1, whereas the national accounts are estimated up to 2002Q4.

Concerning the forecast of GDP growth for the next quarter ($t + 1$)–one quarter ahead from the last release of the national accounts–the simulation is based on the new form of the VAR. According to the results, the GDP growth would continue to rise in 2003Q1 by 0.82 per cent. This compares with a forecast of 1.06 per cent derived from the new VAR.

Table 16.5   Statistics of the models

		RMSE		RRMSFE	RRMSFE
Simulation period	old VAR	AR	new VAR	new VAR *vs* AR	new VAR *vs* old AR
2000Q1–2000Q2	1.32	0.84	1.42	1.69 (6.28) [0.10]	1.08 (0.80) [0.71]
2000Q2–2000Q3	0.40	0.72	0.24	0.48 (−1.03) [0.49]	0.87 (−0.60) [0.61]
2000Q3–2000Q4	0.13	0.97	0.91	0.94 (−0.54) [0.68]	7.02 (2.58) [0.24]
2000Q4–2001Q1	1.53	0.32	0.35	1.09 (8.56) [0.07]	0.23 (−1.01) [0.50]
2001Q1–2001Q2	1.21	0.49	0.37	0.76 (−1.24) [0.43]	0.31 (−4.14) [0.15]
2001Q2–2001Q3	0.78	0.89	0.10	0.12 (−9.32) [0.07]	0.13 (−11.35) [0.06]
2001Q3–2001Q4	1.08	0.69	0.27	0.39 (−1.02) [0.49]	0.25 (−1.13) [0.46]
2001Q4–2002Q1	1.36	0.72	0.52	0.73 (−1.67) [0.34]	0.39 (−1.02) [0.49]
2002Q1–2002Q2	0.85	0.25	0.55	2.16 (1.20) [0.44]	0.65 (−1.20) [0.44]
2002Q2–2002Q3	0.41	0.40	0.56	1.42 (3.37) [0.18]	1.38 (1.13) [0.46]
2002Q3–2002Q4		0.32	0.25	0.79 (−0.76) [0.59]	
Average RMSE			0.52		

Note: Diebold–Mariano t statistics are provided in parentheses. *P*-values are provided in brackets, given that the critical level is 5%. One star indicates that the RRMSFE is not significantly different from 1 at the 1% level.

In order to make an ex post forecast evaluation with two quarters ahead, the two models (VAR versus autoregressive) were re-estimated. The simulation started in 2000Q1by adding one observation each time and keeping the same forecasting horizon. Thus, we came up with 11 dynamic simulations, the last one ending in 2002Q4. Table 16.5 shows the root-mean-squared-errors (RMSE) of the two models as well as those of the old VAR model based on selected components from industry and consumer confidence indicators.

One way to compare the three alternative forecasts is to calculate a relative root-mean-squared forecasting error (RRMSFE), which is the ratio between the root-mean-squared forecasting error of the restricted VAR(1) model and the root-mean-squared forecasting error of the simple autoregressive model. A RRMSFE lower than 1 implies that the out-of-sample performance of the new VAR is better than the performance of the old VAR model and that of the autoregressive model. We then use the Diebold–Mariano test[4] to see whether the RRMSFE is significantly different from 1.

The outcome of the Diebold–Mariano test indicates that in all RRMSFE is significantly different from 1 (see Table 16.5). As we can Table 16.5). As we can see, the new VAR model outperforms both a single equation model and the old VAR in the short run.

Conclusion and future perspectives

This note has outlined how the Principal Component technique can be useful in the short-run economic analysis and forecasting of Euro-area GDP growth. With reference to previous work, the predictive performance of VAR and autoregressive models has been improved by including the first principal component based in all questions from the four main domains (Industry, Consumption, Construction and Retail Trade). Moreover, we showed that the new VAR model outperforms a single autoregressive model in short-term forecasting.

Even if the first principal component removes all the noise factors from the various shocks among the variables to the other components, some improvements have to be made. A distinction between leading, lagging and coincident variables with respect to Euro-area GDP growth is necessary in order to enhance the forecasting performance of our models. Firstly, a combination of a common factor analysis, which will include only the leading variables and VAR models, should be considered in future work. Secondly, concerning all the lagging variables, a phase shift procedure should be performed in combination with the PCA, before we introduce the first principal component within an autoregressive model.

Notes

1   The Industrial (BCSINDU), the Retail Trade (BCSRETA), the Construction (BCSBUIL) and the Consumer Confidence Indicator (BCSCONS) are the four variables introduced.
2   The three components of the Industrial (indu) and the four of the Consumer (cons) Confidence Indicator are based on the balances of opinion in the EU harmonized questionnaire: order books (indu2), stocks (indu4), production expectations (indu5), financial situation over the next 12 months (cons2), general economic situation over the next 12 months (cons4), unemployment over the next months (cons7) and savings over the next months (cons11) are the seven variables introduced.
3   http://europa.eu.int/comm/economy_finance/indicators/businessandconsumersurveys_en.htm
4   The aim of this test is to see whether or not it is possible to discriminate between two forecasting models. Let e_{1t} and e_{2t} denote alternative forecast errors and $d_t = (e_{1t})^2 - (e_{2t})^2$. The Diebold–Mariano test for equal RMSEs is simply formed as a t-statistic on a constant α in the regression $d_t = \alpha + \varepsilon_t$. In general, the closer the RRMSFE is to 1, the more likely the Diebold–Mariano test accepts the hypothesis of same forecast performance. However, this link is not so direct due to a correction of the variance, which is implemented in the Diebold–Mariano test (see Clark, 1999).

References

Marcellino, M., Banerjee, A. and Masten, I. (2003) 'What leading indicators for Euro area inflation and GDP growth?', Working Paper no. 01/2003. Florence: European University Institute.

Linden, S. (2002) 'Assessment of GDP forecast uncertainty', Economic Paper no. 11/02. Bruxelles: European Commission.

De Cabo, G. and Simo, I. (2002) 'A leading consumer confidence indicator for the Euro area', Centro de Estudios Economicos Tomillo, S.L., 11/02.

Grasmann, P. and Keereman, F. (2001) 'An indicator-based short-term forecast for quarterly GDP in the euro area', Economic Paper no. 154. Bruxelles: European Commission.

Zimmermann, K.F. (1996) 'Analysis of business surveys', Working Paper no. 96-17. Munich: Department of Economics.

Part IV

Composite Indicators and Forecasting of Economic Activity

17
A Time-Series Disaggregated Model to Forecast GDP in the Eurozone

Roman Minguez and Antoni Espasa

Introduction

The aim of this chapter is to present a simple approach to forecasting GDP in the Eurozone. In our study, GDP is broken down into two alternative vectors, and the exogenous variables used are GDP lags and the confidence indicators published by the European Commission. A forecasting evaluation over the last 12 observations shows that in forecasting the year-on-year rate of growth for horizons one to four: (1) disaggregation considerably reduces the RMSE for all horizons, (2) the combination of forecasts from demand and production breakdowns improves the results in almost all cases, (3) forecasts from VEqCM models, alone or combined with single-equation transfer function models, are the best options for forecasting one and two quarters ahead, but the differences from the other disaggregated alternatives are small both for these horizons and for three and four quarters ahead. We also show the importance of taking a break in the seasonality of different GDP components into account.

A global econometric model for forecasting GDP in the Eurozone could be considered for our purpose, but the construction and maintenance of this type of model is costly and only large institutions can afford the approach. In fact, global macroeconomic models can be useful for structural and simulation analysis, even when sometimes they are not built by means of econometric methods for estimation and testing, but by calibration techniques. Besides, they may forecast worse than simpler models and much of the literature shows that this is often the case. Univariate time-series models are at the other end of the spectrum of econometric models for GDP. They can forecast accurately on occasions, but they cannot provide an explanation of the factors determining the forecasts and their usefulness for economic policy is very limited; see Granger (2001). We present an intermediate procedure based on the method developed in the *Bulletin of EU* and *US Inflation and Macroeconomic Analysis,* Carlos III University, Madrid.

This method relies on disaggregation, specific and general leading indicators and non-linear structures when required. In the application of this procedure, models with different information sets or different long-term structures can be considered and, in the end, a combined forecast can be constructed if it improves the results. For these cases, Clements and Hendry (1999) indicate that combining could be preferred to encompassing. The starting point in this approach is the consideration that the information set must be enlarged from the univariate system in directions that really increase the information on relevant features of GDP performance, such as trends, seasonality, business cycle fluctuations, and so on. In this context, disaggregation of GDP taking the cointegration relationships between components into account becomes very useful. Likewise, the breakdown of GDP enables the inclusion of specific leading indicators or general indicators with specific parameters in the equation of each component.

In the case of GDP, two alternative ways of breaking down the aggregate in a vector of n components are possible: (a) by items of the final demand, and (b) by production sectors. In the first case, the components are defined in this chapter as: (1) private consumption (PRCO), (2) government consumption (PBCO), (3) gross fixed capital formation (GFKF), (4) changes in inventories (CHIV), (5) exports (EXPO) and (6) imports (IMPO). In the second case the breakdown was: (a) real gross value added in agriculture, forestry, and so on (VAGR), (b) in industry (VIND), (c) in construction (VCON), (d) in private services (VPRS), (e) in public services (VPBS) and (f) net taxes (NTAX). In the next section tests for positive and seasonal unit roots are applied to both vectors. In the demand case, all the components except changes in inventories, which appear to be stationary, can be considered as I(1) with deterministic seasonality. Besides, a seasonal break in 2001 is found for private consumption and GFKF. For this vector, the exogeneity tests lead to a block diagonal VEqCM model with variables (1), (2) and (3) in the first block, (4) in the second and the rest in the third. For the vector of production sectors, all the components can be taken as I(1) with deterministic seasonality, and a seasonal break appears in components (c), (d) and (e). A VEqCM is built for the whole vector. In both cases, demand and production, the models contain European confidence indicators as exogenous variables. The indicators show asymmetric cyclic behaviour and they are modelled using the Markov switching-regimes model proposed by Hamilton (1989, 1990). This type of non-linear model is also built for the imports and exports block of the demand vector.

For both vectors of variables we construct alternative models, discussed later in the chapter, in order to evaluate the forecasting performance of the VEqCM models. These alternatives for all GDP components are ARIMA models and single-equation dynamic models with leading indicators and GDP lags as explanatory variables. In the latter case, for each path forecast at a base point, GDP expectations are computed in a recursive way. We also perform a forecast evaluation of all the models considered, vector, single-equation or univariate models, and the importance of disaggregation appears as a very firm result. Compared with an aggregated ARIMA model for GDP, the disaggregated approach reduces the error variance for horizons one and four by 25 per cent and 80 per cent, respectively.

The main conclusions of the chapter are summarized in a final section.

Modelling and empirical results

In the first place, to determine both the integration order and the type of seasonality (deterministic or stochastic) of each component,[1] following Hylleberg *et al.* (1990), unit-root tests are performed both at zero frequency and at all seasonal frequencies, and combinations of both.[2] The tests are performed with constant, seasonal dummies and trends, even when the trend turns out to be insignificant. Nevertheless, the tests without trend lead to the same conclusions,[3] as follows:

- All GDP components are I(1). In other words, the presence of a unit root at zero frequency is detected, except changes in inventories, which is stationary.
- In most cases, the null hypothesis of the existence of unit roots at seasonal frequencies is rejected, indicating the convenience of deterministic seasonality modelling using dummy variables. The only doubtful cases between deterministic or stochastic seasonality correspond to private consumption and GFKF. However, a more detailed examination of these components shows that there is a possible change in seasonality from the first quarter of 2001, and this is confirmed by a regression model with two sets of seasonal dummy variables. Considering this break-point in the HEGY tests, they also reject the existence of unit roots at seasonal frequencies for the above components. In fact, when the break-point is included in the component models, it is significant in six cases (see column 6 of Table 17.2)

Once both the integration order and the type of seasonality have been determined, components are modelled by VEqCM models of the following type (Johansen, 1995; Harris and Sollis, 2003; Lutkepohl, 2004):

$$\Delta Y_t = \alpha \beta' Y_{t-1} + \sum_{i=1}^{p-1} \Gamma_i \Delta Y_{t-i} + \Psi D_t + U_t \qquad U_t \sim N(0, \Sigma) \qquad (17.1)$$

In equation (17.1) the D_t vector includes the model's exogenous variables (in this case, seasonal dummy variables, step variables (LS) and impulse variables (AO) and economic indicators), relations $\beta' Y_{t-1}$ represent the equilibrium correction mechanisms and the α coefficients measure the influence of deviations from long-run relationships on the evolution of the growth rates of each variable. The Γ_i matrices show the short-term effects on the determination of the variables.

To estimate the above model, we follow a two-stage strategy (Doornik, and Hendry, 2001; Harris and Sollis, 2003; Lutkepohl, 2004), using Johansen tests in a VAR model to determine cointegration rank and estimate equilibrium relations and then re-estimating equation (17.1) with said restrictions. The results[4] of Johansen's trace and maximum eigenvalue tests[5] for VAR supply and demand models show evidence of a single cointegration relation in both cases. The

Table 17.1   Estimated β Coefficients

PRCO	PBCO	GFKF				Trend
1.000 (0.000)	−0.30593 (0.0698)	−0.34712 (0.0172)				−0.0016 (3.22E−4)
VAGR	VIND	VCON	VPRS	VPBS	NTAX	Trend
−2.147 (0.259)	0.889 (0.333)	−4.152 (0.458)	1.000 (0.000)	9.837 (1.432)	2.045 (0.265)	−0.0505 (0.0069)

Table 17.2   Estimated VEqCM models by FIML

	Coef. Coint. Rel.	Lags	VEqCM Indic.	Interv.	Seas. Break	Std. Dev. Eq.
PRCO	−0.312 (0.154)	0	No	LS199301	Yes	0.0048
PBCO	0.401 (0.158)	1,4	No	AO199501	Yes	0.00497
GFKF	1.404 (0.477)	0	0.0988 (0.040)	LS199301	Yes	0.01483

	Coef. Coint. Rel.	Lags	VEqCM Indic.	Interv.	Rupt. Seas.	Std. Dev. Eq.
VAGR	0.079 (0.030)	1,2,3	No	No	No	0.0149
VIND	0.000 (0.000)	0	0.12576 (0.02194)	AO199701	No	0.0123
VCON	0.111 (0.018)	0	No	AO199601	Yes	0.0132
VPRS	−0.013 (0.0076)	1	No	No	Yes	0.0054
VPBS	0.000 (0.000)	1	No	No	Yes	0.0039
NTAX	−0.0714 (0.035)	4	No	LS199301	No	0.0189

Note: Coef. Coint. Rel. shows, for each component, the estimated α coefficient in equation (17.1). In the Interv. column, the AO and LS values represent artificial impulse and step variables included in the equation. The digits indicate year-quarter of the intervention. The Indic. column shows the estimated coefficient of the Indicator for the components in which it is significant. The Seas.Break column indicates whether the seasonal break in 2001Q1 is significant.

estimated β coefficients of both cointegration relations are (standard errors in parenthesis) shown in Table 17.1.

Table 17.2 includes the principal results for the final VEqCM models both for the supply and the demand. The finally estimated VEqCM demand model includes three components (priv. cons., publ. cons., and GFKF), since in the initial complete model both exports and imports and changes in inventories are exogenous and therefore modelled separately. The principal features are: (1) cointegration relations are significant; (2) most of the components have very short dynamics (even non-existent in some cases); and (3) the break-point in the first quarter of 2001 is significant for most components, so it is also propagated in the aggregate GDP. This cannot be explained by a change in the behaviour of economic agents and the break is probably due to a change of method in the determination of the variables.

The univariate modelling of economic indicators is carried out using non-linear MSIH(M)-AR(p) models[6] with changing regimes like the following (see Hamilton, 1989, and Krolzig, 1997):

$$\Delta y_t = v(s_t) + \sum_{i=1}^{p} \phi_i \Delta y_{t-i} + u_t \qquad u_t \sim N(0, \sigma^2(s_t))$$

$$Pr(s_{t+1} = j / s_t = i) = p_{ij} \qquad i, j = 1 \text{ and } 2 \qquad (17.2)$$

The MISH(M)-AR(p) designation proposed in Krolzig (1997, 1998) indicates that they are autoregressive heterokedastic switching Markov models with changing intercept between M different states, two in this case. These autoregressive models enable both the intercept and the variance to depend on a non-observable variable, s_t, which represents the state of the economy. The state transition s_t variable is governed by a stochastic process with stationary and ergodic hidden Markov chain structure. The chosen option of changing the intercept instead of the mean enables gradual instead of instantaneous changes of level (Krolzig, 1997).

Exports and imports are modelled with a MSIH(2)-VAR(2) model (including the export orderbooks indicator as an exogenous variable), which has a slightly better forecasting performance than a linear VAR model[7] between the two components. Finally, for modelling changes in inventories, a first order univariate autoregressive model is used on the level of the variable.

Forecasting exercise

With a view to comparing the forecasts obtained with the different models considered, a forecasting exercise is performed, cutting the initial sample[8] into 12 observations and obtaining forecasts for the year-on-year rate with different forecasting horizons (h = 1, 2, 3 and 4). The models are re-estimated using all the information available at each forecasting time (in which case, for each re-estimate, the sample size must be increased by one observation) and forecasts are calculated for the horizons considered. The comparisons between the roots of the mean-square errors of the forecasts obtained by the previous models and those obtained with a univariate linear model for the aggregate GDP are shown[9] in Table 17.3.

Table 17.3 also includes the GDP forecasts obtained using univariate linear models for each component, and transfer models including the economic indicators and the GDP forecast obtained with the information available to date from an ARIMA model as regressors.[10] To calculate the GDP forecasts required to construct the forecast path of a certain GDP component with a transfer function model, the ARIMA model of the GDP is used to forecast the following observation, $T + 1$, which is used to forecast the GDP components for $T + 1$, and thus obtaining

Table 17.3 Summary of the quotients, in relation to the aggregate GDP, between the roots of the mean-square errors (RMSE) for the year-on-year rate (sample: 2001Q1 to 2003Q4)

	horiz.	GDP disaggregations		
		GDP Mixed	GDP Dem	GDP Sup
UNIV	1	0.96	1.11	0.98
	2	0.63	0.76	0.65
	3	0.46	0.60	0.49
	4	**0.43**	0.54	0.46
TF	1	0.89	1.02	0.92
	2	0.52	0.51	0.59
	3	0.66	0.61	0.77
	4	0.55	0.66	0.64
VEqCM	1	**0.87**	0.91	1.09
	2	0.67	0.82	0.78
	3	0.71	0.93	0.79
	4	0.75	0.99	0.77

hor.	GDP combinations between different models				
	GDP Agr	VEC-UNV	VEC-TF	UNV-TF	VEC-UNV-TF
1	1.00 (0.645E-2)	0.94	0.88	0.89	0.87
2	1.00 (0.957E-2)	0.56	**0.45**	0.52	0.49
3	1.00 (1.070E-2)	0.48	0.58	**0.44**	0.53
4	1.00 (1.192E-2)	0.54	0.62	0.45	0.51

Note: The GDP disaggregations columns correspond to GDP forecasts, disaggregating the demand and production components separately. The GDP Mixed is obtained as a linear combination between GDP Supply and GDP Demand. The GDP combinations are obtained by aggregating the GDP Mixed obtained from each model. A value lower than 1 indicates a lower value of the corresponding RMSE. in relation to the aggregate. The GDP Agr includes the exact RMSE values in brackets. The best forecasts with horizon 1, 2, 3 and 4 are marked in bold type.

a new GDP forecast aggregating the components at $T + 1$, which is considered as observed data. This information is used by the ARIMA model to forecast the GDP for $T + 2$ and the process is repeated.

Besides the GDP forecasts obtained separately by aggregating the supply and demand components, GDP forecasts can also be obtained by combining the two. To obtain the combination's weightings, the root of the mean-square error of the quarter-on-quarter rate is minimized (in order to include more observations) on each forecasting horizon (Diebold, 1998). When we examine the forecast table, we find that the forecast indeed gains by disaggregating and, on many occasions, by combining different models.

Conclusions

The principal conclusions obtained with the above modelling and forecasting are as follows. In general, there is a gain from using GDP forecasts with disaggregate models (of any kind) compared with forecasts obtained with an aggregate model. On many occasions, there is a gain from combining GDP forecasts obtained with different models. In the year-on-year rate for short horizons ($h = 1$), VEqCM models generate forecasts with lower RMSE and the same occurs for $h = 2$ if they are combined with forecasts from transfer function models. For longer horizons, the best combination of VEqCM forecasts is with univariate models, although in this case the disaggregate univariate forecast alone is slightly better.

Although the models employed do not include a theory about the factors determining GDP components, they do provide forecasts on said components and, therefore, on their contribution to GDP growth. This determines which are the most dynamic and which the most sluggish sectors, often providing valuable guidance for economic policy.

Notes

1   All components are in logarithms except changes in inventories.
2   ADF unit-root tests and KPSS stationarity tests have also been performed, seeking the presence of two positive unit roots. However, the existence of a double unit root is rejected for all the components.
3   These tables are available by request from the first author.
4   Calculations are made using the Ox language (Doornik (2001)), integrated in PcGive software (Doornik and Hendry, 2001), and the JMulTi programme developed by Lutkepohl (Lutkepohl and Kratzig, 2003; Lutkepohl, 2004).
5   We also performed the Saikkonen–Lutkepohl cointegration rank test (Saikkonen and Lutkepohl, 2000), which is robust in case of a break-point on an unknown date. The conclusions are similar to those of the Johansen tests.
6   Calculations are performed using the MSVAR programme (Krolzig, 1998) written in Ox language (Doornik, 2001).
7   An equilibrium correction mechanism is not included in the equations, since no cointegration relation is detected between the variables.
8   The complete sample includes data from 1991Q1 to 2003Q4.
9   No forecast comparison test, such as the Diebold-Mariano test, is included, since most of these tests have asymptotic validity and in our case there are only 12 observations available, at most.
10   Logically, the regressors are only added to the equations when they are significant.

References

Clements, M. and Hendry, D. (1999) *Forecasting Non-Stationary Economic Time Series*. London: MIT Press.
Diebold, F. (1998) *Elements of Forecasting*. Cincinnati: South-Western Publishing.
Doornik, J. (2001) *Object-oriented Matrix Programming using Ox.*, 4th edn. London: Timberlake Consultants Press.
Doornik, J. and Hendry, D. (2001) *Modelling Dynamic Systems using PcGive*, Vol. II, 3rd edn. London: Timberlake Consultants Press.
Granger, C. (2001) 'Macroeconometrics. Past and future', *Journal of Econometrics*, 100: 17–19.
Hamilton, J. (1989) 'A new approach to the economic analysis of nonstationary time series and the business cycle', *Econometrica*, 57: 357–84.

Hamilton, J. (1990) 'Analysis of time series subject to changes in regime', *Journal of Econometrics*, 45: 39–70.

Harris, R. and Sollis, R. (2003) *Applied Time Series Modelling and Forecasting*. Chichester: John Wiley.

Hylleberg, S., Engle, R.F., Granger, C.W.J. and Yoo, B. (1990) 'Seasonal integration and cointegration', *Journal of Econometrics*, 44: 215–28.

Johansen, S. (1995) *Likelihood-Based Inference in Cointegrated Vector Autoregressive Models*. Oxford: Oxford University Press.

Krolzig, H.-M. (1997) *Markov-Switching Vector Autoregressions. Modelling, Statistical Inference and Application to Business Cycle Analysis*, Lecture Notes in Economics and Mathematical Systems. Berlin: Springer-Verlag, vol. 454.

Krolzig, H.-M. (1998) 'Econometric modelling of Markov-switching vector autoregressions using MSVAR for Ox', Discussion Paper. Oxford: Oxford University, Department of Economics.

Lutkepohl, H. (2004) 'Recent advances in cointegration analysis', Working Paper no. ECO N 2004/12. Florence: European University Institute.

Lutkepohl, H. and Kratzig, M. (2003) *Applied Time Series Econometrics*. Cambridge: Cambridge University Press.

Saikkonen, P. and Lutkepohl, H. (2000) 'Testing for the cointegrating rank of a VAR process with structured shifts', *Journal of Business and Economic Statistics*, 18: 451–64.

18
Real-Time Detection of the Business Cycle using SETAR Models

Laurent Ferrara and Dominique Guégan

Introduction

Recently, we witnessed the development of new modern tools in business cycle analysis, mainly based on non-linear parametric modelling. Non-linear models have the great advantage to be flexible enough to take into account certain stylized facts of the economic business cycle, such as asymmetries in the phases. In this respect, much of attention has concentrated on the class of non-linear dynamic models that accommodate the possibility of regime changes.

Especially, Markov-switching models popularized by Hamilton (1989) have been extensively used in business cycle analysis in order to describe the economic fluctuations. Among the huge amount of empirical studies, we can quote the papers of Sichel (1994), Lahiri and Wang (1994), Potter (1995), Anas and Ferrara (2002a), Chauvet and Piger (2003), Clements and Krolzig (2003) or Ferrara (2003) as regards the US economy, and the papers of Krolzig (2001, 2004), Krolzig and Toro (2001) or Guégan (2003), as regards the Eurozone economy. Generally, the output of these applications is twofold. The authors aim either at dating the turning points of the cycle, or at detecting in real time the current regime of the economy.

However, a clear distinction must be made between dating and detecting the turning points of the cycle. Dating is an *ex post* exercise for which several parametric and non-parametric methodologies are available. It turns out that simple non-parametric procedures, such as the famous Bry and Boschan (1971) procedure still used by the Dating Committee of the NBER, are more convenient for this kind of work (see Harding and Pagan, 2001, or Anas and Ferrara, 2004, for a discussion on this issue). Real-time detection refers mainly to short-term economic analysis, which is not an easy task for practitioners. Indeed, several economic indicators are released on a regularly monthly basis, or even on a daily basis as regards the financial sector, adding volatility to the existing volatility and thus leading to an inflation of the available information set. Moreover, the data are often strongly revised and the diverse statistical methods, such as seasonal adjustment or filtering techniques, lead to edge effects. In this framework, the statistician has a crucial role to play which consists in extracting the right signal to help the short-term economic diagnosis. The too often quoted word 'data miner' seems to be well-appropriate here. Therefore, real-time economic analysis demands methods with a strong statistical content.

In this respect, Markov-switching models have shown their value in real-time business cycle analysis. Besides this well-known approach, other parametric models have been proposed in the statistical literature to allow for different regimes. Threshold autoregressive (TAR) models (see Tong, 1990) have been used to describe the asymmetry observed in the quartely US real GNP by different authors, such as Tiao and Tsay (1994), Potter (1995) and Proietti (1998) for instance, and using US unemployment monthly data by Hansen (1997). With the TAR model the transition variable is observed: it may be either an exogenous variable, such as a leading index for example, or a linear combination of lagged values of the series. In this latter case, the model is referred to as a self-exciting threshold autoregressive (SETAR) model. This is the main difference with the Markov-switching model whose parameters of the autoregressive data-generating process vary according to the states of the latent Markov chain. These two approaches are complementary because the details investigated are not exactly the same. Nevertheless, a point of interest for the SETAR processes lies in their predictability, see for instance De Goojier and De Bruin (1999) and Clements and Smith (1999, 2000). When dealing with SETAR models, the transition is discrete, but smooth transition is also chosen to study the business cycle by some authors. Thus, we get the so-called STAR model, see for instance Terasvirta and Anderson (1992) and van Dijk, Terasvirta and Franses (2002).

In this chapter we focus on real-time detection of business cycle turning points. Our aim is rather to point out some thresholds under (over) which a signal of a turning point could be given in real-time. We prefer the SETAR approach because a threshold model seems to be attractive in terms of business cycle analysis. Here, we propose a prospective approach as an alternative to other approaches, including, for instance, the use of switching models to detect the business cycle. Thus, in the following we assume that it is possible to adjust a SETAR on the considered data and we do not test this assumption. This approach is based on the following intuition: the existence of two (or more) states inside the data and the possible distinction of these states using the structure of the data, without imposing the existence of another series to explain the split from one state to another.

This chapter is split into two parts. First we introduce the various threshold models and discuss their statistical properties.We especially recall the classical techniques to estimate the number of regimes, the threshold, the delay and the parameters of the model. Then, we apply these models to the Eurozone industrial production index to detect in real time the dates of peaks and troughs for the business cycle. By using a dynamic simulation approach, we also provide a measure of performance of our model by comparison to a benchmark dating chronology.

Lastly, some conclusions and further research directions are proposed in a final section.

Description and inference for SETAR processes

The TAR model introduced in the 1980s was not widely used in applications until recently, primarily because it was hard in practice to identify the threshold variable and to estimate the associated values, and secondly because there was no simple modelling procedure available. Recently some authors have proposed different ways to bypass this problem. In this section we introduce a SETAR model with two regimes and a classical way to estimate its parameters. We assume that it is possible to adjust an AR($p_i, i = 1, 2$) process on each regime. The autoregressive lag p_1 in the first regime may also be different from the lag p_2 in the other regime.

A mean-stationary SETAR $(2, p_1, p_2)$ model can be written in the following form:

$$Y_t = (1 - I(Y_{t-d} > c)) \left(\phi_{0,0} + \sum_{i=1}^{p_1} \phi_{0,i} Y_{t-i} + \sigma_0 \varepsilon_t \right)$$

$$+ I(Y_{t-d} > c) \left(\phi_{1,0} + \sum_{i=1}^{p_2} \phi_{1,i} Y_{t-i} + \sigma_1 \varepsilon_t \right) \qquad (18.1)$$

where $I(Y_{t-d} > c) = 1$ if $Y_{t-d} > c$ and zero otherwise. For a given threshold c and the position of the random variable Y_{t-d} with respect to this threshold c, the process $(Y_t)_t$ here follows a AR(p_1) model or an AR(p_2) model. The model parameters are $\phi_{i,j}$, for $i = 0, 1$ and $j = 1, \ldots, p_k$, and $k = 1$ or 2, the threshold c and the delay d. For each state it is possible to propose more complex stationary models like ARMA(p,q) processes or nonlinear processes (see Guégan, 1994).

The choice of the models in each regime can be made using the procedure proposed by Tsay (1989). As noted above, a major difficulty in applying TAR models is the specification of the threshold variable, which plays a key role in the non-linear structure of the model. Since there is only a finite number of choices for the parameters c and d, the best choice can be made using the Akaike Information Criterion (AIC) (see Akaike, 1974). This procedure has been developed by Tong (1990) and is used by many practitioners dealing with this model. We recall now the main steps for estimation.

Using some algebraic notations, the model (18.1) can be rewritten as a regression model. We denote $I_d(c) \equiv I(Y_{t-d} > c)$, $\Phi_0 = [\phi_{0,0}, \ldots, \phi_{0,p}]'$, $\Phi_1 = [\phi_{1,0}, \ldots, \phi_{1,p}]'$ and $\mathbf{Y}'_{t-1} = [1, Y_{t-1}, \ldots, Y_{t-p}]$, and obtain for the process $(Y_t)_t$, the following representation:

$$Y_t = (1 - I_d(c))\mathbf{Y}'_{t-1}\Phi_0 + I_d(c)\mathbf{Y}'_{t-1}\Phi_1 + ((1 - I_d(c))\sigma_0 + I_d(c)\sigma_1)\varepsilon_t \qquad (18.2)$$

Now, we assume that we observe a sequence of data $(Y_1, \ldots, Y_n)$ from the model (18.2). The equation (18.2) is a regression equation (albeit nonlinear in parameters) and an appropriate estimation method is least-squares (LS). Under the auxiliary assumption that the noise $(\varepsilon_t)_t$ is a strong Gaussian white noise, the least-squares estimation is equivalent to the maximum likelihood estimation.

Since the regression equation (18.2) is nonlinear and discontinuous, the easiest method to obtain the LS estimates is to use sequential conditional LS. We will use this approach here. We recall that conditional least-squares lead to the minimization of:

$$\sum_{Y_{t-d}<c,t=1}^{n} (Y_t - \phi_{0,0} + \phi_{0,1}Y_{t-1} - \cdots - \phi_{0,p_1}Y_{t-p_1})^2$$

$$+ \sum_{Y_{t-d}>c,t=1}^{n} (Y_t - \phi_{0,0} + \phi_{0,1}Y_{t-1} - \cdots - \phi_{0,p_2}Y_{t-p_2})^2 = \min \qquad (18.3)$$

with respect to $\Phi_0, \Phi_1, c, d, p_1, p_2$. Generally, we first assume that the parameters p_1 and p_2 are known.

Chan (1993) proves that, under geometric ergodicity and some other regularity conditions for the process (18.2), the LS parameter estimates of this process have good properties. The threshold parameter is consistent, tends to the true value at rate n and, suitably normalized, asymptotically follows a compound Poisson process. The other parameters of the model are $n^{-1/2}$ consistent and are asymptotically distributed. The limitation of the theory of Chan (1993) concerns the construction of confidence intervals for the threshold c. Indeed, if we denote $\hat{c}$ the LS estimate for c, then Chan finds that $(\hat{c} - c)$ converges in distribution to a functional of a compound Poisson process and, unfortunately, this representation depends upon a host of nuisance parameters, including the marginal distribution of $(Y_t)_t$ and all the regression coefficients. Hence, this theory does not yield a practical method to construct confidence intervals.

The method used here to estimate all the parameters follows Tsay (1989) and Tong (1990). We need to determine the parameters c, d, p_1, p_2. We assume P the maximal possible order of the two subregimes and D the greatest possible delay. The threshold parameter c is chosen by grid-search. The grid points are obtained using the quantiles of the sample under investigation. We use equally spaced quantiles from the 10 (per cent) quantiles and ending at the 90 (per cent) quantiles. Now, for each fixed pair (d, c_i), $0 < d \leq D$, $i = 1, \ldots s$, the appropriate TAR model is to be identified. The AIC criterion is used for selection of the orders p_1 and p_2. In this context, it becomes:

$$AIC(p_1, p_2, d, c) = \ln\left(\frac{1}{n}\sum \hat{\epsilon}_t^2\right) + 2\frac{p_1 + p_2 + 2}{n} \qquad (18.4)$$

where $\hat{\epsilon}_t$ denotes the residuals.

Finally the model with the parameters p_1^*, p_2^*, d^* and c^* that minimize the AIC criterion can be selected. Since for different d there are different numbers of values that can be used for estimation, the following adjustment should be done. With $n_d = \max(d, P)$ it is:

$$AIC(p_1^*, p_2^*, d^*, c^*) = \min_{p_1, p_2, d, c} \frac{1}{n - n_d} AIC(p_1, p_2, d, c) \qquad (18.5)$$

Different algorithms for the parameters estimation of SETAR models are available, references and details can be found in Ferrara and Guégan (2003). Moreover Tsay (1989) proposes a statistic to test the threshold nonlinearity and specify the threshold variable. This test statistic is derived by simple linear regression and its performance is evaluated by simulation. Hansen (1997) considers a likelihood ratio statistic for testing SETAR hypotheses. A Lagrange multiplier test is proposed by Proietti (1998). We can remark that no test has been shown to favour SETAR models or switching models. This matter seems very difficult to settle.

Empirical results

In this section, our aim is to apply a SETAR model to the Eurozone Industrial Production Index in order to detect the low phases of the industrial business cycle referred to as industrial recessions. The application is done in two steps: first we try to find the best SETAR model according to the AIC criterion presented in the previous section and, second, we use this model to detect the periods of each regime. By comparing the results to reference recession dates, we can assess the ability of the model to reproduce the industrial business cycle features.

Data description

The analysis is carried out on the IPI series considered in the paper of Anas *et al.* (2006). This series is a proxy of the monthly aggregate Eurozone IPI for the 12 countries, beginning in January 1970 and ending in December 2002. The data are working-day and seasonally adjusted by using the Tramo-Seats methodology implemented in the Demetra software. Moreover, the irregular part including outliers has been removed.

The original series $(X_t)_t$ is presented in Figure 18.1 as well as its monthly growth rate $(Y_t)_t$ defined by $Y_t = \log(X_t) - \log(X_{t-1})$. The shaded areas in the figure represent the reference industrial recession dates. Several authors have proposed a turning-points chronology for the Eurozone industrial business cycle, by using different statistical techniques and economic arguments. For example, we refer to Anas *et al.* (2006), who propose a classical NBER-based non-parametric approach, and to Artis *et al.* (2004), Krolzig (2004) or Anas and Ferrara (2002b) who apply parametric Markov-switching models. Generally, the industrial recession dates are more or less similar. In fact, it turns out that the Eurozone experienced five industrial recessions: in 1974–75 and 1980–81 due to the first and second oil shocks, in 1981–82 and in 1992–93 due to the American recession and the Gulf war, and lastly in 2000–01 because of the global economic slowdown itself caused by the US recession from March 2001 to November 2001. It is noteworthy that, contrary to a common belief among economists, the Asian crisis in 1997–98 has not caused an industrial recession in the whole Eurozone, but only a slowdown of production. Finally, we retain as a benchmark for our study the dates proposed by Anas *et al.* (2006) and summarized in the first column in Table 18.2.

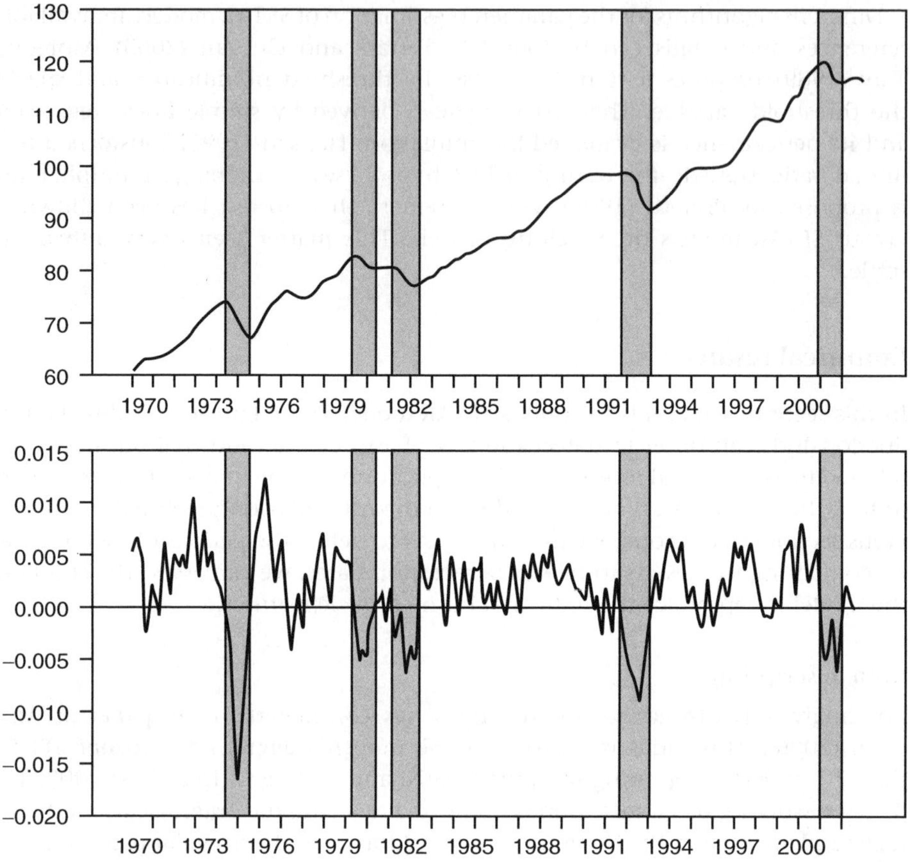

Figure 18.1 Euro12 IPI (top) and its monthly growth rate (bottom), as well as the reference industrial recession periods (shaded areas), from January 1970 to December 2002

To ensure stationarity, we are going to deal with the monthly industrial growth rate $(Y_t)_t$. The unconditional empirical distribution of the IPI growth rate computed by using a non-parametric kernel estimate (with the Epanechnikov kernel) is presented in Figure 18.2. There is a clear evidence of three peaks in the estimated distribution. The lowest peak is due to the negative growth rates during industrial recessions. The intermediate peak seems to be caused by periods of low, but positive, growth rates, experienced for example during the 1980s while the peak corresponding to the highest value is related to periods of fast growth. It is noteworthy that from 1970 to 2002, periods of low growth rates seem to appear more frequently than periods of high growth. Moreover, this empirical distribution is cleary asymmetric (skewness equal to -0.9315) and with heavy tails (excess kurtosis equal to 2.4850). Consequently, the unconditional Gaussian assumption is strongly rejected by a Jarque–Bera test.

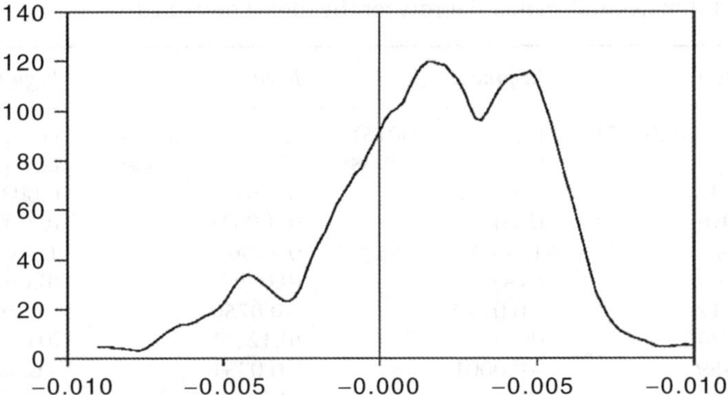

Figure 18.2 Empirical unconditional distribution of the IPI growth rate, from January 1970 to December 2002

Whole-sample modelling

In this subsection we fit various SETAR models to the industrial growth-rate series $(Y_t)_t$; that is, we model the speed of the Eurozone industry. We consider first a two-regime model, the transition variable being successively the lagged series and the lagged differenced series. Then, we consider a multiple regime model by mixing the conditions on these previous series. For each model, we compare the estimated regimes with the reference recession phases in order to assess the ability of the model to reproduce business cycle features (see results in Table 18.2). Only the detailed results related to the third model are presented in this note. Details concerning the other models can be found in Ferrara and Guégan (2003). In the model presented here, we combine the two previous SETAR models in a single model with two transition variables : the lagged growth rate and the acceleration. Therefore, the model possesses four regimes and two thresholds c_1 and c_2. Estimates and their standard errors for the parameters of this model, minimizing the AIC criteria, are given in Table 18.1.

The two thresholds are estimated by using a double loop, but the delays of the model are fixed *a priori* according to the two previous estimated models. Both estimated thresholds are negative but very close to zero. The first regime has an empirical unconditional probability of 0.15 and should be considered at a first sight as a period of recession because the estimated recession dates match the reference recession dates. However, the second regime is also meaningful. Indeed, this second regime possesses an unconditional probability of 0.02: only 7 observations over 385 belong to this state. This is the reason why standard errors of estimates are not available in this regime. Although the frequency of this second regime is very low, this regime is persistent and appears in clusters. In fact, this regime is very interesting because it corresponds to the end of a recession phase when the economy is accelerating again. This regime was detected twice: at the end of the 1974–75 recession and at the end of the 1992–93 recession. Thus, the sum of regime 1 and regime 2 corresponds to the industrial recession phase. The third

Table 18.1 Estimates and standard errors for the model described

	Regime 1	Regime 2	Regime 3	Regime 4
	$[Y_{t-1} < -0.0015]$	$[Y_{t-1} < -0.0015]$	$[Y_{t-1} \geq -0.0015]$	$[Y_{t-1} \geq -0.0015]$
	$[Z_{t-10} < -0.0008]$	$[Z_{t-10} \geq -0.0008]$	$[Z_{t-10} < -0.0008]$	$[Z_{t-10} \geq -0.0008]$
$\hat{\phi}_0$	−0.0040	−0.0070	0.0010	0.0036
	(0.0010)	(NA)	(0.0004)	(0.0005)
$\hat{\phi}_1$	1.1454	1.2803	0.7106	1.3005
	(0.1408)	(NA)	(0.0995)	(0.0660)
$\hat{\phi}_2$	−0.3712	−0.0180	−0.0750	−0.7883
	(0.2076)	(NA)	(0.1216)	(0.0974)
$\hat{\phi}_3$	−0.0359	−0.0001	−0.0331	−0.3321
	(0.1408)	(NA)	(0.1003)	(0.0662)
$\hat{\sigma}_\varepsilon$	0.0019	NA	0.0017	0.0012

Table 18.2 Reference and estimated dating chronologies stemming from the three considered SETAR models

	Reference	Model 1	Model 2	Model 3
Peak	1974M4	1974M6	1974M6	1974M6
Trough	1975M5	1975M5	1975M3	1975M6
Peak	–	1977M3	1976M12	1977M3
Trough	–	1977M6	1977M7	1977M7
Peak	1980M2	1980M4	1980M3	1980M3
Trough	1981M1	1980M10	1980M10	1980M11
Peak	1981 M10	1982M5	1982M6	1982M6
Trough	1982M12	1982 M12	1982M8	1982M12
Peak	1992M1	1992M4	1992M7	1992M4
Trough	1993M5	1993M5	1993M1	1993M6
Peak	–	–	1998M7	–
Trough	–	–	1998M11	–
Peak	2000M12	2001M2	2001M1	2001M2
Trough	2001M12	2001M12	2001M10	2001M12

regime can be considered as a slowdown of the industrial production, that is the industry is below its trend growth rate without being in recession. Lastly, when the series is in the high regime, we can deduce that the industrial growth rate is over its trend growth rate. Actually, regime 3 and regime 4 correspond to the high phase of the industrial business cycle. It appears that only three regimes would be sufficient to describe the industrial business cycle. However, we decide to keep four states because they give a deeper understanding of the industrial business cycle features. As regards the dating results, the model provides almost the same results than the first model, the last recession period being not cut into two parts (see Table 18.2). However, this model presents some non-persistent signals of recession.

Dynamic real-time analysis

In real-time analysis, an economic indicator requires at least two qualities: it must be reliable and must provide a readable signal as soon as possible. Thus, there is a well-known trade-off between advance and reliability for the economic indicators. By using the previous 4-regime SETAR model, we assess if it is possible to have a clear and timely signal for the turning points of the industrial business cycle in a dynamic analysis. We consider the previous IPI series from January 1970 to December 1999, and we progressively add monthly data until December 2002. For each step, we re-estimate the model and we classify the series into one of the four regimes. Thus, by using the conclusions of the whole-sample analysis, if the series lies into regime 1 or regime 2, we can conclude that the industry is in a recession phase. We are aware that a *true* real-time analysis should be done by using historically released data (see for instance Chauvet and Piger, 2003) in order to take the revisions and the edge-effects of the statistical treatments of the raw data into account. However, such series are very difficult to find in economic data bases.

The results of the real-time estimated recession period match with the 2001 recession period estimated in the whole-sample analysis. This fact points out the stability of the model. Indeed, we detect a peak in the business cycle in February 2001 and a trough in December 2001. However, it must be noted that a false signal of a regime change is given in August 2001, but it lasts only one month. Knowing that a signal must be persistent to be reliable, we have to propose an *ad hoc* real-time decision rule. Thus, it is advocated to wait for at least two months before sending a signal of a change in regime. We also note that the exit of the recession is very fast, because the series goes directly from regime 1 in December 2001 to regime 4 in January 2002. Moreover, we observe that the series falls into regime 3 in December 2002.

It is also interesting to consider the evolution of the parameters in a dynamic analysis. In Figure 18.3, the evolution of the thresholds $\hat{c}_1$ and $\hat{c}_2$ is presented. It is striking to observe the change in level of both thresholds during the recession phase. During this phase, thresholds tend to become closer to zero. It is also noteworthy that $\hat{c}_1$ increases slowly from May 2000 to June 2001 but decreases suddently, while, conversely, $\hat{c}_2$ increases suddently in March 2001 but decreases slowly. This feature indicates perhaps an asymmetry between the start and the end of recession and may be exploited later to get a more advanced signal. Lastly, we note that both thresholds are remarkably stable since the end of the recession. Unfortunately, as noted in earlier, there is no practical way to test a change in the thresholds (see, however, Tsay, 1989, and Ip *et al.*, 2003).

Conclusion

We have presented an exploratory analysis of the ability of SETAR models to reproduce the business cycle stylized facts. The results are promising. It appears that the model allows us to identify the turning points of the industrial cycle and can thus be useful for real-time detection. However, a true real-time analysis should

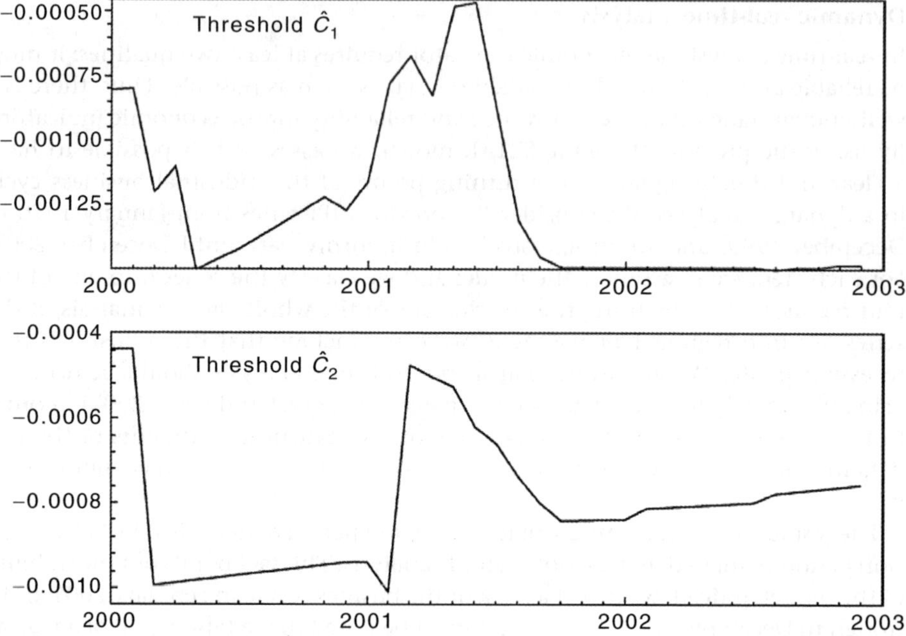

Figure 18.3   Evolution of the real-time estimated thresholds of the 4-regime SETAR model from January 2000 to December 2002

be extended by using historically released data, as used in Chauvet and Piger's (2003) recent paper as regards the US GDP and employment. Unfortunately, such data are not systematically stored in databases and are therefore very difficult to obtain. As another example, business surveys seem to be good candidates for real-time analysis through SETAR models, because they are released quickly and are not generally revised.

References

Akaike, H. (1974) 'A new look at the statistical model identification', *IEEE Transactions on Automatic Control*, 19: 716–22.

Anas, J. and Ferrara, L. (2002a) 'Un indicateur d'entrée et sortie de récession: application aux Etats Unis', watching page no. 58. Paris: Centre d'Observation Economique.

Anas, J. and Ferrara, L. (2004) 'A comparative assessment of parametric and non-parametric turning points detection methods: the case of the Euro-zone economy', in G.L. Mazzi and G. Savio (eds), *Monographs of Official Statistics*. Luxembourg: European Commission, pp. 86–121.

Anas, J., Billio, M., Ferrara, L. and Lo Duca, M. (2006) 'A turning point chronology for the Eurozone classical and growth cycles', this Volume.

Artis, M. Krolzig, H.M. and Toro, J. (2004) 'The European business cycle', *Oxford Bulletin of Economics and Statistics*, 56: 1–44.

Bry, G. and Boschan, C. (1971) *Cyclical Analysis of Time Series: Selected Procedures and Computer Programs*. New York: National Bureau of Economic Research.

Chan, K.S. (1993) 'Consistency and limiting distribution of the least squares estimator of a threshold autoregressive model', *Annals of Statistics*, 21: 520–33.

Chauvet, M. and Piger, J.M. (2003) 'Identifying business cycle turning points in real time', *Review of the Federal Reserve Bank of St. Louis*, March/April: 47–61.

Clements, M.P. and Smith, J. (1999) 'A Monte Carlo study of the forecasting performance of empirical SETAR models', *Journal of Applied Econometrics*, 14: 123–141.

Clements, M.P. and Smith, J. (2000) 'Evaluating the forecast densities of linear and Non-linear models: applications to output growth and unemployment', *Journal of Forecasting*, 19: 255–76.

Clements, M.P. and Krolzig, H.M. (2003) 'Business cycle asymmetries: characterization and testing based on Markov-switching autoregressions', *Journal of Business and Economic Statistics*, 21: 196–211.

Dijk, D. van, Terasvirta, T. and Franses, P.H. (2002) 'Smooth transition autoregressive models – A survey of recent developments', *Econometric Reviews*, 21: 1–47.

Ferrara, L. (2003) 'A three-regime real-time indicator for the US economy', *Economics Letters*, 81: 373–78.

Ferrara, L. and Guégan, D. (2003) 'Detection of business cycles using SETAR models', Preprint, MORA-IDHE, 2003-12, Cachan: Ecole Normale Supérieure.

de Goojier, J.G. and de Bruin, P.T. (1999) 'On forecasting SETAR processes', *Statistics and Probability Letters*, 37: 7–14.

Guégan, D. (1994) *Séries Chronologiques non Liné aires à Temps Discret*. Paris: Economica.

Guégan, D. (2003) 'Point de vue personnel sur le problème de contagion en economie et l'intéraction entre cycle réel et cycle financier', *Research Note*, MORA-IDHE 06-2003, Cachan: Ecole Normale Supérieure.

Hamilton, J.D. (1989) 'A new approach to the economic analysis of non-stationary time series and the business cycle', *Econometrica*, 57: 357–84.

Hansen, B.E. (1997) 'Inference in TAR models', *Studies in Nonlinear Dynamics and Econometrics*, 2: 1–14.

Harding, D. and Pagan, A. (2001) 'A comparison of two business cycle dating methods', unpublished manuscript, Melbourne: University of Melbourne.

Ip, W.-C., Wong, H., Li, Y. and An, H. (2003) 'Testing and estimation of thresholds based on wavelets in heteroscedastic threshold autoregressive models', *Biometrika*, 90: 703–6.

Krolzig, H.M. (2001) 'Markov-switching procedures for dating the Euro-zone business cycle', *Quarterly Journal of Economic Research*, 3: 339–51.

Krolzig, H.M. (2004) 'Constructing turning point chronologies with Markov-switching vector autoregressive models: the euro-zone business cycle', in G.L. Mazzi and G. Savio (eds), *Monographs of Official Statistics*. Luxembourg: European Commission, pp. 147–90.

Krolzig, H.M. and Toro, J. (2001) 'Classical and modern business cycle measurement: the European case', Discussion Paper in Economics no.60. Oxford: University of Oxford.

Lahiri, K. and Wang, J.G. (1994) 'Predicting cyclical turning points with leading index in a Markov-switching model', *Journal of Forecasting*, 13: 245–63.

Potter, S.M. (1995) 'A nonlinear approach to US GNP', *Journal of Applied Econometrics*, 10: 109–25.

Proietti, T. (1998) 'Characterizing asymmetries in business cycles using smooth-transition structural times series models', *Studies in Nonlinear Dynamics and Econometrics*, 3: 141–56.

Sichel, D.E. (1994) 'Inventories and the three phases of the business cycles', *Journal of Business and Economic Statistics*, 12: 269–77.

Terasvirta, T. and Anderson, H.M. (1992) 'Characterising nonlinearities in business cycles using smooth transition autoregressive models', *Journal of Applied Econometrics*, 7: S119–S136.

Tiao, G.C. and Tsay, R.S. (1994) 'Some advances in non-linear and adaptive modelling in time-series', *Journal of Forecasting*, 13: 109–31.
Tong, H. (1990) *Non-Linear Time Series: A Dynamical Approach* . Oxford: Oxford Scientific Publications.
Tsay, R.S. (1989) 'Testing and modeling threshold autoregressive processes', *Journal of the American Statistical Association*, 84: 231–40.

19
Business Survey Data: Do They Help in Forecasting GDP Growth?

*Jesper Hansson, Per Jansson and Mårten Löf**

Introduction

In this chapter we examine whether data from business tendency surveys are useful for forecasting GDP growth in the short run. The starting point is a so-called dynamic factor model (DFM), which is used both as a framework for dimension reduction in forecasting and as a procedure for filtering out unimportant idiosyncratic noise in the underlying survey data. In this way, it is possible to model a rather large number of noisy survey variables in a parsimoniously parameterized vector autoregression (VAR). To assess the forecasting performance of the procedure, comparisons are made with VARs that either use the survey variables directly, use macro variables only, or use other popular summary indices of economic activity. Our DFM-based procedure turns out to outperform the competing alternatives in most cases.

The interest in, and demand for, macroeconomic analyses at high frequencies, most notably forecasts, has increased substantially in recent years. But making analyses and forecasts of high-frequency data is not an easy task. Compared with annual data, data that are observed daily, monthly and quarterly typically display more complicated dynamics, are seasonal, and are – at least as concerns real variables – more frequently revised. One category of data that has the potential of being rather useful in this context is that produced by surveys. Survey data have the advantage of essentially being instantaneously accessible, never being revised, and, furthermore, having little or no measurement errors. The objective of

* We thank Jimmy Miller and seminar participants at the National Institute of Economic Research (NIER), Sveriges Riksbank, and the Ministry of Finance for helpful comments. The views expressed in this chapter are those of the authors and do not necessarily reflect those of Sveriges Riksbank or the NIER.

our study is to exploit whether such data can successfully be used for purposes of forecasting GDP growth.[1]

Our empirical application is based on the Swedish Business Tendency Survey (BTS), which is a large business survey based on questions about economic activity posed to approximately 7,000 different firms in various sectors of the Swedish economy.[2]

Previous research into the forecasting properties of the Swedish BTS has focused on establishing *direct* relationships between the variable to be forecast (typically, the growth rate of industrial production) and the BTS data. The approaches range from simple single-equation models, for example, Bergström (1992, 1993) and Lindström (2000), to Kalman-filter-based updating schemes and sophisticated turning-point analyses, for example, Rahiala and Teräsvirta (1993), Kääntä and Tallbom (1993), Öller and Tallbom (1996), and Koskinen and Öller (2004). A common finding is that only very few BTS variables are useful for macro forecasting, and that the information content in the forward-looking BTS series (expectations regarding the development the next quarter) is particularly weak. One of the main results of our study is that the forecasting performance of the BTS data can be considerably improved if the BTS variables are appropriately filtered prior to forecasting, and thus *indirectly*, rather than directly, related to the variable to be forecast.[3]

The benefits of making use of an indirect, rather than direct, link between the BTS data and the data to be predicted proceed from the fact that changes in the BTS data cannot always be assumed to contain signals that are relevant for activity at the aggregate level. More specifically, it seems likely that idiosyncratic sector-specific changes in a particular series are largely unrelated to the overall state of economic activity. The filtering technique thus entails getting rid of this series-specific 'noise' and only keeping those parts of the data that are common to the series under consideration. As it happens, the proposed filtering procedure also has the property of implying a dimension-reduction framework for the BTS variables. From the forecasting literature it is well known that forecasting approaches using many explanatory variables, and thus many estimated parameters, generate forecasts that quickly become inefficient and unstable. Our proposed procedure addresses this issue by summarizing the observable information of the large BTS data-set by a single common-factor index.

To undertake the filtering of the BTS data we employ a standard so-called dynamic factor model (DFM). Such models have previously been used for similar purposes, but have hardly been applied to survey data. Useful general references include Stock and Watson (1989, 1991, 1999, 2002), Camba-Mendez, Kapetanios, Smith and Weale (1999), Fukuda and Onodera (2001), and Forni, Hallin, Lippi and Reichlin (2000, 2003). The European Commission (2000), Goldrian, Lindbauer and Nerb (2001), and Bruno and Malgarini (2002) are examples of studies that make use of survey data.[4] The DFM, and further issues related to the BTS data, are discussed in the next section.

The forecasting performance of the BTS data filtered by the DFM is investigated using almost-real-time out-of-sample experiments. Here, the idea is that the forecaster takes the estimated common-factor index as given and computes the forecasts as if there is no knowledge about the generating mechanisms of the index. Thus, the forecaster fits a standard dynamic forecasting model, a vector autoregression (VAR). Each VAR consists of the estimated common-factor index and a particular macro variable for which we wish to derive forecasts.

To assess the relative accuracy of the DFM-based VAR forecasts, we make forecast comparisons using three alternative approaches to forecasting GDP growth. These are VARs that use unfiltered BTS variables (that is, that include the survey variables directly without employing the DFM filter); VARs that use information on macro variables only; and VARs that use other popular summary indices of economic activity. Both DFM-based forecasts of the growth rate of real GDP and alternative forecasts of GDP growth are evaluated later in the chapter.

By making comparisons with VARs based on the unfiltered survey data we are able, in terms of forecast precision, to assess the gain made from first applying the DFM to the BTS data (relative to not doing so). That is, we can quantify the effects in forecasting from parsimoniously modelling the noise-reduced BTS series rather than the original series themselves. The comparisons with macro VARs instead enable us to judge how well we do relative to the 'standard' forecasting model. Finally, the comparisons with VARs based on other summary indices of activity allow us to shed some light on the performance of our procedure when holding the gains of dimension reduction constant. Like the DFM procedure, such summary indices have the advantage of enabling the use of very parsimonious forecasting models, without having to give up too much of the relevant forecasting information.

The dynamic factor model

In this section we discuss and estimate the dynamic factor model used to filter the business survey data. The output of this analysis is an estimate of a common-factor index which summarises the co-movements in a broad range of different economic activities such as production, order flows, time of deliveries, employment, and stocks of raw materials and goods. The index is constructed in such a way that it acknowledges that activities occur in different sectors of the economy and that there may be lead–lag relationships between them. Because, the questions of the survey regard both activities in the current and next quarter, the whole analysis is undertaken for two different versions of the index: one coincident (current quarter) and one forward-looking (next quarter).

Specification

Let the n dimensional vector that collects the relevant BTS series be denoted by X_t. It is assumed that the variables in X_t are (stochastically) stationary so that they can be normalised to have mean zero and unit variance. The assumption of stationarity is not restrictive: all BTS series are distinctively cyclical without trends (whether stochastic or deterministic). Standard unit-root tests confirm that all series are stationary $I(0)$.

In the model, X_t is driven by two stochastic components: the unobserved scalar index C_t, which is common to all the variables in X_t, and the equally unobserved n dimensional component I_t, which represents the idiosyncratic movements in the series. The model, in its general form, is:

$$X_t = \gamma(L)C_t + I_t \tag{19.1}$$

$$\phi(L)C_t = \eta_t \tag{19.2}$$

where L is the lag operator such that $L^j y_t = y_{t-j}$ for any vector or scalar variable y while $\gamma(L)$ and $\phi(L)$ are vector and scalar lag polynomials, respectively. The elements in I_t and η_t are the system's disturbances such that idiosyncratic shocks are purely temporary while common shocks may display some persistence. The assumption of a purely temporary process for the idiosyncratic component can be relaxed in favour of more general autoregressive specifications but was found to fit the data well in this particular application.

As it stands, model (19.1)–(19.2) is a standard DFM. As is well-known, it is econometrically unidentified unless restrictions on its feasible set of parameter values are imposed. The following restrictions can be shown to be sufficient for identification: the disturbances in I_t and η_t are mutually and serially uncorrelated; the scalar C_t enters at least one of the variables in (19.1) only contemporaneously; and, the standard deviation of η_t is normalized to unity (or, equivalently, one of the contemporaneous parameters in $\gamma(L)$ is normalized to unity). We then use the Kalman filter together with a numerical optimization routine to obtain maximum likelihood estimates of the unknown parameters and the unobserved components; that is, the common-factor index C_t and the idiosyncratic noise processes in I_t; for details see Harvey (1989).

Although model (19.1)–(19.2) is quite flexible, it is parametric and thus has limitations as concerns the number of variables that it can handle. The feasible set of coincident and forward-looking survey variables that we use is displayed in Table 19.1.

Results

The estimates of the coincident and forward-looking indices obtained by estimating the DFM with the variables listed in Table 19.1 appear in Figure 19.1. The indices are constructed directly from the one-sided estimates of the common factors using either only coincident BTS data or only forward-looking BTS data.[5] Because the DFM is a pure time-series filter, its parameters have no particular interpretation. For this reason, and for expository convenience, we do not explicitly present the estimation results here (although these are of course available upon request). Residual diagnostics (again not shown for purposes of saving space) suggest that the two estimated DFMs by and large have acceptable statistical properties.

The coincident and forward-looking indices estimated from the BTS data appear to accord rather well with common interpretations of cyclical developments in the

Table 19.1   The BTS variables

Activity	Coincident	Forward-looking
Manufacturing industries		
Production	BTVI101	BTVI301
Orders received (domestic)	BTVI105	BTVI305
Orders received (exports)	BTVI106	BTVI306
Time of deliveries	BTVI108	
As-of-now judgement of orderbooks	BTVI201	
Number of workers employed	BTVI203	BTVI308
As-of-now judgement of stocks of raw materials	BTVI208	
As-of-now judgement of stocks of finished goods	BTVI210	
Construction industries		
Construction	BBOA101	BBOA201
Stocks of offers accepted	BBOA102	BBOA202
As-of-now judgement of orderbooks	BBOA104	
Number of workers employed	BBOA106	BBOA204

Note: Each entry gives the code used by the National Institute of Economic Research to denote the particular survey question, see Hansson, Jansson and Löf (2003). The sample runs from 1978Q1–2001Q4 in the case of coincident variables and from 1978Q2–2002Q1 in the case of forward-looking variables.

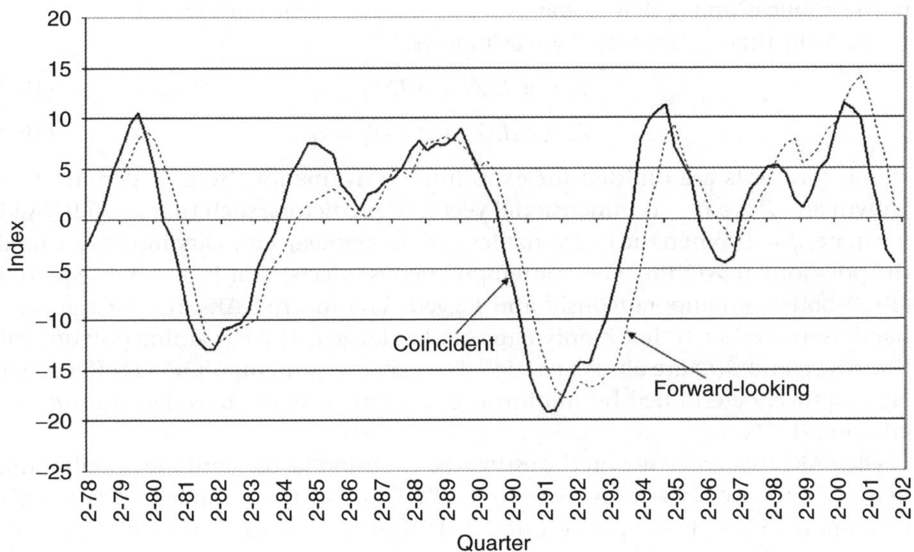

Figure 19.1   One-sided estimates of common factors

Swedish economy over the last two decades (for further discussions see Hansson, Jansson and Löf, 2003). The next issue to be dealt with is to investigate whether this information can also successfully be used for the purpose of out-of-sample forecasting.

Forecasts

In this section we undertake an almost-real-time out-of-sample forecasting experiment that aims at shedding light on how useful the two estimated common-factor indices are for forecasting GDP growth in the short run. The forecasting model throughout is a standard VAR, and evaluations of forecast accuracy are undertaken for four different forecast horizons: one quarter, two quarters, four quarters and eight quarters. To assess the relative accuracy of the DFM-based VAR forecasts, we make forecast comparisons using three alternative approaches to forecasting GDP growth: VARs that use the BTS variables unfiltered, VARs that use macro variables only, and VARs that use other popular summary indices of economic activity. The macro VARs are based on the following feasible set of (stationary) macro variables (in addition to GDP growth): inflation according to headline CPI and the underlying measure UND1X, effective exchange-rate growth, unemployment, employment growth, short- and long-term interest rates and wage inflation.[6] Non-stationary variables in levels are made stationary by using (log) fourth differences.[7] Concerning the arrival of information, we make the assumption that there is an information lag of one quarter for real macro variables (including GDP growth). Hence, when we observe the BTS variables, the other popular summary indices, and the nominal macro variables in quarter t, the real macro variables are only known up to and including quarter $t-1$.[8] This information lag corresponds approximately to the publication lag that prevails today for these particular variables.

The VARs that are estimated are as follows:

$$Y_t = \alpha(L)Z_t + \beta(L)Y_t + \varepsilon_t \tag{19.3}$$

$$Z_t = \tilde{\alpha}(L)Z_t + \tilde{\beta}(L)Y_t + \tilde{\varepsilon}_t \tag{19.4}$$

where constants are omitted for expository convenience. Here, Y denotes GDP growth and Z is a $(q-1)$ dimensional vector of predictors, such that the full VAR is q-variate, $q \geq 2$. When the BTS variables and the popular summary indices are used, the polynomial $\alpha(L)$ includes contemporaneous effects; that is, Z enters equation (19.3) both contemporaneously and lagged. The macro VARs are, on the other hand, restricted such that Z only enters (19.3) lagged. The remaining polynomials $\beta(L)$, $\tilde{\alpha}(L)$, and $\tilde{\beta}(L)$ are always restricted to exclude contemporaneous effects. The lag length is determined by minimising the system-based Bayesian information criterion (BIC).

The VARs that are based on the estimated common factors and the popular summary indices are always bivariate ($q = 2$). Thus, in these models, Z is a scalar containing a single leading indicator of Y. In the case of macro VARs and VARs based on unfiltered BTS variables, we impose the restriction that the variable dimension is at most of fifth order ($q \leq 5$).

The forecasts are computed as follows. The full sample period has 2001Q3 as its last quarterly observation. To undertake the out-of-sample experiments we exclude quarters 1995Q3–2001Q3 (25 observations). Since we wish to derive the forecasts recursively the procedure entails repeated reestimation of equations (19.3) and (19.4) by successively adding observations from the excluded quarters. In each

Table 19.2   Set-up for recursive forecasts of GDP growth using the estimated common factors

	Coincident index (C)	*Forward-looking index (C)*
Sample eq. (19.3)	1978Q4–s, s =1995Q2, …2001Q2	1979Q4-m, m =1995Q2,…,2001Q2
Sample eq. (19.4)	1978Q4-s, s=1995Q3,…2001Q3	1979Q4-m, m =1995Q3,…,2001Q3
Information set	$C_{78Q4}, \ldots, C_s, Y_{78Q4}, \ldots, Y_{s-1}$, s =1995Q3,…,2001Q3	$C_{79Q4}, \ldots, C_{m+1}, Y_{79Q4}, \ldots, Y_{m-1}$, m=1995Q3,…,2001Q3

Note: For each type of recursive model (distinguished by time indices s and m), the table gives the estimation samples and the information set that are used in each forecasting recursion. For example, when C is the forward-looking index, the first recursion estimates equation (19.3) over the sample 1979Q4–1995Q2 and equation (19.4) over 1979Q4–1995Q3. The available information set in this recursion contains GDP growth up to and including 1995Q2 and BTS data up to and including 1995Q4. The forward-looking index has fewer observations than the coincident index due to differences in lag structures, procedures for initial values, and so as, in the DFM.

recursion, we generate forecasts of GDP growth at the one-quarter, two-quarter, four-quarter and eight-quarter horizons. The exact procedure in the case Z in equations (19.3)–(19.4) is the estimated coincident or forward-looking common factors as outlined in Table 19.2.

The analysis of forecast accuracy is mainly based on the out-of-sample (root) mean-squared (forecast) error (RMSE). Under the hypothesis of unbiasedness, the RMSE is simply the standard deviation of the out-of-sample forecast errors. When analysing performance in relative terms, we compute ratios of RMSEs. Under certain circumstances, it is possible to undertake a test of the hypothesis that the relative RMSE equals unity (see Clark and McCracken, 2001, and Stock and Watson, 2001). If this hypothesis is rejected, then we can conclude that there is a statistically significant difference between the performances of the two forecasting models under consideration. But such tests require that the forecasting models that are being compared are nested, that is, are related by a parametric simplification. This does not apply to the models compared in the present analysis, and the distributions of the relative RMSEs are therefore unknown. However, critical values tabulated in previous research may still serve as rules of thumb. For example, the 5 per cent critical values reported by Stock and Watson (2001) indicate that relative RMSEs greater than 1.02–1.04 and smaller than 0.96–0.98 are statistically significant. By this measure, most relative RMSEs reported in this paper are statistically significant.

In our benchmark estimations, we fit all VARs without paying any attention to the models' in-sample performance. To gain some insights into how the analysis is affected if the VARs are required to fulfil criteria of in-sample performance, we repeat all forecasting experiments conditional on the forecasting equations satisfying certain tests of error-term adequacy. We compute three standard tests of model misspecification: the Breusch–Godfrey LM test against autocorrelation; Engle's LM test against ARCH effects; and Chow's parameter stability test. For the in-sample conditioning filter not to be too restrictive, we choose to consider a particular model as having acceptable in-sample properties if it passes at least two of the three error-term tests (at the conventional 5 per cent test error margin). Using in-sample criteria that are too restrictive may entail eliminating models that do not perform very well in sample but nevertheless work well for purposes of out-of-sample forecasting.

GDP-growth forecasts using the estimated common factors

With the two-out-of-three requirement concerning the misspecification tests all VAR models that use the estimated common factors turn out to qualify for the conditional out-of-sample forecasting comparisons. We note that, to the extent that the models do not pass the misspecification tests, it is the parameter stability requirement that seems to be the most difficult criterion to fulfil.[9] This is interesting because the models have been explicitly designed to be (very) parsimoniously parameterized. Thus, although parsimonious, the models still display tendencies of instability. Judging from previous evidence, whether this is a problem or not when it comes to out-of-sample forecasting is unclear. The results in this paper (as is shown below) support the previous finding that in-sample performance is largely unrelated to out-of-sample forecasting accuracy.

Table 19.3 summarizes the properties of the recursive GDP-growth forecasts using various measures of forecast accuracy. Looking first at the reported RMSEs we conclude that forecasts, even at very narrow horizons, are surrounded by a considerable amount of uncertainty. A 95 per cent confidence interval for normally distributed forecast errors at the one- and two-quarter horizons has a width of roughly 4 percentage points. The size of the typical forecast error (as measured by the mean absolute error, MAE) at the one- and two-quarter horizons is in the range 0.8–0.9 percentage points, reflecting the high uncertainty associated with the forecasts. Not surprisingly, all forecasts become successively less accurate as one prolongs the forecasting horizon.

Table 19.3   Forecast-error analysis for bivariate DFM-based VAR models: four-quarter GDP growth

	RMSE	MAE	RMedSE	MedAE	Rank
VAR variables: coincident index					
One-quarter	0.98	0.79	0.59	0.59	1
Two-quarter	1.14	0.93	0.71	0.71	4
Four-quarter	1.80	1.58	1.65	1.64	6
Eight-quarter	2.09	1.96	2.05	2.05	7
VAR variables: forward-looking index					
One-quarter	1.04	0.81	0.71	0.71	2
Two-quarter	1.11	0.87	0.79	0.79	3
Four-quarter	1.59	1.28	1.19	1.19	5
Eight-quarter	2.21	2.08	2.16	2.16	8

Note: Columns one and two give conventional root-mean-squared errors (RMSEs) and mean absolute errors (MAEs). Columns hree and four contain median-based RMSEs and MAEs (RMedSEs and MedAEs).

From a more detailed study of the time paths of the forecast errors it becomes evident that particularly large errors occur when the growth rate is at, or close to, a 'turning point' (in the sense that positive growth switches to negative growth and vice versa). To discern the extent to which the measures of forecast accuracy are influenced by large prediction errors that occur relatively infrequently, Table 19.3 also gives median-based measures of forecast accuracy (called RMedSEs and MedAEs). Comparing the root of the median-squared errors with the usual RMSEs, it can indeed be seen that large errors in the tails of the forecast-error distributions (which translate to the distributions of squared errors being skewed to the right) contribute to significantly worsening the forecasting performance of the procedures. This 'turning-point problem' is typical for linear forecasting models, which are highly influenced by the (average) persistence of the variables in the conditioning set. A non-linear alternative provides a potential solution to the problem, but applying such a framework would go beyond the scope of this paper.[10]

Alternative GDP-growth forecasts

The DFM-based forecasts of GDP growth are compared with various alternative GDP-growth forecasts in Tables 19.4–19.6. The comparisons with unfiltered BTS variables appear in Table 19.4, with macro data in Table 19.5, and with other popular summary indices in Table 19.6. These tables have the same basic format: the entries are relative RMSEs computed for various forecast horizons at which the RMSEs of the DFM-based VARs appear in the denominator so that numbers greater (smaller) than unity mean that the DFM-based VARs outperform (are outperformed by) the alternative forecasts.

Tables 19.4 and 19.5 have further similarities: in these tables, we compare the RMSEs of the DFM-based VARs with RMSEs of alternative forecasts generated by making use of empirical distributions. These distributions are obtained from the forecasts of all possible q-variate VARs given certain feasible conditioning sets (see the discussion above) and the restriction that $q \leq 5$ (including GDP growth). The first two rows in the upper and lower panels of Tables 19.4 and 19.5 construct the relative RMSEs by making use of the medians and means of the RMSE distributions of the alternative forecasts. The interpretation of these numbers is thus that they give a yardstick for assessing the performance of the DFM-based VARs relative to a typical alternative forecast that would obtain when using the BTS data unfiltered (that is, without employing the DFM filter) or making use of macro variables only. The remaining rows in the upper and lower panels of these tables ('Best x-quarter') substitute the central-tendency moments for the optimized RMSEs at the x-quarter horizon, $x = 1, 2, 4, 8$, and report the relative RMSEs that obtain when residually using the same model to derive the forecasts at the other horizons. These numbers thus allow us to undertake a comparison with the best possible forecast at a certain horizon that can be derived using the BTS variables unfiltered or the macro variables (and also to see how well the model used to compute this forecast performs, in relative terms, at other horizons).

Turning first to the results in Table 19.4, it is seen that the DFM filter generally improves the forecasting performance of the VARs. This holds true especially in

Table 19.4 Alternative forecasts of four-quarter GDP growth: relative RMSEs for coincident index and forward-looking index vs. unfiltered BTS variables

	One-quarter	Two-quarter	Four-quarter
Coincident index vs. unfiltered BTS variables			
Median	1.23 (1.20)	1.24 (1.24)	1.08 (1.07)
Mean	1.25 (1.22)	1.25 (1.23)	1.08 (1.08)
Best one-quarter	0.96 (0.96)	1.19 (1.19)	1.09 (1.09)
Best two-quarter	1.06 (1.07)	0.89 (0.92)	0.77 (0.79)
Best four-quarter	1.06 (1.07)	0.89 (0.92)	0.77 (0.79)
Forward-looking index vs. unfiltered BTS variables			
Median	1.23 (1.23)	1.27 (1.28)	1.13 (1.13)
Mean	1.23 (1.23)	1.28 (1.28)	1.13 (1.13)
Best one-quarter	1.11 (1.11)	1.14 (1.14)	0.96 (0.96)
Best two-quarter	1.11 (1.11)	1.14 (1.14)	0.96 (0.96)
Best four-quarter	1.11 (1.11)	1.15 (1.15)	0.95 (0.95)

Notes: All numbers are relative RMSEs. The models that make use of the common-factor index appear in the denominator so that numbers greater (smaller) than unity mean that the models based on the common factor outperform (are outperformed by) the models based the unfiltered BTS variables. In the rows labelled 'Median' and 'Mean' the RMSEs of the models based on the unfiltered BTS variables are central-tendency moments of empirical distributions. The distributions are generated from the forecasts of all possible VAR models of dimension five or less (including the variable to be forecast) using the feasible set of BTS variables outlined in Table 19.1. In the rows 'Best x-quarter' the RMSEs of the models based on the unfiltered BTS variables are optimized such that they are at their minimal at the x-quarter horizon (again making use of the empirical distributions). The numbers in brackets are results that condition the forecasting models on satisfying certain residual diagnostics criteria (see the text for details). The lag lengths of the VARs are determined by minimizing the system-based BIC.

Table 19.5 Alternative forecasts of four-quarter GDP growth: relative RMSEs for coincident index and forward-looking index vs. macro variables

	One-quarter	Two-quarter	Four-quarter	Eight-quarter
Coincident index vs. macro variables				
Median	1.27 (1.26)	1.21 (1.20)	0.92 (0.92)	0.75 (0.76)
Mean	1.28 (1.27)	1.21 (1.21)	0.93 (0.95)	0.76 (0.77)
Best one-quarter	1.16 (1.16)	1.09 (1.09)	0.93 (0.93)	0.86 (0.86)
Best two-quarter	1.23 (1.23)	1.08 (1.08)	0.84 (0.84)	0.84 (0.84)
Best four-quarter	1.31 (1.23)	1.19 (1.08)	0.79 (0.84)	0.82 (0.84)
Best eight-quarter	1.30 (1.41)	1.26 (1.27)	0.93 (1.10)	0.60 (0.63)
Forward-looking index vs. macro variables				
Median	1.20 (1.19)	1.24 (1.23)	1.04 (1.05)	0.71 (0.72)
Mean	1.20 (1.20)	1.25 (1.24)	1.05 (1.07)	0.72 (0.73)
Best one-quarter	1.10 (1.10)	1.12 (1.12)	1.05 (1.05)	0.81 (0.81)
Best two-quarter	1.16 (1.16)	1.11 (1.11)	0.95 (0.95)	0.79 (0.79)
Best four-quarter	1.23 (1.16)	1.23 (1.11)	0.89 (0.95)	0.78 (0.79)
Best eight-quarter	1.23 (1.33)	1.29 (1.31)	1.05 (1.25)	0.57 (0.60)

Note: See the notes to Table 19.4 (except that the empirical RMSE distributions here are generated using macro rather than BTS variables).

Table 19.6   Alternative forecasts of four-quarter GDP growth: relative RMSEs for coincident index and forward-looking index vs. popular summary indices

	One-quarter	*Two-quarter*	*Four-quarter*
Coincident index vs. popular summary indices			
BTS confidence indicator, manufacturing	1.20	1.15	0.94
BTS confidence indicator, construction	1.27	1.23	1.03
Consumer survey, own personal economy	1.15	1.05	0.82
Consumer survey, whole economy	1.14	1.08	0.91
Consumer survey, unemployment	1.15	1.18	1.04
Consumer survey, backward-looking	1.18	1.11	0.89
Activity index (four-quarter change)	1.17	1.05	0.98
Forward-looking index vs. popular summary indices			
BTS confidence indicator, manufacturing	1.13	1.18	1.07
BTS confidence indicator, construction	1.19	1.26	1.16
Consumer survey, own personal economy	1.09	1.08	0.92
Consumer survey, whole economy	1.08	1.11	1.03
Consumer survey, unemployment	1.09	1.21	1.18
Consumer survey, backward-looking	1.12	1.14	1.01
Activity index (four-quarter change)	1.11	1.08	1.11

Note: All numbers are relative RMSEs. The models that make use of the common-factor index appear in the denominator so that numbers greater (smaller) than unity mean that the models on the common factor outperform (are outperformed by) the models based on the other popular summary indices do not pass the residual diagnostics criteria. All models are bivariate VARs, whose lag lengths have been determined using the system-based BIC.

the case of the forward-looking variables. For these variables, the DFM-based VARs outperform the rival models at the one- and two-quarter horizons in all cases, even if the models based on the unfiltered variables are optimised (with respect to the particular forecast horizons).

From the results in brackets, we see that the picture is unaltered when conditioning the forecasting models on their in-sample performance. The difference between the numbers without and within brackets is marginal even though as much as 20–30 per cent of the models are discarded in some cases (coincident data). The finding in previous studies that in-sample performance is largely unrelated to out-of-sample performance is thus confirmed here.[11]

Next, turning to the comparison with macro data (Table 19.5), we find that the DFM approach again outperforms the rival models at all one- and two-quarter horizons. As before, the results are enhanced for the forward-looking data. As expected, the gains from using macro variables increase with the length of the forecast horizon: at the eight-quarter horizon the DFM forecasts never give lower RMSEs than the forecasts based on macro variables. But, the DFM-based models, in several cases, do surprisingly well even at the four-quarter horizon (see the lower panel in Table 19.5).

Finally, the results that compare the DFM-based GDP-growth forecasts with the forecasts of GDP growth based on popular summary indices of activity are in Table 19.6. They are qualitatively similar to those in the previous tables: the DFM forecasts dominate at short horizons and the improvement is somewhat larger for forward-looking variables. One particularly interesting feature of the comparisons with the popular summary indices is that the DFM – except in the case of coincident data at the four-quarter horizon – outperforms the so-called activity index of Statistics Sweden by a relatively large margin (see the last row in each panel in Table 19.6). This is interesting because the activity index is explicitly designed to be a short-run indicator of the growth rate of GDP and in practice used by many of the professional forecasters. Since both indicators are now being analysed and published continuously (see www.scb.se and www.konj.se), future work may make a further contribution by comparing the performance of these indicators in genuine real time.

Concluding remarks

In this chapter we have examined whether data from business tendency surveys are useful for forecasting GDP growth in the short run. The starting point is a so-called dynamic factor model (DFM), which is used both as a framework for dimension reduction in forecasting and as a procedure for filtering out unimportant idiosyncratic noise in the underlying survey data. In this way, it is possible to model a rather large number of noisy survey variables in a parsimoniously parameterized vector autoregression (VAR). To assess the forecasting performance of the procedure, comparisons are made with VARs that either use the survey variables directly, use macro variables only, or use other popular summary indices of economic activity. Our DFM-based procedure turns out to outperform the competing alternatives in most cases.

Our findings relate to the recent research that reports good forecasting performance results for dynamic factor models, for example, Forni, Hallin, Lippi and Reichlin (2000, 2003) and Stock and Watson (1999, 2002). However, in a recent paper, Stock and Watson (2004) find evidence that simple mean combination forecasts (derived from simple indicator regressions augmented with AR terms) outperform DFM-based forecasts in many cases. The simple mean forecasts are found to work well, although the underlying individual forecasts display substantial instability. Our analyses do not comprise an evaluation of a mean combination forecast alternative. The reason for this is that we became aware of the findings of Stock and Watson (2004) after having completed our research. Another limitation of our analyses is that they do not allow for forecasting models that are non-linear. To allow for non-linearities would be interesting, especially since we find that many models suffer from problems of parameter instability and large forecast errors at, or around, turning points. We intend to address these issues in future work.

Notes

1   The forecasting performance for other key macro variables (e.g., inflation, unemployment, employment, wage inflation, interest rates, and the exchange rate) is investigated in a longer version of this chapter, see Hansson, Jansson and Löf (2003).

2 For details about the design of the survey see Hansson, Jansson and Löf (2003) and www.konj.se.
3 One previous analysis that supports the premise that the forecasting performance of the Swedish BTS may be enhanced by filtering techniques is that undertaken by Christoffersson, Roberts and Eriksson (1992). Although these authors do not explicitly favour the kind of filtering procedure that we propose, they show, using methods in the frequency domain, that the BTS series are both noisy at high frequencies and highly collinear. This makes it difficult to directly include them as explanatory variables in a conventional forecasting equation.
4 The models developed in Stock and Watson (1999), Camba-Mendez, Kapetanios, Smith and Weale (1999), and Forni, Hallin, Lippi and Reichlin (2000, 2003) make use of some survey variables but are mainly based on macro variables.
5 We also experimented with models that were based on differences between the coincident and forward-looking variables but such models did not turn out to perform well. The final models include variables BTVI101, BTVI105, BTVI301, BTVI305, BTVI306, BTVI308, BBOA101, BBOA102, BBOA106, BBOA201, BBOA202 and BBOA204 (cf. Table 19.1).
6 UND1X inflation is CPI inflation excluding household mortgage interest expenditure and indirect taxes and subsidies.
7 In Hansson, Jansson and Löf (2003) we also use (log) first differences. This is of some importance but does not affect our results qualitatively.
8 Wage inflation is an exception, however. Since this variable is generated from wage sums and hours worked in the national accounts it is subject to the same publication lag as the real macro variables.
9 This is a general finding that holds true for all forecasting models investigated in this chapter.
10 As mentioned previously, in Hansson, Jansson and Löf (2003) we give a more extensive evaluation of forecasting performance, considering, among other things, forecasts of a number of macro variables. In that analysis we also compare the forecasts of the different macro variables taking into account that they are measured in different scales. This is done using Theil's U (defined as the usual RMSE divided by the standard deviation of the series to be forecast). This measure of forecasting accuracy not only allows us to compare forecasts across series with different scales, but also provides us with a benchmark against the random-walk forecasting model (the criterion being that Theil's U is strictly less than unity). The GDP-growth forecasts evaluated in Table 19.3 all turn out to have a Theil's U well-below unity and thus imply that the DFM-based VAR forecasts always outperform the random-walk forecasts.
11 This is a general finding for the models analysed in this chapter.

References

Bergström, R. (1992) 'The relationship between manufacturing production and different business survey series in Sweden', Working Paper no. 12. Stockholm: National Institute of Economic Research.

Bergström, R. (1993) 'Quantitative production series compared with qualitative business survey series for five sectors of the Swedish manufacturing industry', Working Paper no. 30b. Stockholm: National Institute of Economic Research.

Bruno, G. and Malgarini, M. (2002) 'An indicator of economic sentiment for the Italian economy', Working Paper no. 28/02. Rome: Institute for Studies and Economic Analyses.

Camba-Mendez, G., Kapetanios, G., Smith, R. and Weale, M. (1999) 'An automatic leading indicator of economic activity: forecasting GDP growth for European countries', Discussion Paper no. 149. London: National Institute for Economic and Social Research.

Christoffersson, A., Roberts, R. and Eriksson, U. (1992) 'The relationship between manufacturing and various BTS (business tendency survey) series in Sweden illuminated by frequency and complex demodulate methods', Working Paper no. 15. Stockholm: National Institute of Economic Research.

Clark, T. and McCracken, M. (2001) 'Tests of equal forecast accuracy and encompassing for nested models', *Journal of Econometrics*, 105: 85–100.

European Commission (2000) 'Business climate indicator for the Euro area', (europa.eu.int/comm/economy_finance/indicators/businessclimate_en.htm).

Forni, M., Hallin, M. Lippi, M. and Reichlin, L. (2000) 'The generalized factor model : identification and estimation', *Review of Economics and Statistics*, 82: 540–54.

Forni, M., Hallin, M., Lippi, M. and Reichlin, L. (2003) 'Do financial variables help forecasting inflation and real activity in the euro area?', *Journal of Monetary Economics*, 50: 1243–55.

Fukuda, S. and Onodera, T. (2001) 'A new composite index of coincident economic indicators in Japan: how can we improve forecast performances?', *International Journal of Forecasting*, 17: 483–98.

Goldrian, G., Lindbauer, J. and Nerb, G. (2001) 'Evaluation and development of confidence indicators based on harmonised business and consumer surveys', *EC Economic Paper*, 151. Bruxelles: European Commission.

Hansson, J., Jansson, P. and Löf, M. (2003) 'Business survey data: do they help in forecasting the macro economy?', Working Paper no. 84. Stockholm: National Institute of Economic Research.

Harvey, A. (1989) *Forecasting, Structural Time Series Models and the Kalman Filter*. Cambridge: Cambridge University Press.

Käntä, P. and Tallbom, C. (1993) 'Using business survey data for forecasting Swedish quantitative business cycle variables: a Kalman filter approach', Working Paper no. 35. Stockholm: National Institute of Economic Research.

Koskinen, L. and Öller, L.-E. (2004) 'A classifying procedure for signalling turning points', *Journal of Forecasting*, 23: 197–214.

Lindström, T. (2000) 'Qualitative survey responses and production over the business cycle', Working Paper no. 116. Stockholm: Sveriges Riksbank.

Öller, L.-E. and Tallbom, C. (1996) 'Smooth and timely business cycle indicators for noisy Swedish data', *International Journal of Forecasting*, 12: 389–402.

Rahiala, M. and Teräsvirta, T. (1993) 'Business survey data in forecasting the output of Swedish and Finnish metal and engineering industries: a Kalman filter approach', *Journal of Forecasting*, 12: 255–71.

Stock, J. and Watson, M. (1989) 'New indexes of coincident and leading economic indicators', *NBER Macroeconomics Annual*, 4: 351–93.

Stock, J. and Watson, M. (1991) 'A probability model of the coincident economic indicators', in K. Lahiri and G. Moore (eds), *Leading Economic Indicators: New Approaches and Forecasting Records*. Cambridge: Cambridge University Press.

Stock, J. and Watson, M. (1999) 'Forecasting inflation', *Journal of Monetary Economics*, 44: 293–335.

Stock, J. and Watson, M. (2001) 'Forecasting output and inflation: the role of asset prices', Working Paper no. 8180. New York: National Bureau of Economic Research (revised January 2003, www.wws.princeton.edu/~mwatson/).

Stock, J. and Watson, M. (2002) 'Macroeconomic forecasting using diffusion indexes', *Journal of Business and Economic Statistics*, 20: 147–62.

Stock, J. and Watson, M. (2004) 'Combination forecasts of output growth in a seven-country data set', *Journal of Forecasting*, forthcoming (www.wws.princeton.edu/~mwatson/).

Part V
Turning Points Dating and Detection

20
Business Cycle Analysis with Multivariate Markov Switching Models

Jacques Anas, Monica Billio, Laurent Ferrara and Marco Lo Duca

Introduction

Since the early work of Burns and Mitchell, many attempts have been made to measure and forecast business cycles. Recently, approaches based on time series econometrics, have emerged. The most representative works are the Stock–Watson model which focuses on co-movements among macroeconomic variables, and the univariate regime-switching model developed by Hamilton (1989) which is based on the intuition that turning points and changes in regime are related. Diebold and Rudebush (1996) and Kim and Nelson (1998) synthesized the two approaches allowing for both co-movements among macroeconomic variables and switching regimes.

There is a large literature that uses Markov switching models (MS) to recognize business cycle phases. The starting point of this literature is that there is a relationship between the concepts of changes in cyclical phases and change in regime. Moreover, this relationship has been confirmed by a growing number of empirical studies (Klements and Krolzig, 2003; Krolzig, 2001, 2003; Anas and Ferrara, 2004). Therefore, contractions and expansions are modelled as switching regimes of the stochastic process generating the growth rate of some economic variables. However, some words of caution have to be spent on the MS approach to the business cycle. When using parametric models, such as MS-VAR processes, no *a priori* definition of the business cycle is imposed: by means of the switching approach, different regimes are identified. Indeed, these regimes differ in terms of average growth rates and/or growth volatilities. In many cases the MS approach properly detects the classical cycle phases, but this does not necessarily happen. The model simply detects the presence of different growth rates of the economy, but the regime of low growth could also have a positive mean, in which case the correct detection of the cycle depends on the features of the analysed series. The

MS-VAR approach lets the data describe the features of the different phases of the economy. Thus, the MS approach simply represents the idea that economies are characterized by different phases.

In this chapter we deal with the multivariate extensions of Markov switching models and their reliability in business cycle analysis. We extend basic MS-VAR models (Krolzig, 1997) by introducing a specific Markov chain in each equation of the VAR model. Moreover, we introduce correlated Markov chains which can reveal useful information on the relationship between phases in different countries, and define causality relationships, which can allow more parsimonious representations.

In the next section we deal with simple MS-VAR models with a single Markov chain representing the common cycle (Artis, Krolzig and Toro, 1997) and models with multiple Markov chains (MMS-VAR) which represent country or sector-specific factors. When dealing with multiple Markov chains, we consider different specifications of the transition matrix, involving different hypotheses on the relationship among the specific chains. We then apply the MMS-VAR model to analyse the relationship between cyclical phases of industrial production in the USA and the Eurozone.

Multiple markov switching VAR models (MMS-VAR)

The MS-VAR with a single Markov chain introduced by Krolzig (1997) is the simplest multivariate Markov switching model that can be used in business cycle analysis. Consider the following specification:

$$y_t = \nu(S_t) + \sum_{j=1}^{p} \phi_j(S_t) y_{t-j} + \epsilon_t \qquad (20.1)$$

where y_t is a n-dimensional vector of endogenous variables and $\epsilon_t \sim \aleph(0, \sigma^2(S_t))$ is the vector of the idiosyncratic disturbances. The common latent variable $S_t = 1, \ldots, M$ follows a Markov chain with constant transition probabilities and is assumed to represent the phases of the common cycle. Usually, in business cycle analysis, only the mean (or the intercept) and sometimes the covariance matrix is supposed to depend on the common latent variable, while the other parameters are considered to be constant.

The assumption of a single Markov chain is consistent with the existence of a single common and coincident cycle. However, even if we can hypothesise a common business cycle, empirical analyses often suggest that this cycle could not be synchronised. Using a single Markov chain is undoubtedly a way to aggregate turning points and produce a description of the common cycle phases: in some way, the model finds the turning point that best fits the group of turning points that we can usually observe in a set of different series when there is a change of phase.

To improve the comprehension of the relations among the phases of different economies or sectors and thus to produce a better description of how phases evolve, it is necessary to consider that turning points are not always coincident. This happens when different series are driven by different unobserved factors. In the following we introduce models which explicitly use multiple Markov chains.

Multiple Markov chains

Even if a single business cycle exists in a group of economies (for example the European Monetary Union), there may be no synchronization among the phases of the different economies or among those of different sectors of a single economy. It is then useful to relax the hypothesis that a single Markov chain drives the shifts in all the economies or sectors. In the general case, we can assume that the change in the regime of each series is driven by a specific Markov chain. We then consider a VAR model in which each equation has the following form:

$$y_t = v(S_{it}) + \sum_{j=1}^{p} \alpha_j y_{it-j} + \epsilon_{it}, \qquad \epsilon_{it} \sim \aleph(0, \sigma^2(S_{it})), \quad i = 1, \ldots, n \qquad (20.2)$$

The regime shift of each of the n endogenous variables is driven by a specific Markov chain with M regimes. For estimation purposes, the n specific chains are combined in a single Markov chain with M^n regimes. The regimes of the joint Markov chain are all the possible combinations of the regimes of the specific chains, thus the transition matrix of the joint process contains information on the relationship among the phases of the different series. Hence, the relationships among the phases in different countries are explicitly taken into account and described. Clearly, the number of parameters that have to be estimated rises enormously and this produces serious difficulties in the estimation process. Fortunately, by considering simple constraints based on economic considerations or imposing a dependence structure based on some *a priori* ideas, it is possible to reduce the number of parameters necessary to define the transition matrix. Finally, it is also possible to test whether these constraints are consistent with the data.

Modelling the transition matrix

Markov switching models with specific chains allow us to describe the connections between the phases of cycles in different countries or in different sectors; this is done by making some assumptions on the transition matrix that drives the joint Markov process of all the specific factors. Following Hamilton and Lin (1996), there are four possibilities: common regimes (existence of a unique Markov chain); independent regime; related regimes; or a general specification. These cases allow the description of interesting phenomena but do not give the complete range of possibilities. In the following we propose two additional strategies: to model the transition matrix; to consider dependent and correlated Markov chains (Billio, 2002).

If we assume that there is no relationship among the phases of different economies or sectors, we can use independent Markov chains. In this case the joint process is described by the Kronecker product of the transition matrix of each specific chain. The advantage of this approach is the limited number of parameters to estimate. The hypothesis of independent cycles could be not consistent with the cycle in Europe and often it is not useful when considering different sectors of an economy. Anyway, this specification could be useful if we need to formally test whether or not cycles are related. As an example, it could be useful before extracting a common factor from a group of series. In fact, it is possible to formally test the null of related Markov chains against the alternative of independent Markov chains with a simple Likelihood Ratio test. In this way it is possible to have a selection strategy to choose the variables to be included in the multivariate model.

Concerning the related regime case, the forces that govern both cycles are the same, but are not in phase. Two sub-cases can be considered: the first cycle shifts before so $z_t = s_{t-1}$, and causality is reversed, namely $s_t = z_{t-1}$. Also this type of relation strongly simplifies the transition matrix of the joint process since the number of parameters is simply 2 and it is useful to describe lead or lag relationships among the economies.

In the general specification no *a priori* structure on the transition matrix is imposed. In the case of two series and chains with three regimes (fast expansion, slow expansion and recession), the joint process is characterized by a 9×9 transition matrix.

To reduce the number of parameters it is possible to impose some constraints based on simple economic considerations. For example, it is reasonable to impose that it is not possible that a fast expansion is followed by a recession and vice versa. In this way, we impose that the expected relationship between turning points of different cycles (classical and growth) described by the ABCD approach (see Anas and Ferrara 2004) is respected. First, there will be the growth cycle peak then the business cycle peak, which will be followed by the business cycle trough and the growth cycle trough. If we proceed in this way, the number of parameters to be estimate is naturally reduced; unfortunately, it remains still large and strong convergence problems exist. Consequently, from a practical point of view, we are limited to the analysis of two series with three regimes or three series with two regimes. For this reason this method could be used when dealing with groups of countries.

In general, in a VAR context, the identification of causality relations allows more parsimonious representations. In the literature there are very few attempts to address this issue in MS-VAR models. We propose to describe causality relationships with the Markov chains. This is certainly useful to describe the relationships between leading and lagging countries, or to describe the relation between business surveys and macroeconomic variables. Using this approach it is possible to reduce the number of parameters required to define the transition matrix. Moreover, in a multi-country/multi-sector framework, this type of model allows us to explain the interactions among macro-areas, which is not possible with the independent and common cases presented in the previous section. In particular, if s_t and z_t are two Markov chains and S_t is the resulting joint process, in the general specification we can decompose the transition probabilities of S_t as follows:

$$P(S_t|S_{t-1}) = P(s_t, z_t|s_{t-1}, z_{t-1}) = P(s_t|z_t, s_{t-1}, z_{t-1})P(z_t|s_{t-1}, z_{t-1})$$

We can now define the Granger non-causality for a Markov chain. Let $s^{t-1} = s_{t-1}, s_{t-2}, \ldots, s_0$, *Strong one-step-ahead non-causality (Granger non-causality)*: s^{t-1}

does not strongly cause z_t one step ahead, given z^{t-1} if: $P(z_t|s^{t-1}, z^{t-1}) = P(z_t|z^{t-1})$.

This means that we can assume than s^{t-1} does not strongly cause z_t one step ahead if s^{t-1} contains no information on z_t. Similarly, z^{t-1} does not strongly cause s_t one step ahead, given s^{t-1} if: $P(s_t|s^{t-1}, z^{t-1}) = P(s_t|s^{t-1})$.

As one can see, the non-causality definition involves the marginal conditional distributions. Let us see how we can construct a transition matrix starting from the non-causality definition. Consider specific chains (s_t and z_t) with two states: the independent case requires four parameters while the most general model (see the above general specification) representing $P(S_t|S_{t-1})$ involves 12 parameters to define the transition matrix, since the sum of each row is equal to one. We can also obtain suitable representations with a number of parameters comprised between four and 12. In fact, the following vector represents the four possibilities of the joint Markov chain S_t:

$$X_t = (1, s_{t-1}, z_{t-1}, s_{t-1} z_{t-1})' = (1, s_{t-1})' \otimes (1, z_{t-1})'$$

It is then easy to verify that we can represent the joint probability of s_t and z_t as follows:

$$P(s_t, z_t|s_{t-1}, z_{t-1}) = P(s_t|z_t, s_{t-1}, z_{t-1})P(z_t|s_{t-1}, z_{t-1})$$

$$= \frac{\exp(\alpha_1 W_t)}{1 + \exp(\alpha_1 W_t)} \frac{\exp(\alpha_2 X_t)}{1 + \exp(\alpha_2 X_t)} \tag{20.3}$$

where $W_t = (1, s_t)' \otimes (1, s_{t-1})' \otimes (1, z_{t-1})' = (1, s_{t-1}, z_{t-1}, s_{t-1} z_{t-1}, s_t, s_t z_{t-1}, s_t s_{t-1}, s_t s_{t-1} z_{t-1})'$ and X_t has already been defined.

Now, Y_t and X_t involve respectively eight and four parameters, then we simply have an alternative parameterization of the transition matrix. Such parameterization is very useful since it allows us to simply impose the non-causality restrictions by restricting the transition matrix to be described by a number of parameters comprised between four and 12. In particular, if s^{t-1} does not strongly cause z_t one step ahead, given z^{t-1}, the X_t vector reduces to $X_t = (1, z_{t-1})'$ and the number of parameters reduces to 10. In this setting we can investigate if z_t causes s_t in the Granger sense or the contrary without imposing common states. This can be very useful to understand which series can be useful in predicting the business cycle. Moreover, this type of decomposition allows us to describe all the previous specifications besides other even more interesting cases.

Application: a MMS model for the Eurozone and the US industrial productions

We apply the MMS VAR model with different specifications of the joint transition matrix to the study of the relationships between the industrial production in the USA and the Eurozone. Industrial production data of the Euro-area have been back-calculated starting from a set of national indices; the final sample starts in 1970 and covers up to December 2002. Data have then been pre-treated by using the

Tramo-Seats method in Demetra.[1] For the USA, however, the manufacturing index for major industry groups has been considered; the data-set covers the period from January 1919 to August 2003.

We consider a MMS-VAR model to describe the growth rate over three months of industrial production in Europe and in the USA to detect cyclical phases and analyse the relationships between the two macro areas. Our aim is to simultaneously take into account fluctuations of the business and growth cycles using a single model (see for instance Anas and Ferrara, 2004, for more detailed connections between the two cycles). According to this idea, for both the Eurozone and the USA a specific Markov chain with three regimes is used. The three regimes have the following economic interpretation: (i) low growth regime or Recession (labelled **R**): the regime is usually characterized by a negative average growth rate and it is associated to the classical recessions; (ii) intermediate growth regime or Slow Expansion (labelled **S**): we assume that the growth rate of the economy is below its trend growth rate (low phase of the growth cycle without recession); and (iii) high growth regime or Fast Expansion (labelled **E**): we assume that the growth rate of the economy is above its trend growth rate (high phase of the growth cycle). There is no theoretical reason that guarantees that it is possible to use this interpretation of the regimes, but in empirical applications the relationships between the three regimes and the phases of growth and business cycle are quite strong. Moreover, the use of a three-regime model avoids the recession regime having a positive mean. Even if the detected regimes and phases of the cycle are not perfectly related, we think that to use a three-regime model with this interpretation improves our ability to understand the meaning of regimes. However, it is noteworthy to underline that this interpretation of the three regimes implicitly assumes a constant long-term growth rate over the whole sample period; that is, the estimated growth cycle is the deviation from a linear trend, instead of being computed through a specific filter.

Once the parameters of the model have been estimated, to detect phases we simply assign the observation at time t to the regime with the highest smoothed probability. Concerning turning-points detection, a trough is the last observation of the low-growth regime and a peak is the last observation of the high-growth regime.

To date business and growth cycle phases, we proceed in the following way. Concerning the business cycle, we obtain the smoothed probabilities of an expansion (labelled **EX**) by summing the smoothed probabilities of the second regime (**S**) and the third regime (**E**) and the recession regime (labelled **RE**) is the regime **R** of the starting model. Concerning the growth cycles, we obtain the smoothed probabilities of the under trend phase (labelled **L**) by summing the smoothed probabilities of the first regime (**R**) and the second regime (**S**), while the high regime (labelled **H**) is the regime **E** of the starting model.

Starting from the general model with regime-dependent mean and covariance matrix (no autoregression terms are considered) we reduce the number of parameters by imposing and testing some restrictions. In particular, we set to zero all the transition probabilities with results very close to zero in the first estimation of the model. In Figures 20.1 and 20.2 the detected low phases of the business

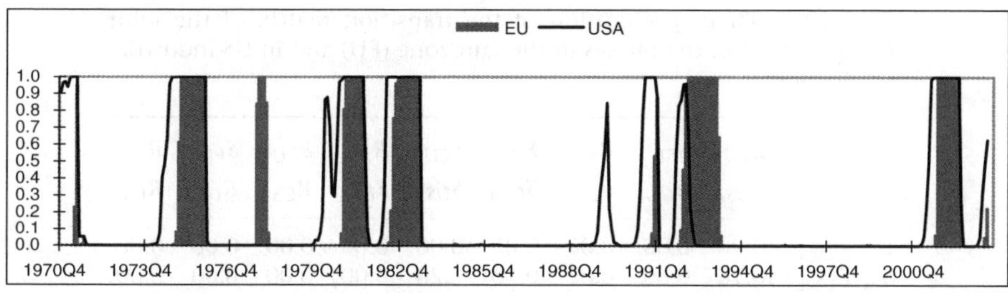

Figure 20.1　Smoothed probabilities of a business cycle recession in the Eurozone (EU) and in the USA

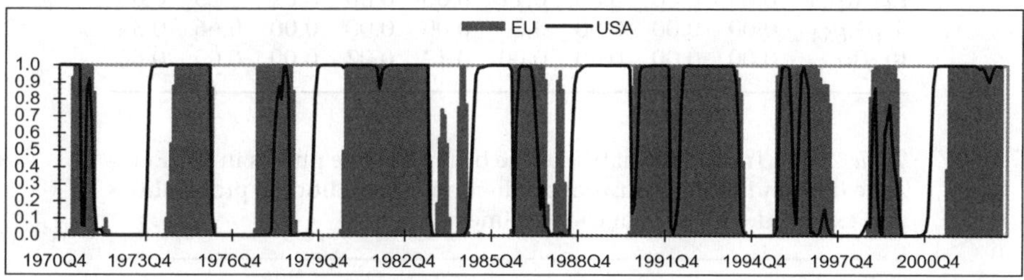

Figure 20.2　Smoothed probabilities of the low phase of the growth cycle in the Eurozone (EU) and in the USA

and the growth cycle are reported for both the areas. In particular, concerning Figure 20.1, it is important to underline the correspondence between regime **R** for the Eurozone and for the USA and the well-known episodes of recession. The first oil shock, the double dip at the beginning of the 1980s, the recession in the USA at the beginning of the 1990s, the Eurozone recession in 1992 and the possible 2001 recession are all well-detected. Moreover, very low uncertainty is associated to the regime classification and by a visual inspection it is possible to note that the USA leads Europe in entering recession.

Both for the business and the growth cycles, the low phases detected with the MMS approach are not erratic but display a very high persistence, hence regimes should be considered informative by policy-makers. Furthermore, by comparing the reference chronology of the growth cycle published by the ECRI for the USA,[2] with the detected phases, it is possible to note that the turning points do not differ significantly.

The most interesting feature of the MMS model is that it allows the estimation of the transition matrix of the joint Markov chain of the phases in the Eurozone and in the USA: this could produce useful information on the relationship between the cycle of the two areas. The final transition matrix is reported in Table 20.1. It is noteworthy that we can accept the equality of zero of most of the transition probabilities: in many rows there are only two or three elements different from zero.

Table 20.1 Final specification of the transition matrix of the joint Markov chain of the phases in the Eurozone (EU) and in US industrial production

	E_{EU} E_{USA}	S_{EU} E_{USA}	R_{EU} E_{USA}	E_{EU} S_{USA}	S_{EU} S_{USA}	R_{EU} S_{USA}	E_{EU} R_{USA}	S_{EU} R_{USA}	R_{EU} R_{USA}
$E_{EU} E_{USA}$	0.90	0.05	0.00	0.05	0.00	0.00	0.00	0.00	0.00
$S_{EU} E_{USA}$	0.18	0.60	0.02	0.00	0.20	0.00	0.00	0.00	0.00
$R_{EU} E_{USA}$	0.00	0.22	0.78	0.00	0.00	0.00	0.00	0.00	0.00
$E_{EU} S_{USA}$	0.00	0.04	0.00	0.88	0.00	0.00	0.08	0.00	0.00
$S_{EU} S_{USA}$	0.03	0.17	0.00	0.00	0.75	0.00	0.00	0.05	0.00
$R_{EU} S_{USA}$	0.00	0.00	0.00	0.00	0.08	0.92	0.00	0.00	0.00
$E_{EU} R_{USA}$	0.00	0.00	0.00	0.11	0.00	0.00	0.64	0.25	0.00
$S_{EU} R_{USA}$	0.00	0.00	0.00	0.00	0.00	0.00	0.00	0.66	0.34
$R_{EU} R_{USA}$	0.00	0.00	0.00	0.00	0.12	0.02	0.00	0.00	0.86

Table 20.2 Transition matrix of the business cycle phases in the Eurozone (EU) and in US industrial production; unconditional probabilities and expected durations of each regime

	EX_{EU} EX_{USA}	RE_{EU} EX_{USA}	EX_{EU} RE_{USA}	RE_{EU} RE_{USA}	*Unconditional probabilities*	*Expected durations*
$EX_{EU} EX_{USA}$	0.97	0.00	0.03	0.00	0.74	30.47
$RE_{EU} EX_{USA}$	0.12	0.88	0.00	0.00	0.05	8.43
$EX_{EU} RE_{USA}$	0.04	0.00	0.75	0.21	0.09	4.00
$RE_{EU} RE_{USA}$	0.12	0.02	0.00	0.86	0.12	7.14

Analysis of the business cycle

Table 20.2 shows the transition matrix of the Markov chain describing the business cycle. Let us start considering the exit of EX_{EU} EX_{USA} regime: this regime is very persistent and its expected duration is 30.5 months; it is striking that the only possible exit from EX_{EU} EX_{USA} is EX_{EU} RE_{USA}, which means that the USA shifted to the recession regime. Moreover, we observe that once we get EX_{EU} RE_{USA}, there is a 84 per cent probability to enter RE_{EU} RE_{USA}, which indicates that both the USA and the Eurozone are in the recession phase with only 16 per cent probability to get back to EX_{EU} EX_{USA}. Since the expected duration of the EX_{EU} RE_{USA} regime is four months, we can conclude that if the USA enters the recession phase, there is a high probability that the Eurozone will follow in four months. The transition matrix clearly indicates a lead of the USA in entering recessions. Finally, we observe that from RE_{EU} RE_{USA} there is an 86 per cent probability of a shift to the EX_{EU} EX_{USA} regime, which means synchronization in exiting the recession and a 14 per cent probability to get to RE_{EU} EX_{USA}, which means that the USA switches in advance. It is striking that, once in RE_{EU} EX_{USA}, the only possible exit is EX_{EU} EX_{USA} which means that the USA drives the recovery. The average lead in this case is 8.5 months.

Table 20.3   Transition matrix of the growth cycle phases in the Eurozone (EU) and in US industrial production; unconditional probabilities and expected duration of each regime

	H_{EU} H_{USA}	L_{EU} H_{USA}	H_{EU} L_{USA}	L_{EU} L_{USA}	*Unconditional probabilities*	*Expected durations*
$H_{EU}H_{USA}$	0.90	0.05	0.05	0.00	0.29	9.89
$L_{EU}H_{USA}$	0.16	0.65	0.00	0.18	0.15	2.90
$H_{EU}L_{USA}$	0.00	0.03	0.92	0.05	0.18	13.28
$L_{EU}L_{USA}$	0.01	0.08	0.00	0.91	0.39	11.17

We can conclude that, both in entering and exiting business cycle recessions, the USA leads the Eurozone or the shifts are synchronized.

Analysis of the growth cycle

Table 20.3 presents the transition matrix of the Markov chain describing the growth cycle. Differently from the business cycle transition matrix, there is no clear evidence of a lead of the USA. Starting from the above trend phase for both areas ($H_{EU}H_{USA}$), there is the same probability to get $H_{EU}L_{USA}$ and $L_{EU}H_{USA}$ and no synchronized shift to the below-trend phase ($L_{EU}L_{USA}$) is possible. From the regimes $H_{EU}L_{USA}$ and $L_{EU}H_{USA}$ it is possible to go to $L_{EU}L_{USA}$ but also to $H_{EU}H_{USA}$, so no clear lead is showed by any area in entering the low phase of the growth cycle. If we consider now the $L_{EU}L_{USA}$ regime, it a synchronized exit to $H_{EU}H_{USA}$ may happen, but in the most of the cases, with an 89 per cent probability, the exit is $L_{EU}H_{USA}$, which means that the USA exits in advance. Once in $L_{EU}H_{USA}$, it is possible to move to $L_{EU}L_{USA}$ again but the exit could also be $H_{EU}H_{USA}$: we can thus conclude that the USA leads the Eurozone in exiting the low phase of the growth cycle or the exit is synchronized. In any case, the Eurozone never leads the USA in exiting the low phase.

The more complex dynamic described by the transition matrix of the growth cycle could be due to the fact that the low phase of the growth cycle is more connected to the area-specific shocks than a recession. In fact, recessions are more synchronized and in most of the cases they seem to be the results of global shocks.

In conclusion, the transition probabilities have to be studied with caution. Some of them may be influenced by the presence of specific cycles, especially those concerning the growth cycle. On the contrary, when the USA shifts in a business cycle recession we expect the Eurozone to follow within a few months. This 'catching-up' effect can be clearly seen if we consider the evolution of the conditional mean of each area to the steady state mean (unconditional mean) given a starting regime. In this way it is possible to note that there is a strong interrelationship between the two areas; in particular, given a starting regime for the Eurozone the evolution of the conditional mean of this area is quite different depending on which is the starting regime for the USA.

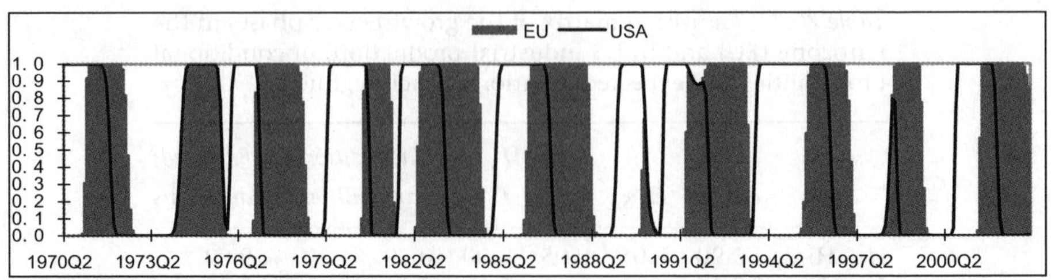

Figure 20.3   Smoothed probabilities of the low phase of the growth cycle in the Eurozone (EU) and in US industrial production (without the trend)

A causality analysis of the Eurozone and US industrial production

To get a more detailed description of the relationship between growth cycles phases in the USA and in the Eurozone, we consider the industrial production indexes without the trend. The trend has been extracted through a two-stage Hodrick–Prescott filter calibrated to maintain all the fluctuations between 1.5 and 8 years (see Artis, Marcellino and Proietti, 2002). To get a representation of the growth cycle phases in terms of Markov chains we implement an MMS-VAR(1) model. This produces a little delay in detecting turning points but in any case the phases are well-described. Starting from the general model with regime-dependent intercept and variances and 12 unrestricted conditional probabilities, we impose some restrictions. In the final specification only the intercepts and the correlation are regime dependent, while the transition matrix is reduced to only six unrestricted elements and correlation are constant across regimes.

Figure 20.3 reports the smoothed probability of being in the low phases of the growth cycle. Comparing Figure 20.3 with Figure 20.2 reporting the classification of the growth cycle derived from the MMS model with nine regimes, it is possible to note that phases are very similar; moreover in Figure 20.3 regimes are less erratic; and as mentioned this is because the nine-regime model involves an approximation assuming a constant trend growth rate.

Concerning the transition matrix, which is reported in Table 20.4, we can evidence some important information. Let us start by considering the exit from the $H_{EU}H_{USA}$ regime: there are two possible exits, $L_{EU}L_{USA}$ (18% probability) and $H_{EU}L_{USA}$ (82% probability). If we move to $L_{EU}L_{USA}$, it means that both areas switch to the low phase but if we go to $H_{EU}L_{USA}$, it means that only the USA shift to the low regime. Moreover, we observe that once we get to $H_{EU}L_{USA}$ we can only exit it by entering in $L_{EU}L_{USA}$. The transition matrix indicates that in most of the cases there is a lead of the USA entering the below-trend phase or at least the shift is synchronized. The same happens in exiting the $L_{EU}L_{USA}$ regime: we have a 21 per cent probability to get $H_{EU}H_{USA}$ and a 79 per cent probability to get $L_{EU}H_{USA}$. In the latter case, the only possible exit is $L_{EU}L_{USA}$, hence the USA again leads the Eurozone or at least the exits from the below-trend phase are synchronized. Finally, given the evidence that the USA lead the change in phase, we tested the null that shifts in the USA do not cause shifts in the Eurozone (*USA NC EU*), and that shifts

Table 20.4 Final specification of the transition matrix of the growth cycle phases in the Eurozone (EU) and in US industrial production (without the trend) and expected duration of each regime

	H_{EU} H_{USA}	L_{EU} H_{USA}	H_{EU} L_{USA}	L_{EU} L_{USA}	*Expected Durations*
$H_{EU} H_{USA}$	0.89	0.00	0.09	0.02	9.14
$L_{EU} H_{USA}$	0.07	0.93	0.00	0.00	13.92
$H_{EU} L_{USA}$	0.00	0.00	0.91	0.09	11.62
$L_{EU} L_{USA}$	0.03	0.11	0.00	0.86	7.33

in the Eurozone do not cause shifts in the USA (*EU NC USA*). As expected, the null *'USA NC EU'* is rejected. However, the null *'EU NC USA'* is also rejected.

Conclusions

In this chapter we have extended the classical MS-VAR approach to the business cycle proposed by Krolzig (1997), introducing multiple Markov chain producing specific shifts in the parameters of each equation of the VAR (MMS VAR). Differently from the MS-VAR approach, which allows the description of the common cycle and the evolution of its phases, the MMS-VAR approach allows us to describe the relationships among cyclical phases of different countries or different sectors.

The MMS-VAR models and their different specifications have been used to analyse the relationship between the industrial cycle in the Eurozone and in the USA. The estimated transition matrix of the MMS model shows that the USA, most of the time, leads the Eurozone in both business and growth cycles. Moreover, we show that there is a strong interrelationship between the two macro areas. In particular, the evolution of the business condition in the Eurozone is strongly affected by the current condition in the USA.

Finally, to evaluate the causality relationship between the growth cycle phases in the two macro areas, we estimated a MMS model for the Eurozone and US industrial productions without the trend components. The US lead is graphically confirmed, but the null of non-causality is rejected in both directions.

Notes

1 No trading day adjustment is used since data are already working and trading days adjusted. Sometimes, the airline model was imposed to avoid a non-parsimonious model or to avoid too many outliers. Similarly, the critical limit for outliers was sometimes fixed to 3.0 to avoid too many outliers. Generally, we avoided the presence of level shift outliers except obviously in the case of the German series. The only outlier found in the Eurozone series is an additive outlier in June 1984.
2 For the Eurozone a reference chronology does not exist for both the growth and business cycles.

References

Anas, J. and Ferrara, L. (2004) 'Detecting cyclical turning points: the ABCD approach and two probabilistic indicators', *Journal of Business Cycle Measurement and Analysis*, 1: 193–226.

Artis, M.J., Krolzig, H.M. and Toro, J. (1999) 'A new approach to decomposition of economic time series into permanent and transitory components with particular attention to measurement of the business cycle', *Working Paper ECO*, 99-24, Florence: European University Institute.

Artis, M.J. and Marcellino, M. and Proietti, T. (2002) 'Dating the Euro area business cycle', *Working Paper*, Florence: European University Institute.

Billio, M. (2002) 'Correlated markov chains', *Mimeo*.

Burns, A.F. and Mitchell, W.C. (1946) *Measuring Business Cycles*, New York: National Bureau of Economic Research.

Clements, M.P. and Krolzig, H.M. (2003) 'Business cycle asymmetries: characterization and testing based on Markov-Switching autoregressions', *Journal of Business and Economic Statistics*, 21: 196–211.

Diebold, F.X. and Rudebusch, G.D. (1996) 'Measuring business cycles: a modern perspective', *The Review of Economics and Statistics*, 78: 67–77.

Hamilton, J.D. (1989) 'A new approach to the economic analysis of non stationary time series and the business cycle, *Econometrica*, 57: 357–84.

Hamilton, J.D. and Lin, G. (1996) 'Stock market volatility and the business cycle', *Journal of Applied Econometrics*, 11: 573–93.

Kim, C.J. and Nelson, C.R. (1998) 'Business cycles turning points, a new coincident index and tests of duration dependence based on a dynamic factor model with regime switching', *The Review of Economics and Statistics*, 80: 188–201.

Krolzig, H.M. (1997) *Markov-Switching Vector Autoregressions. Modelling, Statistical Inference and Applications to Business Cycle Analysis*, Berlin: Springer.

Krolzig, H.M. (2001) 'Markov-switching procedures for dating the Euro-zone business cycle', *Quarterly Journal of Economic Research*, 3: 339–51.

Krolzig, H.M. (2004) 'Constructing turning point chronologies with Markov-switching vector autoregressive models: the euro-zone business cycle', in G.L. Mazzi and G. Savio (eds), *Monographs of Official Statistics*, Luxembourg: European Commission, 147–90.

Krolzig, H.M. and Toro, J. (2001) 'Classical and modern business cycle measurement: the European case', *Working Paper*, Oxford: Institute of Economics and Statistics (www.econ.ox.ac.uk/research/hendry/paper/HMKJTeurosty.pdf).

21
A Turning-Point Chronology for the Eurozone

Jaques Anas, Monica Billio, Laurent Ferrara and Marco Lo Duca

Introduction: why, what and when dating?

In this chapter we aim to construct a turning-point chronology for the Eurozone business and growth cycles. The need for a cycle turning point chronology is now widely recognized by experts and practitioners of economic analysis, but there is no official dating for the whole Eurozone. Various statistical dating techniques have been introduced since the seminal work of Burns and Mitchell (1946) on business cycles, ranging from *ad hoc* rules to recent non-linear time series modelling. In this chapter, we review the diverse Eurozone turning point chronologies, we discuss issues inherent to such a construction and we propose a methodology based on a non-parametric algorithm and diverse criteria assessment, such as duration, deepness, diffusion and synchronization, as well as experts' judgements.

Why dating?

As an example of application, it may help to compare the cycles between nations or to point out links between the cycles and diverse economic aggregates. However, it turns out that the most important use of the turning-point chronology consists in establishing a reference cycle dating for a given country or economic area. Indeed, this reference cycle is often used in empirical studies either to classify economic series (leading, coincident or lagging) or to validate real-time detection and forecasting methods. While there is a reference chronology for the US business cycle, maintained by the Dating Committee of the National Bureau of Economic Research (NBER), there is no such chronology as regards the Eurozone economy. It is obvious that dating is an *ex post* exercise, and in this respect accuracy is a more important criterion than timeliness. Because of the lack of timeliness, dating may not be useful for economic decision-making. As a matter of fact, governments and central banks are very sensitive to indicators showing signs of deterioration in growth to allow them to adjust their policies sufficiently in advance, avoiding more deterioration or a recession. In this respect, timing is important and the earlier the signal, the better. This issue is linked to the 'real-time detection' concept. However, to validate their methods of real-time detection, researchers need a reference turning-point chronology.

What dating?

As our aim is to date cycle turning points, a turning point has to be clearly defined. In this chapter, we define a turning point as a peak or a trough in the economic cycle. This definition in turn implies precision of what we call the economic cycle. In economic literature, two kinds of cycles are generally considered: the *classical business cycle* and the *growth cycle*. The classical business cycle refers to fluctuations in the level of the series while the growth cycle is the deviation to the long-term trend. It should be emphasized that academic literature has focused mainly on the analysis of the classical business cycle. For instance, the NBER gives only a reference chronology for this kind of cycle. In our study we refer to the ABCD approach of both classical and growth cycles proposed in Anas and Ferrara (2004), and we call A the peak of the growth cycle, B the peak of the classical cycle, C the trough of the classical cycle and D the trough of the growth cycle. This approach implies that point A is always before point B and similarly point C is always before point D. This will be a constraint in the construction of the business and growth cycles dating chronologies. A third type of economic cycle is often analysed by practitioners, namely the growth rate cycle. Indeed, some economists talk about a recovery when the GDP growth rate has reached a local minimum. However, the growth rate cycle is subject to very short-term fluctuations due to transitory events making the peaks of this cycle extremely difficult to date, which removes any practical interest for the signal. For this reason, we only focus on the classical and growth cycles in this chapter. If dating the classical business cycle is not so easy, then dating the growth cycle is even more difficult since the series must first be de-trended. Several growth cycle extraction methods have been proposed in the statistical literature, ranging from filtering techniques (Baxter–King, Hodrick–Prescott, Christiano–Fitzgerald...) to parametric modelling, mainly based on state-space and Markov-switching models. However, each method possesses its own advantages and drawbacks and, up to now, it is not very clear which method should be used by practitioners. This supplementary step in the growth cycle dating methodology adds some noise to the signal, since dating depends on the chosen filter (Canova, 1994).

When dating?

There is a substantial delay before announcing the cycle turning points dates in the United States. For example, the July 1990 peak in the classical US cycle was announced by the NBER in April 1991 and the March 1991 trough only in December 1992. Concerning the last classical cycle, the March 2001 peak was announced in November 2001 and the November 2001 trough was announced just after the Dating Committee meeting of July 2003. This delay is certainly due to the idea that the dating should not be revised. In this respect, dating must be as accurate as possible. One issue with the dating process lies in the degree of revision of raw data on which the dating method is applied. We should wait for the last revision of the data, which may be disturbing in the case of GDP. Indeed, GDP figures are constantly revised because of new available surveys and methodological innovations (we refer, for example, to Fischer chain-linked price series in the case of the United States or to the recent revision of national accounts in Japan and United Kingdom). Using series other than GDP may reduce this drawback. But in this case, the availability and the homogeneity of these series over a long period of time are necessary to provide consistent dating through time, which is the main difficulty concerning the Eurozone.

A review of turning-point chronologies for the Eurozone

The construction of a reference turning point chronology raises some issues related to the choice of methods to be used. For instance, starting from a single time series, two different dating procedures can lead to distinct dating results. It may therefore happen that different estimates are available on the market. There is increasing literature relevant to this specific topic, based on comparisons between the results computed by authors and a reference dating chronology. Unfortunately, this literature is specific to the American economy and not the Eurozone, mainly because of the lack of reference chronology. Usually, when a researcher develops a method to estimate the turning point chronology of a given country, the ultimate criteria to assess this method is to compare the resulting dating with a benchmark. However, in our case, we want to construct this reference dating chronology! Therefore, the assessment of diverse dating methods is not obvious. Some properties can help us to compare the methods:

1 Transparency: the dating method must be replicable to every one.
2 Adaptability of the method to different series and countries.
3 Robustness to extreme values and to the sample.
4 The chronology must not be revised through time.

Although an official dating chronology is not yet available, some studies have tried to provide one for the Eurozone cycles. In this section, we present a non-exhaustive review of the various existing chronologies and we discuss the most important issues concerning the choice of the dating methods.

Dating the classical business cycle

Regarding the business cycle, most authors have constructed their chronology based on the Eurozone GDP, either aggregated or country-specific, which appears as the most appropriate univariate time series to be used. This is the reason why the proposed chronologies are generally quarterly, while a monthly dating would be more accurate. For example, Anas (2000) and Harding and Pagan (2001) provide a monthly dating chronology by considering a set of monthly series, such as the industrial production index (IPI) or series related to employment, by reference to the NBER's dating committee. This committee studies four macro-economic series simultaneously to date with non-parametric techniques the classical cycle of the American economy: employment, personal income less transfer payments, volume of sales in the manufacturing and wholesale-retail sectors and IPI. However, there is no measure of monthly aggregate economic activity. Recently, taking the growing available information into account, some authors (for instance Forni *et al.*, 1999, and Watson, 2000) have proposed big data dynamic factor models to construct coincident indexes, with roughly 500 series spanning 500 months. For instance, regarding the Eurozone a recent coincident index called EuroCOIN has been developed by the CEPR (see Altissimo *et al.*, 2001), based on a set of 951 series related to the Eurozone economy.

In the diverse studies, the turning points of the business cycle are either estimated non-parametrically (Anas, 2000; Lommatzsch and Stephan, 2001; or Harding and Pagan, 2001) or parametrically (Artis, Krolzig and Toro, 1999; Krolzig, 2001, 2004; and Anas and Ferrara, 2004). For the most part, non-parametric procedures in turning point dating are based on recognition-pattern algorithms. The most famous one is the Bry and Boschan (1971) procedure, still used in many countries and in academic works when estimating business cycle turning points. Another class of non-parametric dating procedure consists in *ad hoc* rules and experts' claims. For instance, the Conference Board refers to the 3Ds rule to identify turning points (diffusion, deepness, duration) and the Centre for Economy Policy Research (CEPR, 2003) has formed, very recently, a dating committee of eight experts to set the dates of the Eurozone business cycle, based on the NBER experience. However, this class of procedure suffers under a lack of transparency. Apart from these non-parametric approaches, a great number of parametric models have been developed lately to date turning points in the classical business cycle, based mainly on the Markov-switching model popularized in economics by Hamilton (1989) in order to take into account a certain type of nonstationarity inherent to some time series that cannot be caught by classical linear models. In the univariate and multivariate framework, many attempts have been undertaken to provide a Eurozone dating chronology of the business cycle through the MS-AR model and its multivariate generalization introduced by Krolzig (1997). However, in order to establish a reference chronology, the diverse experiences lead to the conclusion that it seems advisable to have an expert analysis based on nonparametric procedure, at least for the business cycle. This is due to the necessary calibration of parametric models on dating and to the lack of robustness to the model to the sample (see Anas and Ferrara, 2004).

Another issue is specific to large economic areas including several national economies. In order to provide a turning-point chronology, is it more appropriate to analyse the economies of each country of the zone (indirect approach) or the whole economy of the zone directly (direct approach)? Regarding the indirect approach, the most difficult part is how to aggregate the multivariate information. Once we get a turning-point chronology for each country of the Eurozone, first of all it is necessary to evaluate whether there is sufficient diffusion of the cyclical movements across countries and whether there is synchronization among these countries. If there is evidence of diffusion and synchronization, then it is necessary to define a way to aggregate that information to provide a chronology for the Eurozone. In practice, it is not so clear how to independently measure the diffusion and the synchronization of the cycles. Several non-parametric measures have been proposed in the literature, but they provide simultaneously an evaluation of diffusion and synchronization. The simplest one is to calculate a diffusion index measuring the percentage of countries that exhibit the same regime (for example a recession) at a certain time t. Other authors (see for example Krolzig and Toro, 2001; Harding and Pagan, 2002; and Artis *et al.*, 2002) compute a concordance index which measures the fraction of time that the cycles of different series are in the same phase (recession or expansion). An algorithm has been proposed by Harding (2004) to cluster various turning points after defining a distance between turning points and a function which measures the centre of tendency of turning points in a cluster. We will use a version of this methodology later in the chapter.

Most of these chronologies start in 1980 and are quarterly because they are based on the GDP. As regards all the dates of peaks and troughs provided by these studies, the results appear to be more or less coherent. The 1974–75 recession due to the first oil shock seems to be clear. Generally, from 1980, three recession periods are detected: 1980–81, 1982 and 1992–93. While the 1992–93 period has been underlined by all the studies with the same accuracy (especially the peak), there is an issue as regards the 1980–81 and 1982 periods. Indeed, both recessions of 1980–81 and 1982 can be seen as a single recession phase, as in Artis, Krolzig and Toro (1999), Krolzig (2004) and CEPR (2003). It is noteworthy that other studies have also considered the issue of business-cycle dating, but only for separate countries and not for the aggregate Eurozone economy (see, for instance, Rabault, 1993, or the Economic Cycle Research Institute).

Dating the growth cycle

The Eurozone growth cycle has been studied much less often compared to the classical cycle, perhaps due to the de-trending problem and to the lack of popularity of this concept. The growth cycle extraction is well-known by practitioners as an intricate issue. Since the introduction of the growth cycle concept by Ilse Mintz of the NBER in 1969, the literature has been very extensive on this topic, but up to now there is no clear recommendation. Several methods have been proposed ranging from the simple linear de-trending method (see for instance Harding, 2004) to the unobserved components approach (Harvey, 1989). One of the most used approaches is the PAT methodology, still in use by the OECD for example (see Zarnowitz and Ozyildirim, 2002). However, most of the recent methods involve bandpass filters which aim at retaining unaltered the cycle stylized facts while removing high and low frequency components. Generally, the movements with a period lower than 1.5 years and greater than six or eight years are disregarded in the spectral domain. The most popular filters, often found in empirical applications, are the Beveridge and Nelson (1981) filter, the Baxter–King and the Hodrick–Prescott filters and the Christiano and Fitzgerald (1999) filter. These filters differ only in the way they approximate the ideal bandpass filter.

In the empirical studies, the estimates are based, most of the time, on the Euro-zone GDP series (only the OECD prefers their CLI index, see Arnaud, 2000, and Arnaud and Hyong, 2001) and the papers differ mainly according to the cycle extraction method. The Hodrick–Prescott filter is used in Vanhaelan *et al.* (2000), the PAT procedure is used by the OECD, and Harding and Pagan (2001) remove a linear deterministic trend from the Eurozone GDP. In Anas (2000), an empirical comparison of the Hodrick–Prescott and Baxter–King filters with an unobservable components model, developed by Harvey (1989), is undertaken. It is worth saying that all these studies have used a non-parametric dating procedure, based on the Bry and Boschan algorithm adapted for quarterly series. On the contrary, Peersman and Smets (2001) have proposed a parametric dating of the growth cycle based on a multivariate Markov-switching model applied to the de-trended IPI of a set of European countries.

Methodology

Several studies have shown the existence of a common Eurozone cycle. Among others, we can quote for instance the paper of Mitchell and Mouratidis (2002) which underlines the common features of the different measures of the growth and business cycles of the Eurozone. Moreover, they show that the synchronization between Eurozone business cycles has increased since the 1980s, which is 'coherent with the emergence of a common Eurozone business cycle'. We can also refer to Artis, Krolzig and Toro (1999) who point out a 'clear evidence of co-movement in output growth among European countries' by using descriptive statistics in the time and frequency domains and by applying different Markov-switching models. Starting from all these previous studies, we first assume the existence of common Eurozone business and growth cycles. Therefore, we can use Eurozone aggregates (for example GDP, IPI and employment) as proxies for the co-movement.

Business and growth cycles are distinct concepts. As the growth cycle is defined by the deviation to the trend, once the trend has been extracted, the peaks A and troughs D of the ABCD approach are not so difficult to locate because of the symmetry of the growth cycle. In this chapter, we consider the 'two-stages' Hodrick–Prescott filter (see Artis *et al.*, 2002) which allows us to design a band-pass filter as the difference of two Hodrick–Prescott de-trending filters, the first one working on higher frequencies (for example 1.5 years) and the second one on lower frequencies (for example six years). However, the business cycle is non-linear and strongly asymmetric, insofar as expansion and recession periods do not present the same stylized facts as regards, for instance, duration, persistence or volatility (see for example Clements and Krolzig, 2004, for a discussion on business cycle asymmetries). Therefore, points B and C are more difficult to locate: the business cycle requires further concepts to be measured.

To start with, we assume the description of Burns and Mitchell (1946) of the business cycle into two regimes: expansions and recessions. We assess the occurrence of a Eurozone recession by measuring the criteria of duration, deepness, diffusion and synchronization across the countries. Starting from a set of candidate turning points provided by the non-parametric algorithm applied to the Eurozone aggregates, we will give a measure of these criteria and say that the Eurozone is in recession if these criteria are simultaneously fulfilled. Duration and deepness are measured starting from the Eurozone aggregated time series (direct approach), while diffusion and synchronization are estimated starting from the specific countries (indirect approach). It is noteworthy that our methodology is a general-to-specific one, insofar as we consider all the candidate turning points of the business cycle provided by the non-parametric procedure and we eliminate them progressively when they do not fulfil one of the criteria.

A non-parametric algorithm

As noted previously, we are in favour of non-parametric procedures instead of parametric ones in the framework of turning points dating chronology. Indeed, it has been shown that the model specification step is an intricate issue and can lead to inappropriate results. First, a set of candidate periods of recession has to be selected on the aggregated series. The non-parametric procedure developed in this section to get a dating chronology on a single time series is based on the following algorithm:

1　Outliers are disregarded in the seasonal adjustment (SA) step executed by the Demetra software.
2　Irregular movements in the series are excluded in the SA step in the case of monthly data. In the case of GDP quarterly data the SA-WDA series is not smoothed out.
3　Determination of a first candidate set of turning points on the time series of interest (y_t) is determined by using the following rule, which is the heart of the Bry and Boschan (1971) algorithm:

$$\text{Peak at}\quad t : \{y_t > y_{t-k}, y_t > y_t + k, k = 1, \ldots, K\}$$
$$\text{Trough at } t : \{y_t < y_{t-k}, y_t < y_{t+k}, k = 1, \ldots, K\},$$

where $K = 2$ for quarterly time series and $K = 5$ for monthly time series.
4　Turning points within six months of the beginning or end of the series are disregarded.
5　A procedure for ensuring that peaks and troughs alternate is developed by using the following rule:

　(a)　in the presence of a double through, the lowest value is chosen
　(b)　in the presence of a double peak, the highest value is chosen.

Deepness and duration assessment

Once the candidate periods have been retained by the non-parametric algorithm on the aggregates, we assess first the criteria of duration and deepness. The duration means that a recession must last 'more than a few months', as noted by the NBER in its seminal definition of a recession, but there is no reference minimum duration. Usually, it is often advocated that for the business cycle a phase of the cycle must last at least six months and a complete cycle must have a minimum duration of 15 months. The deepness refers to the amplitude of the recession. Indeed, as noted by the NBER, a recession is a 'significant decline in activity'. Obviously, the practical difficulty is to assess when the fall of the economy is "significant' enough. To measure this amplitude, we use the following value of deepness, for a recession:

$$Deepness = (X_P - X_T)/X_P \qquad (21.1)$$

where X_P and X_T are respectively the values of the series at the peak and trough of the business cycle to be considered. In the case of normalized indexes, such as the IPI, we simply look at the difference between the values of the series at peak and trough. Moreover, as regards the growth cycle, because of its symmetry, we simply consider the absolute difference for each phase.

To summarize the information on both duration and deepness we assess the measure of what we call severity (denoted by S) of a recession defined by:

$$S = 0.5 \times Deepness \times Duration. \qquad (21.2)$$

This measure is in fact the percentage of loss during the phase of the cycle. This severity measure is also referred in the literature to as the '*triangle approximation*' to the *cumulative movements*; see for example, Harding and Pagan (1999). Note that there is a wide literature concerned with the concept of 'shape' of the cycle, and we refer to the recent paper of Clements and Krolzig (2004) for the diverse definitions of the shape.

Diffusion and synchronization assessment

Once duration and deepness have been estimated for each candidate recession period through the severity index, we assess now their diffusion and synchronization over the countries by considering an indirect analysis. The spatial diffusion means that almost all of the countries have to be affected by the exogenous shock in the case of a recession while the concept of synchronization refers to the timing impact of the exogenous shock which creates leads and lags in cyclical movements of countries. For instance, the industrial growth cycle in 1995 didn't turn into a recession because it was not synchronized (see following section). Indeed, Italy and the Netherlands were in recession later than the other countries. As another example, the 1998 impact of the Asian crisis was not diffused to all the countries in the Eurozone, only Italy and Belgium were affected by an industrial recession.

In this chapter, we introduce a version of the simultaneous measure of diffusion and synchronisation between N cycles introduced by Boehm and Moore (1984) and revisited in Harding and Pagan (2002). Actually, Boehm and Moore (1984) developed an algorithm which tries to mimic the NBER dating procedure by identifying clusters of turning points and applied it to the Australian economy. One of the advantage of this method is to provide as a byproduct a dating chronology of the business cycles, that we call in the remaining *indirect dating*.

First, we compute a dating chronology for each country i, for $i = 1, \ldots, N$, according to the method described in the previous subsection. Then, we define t_{ij}^P (respectively t_{ij}) as j the observation date of the peak (respectively trough) in the country i. We define $d_i^P(t)$ (respectively $d_i^T(t)$) as the distance in time from t to the nearest peak (respectively trough) in the country i. That is, for $i = 1, \ldots, N$ and for

$t = 1, \ldots, T$:

$$d_i^P(t) = \underset{j}{Min} \left| t - \tau_{ij}^p \right| \tag{21.3}$$

In order to aggregate the information relative to the countries, we consider the following statistics, which are the distances to cycle peaks and troughs for the whole Eurozone:

$$d_i^P(t) = \sum_{i=1}^{N} \omega_i d_i^P(T) \tag{21.4}$$

and

$$d_i^T(t) = \sum_{i=1}^{N} \omega_i d_i^T(T) \tag{21.5}$$

where $(\omega_i)_i$ are the weights of the countries in the Eurozone according to a given economic aggregate. We can consider the GDP of the country or the weights given in the national account statistics or in the short-term business statistics. Dates at which $d_i^P(t)$ and $d_i^T(t)$ achieve their local minima can be assumed to be the dates of the centres of a cluster of, respectively, peaks and troughs for the Eurozone. Thus, we get a set of dates t_j^P and t_j^T defined as the estimated indirect dates of peaks and troughs for the Eurozone. Finally, as a measure of the diffusion/synchronization, we choose the following statistic, for the jth peak (respectively trough):

$$DS_j = \frac{1}{d^P(t_j^P)} \times 100 \tag{21.6}$$

For a candidate cycle where there is no local minimum, we set to zero the *DS* measure. Thus, when the value of the *DS* statistic is high we can conclude that the turning point is well-diffused and synchronized; when *DS* is low the turning point is neither diffused nor synchronized; and when *DS* has an intermediate value it means that the cycle is either insufficiently diffused or not synchronized.

As we do not know anything about the probability distribution of these measures of severity and diffusion/synchronization, it is difficult to make statistical inference. In this study, these values serve only as a basis to compare diverse periods of time. The final decision as regards the choice of the dates is done by expert judgements based on a combination of the three following principles:

1 a comparison of direct and indirect dating;
2 an objective of coherence between the turning points of both growth and business cycles (ABCD approach);
3 an objective of coherence between industrial and GDP cycles.

Applications

In this section we propose a dating chronology for both business and growth cycles in the Eurozone, based on IPI and GDP.

A chronology based on the industrial production index (IPI)

The methodology is carried out on the Eurozone aggregated monthly IPI in order to date the industrial business cycle. By applying the non-parametric algorithm to the Eurozone IPI series over the whole period 1970–2002, we first select 10 candidate recession periods. The main economic events since 1970 are present, namely the first oil shock in 1974–75, the second oil shock and its 'double-dip' in 1980–81 and 1981–82, and the 1992–93 recession. Obviously, as no censoring rule is applied, a lot of mini-cycles are also taken into account. For example, the candidate recessions of 1995 and 1996 are only of three months, while the largest candidate recession (16 months) occurred in 1992–93. Note also that the usual censoring rule related to the minimum duration of a complete cycle is always respected, except between the cycle in 1991 and that in 1992–93. This means that one of these two candidate recessions should not be retained at the end of the study. In the recent period, there is a candidate industrial recession in 2001 and a candidate peak in June 2002.

By assessing the duration and the deepness of each candidate recession, summarized by the severity criteria defined by equation (21.2), and by assessing the diffusion and the synchronization of the recessions among the countries through an indirect approach, we finally retain five industrial recession phases in the Eurozone. The dating chronology is shown in Table 21.1 for the IPI business cycle.

The methodology is carried out on the Eurozone aggregated IPI in order to date the growth cycle. First, the industrial growth cycle is estimated through the two-step Hodrick–Prescott filter described earlier, the cut-off frequencies being of 1.5 and 6 years. The growth cycle appears to be symmetric and the peaks and troughs (respectively points A and D in the ABCD approach) seem easier to locate than the business cycle ones. By using the same methodology as previously, we finally retain nine complete growth cycles (from trough to trough) presented in Table 21.2.

A chronology based on Gross Domestic Product

The methodology is carried out on the Eurozone aggregated GDP in order to date the business cycle. By applying the non-parametric algorithm on the Eurozone GDP series over the whole period 1970Q1–2003Q2, we first select four candidate

Table 21.1   Final business cycle chronology for the aggregated Eurozone industrial production

Dates	Peak B	Trough C
1974–75	1974M4	1975M5
1980–81	1980M2	1981M1
1981–82	1981M10	1982M12
1992–93	1992M1	1993M5
2000–01	2000M12	2001M12

Table 21.2 Final growth cycle chronology the aggregated Eurozone industrial production

Dates	Peak	Trough
1971–72	NA	1971M11
1974–75	1974M1	1975M6
1976–78	1976M11	1978M3
1980–81	1980M2	1981M1
1981–82	1981M10	1982M12
1985–87	1985M11	1987M10
1992–93	1992M1	1993M6
1995–96	1995M2	1996M10
1998–99	1998M2	1999M4
2000–?	2000M11	

recessions periods. Here again, we observe that the main economic events since 1970 are described, namely the first oil shock in 1974–75, the second oil shock and its 'double-dip' in 1980–81 and 1981–82, and the 1992–93 recession. Contrary to the IPI, no mini-cycles appear; in fact the GDP is less sensitive to short-term economic shocks. Three of the four candidate recessions last at least three quarters, only the 1982 recession is of one quarter. As regards the recent period, no peak is detected by the algorithm.

As previously, we look simultaneously at the duration and the deepness of each candidate recession, summarized by the severity criteria, to assess the occurrence. The most severe candidate recession is the one due to the first oil shock in 1974–75. In fact, this latter recession is the deepest, its value is twice the 1992–93 one. There is an issue as regards the 1982 candidate recession, because its severity is very low in comparison with the others. We assess then the diffusion and the synchronization of the recessions among the countries through an indirect approach. First, a non-parametric dating procedure is carried out for each of the six considered Eurozone countries. We consider the four main countries (Germany, France, Italy, Spain) since 1970 and Belgium and the Netherlands since 1980. To avoid mini-cycles, we impose a minimum duration of two quarters for each phase of the cycle. The DS measures for the peak and trough of the 1974–75 recession are very strong, because we only consider four countries. However, the recessions in these countries are diffused to all and extremely synchronized, especially the troughs. The measures for the other recession candidates are similar. Especially, the 1982 recession candidate is diffused to four countries out of six, only France and Spain are not affected by this double-dip. Thus, albeit very mild, this candidate recession cannot be dropped from the final selection. As regards the 1992–93 recession, the indirect dating provides exactly the same dates. It is noteworthy that a recession in 2001 appears in the indirect dating. However, the DS measure for the trough is very low. Moreover, it seems to be too soon to be able to confirm this recession, because the GDP figures will certainly be revised. Finally, we retain four

Table 21.3   Final business cycle chronology for the aggregated Eurozone GDP

Dates	Peak B	Trough C
1974–75	1974Q2	1975Q1
1980	1980Q1	1980Q4
1982	1981Q4	1982Q4
1992–93	1992Q1	1993Q1

Table 21.4   Final growth cycle chronology for the aggregated Eurozone GDP

Dates	Peak	Trough
1974–75	1974Q1	1975Q3
1977–78	1977Q1	1978Q2
1979–81	1979Q4	1981Q1
1981–82	1981Q4	1982Q4
1986–87	1986Q1	1987Q2
1991–93	1992Q1	1993Q3
1995–96	1995Q1	1996Q4
1998–99	1998Q1	1999Q1
2000–?	2000Q3	

recession phases based on the Eurozone GDP. The dating chronology is contained in Table 21.3.

The methodology is carried out on the Eurozone aggregated GDP in order to date the growth cycle. First, the GDP growth cycle is estimated through the two-step Hodrick–Prescott filter, the cut-off frequencies being of 1.5 and 6 years. By using the same methodology, we retain eight growth cycles over the period 1970–2000 (see Table 21.4), four of them being followed by a business cycle. Indeed, the growth cycles peaks of 1974, 1979, 1981 and 1992 (points A) were followed by business cycle peaks (points B). The delays between points A and points B are less or equal to one quarter, while the delays between points C and points D are less or equal to two quarters.

Conclusion

In this chapter, we are looking for the dates of the Eurozone business and growth cycles. As a complement to the traditional direct approach based on the study of Eurozone aggregates, the main contribution of this study is to measure the degree of diffusion and synchronization of the cycles among the countries. It seems clear that the Eurozone has experienced four economic recessions since 1970:

1   the first oil shock (1974Q2–1975Q1, 3 quarters);
2 or 3   the second oil shock double-dip (1980Q1–1980Q4, 3 quarters, and 1981Q4–1982Q4, 4 quarters);
4   the 1992–93 recession (1992Q1–1993Q1, 4 quarters). Moreover, we have dated an industrial recession starting in early 2001. Since we found empirically one the period 1970–2000 a full equivalence between industrial recessions and global recessions in the Eurozone, there is a possibility of a recent global recession.

References

Altissimo, F., Bassanetti, A., Cristadoro, R., Forni, M., Hallin, M., Lippi, M., Reichlin, L. and Veronese, G. (2001) 'EuroCOIN: a real time coincident indicator of the Euro area business cycle', CEPR Discussion Paper no. 3108.

Anas J. (2000) 'Le cycle économique Européen: datation et détection', in C. de Boissieu (ed), *Les Mutations de l'Economie Mondiale*, Paris: Economica.

Anas, J. and Ferrara, L. (2004) 'Detecting cyclical turning points: the ABCD approach and two probabilistic indicators', *Journal of Business Cycle Measurement and Analysis*, 1: 193–226.

Anas, J. and Ferrara, L. (2004) 'A comparative assessment of parametric and non-parametric turning points detection methods: the case of the Euro-zone economy', in G.L. Mazzi and G. Savio (eds), *Monographs of Official Statistics*, Luxembourg: European Commission, 86–121.

Arnaud, B. (2000) 'The OECD system of leading indicators: recent efforts to meet users needs', *Paper presented at the 25th CIRET Conference in Paris*, October.

Arnaud, B. and Hyong, E.-P. (2001) 'Comparison of compilation methodologies for the composite Leading indicators of Euro area', *Manuscript*, Paris: OECD.

Artis M. J., Krolzig, H. and Toro, J. (1999) 'The European business cycle', *Working Paper ECO*, 99–24, Florence: European University Institute.

Artis, M. J., Marcellino, M. and Proietti, T. (2002) 'Dating the Euro area business cycle', *Working Paper*.

Boehm, E. and Moore, G.H., (1984) 'New economic indicators for Australia', 1949-84, *The Australian Economic Review*, 4th Quarter, 34–56.

Bry, G. and Boschan, C. (1971) 'Cyclical analysis of time series: selected procedures and computer programs', *Technical Paper*, 20: National Bureau of Economic Research.

Burns, A. F. and Mitchell, W.C. (1946) *Measuring Business Cycles*, New York: National Bureau of Economic Research.

Canova F., (1994) 'De-trending and turning points', *European Economic Review*, 38: 614–23.

CEPR, (2003) *Business Cycle Dating Committee of the Centre for Economic Policy Research*, CEPR, September (www.cepr.org)

Christiano, L.J. and Fitzgerald, T.J. (1999) 'The band pass filter', *Working Paper*, 7257: National Bureau of Economic Research.

Clements M.P. and Krolzig, H.M. (2003) 'Business cycle asymmetries: characterization and testing based on Markov-Switching autoregressions', *Journal of Business and Economic Statistics*, 21: 196–211.

Forni, R., Hallin, M., Lippi, M. and Reichlin, L. (1999) 'The generalized dynamic factor model: identification and estimation', *CEPR Discussion Paper*, 2338.

Hamilton, J. D. (1989) 'A new approach to the economic analysis of non stationary time series and the business cycle', *Econometrica*, 57: 357–84.

Harding, D. (2004) 'Non-parametric turning point detection, dating rules and the construction of the Euro-zone chronology', in G.L. Mazzi and G. Savio (eds), *Monographs of Official Statistics*, Luxembourg: European Commission, 122–46.

Harding, D. and Pagan, A. (1999) 'Dissecting the cycle: a methodological investigation', forthcoming, *Journal of Monetary Economics*.

Harding, D. and Pagan, A. (2001) 'Extracting, analysing and using cyclical information', *Manuscript*: University of Melbourne.

Harding, D. and Pagan, A. (2002) 'Synchronization of cycles', *Working Paper*: Australian National University.

Harvey, A.C. (1989) *Forecasting, Structural Time Series Models and the Kalman Filter*, Cambridge: Cambridge University Press.

Krolzig, H.M. (1997) *Markov-Switching Vector Auto-Regressions. Modelling, Statistical Inference and Applications to Business Cycle Analysis*, Berlin: Springer.

Krolzig, H.M. (2001) 'Markov-Switching procedures for dating the Euro-zone business cycle', *Quarterly Journal of Economic Research*, 3: 339–51.

Krolzig, H.M. (2004) 'Constructing turning point chronologies with Markov-switching vector autoregressive models: the euro-zone business cycle', in G.L. Mazzi and G. Savio (eds), *Monographs of Official Statistics*, Luxembourg: European Commission, 147–90.

Krolzig, H.M. and Toro, J. (2001) 'Classical and modern business cycle measurement: The European case', *Discussion Paper in Economics*, 60: University of Oxford.

Lommatzsch, K. and Stephan, S. (2001) 'Seasonal adjustment method and the determination of turning points of the EMU business cycle', *Quarterly Journal of Economic Research*, 3: 399–415.

Mintz, I. (1969) 'Dating post-war business cycles: methods and their applications to Western Germany, 1950-1967', *Occasional Paper*, 107: National Bureau of Economic Research.

Peersman, G. and Smets, F. (2001) 'Are the effects of monetary policy in the Euro area greater in recessions than in booms?', *Working Paper*, 52, Frankfurt am Main: European Central Bank.

Rabault, G. (1993) 'Une application du modèle de Hamilton à l'estimation des cycles économiques', *Annales d'Economie et de Statistique*, 30: 57–83.

Vanhaelen, J.-J., Dresse, L. and DeMulder, J. (2000) 'The Belgian industrial confidence indicator: leading indicator of economic activity in the Euro area', *Economic Surveys and Data Analysis*, Proceedings of the 25th CIRET Conference in Paris, Paris: OECD.

Watson, M. (2000) 'Macroeconomic forecasting using many predictors', Paper presented at the World Congress of the Econometric Society, August.

Zarnowitz, V. and Ozyildirim, A. (2002) 'Time series decomposition and measurement of business cycles, trend and growth cycles', *Working Paper*, 8736:.National Bureau of Economic Research.

22
Basic Characteristics of the Euro-Area Business Cycle

*Alberto Musso**

Introduction

In this chapter a set of basic stylized facts characterizing Euro-area macroeconomic fluctuations are computed with reference to the deviation cycle (or growth cycle) concept from 1960 to 2003. These stylised facts are discussed and compared to the corresponding ones for the US business cycle. Overall, in addition to a quantification of the basic characteristics of the Euro-area business cycle, it will be seen that, first, the deviation cycle appears to be broadly symmetric, in terms of all of the basic characteristics considered, both in the Euro-area and the USA. Second, compared to the USA, the Euro-area seems to be subject to more frequent fluctuations, on average of shorter duration and milder amplitude. Finally, no clear trend in the evolution of the basic characteristics can be observed over time.

Despite the importance of the phenomenon known as the business cycle it still presents several unexplained features such that many analysts in the profession still regard it largely as a puzzle. Several theories of macroeconomic fluctuations have been proposed (and as a result there exist probably more possible explanations of this phenomenon than cycles can be recorded in the last century), but none has so far been capable of providing a satisfactory comprehensive explanation of business cycles. Nevertheless, the profession seems to have reached a broad agreement from a methodological point of view on how to proceed in the analysis of business cycles. The mainstream research strategy starts from the identification of the stylized facts

* I thank, without implicating, Mike Artis, Fabio Canova, Neale Kennedy, Hans-Joachim Klöckers, Gerard Korteweg, Peter McAdam, and participants in an ECB seminar and the Colloquium for useful comments on various versions of the current chapter and discussions. All remaining errors are of course the sole responsibility of the author. The opinions expressed in this chapter are those of the author and do not necessarily reflect the views of the European Central Bank.

that characterize business cycles, and that therefore need to be explained, with reference to which alternative theories are tested. If a theory is found to outperform the alternatives and reaches a minimum set of criteria, varyingly defined, then it is used as a framework for policy analysis. Following this strategy of research, several studies identifying the main business cycle stylized facts for the US economy have appeared in the past two decades. By contrast, despite the recent publication of a number of studies on business cycles in Europe, a systematic analysis of the main characteristics of the Euro-area cycle is still missing.

The purpose of this note is to contribute to fill this gap by identifying a set of basic characteristics of the Euro-area business cycle, which will be compared to the corresponding ones for the US business cycle. The focus will be on the deviation, or growth, cycle (that is, deviations of real output from trend) and the analysis will cover a period spanning from 1960 to 2003. It should be stressed that over such a long horizon it is to some extent questionable whether it makes sense to refer to an aggregate Euro-area business cycle, at least including the current 12 members. This caveat should of course be taken into account, and the average basic characteristics found over the whole sample period may not necessarily be a robust reference for future developments. Nevertheless, to the extent that also the evolution of these basic characteristics is analysed, the results of this investigation can enhance our understanding of the Euro-area economy along some dimensions, provide a useful reference for the purpose of Euro-area conjunctural analysis, forecasting and policy analysis and can be instrumental in guiding the development of appropriate models of the Euro-area business cycle and selecting among existing ones.

In the past few years a number of studies with a purpose to some extent similar to the current study have appeared. However, a number of them have a different focus, as they either focus on a broader concept of a European business cycle (that is, often including the UK), as opposed to a Euro-area cycle, or analyse exclusively the classical cycle (or sometimes the cycle in the growth rate of the reference series), without discussing the deviation cycle.[1] Among those more closely related to the current study, the majority focus on measures of the deviation cycle, often derived from mechanical filters, which may produce spurious cycles and/or use exclusively industrial production data, thus referring *de facto* to the industrial cycle as opposed to the economy-wide business cycle.[2] Thus, most of the results of the available literature are either not directly relevant for the Euro-area business cycle or are characterized by a low degree of reliability. One notable exception is represented by Artis, Marcellino and Proietti (2004). However, as regards the parts addressing the questions of this chapter, while they consider alternative representations of the deviations cycle, they report the basic characteristics only obtained from a bandpass Hodrick–Prescott filter. Moreover, they focus on a shorter period (starting in 1970), do not provide a comparative perspective with the USA and do not discuss the evolution of the basic characteristics over time (limiting the discussion to average characteristics).

The chapter proceeds as follows. The next section describes the data and methods used in the analysis. We then report on and discuss the basic characteristics of the Euro-area and US business cycles, followed by a final concluding section.

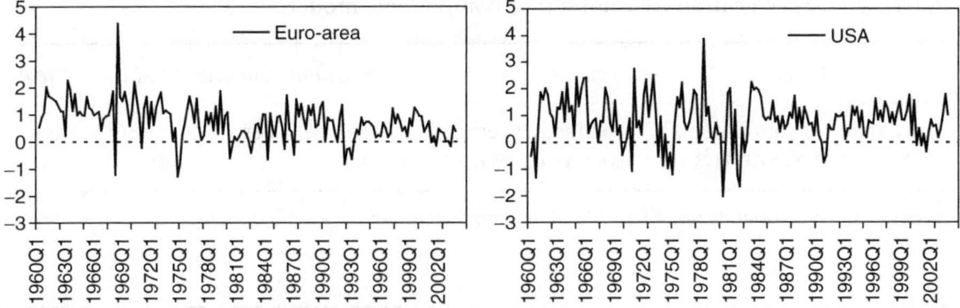

Figure 22.1   Quarterly growth rates
Source: Eurostat, OECD and own calculations.

Data and methods

The main reference series from which the deviation cycle is estimated is represented by quarterly real GDP. For the Euro-area this series is constructed using data from the OECD *Economic Outlook* database, which spans from 1963Q1 to 2003Q4, and extending it back using growth rates based on an aggregate constructed using the OECD *Main Economic Indicators* database from 1960Q1 to 1963Q1.[3] From 1991 these data correspond to the Eurostat ESA 95 official data. For the United States the real GDP data is obtained from the Bureau of Economic Analysis (BEA). The quarterly growth rates of the reference series are shown in Figure 22.1. Apart from an outlier observation in 1968 (due to a spike in the French data resulting from the riots and strikes that took place in France during May of that year), the Euro-area series seems subject relatively milder fluctuations compared to the USA.

In order to estimate the deviation cycle, a univariate unobserved components model was estimated for each real GDP series in levels after taking natural logarithms. The modelling strategy was based on the diagnostics tests, residual graphics and auxiliary residual graphics, following the procedure suggested by Harvey and Koopman (1992) and Harvey (2001). The modelling strategy has been the following. For both quarterly real GDP series, expressed as natural log-levels of the index (with base 1960Q1 = 100), a so-called basic structural time-series model (that is, stochastic level and slope trend, trigonometric seasonal component and irregular component) augmented with a stochastic cycle has been estimated. Once convergence was ensured (if necessary by increasing the number of iterations), the well-specification of the basic general model was checked and possible outliers and breaks was tested using the auxiliary residuals; the significance of the variance of each component was tested and if found not different from zero (implying a deterministic component) the significance of that component was tested. A reduction of the general model was undertaken in steps, always checking for possible residual serial correlation and other signs of misspecification via the available diagnostic tests (available in STAMP, such as the Box-Ljung Q-statistic).[4]

Table 22.1 reports the details of the final models estimated for each economic area. In both cases, the seasonal component was found to be insignificant,

Table 22.1   Specifications of unobserved components models

	Trend	Cycle	Seasonal	Irregular	Outliers	Breaks
Euro-area	smooth trend[a]	stochastic (period 20)	no	yes	1968Q2	no
USA	smooth trend[a]	stochastic (period 20)	no	no	no	no

Source: Own computations. [a] Fixed level and stochastic slope.

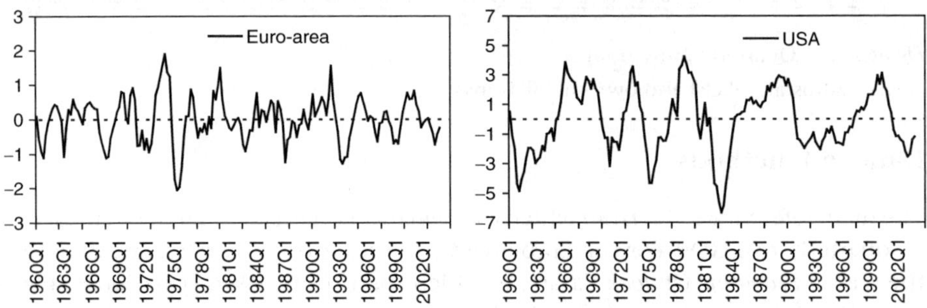

Figure 22.2   Cycles
Source: Own calculations.

signalling the absence of residual seasonality after the seasonal-adjustment implemented by the OECD. Also in both cases the 'smooth trend' representation (that is, fixed level and stochastic slope) was found acceptable. Outliers, detected via auxiliary residuals, were found and corrected for by inserting dummies. The estimated cycles are plotted in Figure 22.2.[5] It can be observed that, as expected on the basis of the original growth rates series, the deviation cycle of the USA exhibits wider fluctuations, although from the mid-1980s the range of fluctuations seems to have become closer to that of the Euro-area.

Some of the basic characteristics that will be discussed are based on a turning-points chronology. Peaks and troughs are defined as local maxima and minima and the cyclical phases, that is upswings and slowdowns, are determined on the basis of these turning points. More precisely, we define upswings as periods starting from the quarter immediately after a troughs and ending with the quarter of the subsequent peak, and slowdowns all other remaining periods (or, as those periods starting from the quarter immediately after a peak and ending with the quarter of a trough). The corresponding sets of peaks and troughs were obtained using the algorithm proposed by Artis, Marcellino and Proietti (2004) applied to each of the cycles (expressed as percentage deviations from trend). This algorithm, based on the theory of Markov chains, consists of a set of rules, including minimum requirements in terms of duration and amplitude of business cycle phases. They can be seen as an extension to quarterly data of the Bry–Boschan algorithm, with the advantage of being more flexible, for example by allowing the imposition of restrictions also in terms of minimum amplitude. More precisely, we have imposed the following restrictions:

1 peaks and troughs must alternate;
2 each phase must last at least two quarters;
3 each cycle must last at least five quarters; and
4 a trough can be located only among quarters of negative (below-trend) values of the cycle and peaks only among positive (above-trend) values.[6]

For the main reference series no threshold for the minimum amplitude was imposed, but a robustness analysis was carried out by also deriving alternative sets of turning points. The latter are derived by imposing that a turning point can only be located among points where the cycle has a minimum magnitude (or distance from the trend), using alternative restrictions from 1 per cent to 5 per cent. This robustness analysis is motivated by the need to assess to which extent minor fluctuations, not all of which may clearly be associated with business cycle fluctuations, may drive the results.

Figures 22.3 to 22.5 show the deviation cycle phases for the Euro-area and the USA derived from the sets of turning points discussed. Slowdowns are shown as shaded areas. For the Euro-area, by imposing the 5 per cent minimum amplitude threshold, various turning points derived from the algorithm without the amplitude criterion disappear. In particular, the 1963/64 and 1989 slowdowns are not classified as such any more, and the two slowdowns of the second half of the 1990s are combined into one. By contrast, for the USA all alternative rules, with or without the amplitude restrictions (up to 5%) determined the same set of turning points.

Basic characteristics of the deviation cycle

Average characteristics

On the basis of the selected turning-points chronology it is possible to compute a set of basic characteristics. These include the average duration, amplitude and

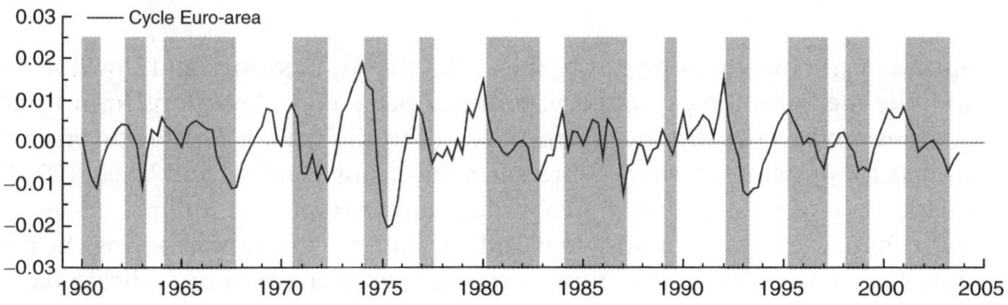

Figure 22.3 Cyclical phases of the Euro-area deviation cycle (basic)

Note: Phases derived without imposing any minimum threshold to cyclical amplitude.

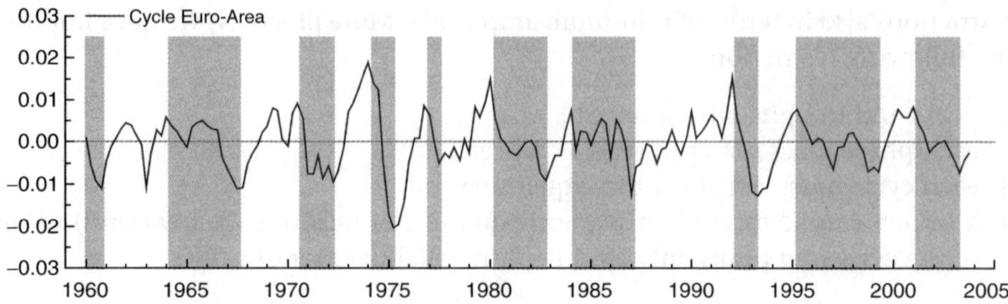

Figure 22.4 Cyclical phases of the Euro-area deviation cycle (alternative)
Note: Phases derived by imposing a 5% minimum threshold to cyclical amplitude.

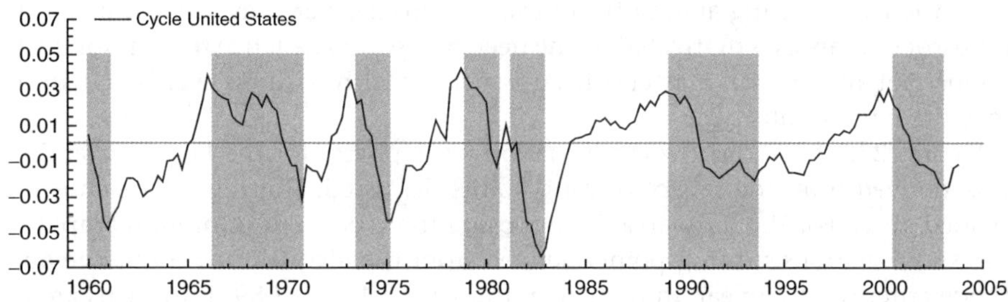

Figure 22.5 Cyclical phases of the US deviation cycle

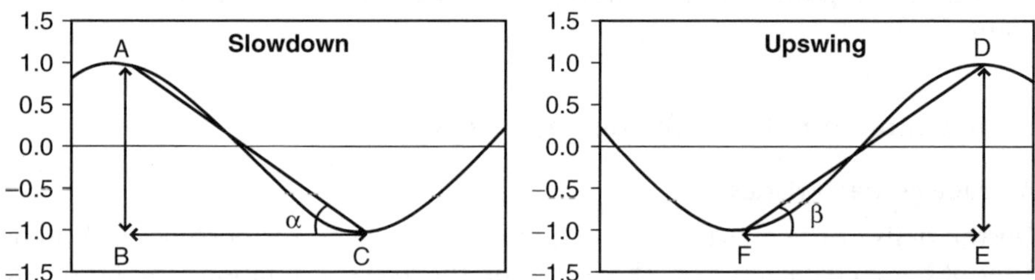

Figure 22.6 Stylized representation of cyclical phases

steepness of the two main phases of the cycle (that is, upswings and slowdowns). Amplitude measures are expressed in terms of percentage deviations from trend, and correspond to the distance from the peak to the trough for slowdowns and vice versa for upswings. Steepness measures, following Harding and Pagan (2001), are derived by dividing amplitude by duration and can be interpreted as the average change (increase for upswings and decrease for slowdown) during the corresponding phase. Figure 22.6 shows a stylized representation of cyclical phases. For slowdowns, represented in the left-hand panel, duration (measured in terms of number of quarters) would correspond to the segment $\overline{BC}$, amplitude to the segment $\overline{AB}$ (measured in terms of absolute value of the deviations from trend, thus in the picture the value would be about 2%) and steepness would correspond to the tangent of the angle α (obtained by dividing $\overline{AB}$ by $\overline{BC}$).

Taking as a main reference for the Euro-area the characteristics derived from the turning-points algorithm without an amplitude censoring rule (which for simplicity will be called the 'basic' reference henceforth), it can be noted that during the sample period considered, the Euro-area experienced about a dozen cycles, that is twice as many as the USA (see Table 22.2). The alternative classification for the Euro-area, based on the algorithm including a 5 per cent minimum amplitude restriction (referred to as the 'alternative' measure henceforth), implies three fewer cycles compared to the basic one, which still corresponds to one-third more frequent fluctuations than in the USA. As a result, it is not surprising that the average duration of cycles in the Euro-area (about four years) is much lower than in the USA (about seven years).

As regards the various measures of the cyclical phases, it can be observed that for the Euro-area the cycle seems to be clearly symmetric. In other words, the average duration, amplitude and steepness of upswings is very similar to those of slowdowns. Thus, on average, both upswings and slowdowns last two years and are characterized by an overall change of almost two percentage points, with an average change per quarter of about one-third of a point. Symmetry also emerges from the alternative chronology for the Euro-area. At the same time, slowdowns seem to be characterized by wider diversity, as signalled by the larger ranges for all three measures. Also for the USA symmetry seems broadly to be a stylized fact, with the possible exception of duration, as slowdowns tend to last on average almost three years, that is one year less than upswings.

Evolution of the basic characteristics over time

Average developments can potentially conceal broad gradual changes over time, as well as be largely influenced by idiosyncratic episodes. Thus, it is important to complement these basic characteristics with representations of the evolution of the various characteristics over time. One way to approach this aspect is to plot the duration, amplitude and steepness of all phases and assess broad trends by visual inspection. Figures 22.7 to 22.10 report the basic characteristics for each cycle and cyclical phase over time for the Euro-area and the USA. The corresponding ones for the alternative Euro-area classification (not shown due to lack of space but available from the author upon request) provide a similar picture compared to the basic classification in terms of broad developments.

As regards durations of cycles and phases, no clear upward or downward trend can be observed over time, neither for the Euro-area nor for the USA. Taking aside specific episodes such as the particularly long slowdown and (peak-to-peak) cycle of the late 1960s in the Euro-area, some broad patterns in terms of gradual change can however be observed. More precisely, in the Euro-area the duration of cycles and phases seems to gradually increase up to the 1980s, and to gradually decrease thereafter (see Figures 22.7 and 22.8). By contrast, for the USA the opposite gradual changes can be observed. For the USA, however, the number of observations is

Table 22.2   Basic characteristics

		Euro-area Basic	USA	Difference EA v. USA	Euro-area Alternative*	Difference EA bas. v. alt.
Frequency				*difference*		*difference*
number of cycles (P to P)		11	5	6	8	3
number of cycles (T to T)		12	6	6	9	3
number of upswings		13	7	6	10	3
number of slowdowns		13	7	6	10	3
Duration (number of quarters)				*difference*		*difference*
cycles (P to P)	average	15	28	−13	20	−4
	minimum	9	10	−1	12	−3
	maximum	27	46	−19	33	−6
cycles (T to T)	average	15	29	−14	20	−5
	minimum	10	10	0	10	0
	maximum	22	44	−22	28	−6
upswings	average	7	17	−9	10	−3
	minimum	4	2	2	5	−1
	maximum	12	27	−15	20	−8
slowdowns	average	7	11	−4	9	−2
	minimum	2	7	−5	3	−1
	maximum	14	19	−5	16	−2
Amplitude (percentage)				*ratio*		*ratio*
upswings	average	1.9	6.8	0.3	2.2	0.9
	minimum	0.9	2.4	0.4	1.5	0.6
	maximum	2.9	9.3	0.3	2.9	1.0
slowdowns	average	1.8	6.4	0.3	2.1	0.9
	minimum	0.6	5.0	0.1	1.2	0.5
	maximum	4.0	7.9	0.5	4.0	1.0
Steepness (percentage)				*ratio*		*ratio*
upswings	average	0.3	0.6	0.5	0.3	1.1
	minimum	0.2	0.2	0.9	0.1	1.3
	maximum	0.5	1.2	0.4	0.5	1.0
slowdowns	average	0.3	0.7	0.5	0.3	1.0
	minimum	0.1	0.3	0.4	0.1	1.3
	maximum	0.8	1.1	0.7	0.8	1.0

Source: Own calculations.

Note: The average and ranges of duration, amplitude and steepness are calculated considering only those phases that fully start and end within the sample. * alternative: derived by imposing a 5% minimum threshold to cyclical amplitude. P = peak; T = trough.

much smaller and therefore it is more difficult to describe these changes as broad (changing) trends.

Also for amplitude no clear trend can be highlighted for neither economic area (see Figure 22.9). For the Euro-area, however, possibly also for this measure a gradual

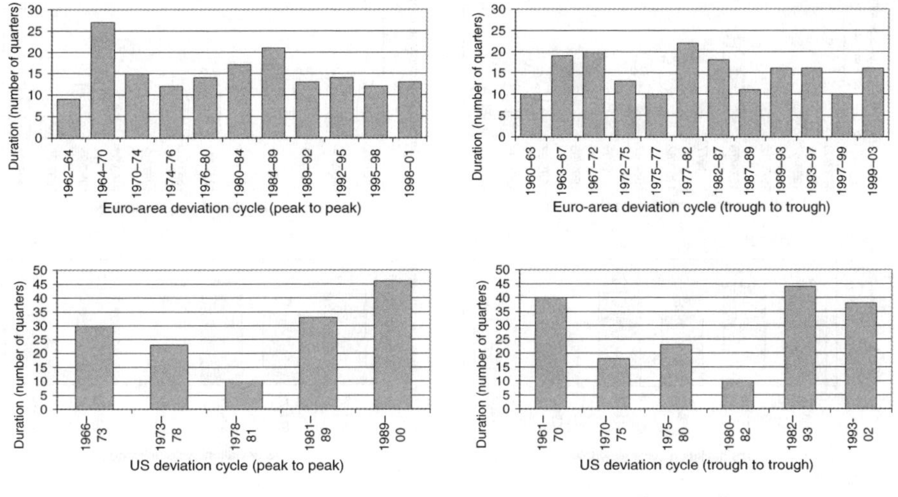

Figure 22.7   Duration of cycles

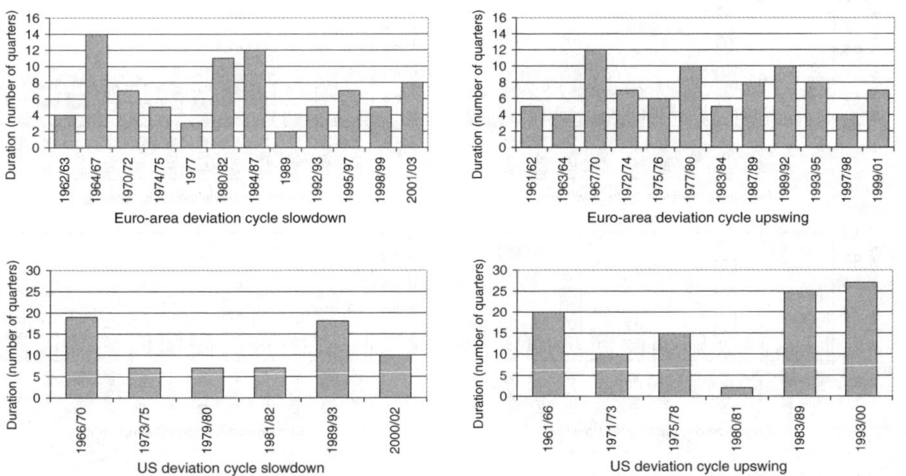

Figure 22.8   Duration of phases

increase up to the late-1970s/mid-1980s and a gradual decrease thereafter can be highlighted. By contrast, for the USA no specific gradual change seems to emerge from the data. It should be noted that the amplitude can be seen as an aspect of volatility. However, volatility is also characterized by other aspects. Therefore, this evidence is not necessarily in contrast with the finding of recent studies that the US cycle has become less volatile since the mid-1980s.[7]

Finally, steepness measures seem to be characterized by a relatively higher dispersion over time, reflecting the specific developments in both duration and amplitude measures (see Figure 22.10). Thus, for the steepness measure it is difficult

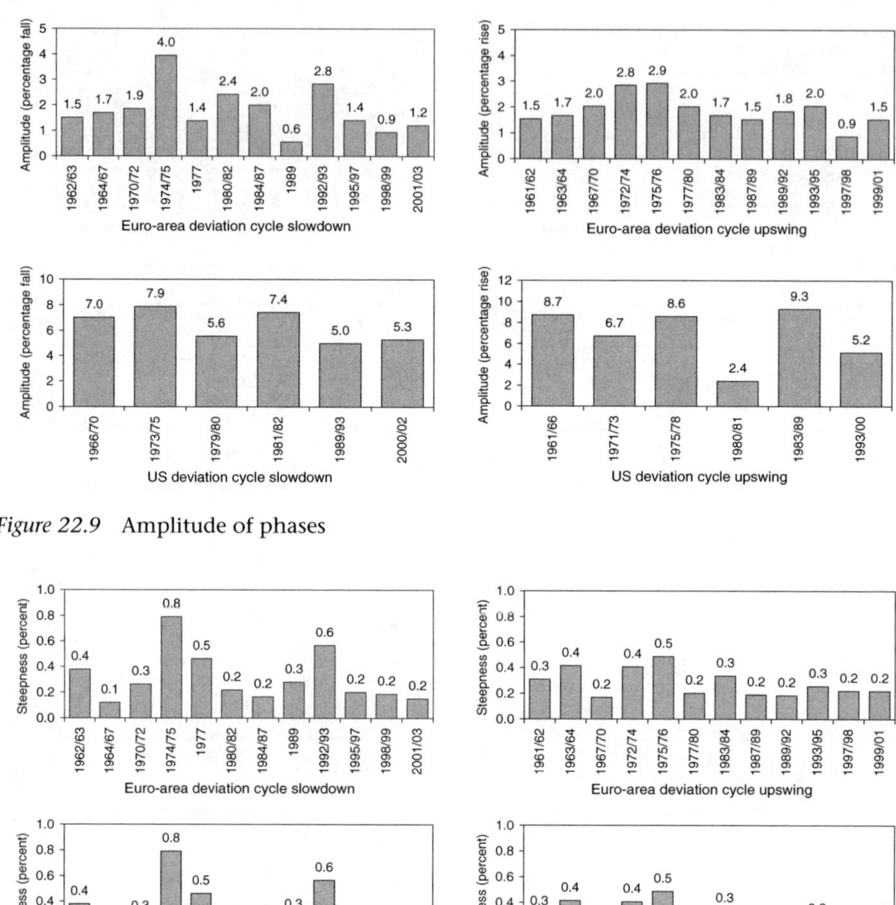

Figure 22.9   Amplitude of phases

Figure 22.10   Steepness of phases

to highlight not only any broad trend, but also gradual changes over time. A possible common feature of these data is the lower steepness that characterizes the most recent cyclical episodes both in the Euro-area and the USA. This can be interpreted as a reduced degree of dynamism, but is also likely to reflect an increased degree of stability of the economies under study.

Complementary aspects of the deviation cycle

A relevant complementary aspect of the deviation cycle is represented by the position of the cycle with respect to the trend, and in particular whether the economy is at a higher or lower level compared to trend. For example, from a

Table 22.3   Additional characteristics

		Euro-area	USA	EA v. USA
Frequency				*difference*
number of periods above trend		12	6	6
number of periods below trend		12	6	6
Duration (number of quarters)				*difference*
above trend	average	8	17	−9
	minimum	2	9	−7
	maximum	13	26	−13
below trend	average	7	16	−9
	minimum	3	9	−6
	maximum	12	26	−14
Amplitude (percentage)				*ratio*
above trend	average	0.9	3.5	0.3
	minimum	0.2	2.9	0.1
	maximum	1.9	4.3	0.4
below trend	average	−1.1	−4.1	0.3
	minimum	−2.0	−6.3	0.3
	maximum	−0.5	−2.1	0.3
Gain (percentage)				*ratio*
cumulated output gain when above trend	average	3.7	29.6	0.1
cumulated output gain when above trend	minimum	0.4	15.2	0.0
cumulated output gain when above trend	maximum	9.0	40.6	0.2
LOSS (percentage)				*ratio*
cumulated output loss when below trend	average	−3.7	−31.3	0.1
cumulated output loss when below trend	minimum	−8.1	−44.7	0.2
cumulated output loss when below trend	maximum	−1.2	−13.8	0.1

Source: own calculations.

Note: The average and ranges of duration, amplitude and gain/loss are calculated considering only those phases that fully start and end within the sample.

monetary policy perspective inflationary pressures would emerge largely (but nor only, as for instance also speed limit effects may be relevant) when the economy is above trend. Note that the classification of cyclical phases from this point of view, which would reduce to two states of above and below trend, does not depend on the turning points chronology, as it depends only on the series representing the cycle. However, the classification of the cycles requires a minimal set of rules to delimit the two regimes. For this purpose, we adopt a minimal set of requirements, consisting of each regime lasting at least two quarters. Thus, isolated quarters of above or below trend within prolonged periods of below or above trend are assumed not to represent interruptions in the regime.

Also from this perspective it can be observed that cycles in the Euro-area are about twice as frequent as in the USA (see Table 22.3). Thus, the average duration of periods above trend and below trend in the Euro-area, which is about two years, is about half that recorded for the USA. Amplitude, measured as the minimum and maximum points in terms of deviations from trend within the corresponding regime, are on average one percentage point in the Euro-area, which is three to four times lower than in the USA. Moreover, regimes tend to be symmetric in both economic areas, as suggested by all measures. The longer duration and higher amplitude of the US regimes on average imply that the average gain and loss of the two regimes, measures as the cumulated output increase and decrease during the corresponding phase, are much higher in the USA, by a factor of about ten. Note that also in this case, no clear trend in the evolution of the two regimes can be observed (see for example Figures 22.3 to 22.5).

Conclusions

Basic characteristics and stylized facts of the business cycle can represent a useful reference for various purposes, including conjunctural analysis, forecasting and model selection. In this study we have identified a set of basic stylized facts of the Euro-area deviation cycle from 1960 to 2003, and discussed it in comparative perspective with respect to the US business cycle.

Summarizing, in addition to a quantification of the basic characteristics of the Euro-area business cycle, the main findings are as follows. First, the deviation cycle appears to be broadly symmetric in terms of all of the basic characteristics considered, both in the Euro-area and the USA. Second, compared to the USA, the Euro-area seems to be subject to more frequent fluctuations, of shorter duration and milder amplitude. Finally, no clear trend in the evolution of the basic characteristics can be observed over time.

Notes

1 For example Artis (2004) Artis, Krolzig and Toro (2004) Krolzig (2001) Krolzig (2004) Krolzig and Toro (2001) and McAdam (2003). Note also that other studies aim at defining a turning-points chronology but do not derive any set of basic characteristics from it (for example, Anas *et al.*, 2006; Anas and Ferrara, 2004; and Mönch and Uhlig, 2004).
2 These include Agresti and Mojon (2003) Döpke (1999) Giannone and Reichlin (2004) and Harding and Pagan (2001). Ross and Ubide (2001) consider several alternative measures of the cycle, including some based on unobserved components models. However, even the model-based approaches they use suffer from some shortcoming. For example, the multivariate unobserved components models (which combine a Phillips-type of relationship and a form of Okun's law) imply that the concept of the cycle under study is the traditional output gap, defined as deviations from the non-inflationary level of output, which is different from the deviation cycle, whose definition does not include any reference to price developments.
3 The aggregate is constructed using real GDP data for all 12 Euro-area countries and fixed GDP weights corresponding to the average weights from 1991 to 2003 from the Eurostat *Annual National Accounts* database. Real GDP data for France before 1963 are from an old vintage of the MEI database. Note that the correlation of the growth rates of the series constructed in this way and the OECD *Economic Outlook* series from 1963 to 2003 is 1.00.
4 All transformations of the data and estimations were carried out using STAMP 6.01 (see Koopman *et al.*, 2000) and Ox 3.00 (see Doornik, 2001).

5 Note that this procedure takes into account the possibility of breaks in the variance and mean of each of the components. Thus, the possibility of breaks in the variability of growth found for some economies, which can affect business cycle association, is allowed for and tested in the current framework. See for example Stock and Watson (2003) for a review of the evidence on breaks in the variability of growth for the G7 economies.

6 Note that rules 2 and 3 are selected as they correspond to the minimum requirements imposed for monthly data in the Bry–Boschan algorithm, which is the most widely diffused algorithm used to locate turning points with monthly data. I thank Tommaso Proietti for kindly making available his Ox codes for the computation of his turning-points selection algorithm.

7 See, for example, the evidence reported in Stock and Watson (2002).

References

Agresti, A.-M. and Mojon, B. (2003) 'Some stylised facts on the euro area business cycle', in *Monetary Policy Transmission in the Euro Area*, I Angeloni, A Kashyap and B Mojon (eds), 2003, Cambridge University Press, Part 1, Chap. 1, pp. 15–35.

Anas, J., Billio, M., Ferrara, L. and Lo Duca, M. (2006) 'A turning point chronology for the Euro-zone classical and growth cycles', this Volume.

Anas, J. and Ferrara, L. (2004) "Detecting cyclical turning points: the ABCD approach and two probabilistic indicators', *Journal of Business Cycle Measurement and Analysis* 1: 193–225.

Artis, M. (2004) 'Is there a European business cycle?', in H. Siebert (ed.), *Macroeconomic Policies in the World Economy*, Heidelberg: Springer.

Artis, M., Krolzig, H.-M. and Toro, J (2004) 'The European business cycle', *Oxford Economic Papers*, 56: 1–44.

Artis, M., Marcellino, M. and Proietti, T. (2004) 'Dating business cycles: a methodological contribution with an application to the Euro-area', *Oxford Bulletin of Economics and Statistics*, 66: 537–74.

Doornik, J.A. (2001) *Ox: An Object-Oriented Matrix Language*, London: Timberlake Consultants Press.

Döpke, J. (1999) 'Stylized facts of Euroland's business cycle', *Jahrbücher für Nationalökonomie und Statistik*, 219.

Giannone, D. and Reichlin, L. (2004) 'Euro-area and US recessions, 1970–2003', in L. Reichlin (ed.), *The Euro-area Business Cycle: Stylized Facts and Measurement Issues*, CEPR.

Harding, D. and Pagan, D. (2001) 'Extracting, analysing and using cyclical information', Paper presented to the CEPR/Banca d'Italia Conference on *Monitoring the Euro-area Business Cycle*, September,.

Harvey, A.C. (2001) 'Testing in unobserved components models', *Journal of Forecasting*, 20: 1–19.

Harvey, A.C. and Koopman, S.J. (1992) 'Diagnostic checking of unobserved components time series models', *Journal of Business and Economic Statistics*, 10, 377–89.

Koopman, S.J., Harvey, A.C., Doornik, J. and Shephard, N. (2000) *STAMP: Structural Time Series Analyser Modeller and Predictor*. London: Timberlake Consultants.

Krolzig, H.-M. (2001) 'Business cycle measurement in the presence of structural change: international evidence', *International Journal of Forecasting*, 17: 349–68.

Krolzig, H.M. (2004) 'Constructing turning point chronologies with Markov-switching vector autoregressive models: the euro-zone business cycle', in G.L. Mazzi and G. Savio (eds), *Monographs of Official Statistics*, Luxembourg: European Commission, 147–90.

Krolzig, H.-M. and Toro, J (2001) 'Classical and modern business cycle measurement: the European case', *Discussion Paper in Economics*, 60, Oxford: University of Oxford.

McAdam, P. (2003) 'US, Japan and the Euro-area: comparing business-cycle features', *Working Paper*, 283, Frankfurt am Main: European Central Bank.

Mönch, E. and Uhlig, H. (2004) 'Towards a monthly business cycle chronology for the Euro-area', *Discussion Paper*, 4377: CEPR.
Ross, K. and Ubide, A. (2001) 'Mind the gap: what is the best measure of slack in the Euro-area?', *Working Paper*, 2001/203, Washington D.C.: IMF.
Stock, J. and Watson, M. (2002) 'Has the business cycle changed and why?', *NBER Macroeconomics Annual*.
Stock, J. and Watson, M. (2003) 'Understanding changes in international business cycle dynamics', *Working Paper*, 9859, New York: NBER.

Part VI
Output Gap Measurement

23
Stability Analysis in ARMA and Unobserved Component Models

*Juan Del Hoyo Bernat and José Luis Cendejas Bueno**

Introduction

The chronology of cycle phases may be obtained from the estimation of the cyclical components in Unobserved Component (UC) models. When instabilities are present in the coefficients of the cycle equation, the chronology obtained may be spurious, and these instabilities will be transmitted to the coefficients of the ARMA reduced form models of the stationary observable variables under study. Therefore, the cyclical equation of the UC model or the derived ARMA model should be tested for instabilities before any use of the estimated model is made. In this chapter, we test for parameter instability in the ARMA and UC models for gross domestic product (GDP) and the industrial production index (IPI) of several European countries, making use of a recursive Wald-type statistic applicable to linear models. To do so, for the case of ARMA models we first linearize the model and, for the case of UC models, we first obtain the Kalman-filtered cyclical component. After these initial steps, the recursive statistic may be applied. The results show that the null hypothesis of constant coefficients cannot be rejected in most of the models studied. An important exception is that of the IPI series computed for the Eurozone. Slight differences in the implied dates of the business cycle are found in the cyclical components uncorrected and corrected for parameter instability.

Since the definition of business cycle given by Burns and Mitchell (1946), many analytical approaches have been used to detect, and eventually to date, the different phases of the business cycle. Some very popular rules are roughly coherent with Burns and Mitchell's definition (for example, two consecutive declines in quarterly GDP to locate a recession), but the complexity of business cycle dynamics

* We are grateful to J.G. Llorente, R.I. Watt, A. García-Ferrer and several participants in the 4th Eurostat-DG-ECFIN Colloquium on Modern Tools for Business Cycle Analysis for their comments and helpful suggestions. Financial support from the Fundación BBVA is acknowledged.

and the desire for a richer phase characterization compel us to design more elaborate tools. With this purpose, time domain and frequency domain filters are widely used to extract unobserved components useful for business cycle analysis. The risk of spurious components due to the automatic implementation of these methodologies has been extensively analysed, for example, by Nelson and Kang (1981), Nelson (1988), Harvey and Jaeger (1993) and Cogley and Nason (1995). Additionally, the literature has noted the subjectivity in trend-cycle decomposition due to *a priori* considerations related, for example, to the degree of smoothness of the trend component or the interval of frequencies selected as specifically cyclical; see, for example, García-Ferrer and Queralt (1998).

Further considerations arise when trend cycle decomposition involves the estimation of parameters. In such cases, parameter instability could lead to several problems mentioned in business cycle analysis. In this context, testing for parameter instability can be necessary to avoid spurious components or inappropriate business cycle chronologies. If breaks are present but ignored, the interpretation and the chronology of the cycle phases, as well as the policy implications, may be misleading.

Additionally, when UC models are employed, the ARMA models directly obtained from the stationary observed variable and those derived from the UC model (that is, the constrained reduced form) should be compatible; see for example Nelson (1988), Watson (1986) and Harvey (1989). In practice, however, the unconstrained ARMA models seem to differ significantly from the constrained ones. A possible explanation for these differences could be that the ARMA or the UC model may have non-constant parameters.

Statistics based on recursive estimations for testing the existence of at least one break in the parameters (with unknown location) are available. Barnejee, Lumsdaine and Stock (1992) focus on linear models, while Andrews (1993) generalizes to nonlinear models. For nonlinear models, Andrews' tests may be quite involved and more burdensome than for linear models. Some apparently simple models, like ARMA, are nonlinear, and therefore the tests devised for linear models to detect if a break has taken place in any of the parameters are not directly applicable. We will show how a Wald-type statistic for testing the existence of at least one break in linear models may be applicable both to ARMA and to UC models by following two-step procedures which differ slightly when applied to ARMA and to UC models.

For ARMA models the two-step procedure starts from the null hypothesis that the ARMA model is well-specified and that their coefficients are constant, as in Del Hoyo and Llorente (2000). Therefore consistent estimates of the model parameters can be obtained. Next, by substituting the perturbations by their consistent estimates in the original ARMA model, an asymptotic equivalent linear model can be obtained that allows the use of the recursive Wald test. As a result of the linearization process, the critical points of the empirical distribution of the derived statistic (under the null of constant coefficients) must be computed for different sample sizes and different location points in the parameter space to know how the empirical critical points differ from the 'true' ones.

For UC models, the unobserved cyclical components are usually modelled as stationary AR equations. Under the null of constant coefficients, it is also possible to show that if in the cyclical equation, the unobserved component is substituted by its Kalman's filtered counterpart, the resulting equation will provide a valid linear equation where we can apply simple recursive tests for parameter instability.

We shall apply a recursive Wald-type statistic to detect parameter instabilities in the cyclical and in the implied ARMA equations of the UC models. We consider two decomposition approaches; first, the classical trend plus cycle decomposition (see for example Clark, 1987), and second, the cyclical trend decomposition (see Harvey, 1985, 1989). The series under study are the GDPs and the IPIs of several European countries.

In the rest of the chapter we proceed as follows. In the next section we briefly present the recursive Wald-type statistic for testing the existence of at least one break in the parameters of a linear model, and the two-step procedures to apply it to ARMA and UC models. We then deal with the estimated models for several European GDP and IPI series. When the recursive test detects substantial parameter instability, we model it with intervention analysis, with some illustrative examples. A final section concludes.

A sequential test for parameter instability in ARMA and UC models

The distribution of the recursive statistics for the case of at least one break with unknown *a priori* date, while not conventional, is known; see Banerjee, Lumsdaine and Stock (1992) for linear models, and Andrews (1993) for nonlinear models. For linear models, it is a simple matter to compute recursive statistics using sub-samples of increasing size in the interval $1 < t_{min} \leq t \leq t_{max} < T$. The recursive estimates derived from linear models allow an easy computation of the recursive statistics to detect break points. Also, by plotting the recursive estimates of the coefficients, valuable information can be obtained on the stability of the coefficients and, in many cases, on the nature of the intervention model to be used to achieve constancy.

Assume that the observations are generated by the model $y_t = X_{t-1}\beta_t + \varepsilon_t$, $t = 2, 3, \ldots, T$, and also that the model is well-specified, in particular that $\beta_t = \beta$ is a $(k \times 1)$ vector of constants. By defining $\lambda = t/T$, $0 \leq \lambda_{min} \leq \lambda \leq \lambda_{max} \leq 1$, we limit the analysis of distributions to the interval $[0, 1]$. The recursive ordinary-least-squares (OLS) coefficients can be written as random elements of $D[0, 1]$, i.e., $\beta(\lambda) = \left(\sum_{t=2}^{[T\lambda]} X'_{t-1} X_{t-1} \right)^{-1} \left(\sum_{t=2}^{[T\lambda]} X'_{t-1} y_t \right)$ for $0 \leq \lambda_{min} \leq \lambda \leq \lambda_{max} \leq 1$. Notice that $\beta(1)$ is the vector with the full sample OLS estimates. The Wald-type statistic used in this chapter to test the hypothesis $H_0: R\beta(\lambda) = r$, where R is a non-stochastic matrix of rank m, $r = R\,\beta(1)$, an $(m \times 1)$ vector, is:

$$F_T(\lambda) = \frac{(R\beta(\lambda) - r)' \left(R \left(\sum_2^{[T\lambda_{max}]} X'_{t-1} X_{t-1} \right)^{-1} R' \right)^{-1} (R\beta(\lambda) - r)}{m\sigma^2(\lambda)} \tag{23.1}$$

where $\sigma^2(\lambda)$ is the recursive estimate of the residual variance. In particular, if we want to test for stability along the sample with respect to $m \leq k$ of the final estimates $\beta(1)$, we represent the statistic by $F(\lambda)^m_{\beta(1)}$. The asymptotic behaviour of the sup $F(\lambda)^m_{\beta(1)}$ is derived applying the Functional Central Limit Theorem and the Central Mapping Theorem (see Stock, 1994). Following Stock (1994), it may be shown that the statistic $F(\lambda)^m_{\beta(1)}$ converges weakly to

$F_T(\lambda)^m_{\beta(1)} \Rightarrow (B_k(\lambda)' \Sigma_X^{-1/2} R' (R\Sigma_X^{-1}R')^{-1} R\Sigma_X^{-1/2} B_k(\lambda))/m \lambda$ where $B_k(\lambda) = W_k(\lambda) - \lambda W_k(1)$ is a k-dimensional Brownian bridge. Therefore, for testing all the coefficients recursively along the sample against the full sample estimators, that is, $R = I_k$ and $r = \beta(1)$, we will obtain $F(\lambda)^k_{\beta(1)} : F_T(\lambda)^k_{\beta(1)} \Rightarrow (B_k(\lambda)' B_k(\lambda))/k \lambda$. By defining $\tilde{F}_T(\lambda)^k_{\beta(1)} = k/(1-\lambda)F_T(\lambda)^k_{\beta(1)} \Rightarrow B_k(\lambda)' B_k(\lambda)/\lambda(1-\lambda)$, the Andrews (1993) statistic is obtained. The statistic to be tabulated is $\max_{\lambda_{\min} \leq \lambda \leq \lambda_{\max}} F_T(\lambda)^k_{\beta(1)} \Rightarrow \sup_{\lambda_{\min} \leq \lambda \leq \lambda_{\max}} B_k(\lambda)' B_k(\lambda)/k\lambda$. It is easy to show that for the case of testing only $m \leq k$ coefficients, the statistic is $\max_{\lambda_{\min} \leq \lambda \leq \lambda_{\max}} F_T(\lambda)^m_{\beta(1)} \Rightarrow \sup_{\lambda_{\min} \leq \lambda \leq \lambda_{\max}} B_m(\lambda)' B_m(\lambda)/m \lambda$. For small sample sizes it is necessary to compute the empirical distribution of the test as we do in the following sections.

ARMA models

The application of equation (23.1) to AR models is straightforward, but for ARMA models[1] the moving average coefficients induce nonlinearities that prevent the direct use of this sequential test. An easy solution[2] to this problem makes use of a two-step procedure to obtain linearity. The first stage assumes the null hypothesis of correct specification of the model and, in particular, that the model coefficients are constant. Under this null, consistent and possibly efficient estimates of the model parameters and perturbations can be obtained. Next, a pseudolinear regression model is obtained by substituting the unknown perturbations by their consistent estimates. Finally, once the model is linear, the recursive Wald test for the detection of breaks may be applied.

Without loss of generality, let y_t follow an ARMA(1,1) model:

$$y_t = \mu + \phi_1 y_{t-1} + \theta_1 \varepsilon_{t-1} + \varepsilon_t \tag{23.2}$$

If e_t is a consistent estimation of ε_t, and $v_t = \varepsilon_t - e_t$, then:

$$y_t = \mu + \phi_1 y_{t-1} + \theta_1 e_{t-1} + (\varepsilon_t + \theta_1 v_{t-1}) = \mu + \phi_1 y_{t-1} + \theta_1 e_{t-1} + (\varepsilon_t + o_p(1))$$

since $v_t = o_p(1)$, then:

$$y_t = \mu + \phi_1 y_{t-1} + \theta_1 e_{t-1} + \varepsilon_t \tag{23.3}$$

Model (23.3) is linear and asymptotically equivalent to model (23.2). Moreover, it can be shown in Del Hoyo, Llorente and Rivero (2003), that the asymptotic distribution of the sup of statistic (23.1) applied to model (23.3), where the unknown perturbation ε_{t-1} has been substituted by its consistent estimation e_{t-1}, converges to the same distribution of the sup of statistic (23.1) applied to model

(23.2). This convergence to the same asymptotic distribution is a particular case of a more general result valid for ARMA(p, q) models in which the lagged unknown perturbations are substituted by their consistent estimates.

However, using the recursive test in (23.3) may distort its size and power. In particular, while the critical points will coincide asymptotically, the approximation to the asymptotic ones will depend on the particular location in the parameter space as well as the actual sample size considered in estimating the coefficients.[3] To illustrate this, we have compared the critical points of the test when applied for ARMA models by simulating AR(1), MA(1) and ARMA(1,1) models.[4] The size of the two-step statistic is quite good, but the power depends on the sample size as well as on the distance between the null and the alternative hypothesis.

UC models

For unobserved component models a two-step procedure may also be used to decide whether the parameters are constant in a similar way as in ARMA models. The procedure first consists of estimating the model parameters consistently, under the null hypothesis of no structural change, using the whole sample. Then, by applying the Kalman filter, an estimable linear equation for the cyclical component is obtained. Once they have been written as linear estimable equations, it will be possible to test for stability of the parameters conditional on the first stage consistent estimates.

The two UC models we employ are the Trend plus Cycle Model and the Cyclical Trend Model. The trend plus cycle model decomposes y_t (in logarithms) as:

$$y_t = T_t + C_t + e_t \tag{23.4}$$

where T_t is the trend component, C_t is the cyclical component, and e_t is the noise series. A commonly used decomposition consists of a trend 'viewed as a nonstationary stochastic process, generally a random walk with drift', and a cycle viewed as 'a stationary process, generally an autoregression' (Nelson, 1988). Following this specification:

$$T_t = \mu + T_{t-1} + \varepsilon_{1t} \tag{23.5}$$

$$\phi_p(L)C_t = \varepsilon_{2t} \tag{23.6}$$

where μ is the drift and $\varepsilon_{1t} \sim$ iid $N(0, \sigma_1^2)$. C_t is cyclical component, which follows $\phi_p(L)C_t = \varepsilon_{2t}$, with $\varepsilon_{2t}; \sim$ $iidN(0, \sigma_2^2)$ and the roots of the autoregressive operator $\phi_p(L)$ lying outside the unit circle.[5] Additional assumptions in the decomposition (23.4) are the following orthogonality conditions between components: $E(e_t\varepsilon_{1s}) = 0$, $E(e_t\varepsilon_{2s}) = 0$, and $E(\varepsilon_{1s}\varepsilon_{2s}) = 0$ for all pair (t, s).[6,7] The decomposition (23.4) is generally considered as the standard trend plus cycle decomposition.

The second decomposition we consider is a cyclical trend model (as in Harvey, 1985). The main difference with respect to the trend plus cycle decomposition is that the trend component is assumed to emerge from the accumulation of the cyclical variation, so in (23.4) the cyclical component must be eliminated. Consequently, in the cyclical trend decomposition we have:

$$y_t = T_t^* + e_t \tag{23.7}$$

$$T_t^* = \mu + T_{t-1}^* + C_{t-1}^* + \varepsilon_{1t} \tag{23.8}$$

$$\psi_{p*}(L)C_t^* = \varepsilon_{2t}^* \tag{23.9}$$

where we employ the asterisk to denote different components with respect to the trend plus cycle decomposition.[8] Stationary conditions on the autoregressive operator $\psi_{p*}(L)$ and orthogonal restrictions also apply.

In both decompositions, a smooth trend component is obtained by assuming that $\sigma_1^2 = 0$. In the estimated models, we impose this restriction given our interest on cyclical behaviour. In the trend plus cycle model this restriction implies a linear deterministic trend.

The state space representations of the trend plus cycle and the cyclical trend decompositions allow maximum likelihood estimation of the parameters and the estimation of the filtered components $T_{t/t}$ and $C_{t/t}$. The smoothed trend and cycle components $T_{t/T}$ and $C_{t/T}$ are obtained conditional on full sample information by means of a fixed interval smoothing algorithm. The smoothed components are commonly used to date business cycle phases, as we shall do later.

Under both decompositions we are interested in analysing whether the parameters in the cycle equation are constant. If the cyclical component C_t were observable the solution would be straightforward by applying the *sup* of statistic (23.1). The problem here is that C_t (or C_{t-1}^* in the cyclical trend decomposition without any substantial change) is unobserved and must be estimated firstly. Del Hoyo, Llorente and Rivero (2003) show that the recursive sup statistics $F(\lambda)_{\beta-1}^m$ applied to (23.6) or (23.9) have the same distribution asymptotically. This result can be proved assuming that we can obtain consistent estimates, uniformly in T, for the model parameters and assuming that the largest eigenvalue of the transition matrix of the state space form is unity; then, if $\tilde{C}_{t|t}^T$ is the filtered cyclical component[9] obtained with the Kalman filter–with T the full sample size and $\tilde{C}_{t|t}$ the unobserved cyclical component–then $\max \max_{t=2,\ldots T} \left| \tilde{C}_{t|t}^T - \tilde{C}_{t|t} \right| \xrightarrow[T\to\infty]{p} 0$ which is a similar situation to the case of estimating the unknown regressors $\left(\varepsilon_{t-1}, \varepsilon_{t-2}, \ldots \varepsilon_{t-p} \right)$ in ARMA models. Again, the size and power of the statistic will depend on the sample size and on the particular region of the parametric space under study; in particular, for parameter values near the non-stationary boundary as obtained in the trend plus cycle decomposition.

Testing for parameter stability for selected European GDPs and IPIs

In this section we first follow the procedure discussed above to detect parameter instabilities in the cyclical components of several European GDPs and IPIs, and

Table 23.1   Wald-type test statistics $sup\ F(\lambda)^m_{\beta(1)}$ for the trend plus cycle models (23.4)–(23.6), the cyclical trend models (23.7)–(23.9) and the ARMA reduced-form models for European GDPs and IPIs

	GDPs			IPIs		
	Trend plus cycle	*Cyclical trend*	*ARMA*	*Trend plus cycle*	*Cyclical trend*	*ARMA*
UK	0.8188	0.5865	0.3103	1.0347	0.9850	1.7404
Germany	1.7743	1.6039	1.8873	1.4030	1.1794	0.6239
France	0.3021	0.3649	0.2067	0.4009	1.6951	1.6829
Italy	0.4537	2.2946	1.3783	0.9306	0.9040	1.0075
Spain	2.7475[*]	3.1467[*]	2.8948[**]	1.9140	4.0036[*]	1.5211
Eurozone	0.1543	0.0566	0.1757	6.7900[***]	5.1546[**]	1.5087
Euro-4 GDP[+]	1.0560	1.3916	3.0227[*]			

Note: Each series corresponds to $y_t = 100 * log(GDP_t)$ or $y_t = 100 * log(IPI_t)$. In the ARMA model, each series corresponds to $y_t = 100 * \Delta log(GDP_t)$ or $y_t = 100 * \Delta log(IPI_t)$ in deviations from the mean. The empirical critical values have been computed by $1,000$ Monte Carlo replications for the sample sizes and parameters values obtained in the estimations. $Sup\ F(\lambda)^m_{\beta(1)}$ is the Wald-type statistic to test the recursive estimations against the full sample estimations. The recursive statistic has been computed with symmetric 15% trimming. The asterisks [*], [**], [***] denote the rejection of the null hypothesis of parameter stability to a significance level of 10%, 5% and 1% respectively. [+] denotes the sum of the GDPs of Germany, France, Italy and Spain in euros.

For the rest of the series the data sources are the National Statistical Offices and Eurostat. Samples for GDP are 1970Q1–2003Q1 for all countries, excluding Spain and Euro-4 1980Q1–2003Q1 and Eurozone 1991Q1–2003Q1. Samples for IPI are 1970M1–2003M4 (UK, Germany), 1970M1–2003M3 (Italy), 1972M1–2003M4 (France), 1975M1–2003M4 (Spain), 1985M1–2003M3 (Eurozone).

then in their implied ARMA models. We start by estimating UC models for the two decompositions presented in the previous section, that is the trend plus cycle and the cyclical trend decompositions. The sup Wald-type statistics $F(\lambda)^m_{\beta(1)}$ for parameter stability in the autoregressive polynomials of the cyclical equations are presented in Table 23.1.[10]

As indicated, once we dispose of the cyclical filtered components it is possible to calculate the $sup\ F(\lambda)^m_{\beta(1)}$ to test for the stability of the autoregressive parameters. In testing for parameter stability, the values presented in Table 23.1 should not be compared directly with those tabulated for very large sample sizes. Instead, under the null hypothesis of no structural change, it is convenient to calculate the empirical distributions of the sup Wald-type statistic for the sample size and the estimated parameters values. This has been done for 1,000 replications in each of the estimated models.[11] By comparing the calculated $sup\ F(\lambda)^m_{\beta(1)}$ for each of the models with the tabulated values, we deduce that we cannot reject the null hypothesis of no structural change in most cases.[12] There are a few exceptions like the Spanish GDP and the Eurozone IPI for the trend plus cycle model, and the Spanish GDP and Spanish and Eurozone IPIs for the cyclical trend model.[13]

If instability in the parameters of the UCM is confirmed, their implied reduced form may also be affected by parameter variation. As mentioned earlier ARMA models are nonlinear and the sequential tests must be performed after obtaining consistent estimates of both the parameters and the perturbations.

From (23.4)–(23.6) and (23.7)–(23.9), the reduced form corresponding to the trend plus cycle and the cyclical trend decompositions can be obtained. When no common factors are present in the AR and MA parts, and applying the restriction that the variance of the trend component is zero ($\sigma_1^2 = 0$), the reduced form of the first decomposition is a restricted ARIMA($p, 1, p + 1$):

$$\phi_p(L)\Delta y_t = \phi_p(1)\mu + \Delta\varepsilon_{2t} + \phi_p(L)\Delta e_t \tag{23.10}$$

The reduced form of the cyclical trend decomposition (23.7)–(23.9), also when $\sigma_1^2 = 0$, corresponds to the restricted ARIMA($p^*, 1, p^* + 1$):

$$\psi_{p*}(L)\Delta y_t = \psi_{p*}(1)\mu + \varepsilon_{2,t-1}^* + \psi_{p*}(L)\Delta e_t \tag{23.11}$$

Given our interest in the autoregressive parameters ARMA models have been estimated the using centred series. The estimations have been performed without restrictions and with a general parametric specification roughly coherent with the two UC models analysed. Again, the *sup* Wald-type test statistic must be evaluated by comparing its value with the empirical distributions. As for UC models, the null hypothesis of no structural change could not be rejected in most cases[14] (except for Spanish GDP and Euro4 GDP). The discrepancies in the rejection of the null hypothesis of parameter stability in the UC models and the compatible ARMA models for the analysed series can be attributed to the low power of the test for the sample sizes and the distances between the null and the alternative hypothesis as we indicated.

In the absence of a power analysis of the *sup* $F(\lambda)_{\beta(1)}^m$ test in UC models, visual inspection of the recursive parameters may offer complementary information to the *sup* statistic. We have plotted the recursive estimates of the autoregressive parameters of some of the UC models in Figure 23.1. These graphs may also contain additional information about how to model parameter instability. The recession periods[15] in these graphs are shaded and the correspondence between recessions and changes in the autoregressive parameters is clear. Although the parameter variation is not substantial in most of the cases, as indicated by the *sup* $F(\lambda)_{\beta(1)}^m$, some stability gains would be possible if we model such abrupt changes in a convenient way (that is by means of regime switching or with intervention analysis).

Some illustrative examples of parameter instability

The computed values of *sup* $F(\lambda)_{\beta(1)}^m$ for UC models and ARMA reduced forms would not allow the null hypothesis of constant coefficients to be rejected in most of the series modelled. Nevertheless, the Spanish GDP and the IPI of the Eurozone show high values for this statistic both in trend plus cycle and cyclical trend decompositions. The graphs of the recursive coefficients in Figure 23.1 seem to confirm this result. To achieve parameter stability we have several modelling

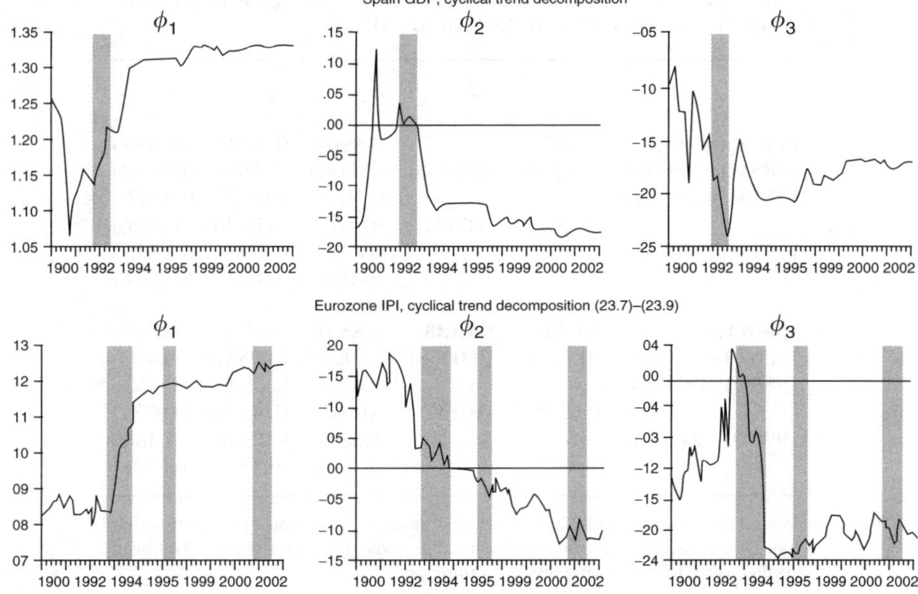

Figure 23.1 Recursive coefficients of some of the UC models of Table 23.1. Shadowed areas denote recession periods according to the criteria of note 16

strategies that consider parameter variation (for example Markov switching models and SETAR models). Intervention analysis can also be useful in some cases.

For illustrative purposes we have modelled the Eurozone IPI with a simple intervention model that allows for variation in the autoregressive parameters from 1991M11 until the end of the sample. This date coincides with the beginning of a recession period located using the smoothed cyclical component of the Eurozone IPI (see note 16). For the case of the Spanish GDP, the second sample period begins in 1991Q1 in which the graph of $\Delta \log(y_t)$ clearly shows a different behaviour. In this case, the *sup* $F(\lambda)^m_{\beta(1)}$ statistic in the ARMA model confirms parameter instability.

Table 23.2 shows that, in both cases, the parameter variation seems substantial. The graphically plotted filtered components of the Spanish GDP and the Eurozone IPI obtained from these estimations show slight differences, but the smoothed component of the Eurozone IPI (see Figure 23.2) displays enough variation to change the dating obtained when the parameter variation in the coefficients is not modelled. In this case, the changes in the dating of the business cycle anticipate on one month the inflexion points (beginnings and endings of recessions) and also signal a possible recession period at the end of the sample. The confirmation of this period as really recessive depends on the data available in the following months (the sample period ends in 2003M3) due to the conditioning of the smoothed component on future information.[16]

Table 23.2   Estimation results with varying autoregressive parameters of the Eurozone IPI and the Spanish GDP

	μ	σ_2^2	ϕ_1	ϕ_2	ϕ_3
Eurozone IPI	0.1525	0.0017	0.8964	0.9139	−0.8654
1985M1–2003M3	(0.0538)	(0.0008)	(0.0065)	(0.0656)	(0.0634)
1985M1–1991M10			0.3016	0.6579	0.0402
	0.1598[+]	0.0038[+]	(0.0058)	(0.0026)	(0.0030)
1991M11–2003M3			0.8894	0.8690	−0.8213
			(0.0253)	(0.0739)	(0.0516)
Spain GDP	0.6083	0.0138	0.8507	0.6816	−0.5496
1980Q1–2003Q1	(0.1414)	(0.0063)	(0.0092)	(0.0531)	(0.0403)
1980Q1–1990Q4			0.8946	0.4440	−0.3526
	0.5976[+]	0.0142[+]	(0.0872)	(0.1199)	(0.0731)
1991Q1–2003Q1			1.0846	0.2583	−0.3680
			(0.2792)	(0.4860)	(0.2621)

Note: The standard deviations are in parenthesis. [+] denotes parameters that have been assumed constant in both subperiods given that the test has been applied only to the autoregressive parameters.

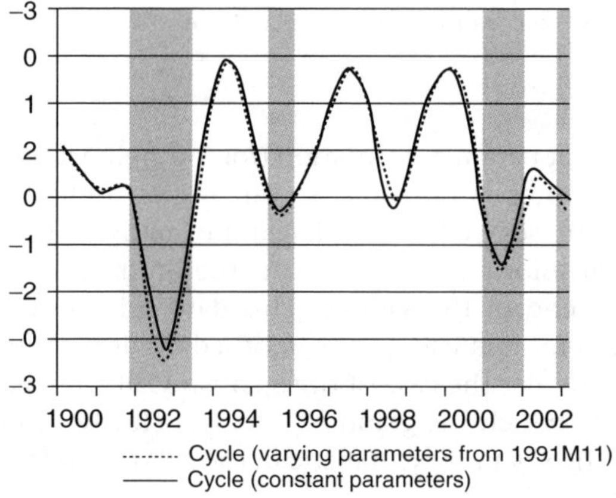

Figure 23.2   Smoothed cyclical components of the Eurozone IPI with and without parameters variation modelled (Cyclical trend decomposition (23.7)–(23.9)). Shaded areas denote recession periods (see note 16) from the constant parameter UC model

Conclusions

When using UC models, the dating of the cycle phases departs from the estimation of the cyclical unobserved components. When the UC model has parameter instability, the estimated cyclical components may be misleading. If instabilities are present in the UC model parameters, they may be translated to the parameters of the ARMA model of the corresponding observed stationary variable. To detect the presence of instabilities in the UC models and ARMA models, we first obtained linear models and then computed a recursive Wald-type test. Since the validity of the results is asymptotic, the combined effect of samples of moderate size and parameters values near nonstationarity may distort the size and power of the recursive Wald test.

When the recursive statistic has been computed for the UC and ARMA models of selected GDPs and IPIs, we have found stability in most of the models analysed. The main exceptions are Spanish GDP and the Eurozone IPI. Once corrected for instabilities, the chronology of the cycle phases of the Eurozone IPI, as given by the smoothed cyclical component, shows small changes that indicate a systematic anticipation for all the phases when comparing to the chronology obtained with the uncorrected cyclical component.

Notes

1 In the Web version of this chapter, we have estimated different ARMA models and obtained the empirical distributions of (23.1) under several null and alternative hypothesis to compute the size and power of the test in those cases.

2 Other solutions also applicable to more complex models; for example transfer function models may be seen in Del Hoyo and Llorente (2000).

3 When the coefficients are close to the nonstationary region or the sample size is not very large, better size and power may be obtained if more efficient initial conditions are used to estimate the perturbations, i.e. backforecasting.

4 The results are presented in the Web version of this chapter.

5 The method may be extended to the autoregressive coefficients of a stationary ARMA model.

6 Orthogonality restrictions are also necessary for identification, see Nelson (1988) and Harvey (1989).

7 The specification (23.4) can be modified to allow a non-constant drift; see Clark (1987), Harvey (1985) and Young (1994). Although in empirical applications, as in Harvey (1985) and Clark (1987), it is often found that the estimated variance of a random-walk drift is very small, reducing this specification to (23.4). We have also tried a random-walk drift component, in most cases obtaining the same result.

8 To simplify notation, we assume the series noise e_t, the trend noise ε_{1t} and the drift μ remain the same in both decompositions (23.4) and (23.5).

9 It is necessary to apply a heteroskedasticity correction of the cyclical component as shown in the Web version of this chapter.

10 The complete estimation results and the graphs of the cyclical components are presented in the Web version of this chapter.

11 The critical values are tabulated in the Web version of this chapter.

12 The graphs of the recursive estimates of the autoregressive coefficients show some instability, but are not statistically significant according to the $sup\, F(\lambda)^m_{\beta(1)}$ statistic.

13 The levels of rejection of the null hypothesis of no structural change for the five cases mentioned was at least 10%.

14 The rejection levels are less than 10%. The critical values are tabulated in the Web version of this chapter.

15 In the GDPs, the criterion to date a recession period has been to consider that a peak (the beginning of a recession) is located in quarter t when $\{\Delta y_t > 0, \Delta y_{t+1} < 0, \Delta y_{t+2} < 0\}$; and a trough (the end of a recession) is located in

quarter t when $\{\Delta y_{t-1} < 0, \Delta y_t < 0, \Delta y_{t+1} > 0\}$. The criterion to date a recession period in the IPIs is the translation to monthly data of the conventional criterion applied to the GDPs. Because the IPIs series are very noisy we have employed as a cyclical signal the smoothed cyclical component $C_{t/T}$ of the estimated cyclical trend UC model. We consider that a peak (the beginning of a recession) is located in month t when $\{C_{t/T} > 0, C_{t+1/T} < 0, \cdots, C_{t+6/T} < 0\}$; and a trough (the end of a recession) is located in month t when $\{C_{t-5/T} < 0, \ldots, C_{t/T} < 0, C_{t+1/T} > 0\}$.

16 New data available confirmed a good portion of the year 2003 as recessive.

References

Andrews, D.W.K. (1993) 'Tests for parameter instability and structural change with unknown change point', *Econometrica*, 61: 821–56.

Banerjee, A., Lumsdaine, R.L. and Stock, J.H. (1992) 'Recursive and sequential tests on the unit root and trend break hypothesis: theory and international evidence', *Journal of Business and Economic Statistics* , 10: 271–87.

Burns, A.F. and Mitchell, W.C. (1946) *Measuring Business Cycles*, New York: National Bureau of Economic Research.

Clark, P.K. (1987) 'The cyclical component of U. S. economic activity', *The Quarterly Journal of Economics*, November: 797–814.

Cogley, T. and Nason, J.M. (1995) 'Effects of the Hodrick-Prescott filter on trend and difference stationary time series. Implications for business cycle research', *Journal of Economic Dynamics and Control* , 19: 253–78.

Del Hoyo, J. and Llorente, G. (1998) 'Stability analysis and forecasting implications', A.-P.N. Refenes, A.N. Burgess and J.E. Moody (eds), *Decision Technologies for Computational Management Science*, London: Kluwer Academic, 13–24.

Del Hoyo, J. and Llorente, G. (2000) 'Recursive estimation and testing of dynamic models', *Computational Economics*, 16: 71–83.

Del Hoyo, J. and Llorente, G. (2001) 'Asset pricing models, specification search and stability analysis', *Computational Economics*, 17: 219–37.

Del Hoyo, J. Llorente, G. and Rivero, C. (2003) 'Changing risk and stochastic volatility models', *Working Paper*, D.pto Economía Cuantitativa: Universidad Autónoma de Madrid.

García-Ferrer, A. and Queralt, R. (1998) 'Using long-, medium-, and short-term trends to forecast turning points in the business cycle: some international evidence', *Studies in Nonlinear Dynamics and Econometrics*, 3: 79–105.

Harvey, A.C. (1985) 'Trend and cycles in macroeconomic time series', *Journal of Business & Economic Statistics*, 3: 216–27.

Harvey, A.C. (1989) *Forecasting Structural Time Series Models and the Kalman Filter*, Cambridge: Cambridge University Press.

Harvey, A.C. and Jaeger, A. (1993) 'Detrending and the business cycle', *Journal of Applied Econometrics*, 8: 231–47.

Nelson, C.R. (1988) 'Spurious trend and cycle in the state space decomposition of a time series with a unit root', *Journal of Economic Dynamics and Control*, 12: 475–88.

Nelson, C.R. and Kang, H. (1981) 'Spurious periodicity in inappropriately detrended time series', *Econometrica*, 49: 741–51.

Stock, J.H. (1994) 'Unit roots, structural breaks and trends', R.F. Engle and D.L. McFadden (eds), *Handbook of Econometrics*, Amsterdam: North Holland, 2739–839.

Watson, M.W. (1986) 'Univariate detrending methods with stochastic trends', *Journal of Monetary Economics*, 18: 49–75.

Young, P.C. (1994) 'Time-variable parameter and trend estimation in nonstationary economic time series', *Journal of Forecasting*, 13: 179–210.

24
Simultaneous Determination of NAIRU, Output Gaps and Structural Budget Balances

Göran Hjelm

Introduction

In this chapter we propose a new approach to estimate Nairu, output gaps and structural budget balances in the same model. A structural VAR model, designed to take the non-stationarity of European unemployment into account, is applied and we provide Swedish evidence and compare with OECD estimates.

Policy-makers and economists of national governments and at the OECD, for example, often focus on three unobservable variables: the Nairu, the output gap, and the structural budget balance. If correctly estimated, all three give crucial information to both politicians and central bankers. Numerous ways have been proposed to estimate these policy variables,[1] but they have, to the author's knowledge, only been estimated simultaneously once before.[2] As we are dealing with the same business cycle that is to be removed from the time series of unemployment, output and the budget balance, we believe that, if possible, the variables in question should be estimated in a single model. One step in this direction is taken by Apel and Jansson (1999a, 1999b), who estimate the Nairu and the output gap in an unobservable components (UC) model. We go a step further and estimate structural budget balances in the same model as well. We propose a structural VAR (SVAR) approach and the Blanchard and Quah (1989) identification method to extract labour market, productivity and business-cycle shocks. The identification is supported by the impulse-response functions and the model (outlined below) is designed to take the non-stationarity of European unemployment into account. The method is applied to Swedish data and compared to the latest OECD estimates. The conclusions are presented in a final section.

The model

SVAR models have previously been used to estimate output gaps (see, for example Cerra and Saxena, 2000, and Scott, 2000). Our model consists of three variables: unemployment (u), GDP (y), and the budget balance (bb, see Figure 24.2 for the u and bb series). Unit-root tests, including those allowing for level shifts (Perron, 1989), suggest that u and y are non-stationary while bb is stationary (see Hjelm, 2003). The stationary vector of the variables at hand is hence: $\Delta x' = [\Delta u\ \Delta y\ bb]^3$ and the structural moving-average representation of the system is given by:

$$\Delta x_t = \mu + C(L)\varepsilon_t \tag{24.1}$$

where $\mu = \overline{\Delta x}$ is a 3×1 vector of constants, L is a lag operator, and $\varepsilon_t' = [\varepsilon_t^{LM}\ \varepsilon_t^{P}\ \varepsilon_t^{BC}]$ is a vector of (by assumption) orthogonal, unobserved structural shocks. For many European countries (including Sweden), we believe that the following identification scheme (including the necessary three assumptions) is a fair description of reality:

1 *Labour market shock* (ε_t^{LM}). Owing to factors like changes in social security systems, demography, and the structure of the labour market, the vertical long-run Phillips curve has shifted in many European countries. This shock corresponds to such shifts and, as the level of GDP is closely related to the labour market, it is allowed to affect both unemployment and GDP in the long run.[4]
2 *Productivity shock* (ε_t^{P}). This shock concerns shifts in the aggregate supply curve due to productivity shocks. While allowing such shocks to have long-run effects on GDP, we assume that there are no long-run effects on unemployment. Hence, our model suggests that, over the long run, the level of unemployment is determined only by the structure of the labour market, not by the development of productivity.
3 *Business-cycle shock* (ε_t^{BC}). This shock is a traditional business-cycle shock and we assume that it has no long-run effects on either unemployment or GDP.

By imposing the three mentioned long-run assumptions, we have the following long-run multipliers ($c(1)$) of the system:

$$\begin{bmatrix} \Delta u \\ \Delta y \\ bb \end{bmatrix} = \begin{bmatrix} c_{11}(1) & 0 & 0 \\ c_{21}(1) & c_{22}(1) & 0 \\ c_{31}(1) & c_{32}(1) & c_{33}(1) \end{bmatrix} \begin{bmatrix} \varepsilon^{LM} \\ \varepsilon^{P} \\ \varepsilon^{BC} \end{bmatrix}$$

where $c_{11}(1)\varepsilon^{LM}$ is the long-run effect of labour-market shocks on Δu, and so on. It is well-known that the identifying assumptions in SVAR-models cannot be tested statistically. We can, however, examine how the variables respond to the shocks. If they respond as we would expect from the labelling of the shocks, support (but no proof) is provided for the identification (and interpretation) of the model. Our model satisfies this criteria for all combinations of variables and shocks (see Figure 24.1).[5] Finally, we obtain our three unobservable variables by calculating the historical decomposition. (i) *Nairu*: what would the unemployment series look like

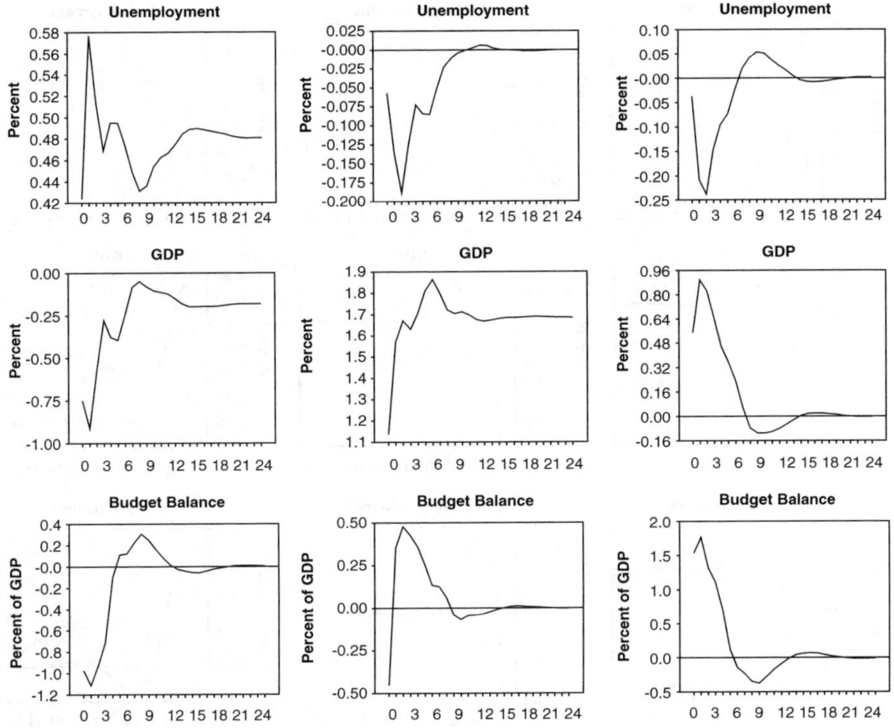

Figure 24.1   Impulse response functions

Left column: (adverse) labour market shock; mid-column: productivity shock; right column: business cycle shock.

in absence of productivity and business-cycle shocks[6]? (ii) *Potential GDP* (y^*): what would the GDP series look like in the absence of business cycle shocks? The output gap is then calculated using the formula: $\left(\frac{y}{y^*} - 1\right) * 100$. (iii) *Structural budget balance* (*sbb*): what would the budget balance series look like in absence of business-cycle shocks?

Swedish evidence and OECD comparison[7]

Yearly data for the period 1950–2004 (including the OECD forecasts for 2003–04) are used.[8] We believe it is unlikely that the data-generating process for unemployment during the 1990s (see the mid-left graph of Figure 24.2) is the same as for the rest of the sample. We therefore include a dummy variable to account for the extreme hump in unemployment.[9] The left column of Figure 24.1 shows the SVAR estimates for the whole period while we concentrate our comments on the right column which compares with the OECD estimates for the period 1980–2004. Beginning with the output gap, the SVAR gap is somewhat less volatile in general (see the upper-right graph of Figure 24.2). From 1993 and onwards, the two gaps

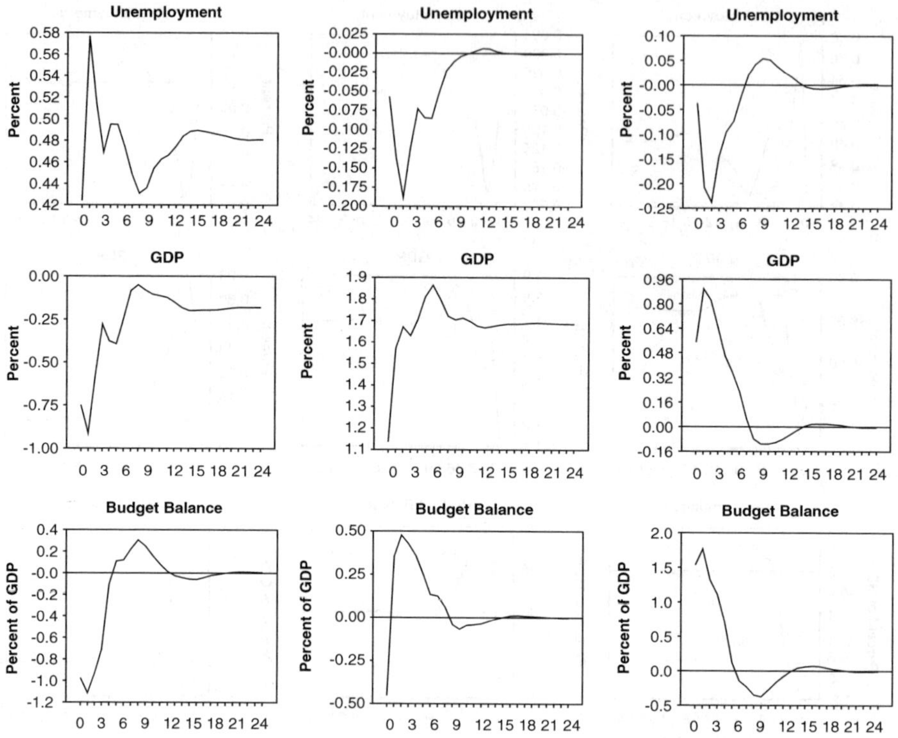

Figure 24.2   Estimates of Nairu, output gap and structural budget balances

Left column: SVAR estimates 1955–2004; right column: comparison between SVAR and OECD estimates 1980–2004.

are rather similar, while the difference is much greater during the 1980s. Which gap is 'best' then? Well, one important usage of output gaps is their ability to predict inflation and, it turns out that the two gaps are similar in this respect.[10]

Turning to the Nairu, both SVAR and OECD implies that actual unemployment was higher than the Nairu in the beginning of the 1980s and during the second half of the 1990s, while unemployment was lower than the Nairu at the end of the 1980s and during the years 2000–02 (see the mid-right graph of Figure 24.2). One can also note that the OECD predicts a considerably higher Nairu for 1986–1991 but the differences are rather small for 1993–2004.

Finally, focusing on the structural budget balance, the SVAR and the OECD give a similar picture, even though there are some important differences (see the bottom-right graph of Figure 24.2). During the 1990s, a larger share of the total deficit is explained by the business cycle in the SVAR-model. When the actual deficit peaked in 1993 (−11.6%), the SVAR-model devotes 4.7 per cent to structural factors while the OECD counterpart is 6.7 per cent. One reason for this result is that the SVAR-model implied a smaller increase in the Nairu which is an important factor determining the size of the structural deficit.

Conclusions

We suggest a new method to estimate Nairu, output gaps and structural budget balances in the same model using a structural VAR (SVAR) approach. We consider this feature important as it is principally the effects of the same business cycle that are to be removed from the three series. The method is designed to take the non-stationarity of European unemployment into account by allowing for labour market shocks to have long-run effects on the unemployment rate and hence the Nairu. Another strength of the proposed method is the possibility of interpreting the time series of structural shocks that are calculated (not shown here, see Hjelm, 2003). For example, the upturn of the economy during the second half of the 1990s was primarily due to favourable labour market and productivity shocks, while the business cycle shocks were mainly negative.

A weakness of the approach is that it requires rather long yearly (quarterly data on the budget balance is generally not available) data series. For many countries, sufficiently long data series of the consolidated budget balance is not (electronically) published by any official source. One has therefore to combine different sources at national statistical offices, a cumbersome procedure if the study is to cover many countries. Despite this weakness, the proposed method could be useful to both governments and research institutes (who have access to sufficiently long data series) as a complement to the existing methods applied by, for example, the OECD. As the three desired series are unobservable, their values are to an important extent a matter of judgement. In this process of judgement, we believe it is wise to use and weigh information arising from several models. The present SVAR-model could arguably be one of these.

Notes

1 The profession seems far from a consensus. See, e.g., Boone (2000), Cerra and Saxena (2000), European Commission (1995), Giorno *et al.* (1995), Richardson *et al.* (2000) and Scott (2000).
2 See chapter 4 in Hokkanen's (1998) thesis for an unobservable components (UC) approach.
3 As the budget balance variable includes negative values, it cannot be expressed in logs. Pre-analysis clearly shows that the models works best when the GDP variable, as the budget balance variable, is expressed in (for GDP, first differenced) levels.
4 As the budget balance is stationary, there are, by definition, no long-run effects on this variable for any of the shocks.
5 u responds positively while y and bb respond negatively to a adverse labour market shock; u responds negatively while y and bb respond positively to a favourable productivity shock; u responds negatively while y and bb respond positively to a favourable business cycle shock.
6 Note that we calculate the Nairu without any explicit information about inflation. Given that the economy (and the variables) are driven by the three structural shocks and that productivity and business cycle shocks have no long-run effect on unemployment, the Nairu can be extracted from the model.

7   The OECD uses three different models to estimate the three unobservable variables (see Giorno *et al.*, 1995, and Richardson *et al.*, 2000). Values are taken from the OECD *Economic Outlook*, various issues.
8   DeSerres and Guay (1995) show that when some shocks only have temporary effects on one of the variables, the VAR representation in general contains an MA term which implies that the number of lags required to generate a fair decomposition of the structural shocks and the dynamics increases. We believe four yearly lags fulfills this requirement in our application.
9   Parallell results not using the dummy can be found in Hjelm (2003). The unemployment variable is in first differences, and the size of the following (highly significant) dummy is therefore determined by the size of the change in unemployment: $D_{1993} = 1$ when $\Delta u \approx 3\%$, $D_{1998} = -0.5$ when $\Delta u \approx -1.5\%$, $D_{1999} = -0.25$ when $\Delta u \approx -0.9\%$, $D_{2000} = -0.25$ when $\Delta u \approx -0.9\%$, zero otherwise.
10 Following Coe and McDermott (1997), we allow for adaptive expectations and estimate $\pi_t = \alpha_0 + \alpha_1 \pi_{t-1} + \alpha_2 gap_{t-1} + \varepsilon_t$, where π and *gap* are inflation and the output gap, respectively. The estimated coefficients for the longest common time period (1968–2004) are (SVAR ordered first): $\alpha_0 = 1.20^{**}, 1.61^{**}; \alpha_1 = 0.80^*, 0.71^*; \alpha_2 = 0.32^{**}, 0.40^*; R^2 = 0.67, 0.71$. '*' and '**' denote significance at the 5 and 10% levels, respectively. See Hjelm (2003) for details.

References

Apel, M. and Jansson, P. (1999a) 'System estimates of potential output and the Nairu', *Empirical Economics*, 24: 373–88.

Apel, M. and Jansson, P. (1999b) 'A theory consistent approach for estimating potential output and the Nairu', *Economics Letters*, 64: 271–75.

Blanchard, O.J. and Quah, D. (1989) 'The dynamic effects of aggregate demand and supply disturbances', *The American Economic Review*, 79: 655–73.

Boone, L. (2000) 'Comparing semi structural methods to estimate unobserved variables: the HPMV and Kalman filters approaches', *OECD ECO/WKP 13*.

Cerra, V. and Saxena, S.C. (2000) 'Alternative methods of estimating potential output and the output gap: an application to Sweden', *Working Paper*, 59, Washington: IMF.

Coe, D.T. and McDermott, C.J. (1997) 'Does the gap model work in Asia?', *IMF Staff Papers*, 44, March, Washington: IMF.

DeSerres, A. and Guay, A. (1995) 'Selection of the truncation lag in structural VARs (or VECMs) with long run restrictions', *Bank of Canada Working Paper*, 95–9.

European commission, (1995) 'Technical note: the Commissions services' method for the cyclical adjustment of government budget balances', *European Economy*, 60, Bruxelles: European Commission.

Giorno, C., Richardson, P., Roseveare, D. and van den Noord, P. (1995) 'Estimating potential output, output gaps and structural budget balances', *OECD ECO/WKP 152*, Paris: OECD.

Hjelm, G. (2003) 'Simultaneous determination of Nairu, output gaps, and structural budget balances: Swedish evidence', *Working Paper*, 82, Stockholm: National Institute of Economic Research, www.konj.se/download/18.165f5065d41637fff177/WP81.pdf.

Hokkanen, J. (1998) 'Estimating structural budget balances with unobservable components', Ch. 4, Phd Thesis, *Interpreting budget deficits and productivity fluctuations*, Economic Studies 42, Uppsala: Uppsala University.

Lütkepohl, H. (1993) *Introduction to Multiple Time Series Analysis*, Berlin: Springer-Verlag.

OECD, *Economic Outlook*, various issues, Paris: OECD.

Perron, P. (1989) 'The great crash, the oil price shock, and the unit root hypothesis', *Econometrica*, 57: 1361–401.

Richardson, P., Boone, L., Giorno, C., Meacci, M., Rae, D. and Turner, D. (2000) 'The concept, policy use and measurement of structural unemployment: estimating a time varying Nairu across 21 OECD countries', *OECD ECO/WKP 23*, Paris: OECD.

Scott, A. (2000) 'Stylized facts from output gap measures', *Discussion Paper Series*, 7: Reserve bank of New Zealand.

van den Noord, P. (2000) 'The size and role of automatic fiscal stabilizers in the 1990s and beyond', *OECD ECO/WKP 3*, Paris: OECD.

25
Density Estimates for Real-Time Eurozone Output Gap Estimates

James Mitchell

Introduction

Output gap estimates calculated in real-time are known to be often unreliable. Recent work has found that, without the benefit of hindsight, it can prove difficult for policy-makers to pin down accurately the current position of the output gap. However, attention has primarily focused on output gap point estimates alone. This chapter considers output gap estimates and their uncertainty more generally. Interpreting real-time output gap estimates as forecasts, we explain the importance of providing measures of uncertainty, *via* interval or density forecasts, around real-time output gap estimates. We illustrate how this can be achieved and note how, *ex post*, the accuracy of these measures of unreliability associated with real-time estimates can be evaluated statistically and a decision then made about their reliability. An application to the Eurozone illustrates the use of these techniques in the context of real-time output gap measurement. Simulated out-of-sample experiments reveal that not only can real-time point estimates of the Eurozone output gap be unreliable, but so can measures of uncertainty associated with them. This provides a serious challenge to both producers and users of output gap estimates.

Policy-makers require output gap estimates in real-time.[1] They do not have the luxury of being able to wait before deciding whether the economy is currently lying above or below its trend level. They have to decide, without the benefit of hindsight, whether a given change to output in the current period is temporary or permanent, that is whether it is a cyclical or trend movement. Their problem can be interpreted as a forecasting one, since these real-time output gap estimates are forecasts, in the sense that they are expectations of the output gap conditional on incomplete information. Only with the arrival of additional information, such as revised historical data and data not available at the time, do the output gap estimates eventually settle down at their 'final' values.[2]

Recent work has found real-time or end-of-sample output gap (point) estimates to be unreliable, in the sense that there is a large and significant revision or forecasting error; see Orphanides and van Norden's (2002) application to the US economy. The revisions associated with real-time estimates are considerable; indeed for the USA they were found to be as large as the output gap estimates themselves. So-called *data* revisions, explained by revisions to published GDP data, were found to be less important than so-called *statistical* revisions. Statistical revisions are explained by the arrival of new data helping macroeconomists, with the advantage of hindsight, better understand the position of the business cycle, and also perhaps revising what model they use to identify and estimate the output gap.

Clearly policy-makers misjudging the position of the business cycle in real-time, or in other words making poor forecasts, can lead to sub-optimal policy-decisions; see Nelson and Nikolov (2001) and Ehrmann and Smets (2003). The findings for the USA therefore, are worrying. Below we find that a similar picture of revisions to output gap estimates emerges when we look at the Eurozone business cycle.

But, should we be surprised by this unreliability? Previous work has largely over-looked this question. With a couple of exceptions to which we turn below, focus has hitherto been on the point forecast – that is on the 'central tendency' of the output gap. But as is well-known from the forecasting literature, forecasts more generally need not be misleading or useless even if point estimates are wrong. Specifically, if the 'final' estimate or outturn falls within the bounds of what was expected in real-time, real-time estimates can remain useful to users. It is therefore imperative to provide users of output gap estimates with not just a real-time point estimate, but an indication of the degree of uncertainty associated with it. If reliable, users can take decisions accordingly, and insure themselves against the possibility of revisions to real-time output point estimates; the weight policy-makers place on real-time output gap estimates should depend on their accuracy. In fact, measures of uncertainty are useful in their own right if interested in analysing, for example, risk and volatility, or the probability of a recession.

Although previous work, such as Orphanides and van Norden (2002) and Camba-Mendez and Rodriguez-Palenzuela (2003), has provided measures of uncertainty associated with output gap estimates, *via* estimated standard errors, as indicated above focus has remained on the point estimates; the quality of real-time output gap estimates has been evaluated primarily by focusing on the degree and nature of *ex post* revisions to output gap point estimates. Typically this has involved examination, for example, both of the correlation between the real-time and final point estimates and the difference between the real-time and final estimates. When presented, measures of uncertainty have been evaluated in specific ways – it has not been made explicit what defines a 'good' measure of uncertainty. This can leave us unclear about the reliability of real-time output gap estimates and their uncertainty.

In this chapter we provide a more general discussion of the importance of providing measures of uncertainty, *via* interval and density forecasts, associated with real-time output gap point estimates. We explicitly relate the computation and evaluation of measures of uncertainty associated with real-time output gap estimates to recently developed techniques from the forecasting literature. By comparison, previous work has left this relationship, at best, implicit and relied on *ad hoc* tests. Camba-Mendez and Rodriguez-Palenzuela (2003) test if the standard error of the real-time estimates is equal to that of the final estimates using what can be interpreted as a test for equal (point) forecast accuracy similar to Diebold and Mariano (1995), while Orphanides and van Norden (2002) actually use a type of Diebold–Mariano test on the second moments of the revision between real-time and final estimates to test if the variability of the revision process is consistent with what was expected *ex post* rather than *ex ante*; for further details see Mitchell (2003). In contrast, we consider real-time (*ex ante*) computation of measures of uncertainty associated with real-time estimates and methods of evaluation that have a clear interpretation and indeed a growing pedigree. The clarity derives from defining what constitutes a 'good', or even 'optimal' (in some respect), interval or density forecast.

The plan of the remainder of the chapter is as follows. The next section illustrates the unreliability of real-time output gap point estimates in the Eurozone; parameter uncertainty is found to be a dominant source of this unreliability. We then turn to whether we should be surprised by this unreliability, and consider how to measure the uncertainty associated with real-time estimates and then evaluate them similarly to how point estimates are evaluated on the basis of their root-mean-squared error (RMSE) against the outturn. The simulated real-time application to the Eurozone is then revisited, indicating and evaluating the degree of uncertainty associated with output gap estimates in real time. A final section offers some concluding comments and discusses the implications of the findings for policy-makers. Further details about the data and models used are given in Mitchell (2003).

The unreliability of real-time output gap point estimates illustrated: an application to the Eurozone

Eurozone data are taken from the ECB's Area Wide Model (AWM) database; see the Appendix for more details.[3] It is expedient in an application to the Eurozone to focus on statistical revisions alone as construction of a 'real-time' data-set is not readily possible; however, see Mitchell (2003) for an attempt.

To illustrate the unreliability of real-time output gap estimates the following experiment is undertaken. Full sample or *final* estimates of the output gap are derived using data available over the (full) sample-period, 1971Q1–2003Q1. Real-time output gap estimates are computed recursively from 1981Q1. This involves using data from 1971Q1–1981Q1, to provide an initial estimation period of 10 years to compute the real-time estimate for 1981Q1.[4] Then data for 1971Q1–1981Q2 are used to re-estimate the output gap (that involves re-estimation of the parameters of the models used to measure the output gap) and obtain real-time estimates for 1981Q2. This recursive exercise, designed to mimic real-time measurement of the

Table 25.1   The unreliability of real-time output gap point estimates for five different output gap estimators: the correlation (r) of alternative real-time and filtered estimates of the Eurozone output gap against the final estimates and the noise-to-signal ratio (*NSR*)

| | *1981Q1–2000Q1* | | | | *1993Q3–2000Q1* | | | |
| | *real-time* | | *filtered* | | *real-time* | | *filtered* | |
	r	*NSR*	*r*	*NSR*	*r*	*NSR*	*r*	*NSR*
Univariate HP	0.273	1.43	0.273	1.43	0.875	1.17	0.875	1.17
Univariate UC	0.600	0.82	0.838	0.64	0.904	0.57	0.898	0.71
Bivariate UC	0.599	0.87	0.941	0.56	0.864	0.70	0.923	0.58
Bivariate HP	0.688	3.31	0.727	1.35	0.585	3.81	0.599	1.87
Trivariate UC	0.760	1.79	0.921	0.57	0.352	2.15	0.795	1.07

output gap, is carried on until data for the period 1971Q1–2000Q1 are used to estimate the real-time output gap for 2000Q1. The last three years are excluded from the real-time simulation to allow for the fact that real-time estimates take time to converge to their 'final' values.[5] What we call the real-time estimate is strictly the *quasi-real* estimate of Orphanides and van Norden (2002).

We illustrate the real-time unreliability of output gap point estimates for five representative output gap estimators; for further details of these estimators see Mitchell (2003). The results are summarized in Table 25.1. Reflecting the fact that these five estimators in Table 25.1 can be interpreted within an unobserved components (UC) framework and that UC models use the data in two ways, as well as considering the real-time estimate, Table 25.1 also examines the filtered estimates (or the *quasi-final* estimates in the parlance of Orphanides and van Norden (2002)).[6] For the univariate HP filter, as the only parameter is chosen *a priori*, clearly there is no parameter uncertainty meaning that the filtered and real-time estimates are equivalent. The reliability of the real-time and filtered point estimates is summarized by their correlation against the final estimates and the noise-to-signal ratio (NSR). The NSR is the ratio of the RMSE of the revision (the difference between the real-time or filtered estimate and the final estimate) to the standard deviation of the final estimate of the output gap. To provide some indication of how sensitive results are to the chosen sample period, Table 25.1 contrasts the performance of the real-time and filtered estimates computed over the period 1981Q1–2000Q1, with those computed over the period 1993Q3–2000Q1. This latter period was chosen as it is after the peak in economic activity in the early 1990s.

Table 25.1 indicates that as the future becomes the present output gap estimates are revised. Real-time point estimates of the output gap in the Eurozone, as in the USA are unreliable, in the sense that there is a large and important revision error. This is reflected by the correlation coefficients, over the period 1981Q1–2000Q1, being in the range 0.27–0.76 and the noise-to-signal ratio exceeding unity for three of the five output gap estimators, and for the remaining estimators being greater than 0.8. Reflecting the importance of *ex post* information in redefining the parameter values, the filtered estimates are more reliable than the real-time estimates: correlation is higher and NSR lower. Parameter uncertainty appears to be a dominant source of the unreliability of real-time estimates.

There is some variation across estimators and the sample period. Comparing the estimators across the period 1981Q1–2000Q1, correlation ranges from 0.27 for the univariate HP measure to around 0.6–0.7 for most of the multivariate measures. In this sense it is encouraging that the move from univariate to multivariate measures of the output gap does lead to real-time estimates better correlated with the final estimates. Adding 'economic information' appears to help. However, the multivariate estimators have higher noise-to-signal ratios than the univariate UC estimator.

This unreliability of real-time point estimates also shows up over the period 1993Q3–2000Q1. Although the univariate estimators are more reliable over this later period than 1981Q1–2000Q1, some of the multivariate estimators appear to be less reliable. This may reflect the fact that they do well at picking up the big movements, such as the boom in the early 1990s, but are worse at picking up more minor movements.

The findings of Table 25.1 beg the question, should we be surprised by this unreliability? To address this question we therefore first take up the challenge of providing, in real time, measures of uncertainty associated with real time (point) estimates of the output gap, *via* interval and density forecasts. Secondly we evaluate them to ascertain whether the unreliability of output gap point estimates is surprising.[7] Could we have anticipated this revision error? Was the revision error to the real-time estimate within the bounds of what we could have predicted in real time? It is important to evaluate whether these measures of uncertainty offer a reliable indication of the degree of unreliability associated with output gap estimates as, otherwise, all that can be said is that the bands are wider for, say, output gap estimate *A* than estimate *B*. Nothing can be inferred about the appropriateness of the bands *per se*.

Uncertainty associated with output gap estimates: density estimates of the output gap

To capture fully the uncertainty associated with the real-time estimates, or forecasts, of the output gap, we construct density forecasts; see Tay and Wallis (2000) for a review of density forecasting. Density forecasts of the output gap provide an estimate of the probability distribution of its possible future values. In contrast, so-called 'interval' and 'event' forecasts provide specific information on forecast uncertainty that can be derived from the density forecast; interval forecasts specify the probability that the actual outcome will fall within a given interval while event forecasts focus on the probabilities of certain events, such as the probability of recession. Density forecasts of inflation in the UK, for example, are now provided each quarter both by the Bank of England in its 'fan' chart and the National Institute of Economic and Social Research (NIESR) in its quarterly forecast. Density forecasts inform the user of the forecast about the risks involved in using the forecast for decision making. Indeed, interest may lie in the dispersion or tails of the density itself; for example inflation targets often focus the attention of monetary authorities to the probability of future inflation falling outside some predefined target range while users of growth forecasts may be concerned about the probability of recession. Moreover, volatility forecasts, as measured by the variance, and other measures of risk and uncertainty, can be extracted from the density forecast.

Questions then arise over how the density forecasts should be constructed. Here we rely on the state-space representation for the output gap estimator (see Mitchell, 2003, for further details). Conditional on Gaussianity (of the disturbances driving the components of the state vector) confidence intervals around the output gap then can be presented given knowledge of the covariance matrix of the estimated state vector.[8] The effects of data revisions and parameter uncertainty could be considered also, but are not here where our aim is simply to stress the importance of providing density estimates for the output gap and suggest how this can be achieved. We then evaluate how well the implied interval and density forecasts perform relative to the outturn (that is, the final estimate). Let $P_{t|t}$ denote the covariance matrix of the output gap at time t, $y^C_{t|t}$, calculated at time t (the output gap is one of the elements of the state vector). Then conditional on Gaussianity confidence intervals can be derived, as can density estimates. The Gaussian density is $N(y^C_{t|t}, P_{t|t})$. We now turn to evaluation of these interval and density forecasts once the final output gap estimate, $y^C_{t|T}$ where $T \to \infty$, has become available.

Evaluation of interval and density forecasts of the output gap

Interval and density forecasts of the output gap are evaluated *ex post* with respect to the outturn, that is the final estimates for the output gap. The interval forecasts are evaluated using the LR tests of Christoffersen (1998). Density forecasts are evaluated in two complementary ways. The first approach reduces the density forecast to an interval forecast and uses the LR test. We focus on the central 50 per cent or inter-quartile-range forecast implied by the density forecast. Secondly, density forecasts are evaluated *ex post* using the probability integral transform; see Diebold., Gunther and Tay (1998).[9] They popularized the idea of evaluating a sample of density forecasts based on the idea that a density forecast can be considered 'optimal' if the model for the density is correctly specified. One can then evaluate forecasts without the need to specify a loss function. This is attractive as it is often hard to define an appropriate general (economic) loss function.

A sequence of estimated density forecasts, $\{p_t(y^C_t)\}_{t=1}^{T}$, for the realizations of the process $\{y^C_t\}_{t=1}^{T}$, coincides with the true densities $\{f_t(y^C_t)\}_{t=1}^{T}$ when the sequence of z_t is independently and identically distributed (*i.i.d.*) with a uniform distribution, $U(0,1)$, where

$$z_t = \int_{-\infty}^{y^C_t} p_t(u)\,du, \,, t = 1, ..., T \tag{25.1}$$

Therefore, to test whether the density forecasts are optimal and do capture all aspects of the distribution of y_t^C one must test whether the z_t are both *i.i.d.* and $U(0,1)$. By taking the inverse normal cumulative density function (CDF) transformation of the $\{z_t\}$ to give, say, $\{z_t^*\}$ the test for uniformity can be considered equivalent to one for normality on $\{z_t^*\}$; see Berkowitz (2001). This is useful as normality tests are widely seen to be more powerful than uniformity tests. For example, consider the Gaussian density forecasts of the output gap computed in real-time, $N(y_{t|t}^C, P_{t|t})$. The probability integral transforms are $z_t = \Phi((y_{t|T}^C - y_{t|t}^C), \sqrt{P_{t|t}})$, that is $z_t = \Phi((y_{t|T}^C - y_{t|t}^C)/\sqrt{P_{t|t}})$. The Berkovitz series $\{z_t^*\}$ are then the scaled revision errors, $(y_{t|T}^C - y_{t|t}^C)/\sqrt{P_{t|t}}$ that are *i.i.d.* $N(0,1)$ under the null. However, testing is complicated by the fact that the impact of dependence on the tests for uniformity/normality is unknown, as is the impact of non-uniformity/normality on tests for dependence.

The uncertainty of real-time output gap estimates in the Eurozone: interval and density forecasts

Figure 25.1 provides a visual indication of the degree of estimated real-time uncertainty for these UC based estimators of the output gap by computing 95 per cent confidence intervals around the point estimates. There are striking differences in the degree of uncertainty (predicted in real-time) associated with the real-time estimates across the alternative estimators of the output gap. As is to be expected, uncertainty is lowest for the Hodrick–Prescott estimator. It is largest for the bivariate Hodrick–Prescott estimator where the degree of uncertainty is, incredibly, large. This reflects the imposition of *a priori* parametric restrictions leading to a poorly defined model, in a statistical sense, where there is considerable uncertainty about the values of the remaining free parameters.

The Gaussian bands are very rarely significantly different from zero; policy-makers on this basis could never be sure about the position of the business cycle. But is the finding that these bands nearly always cover zero, in fact, correctly quantifying the degree of uncertainty associated with real-time estimates. This can be analysed formally using the statistical tests outlined earlier. First, however, it is useful to simply contrast the confidence bands for each measure with the actual outturn (printed in bold face) by looking again at Figure 25.1. There are again important differences across the alternative output gap estimators; the outturn frequently falls outside the 95 per cent confidence bands for the Hodrick–Prescott estimator.

Perhaps not unsurprisingly given the evidence in Figure 25.1, the interval and density evaluation tests (not reported) suggest that the measure of uncertainty does not provide a statistically satisfactory indication of the degree of uncertainty associated with real-time output gap estimates when evaluated against the point estimate for the outturn. There is some evidence to suggest, however, that the measures of uncertainty are less unreliable over the latter period, 1993Q3–2000Q1 – the

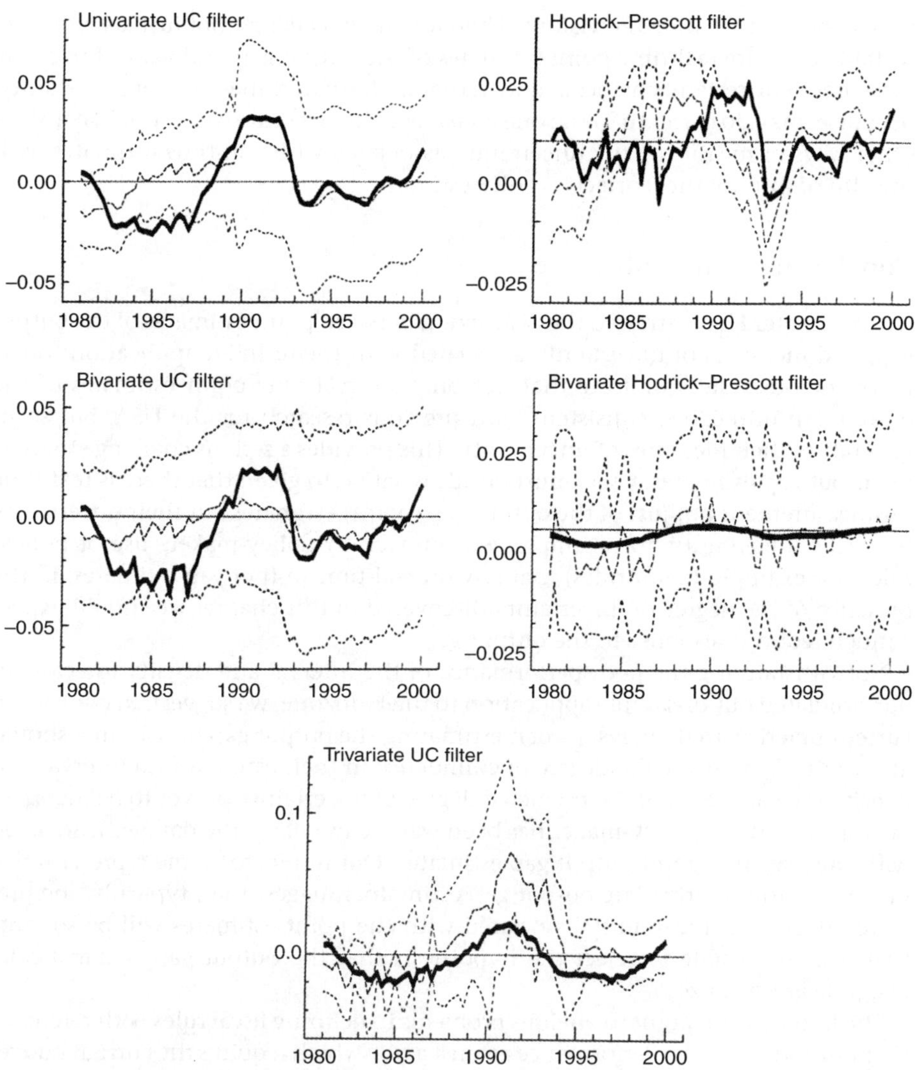

Figure 25.1   Uncertainty associated with real-time estimates using 5 different measures of the output gap: 95 per cent confidence intervals.
Note: final estimate is **bold** face.

p-values for the interval and density evaluation tests tend to be higher. But even over this latter period at least one of the tests rejects the reliability of the particular measure of uncertainty. Reliability of the predicted degree of unreliability associated with real-time output gap estimates requires both the density and interval evaluation tests to be not rejected.

The most common reason for failure of the density forecasts is serial dependence in the first moment of $\{z_t^*\}$. This is consistent with our finding of considerable persistence in the (scaled) revisions. Therefore it appears that not just, as indicated in Table 25.1, are real-time point estimates of the output gap unreliable, but so are measures of uncertainty associated with them. Alternative measures of uncertainty, of course, may do better than the one considered here. Future work should consider other ways of measuring the uncertainty associated with real-time estimates with the aim of finding the 'correct' density estimate.

Concluding comments

In this chapter I have stressed the distinction between point estimates of the output gap, and measures of uncertainty associated with them. In an application to the Eurozone our results indicate that not only are real-time point estimates of the output gap unreliable, consistent with previous research for the USA, but so in general are their measures of uncertainty. This provides a serious challenge to users of output gap estimates. Users must decide what do to given that there is real-time mismeasurement not just of the output gap (point) estimates but their uncertainty too. This uncertainty, for example, will impact on policy-makers use of policy-rules (for example Taylor rules) that rely on real-time output gap estimates; in the presence of the degree of uncertainty discovered in this chapter we should expect a much reduced response to the output gap.

Notwithstanding the poor performance of the interval and density forecasts in our simulated out-of-sample application to the Eurozone, we suggest, in contrast to current practice, that analysts when estimating the output gap in real time should also routinely indicate the degree of confidence in their estimates *via* interval and density forecasts. Even if the predicted degree of uncertainty proves to be incorrect *ex post*, at least the policy-maker has been warned *ex ante* of the dangers associated with the real-time point output gap estimates. Our results for some representative univariate and multivariate output gap estimators suggest that, typically, the predicted degree of uncertainty associated with the point estimates will be so large that it is impossible to reject the hypothesis that the output gap is statistically insignificant from zero.

The findings also point to obvious problems in defining fiscal rules with reference to the economic cycle. Performance against a rule which requires the current budget to be balanced 'over the cycle' cannot be assessed for several years. It is likely that the true position can be established only after at least two or three years. Similarly reforming the Stability and Growth Pact to take account of the cycle, as has been recently suggested in many circles, runs into obvious problems since the cycle cannot be measured accurately on a timely basis.

Appendix: data

Official Eurozone data for GDP, published by EUROSTAT, are available only from 1991. Unfortunately this does not offer a sufficiently long time-series for sensible business cycle analysis. Therefore we take the data from the ECB's Area Wide Model (AWM); see Fagan, Henry and Mestre (2001). We use real GDP data (AWM code: YER). These data are available from 1970Q1–2000Q4. The data are then updated to 2003Q1 using official data from Eurostat (via *New Cronos*). All data are used in their seasonally adjusted form. This means the data have in fact been seasonally adjusted using full-sample information, that of course would not be available to policy-makers in real time. So our results ignore this additional source of uncertainty.

For the multivariate estimators of the output gap, price, unemployment, consumption and investment data are required too. Revisions to these data are less important than for GDP data. Price data are the harmonized index of consumer prices (HICP) . These data are taken from the AWM and updated from 2001Q1 using *New Cronos*.

Notes

1 Since our focus is on the 'growth' business cycle rather than the 'classical' cycle the 'business cycle' and 'output gap' are treated synonymously.
2 Values are never truly final because data revisions and the arrival of new data are a continuous process.
3 Related studies that examine real-time output gap estimates for the Eurozone are Runstler (2002) and Camba-Mendez and Rodriguez-Palenzuela (2003). They ignore data revisions, and in fact use AWM data as in this chapter.
4 We ignore the fact that GDP data are published with, at least, a one-quarter lag.
5 Calculations in this chapter were performed using the GAUSS and Ox (see Doornik (1998)) programming languages. Use was made of the SsfPack module for Ox; see Koopman, Shephard and Doornik (1999)..
6 UC models use the data in two ways in the sense that first they estimate the parameters of the model, and secondly they use these estimates to obtain the smoothed estimates of the output gap that are the final estimates of the output gap.
7 Although Orphanides and van Norden (2002: 578–82) provide measures of uncertainty associated with their final (smoothed) and quasi-final (filtered) estimates they do not present them for real-time estimates.
8 The Kalman filter recursions automatically return estimates of the covariance matrix of the state vector; see Harvey (1989). The diagonal elements of these matrices can then be used to construct the confidence intervals and density estimates.
9 This methodology seeks to obtain the most 'accurate' density forecast, in a statistical sense. It can be contrasted with economic approaches to evaluating forecasts that evaluate forecasts in terms of their implied economic value, which derives from postulating a specific (economic) loss function; see Granger and Pesaran (2000) and Clements (2002).

References

Berkowitz, J. (2001) 'Testing density forecasts, with applications to risk management', *Journal of Business and Economic Statistics*, 19: 465–74.
Camba-Mendez, G. and Rodriguez-Palenzuela, D. (2003) 'Assessment criteria for output gap estimates', *Economic Modelling*, 20: 529–62.
Christoffersen, P. (1998) 'Evaluating interval forecasts', *International Economic Review*, 39: 841–62.
Clements, M. (2002) 'Evaluating the Bank of England density forecasts of inflation', *Discussion Paper*, Warwick: Warwick University.
Diebold., F.X., Gunther, A. and Tay, K. (1998) 'Evaluating density forecasts with application to financial risk management', *International Economic Review*, 39: 863–83.

Diebold, F.X. and Mariano, R.S. (1995) 'Comparing predictive accuracy', *Journal of Business and Economic Statistics*, 13: 253–63.

Doornik, J. (1998) *Object-oriented Matrix Programming using Ox*, London: Timberlake Consultants.

Ehrmann, M. and Smets, F. (2003) 'Uncertain potential output: implications for monetary policy', *Journal of Economic Dynamics and Control*, 27: 1611–38.

Fagan, G., Henry, J. and Mestre, R. (2001) 'An area-wide model (AWM) for the Eu11', Frankfurt am Main: European Central Bank.

Granger, C. and Pesaran, M. (2000) 'Economic and statistical measures of forecast accuracy', *Journal of Forecasting*, 19: 537–60.

Harvey, A.C. (1989) *Forecasting, Structural Time Series Models and the Kalman Filter*, Cambridge: Cambridge University Press.

Koopman, S.J., Shephard, N. and Doornik, J.A. (1999) 'Statistical algorithms for models in state space using SsfPack 2.2', *The Econometrics Journal*, 2: 107–60.

Mitchell, J. (2003) 'Should we be surprised by the unreliability of real-time output gap estimates? Density estimates for the Eurozone', *Discussion Paper*, 225: London: NIESR.

Nelson, E. and Nikolov, K. (2001) 'UK inflation in the 1970s and 1980s: The role of output gap mismeasurement', Working Paper, 148: London: Bank of England.

Orphanides, A. and van Norden, S. (2002) 'The unreliability of output-gap estimates in real time', *The Review of Economics and Statistics*, 84: 569–83.

Runstler, G. (2002) 'The information content of real-time output gap estimates: an application to the Euro area', *Working Paper*, 182: Frankfurt am Main: European Central Bank.

Tay, A. and Wallis, K. (2000) 'Density forecasting: a survey', *Journal of Forecasting*, 19: 235–54.

26
Optimal Bandpass Filtering and the Reliability of Current Analysis

Simon van Norden

Introduction

This chapter shows how existing bandpass filtering techniques and their extensions may be applied to the common problem of estimating current trends or cycles. These techniques give estimates which are 'optimal' given the available data, so their standard errors represent a lower bound on what can be achieved with other univariate techniques. Applications to the problems of estimating current trend productivity growth, core inflation and output gaps are considered. These illustrate the different factors which determine how accurately the underlying trend is measured and the degree to which estimated cycles tend to lead or lag the true cycle.

A common problem in macroeconomics is that of measuring the business cycle, or more generally, of separating long-run trends from short-term movements. A technique which does so may be thought of as a filter, one which is applied to raw economic data prior to analysis. The best known is the Hodrick-Prescott (HP) filter, which has become the benchmark against which all other filters in macroeconomics are compared.[1]

The HP filter is unabashedly arbitrary; it was proposed and adopted largely on the basis that it gave results which 'looked reasonable.' Its use has since been rationalized as an approximate bandpass filter. A bandpass filter is one which isolates movements in a series between a specified upper and lower frequency or duration; movements outside this desired frequency band are eliminated. As commonly used with quarterly economic data, the HP filter eliminates or greatly reduces most long-run movements in the series while preserving those at roughly business cycle frequencies.[2] The result is a detrended series which looks like a business cycle and has served as an agnostic basis for much economic analysis.[3]

Given its preeminent role and its arbitrary nature, the HP filter has been the focus of much emulation and innovation in recent years. Baxter and King (1999) argue in favour of replacing the HP filter with a more exact band-pass filter, arguing that better results come from using a better approximation. Gomez (2001) and Pollock (2000) propose the use of other *ad hoc* filters which are commonly used in engineering and which also approximate bandpass filters.[4] Pedersen (1998) and Kaiser and Maravall (2001) propose extensions or modifications to the HP filter to improve its performance. However, most of this literature has ignored the application to current analysis.

The distinguishing feature of current analysis is that it interprets the most recently available information; the cycle (or trend) of interest is that at the end of the data sample. The dominant focus of the above literature is historical analysis, in which we care mostly about the cycle (or trend) somewhere in the middle of the sample. This distinction is sometimes critical. Most of the analysis in the existing literature is restricted to symmetric filters; to isolate the cycle or trend at time t, such filters use an equal number of observations from before and after t.[5] This precludes their use at the end of sample. Other filters are justified on the basis of their mid-sample properties, but may behave quite differently at the end of sample.[6]

This chapter considers the filtering problem from the perspective of current analysis. Rather than use *ad hoc* approximations to bandpass filters, it shows how to construct one-sided bandpass filters which are optimal in a minimum mean-squared-error sense. Unlike the filters mentioned in the above literature, the optimal filter will vary with the properties of the data series to be filtered. While such filters are little known in macroeconomics, they are not new; the annex of the working paper version of this chapter reviews the contributions of Koopmans (1974) and Christiano and Fitzgerald (1999). This version gives an overview of these optimal filters and applies them to three problems of widespread interest; estimating the current output gap, the current trend growth rate of productivity and the current trend rate of inflation.

Related to the filtering literature discussed above is another one which examines the reliability of filtered estimates of trends and cycles.[7] Since the current analysis filter discussed in this chapter minimizes a MSE criterion, we can relate its reliability to those of other filters examined in this literature. It also establishes an upper bound on the accuracy that any such filters can hope to achieve. Because this bound depends in a complicated way on the properties of the data analysed, we investigate the properties of the optimal filter for the three common problems in current analysis.

The next section provides a non-technical overview of bandpass filtering and the optimal one-sided bandpass filter. I then apply the filter to three common macroeconomic problems of measuring trend and cycles and discuss the results, and a final section summarizes the conclusions and suggests avenues for further research.

An optimal bandpass filter for current analysis

Filters: a primer[8]

A filter may be thought of as an algorithm for processing a time series in order to get a more meaningful statistic; for example the process of averaging measured rainfall at a given location to get 'average' rainfall. We can describe this mathematically as:

$$S = f(\bar{y}) \tag{26.1}$$

where S is our statistic, $\bar{y}$ is our time series and $f(\cdot)$ is our filter. While such processing could be complex, attention often focuses on a particularly simple and tractable case; the *linear time-invariant* filter. Such filters can be described as:

$$S_t = \bar{\beta}\bar{y} = \sum_{i=-\infty}^{\infty} \beta_i \cdot y_{t-i} \tag{26.2}$$

The distinguishing features of such filters are that the weight β_i we put on a particular observation does not depend on t, and that the operation is linear in $\bar{y}$.[9] If we think of y_t as a random error term, the Wold decomposition theorem tells us that this class of filters is related to the class of ARMA process. In this situation, since the properties of $\bar{y}$ are held fixed, the properties of S are determined by $\bar{\beta}$.

We are often particularly interested in the dynamics of S, which may be uniquely characterized via frequency or spectral analysis. The idea is to decompose all the movements in S into cycles of varying frequency and amplitude. Such a unique decomposition exists if S is stationary (and if not, we assume that we can difference it until it is). Furthermore, since cycles of different frequencies are uncorrelated in the long run, the variance of S will simply be the sum of its variances over all frequencies. The relative importance of these different frequencies in the overall variance tells us something about the dynamic behaviour of the series. For example, an i.i.d. error will display a constant variance at all frequencies, while a random walk will have much more variance at low frequencies (long cycles) than at high (short cycles). The function decomposing the total variance by frequency is commonly called the *spectrum* or *spectral density* and is typically shown graphed from 0 (lowest frequencies, infinitely-long cycles) to π (highest observable frequencies, cycles of 2 periods).

The spectrum of S depends on the properties of both $\bar{\beta}$ and $\bar{y}$. To understand the effects of $\bar{\beta}$ we can divide the spectrum of S by that of $\bar{y}$ to define the *squared gain* or *transfer function* of $\bar{\beta}$. Frequencies at which the squared gain is greater than 1 are accentuated in S, while those at which the squared gain is (close to) zero are (nearly) removed from S. The aim of *bandpass* filtering is to choose β to match a particular kind of squared gain function; one which has a gain of 1 over a particular frequency range (l, u) $|0 \leq l < u \leq \pi$ and zero elsewhere. The case where $l = 0$ is called a low-pass filter while $u = \pi$ is called a high-pass filter.

If a filter has the property $\beta_j = \beta_{-j} \, \forall j$ it is called a *symmetric* filter, whereas if $\beta_j = 0 \, \forall j > 0$ then the filter is said to be *one-sided*.[10] Symmetric filters have the property that S will tend neither to lead nor to lag movements in the corresponding components of *y*; the same is not generally true for non-symmetric filters.[11] This effect of non-symmetric filters is called *phase shift* and in general will vary from one frequency to another.

Business cycle filters

Bandpass filtering is an approach to the measurement of trends or cycles in macroeconomics whose appeal rests on two key assumptions:

1 We can agree on some threshold duration such that we wish to interpret movements of longer duration as trends and shorter duration as cycles:
2 Aside from this, we wish to remain fairly agnostic about the economic or stochastic processes generating the data.

In this case we may detrend the data using a low-pass filter (one which passes all frequencies *below* the threshold, that is all durations *above* the threshold) to isolate the trend, or equivalently, use a high-pass filter to isolate the cycle. Two of the three applications we study below use low-pass filters to isolate such trends. The case of business cycles is more complex since we wish to exclude both the trend component and a seasonal/short-lived component. We therefore need a band-pass filter to block both the very long and very short duration movements.

The ideal bandpass filter would have a gain of zero outside the (l, u) interval and a gain of one inside. Deviations from the former condition allow leakage from undesired frequencies, while deviations from the later distort the 'true' cycle present in the data. The unique filter with such properties exists and is given by the formula:

$$B_j = \frac{\sin ju - \sin jl}{\pi j} \quad \text{for} \quad |j| \geq 1 \tag{26.3}$$

One problem with this ideal filter is that we require the sum in (26.2) to go from $-\infty$ to ∞. Truncating this sum at some finite values, say $-N$ and N, results in a approximate filter in which the desired rectangular shape of its squared gain is contaminated by sinusoidal imperfections (see Figure 26.1) Baxter and King (1999) suggest that using values of N as small as 20 in quarterly data gives reasonable results for US business cycles if we adopt the Burns and Mitchell cut-offs of 6 and 32 quarters.

The problem with this approach is that it cannot be used for current analysis. Using $N = 20$ implies that our most recent estimates of the business cycle would be 20 quarters prior to the last quarter for which we had data. One way around this would to use the Baxter–King formula at the end of the sample, simply omitting (that is replacing by zero) the missing observations which are not yet known. As shown in Figure 26.1, this gives poor results, even for large values of N; the resulting filters have a gain which is far from 1, vary considerably over the frequency band of interest, and leak much more of the frequencies outside the desired band. Stock and Watson (1998) use a different *ad hoc* solution. They fit the available time series to a simple AR model, then use forecasts from the fitted model in place of the

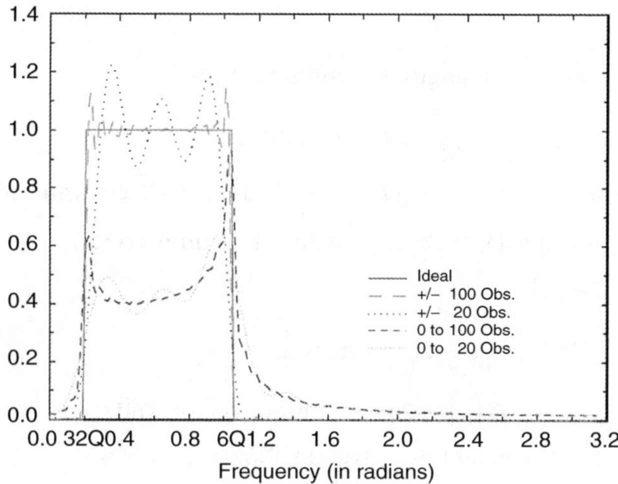

Figure 26.1   Gain^2 for ideal and approximate bandpass filters

required future observations. Unfortunately, they do not provide a justification for this procedure, nor do they examine how closely it approximates the ideal filter.

Another criticism that has been made of this approach is that even if the filter we use has a gain function which is close to that of the ideal filter, this need not imply that the series it produces will be a good approximation of the ideally filtered series.[12] The problem is that many economic series display a 'Typical Granger Spectral Shape'; the density in their spectrum is highly concentrated at the lowest frequencies. This in turn means that for bandpass or high-pass filtering (for example for measuring business cycles), we care much more about how well we approximate the ideal filter at low frequencies than at high frequencies.[13]

Optimal current-analysis filters

To adapt the bandpass filtering approach to a current analysis context, we would like to have some optimal filter $\{\widehat{B}_j\}$ which minimizes:

$$
E\left[\sum_{j=0}^{T-1} \widehat{B}_j \cdot y_{T-j} - \sum_{j=-\infty}^{\infty} B_j \cdot y_{T-j} \right]^2 \tag{26.4}
$$

In other words, given T observations on the series we wish to filter $\{y_t\}$, the optimal filter will give us the minimum mean-squared error (MSE) estimate of what the ideal filter would give us with data from ∞ to $-\infty$ This problem has a unique solution under fairly standard conditions.[14] In the case where $\{y_t\}$ is stationary, we find that:

$$
\overline{\beta} = \overline{\sum_y}^{-1} \cdot \overline{B}^{-1} \cdot \overline{\sigma}_y \tag{26.5}
$$

where

$$\overline{\beta} = \left[\widehat{B}_0, \widehat{B}_1, \ldots, \widehat{B}_{T-1}\right]', \text{ a length } T \text{ column vector;}$$

$$\overline{\Sigma_y} = \left[\overline{\sigma}_{y,0}, \overline{\sigma}_{y,1}, \ldots, \overline{\sigma}_{y,T-1}\right]'', \text{ a } T \times T \text{ matrix;}$$

$$\overline{\sigma}_{y,j} = \left[\overline{\sigma}_y(-j), \overline{\sigma}_y(-j+1), \ldots, \overline{\sigma}_y(T-1-j)\right]', \text{ a length } T \text{ column vector;}$$

$$\overline{\sigma}_y = \left[\overline{\sigma}_y(-q), \overline{\sigma}_y(-q+1), \ldots, \overline{\sigma}_y(q)\right]', \text{ a } 2q+1 \text{ column vector;}$$

$$\overline{\sigma}_y(q) = cov\left(y_t, y_{t+q}\right);$$

$$\overline{B} = \left[\widehat{B}^0, \widehat{B}^1, \ldots, \widehat{B}^{T-1}\right]' \text{ a } T \times 2q+1 \text{ matrix;}$$

$$\widehat{B}^j = \left[B_{j-q}, B_{j-q+1}, \ldots, B_{j+q}\right]' \text{ a } 2q+1 \text{ column vector; and}$$

B_j is the weight of the ideal filter, given by (26.3).

In general, these optimal weights depend on (a) the number of observations T, (b) the dynamics of our series y_t, as measured by its autocovariances, and (c) the ideal weights B_j from (26.3). Furthermore, they have an intuitive interpretation as the solution to a regression problem; one where we regress the doubly infinite set $\left\{B_j \cdot y_{T-j}\right\}$ on our T observations $\overline{y}$. The resulting coefficients are our optimal weights, and therefore our minimization problem (26.4). simply seeks to minimize the variance of the regression residuals.[15]

We can better understand this formula and the above intuition if we consider two special cases. First, suppose that y_t is identically and independently distributed. This means that $\sigma_y(l) = 0$ for all $l \neq 0$, so we may set $q = 0$. This makes $\overline{\sigma}_y$ a scalar, equal to the variance of y, and $\overline{\Sigma}_y$ is simply the identity matrix times this variance. This means that (26.5) further simplifies to $\overline{\beta} = \left[B_0, \ldots, B_{T-1}\right]'$. Put another way, in this case the optimal solution is simply a truncated version of ideal weights, precisely the same solution which was seen to give very poor results in Figure 26.1.

Now suppose that y follows a stationary MA(Q) process. Since its autocovariances will be zero for leads and lags greater than Q, this again effectively determines q in (26.5). However, suppose that instead of using the optimal weights, we use the Stock and Watson approach of padding our T observations with Q forecasts/backcasts from the MA model at each end of the sample, then using the Baxter–King approximate filter with $N = Q$. The estimate from this two-step *ad hoc* procedure will be identical to the estimate from our optimal filter. This is because the optimal weights given in (26.5). reflect both the weights used to form forecasts/backcasts at the ends of the available sample, as well as the weights which the Baxter–King filter would place on them. Put another way, (26.5) implies that the Stock–Watson two-step procedure will give optimal estimates at the end of sample provided that (1) we use the 'right' forecasting model to pad our data, and (2) we pad our sample until our forecasts have converged to zero.

Another feature of (26.5) is that it lets us solve for the minimum value of (26.4). This is useful, since it tells us how well our best end-of-sample estimates can approximate the ideal estimates. The general solution is given by:

$$E\left[\sum_{j=-\infty}^{\infty} B_j \cdot y_{T-j}\right]^2 - E\left[\sum_{j=0}^{T-1} \widehat{B}_j \cdot y_{T-j}\right]^2 \tag{26.6}$$

In the above case where y is *i.i.d.*, this reduces to:

$$\left(\sum_{j=-\infty}^{\infty} B_j^2 - \sum_{j=0}^{T-1} B_j^2\right) \cdot \sigma_y^2 = \left(\sum_{j=-\infty}^{-1} B_j^2 - \sum_{j=T}^{\infty} B_j^2\right) \cdot \sigma_y^2 \tag{26.7}$$

Applications

We now examine the performance of the optimal filter by applying it to three problems of common interest; estimating the current output gap, the current trend growth rate of productivity and the current trend rate of inflation. The first of these differs from the other two in that we analyse the raw data in levels, not growth rates, and that we seek to isolate the intermediate frequencies rather than the low frequencies. Because the optimal filter is a function of the dynamic properties of the series analysed, our results can be expected to differ across applications.

The output series (Y_t) is the natural logarithm of Eurozone real GDP for the period 1991Q1 to 2003Q2. The inflation series (π_t) is the monthly difference of the natural logarithm of the Eurozone Harmonized Index of Consumer Prices (seasonally adjusted) covering the period January 1995 to August 2003. The pro-ductivity series (Q_t) is the difference of the natural logarithm of quarterly data on real GDP per person employed from 1991Q1 to 2003Q2. Note that deterministic components were removed from all three series prior to analysis. In the case of Q_t the series were demeaned; for Y_t and π_t a deterministic linear trend was also removed.

For each series, two different estimates of the autocovariance functions $\sigma_y(q)$ were then constructed. The first fit a low-order ARMA model to the data (Table 26.1), then used the estimated parameters of the ARMA model to calculate the implied

Table 26.1   Estimated ARMA models

Series	Q_t	π_t	Y_y
# AR parameters	1	1	1
ρ	0.401	0.904	0.882
# MA parameters	0	0	2
$\sum \theta_i$			0.380
$\sigma^2 \cdot 10^6$	10.38	3.45	26.18
# Observations	49	92	50
Frequency	Quarterly	Monthly	Quarterly

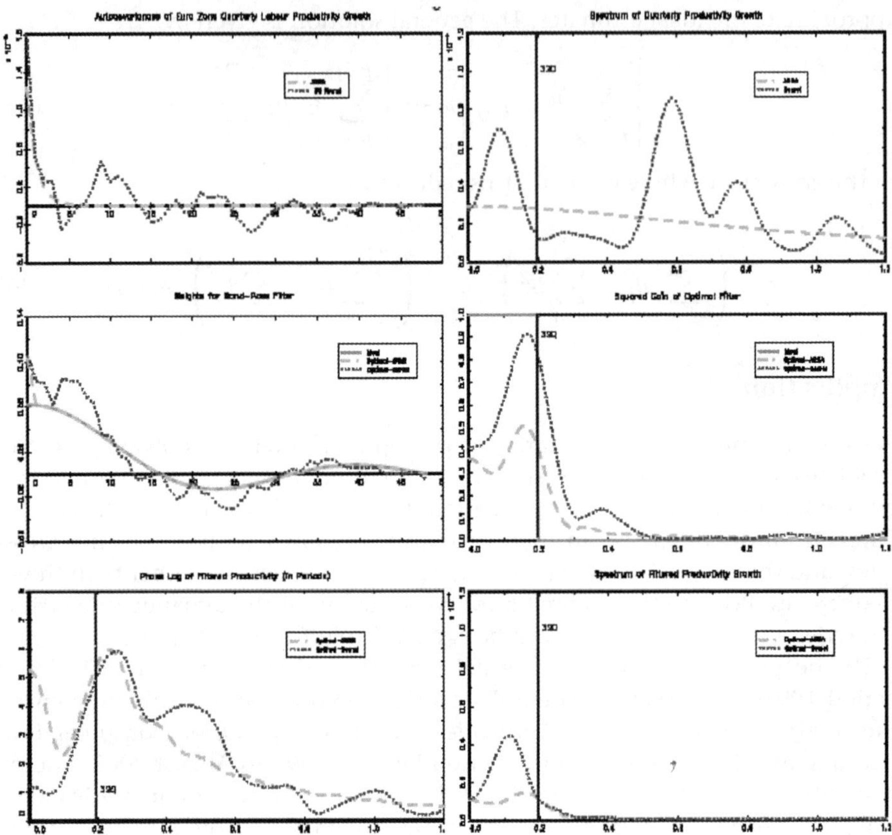

Figure 26.2   Eurozone labour productivity growth

covariances.[16] The second used a nonparametric kernel estimate.[17] In both cases, each data sample of N observations was used to calculate $N - 1$ autocovariances. The two approaches gave sometimes similar estimates, as shown in the top-left panel of Figure 26.2 through Figure 26.4, with the non-parametric kernel tending to capture somewhat more complex and persistent dynamics. The second panel (top-right) in each of these figures shows the corresponding spectrum for each series.

The dynamics of the three series look quite different. Quarterly productivity growth shows little persistence and is close to white noise; its ARMA spectrum is nearly flat and the kernel-estimated spectrum shows no clear tendancy to rise or fall as the frequency increases. Output shows slowly decaying autocovariances, consistent with estimated autoregressive roots of nearly 0.95. Its spectrum displays the typical Granger shape, with density powerfully concentrated in the low frequencies. Monthly inflation falls between these two extremes, with the dynamics of its ARMA approximation showing less persistence that those of the

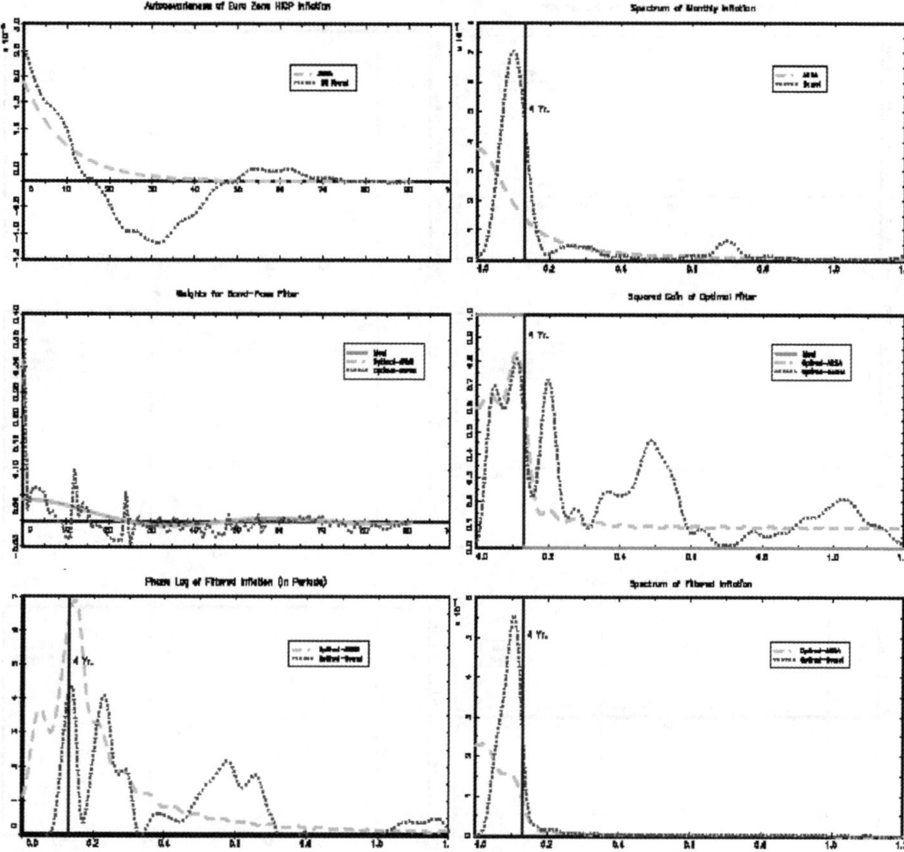

Figure 26.3   Eurozone HICP inflation

non-parametric kernel estimate.[18] The result is two very different-looking spectra, with the ARMA-based estimate looking quite flat, but the kernel-based estimate showing even more concentration in the low frequencies than the spectrum for output growth.

Filtering productivity growth

Trends in productivity growth are the subject of considerable analysis, with interest in current trends having intensified in recent years. While it is widely acknowledged that labour productivity is procyclical, most analysis of productivity growth does little to explicitly separate its trend and cyclical components beyond examining averages of growth rates over several years. It would therefore be useful to construct optimal estimates of current trend productivity, as well as to know how reliable such estimates may be. This is precisely what the results from the previous section now enable us to do.

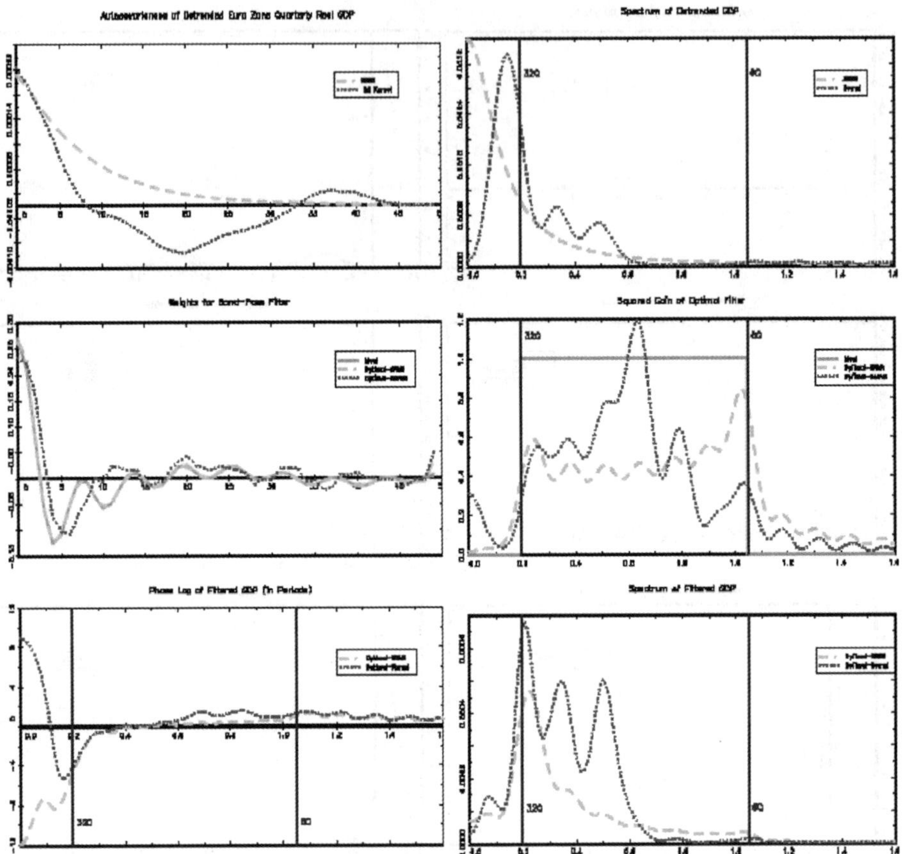

Figure 26.4   Eurozone detrended real GDP

Since we are trying to remove business cycle influences from productivity growth, we adopt the Burns–Mitchell–Baxter–King characterization of these cycles as having durations of up to eight years in length. Our ideal filter for quarterly data is therefore a symmetric lowpass filter which blocks all frequencies above $\pi/16$. This together with the results presented earlier are all we need to construct the optimal filter. Its properties are described in Figure 26.2 and Table 26.2. The third panel in Figure 26.2 (middle row, left column) compares the weights of the optimal and ideal filters. In the case of the ARMA model, the two are almost identical. This is because the ARMA model implies quarterly productivity growth is almost serially uncorrelated; this is almost the simple case discussed earlier (pp. 325–7). The weights for the kernel model are similar, but die away more slowly and are somewhat more volatile, reflecting the somewhat greater persistence in the series which the kernel detects.

Panels 4 and 6 in Figure 26.2 (right column, middle and bottom rows) compare the spectral properties of the three filters and the two optimally-filtered series. The gain of the optimal kernel filter shows a pattern similar to that shown in Figure 26.1 for other truncated ideal filters; the biggest difference being the absence of a lower bound on the filter.[19] The optimal ARMA filter has a somewhat similar shape, but tends to have a lower squared gain at most of the frequencies shown. Note that the kernel filter has a particularly high gain at the start of the stop band (about 0.8 near $\omega = 0.2$); this is roughly double the corresponding squared gain for the ARMA filter. This difference is to be expected given the peaks and valleys of the kernel-estimated spectrum in these ranges; there is a dip in the density around $\omega = 0.2$ and so leakage in this area is less important for the kernal filter than for the ARMA filter.

Multiplying the spectral density at a given frequency from panel 2 by the squared gain at that frequency from panel 4 gives us the spectrum of the filtered series shown in Panel 6. In contrast to the relatively flat spectra shown in panel 2, our low-pass filters have succeeded in powerfully concentrating the spectrum of the filtered series over the desired frequencies. At the same time, however, the imperfections of the optimal filters are clearly visible; the spectral density at the low frequencies is much less than that in the raw data, and the ARMA-filtered spectrum has a small artificial peak at the cutoff frequency, which implies a modest, but spurious, cycle in the filtered series.

The overall performance of the filter across all frequencies is summarized by the statistics presented in Table 26.2. The variance of the raw series (line 1) is simply the area under the spectra shown in panel 2 of Figure 26.2.[20] Similarly, the variance of the ideally filtered series (line 2) is the area under those spectra lying between frequencies 0 and $\pi/16$. In this case, the ideally-filtered trend accounts for under 20 per cent of the total variance of the observed series. The optimally-filtered estimate of that trend captures between half and three-quarters of the variance of the ideal trend. The difference between the ARMA and Kernel models becomes more apparent when this is expressed in terms of correlations and noise–signal

Table 26.2   Optimal filter for productivity growth trends

Statistic		*ARMA model*	*Kernel model*
1	Variance of raw series $(x)^a$ 106	12.37	17.90
2	Variance of ideally filtered series $(x)^b$ 106	1.78	2.81
3	Variance of optimally filtered series $(x)^c$ 106	0.99	2.08
4	MSE of filtered estimate $(x)^d$ 106	0.79	0.74
5	Correlation with ideal estimate^e	0.745	0.859
6	N/S ratio^f	0.799	0.355
7	Mean phase lag (quarters)^g	3.862	2.435

[a] Differences between the ARMA and kernel estimates of the variance are due to approximations in the construction of the theoretical autocorrelations of the ARMA model; the kernel estimates precisely match the sample variance of the series. [b] Calculated as the integral of the spectral density over the interval $[-u, u]$. [c] Calculated as the integral of the spectral density over the interval $(-\pi, \pi]$. [d] Calculated as (2) - (3). [e] Calculated as $\sqrt{(3)/(2)}$. [f] Calculated as (4)/(3). [g] Calculated as the integral of the product of the phase lag and the spectral density of the filtered series.

(N/S) ratios. Here we see that the Kernel model implies an N/S ratio less than half that of the ARMA model, as well as an 86 per cent correlation with the ideal estimate compared to 74.5 per cent for the ARMA model.

The fifth panel of Figure 26.2 (bottom row, left column) shows the degree of phase lag implied by the filters. The last row of Table 26.2 shows the mean phase lag, which simply uses the spectral density of the filtered series (the sixth panel in Figure 26.2) to produce a weighted average lag for the filtered series. We see that the phase lag is positive at all the frequencies shown, increasing as we move from the highest frequencies to those near the cutoff. However, these frequencies have little weight in the filtered series, whose density is concentrated in the pass-band below the 32Q cutoff. Here, the phase lag varies across the two estimates, with that for the kernel estimate dropping from a high of about 5 periods to a low near 1. The ARMA estimate gives a larger lag than the kernel estimate everywhere in the pass band, with the difference becoming larger as the frequency approaches zero. As a result, the mean phase lag is almost a full year (see Table 26.2) for the ARMA estimate but only just over half a year for the kernel estimate.

Filtering inflation

As the objective of price stability has moved to the forefront of monetary policy formulation throughout much of the world over the past decade and a half, more attention has been given to the question of how to measure and monitor progress towards this goal. Most monetary authorities propose a modified (or 'core') measure of inflation which aims to capture persistent trends in inflation or inflationary pressures.[21] It would therefore be of interest to use bandpass filters to construct optimal measures of current trends in inflation, where these trends are again defined using a low-pass filter. The appropriate cut-off frequency to use for such a filter is debatable; for the example we study in this section a frequency of $\pi/24$ (corresponding to cycles lasting 48 months) is used in order to give seasonal influences and short-run nominal shocks ample time to dissipate. Results are presented in Table 26.3 and Figure 26.3.

The third panel (left column, middle row) in Figure 26.3 shows us that the optimal weights now put a much higher weight on the most recent observations

Table 26.3   Optimal filter for inflation trends

Statistic		ARMA model	Kernel model
1	Variance of raw series ($\times 10^6$)	18.86	25.05
2	Variance of ideally filtered series ($\times 10^6$)106	11.00	16.01
3	Variance of optimally filtered series ($\times 10^6$)106	8.63	12.80
4	MSE of filtered estimate ($\times 10^6$) 106 2.37	2.37	3.21
5	Correlation with ideal estimate	0.886	0.894
6	N/S ratio	0.275	0.251
7	Mean phase lag (months)	3.33	0.68

See notes for Table 26.2.

than the ideal weights. Again, the ARMA-model weights converge much more quickly to the ideal weights than the kernel model, presumably reflecting the greater persistence in the kernel-estimated dynamics.

The fourth panel (right column, middle row) shows that the gain functions of the optimal filters are again different from that of the ideal filter in several respects. The gain function for the ARMA filter again resembles the shape we encountered in Figure 26.1, with a gain of less than 0.5 for most of the pass band, and a gain near 1 for only a narrow band near the cutoff frequency. Although the gain drops sharply beyond that point, it stays significantly above zero for the rest of the graphed frequency range. The gain of the kernel filter resembles that of the ARMA filter over the pass band, with the exception of a near-zero gain at frequency zero. Outside the pass-band, however, there are multiple peaks with gains close to or exceeding 50 per cent.

The sixth panel (right column, bottom row) shows that despite the apparently irregular gain functions, both of the resulting filtered series capture most of the density of the raw series at the low frequencies and have a very sharp drop in density at the cutoff frequency, with very little density at the higher frequencies. This reflects the fact that both filters have sharp drops in gain at the cutoff frequency, and that the potentially large leakage they allow from much higher frequencies is relatively unimportant due to their lack of importance in the original spectrum. Similarly, we may note that the variable gain of the kernel filter within the pass-band does not appear to greatly distort the spectrum of inflation within this band. This is because peaks in the raw spectrum correspond to frequencies around which the gain is not far from 1, while areas of particularly low gain in the passband correspond to troughs in the raw spectrum.

Table 26.3 confirms the relatively good performance of the optimal filter for both the ARMA and kernel-based models. Both give estimates which have correlations of over 88 per cent with the true trend rate of inflation, and their noise–signal ratios are both under 30 per cent. This improved performance is consistent with the basic intuition we saw earlier (pp. 325–7), that persistence tends to improve the quality of current estimates of the trend. We can understand this in terms of the Stock–Watson two-step procedure; the more persistent a series is, the better we are able to forecast it and therefore the better we approximate the ideal filter.

Another way to understand these results is to recall that as persistence increases, the spectrum of our data series becomes increasingly concentrated in the lowest frequencies. Since our goal is to design a low-pass filter, this in turn reduces the importance of leaking higher frequencies, allowing us to increase the average gain of the optimal filter and thereby better approximate the ideal filter.

Although the phase lag of these filters varies by frequency, the lags are smaller than in the productivity growth case and rarely exceed half a year (6 months). The lag for both filters peaks at the cutoff frequency and for the kernel filter it then quickly falls to zero in both directions. As a result, its mean phase lag is a trivial 0.68 months. Phase lag for the ARMA filter falls off more gradually, however, resulting in a mean lag of just over one quarter.

Table 26.4 Optimal filter for business cycles

Statistic		ARMA model	Kernel model
1	Variance of raw series ($\times 10^6$)	211.3	224.2
2	Variance of ideally filtered series ($\times 10^6$)106	60.72	92.51
3	Variance of optimally filtered series ($\times 10^6$)106	38.02	63.53
4	MSE of filtered estimate ($\times 10^6$) 106 2.37	22.70	28.98
5	Correlation with ideal estimate	0.791	0.829
6	N/S ratio	0.597	0.456
7	Mean phase lag (quarters)	−2.43	−0.70

See notes for Table 26.2.

Filtering GDP

Optimal filters for business cycles and their properties are described in Figure 26.4 and Table 26.4. Unlike the two previous filters we have considered, this is a band-pass rather than a low-pass filter, and it uses the values suggested by Baxter and King ($\pi/16, \pi/3$) to define the frequencies of interest.

Panel 3 (left column, middle row) of Figure 26.4 shows that the optimal ARMA weights are indistinguishable from the ideal weights, while the kernel weights resemble the ideal weights in many respects. Panel 4 (right column, middle row) shows that the squared gain of the optimal ARMA filter again resembles the patterns we saw in Figure 26.1, but that for the kernel filter it is different in some important respects. It has a non-trivial gain at zero frequency, a pronounced peak (with a gain > 1) in the middle of the pass-band and very low gain as it approaches the high-frequency cutoff. However, it closely resembles the squared gain of the ARMA filter near the low-frequency cut-off and above the high-frequency cutoff.

Panel 6 (right column, bottom row) shows that both filtered series have effectively blocked the high-frequency part of the original spectrum, but that both seem to pass significant amounts at the lowest frequencies. Results in Table 26.4, similar for both models, apparently reflect this low-frequency leakage. The correlation of optimal and ideal filter estimates is about 80 per cent, and the noise–signal ratio ranges from 46 per cent for the kernel model to 60 per cent for the ARMA model.

Phase lag for these models is small for most frequencies with the exception of those below the lower cutoff, where it becomes positive and large (peaking with a lag of over two years) for the kernel model, and negative (that is a phase *lead*) and large (peaking at three years) for the ARMA model. However, the relatively low spectral density of the filtered series in this region greatly reduces their overall impact. As shown in Table 26.4, mean phase lag is negative for both series, with a lead of roughly two and a half quarters for the ARMA model and less than one quarter for the kernel model.

Estimates of the reliability of output gaps are of particular interest for the design of optimal monetary policies. It is therefore of interest to compare the above results with other recent estimates in the literature.

Christiano and Fitzgerald (1999) solve roughly the same optimal filter problem solved in this paper.[22] However, on the basis of experiments with models in the IMA$(1, q)$ class, they conclude that most economic time series can be nearly optimally filtered if we assume that they are random walks and solve for the corresponding approximately optimal filter.[23] In that case, the filter weights become functions of only the cutoff frequencies and the sample size. They calculate that the correlation between their nearly optimal filter and the ideally filtered measure of the business cycle is roughly 0.65 and that the noise–signal ratio is 0.77.[24] This is a lower correlation than we find for either model, while their noise–signal ratio is higher.

Orphanides and van Norden (1999, 2002) and Cayen and van Norden (2002, 2004) study other filters which do not have optimal bandpass properties but are nonetheless used to measure business cycles. They compare the rolling estimates produced when such filters are applied at the end of sample to historical estimates produced after many subsequent years of data are available.[25] The size of this revision in estimated business cycles corresponds to the difference between our ideal and optimal filter estimates. Using US data, Orphanides and van Norden (1999) find correlation coefficients ranging from 0.63 to 0.96, depending on the model used.[26] Cayen and van Norden (2004) use a comparable sample of Canadian data and finds correlation coefficients for the same models ranging from 0.70 to 0.96; Cayen and van Norden (2002) examined a smaller sample and reported results ranging from 0.70 to 0.84.[27] We can also reconstruct noise–signal ratios for Orphanides and van Norden (1999) based on the ratio of the reported standard deviation of the revisions to the standard deviation of the final measure of the output gap. These figures are reported in Table 26.5; the values range from 0.34 to 0.79.

While it may appear counter-intuitive that non-optimal models appear sometimes to give better correlations or noise–signal ratios than the optimal measures developed in this chapter, it should be remembered that the two are not strictly comparable since their definitions of trend and cycle differ. However, these results suggest that the optimal frequency-based techniques should not be expected to give markedly more accurate estimates than other sophisticated time-series methods.

Table 26.5 Reconstructed noise–signal ratios from Orphanides and van Norden (1999)

Model	Errors^a (1)	Final^b (2)	Noise/signal $= (1)/(2)$
Clark	1.11	2.11	0.53
Harvey–Jaeger	1.22	1.55	0.79
Watson	1.16	3.44	0.34

^{a} Figures are the reported standard deviations for Final – QuasiFinal revisions, taken from Orphanides and van Norden (1999) table 26.4, p. 36. ^{b} Figures are the reported standard deviations for final output gaps, taken from Orphanides and van Norden (1999) table 1, p. 32.

Conclusions

The derivations contained in the annex of the working paper version of this chapter show how to construct optimal bandpass filters for them ARIMA models commonly used with macroeconomic time series. Together with the above applications of such filters, this produces several interesting results.

First, it illustrates how the accuracy of such filters may vary considerably. When a series has little or no predictability, as is the case for the ARMA model of productivity growth, this limits our ability to measure the current long-term trend. We found therefore that current estimates of trend productivity growth based on the ARMA model have correlations of about 75 per cent with comparable estimates constructed with the benefit of hindsight; put another way, their noise–signal ratio is about 80 per cent. The ARMA model therefore implies that the measurement of productivity trends is the most difficult of the three problems considered in this paper. The kernel model suggests that productivity trend measurement is substantially easier, however. Reconciling these results is left to future work.

The results for inflation illustrate how increased predictability improves our measurement of current trends. Both of the models we examined imply that current inflation trends can be measured with considerable accuracy, giving about 90 per cent correlations with the best *ex post* measures and noise–signal ratios just above 20 per cent.

Persistence acts as a double-edged sword, however, when we seek to measure current cycles, as shown by the results for business cycle measurement. On the one hand, it improves the amount of information available about the future of the series, thereby reducing the difference between current and future estimates of trend. On the other hand, by increasing the relative amount of noise to be filtered out, it increases the potential effects of leakage and therefore of measurement error. In the case of business cycle measurement, we see that optimal filters do not perform especially well; their correlations and noise-signal ratios are similar to those for productivity growth.

The results for business cycle measurement are somewhat surprising in light of previous work examining the performance of non-frequency-based models of trend and cycles. Comparison of these results seems to show that the latter will in some cases perform as well or better than the optimal methods analysed here. The comparisons are potentially misleading, however, since the definitions of trend and cycle are not comparable across models. The previous work also focused on models in which output was assumed to follow a stochastic trend rather than the deterministic trend assumed here. A reconciliation of these results should examine the extent to which the results for frequency-based filters are sensitive to the assumption of trend-stationarity.

More generally, the sensitivity of optimal filters to the assumed dynamics of the data series requires further evaluation. This would allow a closer scrutiny of Christiano and Fitzgerald's (1999) claim that the assumption of random-walk dynamics is adequate for most macroeconomic time series, which is a potentially important simplification for applied work. It would also have implications for the accuracy with which business cycles may realistically be measured. The only source of error considered in this chapter's analysis is the extent to which estimated cycles will be revised as new observations become available. As noted in Orphanides and van Norden (1999, 2002), other sources include estimation error in the autocovariance function, data revision and model misspecification. The results presented above should therefore be viewed as lower bounds on the total measurement error in frequency-based estimation of current trends and cycles.

Notes

1   Its current popularity stems from its use in the seminal working paper Hodrick and Prescott (1977), finally published as Hodrick and Prescott (1997), although the technique dates from the 1920s.
2   In practice, business cycles are defined to have durations between 6 and 32 quarters. This definition gained popularity after Baxter and King (1999) cited Burns and Mitchell (1947) as characterizing business cycles in this way. It is useful to remember that these numbers are not written in stone; Stock and Watson (1998) quote Burns and Mitchell (1947: 3) as stating that business cycles vary in duration '... from more than one year to ten or twelve years.'
3   The claim that HP-filtered output 'looks like' a business cycle is a popular misstatement. Business cycle measurement and analysis, since its infancy, has used the HP filter (or even simpler moving-average filters which produce similar results.) It is therefore probably more accurate to say that the output of these filters have *defined* what we think of as business cycles. See Morley, Nelson and Zivot (1999).
4   Both examine Butterworth filters, of which they note the HP filter is simply a special case.
5   Baxter and King (1999), for example, suggest reserving about five years of data from each end of the sample to provide the necessary leads and lags.
6   The HP filter is a case in point. Comparisons to bandpass filters are based on its symmetric MA representation, which is a limit the filter approaches in the middle of a large sample. Its representation at the end of sample is quite different; see St. Amant and van Norden (1997).
7   Examples of this include Setterfield *et al.* (1992), Staiger, Stock and Watson (1997), Orphanides and van Norden (1999, 2002) and Cayen and van Norden (2002).
8   This section provides an intuitive introduction to the filtering terms used in the rest of this chapter. It may be skipped without loss of continuity by those familiar with spectral analysis.
9   Several well-known filters do not belong in this class. Examples include the HP filter (where the weights vary with t) and the Hamilton filter for the probability of being in a particular regime (which is a non-linear function of $\bar{y}$).
10   The only one-sided symmetric filter is the trivial filter which just multiplies y_t by a constant; we'll typically ignore that special case and talk as if these two classes are mutually exclusive.
11   For example, consider the difference between a centre-weighted and a one-sided moving average.
12   For example, see Guay and St. Amant (1997).
13   Pedersen (1998) re-examines HP filters from this perspective and suggests alternatives to the traditional value of 1,600 for its smoothing parameter.
14   The annex of the working paper version of this chapter gives solutions for the case of ARIMA(p, d, q) processes ($-1 < d < 3$) and surveys related contributions in the literature.

15 This interpretation is developed further in the annex to the working paper, particularly in section 2.1.
16 The *ARMABIC3*() procedure from the COINT module for GAUSS by Ouliaris and Phillips (1995) was used for estimation and model selection. This uses the BIC criterion for model selection and a 2 or 3-stage Hannan–Rissanen iterative estimation procedure.
17 The results presented here use the quadratic-spectral kernel (without the data-dependent bandwidth selection). Limited experimentation suggested that the results were not sensitive to this choice.
18 ARMA model selection for the CPI data was problematic. It is doubtful that the MA(12) adequately captures the persistence of inflation, since this would imply that inflation shocks completely die out in 12 months.
19 To understand why a filter with a gain everywhere less than 1 may still be optimal, consider the effect of scaling all the filter weights by some constant $k > 1$. This has the effect of scaling the squared gain everywhere by k^2. In the case of the ARMA filter, this will reduce the difference between its gain and that of the ideal filter at frequencies below the cutoff frequency (i.e. reducing compression), thereby improving the estimate. However, this benefit is counterbalanced by the effect of increasing the difference between the two filters at frequencies above the cutoff (i.e. increasing leakage). The optimal scale is the one at which the marginal benefits at some frequencies of a change in scale are exactly equal to the marginal costs at all other frequencies.
20 Strictly speaking, it is twice that area, since the full spectrum is symmetric about 0; the figure shows only half that range. This applies to the analysis of subsequent rows in this table as well.
21 Unlike the techniques examined in this chapter, many other approaches to measuring core inflation rely on the analysis of disaggregated price movements.
22 See the annex to our working paper for a discussion.
23 The fact that they use low-order IMA models presumably guarantees that the optimal weights and their approximate weights will differ only for the last few observations, and even then not very much. It would be interesting to see whether the usefulness of the random-walk approximation would be sustained if kernel or ARIMA models were used instead to derive optimal filters.
24 The correlation is taken from the end-point of the graph in the left column, middle row of their figure 6, while the signal–noise ratio is given in the discussion on p. 21 in Christiano and Fitzgerald (1999). Note that their bandpass filter is set to pass all cycles with durations from 2 to 8 years versus the 6 to 32 quarters used here.
25 In the terminology of these papers, these are the Final and the QuasiFinal estimates. The Final – QuasiFinal revision is a better analogue to the estimation error considered in this chapter since both ignore the role of uncertainty in the underlying data-generating process.
26 Orphanides and van Norden (1999), table 1, p. 32. Results are correlations between Quasi-Final and Final estimates for the Watson, Clark and Harvey–Jaeger Models.
27 Cayen and van Norden (2004), table 2, p. 40. Cayen and van Norden (2002), table 1, p. 25.

References

Baxter, M. and King, R.G. (1999) 'Measuring Business Cycles: Approximate Band-Pass Filters for Economic Time Series', *The Review of Economics and Statistics*, 81: 575–93.
Burns, A.F and Mitchell, W.C. (1947) *Measuring Business Cycles*, New York: NBER.
Cayen, J.-P. and van Norden, S. (2002) 'La fiabilité des estimations de l'écart de production au Canada', *Working Paper*, 2002-10, Ottawa: Bank of Canada.

Cayen, J-P. and van Norden, S. (2004) 'The reliability of Canadian output gap estimators', *Mimeo*, Prepared for Bundesbank Conference on Real-Time data, Eltville.

Christiano, L.C. and Fitzgerald, T.J. (1999) 'The band pass filter,' *Working Paper*, 99-06, Cleveland:Federal Reserve Bank of Cleveland (also published as NBER Working Paper 7257).

Cogley, T. and Nason, J.M. (1995) 'Effects of the Hodrick-Prescott filter on trend and difference stationary time series: implications for business cycle research,' *Journal of Economic Dynamics and Control*, 19: 253–78.

Den Haan, W.J. and Sumner, S. (2001) 'The comovements between real activity and prices in the G7', *Working Paper*, 2001-05, San Diego: University of California, Department of Economics.

Gerlach, S. and Smets, F. (1997) 'Output gaps and inflation: unobservable components estimates for the G-7 Countries', *Mimeo*, Basel: Bank for International Settlements.

Gomez, V. (2001) 'The use of butterworth filters for trend and cycle estimation in economic time series," *Journal of Business and Economic Statistics*, 19: 365–73.

Guay, A. and St. Amant, P. (1997) 'Do mechanical filters provide a good approximation of business cycles?', *Technical Report*, 78, Ottawa: Bank of Canada.

Harvey, A.C. (1985) 'Trends and cycles in macroeconomic time series', *Journal of Business and Economic Statistics*, 3: 216–27.

Harvey, A.C. and Jaeger, A. (1993) 'Detrending, stylized facts and the business cycle', *Journal of Applied Econometrics*, 8: 231–47.

Hodrick, R. and Prescott, E. (1997) 'Post-war business cycles: an empirical investigation', *Journal of Money, Credit, and Banking*, 29: 1–16. (Working paper version cited as Hodrick and Prescott 1977.)

Kaiser, R. and Maravall, A. (2001) *Measuring Business Cycles in Economic Time Series*, forthcoming.

Koopmans, L.H (1974) *The Spectral Analysis of Time Series*: Academic Press.

Kuttner, K.N. (1994) "Estimating potential output as a latent variable," *Journal of Business and Economic Statistics*, 12: 361–68.

Morley, J., Nelson, C. and Zivot, E. (1999) 'Why are Beveridge-Nelson and unobserved-component decompositions of GDP so different?', *Mimeo* : University of Washington.

Orphanides and van Norden, S. (1999) 'The reliability of output gap estimates in real time', *FEDS Discussion Paper*.

Orphanides and van Norden, S. (2002) 'The unreliability of output gap estimates in real time', *The Review of Economics and Statistics*, 84: 569–83.

Ouliaris, S. and Phillips, P.C.B. (1995) *Coint 2.0: GAUSS Procedures for Cointegrated Regressions*, distributed by Aptech Systems.

Pedersen, T.M. (1998) 'The Hodrick-Prescott filter, the Slutzky effect, and the distortionary effect of filters', *Discussion Paper* , 98/09, Copenhagen: University of Copenhagen, Institute of Economics.

Pollock, D.S.G. (2000) 'Trend estimation and de-trending via rational square-wave filters', *Journal of Econometrics*, 99: 317–34.

St. Amant and van Norden, S. (1997) 'Measurement of the output gap: a discussion of recent research at the Bank of Canada', *Technical Report*, 79, Ottawa: Bank of Canada.

Schleicher, C. (2001) 'Approximate bandpass filters for ARIMA models', *Mimeo*: University of British Columbia.

Setterfield, M.A., Gordon, D.V. and Osberg, L. (1992) 'Searching for a will o' the wisp: an empirical study of the NAIRU in Canada', *European Economic Review*, 36: 119–36.

Staiger, D., Stock, J.H. and Watson, M.W. (1997) 'The NAIRU, unemployment and monetary Policy', *Journal of Economic Perspectives* , 11: 33–49.

Stock, J.H. and Watson, M.W. (1998) 'Business cycle fluctuations in U.S. macroeconomic time series', *Working Paper*, 6528, New York: NBER (prepared for *The Handbook of Macroeconomics*, J.B. Taylor and M. Woodford (eds)).

Part VII
Monetary Policy and Business Cycles

27
Monetary and Fiscal Policy Transmission in the Euro-Area: Evidence from a Structural VAR Analysis

Bas van Aarle, Harry Garretsen and Niko Gobbin

Introduction

In this chapter we study the transmission of monetary and fiscal policy in the Euro-area, through a structural VAR (SVAR) analysing of monetary and fiscal policy transmission. The SVAR model of the Euro-area is compared with equivalent SVAR models for the USA and Japan. This exercise is useful in assessing the effects of monetary and fiscal policy on the aggregate EMU economy and also to have a comparison with two other major economies. Attention is also paid to interaction of macroeconomic policies.

Economic and Monetary Union (EMU) has led to a new framework of monetary and fiscal policy in the European Union (EU). It has also stimulated a renewed interest in the design, implementation and transmission of monetary and fiscal policy in Europe. A successful design and implementation of the common monetary policy by the ECB requires a detailed knowledge of the effects of the common monetary policy on the Euro-area economy. Also, the effects of fiscal adjustments in the Euro-area have received considerable interest recently since EMU imposes a set of fiscal stringency requirements in the form of the Stability and Growth Pact. As a result, EMU has stimulated a considerable academic literature on the transmission of monetary and fiscal policy in the Euro-area.

One of the recent approaches to analyse the transmission of macroeconomic policies to macroeconomic variables adopts the vector autoregression (VAR) methodology. In this chapter we analyse the macroeconomic effects of monetary and fiscal policies in the Euro-area using a structural VAR (SVAR) approach to estimate the short-run and medium-term effects of monetary and fiscal policy innovations and demand and supply shocks. Insight into the possible effects of fiscal policy adjustments in the EMU is not only important in itself, but it can also be useful to assess the implications of fiscal adjustments for the common monetary policy and in the context of the Stability and Growth Pact.

The effects of macroeconomic and macroeconomic policy shocks are estimated for the Euro-area and a comparison with the USA and Japan is carried out. The estimations also enable us to analyse the important aspect of monetary and fiscal policy interaction and to analyse the relations between government revenue and government spending policies. Our study contributes to the literature on monetary and fiscal policy analysis by integrating the literature on monetary SVARs and that on fiscal SVARs into one framework in which both are analysed simultaneously.

The chapter is structured as follows: in the next section we take a brief overview of the literature on monetary and fiscal policy SVARs, before estimating the SVAR of monetary and fiscal policy in the Euro- area to compare the results with the USA and Japan. The concluding section summarizes the main results from the analysis.

Macroeconomic analysis using SVARs: a brief overview

Structural VAR models impose identifying restrictions on an ordinary VAR model to infer structural shocks from it. Its workings can be briefly summarized as follows. Assume that an unrestricted VAR model:

$$x_t = A(L)e_t \tag{27.1}$$

is estimated – written here in moving average form – where x is a vector of covariance stationary (macroeconomic) variables, $A(L)$ a polynomial matrix of lag length l, L the lag operator and e a vector of reduced-form innovations in the elements of x with variance-covariance matrix $E(e_t e_t^T) = \Sigma$. These reduced-form innovations are likely to be correlated and can, therefore, not necessarily be interpreted as purely structural innovations. To remedy this, the SVAR approach relates the vector x to a vector of structural innovations, u:

$$x_t = B(L)u_t \tag{27.2}$$

where $B(L)$ is a polynomial matrix. In this SVAR, u is a vector of serially and contemporaneously uncorrelated, normalized structural residuals with $E(u_t u_t^T) = I$. From (27.1) and (27.2) it follows that the vector of reduced form innovations can be represented as a linear combination of the structural residuals, that is $e_t = Cu_t$ with $CC^T = \Sigma$. As a result, $A(L)C = B(L)$, enabling the identification of the structural innovations from the reduced-form innovations of the reduced form VAR. $C(L)$ is a lag polynomial where the Cs are coefficient matrices at the respective lags of the errors. In this way the structural form (27.2) can be obtained from the estimates of the reduced-from representation (27.1), provided that the transformation matrix C is of full rank.

The structural VAR model (27.2), in other words, imposes identifying restrictions upon VAR estimates (27.1) to recover structural innovations from the estimated VAR. The identification is achieved in practice by imposing identifying short or long-run restrictions. The advantage of using long-run restrictions is that in many instances, economic theory provides more guidance about long-run relationships than about short-run dynamics. Short restrictions impose typically that the impact effect of a given shock on a certain variable is null, which can be achieved by setting the appropriate elements in $C(0)$ to zero. Long-run constraints impose typically that there is no long run effect of a shock on a variable, which is achieved by setting the appropriate elements of $C(1)$ to zero. In order to identify exactly a VAR model of n endogenous variables, $(n^2 - n)/2$ restrictions need to be imposed in the structural model (27.2).

A number of studies use a SVAR approach to analyse the transmission of monetary policy in E(M)U countries; for example Monticelli and Tristani (1999) use a SVAR model of the Euro-area to study the transmission of aggregate demand shocks, aggregate supply shocks and monetary policy innovations. Garcia and Verdelhan (2000) study the fiscal and monetary policy transmission mechanisms in the Euro-area. Supply shocks, nominal shocks, fiscal policy shocks and monetary policy shocks are identified and their impacts on the Euro-area economy assessed. Dalsgaard and de Serres (2000) estimate a SVAR model for 11 individual EMU countries.

A SVAR model of the Euro-area

In this section, SVAR models of monetary and fiscal policy transmissions are estimated, and the estimated SVAR model of the Euro-area is compared with SVAR models for the USA and Japan. The vector x of macroeconomic variables that are included in the SVAR analysis consists of real output, real government revenue, real government spending, short-term interest rates and prices. These variables were collected for the Euro-area aggregate, Japan and the USA for the period 1980Q1–2001Q4, whenever available. Before estimating and analysing the SVAR models it is of interest to summarize the observed adjustments of these variables over time, as in Figure 27.1.

The graphs illustrate the well-known business-cycle patterns with hampered growth in the early 1980s and 1990s and subsequent improvements. Another well-observable fact is the gradual decline of inflation and interest rates during the 1980s after which they start to fluctuate around a modest average. The considerable variation in the fiscal growth rates suggest a large number of fiscal adjustments both on the revenue and spending side during this period. The Euro-area (and also the USA) experienced a period of fiscal retrenchment since 1994, as witness low growth rates of government spending and higher growth rates of government revenues. The picture of Japan is more or less opposite: growth of revenues exceeded the growth of government until 1991, since then a period with high spending growth and increasing deficits and government debt occurred.

It is appropriate to check that all series included in the SVAR model are (approximately) stationary. It turns out that in practically all cases real output, the price level, the interest rate, real government spending and real government revenue are integrated of order one but that their quarterly growth rates are stationary. Consequently, the SVAR model contains real output (GDP) growth, Δy,

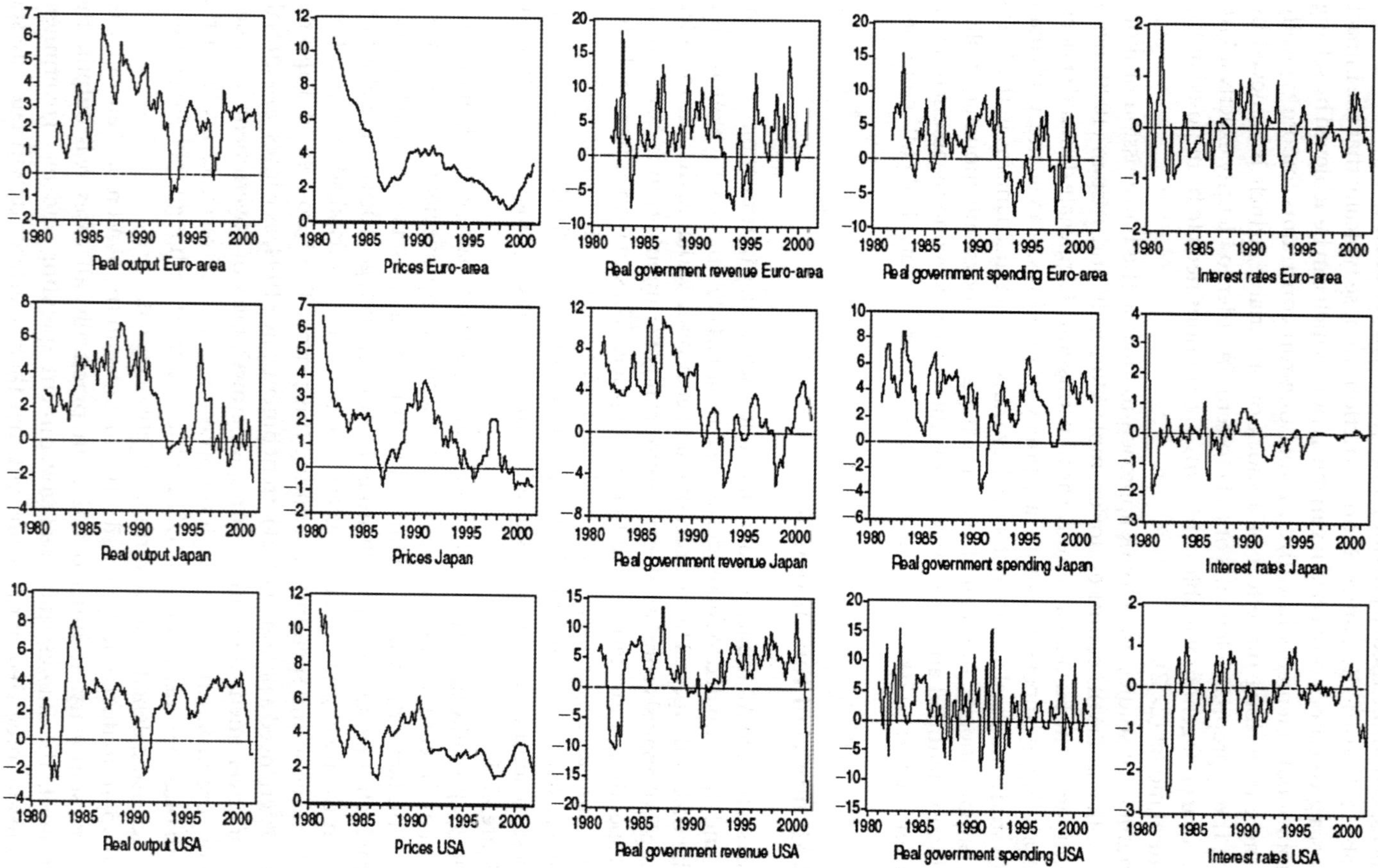

Figure 27.1   Annual percentage rate of change of real output, prices, real government revenue, real government spending and interest rates

real government revenue growth, Δt, real government spending growth, Δg, the change in the short-term interest rate, Δi, and (CPI) inflation, Δp, as endogenous variables. It is driven by five structural shocks: an aggregate supply shock, u^s, a shock to government revenues, u^t, a government spending shock, u^g, a monetary shock, u^m, and an aggregate demand shock, u^d:

$$\begin{bmatrix} \Delta y \\ \Delta t \\ \Delta g \\ \Delta i \\ \Delta p \end{bmatrix} = B(L) \begin{bmatrix} u^s \\ u^t \\ u^g \\ u^i \\ u^d \end{bmatrix} \tag{27.3}$$

Up to four lags of all endogenous variables are included in the estimation of all the VAR models in the chapter. The oil price, a constant, a trend and seasonal dummies are included as exogenous variables in the VAR. The oil price is expressed in domestic currency to take into account exchange rate fluctuations against the US dollar.

In a way, the VAR part estimates a reduced form model of output, government revenue and government spending, interest rates and prices. The VAR estimations for the interest rate, government revenues and government spending equations could be interpreted as systematic (or automatic) or anticipated monetary and fiscal policy responses to the endogenous variables in the VAR (sometimes also interpreted as policy rules). Taken together, the estimated relations between the endogenous variables included in the VAR model determine how the identified structural shocks are transmitted in the model. The structural monetary, government revenue and government spending shocks in this interpretation represent unanticipated monetary and fiscal policy innovations.

To identify the structural innovations from the VAR model, ten identifying restrictions are required. These are:

1 real government revenue shocks do not have a permanent effect on real output;
2 real government spending shocks do not have a permanent effect on real output;
3 real government spending shocks do not have a permanent effect on real government revenue;
4 monetary shocks do not have a permanent effect on real output;
5 monetary shocks do not have a permanent effect on real government revenue;
6 monetary shocks do not have a permanent effect on real government spending;
7 demand shocks do not have a permanent effect on real output;
8 demand shocks do not have a permanent effect on real government revenue;
9 demand shocks do not have a permanent effect on real government spending; and
10 demand shocks do not have a permanent effect on the interest rate.

These restrictions can already be discerned from the ordering of our variables in (27.3). Most of these restrictions are also found in other SVAR analyses with monetary and/or fiscal policy instruments. Ideally, one would like the identifying restrictions to follow strictly from the properties of a small theoretical model of monetary and fiscal policy. In the literature often a small AD-AS model is constructed to motivate the identifying restrictions here (see for example Blanchard, 1989, and Gali, 1992, for a discussion). Most of the above restrictions will hold in that framework but a further elaboration is omitted here for space considerations.

From the estimated SVAR models, impulse response functions can be calculated which show the effects of supply, demand and macroeconomic policy innovations on output, government revenue, government spending, interest rates, and inflation. Figure 27.2 provides the estimated impulse response functions for the EMU12, Japan and the USA.

The graphs show the accumulated effects on the endogenous variables in the VAR model – the quarterly growth rates of real output, real government revenue, real government spending, nominal interest rates and prices – to structural, one-standard-deviation shocks. Note that a response of 0.001 (0.01) corresponds with a 0.1% (1%) change in the variable of interest. These accumulated effects on growth rates give us also the effects we are especially interested in: the effects in each period on the levels of the endogenous variables. Also, we can directly trace the implications of the restrictions we have imposed. For example, imposing that government spending shocks do not have a permanent effect on real output will show up in the graphs as a zero accumulated effect in the long run in the impulse response function of structural shocks on the growth rates of the endogenous variables. Because of the accumulation over time of these effects, this at the same time implies that the long-run effect of the real government shock on the level of real output equals zero.

Supply shocks result in an increase in real output and a drop in prices. Demand shocks also have a positive effect on output but increase prices. In the long run they have, by assumption (cf. restriction 7), no effect on real output. In the case of Japan and the USA the output effect of demand shocks appears to be smaller and more short-lived than in the Euro-area. The effect on prices is also a bit stronger in the Euro-area.

The effects of fiscal policy innovations are small in size and more diverse. Not in all cases the perhaps expected Keynesian type response does not occur, for example, a positive innovation to government spending does not necessarily increase output (Japan and the USA) and a positive revenue impulse does not necessarily induce a reduction in output (the USA). An explanation could be that the Keynesian effects of fiscal adjustments are outweighed by non-Keynesian effects.

In the case of monetary policy innovations we observe small negative effects of interest rate increases on output in the Japan, but in the Euro-area and the USA such a negative effect is absent. The interest rate innovation seems – if anything – to increase prices rather than to reduce them. This last result is in line with many other

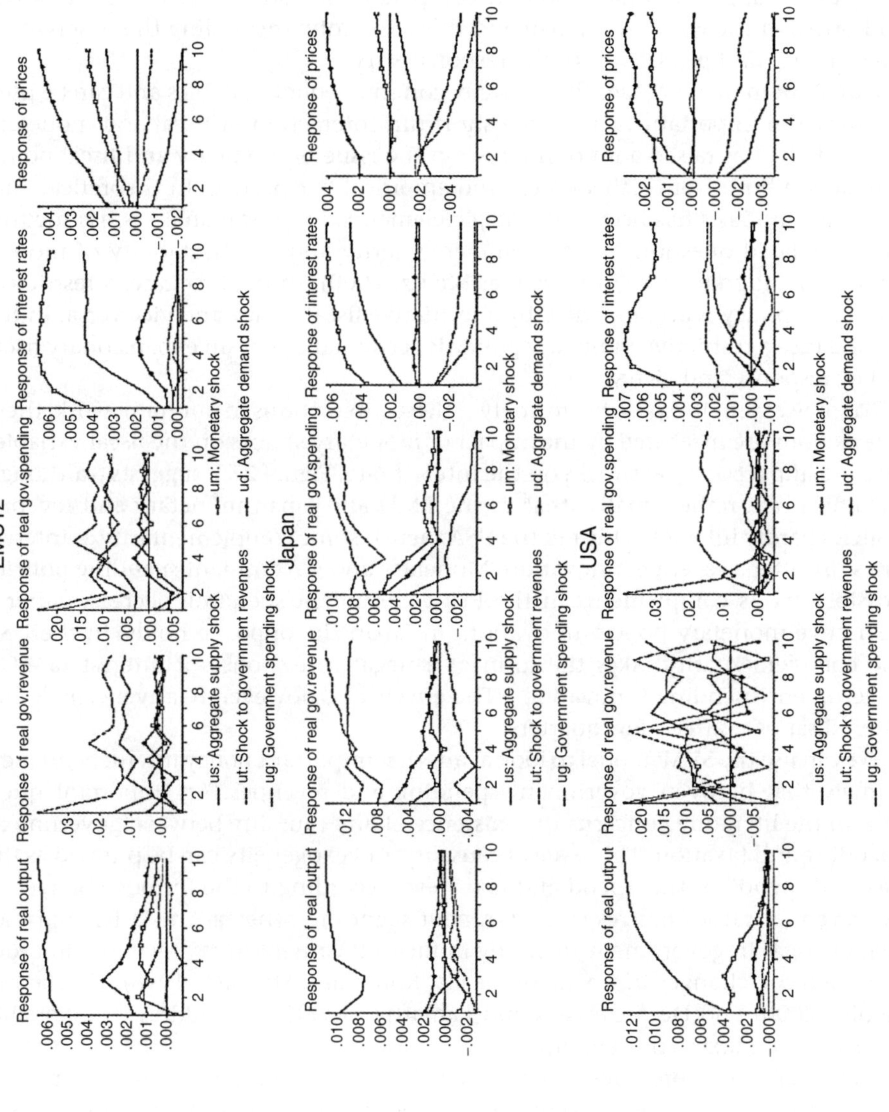

Figure 27.2 Impulse response functions SVAR models of Euro-area, Japan and the USA

VAR studies on the monetary transmission process (known as the 'price-puzzle') and leaves considerable doubt about the effectiveness of interest rate policies to control inflation.

All in all, the effects of demand and supply shocks on output and prices seem to be comparable in the Euro-area, Japan and the USA. Also, the macroeconomic policy innovations appear to induce broadly comparable adjustment dynamics of output and prices in the Euro-area, Japan and the USA, notwithstanding the observation that the size and persistence of the response vary.

Our SVAR model includes three macroeconomic policy variables and can be used to study the important issue of the short-run interaction of fiscal and monetary policy. EMU has raised a lot of interest on the issue of monetary and fiscal policy interaction both from a theoretical and empirical perspective. In theoretical analysis the emphasis has been on strategic elements. Empirical analysis has focused on the related question on the complementarity and substitutability of monetary and fiscal policy (see in particular Mélitz, 2000). In the first case, a restrictive monetary policy is accompanied by a restrictive fiscal policy and vice versa. In the second case a restrictive monetary policy is accompanied by an expansionary fiscal policy response and vice versa.

To some extent it is possible to analyse these interactions in our framework: these interactions are measured by the impact of monetary shocks on the fiscal variables and the impact of fiscal shocks on the interest rate. Figure 27.2 suggests – although the effects are rather small – that in the EMU and Japan monetary and revenue policies hardly interact, whilst in the USA there is some complementarity as interest rates rise after a revenue innovation. Monetary and government spending policies possibly act as complements in the EU: government spending decreases after a restrictive monetary policy innovation. In Japan the opposite holds. In the USA the complementarity takes the form of a negative response of interest rates to government spending innovations. The effects are, however, relatively small and often disappear after a few quarters.

We can use the SVAR model to look at another important policy interdependency, namely that between government spending and revenues. An important question in the literature concerns the existence of any causality between government spending and taxation. This issue of causality and exogeneity can be phrased as the 'tax and spend' vs. the 'spend and tax' view. According to the former, changes in tax revenues cause changes in government spending, whereas the latter supposes that changes in government spending induce adjustment in tax revenues in order to match the changes in financing needs. Koren and Stiassny (1998), Garcia and Henin (2000) and De Arcangelis and Lamartina (2001) also address the possible links between taxes and spending.

Figure 27.2 also provides some – albeit rough – information on this interaction between government revenue and spending. It turns out that a government revenue impulse goes along with an increase in government spending in the EU and Japan, and that government spending reduces government revenue in the case of Japan. Taken together, this would favour at first sight the 'tax and spend' hypothesis over the 'spend and tax' hypothesis. Note, however, that the restriction that we have imposed that there is no long-run effect from spending innovations on revenue rules out any impact in the long run from spending on taxation. There does not seem to be a clear causality between government revenue and spending in the case of the USA.

Conclusion

The transmission of monetary and fiscal policies is a very important issue in the analysis of macroeconomic policy in the EMU. In this chapter we have used a structural VAR model to analyse the transmission of monetary and fiscal policy in the Euro-area. This model has allowed us to trace the effects of structural supply and demand shocks and macroeconomic policy innovations on real output, prices, interest rates and fiscal balances. Attention was also devoted to the interaction of monetary and fiscal policies, to the interaction between government spending and government revenues and the role of financial markets. The estimated adjustments in the Euro-area to the various structural shocks are by and large found to be comparable with the effects observed in the case of Japan and the USA.

References

Blanchard, O. (1989) 'A traditional interpretation of macroeconomic fluctuations', *The American Economic Review*, 79: 1146–64.
Dalsgaard, T. and de Serres, A. (2000) 'Estimating prudent budgetary margins for EU countries: a simulated SVAR model approach', *OECD Economic Studies*, 30: 115–47.
De Arcangelis, G. and Lamartina, S. (2001) 'Fiscal and policy regimes in some OECD countries', *Mimeo*.
Gali, J. (1992), 'How well does the IS-LM model fit post-war U.S. data', *Quarterly Journal of Economics*, 107: 975–1009.
Garcia, S. and Verdelhan, A. (1999), 'Impact of the monetary and fiscal shocks in the Euro-area', *Mimeo*.
Garcia, S. and Hénin, P. (1999), 'Balancing budget through tax increases or expenditure cuts: is it neutral?', *Economic Modelling*, 16: 591–612.
Koren, S. and Stiassny, A. (1998), 'Tax and spend, or spend and tax? An international study', *Journal of Policy Modeling*, 20: 163–91.
Mélitz, J. (2000), 'Some cross-country evidence about fiscal policy behavior and consequences for EMU', *Mimeo*.
Monticelli, C. and Tristani, O. (1999), 'What does the single monetary policy do? A SVAR benchmark for the European Central Bank', *Working Paper*, 2, Frankfurt am Main: European Central Bank.

28
Business Cycle Fluctuations in the Euro-Area

Nuno Cassola and Claudio Morana

Introduction

In this chapter we investigate empirically the causes of business cycle fluctuations in the Euro-area by means of a small-scale macroeconometric model, allowing for interactions between nominal variables – nominal short (i) and long (l) interest rates and inflation (π) – and real variables – real output (y), real M3 balances (rm) and real stock market prices (f). The analysis is carried out in the framework of the vector-error-correction model (VECM) and common-trends model (CT), which allow the estimation of the long-run relationships linking the variables, the identification of the permanent and transitory shocks and the decomposition of the processes in trend and cyclical components.

Our main findings are as follows. Firstly, coherent with the classical dichotomy, we find evidence of long-run separation between real and nominal variables, which is however not complete due to their interactions in the short term. Secondly, while productivity shocks are the main determinant of output fluctuations in the long term, aggregate demand shocks are the most important contributing element in the short term. In particular, aggregate demand shocks have been the most important determinant of cyclical dynamics in the Euro-area in the late 1980s and early 1990s, while productivity shocks have been the most important in the late 1990s and 2000. Thirdly, inflation dynamics reflects the setting of the policy interest rate in the short term and the evolution of excess nominal money growth in the long term. Finally, liquidity preference shocks are the most important determinant of the fluctuation in real stockmarket prices in the short term, while productivity shocks are their main source in the medium to long term.

The chapter is organized as follows. In the next sections we present the data and the econometric results of cointegration and common trends analysis, with a final concluding section.

The data

In this study, quarterly data from 1980Q1 through 2000Q4 are used. As a measure of M3, quarterly averages of the month-end stocks of M3 are used (source: ECB database, in millions of euros, seasonally adjusted). Until 1997Q3, M3 data are based on stocks; from 1997Q4 on flow statistics. Nominal and real GDP until 1994Q4 is calculated based on the ESA79 system of national accounts. From 1995Q1 the series is extended using ESA95 quarter-over-quarter growth rates. Nominal GDP is in millions of euros and has been seasonally adjusted and converted to euros via the irrevocable fixed conversion rates of 31 December 1998. The real and nominal GDP series are used to construct the GDP deflator. Short-term rates are three-month money market interest rates and long-term interest rates are 10-year government bond yields or close substitutes. From 1999 onwards the EURIBOR is used as the three-month money market rate. Interest rates are measured as averages of the respective euro-11 interest rates using GDP weights at purchasing power exchange rates in 1995. Except interest rates, all data are in logs. The underlying national series are taken from the macroeconomic database provided by the BIS. The stockmarket index is taken from Datastream (TOTMKEM). We took the benchmark series expressed in USD and converted it into EUR using a synthetic USD/EUR exchange rate series. As a caveat, it should be noted that the resulting stockmarket series does not have the same aggregation scheme used to construct Euro-area output, inflation and monetary series.

Empirical results

Cointegration analysis

As indicated in Table 28.1, the null of no cointegration can be rejected, at the 5 per cent significance level, in favour of the alternative hypothesis of four cointegrating vectors. The identification structure selected is also not rejected by the data at the 5 per cent significance level.

According to imposed restrictions, the identified long-run relationships in Table 28.2 can be interpreted as a long-run money demand equation, a term structure relation, a Fisher parity relation and a long-run relationship between the real stockmarket index and real output. An interesting feature of the identified cointegration space is long-run separation as defined by Konishi and Granger

Table 28.1   Cointegration tests

Eigenvalue:	0.3815	0.2896	0.2581	0.1842	0.1533	0.0000
Hypothesis:	$r = 0$	$r \leq 1$	$r \leq 2$	$r \leq 3$	$r \leq 4$	$r \leq 5$
λ_{TRACE}	120.8**	81.85**	54.15*	29.97*	13.48	0.0066
95% crit. value	94.2	68.5	47.2	29.7	15.4	3.8

* Significant at the 5 per cent level.
** Significant at the 1 per cent level.

Table 28.2   Estimated cointegrating vectors

y	f	rm	i	l	π
-1.4273		1			
(0.0206)		$(-)$			
			-1	1	
			$(-)$	$(-)$	
			1		-1.5937
			$(-)$		(0.1252)
-4.6884	1				
(0.3712)	$(-)$				

(1992). In fact we can separate the cointegration space into two blocks, one involving only real variables $\{y_t, rm_t\}$ and $\{y_t, f_t\}$, and the other including only nominal variables, $\{i_t, l_t\}$ and $\{\pi_t, i_t\}$, each block of variables being driven by a different common stochastic trend. This is an important result that can be taken as evidence of long-run monetary neutrality. Separation is, however, not complete, since nominal and real variables interact in the short run (see Cassola and Morana, 2002).

Common trends analysis

The presence of four cointegration relations between the six variables in the system implies that there are two distinct sources of shocks having permanent effects on some of the variables. Based on the theoretical framework, we interpret the permanent shocks as being a productivity shock (ψ_θ) and a nominal shock (ψ_β). As argued in Cassola and Morana (2002), the latter bears the interpretation of an excess nominal money growth shock. One identifying restriction imposed is a long-run monetary neutrality condition; that is, we assume that the permanent nominal shock does not have a long-run impact on real GDP. This restriction ensures exact identification of the permanent innovations, and it is supported by the finding of long-run separation between real and nominal variables pointed out by cointegration analysis. Moreover, the exact identification of the transitory innovations requires the imposition of six additional restrictions on the instantaneous impact Γ_0 matrix. The imposed restrictions mean that: (1) the shock to the term structure (v_{TS}) does not have a contemporaneous impact on output, inflation and real balances; (2) the liquidity preference shock (v_{SM}) does not have a contemporaneous impact on output and inflation; (3) there is an underlying temporary shock to output (v_{AD}) (interpretable as a demand shock) that does not have a contemporaneous impact on inflation; and (4) the shock to the Fisher relation (v_{FH}) has a contemporaneous impact on all variables (see Cassola and Morana, 2002, for additional details).

Consider, for the sake of exposition, three dimensions of the forecast horizon: short-term (below one year), medium-term (three years) and long-term (above five

Table 28.3   Forecast error variance decomposition: short term

	1 quarter						1 year					
	τ_θ	τ_β	v_{TS}	v_{SM}	v_{AD}	v_{FH}	τ_θ	τ_β	v_{TS}	v_{SM}	v_{AD}	v_{FH}
y	0.05	0.05	0.00	0.00	0.86	0.04	0.05	0.04	0.00	0.01	0.88	0.02
f	0.25	0.16	0.04	0.44	0.10	0.01	0.46	0.12	0.11	0.17	0.06	0.08
rm	0.10	0.06	0.00	0.23	0.12	0.49	0.28	0.02	0.00	0.28	0.14	0.28
i	0.42	0.18	0.26	0.00	0.03	0.11	0.32	0.37	0.09	0.00	0.15	0.07
l	0.33	0.25	0.15	0.00	0.04	0.23	0.29	0.47	0.07	0.00	0.07	0.10
π	0.02	0.24	0.00	0.00	0.00	0.74	0.13	0.47	0.01	0.00	0.01	0.38

Table 28.4   Forecast error variance decomposition: medium term

	3 year						5 year					
	τ_θ	τ_β	v_{TS}	v_{SM}	v_{AD}	v_{FH}	τ_θ	τ_β	v_{TS}	v_{SM}	v_{AD}	v_{FH}
y	0.34	0.08	0.01	0.01	0.53	0.03	0.69	0.04	0.00	0.00	0.25	0.02
f	0.72	0.06	0.04	0.08	0.05	0.05	0.78	0.04	0.03	0.05	0.06	0.04
rm	0.43	0.02	0.01	0.10	0.35	0.09	0.73	0.02	0.00	0.04	0.17	0.04
i	0.24	0.60	0.02	0.00	0.12	0.02	0.17	0.73	0.02	0.00	0.07	0.01
l	0.18	0.74	0.02	0.00	0.03	0.03	0.13	0.82	0.01	0.00	0.02	0.02
π	0.15	0.65	0.01	0.00	0.02	0.17	0.12	0.75	0.00	0.00	0.02	0.11

years) – see Tables 28.3–28.4. From the forecast error-variance decompositions the following facts are worth noting.

First, depending on the forecast horizon there is a marked difference between the factors that explain variability. In the short to medium term aggregate demand shocks are the main source of output variability (88% at 1 year; 53% at 3 years), while productivity shocks are the main source of output variability in the long term (about 70% already at 5 years). In the short term, shocks to the Fisher relation are the main source of inflation variability (74% at 1 quarter), while the nominal permanent shock is the main source of inflation variability in the medium to long term (65% at 3 years; 75% at 5 years). Thus, the forecast error-variance decompositions of output and inflation illustrate some 'textbook' features of our model: productivity driving trend output and aggregate demand shocks deviating output from the trend; inflation reflecting both dimensions of monetary policy (interest rates in the short term; excess money growth in the long term). Liquidity preference shocks are the most important determinant of real stockmarket price index volatility in the short term (44% at 1 quarter), whilst productivity shocks are the main source of stockmarket variability in the medium to long term (72% at 3 years; 78% at 5 years). In the short term, shocks to the Fisher relation are the main source of real M3 variability (49% at 1 quarter), while the productivity shock is the main source of real M3 variability in the medium to long term (43% at 3 years; 73%

at 5 years). However, in the short to medium term, aggregate demand and liquidity preference shocks are also important explanatory factors for real M3 variability. Short- and long-term interest rates seem to share the same underlying factors of variability displaying an interesting 'reversal' in causal factors: in the short term the productivity shock is the main source of variability (42% and 33% at 1 quarter; short- and long-term interest rates respectively), whilst the nominal permanent shock is the main source of variability in the medium to long term (60% and 74% at 3 years, for short- and long-term interest rates, respectively). Thus, the forecast error variance decompositions of interest rates illustrate another 'textbook' feature of our model: due to 'price-stickiness' short-term changes in interest rates are also changes in real interest rates and are thus to some extent related to productivity changes. In the long term nominal interest rates fully reflect anticipated inflation.

Second, depending on the type of variables there is a marked difference between the factors that explain variability: in the short term the behaviour of real variables is more heterogeneous than the behaviour of nominal variables. In terms of forecast error-variance decomposition the separation between the real and the nominal sides of the economy is already apparent at the five years horizon. In fact, at that horizon the productivity shock is the main factor explaining variability of output, real stock prices and real M3 (69%, 78% and 73%, respectively); in contrast, at that horizon, the permanent nominal shock is the main factor explaining variability of short- and long-term interest rates and inflation (73%, 82% and 75%, respectively). However, in the short term, variability of real variables is explained by different factors: output by aggregate demand shocks, stockmarket by liquidity preference shocks, and real balances by Fisher equation shocks. On the nominal side, volatility of interest rates is mainly explained by the same shock (productivity). However, in the short term, inflation variability is explained by a different factor (Fisher equation shock).

A closer look at cyclical dynamics

Following Warne (1993), given a vector of $n\ I(1)$ cointegrated variables of interest $\mathbf{x}_t$, the common trends representation of Stock and Watson (1988) in structural form can be written as:

$$\mathbf{x}_t = \mathbf{x}_0 + \mu t + \Gamma(1) \sum_{j=0}^{t-1} \varphi_{t-j} + \Gamma^*(L)\varphi_t$$

$$= \mathbf{x}_0 + \mu t + \Gamma_g \sum_{j=0}^{t-1} \psi_{t-j} + \Gamma^*(L)\varphi_t \tag{28.1}$$

where $\varphi_t \equiv \begin{bmatrix} \psi_t & \upsilon_t \end{bmatrix}' \sim I.I.D.(\mathbf{0}, \mathbf{I}_n)$, with ψ_t and υ_t subvectors of structural shocks of k and r elements respectively, where $r < n$ is the number of cointegrating vectors, and $\Gamma(1) = \sum_{j=0}^{\infty} \Gamma_j$, $\Gamma^*(L) = \sum_{j=0}^{\infty} \Gamma_j^* L^j$, $\Gamma_j^* = -\sum_{i=j+1}^{\infty} \Gamma_i$, where Γ_i are matrices of parameters in the structural Wold vector moving-average (VMA) representation. In the structural common trends representation only k shocks (the permanent shocks ψ_t) are cumulated in the trend component. The behaviour of the variables in $\mathbf{x}_t$ induced by permanent disturbances may then be computed as:

$$\mathbf{x}_t^p = \mathbf{x}_0 + \mu t + \Gamma_g \sum_{j=0}^{t-1} \psi_{t-j} \tag{28.2}$$

while the cyclical components is:

$$\mathbf{x}_t^c = \Gamma^*(L)\varphi_t \tag{28.3}$$

This is the Beveridge–Nelson–Stock–Watson trend-cycle decomposition of $\mathbf{x}_t = \mathbf{x}_t^p + \mathbf{x}_t^c$. Note that the cyclical component is determined by all the innovations in the system, both permanent and transitory. This implies that permanent innovations also induce transitory dynamics. A structural version of the Proietti (1997) decomposition can be computed by rewriting the vector of cyclical components as:

$$\mathbf{x}_t^c = \Gamma^*(L)\varphi_t = \Gamma_1^*(L)\psi_t + \Gamma_2^*(L)\upsilon_t \tag{28.4}$$

The vector $\Gamma_1^*(L)\psi_t$ gives the contribution of permanent innovations to the overall cycle (dynamics along the attractor), while the vector $\Gamma_2^*(L)\upsilon_t$ measures the contribution of the transitory innovations to the overall cycle (dynamics towards the attractor). Differently from the Proietti decomposition, the latter approach allows assessing the contribution of each structural shock to cyclical fluctuations separately, and is therefore more informative from an economic point of view.

Table 28.5 reports the correlation matrix of the overall cyclical components.

The cyclical components are all positively correlated except the stockmarket cycle which is negatively correlated with the other cycles. The highest contemporaneous correlation is between the cyclical components of output and real balances, followed by the relatively high correlations (in absolute value) between stockmarket and real balances cyclical components and between the stockmarket cycle and the long-term interest rate cycle. Also noticeable is the high positive correlation between the short-term interest rate cycle and the output cycle. The correlations seem to have been stable in the sample period.

Historical decompositions into dynamics towards the attractor (DTA; disequilibrium dynamics) and dynamics along the attractor (DAA; equilibrium dynamics)

Table 28.5   Cyclical components: correlation matrix

	y	*f*	*rm*	*i*	*l*	*π*
y	1					
f	−0.41	1				
rm	0.83	−0.72	1			
i	0.52	−0.42	0.59	1		
l	0.12	−0.62	0.27	0.53	1	
π	0.25	−0.30	0.24	0.12	−0.14	1

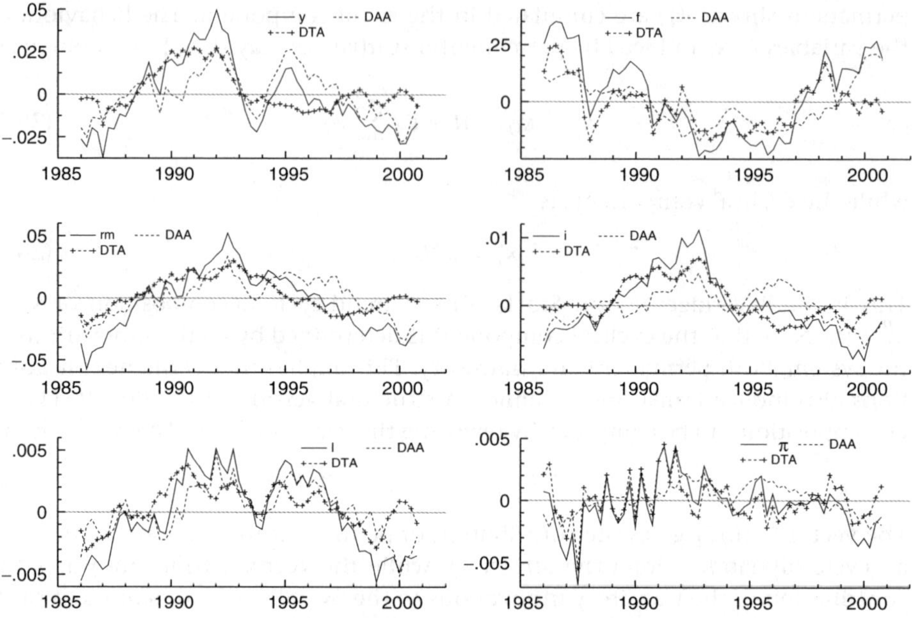

Figure 28.1   Decomposition of the overall cycle in dynamics towards the attractor (DTA) and dynamics along the attractor (DAA)

Notes: Abbreviations are: output (y), stockmarket index (f), real money balances (rm), short-term interest rate (i), long-term interest rate (l), inflation (π).

Table 28.6   Cyclical components: correlation matrix

Variable	DAA					
DTA	y	f	rm	i	l	π
y	–	−0.72	0.91	0.86	0.85	0.84
f	0.04	–	−0.87	−0.87	−0.89	−0.90
rm	0.66	−0.55	–	0.87	0.82	0.90
i	0.77	−0.11	0.82	–	0.95	0.85
l	0.56	−0.60	0.75	0.53	–	0.83
π	0.43	−0.02	0.19	0.33	−0.73	–

are shown in Figure 28.1. Table 28.6 reports the correlation matrices of each cycle explained by the two components.

An interesting result is the change in the magnitude of the correlation between the cyclical components of the short-term interest rate and inflation: the correlation of the DAA is much stronger than that of the DTA. To understand this result recall that both permanent shocks imply a short-run positive correlation between inflation and (nominal) interest rates. However, the transitory Fisher equation shock, which we interpret as capturing monetary policy 'surprises', implies a negative short-run correlation between inflation and the short-term interest rate. It is this effect that explains the lower correlation in the DTA, which nevertheless remains positive due to the effect of aggregate demand shocks on both variables. Note that the correlation of inflation and long-term interest rate changes sign because the impact of aggregate demand shocks is less important to explain the variability of the long-term interest rate than of the short-term interest rate.

One conclusion that can be drawn is that monetary policy was countercyclical, also given the high positive contemporaneous correlation between the DTA of short-term interest rate and output (and real M3 balances). In this sense the negative correlation between the inflation and the stockmarket cycles can also be explained by the countercyclical nature of monetary policy.

There are two distinct phases of the output cycle in 1986Q1–2000Q4: an expansionary phase, from 1986 until 1992, and a contractionary phase, from 1993 until 2000. Given the high contemporaneous correlations of all cyclical components the same classification applies to the other variables (the stockmarket cycle has an opposite sign). As illustrated in Figure 28.1 both the DAA and the DTA were important factors in explaining cyclical dynamics of all variables. However, the DTA played a more important role in the expansionary phase, particularly in 1989–91, whereas the DAA played a greater role in the contractionary phase, especially in 1999–2000. Thus, one can conclude that disequilibrium factors (temporary shocks) were the most important determinants of cyclical dynamics in the Euro-area in the late 1980s and early 1990s, whereas equilibrium factors (permanent shocks) were the most important determinants of cyclical dynamics in the euro area in the late 1990s and 2000.

Conclusions

We have investigated empirically the sources of business cycle fluctuations in the Euro-area over the period 1980–2000. Our main findings are as follows. Firstly, coherent with the classical dichotomy, we find evidence of long-run separation between the real and nominal side of the economy, which is however not complete due to interactions of real and nominal variables in the short term. Secondly, while productivity shocks are the main determinant of output fluctuations in the long term, aggregate demand shocks are the main contributing element in the short term. In particular, aggregate demand shocks have been the most important determinant of cyclical dynamics in the Euro-area in the late 1980s and early 1990s, while productivity shocks were the main determinants in the late 1990s and 2000. Thirdly, inflation dynamics reflects the setting of the policy interest rate in the short term (Fisher parity shocks) and the evolution of excess nominal money growth in the long term. Finally, liquidity preference shocks are the most important determinant of fluctuations in real stockmarket prices in the short term, while productivity shocks are their main source in the medium to long term.

References

Cassola, N. and Morana, C. (2002) 'Monetary policy and the stock market in the Euro area', *Working Paper*, 119, Frankfurt am Main: European Central Bank.

Konishi, T. and Granger, C.W.J. (1992) 'Separation in cointegrated systems', Mimeo, San Diego: University of California.

Proietti, T. (1997) 'Short-run dynamics in cointegrated systems', *Oxford Bulletin of Economics and Statistics*, 59: 403–22.

Stock, J.H. and Watson, M.W. (1988): "Testing for common trends', *Journal of the American Statistical Association*, 83: 1097–107.

Warne, A. (1993) 'A common trends model: identification, estimation and inference', *Seminar Paper*, 555: Stockholm University.

29
Measuring the 'Financing Gap' of European Corporations: An Update

*Federico Galizia**

Introduction

The 'financing gap' measures external funding needs of the corporate sector as the difference between gross capital formation and savings. Taking advantage of the recent release of data in the ESA95 standard, this chapter assembles a set of stylized facts about the corporate financing gap for the largest European economies (annual frequency from Eurostat *New Cronos* database) and for the Euro-area as a whole (quarterly frequency from the European Central Bank). The results update and are consistent with previous findings from data in the ESA79 standard, which cover the period 1970–97. In particular we find that (1) a large majority of investment remains funded from internal sources, and (2) bank lending is the principal source of external finance. However, the fact that (3) loans to corporations tend to overshoot the financing gap during an upturn emerges more clearly in the recent cycle than it did in previous ones.

The 'financing' or 'savings gap' is generally defined as the difference between capital formation and savings of the corporate sector over a given period and measures the external funding requirements. The interpretation of this measure is straightforward; for a given level of capital formation, whatever funds the corporate sector cannot generate from internal sources (retained earnings or cash flow), it has to raise from other sectors. These funds come typically in the form of loans from the banking sector, trade credit from the rest of the world, issues of shares and corporate bonds placed with households, the financial sector and the rest of the world.

---

* The views expressed in this chapter are exclusively those of the author and do not necessarily represent those of the European Investment Bank.

The goal of this chapter is to provide a basis for further research by establishing a set of stylized facts on the flows of investment and savings of European corporations, as well as key financial sources and uses of funds. The analysis originates and partially relies on a companion study, entitled 'The Savings Gap of European Corporations: A first look at the available data', which is also published in this volume.[1] Based on recently released data, published by Eurostat in the ESA 95 standard, covering EU countries, as well as aggregate flow of funds data for the Euro-area published from the European Central Bank, we update and confirm the evidence in the companion paper (which was based on analogous data previously compiled by Eurostat following the ESA 79 standard, and covering the period 1970–97). A potential interpretation of the key stylized facts is set forward, which can be summarized along two main lines of reasoning. On the one hand, cyclical analyses detect a marked increase in bank credit as well as share and bond issues at the end of the last decade, in coincidence with a more dynamic investment environment in Europe. On the other hand, long-term analysis of the corporate cash flows suggests a more prudent assessment. Currently, not unlike the 1970s, the large majority of corporate investment (gross fixed capital formation) is internally financed, with external funds contributing at best to a small fraction of investment. Moreover, traditional bank lending still constitutes the bulk of external funds. Underlying these competing (but also potentially complementary) economic hypotheses is the deeper question of whether corporate finance is demand-driven, in the sense that higher capital formation induces increased offers of financial sources, or instead is supply-driven, so that increased availability of credit in general induces companies to invest more.

In the next section we quantify the financing gap and summarize well-known evidence on the structure of sources and uses of funds by the corporate sector. This is followed by an interpretation of the developments over the business cycle, with special emphasis on the current phase. The final section concludes, by summarizing the key stylized facts supported by data available so far and thus motivating the need for continued improvement of data coverage at a quarterly frequency. Fortunately, such efforts are already under way.

A bird's-eye view of corporate finance in Europe

In the *National Accounts by Institutional Sector*, the corporate financing gap is found under the name of *net borrowing*. The latter takes into account not only the difference between gross capital formation and savings of non-financial corporations, but also transfers to this sector. Figure 29.1 (drawn simply by dividing net borrowing by gross capital formation in each country-year data point and by taking arithmetic averages of the results) is meant to offer an overall view of the financing needs of European corporations in the five largest EU countries over the last three decades. This figure supports the conclusion that in recent years a large majority of investment is internally financed. In the following paragraphs, we present a brief historical summary on the evolution of the financing gap; we

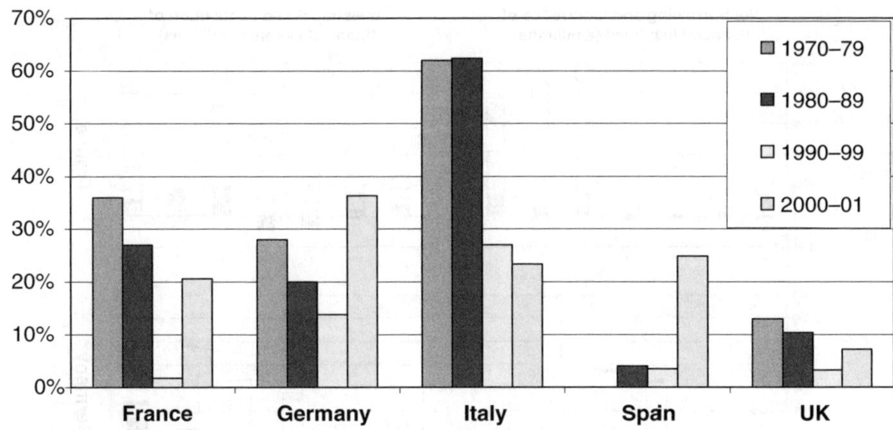

Figure 29.1   Financing gap as percentage of capital formation
Source: Eurostat ESA79 and ESA95 accounts.

argue that it is largely financed via bank lending; and conclude by taking a closer look at this form of financing.

A summary of the historical evolution of the financing gap

The companion study 'The Savings Gap of European Corporations' presents a more detailed historical as well as cyclical perspective of the evolution in the corporate financing gap until the mid-1990s, as it was determined by the specific evolution of savings and investment flows. A summary and an update are provided in Figure 29.1, showing that at one extreme, companies in the UK have always been and are almost entirely self-financed. At the other extreme Italian companies covered on average half of their investments from external sources.[2] French and German companies are in the middle, with financing gaps averaging three-quarters of investment, but important variations over time.

Over time, starting in the 1970s and until the mid-1990s, most countries saw a progressive reduction of investment as a percentage of GDP, while corporate savings remained stable or were increasing slightly. Such dynamics de facto implied a disappearing financing gap in France and the UK, while halving it in Italy. In Germany the decline in the gap was more limited, due to its post-unification investment boom. However, the tendency to lower gaps has been reversed in the second half of the 1990s, in correspondence to a generalized investment-led growth. Especially in Germany, France and Spain, the gap was 20 percentage points larger in 2000–01 than during the previous decade. Still, a simple arithmetic average across countries would indicate that over three quarters of corporate investment in Europe remain internally financed.

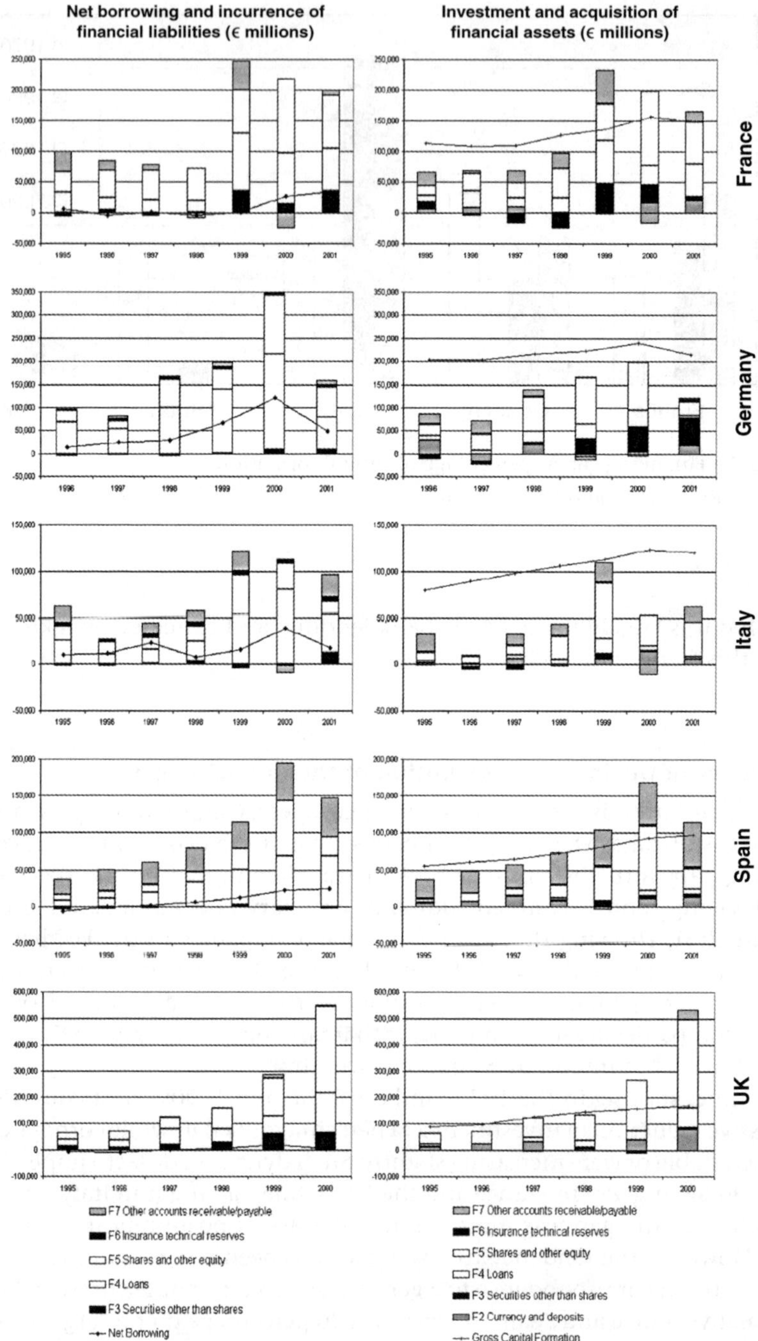

Figure 29.2 Financial transactions and investment of non-financial corporations
Source: Eurostat Financial and Sector Accounts ESA95.

By exclusion, bank lending is the principal external source of corporate funding

For the same set of countries, Figure 29.2 represents the main financial sources ('incurrence of financial liabilities') and uses ('acquisition of financial assets') of funds starting in the mid-1990s. The figures are in millions of euros and for ease of reference the financing gap is plotted as a line in the sources graph, and, similarly, gross capital formation is plotted in the uses graph for each country. Looking at the graphs in the left column, the relation between the financing gap and the incurrence of financial liabilities is remarkably weak, as the latter is several orders of magnitude bigger than the gap. The explanation comes from the set of graphs on the right, showing that the acquisition of financial assets is of the same order of magnitude as investment. A closer look at each main category of financial sources and uses is clearly needed in order to understand the economic determinants of such flows.

Share and bond issues still play a minor role in aggregate corporate finance. Throughout the second half of the 1990s and until the recent stockmarket crash, the corporate sector as a whole has purchased more shares than it has issued. In part, this is explained by the difficulty in consolidating intra-sector transactions, and the ensuing potential double counting of such issues as both sources and uses of funds by the corporate sector.[3] Another explanation comes from sizable cross-border acquisitions in a number of sectors (notably telecommunications, but also car manufacturers, utilities, energy), which involved both European and US companies. In any case, it is well-known that financing via share issues is limited to listed companies – particularly the larger ones – and that such companies represent only a fraction of the overall corporate sector. Figure 29.2 also shows that *issues of bonds* were very limited in all countries, including the UK, arguably the most developed corporate bond market in the EU over the period covered. Another source of funds that is important for a single company, but not on aggregate is *trade credit*. Figure 29.2 shows that especially in Spain, but also in France and Italy, 'other accounts payable' represents a significant fraction of total financial sources. However, 'other accounts receivable' represents as significant a fraction of total financial uses, and what is a 'payable' for one company is a 'receivable' for another, which would disappear with consolidation across the corporate sector at a country level, and even more at a European level. The only remaining major source of aggregate funding for the corporate sector is thus *bank credit*, as shown in Figure 29.2, amounting to from one-third to half of total sources across different countries and years.

The role of bank lending is however limited by other factors

The logic outlined above, that, by exclusion, the financing gap of European corporates is filled via bank lending, is weakened by three main considerations. Firstly, at least half of bank lending is for short-term maturities and is counterbalanced by a significant build-up of cash ('currency and deposits' in Figure 29.3). Secondly, corporations are net creditors of households because they extend

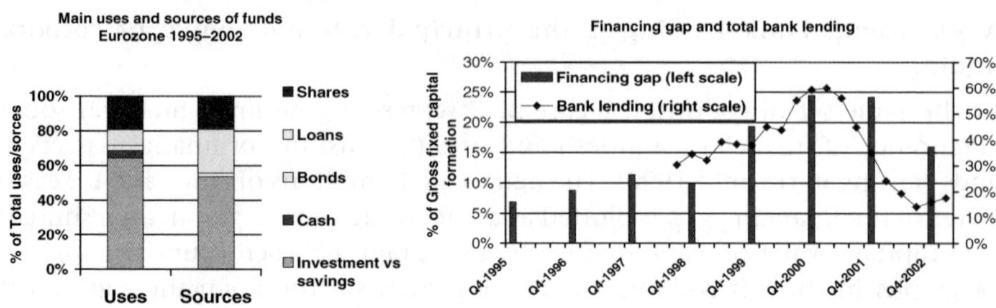

Figure 29.3   Eurozone: financing gap, uses and sources of funds and bank lending
Source: European Central Bank.

consumer credit (automobiles manufacturers, retail distributors), and of the public
sector (construction companies). Such credits in turn need financing. Thirdly, in
some countries corporate pension plans and/or severance grants are administered
in such a way to provide a net source of funds to the corporate sector.[4] One is
forced to deduce that bank credit – even medium to long-term – ends up financing
quite a limited share of corporate investment. This conclusion is also supported by
analysis of earlier periods and by company-level data to be found in the companion
paper.

Insufficient supply of funds or scarce demand?

The long-term historical perspective should illuminate recent events, particularly
the investment and stockmarket boom at the turn of the millennium and the current crisis. We have already mentioned that corporate investment – as a fraction
of GDP – followed a declining trend until the mid-1990s, while corporate restruc-
turing and cost-cutting efforts maintained stable or slightly increasing profits. In
some countries, France in particular, the equity base of the corporate sector has
been reinforced; in Italy, it has stabilized.[5] Such a tendency was however reversed
in the second half of the 1990s and notably at the turn of the millennium, unfortunately with negative consequences on the business cycle. Corporate investment
as a fraction of GDP increased significantly in all countries from 1993–94 until
2000. In the presence of stable corporate savings, the financing gap progressively
widened, and this was reflected in rapid growth in the sources of funds for the
corporate sector, being then bank credit, shares or bond issues.

A strong supply of funds to corporates characterized the 'roaring 1990s'

However, Figure 29.2 demonstrates that the absolute amount of sources of funds
was a multiple of the financing gap. For instance, in Germany, total financial
sources amounted to over € 350 bn, compared to a financing gap of € 120 bn.
Other than for special needs (for example, payment of UMTS licences) such an
abundance of financial sources has been used to invest in financial assets or to
fund acquisitions in Europe and beyond. These annual datasuggest that, in the

presence of a renewed demand of funds for both real and financial investment, banking and financial markets have responded making abundant funds available.

Recently published Euro-wide data from the ECB also support the thesis that availability of financial sources, particularly bank credit, overshot the financing gap in the late 1990s. The left panel in Figure 29.3 summarizes total sources and uses of funds. Consistently with the analysis in the previous section, issues and purchases of shares balance each other out and the same applies to bonds. Thus loans are left to cover the financing gap, as well as holding of cash and loans to other sectors. The right panel of the figure further demonstrates the point by plotting the annual financing gap for Euro-area corporations alongside a moving average of quarterly expansion in bank lending to corporates (at an annual rate to ensure comparability). At the business cycle peak in 2000, while the corporate financing gap amounted to 25 per cent of total gross fixed capital formation, bank lending provided finance exceeding twice that amount, at 60 per cent. Quite interestingly the phenomenon reversed over 2001 and 2002, with the financing gap decreasing by a third (from 25% in 2000 to 16% in 2002) against our indicator of lending decreasing by three quarters (from 60% in 2000 to 16% in 2002). Thus, at the end of 2002, bank lending appeared to be more or less in line with the financing gap. This point deserves some further elaboration.

Are current credit markets characterized by scarce demand or scarce supply?

There are at least two sets of reasons currently limiting the willingness of European corporations to invest. Firstly, investment is the most volatile component of GDP, often the first to drop at the onset of a recession. Available data confirm that this is indeed happening. Secondly, the ample volume of debt, which was accumulated in the last few years in order to finance both an investment and an acquisition boom, has become particularly difficult to sustain during a bear market, due to reduced value of corporate assets. Based on such considerations, most economists attribute the current slowdown in bank lending to demand factors.

The possibility of a drop in credit supply should also not be overlooked, as the deterioration in both corporate and bank balance sheets may reduce the latter's willingness to lend, and possibly lead to a flight to quality and credit rationing. Since both credit demand and supply depend on cyclical factors and should be expected to co-move, we are unable to distinguish between the two competing (but also complementary hypothesis) based on aggregate data. What we find most interesting is the potential to use the quarterly data on corporate loans compiled by the ECB in order to forecast evolutions of the corporate financing gap, which is currently measured solely at annual frequencies.

Conclusions and agenda for future research

In coincidence with the adoption of the euro and the ever-closer integration of the European economies, important progress has been realised in the collection of flow of funds data. The researcher now has available a much richer and consistent set of information compared to even a couple of years ago. In particular:

1 Aggregate sector-level information is assembled in the *New Cronos* Database, published by Eurostat. The corporate sectors of the largest European countries, notably Germany, France, the UK, Italy and Spain (EU5 henceforth) are covered at annual frequency. Annual data on the saving, investment and financing of Euro-area non-financial corporations are published by the ECB. Adoption of the ESA 95 standard has greatly enhanced comparability across countries. Due to issues of comparability between this standard and the former ESA 79,[6] this chapter only uses ESA 95 data, while a detailed historical analysis using ESA 79 data is found in a companion paper 'The Savings Gap of European Corporations'.
2 Coverage, at quarterly frequency, of amounts outstanding as well as financial transactions in financial assets and liabilities by the corporate sector are published by the National Central Banks at country level and in aggregate for the Euro-area by the ECB. For a disaggregate view of the corporate sector the companion paper relies on two company-level sources:
3 financial reports (including cash-flow statements) for companies that are listed on a European stockmarket are collected in the Worldscope database from Bureau Van Dijk and Disclosure, again at annual frequencies;
4 assets and liabilities (but not cash-flows) of both listed and not listed companies are analysed by the European Committee of Central Balance Sheet Data Offices (ECCB) and collected in the BACH and European Sectoral References databases.

While results from such a disparate set of sources are not immediately comparable, they are complementary and do provide consistent information, especially concerning the business cycle dynamics. Accordingly, the nature of this study, and its companion one, was that of a 'first step'. Primary concern is about getting stylized facts right, by assembling and comparing evidence from several sources. Since this first step already implies a sizeable amount of work we chose to restrict attention to a descriptive analysis and only suggest a preliminary explanation of what is observed. Interpretation will follow as a topic of further research. The key findings are as follows:

1 While notable differences exist among countries and time periods, internal finance is the principal source of funds for the corporate sector in the largest European economies, covering in recent periods less than three quarters of investment. The importance of internal finance has been increasing from the 1970s through the mid-1990s, in coincidence with a slowdown in investment and stable to increasing savings. Current levels of internal finance are lower and close to long-term averages.
2 If one abstracts from privatization and stockmarket boom episodes, loans are the principal source of external finance, followed by trade credit. On average, half of the loans are short-term and are offset by the presence of cash balances in the sector's accounts. Similarly, accounts payable are largely offset by accounts receivable from households and the public sector. Bond issues are minimal.

3 Analysis of yearly flows shows that the savings gap can vary enormously over the business cycle. Notably, the financing gap attained its lowest level in the mid-1990s in all countries, to rebound strongly towards the long-term average of three quarters of investment by the end of the millennium. A reversal followed, chiefly determined by shrinking investment.

Notes

1 Extended versions of both studies are available on www.eib.org/efs/reports.htm and http://europa.eu.int/comm/eurostat
2 Such a notable role of external finance in Italy is partly explained by a system in which a significant fraction of the corporate sector was state-owned and financed by state-owned banks. Substantial privatizations of banks and corporations in the 1990s thus significantly reduced the financing gap.
3 As most countries do not publish consolidated data for the corporate sector, for comparability across countries, non-consolidated data are used in Figure 29.2
4 This reasoning could however be turned on its head, and pension plans become a net use of funds by the corporate sector as payment of accrued benefits begins to exceed receipts.
5 The point is covered in more ample detail in the companion paper "The Savings Gap of European Corporates", also relying on studies by the European Committee of Central Balance Sheet Offices.
6 In Germany, the housing activities of private households are included as part of the corporate sector in the ESA 79 accounts.

Reference

Galizia, F. (2001) 'The savings gap of European corporations: a first look at the available data', *Economic and Financial Reports*, 2001/01, Luxembourg: European Investment Bank (with T. Steinberger); also as (2004): *Working Papers and Studies*, Luxembourg: Eurostat.

30
The 'Savings Gap' of European Corporations: A First Look at the Available Data

Federico Galizia with Thomas Steinberger*

Introduction

The 'savings' or 'financing gap' measures external funding requirements of the corporate sector as the difference between gross capital formation and savings. Stylized facts on the corporate financing gap for the main European economies are based on two sources of data: country-level flow-of-funds in the ESA 79 format, covering the period 1970–97; and firm-level cash-flow statements for listed corporations over the period 1989–99. Key findings are as follows: (1) Despite notable differences among countries and across time periods, retained earnings are the principal source of funds for non-financial corporations. The importance of internal financing has increased through the mid 1990s, in coincidence with a gradual slowdown in investment. (2) Loans dominate the sources of external finance, equity issues are a second sizable source while bond issues are minimal. (3) Among listed companies, the smallest display the fastest growth and the highest savings gap, while the largest rely mostly on internal finance. (4) Variation of the savings gap over the business cycle dwarfs differences across countries.

The savings gap for the corporate sector within a country is measured as the difference between corporate investment and retained earnings flows, and it determines the amount of funds that need to be raised from other sectors. Applied macroeconomists monitor thegap as a synthetic indicator of the interacting

---

* The views expressed in this chapter are exclusively those of the author and do not necessarily represent those of the European Investment Bank. Thomas Steinberger collaborated in the first phase of the project as a consultant. His excellent contribution is gratefully acknowledged, but all errors and omissions remain the sole responsibility of this author.

movements in business profits, investment and credit that are at the center of business cycles. Accordingly, the terms 'flow-of-funds cycle' or 'credit cycle' are sometimes used (see Zarnowitz, 1999, and Eckstein and Sinali, 1986). In finance, fixed income analysts have found the savings gap to have strong predictive power in modelling corporate bond spreads (Bevan and Garzarelli, 1999).

In the USA, the Federal Reserve has been publishing quarterly flow of funds figures for the non-financial non-farm corporate sector since at least 1952; Compustat is a rich source of quarterly company-level cash-flow data for listed companies. Unsystematic coverage and unavailability of data at quarterly frequencies has greatly hindered analysis of investment and credit cycles in Europe. This chapter assembles evidence from disparate flow-of-funds information, considering both aggregate and firm-level data, in order to characterize the savings gap. Historical sector-level information in the ESA79 standard is published by Eurostat in the *New Cronos* Database. Notably, the corporate sectors[1] of the largest European countries, Germany, France, the UK, Italy and Spain (EU5 henceforth) are covered at annual frequencies from 1970 to 1997. Firm-level cash-flow information is provided in the Worldscope database from Bureau Van Dijk and Disclosure, again at annual frequencies, for companies that are listed on a European stock exchange. While not immediately comparable, aggregate and firm-level data are complementary and do provide consistent information, especially concerning the business cycle dynamics. In the next section we present a historical perspective of the savings gap at a sector level, followed by a discussion of the way in which it has been financed. Still using company-level information, we the describe the business cycle behaviour of the savings gap and discuss the way in which the gap is financed across different countries and size classes. A final section concludes. A companion paper in this volume, 'Measuring the Financing Gap of European Corporations. An Update', updates the aggregate analysis, based on recently released Eurostat data in the ESA95 standard. For more detailed information on the data as well as supplementary tables, which have not been included to comply with space limitations, the reader is invited to consult the working paper version of this work.

Aggregate investment, savings and borrowing flows

Figure 30.1 plots corporate investment and savings flows by country,[2] based on the ESA79 *Capital Account*, which includes harmonized sector-level flow-of-funds data at annual frequencies. The data shown are averaged over the last three decades. Savings are sufficient to cover a majority of investment in all countries. UK and Spanish companies are able to finance almost all of their investment internally. Italian, German and to a lesser extent French companies have instead to rely on significant flows of external finance. These averages conceal evolutions in investment that took place over time. With the exception of Germany, corporate investment as a percentage of GDP decreased steadily through the mid-1990s. Corporate savings dynamics were less uniform, generally showing a stable to increasing pattern. The combined effect of lower investment and higher savings resulted in significantly lower needs for external finance in Italy, France and the

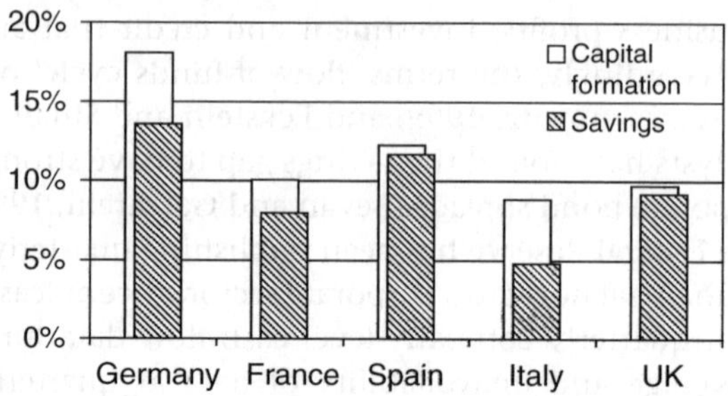

Figure 30.1   Average corporate investment and savings 1970–97, percentage of GDP
*1980–97

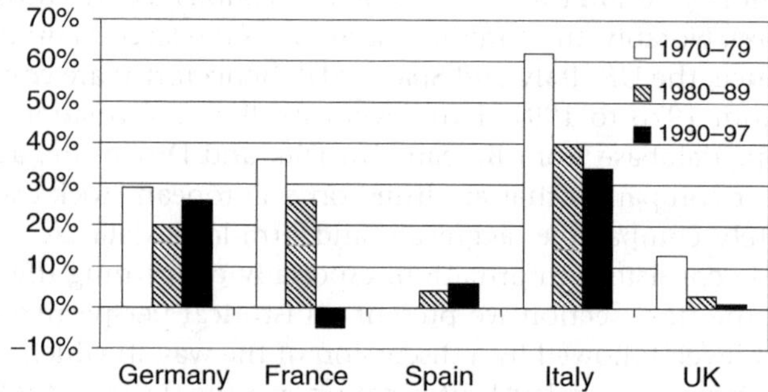

Figure 30.2   Average savings gap, percentage of gross corporate capital formation

UK over time, as illustrated by the savings gap measures in Figure 30.2. In 1990–97, the last period for which data in the ESA79 standard are available, Italy and Germany are the only countries whose corporate sectors made use of a significant share of external finance. The financing gap was very small in Spain and the UK, and France was running a surplus.

How is the aggregate savings gap financed?

The Eurostat ESA79 *Financial Accounts* detail the net increase in financial assets and in financial liabilities for the corporate sector. A net increase in financial liabilities is a source of funds, additional to the internal funds or savings described in the last section, while a net increase in financial assets is a use of funds, in addition to capital formation. The main financial liabilities are loans (both short-term and medium/long-term), bonds and shares. The main assets are again loans (to other sectors, like consumer credit or trade credit owed by foreign companies), bonds (typically government, bank and insurance bonds held by the non-financial corporate sector), shares (of foreign companies), deposits and other short-term investments (referred to as 'cash').

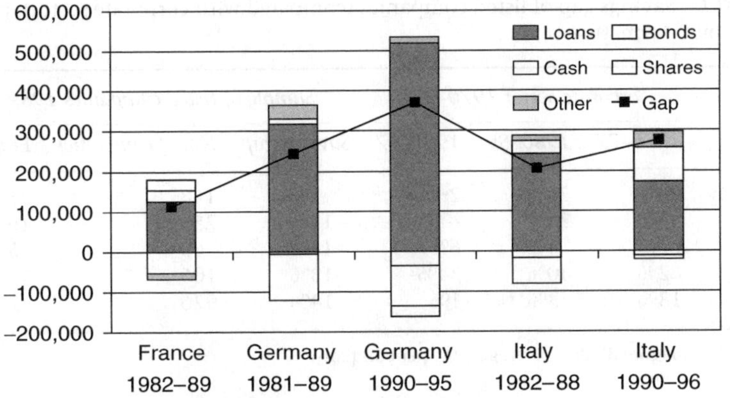

Figure 30.3   Composition of the financing gap, millions

Harmonized data on the flows of funds for the corporate sector are available over the period 1982–96 for the five largest EU economies (1981–95 in the case of Germany). Since the accounts are drawn on a non-consolidated basis, we net financial assets out of the corresponding financial liabilities.[3] Thus, apart from statistical discrepancies, the increase in financial liabilities of the corporate sector equals the sum of the financing gap plus the increase in cash holdings. Figure 30.3, drawn for the countries/periods for which the savings gap is most important, shows that most of the gap is covered by an increase in loans. Bond finance does not play a significant role. Equity issues are important in Italy especially in the 1990s, a period in which several large public sector entities were incorporated and gradually privatised. In all three countries external funds are used to finance cash holdings of the sector, in the form of deposits, bills and short-term bonds.

Analysis of the savings gap across different firm sizes and the business cycle

Cash flow statements for listed companies provide information on capital expenditures as well as retained earnings of each firm, which measure respectively investment and savings. The interest of comparing the savings gap for listed companies with aggregate data is twofold. Firstly, size heterogeneity is often associated to differing patterns in corporate investment and borrowing between large and small companies.[4] Since in several countries small-unlisted companies account for a majority of investment, aggregate data may conceal different dynamics that characterize, especially, large listed companies. Secondly, the dynamics of listed companies might in some cases provide a leading indicator of the evolution of the savings gap over the cycle.

Based on an unbalanced panel extracted from the WorldScope database and covering the period 1989–99, the country breakdown of the savings gap for listed companies is presented in Table 30.1. Savings gapsfor listed companies

Table 30.1   Savings gap of listed companies (compared with corporate sector), per cent of gross capital formation

	Corporate sector 1970–97*			Sample of listed companies 1989–99**		
	1970–79	*1980–89*	*1990–97*	*Savings gap*	*No. of companies*	*Employees****
Germany	29%	20%	26%	1%	148	25,500
France	36%	26%	−5%	−11%	250	16,336
Spain	n.a.	4%	6%	−11%	60	5,860
Italy	62%	40%	34%	−13%	105	12,445
UK	13%	3%	1%	14%	976	7,330

Notes: * From Figure 30.2; ** averages, *** per company.

in continental Europe are significantly smaller than for the aggregate corporate sector. In fact, companies listed in Italy, France and Spain generate internal funds in excess of investment. UK listed companies, on the contrary, display a positive gap, which is also higher than the corporate sector as a whole. Perusal of the summary statistics in Table 30.1 suggests that these differing patterns could depend on the largest companies being the ones running the smallest gaps. Take German listed companies, the largest in our sample as measured by number of employees. Their average savings gap is only 1 per cent, against 26 per cent for the corporate sector on aggregate; this is consistent with the findings of Sauvé and Scheuer (1999) that the largest German companies use much less external finance than their smaller counterparts. On the other hand, UK listed companies are smaller on average and display a savings gap which is higher than the aggregate.[5] In order to check this interpretation, we extend the sample to include all companies listed on EU15 stock exchanges, provided they report cash-flow information on the main variables of interest in any given year.

Size classes are defined in Table 30.2, based on the average number of employees in the years over which each company has been active. It is noteworthy to observe that the smallest size class, companies with less than 100 employees, have expanded at a rate (11% per year) that is three times faster than the average (4% per year).

Table 30.3 details the savings gap and the sources of finance for each class. It confirms our hypothesis that the savings gap decreases on average as company size increases. Smaller companies are the ones that make the largest use of external borrowing and that issue the largest proportion of shares as a proportion of their capital formation. A natural interpretation is that smaller companies are also younger and are growing at a faster pace compared to larger, mature companies. While large companies are more likely to generate stable and sizeable cash flows to finance investment, smaller ones need to rely to a larger extent on external sources. We should also mention that listed companies (small and large alike) are less likely than unlisted ones to suffer from asymmetric information problems related to their ability of raising external finance. Thus, thecommon perception of small

Table 30.2   Definition of size classes by average number of employees, EU15

Name	Class definition based on average no. of employees	Average no. of companies in the sample	Average no. of employees	Average employee growth rate
Size class 1	Less than 100	84	48	11%
Size class 2	Between 100 and 500	429	269	3%
Size class 3	Between 500 and 2000	612	1,035	4%
Size class 4	Between 2,000 and 10,000	504	4,486	4%
Size class 5	Above 10,000	375	43,499	4%
Total	All	2,004	5,986	4%

Table 30.3   Corporate sample: net external financial sources 1989–99, per cent of gross capital formation

	Gross MLT borrowing	Repayment of long term debt	Net short term borrowing	=Total net borrowing	Net share proceeds	Net other sources	Cash and other investments	Savings gap
Size class 1	49%	−22%	−4%	23%	58%	2%	−21%	61%
Size class 2	43%	−32%	−5%	6%	41%	3%	−17%	33%
Size class 3	50%	−38%	−2%	11%	21%	0%	−14%	17%
Size class 4	51%	−37%	−2%	12%	13%	−1%	−10%	14%
Size class 5	43%	−36%	−1%	6%	8%	1%	−14%	0%

companies as financially constrained and mostly reliant on internal finance for their investment needs is potentially less relevant to our sample.

It was shown in the first section that the savings gap followed a downward trend over the past three decades. In Figure 30.4, we have plotted the annual dynamics by country and by size class. Volatility over time of the savings gap is very high, and it dwarfs cross-country differences as well as, to some extent, cross sectional ones. Each country graph also plots the GDP growth rate, suggesting that savings gaps grow at the beginning of a slowdown and decline quickly as the slowdown persists. The observation is consistent with standard beliefs about the business cycle. Corporate savings (that is profits) are the first to be hit in a slowdown, while fixed investment decisions made in the past are still given course and the inventory component of investment increases. Subsequently, fixed investment as well as production and inventories are reduced and the gap falls, often sharply. The chart also shows the evolution over time of the savings gap for listed companies in each country. Turning points for these samples appear to lead the aggregate.

Conclusion

The overwhelming conclusion of this chapter is that corporate investment is mostly financed through internal sources. Even in a country like Italy, whose

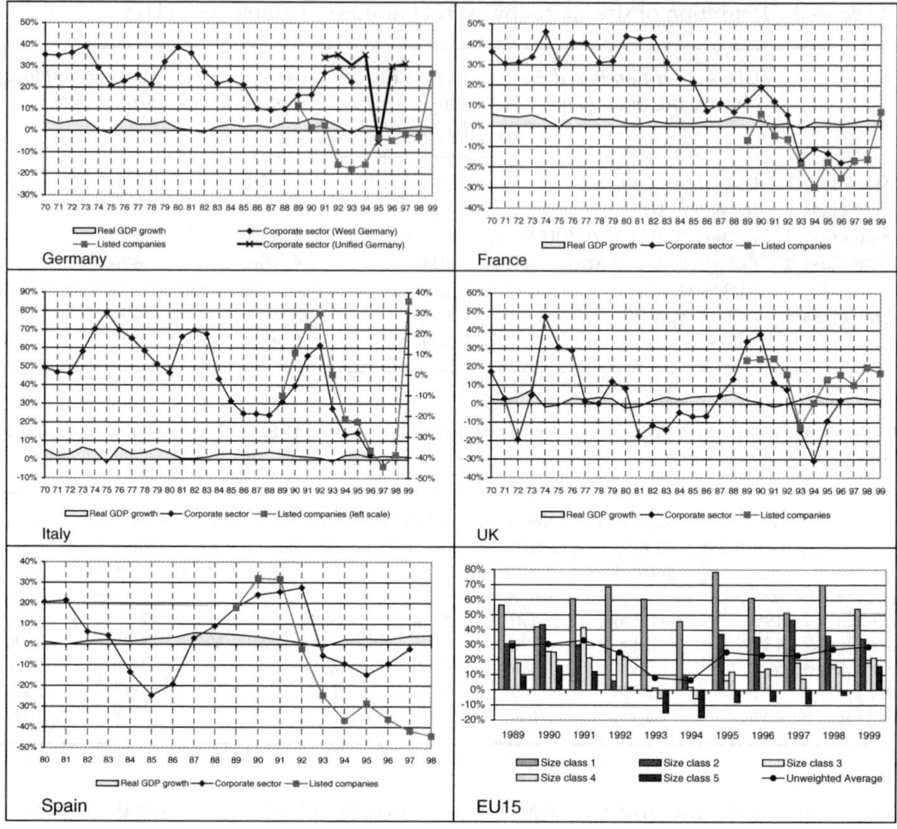

Figure 30.4 Corporate savings gap and the business cycle per cent of gross capital formation; percentage growth

corporations financed over half of their investment externally in the 1970s, firms have dramatically reduced reliance on external sources. The observation is somewhat counterintuitive. Financial markets have developed impressively over the same period and one would expect that more sophisticated financial markets should free companies from overreliance on internal cash flows. On aggregate this is not the case. In continental Europe, listed companies are the ones making the least use of external finance, while one would expect exactly the opposite. The general conclusion is further supported if one computes the time-correlation between savings and investment at a corporate sector level. Correlation is quite high for the largest economies in continental Europe, and in particular for Germany (61%) and Italy (52%). It is lower for Spain (33%) and France (26%), while perhaps not surprisingly is negative for the UK (−21%). Exploring the implications of these stylized facts in the context of existing theories of investment and capital structure should make for an interesting research agenda. Some additional perspective is provided by a companion study in this volume entitled 'Measuring the Financing Gap of European Corporations. An Update'.

Other stylized facts emerge from the analysis. Firstly, external finance is mostly in the form of loans. The working paper version of this article contains evidence on the maturity structure of these loans, showing that, outside Germany and France, short-term loans prevail. Share issues are the second source of external finance, although smaller than loans, while bond issues appear negligible over the period covered. Secondly, when data for listed companies are analysed, one finds the smallest companies displaying the fastest growth and the highest savings gap. At the other extreme, the largest companies rely almost entirely on internal finance. This latest finding is at odds with a commonly held view that small companies are credit-constrained and need to rely on internal finance. Further research should try to reconcile such a view with the facts, ideally distinguishing between listed and unlisted companies. Finally, variation of the savings gap over the business cycle is way more important than variation across countries or size classes (or sectors, as shown in the working paper version of this article). High variability over time in corporate savings and investment is at the origin of this time series behaviour. Further research should model these two components separately, possibly embedding them into a macro-economic model.

Notes

1 European system of integrated economic accounts ESA (1978), pp. 26–7, defines the corporate sector as follows. 'The sector non-financial corporate and quasi-corporate enterprises (S10) consists of enterprises which are institutional units – i.e. enterprises whose distributive and financial transactions are distinct from those of their owners – and which are principally engaged in the production of goods and non-financial market services.' Public corporations and enterprises are included provided they are 'recognized as independent legal entities and are principally engaged in the production of goods and non-financial market services.'

2 For an analysis of aggregate investment see Catinat *et al.* (1987) and European Commission (2001). To simplify the analysis in this chapter, the figures for gross savings include capital transfers from other sectors (mainly government subsidies) and are net of capital transfers to other sectors (mostly taxes paid to the government). Net purchases of land and intangible assets are included into gross capital formation.

3 The reader will find a discussion of gross flows for all countries, as well as an illustration of the maturity compositions of the increase in loans in the working paper version of this article. Evidence from a large sample of companies studied by the European Committee of Central Balance Sheet Offices, showing consistent patterns with the ones expected from the observed flows, is also presented.

4 Fazzari, Hubbard and Petersen (1989) and Gilchrist and Himmelberg (1992) find that, possibly because of financing constraints, investment for small companies is more sensitive to the availability of internal finance than is the case for large companies. Gertler and Gilchrist (1994) show that small companies are forced to reduce their borrowing during a recession, while large companies are able to expand their use of debt in order to compensate for lower internal funds. However, the interpretation of excess investment-cash-flow sensitivities as a useful indicator of financing constraints has been called into question by Kaplan and Zingales (2000). Bond *et al.* (1997), comparing companies in

the UK, Belgium, France and Germany, find that investment by UK companies is more sensitive to internal sources than it is the case for the European companies. Focusing on German companies, Stöss (1996) fails to find any discrimination of smaller enterprises by German banks.
5   Listed Spanish companies are smaller than UK ones on average and still they run a negative savings gap. However, the Spanish sample is much smaller (only 60 companies on average) and the weighted average much more likely to be dominated by a few large companies running negative gaps than it is the case for the UK (almost 1,000 companies in the sample).

References

Bevan, A. and Garzarelli, F. (1999) 'Corporate bond spreads and the business cycle: introducing GSSPREAD', *Goldman Sachs Working Paper*.

Bond, S.R., Elston, J.A., Mairesse, J. and Mulkay, B. (1997) 'Financial factors and investment in Belgium, France, Germany and the UK: a comparison using company panel data', Working Paper no. 5900. New York: National Bureau of Economic Research.

Catinat M., Cawley, R., Ilzkovitz, F, Italianer, A. and Mors, M. (1987) 'The determinants of investment', *European Economy*, 31: 5–60.

Ekstein, O and Sinai, A. (1986) 'The mechanisms of the business cycle in the postwar era', in R.J. Gordon (ed), *The American Business Cycle*, Chicago: The University of Chicago Press

European system of integrated economic accounts ESA, November 1978 Second Edition.

Eurostat, *European system of Accounts: ESA 1995*.

European Commission (2001) 'The determinants of investment: an overview for the EU and the US', *Technical Note from the Commission Services*.

Fazzari, S., Hubbard, M.R.G. and Petersen, B.C. (1998) 'Financing constraints and corporate investment', *Brookings Papers on Economic Activity*, 141–95.

Feldstein, M and Horioka, C. (1980) 'Domestic savings and international capital flows', *The Economic Journal*, 90: (June), 314–29.

Galizia, F., (2001) 'The savings gap of European corporations: a first look at the available data', *Economic and Financial Reports*, 2001/01, Luxembourg: European Investment Bank. (With T. Steinberger), also as (2004): *Working Papers and Studies*, Luxembourg: Eurostat.

Galizia, F. (2003) 'Measuring the financing gap of European corporations. an update', *Economic and Financial Reports*, European Investment Bank, 2003/02. Also (2004): *Working Papers and Studies*, Eurostat.

Gertler, M and Gilchrist, S. (1991) 'Monetary policy, business cycles and behavior of small manufacturing firms', *Quarterly Journal of Economics*, 109: (May), 309–40.

Gilchrist, S and Himmelberg, C.P. (1995) 'Evidence on the role of cash flow for investment', *Journal of Monetary Economics*, 36: 541–72.

Kaplan, S.N and Zingales, L. (2000) 'Investment-cash flow sensitivities are not valid measures of financing constraints', *Quarterly Journal of Economics*, (May).

Sauvé, A and Scheuer, M. (eds) (1999) *Corporate Finance in Germany and France*, Joint Research Project of the Deutsche Bundesbank and the Banque de France.

Stöss, E. (1996) 'Enterprises' financing structure and their response to monetary policy stimuli. An analysis based on the Deutsche Bundesbank's corporate balance sheet statistics', *Deutsche Bundesbank Discussion Paper*, 9/96.

Zarnowitz, V. (1999) 'Theory and history behind business cycles: are the 1990s the onset of a golden age?', *Journal of Economic Perspectives*, 13: (2 Spring), 69–90.

31
Explaining the Time-Varying NAIRU in the Euro-Area

*Camille Logeay and Silke Tober**

Introduction

There is no consensus as to what caused the significant increase in the unemployment rate in Europe since the early 1970s. Although there is ample evidence that institutional changes in the early 1970s contributed to the increase in the Nairu and thereby also pushed up actual unemployment, there seem to be limits to what these factors can explain.[1] By using a state-space model to estimate the Nairu in the Euro-area since 1975 and to gauge the effect of certain exogenous variables we hope to contribute to this debate. We tested the effect of three other exogenous variables that find mention in the literature: wage wedge, productivity slowdown and real short-term interest rates. The novel approach of applying the Kalman-filter technique with explicit exogenous variables allows us to quantify the effect of changes in these variables on the Nairu. We find that all three variables have a significant effect, the largest being the one of the real interest rate with a coefficient of 0.4.

The magnitude of the effect of real interest rates on the Nairu is also found in other studies. In these studies the authors do not refer to it as the effect of real interest rates on the Nairu, but rather the long-term effect of real interest rates on unemployment. However, this is the same thing given that the unemployment gap is zero in the long run. Fitoussi, Jestaz, Phelps and Zoega (2000) for example find that a one percentage point increase in real long-term interest rates causes a long-term increase in the unemployment rate by one-quarter of a percentage point – somewhat smaller than the 0.4 percentage points arrived at in our study. Similarly, Nickell, Nunziata, Ochel and Quintini (2002) and IMF (2003, chap. 4) calculate a long-term effect of 0.2 per cent. Blanchard and Wolfers (2000) come up with half a

* Research for this study was financially supported by the German government. Gustav Horn, Ulrich Fritsche, Werner Röger and Michael Pflüger offered valuable comments for which we are grateful.

379

percentage point. Our approach has the advantage of allowing us to take account of the time-series properties of the variables analysed and not requiring us to resort to somewhat arbitrary longer-term averages of real interest rates to determine their longer-term effect on unemployment.

Fitoussi, Jestaz, Phelps and Zoega (2000), Ball and Mankiw (2002), Ball (1999) and Blanchard and Katz (1997) relate the marked increase in unemployment and the fact that it remained high to the restrictive stance of monetary policy. In the approach presented here, a long-term effect of monetary policy on the Nairu requires the rejection of the Fisher relation. This is because symmetry is assumed by design. If the Nairu is found to increase as a reaction to a rise in real interest rates it will decline by the same amount once real interest rates fall to their initial level.

The remainder of the chapter is structured as follows: In the next section we sketch the way in which we apply the Kalman-filter technique and discuss the properties of the data used. We then present the outcome of the Kalman-filter regression of the Euro-area Nairu using explicit exogenous variables. A final section concludes.

Modelling the Nairu and the Phillips curve for the Euro-area

The Kalman-filter technique (state-space modelling) offers a fruitful approach to estimating the Nairu because it is designed to identify an unobservable variable – like the Nairu – on the basis of assumptions made about the econometric properties of the variable and the economic interrelation between this variable and other observable variables.[2] In what follows we model the Nairu as a nonstationary trend and estimate it simultaneously with a Phillips curve, the latter being the relationship through which the unemployment gap – the deviation of actual unemployment from the Nairu – affects inflation. We use a procedure presented by Kuttner (1994).

The Phillips curve is derived from two equations: a wage-setting equation (31.1) and a price-setting equation (31.2) (Layard, Nickell and Jackman 1991: 361–96).

Wages (w) are dependent on adaptive price expectations ($p^{cpi,e}$), labour productivity ($prod$), some long-term wage-push variables (Z^W), such as the wage wedge or institutional changes, and on the general conditions in the labour market that are here proxied by the unemployment rate (u):

$$\Delta w_t = \Delta p_t^{cpi,e} + \alpha_2 \Delta prod_t - \beta_0 u_t + \delta_w Z_t^W + \epsilon_t \tag{31.1}$$

Prices are determined by marginal costs and supply shocks, the latter being proxied by the oil price (p^{oil}) for the short-term horizon and by (Z^p) for the long-term horizon. This latter variable includes for example the real short-term interest rate, the changing conditions of competition, and so on:[3]

$$\Delta p_t^{cpi} = \Delta w_t - \beta_2 \Delta prod_t + \delta_1 \Delta p_t^{oil} + \delta_p Z_t^p + \epsilon_t' \tag{31.2}$$

The Phillips curve is obtained by putting the wage equation (??) into the price equation (31.2):

$$\Delta p_t^{cpi} = \pi_t = \pi_t^e + (\alpha_2 - \beta_2)\Delta prod_t - \beta_0 u_t + \delta_1 \Delta p_t^{oil} + (\delta_w Z_t^W + \delta_p Z_t^p) + v_t \tag{31.3}$$

The long-run solution ($\pi_t = \pi_t^e$; $\Delta p_t^{oil} = v_t = 0$; $\Delta prod_t = \overline{\Delta prod_t}$) yields to the Nairu ($u_t^*$):

$$u_t^* = \frac{(\alpha_2 - \beta_2)\overline{\Delta prod_t} + (\delta_w \mathbf{Z}_t^w + \delta_p \mathbf{Z}_t^p)}{\beta_0} \tag{31.4}$$

Expectations are modelled as a backward-looking process: $\pi_t^e = \gamma \pi_{t-1}$. The choice of adaptive expectations can be justified on the grounds that employees try to compensate for past losses in purchasing power and that the model yields good results under this assumption ($\gamma \in [0, 1]$).[4]

The Phillips curve is then:

$$\pi_t = \gamma \pi_{t-1} + (\alpha_2 - \beta_2)(\Delta prod_t - \overline{\Delta prod_t}) - \beta_0(u - u^*)_t + \delta_1 \Delta p_t^{oil} + v_t \tag{31.5}$$

The key idea of our Kalman-filter approach is to divide the unemployment rate (u) into two components: the unemployment gap ($u - u^*$) and the Nairu (u^*). Both components are unobservable. But by assumption, the unemployment gap significantly influences inflation. The Nairu indicates how much an economy can and must grow in order to prevent both inflationary and deflationary tendencies. The Kalman filter uses this economic relationship embodied in the Phillips curve as well as the assumed statistical properties of both components to extract both unobservable variables from the data.

The state-space model is written below. The first three equations (31.6 to 31.8) specify the stochastic properties of the unobserved variables (state equations). In our model the unemployment gap is modelled as an AR(2) process and the instationarity of the Nairu as a local linear model. A local linear model is more general than the random-walk approach in that it allows one to model the Nairu either as an I(1)-variable or as an I(2)-variable. In addition, it is possible to test whether the random-walk asssumptions are too restrictive which turned out to be the case here. The Nairu is therefore modelled as a random walk with a stochastic drift, that is as an I(2)-variable. The modelling of the Nairu as an integrated random walk should not be interpreted in economic terms. As in Denis, McMorrow and Röger (2002) and Fabiani and Mestre (2001) it is a frequently found chracteristic that may be induced by the smoothness of the data resulting for example from seasonal adjustment. The term 'implicit' in equations (31.7) and (31.9) refers to the part of the Nairu that is not explicitly explained by exogenous variables; in our case this includes, for example, institutional factors. ($\mathbf{Z}_t^{nairu}$) contains those variables affecting the Nairu that are made explicit here. The fourth equation (31.9) is a definition, defining the unemployment rate as the sum of the unemployment gap and Nairu. The last equation (31.10, observation equation) is the Phillips curve that describes the interrelation between the unobserved unemployment gap and the observed inflation rate. $\mathbf{X}_t^{phillips}$ contains exogenous variables that explain the development of inflation rate (lags of inflation, labour productivity growth and the oil price in first differences).

$$(u - u^*)_t = ar_1(u - u^*)_{t-1} + ar_2(u - u^*)_{t-2} + \epsilon_t^{ugap} \tag{31.6}$$

$$NAIRU_t^{implicit} = NAIRU_{t-1}^{implicit} + trend_t + \epsilon_t^{nairu} \tag{31.7}$$

$$trend_t = trend_{t-1} + \epsilon_t^{trend} \tag{31.8}$$

$$u_t = (u - u^*)_t + (NAIRU_t^{implicit} + \delta Z_t^{nairu}) \tag{31.9}$$

$$\pi_t = -\beta_0(u - u^*)_t + \gamma X_t^{phillips} + \epsilon_t^{\pi} \tag{31.10}$$

$$memo : u_t^* = NAIRU_t = NAIRU_t^{implicit} + \delta Z_t^{nairu}$$

The Nairu is estimated for the aggregate Euro-area rather than for the individual countries. The latter has the disadvantage that the interdependence between economic developments in the individual countries is not taken into account unless one has multi-country models. However, the indirect method has the advantage that existing differences in institutions and transmission mechanisms of shocks can be taken into consideration. Most of the data used are provided by the database of the ECB's Area Wide Model (AWM).[5] The data is seasonally adjusted and refers to the Euro-area with 12 member states, that is, Germany, France, Italy, Spain, the Netherlands, Austria, Portugal, Finland, Ireland, Belgium, Luxembourg and Greece. The time series for the price of oil (Brent, US dollar) is taken from the IMF's International Financial Statistics; the series for a synthetic euro was constructed using the exchange rate series for the 12 member states provided by the IMF; the weights correspond to each country's share in the Euro-area's real GDP in 1995. Table 31.1 below and Figure 31.3 in the Appendix provide a synopsis of the data. Table 31.3 in the Appendix provides the results from unit-root tests.

Table 31.1   Description of the data

Abbreviation	Name	Integration order*
$inflation_{yoy}$	Inflation rate; year-on-year growth rate of HICP in %	I(1)
alq	Unemployment rate (standardized) in %	I(1)
dlprod	Quarter-on-quarter growth rate of labour productivity (real GDP/employment) in % p.a.	I(1)
oil	Oil price in euros (1995 = 100)	I(1)
$dloil_{yoy}$	Year-on-year growth rate of the oil price in euro in %	I(1)
realzins	Real interest rate; nominal short-term (3-months) interest rate minus $inflation_{yoy}$	I(1)
wedge	Wage wedge in % of gross wages[b]	I(1)

* The test results are presented in the appendix.
[b] Includes income tax and social security contributions of both employers and employees.

Table 31.2   Output of the Kalman-filter estimation with exogenous variables: maximum likelihood estimates and statistics, 1975Q1–2001Q4 (108 obs.)

Variables	Coefficients	s.e.	t-stat
State equations			
AR1	1.9479		
AR2	−0.9700	lower bound reached	
$Var(\epsilon^{nairu})$	6.90E-03		
$Var(\epsilon^{trend})$	1.73E-03	< 3.E-03	not binding
$Var(\epsilon^{ugap})$	4.03E-04		
hp_dlprod(−4):	−0.3222	0.1664	−1.9355
hp_realzins(−5):	0.4007	0.2303	1.7401
wedge(−1)	0.1679	0.0907	1.8519
Phillips curve (observation equation)			
Intercept	–	–	–
unemployment gap	−0.1488	0.0627	−2.3731
$inflation_{yoy}(-1)$	1.1715	0.0359	32.623
$inflation_{yoy}(-4)$	−0.5324	0.0818	−6.5089
$inflation_{yoy}(-5)$	0.3365	0.0693	4.8529
$dloil_{yoy}(0)$	0.0001	0.0000	3.2180
$dloil_{yoy}(-8)$	0.0001	0.0000	4.5077
Innovation var	9.11E-02		
−2∗log-likelihood:	−309.2833	LR-stat=12.364> $\chi^2(3)$	
Residual diagnostics			
State equations			
Ljung–Box Q(4) stat. = 7.5703		p-value = 0.1086	
Jarque–Bera stat. = 1.1229		p-value = 0.5704	
Phillips curve			
Ljung–Box Q(4) stat. = 3.1829		p-value = 0.5277	
Jarque–Bera stat. = 2.0026		p-value = 0.3674	

Kalman-filter estimate of the Nairu using explicit exogenous variables

The Kalman-filter estimate is produced with the programme GAP (2.2) developed by the European Commission.[6] The results are reported in Table 31.2. The first part of the output table refers to the three state equations (31.6–31.8), the second part to the Phillips curve (equation 31.10).

We explicitly tested for three exogenous variables: the short-term real interest rate, the wage wedge and productivity growth. For the short-term real interest rate and productivity growth an HP-filter ($\lambda = 100$) was first applied to avoid capturing small and erratic deviations (see Figure 31.1). Productivity can affect the Nairu via its influence on wages and prices and was found to be significant in Nairu estimates for the United States (Stiglitz, 1997). The wage wedge proxies the supply side influence of fiscal policy on the Nairu, the real interest rate is interpreted as a proxy for the effect of monetary policy.

The short-term real interest rate is the difference between the short-term nominal rate and inflation. Inflation is calculated as year-on-year changes of the consumer

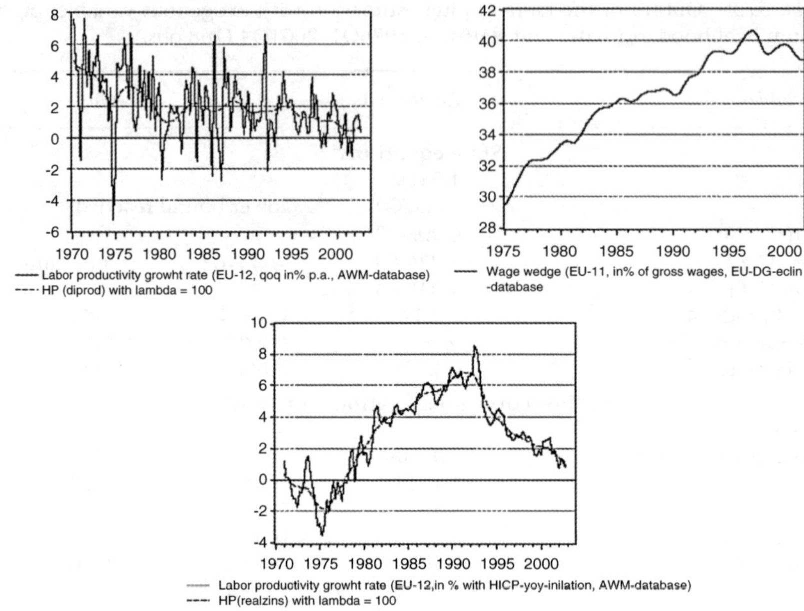

Figure 31.1   Potential exogenous variables affecting the Nairu

price index (y-o-y inflation rate). A positive lagged effect of real interest rates on the Nairu can be expected: an increase in real interest rates lowers investment, consumption and – through its influence on the exchange rate – exports. The full impact including multiplier effects should only be felt after more than one year.[7] An analogous reaction is assumed in the case of a decline in real interest rate.

The wage wedge is calculated as the percentage share of income tax and social security contributions of employees and employers in gross wages.[8] A positive sign is to be expected as an increase in the wage wedge implies an increase in labour costs which in themselves increase the equilibrium level of unemployment.[9]

As the measure for productivity we use labour productivity (real GDP divided by total employment) already tested for in the Phillips curve. Productivity can affect the Nairu if wages and prices do not fully adjust in line with it. For example, if wages do not reflect a given slowdown in productivity growth they give rise to inflationary pressures. Either firms are then able to raise prices accordingly, so that inflation increases without changing the rate of unemployment; or firms are unable to raise prices – due to high competition and/or low demand – in which case inflation will remain unchanged but unemployment will rise. Both cases imply an increase in the Nairu so that one would expect the coefficient to be negatively signed.

All three variables were found to be significant when tested for separately and when tested for together. The coefficients were similar in both cases. Consequently the model presented here includes all three exogenous variables.

The level of the real interest rate in the Nairu equation is significant at lag 5, the coefficient being 0.4. A one percentage point increase in the real interest rate thus raises the Nairu by 0.4. Given that the real interest rate in the Euro-area increased by about 7.5 percentage points from 1975 until 1992, according to this model 3.0 percentage points of the increase in the Nairu – and thus 43 per cent of the increase in the Nairu observed in this period (7 percentage points) – is explained by the increase in real interest rates.

Productivity growth is significant at lag 4. The coefficient is –0.3. A slowdown in the speed of productivity improvements by 1 percentage point therefore causes the Nairu to increase by 0.3 percentage point.[10] We interpret it to mean that wages adjust to changes in productivity to a great degree but not fully. The decrease in productivity growth by 0.7 percentage point from 1975 to 1992 can according to this estimate explain an increase in the Nairu by 0.2 percentage point.

The coefficient of the wage wedge is estimated as 0.2 (lag 1) implying that a one percentage point increase in this variable raises the Nairu by 0.2 percentage point.[11] Between 1975 and 1992, 1.4 percentage points of the increase in the Nairu can be attributed to the 8.3 percentage point increase in the wage wedge during this period.

The AR-coefficients of the state equation (unemployment gap) imply a cycle length of 10.5 years.[12] The residuals can be interpreted as white noise. The normality test for residuals is accepted for the state equation and the Phillips curve at the 10 per cent level.

The sum of the coefficients of the lagged endogenous variable is 0.9756. The unemployment gap has a significant negative effect (coefficient = – 0.15; *t*-statistic = – 2.37). Figure 31.2 presents the estimated Nairu and unemployment gap for the Euro-area.

Conclusion

Our econometric analysis supports the hypothesis that the Euro-area's Nairu varies over time. Given the lack of comparable data on labour market institutions we

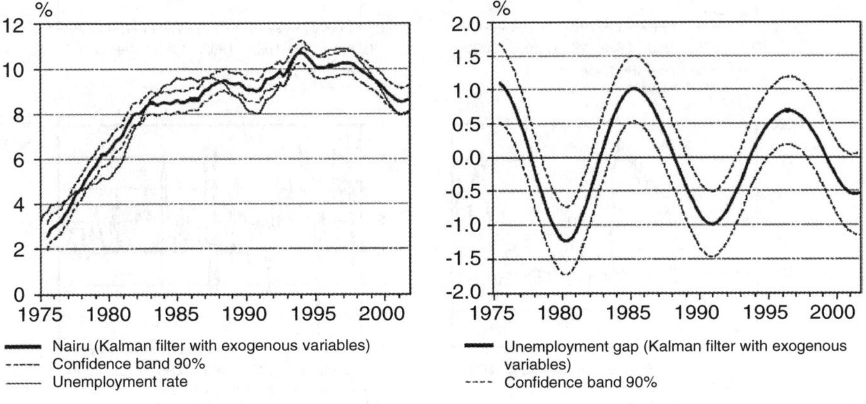

Figure 31.2 Kalman-filter estimate of Nairu and unemployment gap in the Euro-area

chose an econometric technique that does not require such detailed information. The Kalman-filter estimates a time-variable Nairu using information provided by the simultaneously estimated Phillips curve without requiring the individual determinants of the Nairu to be specified. They are implicitly contained in the estimation. It furthermore offers the possibility of specifying individual exogenous variables and quantifying their effect. Short-term real interest rates proved to have a significant influence on the Nairu as did the wage wedge and productivity growth.

Our econometric analysis produced the following results: The Nairu in the countries of the Euro-area rose from around 2.7 per cent in 1975 to 10.5 per cent in 1994; in 2001 the Nairu was 8.6 per cent.[13] A change in the short-term real interest rate by 1 percentage point leads to a change in the Nairu by 0.4 percentage points. Increases in the wage wedge and productivity growth by one percentage point change the Nairu by 0.2 percentage points and −0.3 percentage points, respectively.

The increase in the Nairu between 1975 and 1992 was largely caused by the change in real interest rate (+7.5 percentage points) and the wage wedge (+8.5 percentage points). According to our estimate, these two factors can explain 4.4 percentage points of the 7 percentage-points increase in the Nairu during that period. Since the mid-1990s the real interest rate has come down substantially, in part reversing its effect on the Nairu. In contrast the wage wedge has remained high.

Appendix

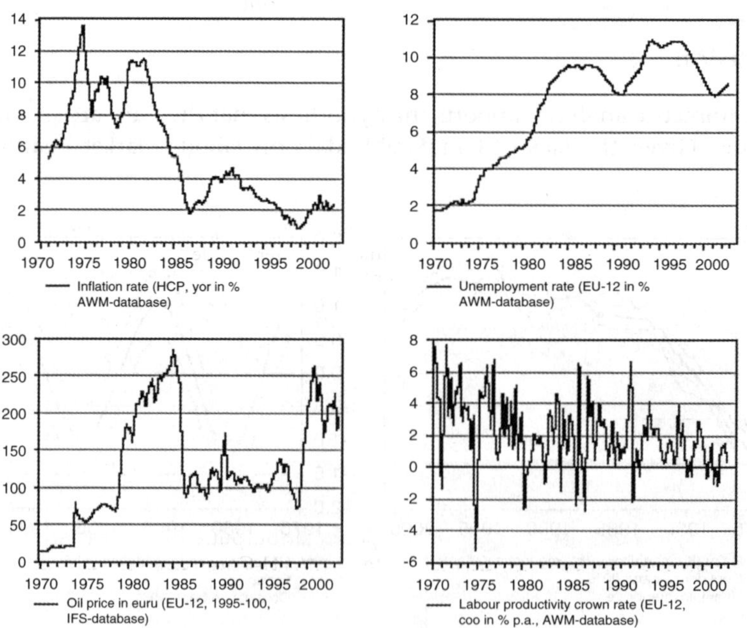

Figure 31.3   Presentation of the data

Table 31.3 Unit-root tests

Variable	Sample	Test type[a]	Lag-length [b]	Deter-ministic	Test-stat	Test-prob[c]
inflation$_{yoy}$	1970–2002	ADF	10	c	−1.47	0.543
		ADF	6	c	−1.37	0.595
		ERS	10	c	−1.57	***
		ERS	6	c	−1.43	***
ur	1970–2002	ADF	5	c	−1.92	0.321
		ADF	2	c	−1.93	0.319
		ERS	5	c	−0.18	***
		ERS	2	c	−0.22	***
oil	1970–2003	ADF	4	c	−2.08	0.254
		ADF	0	c	−1.88	0.34
		ERS	5	c	−0.57	***
		ERS	0	c	−0.71	***
dlprod	1970–2002	ADF	0	c	−9.6	0
		ERS	9	c	0.18	***
		ERS	3	c	−1.18	***
		ADF	0	c,trend	−10.66	0
		ERS	9	c,trend	−1.45	***
		ERS	1	c,trend	−4.93	
realzins	1970–2002	ADF	12	c	−1.61	0.473
		ADF	0	c	−1.43	0.568
		ERS	12	c	−1.37	***
		ERS	0	c	−1.33	***
		ADF	12	none	−0.95	0.302
		ADF	0	none	−1.02	0.277
wedge	1970–2001	ADF	10	c	−2.72	0.074
		ERS	12	c	−0.63	***
		ERS	8	c	−0.3	***
		ADF	10	c, trend	−0.6	0.977
		ERS	12	c, trend	−0.98	***
		ERS	10	c, trend	−0.46	***

[a]ADF: Augmented-Dickey-Fuller test; ERS: Elliott-Rothenberg-Stock DF-GLS test. [b]The lag-length was choosen along AIC and SC criteria; when they indicate different lag-lengths, both are reported. [c] *, **, *** = accept H_0 at 1 per cent, 5 per cent, 10 per cent

Notes

1 See Nickell, Nunziata, Ochel and Quintini (2002), Machin and Manning (1999: 3107), and Blanchard and Katz (1997: 68).
2 Kalman-filter estimates of the Nairu of the OECD are found in Turner, Boone, Giorno, Meacci, Rae and Richardson (2001); for the IMF see Laxton, Isard, Faruqee, Prasad and Turtelboom (1998) and IMF (2001) as well as Masi (1997) for the different methods used by the IMF to estimate the Nairu and potential output. Denis, McMorrow and Röger (2002) provide the Kalman-filter estimate of the EU-Commission.
3 By including the price of oil in the Phillips curve we eliminated the effect of the oil price on inflation. Turner, Boone, Giorno, Meacci, Rae and Richardson (2001: 171–216) and IMF (2001) do pretty much the same. They, however, put the real oil price as well as additional supply shocks, such as real import prices, into the Phillips curve. Otherwise an

increase in inflation due to an oil price shock would be attributed to the unemployment gap and would imply an increase in the Nairu given unchanged unemployment. It follows that in the Kalman-filter regression the effect of oil price changes on inflation is also eliminated. We do not however thereby eliminate the effects of oil price changes on the Nairu but only those on inflation: if the change in relative prices resulting from an oil price shock cause the Nairu to increase – either because real wages so not adjust accordingly or productive capacities are reduced – this increase will show up in our estimate. The rationale for eliminating the direct effect of the oil price is that a price level jump due to an adverse supply shock cannot be prevented by a central bank, not even if it acted very restrictively. In, the economic profession it has furthermore become common sense that central banks should not react to supply shocks – cf. Ball and Mankiw (1995), Shapiro (1994) and Taylor (1996: 191–5).

4   See Mankiw (2001: C58f). The sum of the coefficients of lagged inflation are not set equal to zero; for a discussion of this assumption see Sargent (1971) and Hall (1999).

5   Fagan, Henry and Mestre (2001). The data constructed by Fagan, Henry and Mestre (2001) can be found under http://www.ecb.int; A revised and updated version was directly obtained from the authors.

6   The programme is available free of charge under http://webfarm.jrc.cec.eu.int/. Questions concerning the programme can be addressed to the authors of this chapter or to christophe.planas@jrc.it and alessandro.rossi@jrc.it (The European Commission, Joint Research Centre, Italy).

7   For a recent summary of the timing of monetary policy effects in the Euro-area using different models, see European Central Bank (2002: 43–53). Symmetry is an implicit assumption. Should the effect of interest rate changes in fact be asymmetric if monetary policy is expansionary or restrictive, the modelling here would imply an averaging of both coefficients. Testing for asymmetry promises to be a fruitful endeavour for future research, especially given recent findings of the ECB to this effect.

8   The time series is taken from the European Commission's database.

9   To the extent that not only wages but also social security contributions are included, a lower real employee wage is theoretically probable so that labour costs would not increase; see Blanchard and Wolfers (2000: 13).

10   This is similar to the -0.34 percentage point in IMF (2003), but smaller than the effects found in Fitoussi, Jestaz, Phelps and Zoega (2000) (-1.1) and Blanchard and Wolfers (2000) (-0.7).

11   This largely corresponds to the coefficient found by OECD (1999).

12   The formula for calculating the cycle length is given in Jaeger and Parkinson (1994, p. 338).

13   Like ours, most other economic regressions show a marked reduction in the Nairu since 1996; see for example IMF (2001: 4). IMF (2001: 8) uses the Kalman-filter technique (without explicit exogenous variable) to derive a no-supply-shock Nairu that has hovered around 9.5% since the first quarter of 1983 and a Nairu with supply shocks that increased from 8.5% (1983) to almost 11% in 1994 and then slowly diminished to reach slightly more than 8% in the year 2000. The OECD's Nairu (without supply shocks, Turner, Boone, Giorno, Meacci, Rae and Richardson, 2001) climbs from 5.5% in 1980 to 9.2% in 1995 and then falls to reach 8.8% in 1999.

References

Ball, L. (1999) 'Aggregate demand and long-run unemployment', *Brookings Papers on Economic Activity*, 2: 189–251.

Ball, L. and Mankiw, N.G. (1995) 'Relative-price changes as aggregate supply shocks', *The Quarterly Journal of Economics*, 110: 161–93.

Ball, L. and Mankiw, N.G. (2002) 'The NAIRU in theory and practice', *Journal of Economic Perspectives*, 16: 115–36.

Blanchard, O. and Katz, L.F. (1997) 'What we know and what we do not know about the natural rate of unemployment', *Journal of Economic Perspectives*, 11: 51–72.

Blanchard, O.J. and Wolfers, J. (2000) 'The role of shocks and institutions in the rise of European unemployment: the aggregate evidence', *The Economic Journal*, 110: C1–33.

Denis, C., McMorrow, K. and Roger, W. (2002) 'Production function approach to calculating potential growth and output gaps – Estimates for the EU Member States and the US', *Economic Papers*, 176, Bruxelles: European Commission.

European Central Bank (2002) 'Recent findings on monetary policy transmission in the Euro area', *Monthly Bulletin*, October, Frankfurt am Main: ECB, 43–53.

Fabiani, S. and Mestre, R. (2001) 'A system approach for measuring the Euro area NAIRU', Working Paper no. 65, Frankfurt am Main: European Central Bank.

Fagan, G., Henry, J. and Mestre, R. (2001) 'An area-wide model (AWM) for the Euro area', Working Paper no. 42, Frankfurt am Main: European Central Bank.

Fitoussi, J.-P., Jestaz, D., Phelps, E.S. and Zoega, G. (2000) 'Roots of the recent recoveries: labor reforms or private sector forces?', *Brookings Papers on Economic Activity*, 1: 237–311.

Hall, R.E. (1999) 'Comment on Estrella and Mishkin', in J.B. Taylor (ed), *Monetary Policy Rules*, Chicago: The University of Chicago Press, 431–35.

International Monetary Fund (2003) *World Economic Outlook – Growth and Institutions*, Washington D.C.: Internationl Monetary Fund.

International Monetary Fund (2001) 'Monetary and exchange rate policies of the Euro area: selected issues', *Country Report*, 1/201, Washington D.C.:Internationl Monetary Fund.

Jaeger, A. and Parkinson, M. (1994) 'Some evidence on hysteresis in unemployment rates', *European Economic Review*, 38: 329–42.

Kuttner, K.N. (1994) 'Estimating potential output as a latent variable', *Journal of Business & Economic Statistics*, 12: 361–68.

Laxton, D.M., Isard, P., Faruqee, H., Prasad, E.S. and Turtelboom, B. (1998) 'Multimod Mark III: the core dynamic and steady state model', Occasional Paper no. 164, Washington D.C.:Internationl Monetary Fund.

Layard, R., Nickell, S. and Jackman, R. (1991) *Macroeconomic Performance and the Labour Market*, Oxford: Oxford University Press.

Machin, S. and Manning, A. (1999) 'The causes and consequences on long-term unemployment in Europe', in *Hanbook for Labour Economics* , in O.C. Ashenfelter and D. Card (eds), vol. 3C, Ch. 47, Amsterdam: North-Holland, 3085–139.

Mankiw, N.G. (2001) 'The inexorable and mysterious trade-off between inflation and unemployment', *The Economic Journal*, 111: C45–61.

Masi, P.R.D. (1997) 'IMF estimates of potential output: theory and practice', *Staff Studies for the World economic Outlook*, Washington D.C.:Internationl Monetary Fund, 40–6.

Nickell, S., Nunziata, L., Ochel, W. and Quintini, G. (2002) 'The Beveridge curve, unemployment and wages in the OECD from the 1960s to the 1990s', in P. Aghion, R. Frydman, J. Stiglitz and M. Woodford (eds), *Knowledge, Information, and Expectations in Modern Macroeconomics: In Honour of Edmund S. Phelps*, Ch. 19, Princeton: Princeton University Press, 394–440.

OECD (1999): *Employment Outlook*, Paris: OECD.

Sargent, T.J. (1971) 'A note on the accelerationist controversy', *Journal of Money, Credit, and Banking*, 3: 721–25.

Shapiro, M. D. (1994) 'Supply shocks in macroeconomics', in P. Newman, M. Milgate and J. Eatwell (eds), *The New Palgrave Dictionary of Money and Finance*, London: MacMillan, 611–15.

Stiglitz, J. (1997) 'Reflections on the natural rate hypothesis', *Journal of Economic Perspectives*, 11: 3–10.

Taylor, J.B. (1996) 'How should monetary policy respond to shocks while maintaining long-run price stability: conceptual issues', in Federal Reserve Bank of Kansas City (ed), *Achieving Price Stability* (Symposium Proceedings, Jackson Hole, Wyoming), 181–95.
Turner, D., Boone, L., Giorno, C., Meacci, M., Rae, D. and Richardson, P. (2001) 'Estimating the structural rate of nnemployment for the OECD countries', *OECD Economic Studies*, II(33), Paris: OECD, pp. 171–216.

32
Asymmetries and Credibility in Monetary Policy for the Euro-Area

*Kostas Mouratidis**

Introduction

In this chapter I utilize the Markov regime-switching modelling framework to study the credibility of monetary policy by taking into account the asymmetric behaviour of central banks in eight member countries of the European Monetary System (EMS) throughout its life, that is from 1979 to 1998. Moreover, I examine the implications of this analysis for the Euro-area by applying a Markov regime switching model using Euro-area data. Eight countries are examined: Austria, Belgium, Finland, France, Italy, the Netherlands, Portugal and Spain. In addition, Germany and the USA are used as benchmark cases. A number of other studies have investigated the issue of credibility during the EMS period (see for example, Arestis and Mouratidis, 2003; Dahlquist and Gray, 2000). One of the main conclusions of this body of literature is that monetary policy may go through different stages of credibility through time, in a way that it is perceived to be credible in some circumstances and may lack credibility on other occasions. It is, thus, appropriate to use the Markov regime-switching modelling framework to study this phenomenon.

We begin, in the section that follows, with the theoretical and empirical underpinnings of credibility in the EMS. The empirical methodology adopted is explored in the subsequent section, with the empirical findings reported and discussed in the penultimate section. The final section summarizes and concludes.

* I would like to thank Martin Weale, James Mitchell, Joseph Byrne and Andrea Cipollini for very useful comments and suggestions.

Theoretical underpinnings

In recent years, most explanations of positive average inflation rates are based on the time-inconsistency problem which induces an inflation bias. The solution to the inflation bias is achieved in the form of lost reputation in a repeated game version of the basic Barro–Gordon (1983a, 1983b) model. This behaviour of a central bank raises the issue of the public's uncertainty in relation to the 'type' of central bank (see, for example, Backus and Driffill, 1985; Ball, 1995). More concretely, there is uncertainty as to whether the central bank prefers to stabilize inflation variability (that is, the 'dry' type of central bank), or to stabilize output-gap variability (that is, the 'wet' type of central bank).

We adopt this assumption in what follows, along with a theoretical argument stressed by Cukierman (1999), namely that central bank preferences are asymmetric and depend on the state that the economy is in. If the economy is in expansion, central banks react more to inflationary pressures than in recession. Alternatively, the central bank is less reactive to the deviation of output gap from its target level when the economy is in recession than in expansion.

In what follows, we measure the uncertainty regarding the type of central bank as a deviation of the interest rate policy from a target level, where this target is the interest rate of a country with low inflation reputation (Ball, 1995). Giavazzi and Pagano (1988) argue that during the 1980s, the EMS countries designated the Bundesbank as their 'dry central bank' by pegging their exchange rate to the German mark, themselves becoming the 'wet central banks'. In our case the domestic interest rate is the interest rate of each of the nine individual countries and the target interest rate is the German interest rate. We, thus, use Germany to represent the dry type of central bank and the nine countries to represent the wet type of central bank.

Econometric methodology

We use two MRS-BVAR models: the first draws on the relationship between the interest rate differential and inflation; and the second draws on the relationship between the interest rate differential and output gap. The estimation procedure of the MRS-VAR model is an extension of the basic VAR model. The most general specification of a M-state MRS(M)-VAR model can be presented as follows:

$$y_t = v(s_t) + A_1(s_t)y_{t-1} + A_2(s_t)y_{t-2} + \ldots + A_p(s_t)y_{t-p} + \sum u(s_t) \qquad (32.1)$$

where $s_t = 1, 2 \ldots m$ is a $(m \times 1)$ vector of state variable, $u \sim NID(0, I_n)$, $\sum(s_t)^{1/2}$ is the square root of state dependent variance covariance matrix and $A_i(s_t)$ is a state dependent $(n \times n)$ matrix of the autoregressive coefficients at $i-th$ lag.[1] In our case, A is a (2×2) matrix, and the order of the VAR is one.

The MRS-VAR are reduced-form models, and, therefore, no structural interpretation can be given to the coefficients of output-gap and inflation on the interest rate differential. However, the significance of these variables in the equations of interest rate differential is based on sometheoretical models regarding the effects of inflation expectations on economic growth, and the uncertainty surrounding the type of central bank behaviour. This leads to certain conclusions about the preferences of the central bank. In particular, high inflation expectations increase the ex-ante nominal interest rate which affects negatively economic growth. Under such circumstances, the incentive of monetary authorities to inflate become stronger. In the framework of Ball (1995) concerning the uncertainty in terms of the type of central bank, this means that in the high volatility regime the risk premium for the wet type of central bank to deviate from the policy pursued by the dry type, is so intense that it prefers to reveal its identity as a wet type.[2] Under such circumstances where inflation expectations affect policy-makers' preferences and, therefore, the risk premium to deviate from a low inflation country, we interpret evidence of the significance of inflation and the output gap in the equation of interest rate differential in the following way.

In the low credibility regime (that is, high volatility regime), the wet type of central bank has an incentive to inflate. Therefore, in this regime we expect the central bank under consideration to deviate from the German monetary policy emphasising more domestic issues such us growth and unemployment than credibility gains. Output-gap, then, is expected to be significant in the low credibility regime. This is also consistent with the asymmetric behaviour of the central bank. In particular, within this framework the central bank reacts stronger to the deviation of the output gap from its target, in recession than in expansion. Assuming that the high volatility regime is associated with recession, we expect the effect of the output gap on the interest rate differential to be stronger in the high volatility regime than in the low volatility regime. Alternatively, if in the high volatility regime the output gap is not significant, but inflation is significant, then monetary authorities put more weight on inflation than on the output gap. When both inflation and output gap are significant in the high volatility regime, then the credibility of monetary policy regarding the objective of price stability, depends on whether the coefficient of inflation is higher than the coefficient of the output gap. If the coefficient of inflation is higher than the coefficient of output-gap variability, then monetary policy is considered credible regarding the stabilization of inflation.

In the high credibility state (that is, low volatility regime), the output gap is expected to be insignificant. This is so because in a free-shock environment the wet type of central bank has no incentive to deviate from the low inflation policy pursued by the dry type of central bank. Therefore, monetary authorities will react to deviation of inflation from its target level. This is also in line with the asymmetric behaviour of the central bank, which prefers to be more reactive to deviation of inflation from its target in expansion than in recession. Using the assumption that expansion is associated with the low volatility regime, we expect inflation variability to have stronger effects on the interest rate differential in the low volatility regime, than in the high volatility regime. However, if output-gap variability is significant in the high credibility regime, while inflation variability is not, then the monetary authority prefers to stabilize the output-gap variability. Finally, if inflation variability and output-gap variability are significant at the same time in the high credibility state, then we compare the size of their coefficients to reach a conclusion regarding policy preferences.

Data and data sources

We employ monthly data for interest rates, inflation and industrial production for the nine EMU countries included in our sample. The interest rate data were taken from line 60b of the International Financial Statistics database (Datastream). They are monthly averages of day-to-day money rates defined by the IFS as the rate at which short-term borrowing is effected by financial institutions. The Consumer Price Index (CPI) is taken from line 64 and industrial production from line 66 of the same publication. Data are used over the whole period of the EMS, that is from March 1979 to December 1998. Exceptions are the cases of Luxemburg and Portugal where data are available from January 1986 and January 1983 respectively.

The annualized inflation and output gap are measured by $(CPI\text{-}CPI_{12})/CPI_{12}$ and $(IP\text{-}IP_{12})/IP_{12}$ respectively, where CPI is the consumer price index, and IP stands for industrial production; the subscript denotes the lag order. We use the 12-order difference mainly because central banks concentrate on the annual inflation rate. The output-gap series have been measured by assuming that the trend follows a random walk plus drift process. We also experimented with the following additional assumptions relating to the trend: (1) a smooth stochastic process uncorrelated with the cyclical component (Hodrick–Prescott detrending method); (2) a log-linear trend; and (3) a linear deterministic trend uncorrelated with the cyclical part. The empirical results under different measures of output gap were qualitatively similar.

Modelling strategy

We specify a model where the autoregressive coefficients and the variance–covariance matrix are state-dependent, while the state vector follows a Markov process.[3] In this general MRS-BVAR model, an increase in the number of states leads to a statistical model with an excessively large number of coefficients. This makes the estimation difficult and problems of convergence of the MLE arise. Moreover, a number of lags higher than one, does not increase the value of the likelihood function. We, therefore, retain only one lag. It is for these reasons that we retain eventually a first-order Bivariate model with two regimes, MRS(2)-BVAR(1).

General observations

We begin this section by clarifying the coefficients in Tables 32.1–32.4. In Tables 32.1 and 32.2, the estimated equations describe the relationship between the interest rate differential and inflation. In Tables 32.3 and 32.4, the estimated equations refer to the relationship between the interest rate differential and the output gap. The subscripts of each coefficient have the following meanings. The first subscript before the dot indicates the equation and the second the

Table 32.1   Parameters estimates and related statistics for MS(2)-BVAR regime-switching model: inflation

Par.	Austria	Belgium	France	Finland	Italy
$c_{10,1}$	0.020 [0.172]	−0.017 [0.731]	0.060 [0.035]	0.009 [0.069]	−0.095 [0.000]
$\alpha_{11,1}$	0.727 [0.000]	0.624 [0.000]	0.959 [0.000]	0.966 [0.000]	0.962 [0.000]
$\alpha_{12,1}$	−0.509 [0.058]	−1.334 [0.581]	−2.774 [0.007]	1.861 [0.000]	4.133 [0.000]
$c_{10,2}$	0.080 [0.216]	−0.266 [0.205]	−0.872 [0.080]	0.183 [0.480]	0.773 [0.000]
$\alpha_{11,2}$	0.747 [0.000]	0.596 [0.000]	0.325 [0.048]	0.769 [0.000]	0.981 [0.000]
$\alpha_{12,2}$	−1.117 [0.523]	−11.02 [0.010]	−20.96 [0.006]	0.990 [0.848]	1.120 [0.518]
$c_{20,1}$	0.009 [0.003]	0.0009 [0.270]	0.0004 [0.130]	0.020 [0.0001]	0.0006 [0.202]
$\alpha_{21,1}$	0.001 [0.439]	0.0007 [0.339]	−0.0003 [0.008]	0.0001 [0.958]	0.0002 [0.975]
$\alpha_{22,1}$	0.716 [0.000]	0.937 [0.000]	0.944 [0.000]	0.786 [0.000]	0.979 [0.000]
$c_{20,2}$	0.0002 [0.579]	0.001 [0.091]	−0.0001 [0.842]	−0.003 [0.084]	−0.006 [0.925]
$\alpha_{21,2}$	−0.0001 [0.630]	0.0006 [0.0009]	−0.0007 [0.684]	0.002 [0.001]	−0.0009 [0.932]
$\alpha_{22,2}$	0.980 [0.000]	0.998 [0.000]	1.007 [0.000]	1.012 [0.000]	1.176 [0.000]
$\Sigma_{11,1}$	0.184 [0.000]	0.022 [0.000]	0.054 [0.000]	0.235 [0.000]	0.179 [0.000]
$\Sigma_{12,1}$	0.015 [0.000]	−0.0007 [0.691]	−0.00005 [0.192]	0.014 [0.000]	0.00007 [0.390]
$\Sigma_{22,1}$	0.001 [0.000]	0.0007 [0.000]	0.00006 [0.001]	0.0009 [0.000]	0.00007 [0.000]
$\Sigma_{11,2}$	0.178 [0.856]	1.485 [0.000]	3.869 [0.000]	0.286 [0.056]	2.750 [0.000]
$\Sigma_{12,2}$	0.0001 [0.008]	0.0004 [0.901]	−0.002 [0.003]	−0.014 [0.114]	−0.044 [0.035]
$\Sigma_{22,2}$	0.00007 [0.000]	0.0001 [0.000]	0.000004 [0.000]	0.00002 [0.264]	0.001 [0.003]
p_{12}	0.017 [0.016]	0.040 [0.071]	0.063 [0.002]	0.0432 [0.000]	0.016 [0.114]
p_{21}	0.334 [0.000]	0.031 [0.036]	0.304 [0.0001]	0.0435 [0.124]	0.583 [0.000]
LogLik	756.45	916.959	1053.04	844.17	985.64

Notes: 1.) *P*-values are reported in squared brackets; 2.) Inflation on the title indicates that the estimation has been implemented for the case where inflation is used as a regressor

regressor under consideration. The subscript after the dot indicates the regime. The coefficient $c_{i0.1}$ denotes the constant coefficient in the $i = 1, 2$ equation in the first regime (that is, high credible regime); the coefficient $ij.1$ is the coefficient of the $j = 1, 2$ regressor in the $i = 1, 2$ equation in the first regime. Similarly, $c_{i0.2}$ is the constant coefficient in equation $i = 1, 2$ in the second regime (that is, low credible regime); and $ij.2$ the coefficient of $j = 1, 2$ regressor in the second regime. The variance–covariance matrix $ij.1$ denotes the covariance between $i = 1, 2$ and $j = 1, 2$ in the first regime, and the variance–covariance matrix $ij.2$ is the covariance matrix in the second regime. The transition probability p_{12} denotes the

Table 32.2 Parameters estimates and related statistics for MS(2)-BVAR regime-switching model: inflation

Par.	Netherlands	Portugal	Spain	Euro-area
$c_{10,1}$	−0.071 [0.186]	−0.091 [0.058]	0.100 [0.236]	−0.190 [0.069]
$\alpha_{11,1}$	0.820 [0.000]	0.992 [0.000]	0.957 [0.000]	0.641 [0.000]
$\alpha_{12,1}$	3.758 [0.067]	0.357 [0.806]	0.418 [0.877]	8.668 [0.013]
$c_{10,2}$	−0.501 [0.010]	0.778 [0.323]	1.497 [0.092]	−0.113 [0.080]
$\alpha_{11,2}$	0.598 [0.000]	0.629 [0.000]	0.804 [0.000]	0.129 [0.000]
$\alpha_{12,2}$	9.893 [0.011]	21.13 [0.002]	2.518 [0.813]	3.494 [0.191]
$c_{20,1}$	0.002 [0.000]	−0.0006 [0.388]	0.0008 [0.154]	0.008 [0.052]
$\alpha_{21,1}$	−0.001 [0.013]	−0.0003 [0.302]	0.0001 [0.232]	−0.001 [0.200]
$\alpha_{22,1}$	0.910 [0.000]	1.048 [0.000]	0.965 [0.000]	0.845 [0.000]
$c_{20,2}$	−0.0009 [0.360]	0.008 [0.856]	0.0006 [0.802]	−0.005 [0.000]
$\alpha_{21,2}$	0.0001 [0.746]	−0.0002 [0.299]	0.0001 [0.561]	0.008 [0.000]
$\alpha_{22,2}$	1.004 [0.000]	0.986 [0.000]	0.969 [0.000]	0.908 [0.000]
$\Sigma_{11,1}$	0.041 [0.000]	0.064 [0.000]	0.170 [0.000]	0.351 [0.000]
$\Sigma_{12,1}$	0.0005 [0.896]	−0.0004 [0.703]	−0.00007 [0.550]	0.002 [0.000]
$\Sigma_{22,1}$	0.0005 [0.000]	0.00001 [0.000]	0.00001 [0.000]	0.00003 [0.000]
$\Sigma_{11,2}$	0.313 [0.000]	5.787 [0.000]	6.181 [0.000]	3.041 [0.056]
$\Sigma_{12,2}$	0.00001 [0.948]	−0.0003 [0.074]	−0.001 [0.617]	−0.033 [0.000]
$\Sigma_{22,2}$	0.00008 [0.000]	0.00005 [0.002]	0.00001 [0.000]	0.0004 [0.264]
p_{12}	0.040 [0.055]	0.083 [0.005]	0.015 [0.103]	0.019 [0.008]
p_{21}	0.104 [0.014]	0.103 [0.029]	0.041 [0.033]	0.025 [0.000]
LogLik	756.45	916.959	829.98	511.64

See notes To Table 32.1.

transition from the high credible regime to the low credible regime. The transition probability p_{21} is the transition from the low credible regime to the high credible regime.

The model is a reduced form and we concentrate only on the significance of the information variables in the equations of interest rate differential. In all the cases reported in Tables 32.1–32.4 there are three main characteristics that separate the two regimes. First, in the majority of cases the variance of the interest rate differentials in the low credible regime (that is, $\Sigma_{11,2}$) is many times greater than that in the high credible regime ($\Sigma_{11,1}$). Second, subject to some exceptions, the coefficient of the lagged value of the interest rate differential isgreater in the high

Table 32.3 Parameters estimates and related statistics for MS(2)-BVAR regime-switching model: IP

Par.	Austria	Belgium	France	Finland	Italy
$c_{10,1}$	0.051 [0.270]	−0.044 [0.067]	0.018 [0.498]	−0.027 [0.061]	−0.129 [0.036]
$\alpha_{11,1}$	0.775 [0.000]	0.651 [0.000]	0.989 [0.000]	0.996 [0.000]	1.010 [0.000]
$\alpha_{12,1}$	0.029 [0.805]	0.197 [0.722]	0.501 [0.464]	0.637 [0.000]	0.479 [0.483]
$c_{10,2}$	0.164 [0.997]	−0.526 [0.003]	−1.116 [0.011]	0.135 [0.145]	0.973 [0.078]
$\alpha_{11,2}$	0.920 [0.985]	0.648 [0.000]	0.632 [0.000]	0.970 [0.000]	0.847 [0.000]
$\alpha_{12,2}$	0.300 [0.999]	−4.275 [0.463]	−2.385 [0.820]	−3.321 [0.251]	7.132 [0.190]
$c_{20,1}$	0.036 [0.000]	0.001 [0.001]	0.007 [0.000]	0.004 [0.136]	0.013 [0.014]
$\alpha_{21,1}$	−0.029 [0.000]	0.0008 [0.000]	0.0008 [0.063]	0.0003 [0.958]	−0.0001 [0.162]
$\alpha_{22,1}$	−0.001 [0.905]	0.954 [0.000]	0.743 [0.000]	0.875 [0.000]	0.628 [0.000]
$c_{20,2}$	0.073 [0.999]	0.0006 [0.332]	−0.006 [0.126]	0.017 [0.000]	−0.030 [0.016]
$\alpha_{21,2}$	−0.059 [0.999]	0.0007 [0.776]	−0.003 [0.762]	0.001 [0.384]	0.004 [0.048]
$\alpha_{22,2}$	−0.414 [0.999]	0.987 [0.000]	0.761 [0.000]	0.182 [0.097]	0.495 [0.001]
$\Sigma_{11,1}$	0.171 [0.000]	0.020 [0.000]	0.051 [0.000]	0.016 [0.000]	0.106 [0.000]
$\Sigma_{12,1}$	−0.001 [0.584]	0.002 [0.002]	0.0001 [0.811]	−0.0001 [0.706]	−0.001 [0.241]
$\Sigma_{22,1}$	0.002 [0.000]	0.0002 [0.000]	0.0002 [0.000]	0.0008 [0.000]	0.001 [0.000]
$\Sigma_{11,2}$	0.839 [0.992]	1.511 [0.000]	4.479 [0.000]	0.254 [0.000]	1.334 [0.002]
$\Sigma_{12,2}$	0.050 [0.999]	−0.0003 [0.514]	−0.016 [0.005]	−0.001 [0.575]	−0.002 [0.580]
$\Sigma_{22,2}$	4.161 [0.994]	0.00002 [0.000]	0.0003 [0.000]	0.0006 [0.000]	0.0005 [0.005]
p_{12}	0.047 [0.077]	0.047 [0.077]	0.072 [0.001]	0.053 [0.031]	0.052 [0.013]
p_{21}	0.033 [0.052]	0.031 [0.052]	0.031 [0.000]	0.089 [0.022]	0.275 [0.013]
LogLik	354.49	845.469	639.65	657.68	506.65

See notes to Table 32.1. Inflation on the title indicates that the estimation has been implemented for the case where industrial production is used as a regressor.

credible regime (that is, $\alpha_{11.1}$) than in the low credible regime ($\alpha_{11.2}$). Also, the transition probability from the low credible regime to the high credible regime (p_{21}) is higher than the transition probability from the high credible regime to the low credible regime (p_{12}). This implies that high credible regimes are more persistent than low credible regimes. Third, in the majority of cases, the covariances $\Sigma_{12.i}$ and $\Sigma_{21.i}$ (with $i = 1, 2$) are both equal to zero. This result does not indicate that there is no relationship between the two variables, since $\alpha_{12.i} \neq 0$. However, it implies that the unobserved state variables for each equation in the BVAR-MRS model are not perfectly correlated.

Table 32.4   Parameters estimates and related statistics for MS(2)-BVAR regime-switching model: IP

Par.	Netherlands	Portugal	Spain	Euro-area
$c_{10,1}$	−0.019 [0.348]	−0.077 [0.127]	0.041 [0.749]	0.0182 [0.525]
$\alpha_{11,1}$	0.908 [0.000]	0.989 [0.000]	0.979 [0.000]	0.977 [0.000]
$\alpha_{12,1}$	0.168 [0.680]	0.169 [0.454]	−0.590 [0.618]	0.016 [0.000]
$c_{10,2}$	−0.191 [0.007]	2.205 [0.007]	1.491 [0.000]	0.309 [0.134]
$\alpha_{11,2}$	0.576 [0.000]	0.712 [0.000]	0.809 [0.000]	0.872 [0.000]
$\alpha_{12,2}$	−12.84 [0.014]	−3.990 [0.226]	7.704 [0.350]	0.022 [0.435]
$c_{20,1}$	−0.017 [0.000]	−0.005 [0.722]	−0.003 [0.001]	−0.118 [0.136]
$\alpha_{21,1}$	0.001 [0.770]	0.003 [0.244]	0.0004 [0.004]	0.078 [0.022]
$\alpha_{22,1}$	0.317 [0.000]	0.851 [0.000]	1.027 [0.000]	0.913 [0.000]
$c_{20,2}$	−0.026 [0.000]	0.024 [0.372]	0.004 [0.000]	−1.084 [0.114]
$\alpha_{21,2}$	−0.005 [0.256]	−0.004 [0.116]	−0.0002 [0.017]	0.422 [0.084]
$\alpha_{22,2}$	−0.140 [0.424]	0.698 [0.000]	0.959 [0.000]	0.706 [0.000]
$\Sigma_{11,1}$	0.051 [0.000]	0.061 [0.015]	0.117 [0.000]	0.028 [0.000]
$\Sigma_{12,1}$	−0.001 [0.026]	0.002 [0.419]	−0.0003 [0.032]	−0.009 [0.337]
$\Sigma_{22,1}$	0.001 [0.000]	0.007 [0.000]	0.00001 [0.000]	0.376 [0.000]
$\Sigma_{11,2}$	0.447 [0.000]	5.892 [0.000]	5.124 [0.000]	0.146 [0.000]
$\Sigma_{12,2}$	−0.0003 [0.912]	0.0178 [0.320]	−0.001 [0.074]	0.026 [0.605]
$\Sigma_{22,2}$	0.007 [0.000]	0.006 [0.003]	0.00001 [0.000]	1.480 [0.000]
p_{12}	0.012 [0.092]	0.081 [0.022]	0.063 [0.002]	0.071 [0.058]
p_{21}	0.090 [0.091]	0.095 [0.134]	0.304 [0.0001]	0.235 [0.007]
LogLik	756.45	112.831	802.96	−21.385

See notes to Table 32.3.

Detailed discussion of results by country

The second column of Table 32.1 indicates that in case of Austria inflation is significant only in the high credible state (that is, $\alpha_{12.1}$). This is consistent with the theory of state-dependent behaviour of central banks. This implies Austrian monetary authorities followed a policy consistent with the objective of price stability, and this is reinforced by the evidence that output-gap variability is insignificant in all states (see the second column of Table 32.3).

In Belgium inflation is significant only for the high volatility regime (that is, $\alpha_{12.1}$ in Table 32.1). Moreover, the output gap is not significant in any state. These results show the determination of Belgian authorities to meet the objective of price stability stated in Article 3 of the Maastricht Treaty. The third column of Table 32.1 show that in the case of France inflation is significant in both regimes.

In contrast to our theoretical priors, the effects of inflation are stronger in the low credibility state than in the high credibility state (that is, $\alpha_{12.1} < \alpha_{12.2}$). This indicates that the unobserved state variable of inflation is independent of the unobserved state variable of interest rate differential. In general, the results for France show that monetary policy in this country puts a strong emphasis on the objective of low and stable inflation. This is reinforced by the evidence that output-gap variability is insignificant in all states (see the fourth column of Table 32.3).

In Finland, both inflation and the output gap are significant only in the high credible state. Regarding the output gap there is inconsistency between the theory induced by Cukierman (1999) and the evidence that is significant only in the high credibility state. The last columns of Tables 32.1 and 32.3 show that in the case of Italy only inflation in the high credibility state is significant. In the case of the Netherlands, inflation is significant in both regimes and the output gap in the low credibility regime (see $\alpha_{12,1}$ and $\alpha_{12,2}$ in Tables 32.2 and 32.4). It is interesting to note that the coefficient of inflation is higher in the low credibility than in the high credibility state, and that the coefficient of output gap in the low credibility state is higher than the corresponding coefficient of inflation. This implies that Dutch monetary policy emphasizes more deviation of output from its trend than inflation from its target.

In Portugal, only inflation is significant in the low credibility state (that is, coefficient $\alpha_{12.2}$ in the third column of Table 32.2). The fact that the output gap is not significant in any state, shows the determination of the central bank to stabilize inflation irrespective of the cost that this policy implies for the output gap. In Spain, none of inflation and output-gap coefficients are significant in any regime (see column 5, Tables 32.2 and 32.4 respectively). Spanish monetary authorities adopted a flexible inflation target accompanied by better communication to the public. They, thus, managed to increase flexibility and transparency, without experiencing any cost in terms of credibility, higher inflation and even exchange rate instability.

In general, on results show that the monetary policies followed by the eight EMU countries during the EMS period were consistent with the objective of price stability induced by the ECB. In particular, in the majority of the cases inflation had significant effects on the interest rate differential while this was not the case for the output gap. We extended this study to examine the implication of these results for the Euro-area, applying the MRS-BVAR model to Euro-area data. However, in this case we don't use Germany as the dry type of central bank but the USA. Therefore, we use the interest rate differential between the Euro-area interest rate and the interest rate of the USA.[4] The sample of data start from January 1986 to August 2002, because Euro-area data of short-term interest rates are only available from January 1986. Moreover, we use producer prices data instead of CPI to compute Euro-area inflation, because data of the Harmonized Index of Consumer Prices (HICP) for the Euro-area are only available after 1990. Producer price index data were taken from *New Cronos*, Eurostat, based on ESA95 National Accounts.

The last columns of Tables 32.2 and 32.4 show that both inflation and the output gap are significant in the high credibility state. However, the coefficient of inflation is much higher than that of the output gap. Therefore, monetary policy for the Euro-area was more inclined to correct deviation of inflation from its target than output from its trend.[5] This is in line with the findings from the analysis of individual countries.

Conclusions

We have used two different MRS(2)-BVAR(1) models to analyse the credibility of monetary policy in a subset of EMU countries and for the Euro-area. In the first specification we use a MRS(2)-BVAR(1) model between the interest rate differential of individual EMU countries and the German interest rate and inflation. In the case of the Euro-area we use the interest rate differential between the Euro-area short-term interest rate and the interest rate of the USA. In the second model we use a MRS(2)-BVAR(1) model between the same interest rate differential and the output gap.

The evidence adduced indicates the existence of asymmetric effects, with the output gap and inflation having different effects in each state. In general, results from the analysis of the eight EMU countries show that in the majority of cases inflation had significant effects on the interest rate differential, while the output gap found no significance. Under such circumstances the objective of price stability induced by the ECB will not be in contrast to the national preferences of any individual country. Moreover, we also studied whether the results from individuals countries were in line with the results of an analysis based on Euro-area data, and estimated monetary policy preferences for the Euro-area. Evidence from the Euro-area analysis was consistent with those of individual countries. In particular, the effects of inflation on the interest rate differential were stronger than the effects of the output gap.

Notes

1 Krolzig (1997) describes some particular specifications of MRS-BVAR models where the autoregressive parameters, the mean or the intercept are state dependent and the error term is homoscedastic or heteroscedastic.
2 Ball (1995) shows that the wet type of central bank sets inflation equal to zero so long as supply shocks are absent, and inflates at the discretionary level (see text for its meaning) when supply shocks occur.
3 For a detailed discussion regarding the reason that we allow all coefficients to be state-depedent see Arestis and Mouratidis (2003).
4 The Euro-area interest rate is the three-month money market rate taken from Datastream. The interest rate for the USA is the three-month certificate of deposit rate taken from the OECD database.
5 Here, we have assumed a zero inflation as a target level.

References

Arestis, P. and Mouratidis, K. (2003) 'Credibility of EMS interest rate policies: a Markov regime-switching approach', *The Manchester School*, forthcoming.

Ball, L. (1995) 'Time-consistence and persistence changes in inflation', *Journal of Monetary Economics*, 36: 329–50.

Barro, R.J. and Gordon, D.B. (1983a) 'A positive theory of monetary policy in a natural rate model', *Journal of Political Economy*, 91: 589–610.

Barro, R.J. and Gordon, D.B. (1983b) 'Rules discretion, and reputation in a model of monetary policy', *Journal of Monetary Economics*, 12: 101–21.

Backus, D.K. and Driffill, J. (1985) 'Inflation and reputation', *American Economic Review*, 75: 530–38.

Cukierman, A. (1999) 'The inflation bias result rivisited', Working Paper n. 38–99, Tel Aviv University.

Giavazzi, F. and Pagano, M. (1988) 'The advantage of tying one's hand, EMS discipline and central bank credibility', *European Economic Review*, 32: 1055–82.

Krolzig, H-M. (1997) *Markov-Switching Vector Autoregressions: Modelling, Statistical Inference, and Application to Business Cycle Analysis*, Berlin: Springer.

Index

In transcribing the Cartwright Papers, I have wherever possible kept spelling and sentence structure true to Cartwright's version. Throughout the papers Cartwright's spelling of a word can vary, as in *length* and *lenth, asunder* and *assunder,* or *cayenne, kayan,* and *kayane.* Some minor changes in the transcription were made; Cartwright's handwritten gothic "ß" and "f" have been replaced with a single or double "s," while apostrophes, which he used inconsistently, have been inserted to show possessives. The letter "t" is often uncrossed, and "r" can resemble any number of letters. In these and similar cases where the word choice is obvious but Cartwright's penmanship wanting, the correct letter has been inserted.

Eighteenth-century spelling and syntax differed in some respects from today's, as in the inconsistent capitalization of proper nouns and the longer sentences. Where Cartwright's meaning is uncertain, I leave it up to the reader to venture an interpretation. Where his spelling diverges widely from today's, I have left the original followed by "[*sic*]" to show that the transcription follows the original. Sometimes it was not possible to transcribe a word with certainty. Where I felt relatively secure in offering a transcription, the suggested word is shown in square brackets. Some words were unreadable due to ink smudges, poor penmanship, or paper damage. In these instances a question mark in square brackets, "[?]," indicates that I haven't given a suggestion. Overall, Cartwright's sentences are often lengthy and have unusually placed commas. He used hyphens with abandon, and many entries give the impression of having been written in haste. The transcription stays true to this style, and Cartwright's intended meaning is generally not too elusive.

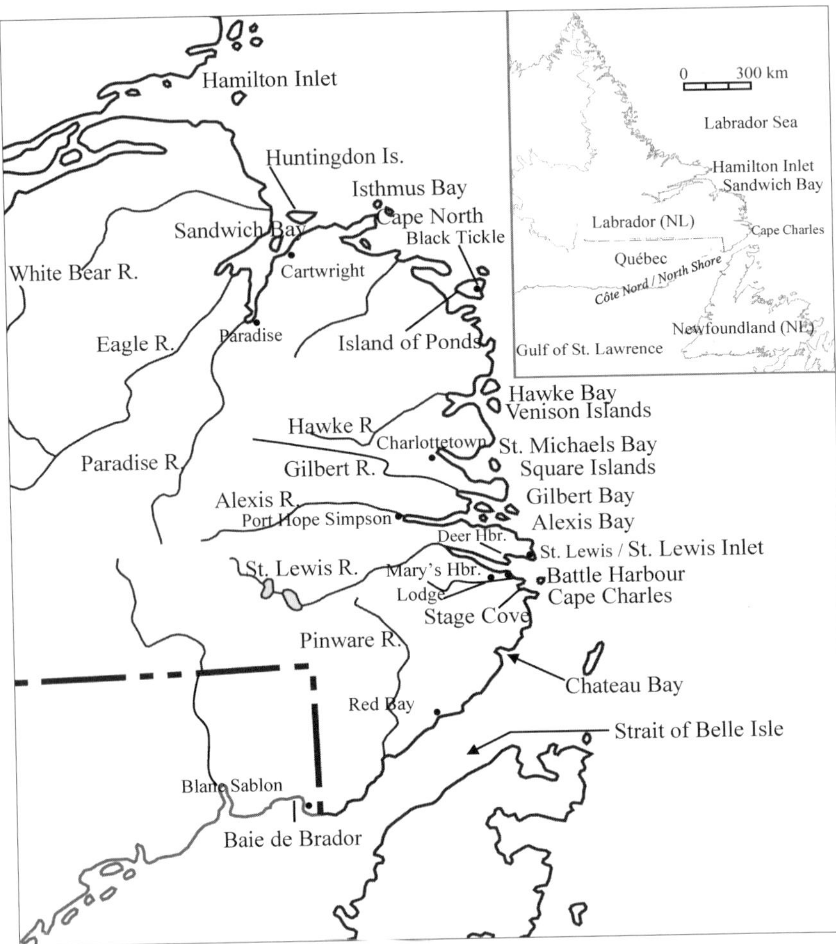

Fig. 2   Map of southern Labrador, showing place names

Nord, or the Gulf coast refer to the coastline from Blanc Sablon south and westward along the northern shore of the Gulf of St Lawrence. These regions and other places mentioned in the text are shown on the map of figure 2. George Cartwright named much of the south-central coast in the 1770s, including many of the hinterland ponds and hills where he hunted and trapped. Today many of his coastal toponyms continue to be in use, although the majority of his inland names are forgotten.